FOR DUMMIES

The fun and easy way™ to travel!

U.S.A.

 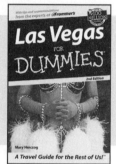

Also available:

America's National Parks For Dummies

Arizona For Dummies

Boston For Dummies

California For Dummies

Chicago For Dummies

Florida For Dummies

Los Angeles & Disneyland For Dummies

New Mexico For Dummies

New Orleans For Dummies

New York City For Dummies

San Francisco For Dummies

Seattle For Dummies

Washington, D.C. For Dummies

RV Vacations For Dummies

Walt Disney World & Orlando For Dummies

EUROPE

Also available:

England For Dummies

Europe For Dummies

Ireland For Dummies

London For Dummies

Paris For Dummies

Scotland For Dummies

Spain For Dummies

OTHER DESTINATIONS

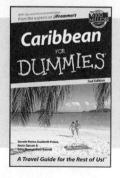

Also available:

Bahamas For Dummies

Honeymoon Vacations For Dummies

Mexico's Beach Resorts For Dummies

Vancouver & Victoria For Dummies

Available wherever books are sold.

Go to www.dummies.com or call 1-877-762-2974 to order direct.

WILEY

RV Vacations FOR DUMMIES®
2ND EDITION

by Shirley Slater & Harry Basch

WILEY

Wiley Publishing, Inc.

RV Vacations For Dummies,® 2nd Edition
Published by
Wiley Publishing, Inc.
111 River St.
Hoboken, NJ 07030-5774
www.wiley.com

For general information on our other products and services or to obtain technical support, please contact our Customer Care Department within the U.S. at 800-762-2974, outside the U.S. at 317-572-3993, or fax 317-572-4002.

Wiley also publishes its books in a variety of electronic formats. Some content that appears in print may not be available in electronic books.

Library of Congress Control Number: 2004103170

ISBN: 0-7645-4442-X

Manufactured in the United States of America

10 9 8 7 6 5 4 3

2B/QR/QW/QU/IN

WILEY

About the Authors

Shirley Slater and **Harry Basch** are a husband-and-wife travel-writing team whose books, articles, and photographs have been published internationally over the past 25 years. Former stage, film, and television actors, they have written their syndicated column "Cruise Views" for the *Los Angeles Times* and other major newspapers for more than 20 years, produced six annual editions of the *North American Ski Guide* for Prodigy Computer Services, and written *Shirley and Harry's RV Adventures* (a monthly newsletter) plus four books on worldwide cruising.

In 1990, at the 60th World Travel Congress in Hamburg, Germany, the authors were only the third writers (and the first freelancers) to receive the prestigious Melva C. Pederson Award from the American Society of Travel Agents for "extraordinary journalistic achievement in the field of travel."

On assignment for publications as diverse as *Bon Appétit* and *Travel Weekly,* they have covered 188 countries by barge, elephant back, hot-air balloon, luxury cruise ship, cross-country skis, paddle-wheel steamer, and supersonic aircraft, but their favorite method of transportation is by RV. In their former 27-foot Winnebago Brave motorhome and their new 36-foot Itasca Sunflyer, they have logged more than 100,000 miles traveling across the United States, Canada, and Mexico. Aboard other RVs — from mini-motorhomes to 36-foot widebodies with slideouts — they have traveled an additional 60,000 miles exploring the back roads and campgrounds of America. These journeys are all based on the authors' personal experiences.

They're the authors of three editions of *Frommer's Exploring America by RV* and appear on informational RV videos featured at `www.rvtv direct.com`.

Dedication

To Christopher and Eugenia, who are just starting out.

Authors' Acknowledgments

We would like to thank the following people for their invaluable assistance and information that led to the creation of this book. First of all, our wonderful and patient editor, Lisa Torrance Duffy; Dave Humphreys at RVIA and his knowledgeable associates Gary LaBella, Christine Morrison, Nancy White, and Alan Piercy; Sheila Davis, PR director of Winnebago Industries; B. J. Thompson & Associates; Frank Gilanelli of Barton-Gilanelli & Associates; Fran Conners and Jon Tancredi; and Marcia Schnedler, who first suggested we write an RV book.

Publisher's Acknowledgments

We're proud of this book; please send us your comments through our Dummies online registration form located at www.dummies.com/register/.

Some of the people who helped bring this book to market include the following:

Editorial

Editors: Lisa Torrance Duffy, Tim Gallan

Copy Editor: E. Neil Johnson

Cartographer: Roberta Stockwell

Editorial Manager: Christine Meloy Beck

Editorial Assistant: Melissa S. Bennett

Senior Photo Editor: Richard Fox

Front Cover Photo: John Warden / Getty Images

Back Cover Photo: Suzanne & Nick Geary / Getty Images

Cartoons: Rich Tennant, www.the5thwave.com

Production

Project Coordinator: Ryan Steffen

Layout and Graphics: Stephanie D. Jumper, Michael Kruzil, Lynsey Osborn, Julie Trippetti

Proofreaders: Laura Albert, Andy Hollandbeck, Carl Pierce, Dwight Ramsey, TECHBOOKS Production Services

Indexer: TECHBOOKS Production Services

Publishing and Editorial for Consumer Dummies

Diane Graves Steele, Vice President and Publisher, Consumer Dummies

Joyce Pepple, Acquisitions Director, Consumer Dummies

Kristin A. Cocks, Product Development Director, Consumer Dummies

Michael Spring, Vice President and Publisher, Travel

Brice Gosnell, Associate Publisher, Travel

Kelly Regan, Editorial Director, Travel

Publishing for Technology Dummies

Andy Cummings, Vice President and Publisher, Dummies Technology/General User

Composition Services

Gerry Fahey, Vice President of Production Services

Debbie Stailey, Director of Composition Services

Contents at a Glance

Maps at a Glance

Table of Contents

Introduction

. . . .

*C*ongratulations! After looking at all those RVs — recreation vehicles — rolling down the highway and wondering what driving one would be like, you decided to find out. You're probably like us — a few years ago, an RV vacation never crossed your mind.

But as the world grows louder and closer, and job stresses pull you in all directions, you find yourself yearning for meaningful time alone with those closest to you. At the same time, you want some control over your life and a sense of self-sufficiency. That's what an RV vacation can give you.

As travel writers, we spent the past 25 years visiting the most exotic parts of the world. Today, when we travel abroad, we look forward to going back home, unpacking the sequins and tuxedos, and heading out for a back roads getaway in our motorhome. Our trip may be for only a weekend or an entire glorious month, but the experience recharges our souls, rejuvenates our bodies, and reinvents our relationship.

How can a specialized motor vehicle do all this? You may well ask. Well, that's what this book is about. Now, we can go out to see our world and take all the comforts of home — kitchen, bathroom, dressing room, sofa, refrigerator, and TV/VCR — along with us. We can park our RV by the sea one day and on top of a mountain the next, but we're always at home.

On the road, we meet families with small children, independent young couples who bring their offices along and work on the road, pet owners who don't want to separate from their animals on vacation, retirees who want to putter around discovering America gradually, fussy diners who don't want to down another fast-food franchise meal, fussy sleepers who don't want to lie awake wondering who slept in their bed the night before, and the disabled or diet-bound who know that their specialized adjustments in the RV enable them to travel safely and securely.

About This Book

In the first chapters of this book, we tell you everything that you ever wanted or need to know about RVs and RVing, filtered through our hands-on experience and total lack of knowledge when we started RVing a decade ago. Then we give you an insider's look at some of our favorite drives particularly suited for RVs in what we have discovered to be the most diverse, beautiful, and exciting travel venue in the world — the United States of America. And, finally, we offer some timely tips that make all this travel easier.

Throughout the drives — 14 in all — we give you the information you need to find your way and point out only the highlights rather than every musty museum or historic home. We share some of our favorite campgrounds with you, and because, in most cases, you're carrying your own kitchen, we steer you to places where you can pick up local produce, regional delicacies, or special takeout meals to pick up and eat later.

Use *RV Vacations For Dummies* as a reference guide. You can, of course, start at the first page and read all the way through to the end. Or if you're a more experienced RVer, you can flip to our favorite drives, and start checking out the itineraries. The main thing is that you can move around from chapter to chapter, picking and choosing what interests you.

You won't find much in this book about repairing a malfunctioning RV. We learned early on to leave that to the experts. Although through the years, we've acquired a few handy maintenance tips that we pass on to help you and your RV stay in shape and cut down on repair bills.

Please be advised that travel information is subject to change at any time — this is especially true of prices. We, therefore, suggest that you write or call ahead for confirmation when making your travel plans. The authors, editors, and publisher can't be held responsible for the experiences of readers while traveling. Your safety is important to us, however, so we encourage you to stay alert and be aware of your surroundings. Keep a close eye on cameras, purses, and wallets, all favorite targets of thieves and pickpockets. And always lock your vehicle in or out of campgrounds.

Conventions Used in This Book

To keep this book from being longer than the Harry Potter series, we use a number of abbreviations in the driving and campground sections.

Campground amenities:

- ✔ CATV Cable TV hookup
- ✔ SATV Satellite TV hookup

Credit cards:

- ✔ AE American Express
- ✔ DISC Discover
- ✔ MC MasterCard
- ✔ V Visa

Road names:

> ✔ I- # Interstate Highway
>
> ✔ SR # State Road
>
> ✔ CR # County Road
>
> ✔ FM # Farm to Market Road

We divide campgrounds into two categories — our personal favorites and those that don't quite make our preferred list but still get our hearty seal of approval. Sometimes those on the second list may offer more amenities than our favorites — such as whirlpool spas and line dance lessons.

We also use some general pricing information to help you as you decide where to camp. The following system of dollar signs is meant to be a guideline only and suggests the range of costs for one night in a campground.

Cost	Campground
$	Up to $10
$$	$11 to $20
$$$	$21 to $30
$$$$	$31 to $40
$$$$$	$41 and more

Foolish Assumptions

As we wrote this book, we made some assumptions about you and what your needs as an RVer may be. Here's what we assumed about you.

> ✔ You may be an inexperienced RVer looking for some advice about what RVs are and what RVing is all about.
>
> ✔ You may be an experienced RVer looking for new experiences, new attractions, new roads to conquer, and don't want to miss a good bet.
>
> ✔ You're not looking for a book that provides all the information available about RVing or that lists every campground, attraction, or food venue available to you. Instead, you're looking for a book that focuses on the most important information and the best or most unique experiences as you travel the highway.

If you fit any of these criteria, then *RV Vacations For Dummies* gives you the information you're seeking!

How This Book Is Organized

Although broken into six parts, the book consists of three major sections. Parts I and II provide the how-to info that you need to get started before you hit the road. Parts III, IV, and V include 14 fabulous driving itineraries, each in a different part of the United States. And, finally, Part VI gives you the lowdown on the country's best campgrounds and zany attractions for RVers who want to explore beyond our itineraries.

Part I: Getting Started

What is an RV and what is RVing? You find out in this part, and you see why we think it's the greatest thing since sliced bread. We tell you where to go and when, what types of RVs are out there and how to choose the best one for you, how to plan ahead for renting or buying an RV, and how to budget your expenses.

Part II: Ironing Out the Details

After you get an RV, what are you going to do with it? This part includes tips for getting started — what to plan for, how to be prepared, and what you need to know about packing, cooking in your RV, campgrounds, and more.

Part III: Exploring the East

In Chapters 11 through 15, we explore the eastern United States by RV. The driving routes in each chapter offer a variety of scenery and activities, and each includes at least one designated scenic roadway, sightseeing attraction, or national park. Two routes — **The Coast of Maine: Lobster Land** and **The Gulf Coast: Tallahassee to New Orleans** — follow the sea. **Blue Ridge Mountains: Skyline Drive and Blue Ridge Parkway** brings together two great American roadways with the Great Smoky Mountains National Park — all without the hassle of commercial traffic. **Western New York: Cooperstown to Niagara Falls** lets you see a museum for baseball greats (some fans allow three days to see it all) and witness the power of Niagara Falls. **The Natchez Trace: Natchez, MS, to Nashville, TN,** takes you through the old and new South, past the birthplaces of such icons as Elvis Presley, W.C. Handy, and Oprah Winfrey. We share our favorite campgrounds and cafes along the way.

Part IV: Discovering Mid-America

Chapters 16 through 19 take you through the heartland with a choice of four itineraries, at least one of which should be within a reasonable driving time from a Midwestern home base. **Texas Hill Country:**

Bluebonnets and Barbecue tells you when to catch the optimum wild-flower shows and where to taste the best barbecue. The **Heart of Ohio: A Circle Around Circleville** carries you on a loop from aviation history to rock-and-roll, with a pause in the world's largest Amish community. **Northern Minnesota: Paul Bunyan Country** visits an American icon that delights kids of all ages, takes you to the source of the great Mississippi River, and leads you to North America's largest shopping mall. **The Ozarks and Branson: Hot Springs to Springfield** lets you in on how to get good deals in an area that's the second most popular travel destination in the United States.

Part V: Seeing the West

In Chapters 20 through 24, we follow the trail of American icons through some of the world's most dazzling scenery. **Montana and Wyoming: Tracking Buffalo Bill** follows the famous showman through Yellowstone National Park and to the town of Cody, Wyoming, named for him. **New Mexico: Billy the Kid Meets E.T.** lets you visit a notorious real-life cowboy and the alien visitor from the film *E.T.* (whose space alien relatives may have dropped in on Roswell, New Mexico, a few years ago). **The Oregon Coast: California to Washington** combines scenery with seafood, taking you beachcombing, kite-flying, and wine-tasting, while **California Coast: Malibu to Monterey** explores what some people (including the authors) think is the most beautiful place on earth. **Route 66: OK to LA** follows the famous road (what's left of it) and digs out some little-known and big-name landmarks along the way.

Part VI: The Part of Tens

The Part of Tens highlights campgrounds and destinations beyond the itineraries in this book. We know that after RVers get started, they soon want to travel more and more. This part includes the ten best **winter getaways for snowbirds,** fascinating **factory tours** where you can watch the manufacture of everything from Crayolas to Jelly Bellies (and get free samples), and **offbeat museums** saluting Jell-O, Lucille Ball, Spam, UFOs, and mustard.

Appendix and worksheets

Here are the plain facts you need to complete the final details for your RV vacation, including toll-free telephone numbers and Web sites to expand your research. We also include a list of common RV and campground terms and some yellow worksheets to help you with budget planning, selecting an RV, choosing a campground, organizing your schedule, and creating itineraries.

Icons Used in This Book

 This icon pegs the best bargains and money-saving tips for your RV vacation, from where to buy gas or groceries to campgrounds that represent a good buy for the buck.

 Look out for tourist traps, scams, and rip-offs when you see this icon, which also saves you money by pointing out places that aren't worth the price of admission in our opinion. We give the warning; the rest is up to you.

 This icon is to let you know when something special is available for the younger set; this helps cut down on the "Are we there yet?" syndrome.

 Accompanying this icon are special warnings for RVers, whether you face a low bridge ahead or a difficult parking situation.

 For hints, tips, or insider advice to make your trip run more smoothly, look for this icon. Although the point of a travel guide is to serve as one gigantic "tip," this icon singles out little nuggets of knowledge that may be new to you.

This icon tells you when special sights along the way may take you off the direct route. Follow the detour to discover special places and experiences.

Where to Go from Here

To the freedom of the open road. How you want to use this guide is up to you. You can start from the book's beginning and read straight through, or you can start anywhere in between and extract information as you want or need it. Throughout, think of us as your guides. We'll help you pick out your RV, stock it with your favorite supplies, and choose when and where you want to travel. With your RV as home and all the highways of America as your open road, you can be king or queen of the world.

Part I
Getting Started

"Well, this thing is starting to <u>melt</u>! Shoot! Those people we bought it from way up north never said anything about their motorhomes melting!"

In this part . . .

You like being outdoors, sitting around a campfire, hiking in the wilderness, and breathing in the fresh air — the pure freedom of getting away from it all. But you don't relish sleeping on the rocky ground, cooking over an open fire, and washing up in icy water. You're ready for RVing.

In this part, we give you several reasons for hitting the open road in an RV — just in case you're not yet convinced. Then we get down to basics, discussing where to go and when, what types of RVs are out there, and how to choose the best one for you, how to plan ahead for renting or buying an RV, and how to budget your expenses.

Chapter 1

Discovering the Best of RVing

*W*hen we first discovered RVing, we couldn't believe how perfectly the experience fit our lifestyle, how comfortable and convenient it is, and how liberating it makes travel. After less than two weeks on the road, we began plotting ways to buy and keep the motorhome we'd rented. (To be honest, we also didn't look forward to unpacking when we got home.)

To help us with our first RV experience, we looked for a book like this. Because we couldn't find one, we wrote this book for you.

Being Your Own Boss

Freedom! If you want to sum up RV travel in one word, that's it. You're freed from fighting the battle of airports, from arriving at hotels only to find that your reservation was lost or your room isn't ready, and from waiting an hour past your reservation time at a restaurant or tipping the host to get a better table. In your RV, you're the boss. You go where you want to go, when you want to go, and at whatever pace you please. That's *FREEDOM!*

Discovering Something for Everyone

The 14 drives described in this book offer something for everyone, whether you're a couple, single, retiree, honeymooner, graduate student, or teacher on sabbatical. Each drive is outlined for a comfortable 7- to 14-day vacation, but within each is a shorter, weekend version that gives you the essence of the experience in a short, affordable getaway.

For families with children, the drives include a wealth of show-and-tell and how-I-spent-my-summer-vacation material, from discovering how baseball was invented at the **National Baseball Hall of Fame** in Cooperstown, New York (Chapter 12), and seeing curious rock formations underground at **Carlsbad Caverns National Park** in Carlsbad, New Mexico (Chapter 21), to finding out why President William McKinley always wore a red carnation at the **McKinley Museum** in Canton, Ohio (Chapter 17). Kids remember the McKinley story because they hear it from the animatronic version of the man himself. Families who want to explore beyond the drives in this book, can seek out factory tours showing kids such wonders as how **Crayola crayons** and **Jelly Belly jellybeans** are made (Chapter 26).

Hikers and bikers can pinpoint state or national parks with great walking and bicycle trails. The **Oregon Dunes National Recreation Area** (Chapter 22) is just one of the many parks in that state with hiking trails that skirt the coast. Cyclists can take advantage of 45 miles of carriage roads in Maine's **Acadia National Park** (Chapter 11) or wooded roads regularly closed to traffic in **Great Smoky Mountains National Park** (Chapter 13) on the Tennessee–North Carolina border. Best of all, after a day of breaking a sweat, you can return to a comfortable RV bed instead of an air mattress on the ground.

Do you want to settle into the driver's seat and just cruise? We have the roads for you. Scenic highways such as the **Blue Ridge Parkway** and **Skyline Drive** (Chapter 13), **Natchez Trace** (Chapter 15), and California's **Pacific Coast Highway** (Chapter 23) were built for slow, easy driving and frequent stops to admire the view or set out a picnic. For a slice of Americana, drive what remains of old **Route 66** between Oklahoma and California (Chapter 24).

For more of what makes America unique, look no farther than the country's colorful icons. New Mexico brings Billy the Kid to life again along the **Billy the Kid National Scenic Byway** (Chapter 21), while **Buffalo Bill Center** in Cody, Wyoming, celebrates yet another figure from the American West (Chapter 20). From folklore and the imagination come Minnesota's **Paul Bunyan** (Chapter 18), who pops up in living color by the side of the road in Bemidji and Akeley.

For delicious tastes of America, sample fresh-from-the-sea **Maine lobster** with melted butter (Chapter 11), **Texas barbecued brisket** smoky from the grill (Chapter 16), **Santa Maria barbecue** along California's Central Coast (Chapter 23), succulent **shrimp and oysters** around the Gulf Coast (Chapter 14), **Virginia country ham** on a fresh-baked biscuit (Chapter 13), or **New Mexico's spicy chile** dishes (Chapter 21).

Music lovers can tap their toes to the rich sounds of America. Enjoy authentic mountain music at the **Ozark Folk Arts Center** or pop/country music productions in **Branson** (Chapter 19), hear funky blues and soul at the **Alabama Music Hall of Fame** or visit the birthplaces of **W.C.**

Handy and **Elvis Presley** (Chapter 15), and listen to rock in all its forms at Cleveland's **Rock and Roll Hall of Fame and Museum** (Chapter 17).

Good sports find great entertainment in Cooperstown's **National Baseball Hall of Fame** (Chapter 12) with its gloves, bats, and uniforms from famous players; the **Mississippi Sports Hall of Fame and Museum** (Chapter 15) where you can make like a sports announcer and tape your own play-by-play commentary; and the **United States Hockey Hall of Fame** (Chapter 18) where you can take shots at an electronic goalie.

Remembering Our First RV Journey

We encountered RVs for the first time during our years as actors in the film and television industries, where the self-contained vehicles are used as dressing rooms. At first, we didn't even realize they moved. But when we had a writing assignment that involved traveling across the United States, we rented a motorhome and discovered plenty the hard way. This section contains some excerpts from our road diary on our very first RV journey. As you can tell, our initial trip was rough, but soon we learned to master the details. Why do we share this with you? Because if we can do it, anybody can.

> **August 14:** The day before we're scheduled to leave, we lay out newspaper sections on the floor of our apartment folded to fit the measurements of the RV's cupboards. Then we set out the items that we intend to put in those places and pack them in a box labeled for that section.
>
> **August 15:** Unfortunately, life isn't that rational and orderly. On packing day, we're forced to double-park in our crowded urban neighborhood and relay boxes of books, cartons of pots and pans, and hangers of clothes back and forth from our apartment to the street. We both keep a constant watch so that nothing is stolen. We dump the gear in the RV anywhere there's space, which mostly is on the plastic-wrapped mattress and in the bathroom shower.
>
> When we set out, the soothing noise from the air conditioner drowns out many of the small crashes and thuds from the back as our possessions settle in on their own, with only an occasional loud thunk making us glance furtively backward.
>
> Exhausted, we agree that it's time to stop. Just in front of us, between the gas station and the freeway, is an RV campground. Although we can see the sign, we cannot figure out how to get to it, because a used car lot and a strip mall are in the way.
>
> At about this point, we give up the fantasy of waking to birdsong and the breeze wafting through the pine trees.

Not far away, we find a second campground and something better than birdsong — a space called a *pull-through,* which means we can drive the motorhome in one side, plug in the electrical cord, then drive out the other side the next morning without backing up — something we haven't exactly learned how to do yet.

Stunned, almost stupid with exhaustion, we microwave some soup for dinner, wash the dishes, close the blinds and curtains, and move back to the bedroom to make the bed. Clearing it is easier than we expect, because most of the gear piled on the bed already has fallen onto the floor. We raise the mattress to remove its plastic cover, and the hinged supports on the base of the bed lock into the open position, leaving the bed firmly set at a rakish 45-degree angle. By this time, we're so tired that we probably could've slept on it that way, but we get out the toolbox and unscrew the supports, so we can flatten the mattress again. Somehow we manage to simultaneously make the bed and fall asleep in it. . . .

August 20: We get lost in Kansas City looking for Arthur Bryant's barbecue restaurant, so once again darkness has fallen by the time we check into a small RV campground in the neighboring town of Independence, where a kindly campground manager with a flashlight loans us a sewage hose (because ours is too short for the hookup) and talks us step-by-step through the dumping procedure for the holding tanks, which by now have reached their capacity. The same helpful manager shows us where to push a black button that activates the TV set. Harry, I don't think we're in Kansas any more.

September 1: A great comfort can be found in riding along listening to the sounds in the motorhome behind us. We recognize the sharp clatter of the cutlery drawer suddenly swinging open, the more subdued sounds of the mug of wooden utensils spilling onto the stove top, the rolling thud of the canned food swaying back and forth in its bin, the rattle when the bedroom blinds come unhooked from their pins and randomly sway, the bump when a camera forgotten and left on a chair falls onto the floor.

After repairing the bed supports, the bed develops a mind of its own and pops up occasionally while we're in transit as if to have a look around.

September 15: We drive into Yellowstone, suddenly aware of how special it is to travel in a motorhome like this with wide scenic views through the big windows from comfortable high seats, as if looking down from a bus. Huge herds of bison shamble around in the roadway, in no hurry to move along, and our vantage point is ideal for photographing them. We stop for lunch by the Yellowstone River in a grove of trees, their leaves turned golden, and for the first time, talk about perhaps buying a motorhome of our own.

September 27: Partly because we despair of ever having to unpack, we buy the motorhome from the dealer, driving off with the feeling that we're now full-fledged RVers.

Uncovering the Myths about RVing

Because we enjoy RVing so much, we shudder upon hearing the frequent misuse of terms, the leaping to conclusions, and frequent clichés from the uninformed, some of whom are TV newscasters. In the following list, we set the record straight.

- ✔ The cliché of the **RV lifestyle** turns off many likely candidates of RV travel. Some believe that after you join the ranks of RV vacationers, you sit around a campfire in groups swapping yarns or head off with a caravan of other RVs to some scenic area. Not that anything is wrong with that, but if you're like us, you take RV vacations to spend time alone with each other.

  We've discovered that as many RV lifestyles exist as RVers. You can match your own lifestyle to the type of RV you select, your choice of destination, and the pace of your journey.

- ✔ A **mobile home** is not an RV. Mobile homes are manufactured housing (they used to be called house trailers), which are towed by large trucks and escort vehicles from the factory or dealer to the homeowner's lot. (The lots are often part of what used to be called a trailer court.) After set in place on these lots, mobile homes rarely move again. **Motorhomes,** on the other hand, are recreation vehicles that move frequently along the highways and back roads of America. Motorhomes take their occupants on vacation to the mountains, the seashore, special events, or to visit friends and relatives in other parts of the country.

- ✔ Likewise, a **Winnebago** is only one of many brands of RVs on the market. Winnebagos are manufactured by Iowa-based Winnebago Industries. And although all Winnebagos are RVs, not all RVs are Winnebagos. The misuse of the term is similar to that of referring to all refrigerators as Frigidaires or to all vacuum cleaners as Hoovers.

- ✔ In a magazine story by a fellow travel writer, we read a reference to RVers as "wheezing geezers willing to take a short walk from motorhome to overlook." Puh-leeze, wheeze us no geezers! Recent studies show that the **average RV owner** is 49 years old, married with children, owns a home, and has a household income of around $56,000 a year. Studies predict that the average owner during the next decade will be college educated and younger than the age of 45.

- ✔ Well-meaning environmentalists like to say that unlike backpacking and tent camping, RVing pollutes the environment and guzzles gas and water resources. As graduates from the ranks of backpackers and tent campers, we count ourselves among the 98% of all RVers in a recent RVIA (Recreation Vehicle Industry Association) poll that practice one or more forms of **"green" RVing.**

In our case, our low-flow toilet and quick showers use much less water than public facilities in parks and campgrounds. All our wastewater goes into holding tanks to be properly disposed of at a sanitary dump station, rather than being poured onto the ground or into streams. We never build campfires that leave layers of pollution hanging in the atmosphere, because we can keep warm and cook food in our RVs. We don't dig up the ground, hang clotheslines from trees, or toss away paper plates and plastic utensils after every meal. We use real dishes and silverware.

Ten personalities ideal for RVing

So is RVing for you? See whether you fit any of these personality types.

Garbo Gourmets: Alone together luxuriating in the best that life can offer, these epicures carry their own wines and food, sleep in their own beds, and select their own surroundings by serendipity.

Sportsmen: Skiers, fishermen, surfers, golfers, and mountain bikers get into the heart of the action with all the comforts of home.

Weekenders: The stressed-out get out of the rat race and into the countryside to delete the pressures of the workweek from their hard drives.

Families on Vacation: Offsetting the pricey amusement park, these families think of their motorhome as their own budget hotel and round-the-clock, self-serve restaurant. For the kids, RVing means no more "Are we there yet?," "I have to go potty!," or "I'm hungry!" Everything is here.

Eco-Tourists: Getting back to nature the easy way, eco-tourists bird-watch at dawn and spot wildlife during twilight. Photography and hiking lay fewer burdens on Mother Earth than heavy hotel and resort infrastructures.

The Ultimate Shoppers: Hitting all the antiques shops, estate sales, and the world's biggest swap meets, shoppers enjoy comfort and style with room to take home all the treasures easily in the RV.

Pet-Lovers: Taking Fifi and Fido along for the ride and enjoying their company, animal lovers avoid facing rebellious and destructive pets after a spell of boarding them in a kennel.

Disabled Travelers: A customized RV can open up the world with familiar and accessible surroundings.

Special-Events Attendees: Tailgating for a football game, hitting a jazz festival or an arts festival on the spur of the moment, RVing fans sidestep overbooked hotels and restaurants and invite friends in for a meal.

Relatives: Visiting family and friends, RVers can take along their own bed and bathroom. When parked at home, RVs provide an extra guest room with bath.

Chapter 2

Choosing the Itinerary and Season for You

In This Chapter

▶ Matching the drives to the seasons

▶ Discovering what each drive has to offer

▶ Finding out who should go where — and who shouldn't

T he 14 RV vacation drives that we present for you in this book explore different regions of the contiguous United States with its diverse four-season weather, so certain drives are best during certain seasons. In this chapter, we suggest the best season for each drive and how much time to schedule. We also let you know when traffic is light or heavy and discuss rewards and drawbacks of each itinerary for certain types of travelers.

Revealing the Secrets of the Seasons

Summer is the most popular vacation time for families because the kids are out of school. But for RVers looking for more solitude and milder weather, **spring** and **fall** may be preferable. In the southernmost parts of the United States, **winter** is best for its mild, sunny weather, but in resort areas, prices can climb with popularity, peaking between Christmastime and the weekend of President's Day.

In RV parlance, retirees from northern regions fleeing winter weather are known as **snowbirds,** and they're warmly welcomed in the south, particularly southern Texas along the Rio Grande, along the Gulf of Mexico from Florida to Louisiana, in southern Arizona and New Mexico, and in the California deserts. Snowbirds usually flee the Northeast, Midwest, or Northwest when the first cold weather hits, spend the winter months in the sun, and then head back north in spring.

Summer is prime time almost everywhere in the North, but it's too hot for optimum comfort in the snowbird winter retreats of the South.

Off-season means smaller crowds and lower prices, but it also can mean that some campgrounds, restaurants, and shops are closed. In each driving chapter, we list opening and closing dates for seasonal campgrounds and attractions, so pay close attention if your trip is scheduled during transitional months, such as April or October.

Traffic almost always is heavy on the interstate highways. On the first and last days of a holiday weekend, the highways, and even some back roads, are more crowded than usual. Smart RVers often opt to stay over an extra night at the campground to avoid the rush and drive home after most people already have returned to work.

Scoping Out Your Perfect RV Vacation

We had enough trouble narrowing down our favorite RV drives to the 14 in this book to know that you'll have trouble choosing among them. The following sections offer a rundown of each drive, including what you can see, the best times to go, who should go, who shouldn't go, and how much time to allow. In the "Getting There" sections of each drive, we suggest a starting point, and distance references begin there; however, you can jump in at any point along the drive and do what you please.

Obviously, some geographic areas we describe are closer to you than others. So if you plan to rent an RV for your vacation, take note that you don't have to rent one close to home. With nationwide rental companies (see the Appendix), you can fly to another part of the country and rent your RV there.

Regardless of your starting point, consider planning a route that enables you to visit friends or relatives en route along your drive. They'll be glad to see you, because you're carrying your own bedroom and bathroom.

The Coast of Maine: Lobster Land

This drive follows Maine's rocky coastline along local roads and state highways, which sometimes are narrow and winding. Campgrounds are scenic and tree-shaded; the sites at many are small and narrow. Overall, you find high to moderate prices for goods and services.

- ✓ **Best time to go:** Summer and early fall.
- ✓ **Who should go:** Couples, families, retirees, lobster lovers, antiques shoppers, scenery buffs, and people who can plan ahead to reserve campgrounds for July and August.
- ✓ **Who should not go:** Anyone who gets nervous backing into narrow, tree-lined campsites.

✔ **How far/how long:** Although the drive is only 225 miles, you need ten days to really relax and enjoy it.

✔ **Scenery:** Coastal views with rocks, crashing waves, lighthouses, lobster pots, and fishing boats.

✔ **Sightseeing:** Art museums, Acadia National Park, and trolley and transportation museums.

✔ **Food:** Fresh lobster, clams, chowder, and blueberry muffins.

✔ **Shopping:** Freeport factory outlets, teddy bear workshops, whirligig lawn ornaments, and antiques.

✔ **Offbeat:** The Moxie soft drink bottling company and museum in New Lisbon.

Western New York: Cooperstown to Niagara Falls

Highlights include the crashing, roaring waters of Niagara Falls and surprisingly scenic rolling green hills dotted with vineyards around the Finger Lakes. You encounter much history and several hands-on museums, plenty of good campgrounds, and high to moderate prices for goods and services.

✔ **Best time to go:** Anytime it isn't snowing. Late spring and early autumn are less crowded than summer.

✔ **Who should go:** Baseball fans, *I Love Lucy* nuts, feminists, honeymooners, photographers, player piano owners, couples, families, and those who know what a kazoo is.

✔ **Who should not go:** Anyone who doesn't like Buffalo wings, hot dogs, and roast beef sandwiches.

✔ **How far/how long:** The drive is 725 miles; allow a week or more.

✔ **Scenery:** Niagara Falls, the Finger Lakes, the Erie Canal.

✔ **Sightseeing:** The National Baseball Hall of Fame, a carrousel factory, the Corning Glass Museum, the George Eastman House and International Museum of Photography, the Mark Twain study, the National Women's Hall of Fame, and Women's Rights National Historic Park.

✔ **Food:** Buffalo wings, beef on weck (a German caraway seed bun encrusted with coarse salt) sandwiches, grape pie, fresh cheese curds, Italian breads and biscotti, Ted's red hots, and Nick Tanou's garbage plate.

✔ **Shopping:** Glassware at Corning and Steuben, New York State cheese, and American antiques.

✔ **Offbeat:** The Jell-O Gallery museum in LeRoy.

Blue Ridge Mountains: Skyline Drive and Blue Ridge Parkway

This leisurely, classic drive — avoiding commercial traffic, billboards, fast-food chains, and gas stations — offers frequent opportunities to pull off the highway for short nature walks and many chances to leave the parkway for small towns with gas stations and cafes. Parkway campgrounds don't provide hookups and sometimes take no advance reservations. Prices are moderate to low-moderate.

- **Best time to go:** Spring, summer, and fall, with spring the least crowded. The roads usually are open in winter but the season's heavy fogs and sometimes icy roadways can be dangerous.

- **Who should go:** Nature and scenery lovers, collectors of American crafts, Civil War buffs, lovers of home cooking, families, couples, and retirees.

- **Who should not go:** Anyone too impatient to stay within the parkway speed limit, which is 45 mph.

- **How far/how long:** The route covers 643 miles; allow one to two weeks to have plenty of time for camping and hiking.

- **Scenery:** Rolling hills and wooded hillsides, great shows of bloom, especially dogwood, rhododendron, and mountain laurel in springtime and autumn leaves in fall.

- **Sightseeing:** Great Smoky Mountains National Park, Shenandoah National Park, Manassas, Dollywood amusement park, and the Museum of American Frontier Culture.

- **Food:** Southern-style home cooking with country ham, fried chicken, hot biscuits, and a big selection of cooked vegetables, homemade relishes, pound cake, banana pudding, buttermilk pie, chess pie, and rich layer cakes.

- **Shopping:** American crafts, especially handmade quilts, wood furniture and wooden toys for children, pottery, and rag rugs.

- **Offbeat:** Snappy Lunch in Mount Airy, North Carolina, where TV's Andy Griffith ate in real life and in TV's *Mayberry RFD*.

The Gulf Coast: Tallahassee to New Orleans

You can stroll along the coast's white sand beaches, fine and soft as powdered sugar. Scarlett O'Hara would feel right at home among the region's antebellum mansions. Other highlights include an abundance of fresh seafood at bargain prices, Vegas-style casinos, and plenty of campgrounds, and good takeout food. Prices are low-moderate to low.

✔ **Best time to go:** Early spring when the azaleas and camellias are blooming. Although the area is enjoyable year-round, summer temperatures can get hot.

✔ **Who should go:** Anyone who's never had enough shrimp to eat, beach lovers, history buffs, garden growers, families, couples, students, retirees, and snowbirds.

✔ **Who should not go:** Anyone who thinks Florida is famous only as a home of Mickey Mouse.

✔ **How far/how long:** The drive is 610 miles; allow three to seven days. This itinerary connects easily to the Natchez Trace drive in Chapter 15, if you have more time.

✔ **Scenery:** Seacoast with rolling surf and gleaming white sand beaches, antebellum homes and gardens, and trees festooned with Spanish moss.

✔ **Sightseeing:** Bellingrath Gardens, Gulf Islands National Seashore, Pensacola's Blue Angels, and Battleship USS *Alabama*.

✔ **Food:** Shrimp, shrimp, shrimp, fried, boiled, in the shell or out; fresh Apalachicola oysters; fresh crabmeat in crab cakes and salads; po' boy sandwiches; fried chicken; boiled peanuts; gumbo; smoked mullet; grouper burgers; and pecan pie.

✔ **Shopping:** Superfresh seafood from Joe Patti's in Pensacola or handmade farm cheeses from Alabama's Sweet Home Farm.

✔ **Offbeat:** Film locations for *Tarzan* and *Creature from the Black Lagoon* in Wakulla Springs State Park.

The Natchez Trace: Natchez, MS, to Nashville, TN

Closed to commercial traffic, the Natchez Trace offers easy driving on good roads. You find plenty of campgrounds (but not all have hookups) and restaurants serving huge portions of food. Prices are low-moderate to low.

✔ **Best time to go:** Early spring when weather is mild and showy azaleas are in bloom and antebellum homes are open to visitors. The Natchez Trace can be traveled any time of year, but winter can be rainy and sometimes chilly, and summers are hot.

✔ **Who should go:** Southern-cooking aficionados, Civil War buffs, Elvis and Oprah fans, antiques collectors, country music buffs, couples, families, and retirees.

✔ **Who should not go:** Hotshots who won't honor the 50-mph speed limit along the Natchez Trace.

✔ **How far/how long:** 500 miles; allow three to seven days.

✔ **Scenery:** Meadows and gentle, wooded hillsides, Tupelo swamps with trees knee-deep in water, and small towns where time has stopped.

✔ **Sightseeing:** Alabama Music Hall of Fame, Elvis and Oprah birthplaces, Mississippi Sports Hall of Fame, and Vicksburg National Military Park.

✔ **Food:** Country ham, grits and gravy, fried dill pickles, fried catfish with hush puppies, candied yams, white beans with ham, plenty of iced tea, and blackberry cobbler.

✔ **Shopping:** Crafts created by local Choctaw and Chickasaw weavers, including baskets, quiltwork handbags, and pottery.

✔ **Offbeat:** Key Underwood Coon Dog National Memorial Park, the world's only cemetery for raccoon-hunting hound dogs.

Texas Hill Country: Bluebonnets and Barbecue

A big state with decent roads and friendly people, Texas is very RV-friendly and offers good campgrounds with hookups in the state parks and uncrowded driving outside major cities. Prices are moderate to low-moderate for goods and services.

✔ **Best time to go:** When the wildflowers bloom in spring, usually between the end of March and mid-May, but comfortable year-round.

✔ **Who should go:** Couples, families, retirees, barbecue nuts, wildflower aficionados, and country music fans.

✔ **Who should not go:** Anyone who can't sing along to "Luckenbach, Texas."

✔ **How far and how long:** Allow at least a week for the 400 miles, round trip from San Antonio.

✔ **Scenery:** Hills covered with wildflowers, rocky canyons, colorful German villages, and San Antonio's River Walk.

✔ **Sightseeing:** Wildflowers, LBJ country, San Antonio, and the Alamo.

✔ **Food:** Texas barbecue, mostly beef with sizzling hot sausages; Tex-Mex; German food; country-fried steak; fried chicken; fresh peaches; and Blue Bell ice cream.

✔ **Shopping:** Cowboy boots, Texas wine, amd German beer mugs.

✔ **Offbeat:** Bats under the Congress Avenue Bridge in Austin.

The Heart of Ohio: A Circle Around Circleville

On this drive, you can spend time in Ohio's rural areas and small towns and stop in cities only to visit the must-sees, such as Cleveland's Rock and Roll Hall of Fame and Museum, Cincinnati's Museum Center, and Dayton's United States Air Force Museum. Plenty of campgrounds line the route. Prices are high-moderate to moderate.

- ✔ **Best time to go:** Summer is the best time to see Ohio, but spring and fall are less crowded.

- ✔ **Who should go:** Hikers, bicyclists, rock fans, families, couples, retirees, and fans of things presidential. Ohio is home to eight presidents — Ulysses S. Grant may be the most famous.

- ✔ **Who should not go:** Anyone who can't name one of the seven others — McKinley, Harding, Hayes, Harrison, Harrison (there were two of them, William and Benjamin), Garfield, and Taft.

- ✔ **How far/how long:** 1,000 miles, a week to ten days.

- ✔ **Scenery:** American Midwestern farmland, at its most scenic in the Amish country; Native American earthworks, such as the Serpent Mound; and the meandering Ohio River.

- ✔ **Sightseeing:** Historic villages staffed with costumed interpreters, the National Road Museum, the Portsmouth Floodwall Murals, the Hoover Historical Center vacuum cleaner museum, the James Thurber home and museum.

- ✔ **Food:** Amish all-you-can-eat spreads that offer chicken, ham, and roast beef as the main course; homemade breads and pies; Cincinnati chili; homemade noodles; sauerkraut; popcorn; and cracker pudding.

- ✔ **Shopping:** Baskets, handcrafted Amish furniture, quilts, Amish cheeses, hand-dipped chocolates, and nonelectrical appliances, such as wringer washing machines and hand-cranked coffee mills.

- ✔ **Offbeat:** The world's largest cuckoo clock at Alpine Alpa in Wilmot.

Northern Minnesota: Paul Bunyan Country

The North Woods lake country, with vast stretches of woods and water, offers fishing, hiking, and canoeing, and plenty of campgrounds. Prices are moderate.

- ✔ **Best time to go:** Summer offers the warmest weather, but late spring and early autumn also are good times. Only the hardy need visit in winter.

- ✔ **Who should go:** Fishermen and other outdoor enthusiasts, shoppers (the area sports the nation's biggest mall), families with kids who want to pose with Paul Bunyan, retirees looking for inexpensive summer escapes, and fans of Judy Garland and Bob Dylan.

- ✔ **Who should not go:** Anyone who can't tolerate mosquitoes, which are at their worst in the northern lakes in late spring and early summer. (Mosquito-phobes can wear *bug hats* — pith helmets with veils of mosquito netting.)

- ✔ **How far/how long:** 357 miles for the basic tour to Fargo, 514 if you start at the Mall of America instead of Duluth; allow a week.

- ✔ **Scenery:** Evergreens, hardwood trees, lakes, uncrowded roads, shore of Lake Superior, and Mesabi Iron Range.

- ✔ **Sightseeing:** Headwaters of the Mississippi River, Great Lakes Aquarium, Ironworld Discovery Center, Judy Garland Museum, the Greyhound Bus Origin Center museum, the International Wolf Center, and the United States Hockey Hall of Fame.

- ✔ **Food:** Bratwursts and sausages of all sorts, Cornish pastries, stuffed cabbage, pickle on a stick, wild rice, fresh walleye pike, fresh-picked blueberries and raspberries in season, *potica* (walnut-filled pastry roll), and Widman's *Chippers* (chocolate-covered potato chips).

- ✔ **Shopping:** The Mall of America in Bloomington, the largest shopping mall in North America.

- ✔ **Offbeat:** The giant Paul Bunyan statue in Akeley, with his hand lowered so people can sit in it for photos.

The Ozarks and Branson: Hot Springs to Springfield

You can drive miles through the rugged, tree-clad Ozarks between towns or farms. Roads are sometimes winding and narrow, but the scenery is lovely and so are the mountain crafts for sale. The musical capital of Branson, Missouri, is the second most popular tourist destination in the United States (after Orlando). Campgrounds are everywhere and state parks usually offer hookups. Prices are low-moderate to low, with goods and services cheaper in the Ozarks than in Branson itself.

- ✔ **Best time to go:** Spring when dogwoods are in bloom or fall when the leaves begin to change. Summer can be hot and crowded.

- ✔ **Who should go:** Fans of country music and American crafts, born-again Christians, New Age music buffs, retirees, families, couples, canoers and river rafters, spa devotees, collectibles lovers, and Victorian architecture aficionados.

✔ **Who should not go:** Anyone who hates country music, fried catfish, and fried chicken.

✔ **How far/how long:** 700 miles, allow one to two weeks, round trip from Hot Springs.

✔ **Scenery:** Ruggedly beautiful in the mountains with pretty, small towns, such as Eureka Springs.

✔ **Sightseeing:** Branson's 35 or so live music theaters, Eureka Springs' Victorian houses and antiques shops, Bass Outdoor World, Hot Springs National Park, Buffalo National River Park, and Ozarks Folk Arts Center.

✔ **Food:** Smoked meats and country ham, fried chicken, fried catfish and hush puppies, barbecue, and fried apple pies.

✔ **Shopping:** Antiques, country ham, and silly hillbilly souvenirs.

✔ **Offbeat:** Lambert's, "the home of the throwed roll," where servers toss hot homemade rolls to your table.

Montana and Wyoming: Tracking Buffalo Bill

Some of the most spectacular mountain scenery in the world lines this drive through regions where cattle outnumber people three to one. You find a world-class museum dedicated to Buffalo Bill and uncrowded campgrounds with wide-open spaces (except at Yellowstone). Prices are moderate to low-moderate.

✔ **Best time to go:** Early fall from Labor Day to early October, but late spring and summer also are pleasant.

✔ **Who should go:** Lovers of the outdoors, cowboy fans, Western history buffs, families, couples, and retirees looking for a summer hideaway.

✔ **Who should not go:** Anyone who hates traffic jams should avoid Yellowstone in summer. (We suggest an alternate route to avoid the park at that time.)

✔ **How far/how long:** 772 miles, allow two weeks.

✔ **Scenery:** *National Geographic* comes to life with mountain vistas you won't believe; Yellowstone's geysers, waterfalls, and wildlife.

✔ **Sightseeing:** Yellowstone National Park, the Beartooth Highway, the Chief Joseph Highway, the Little Bighorn Battlefield National Monument, and the Grizzly Discovery Center.

✔ **Food:** Rainbow trout, burgers and steaks from beef and buffalo, homemade pies and rolls and gargantuan cinnamon buns, and meatloaf and Mexican dishes.

✔ **Shopping:** Museum shops, such as the one in the Buffalo Bill Center, stock outstanding Western craft items; antiques; Western clothing and artifacts.

✔ **Offbeat:** Betting on the pig race at Bear Creek Downs near Red Lodge, Montana.

New Mexico: Billy the Kid Meets E.T.

Old West scenery of red rock canyons, mesas, buttes, rocks, and deserts fills your windshield in New Mexico. Uncrowded highways and scenic campgrounds are common. Prices are low-moderate to low.

✔ **Best time to go:** Spring and fall, but any time of year is acceptable, including winter. Summers can be hot in desert areas.

✔ **Who should go:** Alien trackers looking for a close encounter, history buffs interested in Native American culture, turquoise jewelry collectors, pottery collectors, chile-heads, families, couples, retirees, and snowbirds.

✔ **Who should not go:** Urbanites who get spooked when surrounded by plenty of empty space.

✔ **How far/how long:** 943 miles, allow two weeks.

✔ **Scenery:** Red rock canyons and sagebrush, misty blue hills and snow-capped peaks in the distance, and glistening white sand dunes and desert.

✔ **Sightseeing:** Carlsbad Caverns National Park, International Space Center in Alamogordo, International UFO Museum and Research Center in Roswell, and White Sands National Monument.

✔ **Food:** New Mexico cuisine blending the foods of Mexico and Pueblo Indians (try fried breads turned into Indian tacos or sopapillas filled with honey); anything with chiles, particularly soupy red and green chile stews; chicken-fried steak; and home-made tortillas.

✔ **Shopping:** Cowboy boots, silver and turquoise jewelry, Pueblo pottery, hand-woven rugs.

✔ **Offbeat:** Meeting (and buying) E.T. replicas at Roswell's UFO Museum.

The Oregon Coast: California to Washington

This stretch of coast offers beachcombing on uncrowded beaches with twisted driftwood, rocks, and surf. Although crowded on summer weekends, a generally good highway passes through the middle of most of the beach towns. You find wonderful local wines, cheeses, and seafood, and scenic state parks with hookups in this RV-friendly region. Prices for goods and services are high-moderate to moderate.

- ✔ **Best time to go:** Summer has the best weather and the least rain, but you can drive the coast year-round.

- ✔ **Who should go:** Laid-back people who like casual clothes, boutique breweries, beachcombing, hiking, and biking; kite-flyers; sandcastle builders; families with children; romantic couples; and retirees looking for a quiet hideaway.

- ✔ **Who should not go:** The uptight, the dressed up, or the fussy and demanding.

- ✔ **How far/how long:** 365 miles plus an optional add-on peninsula in Washington state; allow a week.

- ✔ **Scenery:** High sculpted sand dunes; rocky beaches with heavy surf and driftwood; and friendly, sometimes funky, little beach towns and fishing villages.

- ✔ **Sightseeing:** Sea Lion Caves, Oregon Coast Aquarium, Oregon Dunes National Recreation Area, Tillamook Cheese Factory, Columbia River Maritime Museum, and the Lewis and Clark winter quarters.

- ✔ **Food:** Fresh seafood, dig-your-own clams, Tillamook cheddar, Bandon cheddar, Blue Heron Brie, smoked fish, local cranberries, Umpqua Dairy ice cream, clam chowder, and fried oysters.

- ✔ **Shopping:** Cheeses, myrtlewood salad bowls, and smoked salmon.

- ✔ **Offbeat:** The snake-headed, insect-devouring carnivorous plants at Darlingtonia State Botanical Wayside.

California Central Coast: Malibu to Monterey

Along the Pacific Coast Highway, you can listen to the distant barking of sea lions above the ocean's roar and drive along cliffs overlooking the rocks far below. You find frequent scenic turnouts and good roads, except when rockslides or mudslides block the highway during storms. Campgrounds are frequent but also heavily occupied throughout the year. Prices are high-moderate to moderate.

- ✔ **Best time to go:** Anytime, but expect some coastal fog in summer and winds and occasional storms in winter. We prefer February and March, September and October.

- ✔ **Who should go:** People who can make campground reservations in advance; spur-of-the-moment RVers who can make do with what's left; and families, retirees, and romantic couples.

✔ **Who should not go:** White-knuckled drivers. If you do go, follow our suggested south-to-north route, which puts you and your RV on the cliff side of the highway rather than the ocean side.

✔ **How far/how long:** 340 miles; allow three or four days to see all the attractions.

✔ **Scenery:** Dizzying overlooks above the pounding surf, treeless green hillsides and meadows that turn golden in summer, and elegant arched bridges spanning chasms.

✔ **Sightseeing:** The Big Sur coast, trees and bushes covered with monarch butterflies, old Spanish missions, the Getty Museum, the Hearst Castle at San Simeon, a splendid museum for John Steinbeck, and Monterey Bay Aquarium.

✔ **Food:** Cal-Mex cooking; real hamburgers; Santa Maria tri-tip roast beef with pinquito beans; the world's most famous taco stand, endorsed by Julia Child; Danish pastries in Solvang; and split-pea soup in Buellton.

✔ **Shopping:** Danish souvenirs in Solvang; out-of-date maps to movie star homes in Malibu; wineries around Santa Barbara, and antiques and collectibles in Cambria and Cayucos.

✔ **Offbeat:** Pieces of the 1920s movie set for Cecil B. DeMille's original version of *The Ten Commandments* (he remade the movie in the 1950s) buried under the sand dunes at Nipomo.

Route 66: OK to LA

You can visit what's left of old Route 66, long ago replaced by I-40, but popular again with back-road explorers. Bonus discoveries include Burma-Shave signs, the wild burros of Oatman, and the corn dog inventor. Road conditions vary widely so ask locally about present passability. Plenty of campgrounds and fast-food outlets line I-40. The prices are moderate.

✔ **Best time to go:** Spring and fall. Summer is hot in some areas. Winter brings the possibility of snow around Flagstaff.

✔ **Who should go:** Baby Boomers who remember family road trips in the 1950s and 1960s; anyone who remembers the lyrics of the song.

✔ **Who should not go:** Anyone who's going to complain about potholes instead of admiring faded billboards and defunct gas stations.

✔ **How far/how long:** 1,435 miles, allow at least seven days.

✔ **Scenery:** Extremely varied, with grassy prairies and ranch country around Tulsa, the windswept Texas panhandle, the rose-colored desert of New Mexico, the sun and golden sand of California's Mojave beginning in Arizona, the highs of San

Bernardino Mountains, the lows of San Gabriel Valley, the sprawl of Los Angeles, and the rolling surf of the Pacific Ocean at Santa Monica.

✔ **Sightseeing:** Grand Canyon National Park, Acoma Pueblo, National Cowboy Hall of Fame, Calico ghost town, Will Rogers Memorial Museum, Petrified Forest and Painted Desert, Oklahoma Route 66 Museum, Cadillac Ranch, and the Roy Rogers/Dale Evans Museum.

✔ **Food:** Onion-fried hamburgers, buffalo burgers, hillbilly chicken, sourdough biscuits, chicken-fried steak, corn dogs, and beef jerky.

✔ **Shopping:** Minnetonka moccasins at roadside trading posts, and truly tacky souvenirs at Barstow Station.

✔ **Offbeat:** Exotic World, the Burlesque Hall of Fame, in California's high desert country.

Chapter 3

Selecting Your RV

. . . .

In This Chapter

▶ Getting the lowdown on different types of RVs

▶ Deciding which type is best for you

▶ Calculating costs for each type of RV

. . . .

*H*ow you like to travel, where you want to go, and how many other travelers accompany you must be considered when selecting an RV. Carefully consider the pros and cons of each type before going out to look at options to rent or buy.

For definitions of the RV lingo used in this chapter, check out the Appendix. For information on renting and buying, see Chapter 4.

Getting to Know the RV Types

Based on locomotion, RVs break down into two basic types — **towable vehicles** and **motorized vehicles.**

Towable vehicles, such as **folding camping trailers, travel trailers,** and **fifth-wheel travel trailers,** are living units that can stand alone in camp but must be hitched up to motor vehicles to travel. **Truck campers,** which are compact living units designed to fit atop the bed and cab of a pickup truck, also are part of the towable team.

Motorized vehicles are the ones that travel under their own power rather than depending on a separate motorized unit for locomotion. Motorized RVs include **motorhomes** (sometimes called Type-A RVs) and **van campers** (sometimes called Type-B RVs), both of which are self-contained units built on a truck or van chassis with living, sleeping, cooking, and bathroom facilities accessible from the driver's area without leaving the vehicle. The cabover bed or storage unit that overlaps the cab of the truck distinguishes the **mini-motorhomes,** also called Type-C RVs. The dividing line between mini-motorhome and camper van is becoming more and more blurred as more van-style compact units fitted with all the necessities for self-contained camping appear on the market.

Along with our definitions of each RV type in this chapter, we also give you the average vacation cost for a family of four for 2, 7, and 14 nights of travel. By comparison, a family of four, traveling in their personal car, staying at motels or hotels, and eating most of their meals in restaurants, spends an average of $360 for 2 nights, $1,360 for 7 nights, and $2,500 for 14 nights. The cost of an RV vacation is often more than 50% less.

Folding camping trailers

In most cases, the family car can pull these neat little units; a sport utility vehicle or station wagon certainly can do the job. Affordable, open, and airy, these lightweight RVs are the closest thing to tent camping. (See Figure 3-1.) They fit into a carport or garage and are easy to hook up, tow, and store. From a compact trailer, the RV unfolds upward to standing-room height with side walls that slide out to form two screened, covered wings, each containing a double bed area.

Figure 3-1: Folding camping trailer.

The center section has a solid floor that supports cooking, dining, and lounging areas. Some convert to provide even more sleeping space on a sofa or dinette and optional toilet and shower facilities. Some models are equipped with heating and air-conditioning options, and most have a gas stove that can be used inside the unit or plugged into outside connections.

Unit cost

Generally, the least expensive of the RVs, folding camping trailers are priced from **$3,600 to $18,000,** and may sleep as many as eight. The average price is about **$5,483.** Although early folding camping trailers had canvas and/or screen sides, newer models also offer the option of vinyl or even hard siding of lightweight aluminum.

Budget-minded young families with small children, tent campers who seek a bit more luxury without giving up the canvas-and-campfire ambience, and even veteran RVers seeking a simpler travel lifestyle enjoy these vehicles.

Vacation costs

In a study commissioned by the Go Camping America Committee, the average, national vacation costs for a family of four traveling in their personal automobile, towing a folding camping trailer, staying at campgrounds, and preparing the majority of their meals in the RV, came to $149 for 2 nights, $483 for 7 nights, and $889 for 14 nights.

Pros and cons

Folding camper trailers have the following advantages:

- ✔ **Easy to tow, good gas mileage, and lower wind resistance.** Goes anywhere the family car can go, and it stays behind in camp while the family explores by car.

- ✔ **Lavish living for the cost.** These trailers may contain many options found in more expensive RVs — air-conditioning, heating, toilet facilities, three-way refrigerators, awnings, and even roof racks to carry boats or bicycles atop the folded unit.

- ✔ **Easy to store.** Garage or carport can handle the storage; folded, these units measure from 5 to 19 feet long and usually are less than 60 inches high.

But keep these negatives in mind:

- ✔ **Not always convenient.** Most use a hand-crank system for raising and lowering, which is simple when the weather is nice but tricky in the rain when you're trying to keep wing mattresses dry.

- ✔ **Limited on-road access.** The unit is not usable when you're underway unless you crank it open at rest stops. Some models have front storage units that you can access when the unit is folded, but kitchen and toilet facilities are available only when the rig is fully set up.

- ✔ **May mildew when wet.** If a canvas unit is closed when wet, it must be unfolded at home and dried out completely before it is stored; otherwise, it can mildew. Vinyl units can simply be wiped dry.

- ✔ **Limited toilet facilities.** Some models contain neither toilet nor shower facilities, nor do they offer them only as an option. Most contain a storage area for a portable toilet that has to be removed and emptied manually — you have to camp in areas that have public toilets and showers.

Truck campers

If you already own a pickup truck, the easiest and least expensive RV may be a truck camper (see Figure 3-2), a unit that slides onto the bed of a pickup, sometimes overhanging the cab or the rear of the vehicle.

Most models sleep two to six people. Because the unit slides on and off, the truck continues to be useful as a hauling and transportation vehicle without the camper.

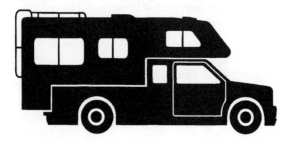

Figure 3-2: Truck camper.

Sportsmen like the rugged outdoorsy capability of truck campers, because they can remove the camper and set it up in camp, and then use the truck to go to and from ski areas, fishing holes, or trailheads. You can also tow a boat, snowmobile, or horse trailer behind a truck camper — something not permitted with other towables.

Low-profile pop-up models are available, as are units that have optional electrical systems to load and unload the camper from the truck bed.

Units range from 7 to 18 feet in length with a cabover bed extending over the pickup's cab. Truck campers usually are equipped with a small bathroom and kitchen unit. Sofa or dinette built-ins may convert to form a second sleeping area, but the beds usually are fairly short. A step leads from the lower floor area up to the cabover bed.

Unit cost

Most models cost between **$3,800 and $24,000,** with the average price about **$14,490.**

Buyers of truck campers need to plan to spend extra time matching camper to pickup in categories such as weight, tow bar, and other essentials.

Vacation costs

In a cost comparison survey, a family of four traveling with a light-duty truck and truck camper, staying in campgrounds, and preparing most of their meals at campsites, spends $160 for 2 nights, $575 for 7 nights, and $989 for 14 nights.

Pros and cons

Truck campers have the following advantages:

✔ **Economical.** Cheaper to buy, maintain, and operate than most other towables, with better gas mileage.

✔ **Versatile.** The camper unit can be removed and stored at home or set in place at the campground, so the truck can be used for utility. With a self-contained camper and a four-wheel-drive truck, you can go almost anywhere.

✔ **Durable.** Most models are made to endure tougher road conditions than other towables.

✔ **Passenger convenience.** In most states (except Maine, Mississippi, New Hampshire, New Mexico, North Dakota, Pennsylvania, and Wisconsin), passengers are permitted to ride inside a truck camper. California permits passengers to ride inside only if communication is possible with the driver and if the door can be opened from both inside and outside.

But keep in mind the downside:

✔ **Floor space is limited.** Two adults can't move around freely inside the unit at the same time. However, some new models have slide-outs that expand the living area.

✔ **May be hard to handle.** Weight distribution and a higher center of gravity often mean more difficulty handling these units on the road.

Travel trailers

Vans, autos, or pickup trucks can tow these soft- or hard-sided RVs, depending on the weight of the unit (see Figure 3-3). They sleep from two to eight people, range from 10 to 40 feet long, and usually contain full bath and kitchen facilities. Models come in traditional box shape, teardrop shape, and a hard-sided telescoping unit that can be lowered for towing and storage and raised for campground living.

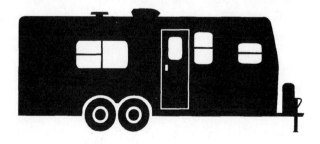

Figure 3-3: Travel trailer.

Slideouts (a portion of the vehicle that slides open when the RV is parked to expand the living area) add more walking-around room inside; today's models may offer as many as three slideouts. Campgrounds with narrow sites may prohibit RVs from using slideouts. Ask about this restriction before checking in.

Before choosing a travel trailer to be towed behind a vehicle that you already own, check that vehicle's weight limit. Remember that you'll be adding food, water, clothing, books, and sports gear — be sure your tow vehicle is capable of handling it all.

Unit cost

Prices for travel trailers range from **$9,500 to $76,000,** with an average cost of about **$15,336.**

Vacation costs

A family of four traveling in their personal car or light truck, towing a travel trailer, and staying in campgrounds, where they prepare most of their meals, spends an average of $160 for 2 nights, $850 for 7 nights, and $1,000 for 14 nights.

Pros and cons

Travel trailers offer the following pluses:

- **Easy to unhitch.** Travel trailers can be unhitched at the campsite, releasing the tow vehicle for local errands and touring.

- **Versatile.** Choose from various floor plans, furniture, colors, and cabinet finishes. Some models have two doors; some offer a forward bedroom and rear bunkhouse design to sleep the whole family without converting sofas and dinettes into beds.

- **Can be pulled by most vehicles.** Thanks to a variety of tow-package options, travel trailers can be pulled by 4-by-4s, SUVs and light trucks, full- and mid-size cars, station wagons, and minivans.

But note these disadvantages:

- **Can be hard to handle.** Handling a travel trailer, especially when backing up, takes extra skill until you get the knack.

- **Not always convenient.** Wind resistance is greater with travel trailers than with other towables, and hitching or unhitching can be a nuisance in bad weather.

- **Costs more in tolls.** Road tolls based on axles are higher for travel trailers and fifth-wheels than they are for other towables.

Fifth-wheel travel trailers

The most luxurious of the towables, fifth-wheels (Figure 3-4) are popular with full-time RVers and snowbirds because of their ease of maneuvering and towing, generous storage areas, large living spaces, and home-like design. The raised forward section that fits over the truck bed allows a split-level design and is usually allotted to bedroom space.

Figure 3-4: Fifth-wheel travel trailer.

Numerous floor-plan, decor, and furnishing options are available. Many offer up to three slideouts that further expand the living space. Fifth-wheels often include washer/dryer, bedroom TV, entertainment or computer center, or even a kitchen island. Fifth-wheels are from 22 to 40 feet long.

Unit cost

Fifth-wheels sell from **$12,000 to $102,000** and up, with an average cost of around **$28,165.**

Vacation costs

A family of four traveling in their personal car or light truck towing a travel trailer and staying in campgrounds, where they prepare most of their meals, spends an average of $160 for 2 nights, $550 for 7 nights, and $1,000 for 14 nights.

Pros and cons

Fifth-wheels offer the following advantages:

✔ **Maneuverability and towability.** Fifth-wheels are easier to handle than travel trailers because the hitch is in the bed of the truck with less vehicle trailing behind. This setup also creates a shorter turning radius.

✔ **Easy to unhitch.** Like the other towables, the fifth-wheel can be unhitched and left at the campsite, thus leaving the truck free for touring or shopping in the area.

✔ **Extra storage in your pickup.** The truck bed still can be used for storage with the addition of a pickup bed cover.

But keep in mind these negatives:

✔ **Can't carry passengers on the road.** Passengers aren't permitted to ride in the fifth-wheel in 29 states.

✔ **Limited headroom.** In many forward bedroom models, except those labeled "high profile," anyone more than six feet tall cannot stand up straight in that part of the unit.

✔ **No entry from towing vehicle.** As with all towables, you have to exit the towing vehicle and go outdoors to enter the RV, an inconvenience in bad weather.

Van campers (Type B)

Also called Type-B motorhomes (Figure 3-5), these van conversions are built within the framework of a van but with raised roofs or lowered floor sections that enable passengers to stand upright at least in the center of the vehicle. Galleys, freshwater hookups, sleeping and dining areas that convert to beds, even toilets and showers are available in these versatile vehicles.

Figure 3-5: Van camper (Type B).

Ranging from 18 to 22 feet in length, van campers sleep from two to four people by turning the sofa or dinette into a double bed and converting the two rear seats into single beds. This design can also carry four to six adults as a weekday commuter vehicle.

Unit cost

Van campers sell from **$42,000 to $73,000,** with an average cost of around **$60,116** — comparable in price to an entry-level motorhome.

Custom van conversions also are readily available from a number of manufacturers at an average price of around **$28,500.** For a complete list of manufacturers who make van conversions, contact RVIA (see Appendix).

Vacation costs

A family of four using their own van camper or van conversion, staying in campgrounds, and preparing most of their meals in camp, spends an average of $165 for 2 nights, $550 for 7 nights, and $1,025 for 14 nights.

Pros and cons

Van campers offer the following pros:

- **Multipurpose use.** These RVs double as a second car.
- **Easy to drive and park.** Van campers go anywhere a passenger car can, including places where larger RVs may be restricted, and can fit into tent and RV spots in campgrounds.
- **Good gas mileage.** Van campers usually get much better mileage than motorhomes or mini-motorhomes.
- **Cozy (the good kind).** Self-contained van campers mean you don't have to leave the vehicle to use any of the facilities.

But keep these cons in mind:

- **Cozy (the bad kind).** Although a van camper can sleep four people, they'd better be very good friends. The arrangement is best for a couple with one or two small children. The living area is very tight for a family to spend a rainy day inside.
- **Racks up extra miles.** Because the van doubles as a second car, the greater mileage accrued by selling time may make it harder to sell or trade than a larger motorhome.
- **Not easy to set up.** Making up some of the optional beds in these vans can knock your back out — even before you lie down.
- **Limited storage space.** You must carry fewer clothes and supplies and make more frequent laundry and grocery stops; the minirefrigerator inside doesn't always have a freezer compartment.

Mini-motorhomes (Type C)

Familiar, convenient, and affordable, the Type-C motorhome (Figure 3-6) packs plenty of living into a compact space. Also called mini-motorhomes, the units are built on truck or van chassis and usually range in length from 19 to 31 feet long. Slideouts, widebody designs up to 102 inches across, and diesel engine options are available. Low-profile models can be telescoped to less than eight feet high for travel and storage.

Figure 3-6: Mini-motorhome (Type C).

Normally, a cabover bed is above the driver's seat, while a sofa turns into a second bed. A dinette, kitchen, and bathroom complete the interior. Some models have an additional bedroom and an entertainment center in the cabover space.

Unit cost

Type Cs are priced from **$48,000 to $139,000** or more, with the average price around **$58,840.**

Vacation costs

A family of four traveling in their own mini-motorhome, staying in campgrounds and preparing most of their meals in camp, spends an average of $200 for 2 nights, $650 for 7 nights, and $1,100 for 14 nights.

Pros and cons

Mini-motorhomes offer the following advantages:

- ✔ **Easy to drive.** Type Cs are more maneuverable for beginning RV drivers than the longer Type-A motorhomes.

- ✔ **Comfortable and compact.** Mini-motorhomes are as livable as larger motorhomes but take up less parking and campground space.

But keep these disadvantages in mind:

- ✔ **So-so sleeping accommodations.** The cabover bed doesn't appeal to claustrophobic adults, but kids love it. Except in units that have a rear bedroom, the sleeping accommodations are less private than in the Type-A motorhome when more than two people are traveling.

- ✔ **Limited driving visibility.** Because of the overhang from the cabover bed, visibility is limited to that of a normal-size windshield. Most Type-A motorhomes, on the other hand, provide large, panoramic windshields.

> ✔ **Limited gas mileage.** Based on our experience, with the exception of lightweight models, Type-C mini-motorhomes get about the same gas mileage as a Type A of comparable length.

Motorhomes (Type A)

A self-propelled motor-vehicle chassis with a living unit built on its frame, the Type-A motorhome (Figure 3-7) offers the widest range of choices in the entire RV fleet, from small, 22-foot, fully equipped entry-level vehicles to enormous, 45-foot, buslike widebody coaches with slideouts, icemakers, washer/dryers, richly appointed furnishings, and marble bathrooms.

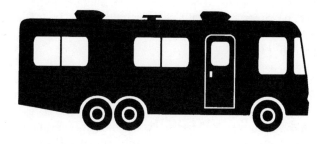

Figure 3-7: Motorhome (Type A).

Decor can vary from the old-fashioned but tough velour fabrics in slate blue or green in the lower-priced vehicles to cushy white leather furniture, brass trim, wood parquet floors, mirrored ceilings, and sculpted area rugs.

A fairly standard entry-level 28-foot model contains cockpit seats that swivel, a sofa and dinette — either of which can be made into a bed, a bath, and rear bedroom with an option of queen or twin beds.

Unit cost

Motorhomes are priced from **$57,000 all the way up to $1,400,000** for the most deluxe models, with the average around **$135,805.**

Vacation costs

A family of four traveling in their own motorhome, staying in campgrounds and preparing most of their meals in camp, spends an average of $200 for 2 nights, $680 for 7 nights, and $1,100 for 14 nights.

Pros and cons

A Type A motorhome offers the following pros:

- ✔ **Always accessible from the front seats.** In a Type A motorhome you can pull over to fix lunch, use the bathroom, or take a quick nap by the side of the road or in a parking lot without going outside.

- ✔ **Bigger windshield and windows than the Type C.** The Type A offers more visibility when traveling, more light inside, and better vantage points for photographs than the Type C.

- ✔ **Livability.** A big, open sense of space and luxury makes this the most comfortable of the motorized RVs.

- ✔ **No setup required.** In most Type A's, living and sleeping areas are set up and ready for two people. For sleeping more than two people, however, a sofa or dinette usually has to be made up.

But keep in mind these cons:

- ✔ **It's your only transportation.** Unless you're towing a car, a Type-A motorhome has to be unplugged and moved if you need to go shopping or sightseeing away from the campground.

- ✔ **Tough to maneuver.** The larger Type-A motorhomes have difficulty maneuvering in narrow city streets with heavy traffic and are tough to park almost everywhere except mall and supermarket parking lots. Height and width limitations prohibit you from entering most parking garages and can present problems in clearing low overhanging roofs and narrow tunnels or bridges.

- ✔ **Low mileage.** Gas mileage is quite low, usually less than ten miles to the gallon.

- ✔ **Sometimes too big for parks and campgrounds.** Choosing a size to match your travel style is critical in this category because larger units can't be accommodated in some rustic campgrounds and aren't permitted to enter certain roadways and campgrounds in some national parks.

Selecting the RV for You

This section helps you narrow down the choices so that you can match an RV to your lifestyle and needs.

Matching an RV to your lifestyle

When selecting an RV that's right for you, you need to consider the kind of vacation you want to take and the level of comfort you desire.

If you want a close-to-nature experience but a good mattress for your aching back, check out the **folding camping trailer.** Each of two side panels slides out to hold a large mattress, and the screen windows and canvas roof provide a feel that's closer to the outdoors.

When you're venturing down rough roads in potentially extreme weather on a hunting or fishing trip, the **truck camper** may be the right choice. This efficient hard-sided unit fits into the bed of an existing truck and can be removed and set up to stand alone at a campsite.

If you want a relatively small, easy-to-handle RV that you can store in the driveway or garage at home, consider a **camper van.** You can purchase one as a camper or as a van that has been converted to a camper. One big advantage: These RVs double as commuter vehicles.

For camping conditions that approximate home comfort, **travel trailers, fifth-wheels,** and **motorhomes** offer the optimum in comfort but also are the largest and most expensive RVs. Pricing ranges from an entry-level motorhome in the $50,000 bracket to an elegant bus-type motorhome that can cost up to $1 million.

Asking yourself ten questions

These questions get down to the basics — how many people do you need to accommodate, how much privacy do you want, what are your storage needs, and more.

1. **Do I already have part of an RV unit?**

   If you have a pickup, for example, depending on its size, you're already capable of handling a towable, such as a travel trailer, truck camper, or fifth-wheel. Most family cars can pull a small travel trailer or folding camping trailer.

2. **How many people does the RV need to accommodate on a routine trip?**

   You find a big difference between a salesman's estimate of how many people a vehicle can sleep and the reality of the number of adults and children the unit can comfortably and conveniently accommodate. Some people dislike the idea of making a bed out of a sofa or dinette night after night during a vacation. Others don't want someone climbing over them in the middle of the night to go to the bathroom.

3. **How will I be using the vehicle?**

   People who like to stay in one place, say a country club–type private campground with swimming pools and putting greens, want a more luxurious vehicle than campers who want to go out in the woods in a national park or forest, build a campfire, and cook out-doors. Travelers who want to stop at a different campground every night while touring a large region need to give priority to ease of setting up camp and fuel efficiency. Snowbirds who want to stay in one place without hookups for a long time need to look for greater capacity in water storage and holding tanks.

4. **Which is more important, generous living space in the vehicle or more flexible handling, parking, and roadway options?**

   In making a decision on vehicle size, one foot in length or four inches in width can make a tremendous difference in the long run. Spend plenty of time mentally moving around in the floor plan or even physically moving around in the vehicle at the dealer or the RV show to assess its livability. Know your size requirements before setting out to look at vehicles, especially if you're consider-ing a motorhome; you'll save a lot of time on the lot.

5. **How important is personal privacy?**

   Some types of RVs offer more solid-door privacy areas than others. In particular, the shower and toilet facilities in folding camping trailers or camping vans (when they're provided at all) may offer minimum privacy, while travel trailers, fifth-wheels, motorhomes, and some truck campers provide facilities in com-pletely closed-off areas. Sleeping facilities also may be open or shielded with curtains rather than doors, which is true of many folding camping trailers, truck campers, and even Type-C mini-motorhomes.

6. **What kind of fuel, gasoline or diesel, do I want the vehicle to burn?**

   The general consensus is that diesel engines cost more on initial purchase but less in the long run to operate. Some complain about the high cost of oil and filters for diesel engines. Diesel engines usually seem quieter in the cockpit than gasoline engines because they're positioned in the rear of the vehicle.

7. **Will I be happy with a standard "off-the-rack" model RV, or do I want some special features and options?**

   Manufacturers are coming up every year with new toys and gim-micks for today's younger market. High-tech elements, such as computer stations, satellite dishes, and electronic navigational systems, have joined rearview backing cameras and slideouts as common optional equipment.

8. **How often will I use the vehicle?**

   Some RV owners in cold climates have to winterize and store the RV, while others use it year-round, either driving south for the winter, going skiing or winter camping, or just living in or near mild climates. (If you think you'll use your RV only once a year for a two-week family vacation, renting, rather than buying an RV may be cheaper.)

9. **Where will I store the vehicle?**

City-dwellers like us must rent storage space for our vehicles. Even suburbanites, however, can face parking regulations that forbid keeping an RV in the driveway or on the street in front of the house. Owners with a large garage may consider folding camping trailers, truck campers, or telescoping travel trailers that are compact enough to store inside. Some travelers who like to visit the same park or campground year after year may want to store the vehicle permanently at the vacation location.

10. **How much money can I spend?**

Budgeters and young families starting out often begin by buying an entry-level RV in whichever type category they want. With sticker shock being a strong factor these days, more and more manufacturers are offering lower-priced models in all categories. Previous RV owners often, but not always, look toward buying a larger, newer, and more expensive model. A few choose instead to downgrade for a simpler travel lifestyle. In many cases, interest paid on your loan to purchase an RV is tax deductible as a second home. For more info about buying an RV, see Chapter 4.

Chapter 4

Planning Your Budget

. . . .

In This Chapter

▶ Calculating a budget

▶ Finding out how to get the lowest rental rate

▶ Shopping for your RV

. . . .

*I*f Congress can spend weeks talking about budgets, you can spend a few minutes looking over some basic information, tips, and how-to instruction for planning the budget for your upcoming RV trip. Here are some pointers.

Adding It Up: Your Vacation Budget

Projecting exactly how much you'll spend is difficult, if not impossible. The **Making Dollars and Sense of It** worksheet at the back of this book and the information in this chapter can help you develop fairly sound parameters for your budget.

Transportation

The cost of transportation — renting an RV, buying an RV, filling the gas tank, and maintaining your RV — is the biggest chunk of your budget. For information on **renting and buying,** see "Testing the Waters: RV Rentals" and "Taking the Plunge: RV Purchases" later in this chapter.

Even after you own an RV, you still must pay attention to the cost of filling the gas tank and maintaining the vehicle in top working order. And you'll want to prorate your annual maintenance costs, insurance, license, lubes, and minor repairs while also crediting any tax benefits that you may receive from depreciation and loan interest payments.

The cost of **gas** depends on how much time you plan to spend on the road. Your gas price per day goes down considerably if you spend some days hiking, fishing, or doing local sightseeing. To get an estimate, drive yourself mentally through your trip, adding up the mileage as you go based on the estimates in this book. Next, settle on a per-gallon price for gas. You can take an average figure per gallon from your local service station. Knowing the exact price of gas in the future or even two or three states down the road is impossible. Divide the daily mileage or the total trip mileage by the estimated miles per gallon your RV gets, and you can get an idea of how many gallons you'll use per day or for the entire drive. For our tips on saving money on fuel costs, see Chapter 6.

Maintenance costs vary according to the type of RV you have. Of course, a towable has less motor-related costs than a motorhome. However, your towing vehicle may require some maintenance. A rental unit should be in tip-top condition when you pick it up, so maintenance costs will be minimal. If you own your RV, you face the usual road costs — we've had roofs blow off, windows shatter, and tires blow. Your warranty or RV insurance can cover such incidents.

Along with regular engine and vehicle upkeep on a long haul, spend that little bit of extra money on RV service when necessary. The added expense saves money in the long run.

Be aware that when you travel on back roads, you not only drive slower (not a bad idea when sightseeing), but you also avoid the **toll roads** that charge fees based on the number of axles on your rig. **Parking** charges may double or triple for RV drivers. Our 36-foot motorhome takes up two parking meters and both must be fed. Parking lots may charge additional fees depending on the size of your rig.

RV and camping supplies

Most RV and camping supplies can be purchased at your local supermarket. Specialty items, such as storage tank deodorizers, biodegradable toilet paper, and other RV items, can be found in RV stores, such as Camping World or auto supply shops. For a list of essentials, see Chapter 6 or the Cheat Sheet in the front of this book.

Campgrounds

A family of four can vacation in a family campground for less than $200 per week, and a snowbird can spend the entire winter in a full-service, warm-climate resort for less than $2,000, according to the National Association of RV Parks and Campgrounds. To determine your expenses, add up the costs of campground fees for each night that you're spending on the road. See the campground sections of this book for relevant fees.

For tips on saving money on campground costs, see Chapter 9.

Food

A great moneysaving feature of RVs is being able to carry and prepare your own food rather than eating in restaurants. Even buying takeout lunches or making picnics at lunch stops keeps the price lower than eating inside a restaurant. Figure on spending one-fourth to one-third more than you'd spend at home on food, allowing for splurges and snacks on the road.

For tips on trimming food costs on the road, see Chapter 8.

Attractions and activities

We list admission fees for attractions and activities throughout this book. You can easily include the must-sees and maybes in your budget and leave out the ones that don't interest you. We also recommend free attractions that you can visit at the last minute without affecting the bottom line.

Shopping and entertainment

Budgeting for something as personal as shopping is difficult, unless, of course, you're completely honest about your own weaknesses. We buy only what we really need plus some discounted items, such as candies from the factories that make them or one-of-a-kind artworks from the artists themselves. Figure it out. The good thing about a large RV, that it can accommodate large souvenirs, also can be the bad thing.

Because we like to do all our sightseeing throughout the day and spend evenings at home in the campground, our entertainment costs are minimal. Many campgrounds offer free movies or live music during summer. If you're taking the Ozarks and Branson drive in Chapter 19, however, factor in the cost of buying tickets to one of the shows — the highlight of that itinerary. We give average show prices in that chapter. Matinees usually are less expensive than evening shows, although ticket prices in Branson generally are not as high as those for other major venues, nationally.

Testing the Waters: RV Rentals

For our first RV experience, we leased a 27-foot motorhome for six weeks. We'd rented the unit for a book assignment that required us to visit more than a hundred remote ski areas across the United States. If we'd rented the RV for only a weekend, we'd probably have returned it and said RVing was not for us. (See the excerpt from our road diary in

Chapter 1.) However, three or four weeks into the journey, we decided that not only was RVing fun, but that we also had to have that very motorhome. So we bought it from the dealer, and drove it for 50,000 miles before deciding to move up to a larger vehicle. We now own a 36-foot widebody motorhome with two slideouts — and 40,000 miles on the odometer since January 2000.

When to rent

If you don't already own an RV, you need to rent or buy one for your trip. But how do you decide which way to go? In the following circumstances, renting an RV makes the most sense when:

- Setting out on your very first RV journey.
- Thinking about replacing your current RV with a different type.
- Taking your family on only a two-week vacation once a year and wanting to do so in an RV. That way you can test drive different models every year, and when the time comes to buy, you'll know what you want.
- Wanting to travel for several weeks from a location that's far from home. Fly-and-drive packages are available from several rental companies. (See the Appendix for a list of companies that rent RVs.)
- Wanting to drive along a rough or rugged stretch of road without subjecting your own RV to wear and tear.
- Wanting to travel a long haul, such as Route 66, in only one direction.

How to rent

Several companies rent RVs. To find one near you, see our recommendations in the Appendix, log on to the Recreational Vehicle Rental Association's Web site at www.rvra.org, or look in the local Yellow Pages.

Make reservations for your RV three months in advance especially for use during holiday periods and peak travel seasons when tourists from Europe, Australia, and New Zealand like to rent them for visits to national parks in the United States or drives along the coast of California. During the off-season, however, you may be able to book a spur-of-the-moment rental for a few days or a week, especially from a nearby dealer.

The most common unit available is the motorhome — either the larger Type-A or the Type-C mini-motorhome (see Chapter 3 for definitions) — which accounts for 90% of all rentals.

Prices begin around $875 a week. For tips on negotiating the figure, see the next section, "How to get the best rate." Keep in mind, however, that your rental rate doesn't include:

- ✔ **The use of the generator.** You need the generator, however, only for operating ceiling air conditioner, microwave oven, and TV in places without electrical hookups. When you return the RV, the dealer reads the generator counter, which usually is located by the on/off switch, to find out how much time you logged.

- ✔ **A supply of certain furnishings.** Some companies offer a furnishings package with bedding, towels, dishes, cooking pots, and utensils for a flat price of about $85 per trip. Others offer add-on kits containing power cords and hoses, plastic trash bags, toilet chemicals, and a troubleshooting guide. Sometimes purchasing these packages, or bringing items from home, makes more sense than spending vacation time searching for them. So you know what's needed, get a detailed list of what's included in your rental from the company.

- ✔ **Connections for travel trailers.** When you find a company that rents travel trailers, you may find that it requires you to furnish your own tow vehicle, hitch, and electrical hookups on the tow vehicle.

- ✔ **Insurance.** Insurance on a rental RV normally isn't covered on your personal automobile insurance, so ask your insurance agent for a binder that extends your coverage to the RV for the full rental period. Many dealers require the binder before you can rent a vehicle.

Most rental centers request a cleaning deposit, which isn't returned if you bring the vehicle back with the holding tanks full or the interior dirty or damaged. Some companies also offer free airport pickup and return if you notify them of your flight number and estimated arrival time.

At the dealership, be sure the dealer demonstrates all the components and systems of the RV you're renting. Take careful notes. As is true with rental cars, check for dents and damage from previous use before leaving the lot.

Be sure you're provided with a full set of instruction booklets and emergency phone numbers in case of a breakdown. Having a 24-hour emergency 800 number to call in case of a problem is best.

If you fall in love with your rental vehicle (the way we did ours), you may be able to negotiate a purchase price that subtracts your rental fee from the total. You can get a good deal if the vehicle is a couple of years old, because most dealers get rid of vehicles after two or three years.

How to get the best rate

For the best rental rate, follow these five tips:

✔ Check prices with several companies before making a decision. Establish exactly what the lowest-priced rental includes, such as free miles, the price per mile beyond the daily or weekly limit, amenities such as dishes and linens, and breakdown service. Organize your data using the **Renting the Right Rig** worksheet in the back of this book.

✔ Try to plan your trip during the off-season or *shoulder season,* the period between the most popular and the least popular travel times. The times of year for these seasons vary depending on the area you're renting from.

✔ Find out in advance whether your own automobile insurance agent covers your rental insurance for an RV. Your agent usually can provide a cheaper rate than the rental company.

✔ Try to plan your trip in a loop trip with the rental agency serving as the starting and ending point, so you can avoid drop-off charges.

✔ Negotiate based on selection. The more RVs a rental company has, the wider your range of choices, but if you're flexible about what sort of rig you rent, you may be able to negotiate a better price when the selection is limited.

Taking the Plunge: RV Purchases

Buying an RV is a big moment and certainly not a time for a fast-talking salesman to steer your emotions into a hasty purchase. Use the **Buying the Right Rig** worksheet in the back of the book to list the amenities that you want to include in your purchase and make comparisons with a variety of manufacturers and dealers.

For a first-time buyer, renting an RV of the type you're thinking about buying can be a big help in making up your mind. Just be sure to allow enough time to get comfortable with the RV. A week is the minimum; two weeks are better. You need enough time to relax into the day-to-day logistics of handling the RV on the road and hooking it up in the campground to evaluate the design properly. For more tips on selecting the right RV for you, see Chapter 3.

An **RVIA Seal,** clearly affixed near an RV's doorway, certifies that the vehicle complies with 500 specifications established under the American National Standards Institute for fire and safety, plumbing and electrical systems, and liquid propane gas systems. The Recreation Vehicle

Industry Association, representing builders of more than 95% of all RVs sold in the U.S., makes periodic unannounced plant inspections to ensure that members maintain acceptable levels of compliance.

Why go to an RV show?

When the bug to buy an RV first strikes, one of the best places to look is at an annual national or regional RV show, which usually take place during the winter months. They make especially safe hunting grounds for three types of people:

- ✔ Looky-loos who have no idea what they want but aren't about to succumb to the first smooth-talking salesman they encounter
- ✔ Well-researched potential buyers who know exactly what they want and are ready to make a deal
- ✔ RV owners who want to see the latest technical and design innovations but basically are happy with their existing vehicles

What you get for the price of admission to an RV show is a chance to compare different types of RVs, different brands, and different models. Salesmen on site are happy to spend time answering your questions, handing out brochures with floor plans and operating statistics, and pointing out features that distinguish their particular vehicles.

The action gets hot and heavy during the last day or two of a show when prices may be reduced and stumbling across an offer that you can't refuse is possible. On the other hand, if you're susceptible to sales talk, tread carefully or you may be driving a brand-new RV home from the show — not that there's anything wrong with that.

For a free listing of RV shows, contact the RVIA, or watch local newspaper or TV ads for a show in your area.

How to deal with dealers

Check the Yellow Pages for local RV dealers and spend an afternoon walking around the lot looking at various types of vehicles and mentally moving into them. The dealer usually can give you a brochure that details all the features, floor plans, and specifics to take home and study.

Every dealer has a number of previously owned vehicles that they've taken as trade-ins or they're selling for other owners. Generally, a used vehicle can be one-third to half the price of a new model. Purchasing from a reputable dealer improves the chance that the RV is in good condition and gives you some place to come back to if you have a problem later. For a few issues to keep in mind, see the sidebar, "Buyer beware: Used RVs," later in this chapter.

Don't worry about taking up a salesman's time if you're not yet ready to buy. Sooner or later you will be, and dealers are accustomed to the allure of a new yet unfamiliar RV to wannabe and veteran owners.

Expect the best buys in December and January, when dealers want to get the previous year's still-new models off the lot to make room for the new year's models. Ask to be put on dealers' mailing lists for any sales that they may have in the future.

Where not to shop for an RV

Avoid parking lot and campground "distress" sellers who give you a spiel about bad luck and desperate need for cash. A nationwide group of con artists calling themselves "Travelers" make a big profit selling cheaply made travel trailers, which also serve as living quarters and office headquarters for numerous other scams.

Be extremely careful buying from any private party unless you're familiar with the RV and can make a clear-eyed evaluation of it before signing the deal. If the RV looks beat up and shows wear and tear inside and out, walk away. Chances are, if the owner has treated the superficial areas badly, the critical working systems that you can't see also are flawed. Remember, with motorized vehicles, you're buying both a used car and a used house.

Buyer beware: Used RVs

Before buying a used RV, you want to protect yourself from making the wrong purchase. Consider the following five precautions before you buy:

- ✔ **Take a long test drive.** Watch gauges closely and check out all systems personally from toilet flush to water pump and heater. Look particularly for dry rot in any areas with wood or water stains that may be signs of leaks.

- ✔ **Ask questions.** Ask the owner direct and specific questions about all systems in the vehicle.

- ✔ **Have the RV inspected.** Ask a knowledgeable friend, or better still, hire an RV mechanic to look at the vehicle.

- ✔ **Check the book value of the unit.** Look at the current value in a Kelley or NADA blue book; your bank's loan officer should have current copies.

- ✔ **Shop around.** Visit at least one other dealer's lot to check comparable models and prices.

How to finance your purchase

For a description of RV types and costs, see Chapter 3. Because RV buyers generally are considered more reliable for a loan than car buyers (only 1.39% of all RV loans are delinquent), loans are easier to get. Check with banks, savings and loan associations, finance companies, credit unions, or the RV dealer. Loans for big new RVs typically range from 10 to 12 (and even 15) years, and many lenders ask for a 20% down payment or less. A few lenders may require a 25% down payment. Financing packages for used RVs can run up to eight years. Interest on the loan is deductible as second home mortgage interest, as long as the unit contains basic cooking, sleeping, and toilet accommodations.

Chapter 5

Planning Ahead for Special Travel Needs

. . . .

In This Chapter

▶ Taking the kids, cats, and dogs

▶ Freewheeling for the handicapped

▶ Hitting the road senior-style

▶ Meeting up with other RVers

. . . .

*W*hen we say RVing is for everybody, we mean it. No other form of travel adjusts so readily to any sort of special need.

RVing with Kids

RV vacations are family friendly in the extreme. We can start with the usual reasons: RVing is a cheap and convenient way of taking the whole family on vacation. In most cases, having the kitchen and bathroom with you makes the "I'm hungry" and "I have to go potty" whines easier to deal with, and traveling together comfortably as a family fosters closeness and communication. The simple truth is that *kids love RVing and camping.*

Veterans of family RV travel suggest involving children in the planning stages, rotating seats in the car or RV en route to the campsite, and assigning regular duties at the campsite. Older children can be responsible for packing certain items for the trip and handling last-minute duties at home, such as locking doors and windows or removing perishable food from the refrigerator.

Even infants can go camping happily. Experts recommend carrying a toddler in a backpack carrier and an infant in a frontpack carrier — both are made specifically for hiking. Bring along a folding stroller and playpen, mosquito netting, and a baby guardrail for the bed to use while in camp. A baby seat that clamps to a picnic table also enables a small child to join the rest of the family at meals.

Packing sunscreen to protect children's delicate skin is essential, and so is bringing along a gentle insect repellant.

For more tips on traveling with kids, check out these Web sites:

- ✔ **Family Travel Network** (www.familytravelnetwork.com) offers travel tips and reviews of family friendly destinations, vacation deals, and campgrounds.
- ✔ **Family Travel Files** (www.thefamilytravelfiles.com) provides an online magazine and advice on camping, cruising, and journeying domestically or abroad with kids.

For information on traveling with other families, see the listings under "RV clubs," later in this chapter.

RVing with Pets

As you travel, you meet many RV owners who favor their particular brand of travel because they can take their pets along with them. The Travel Industry Association of America (TIAA) says 6% of all traveling dog owners take their pets with them on vacation, while only 1% of cat owners do. We're willing to bet that some 50% of all dog owners (and probably 25% or more of cat owners) take their pets along on their RV vacations.

Always check campground information in advance to make sure that pets are permitted. Some campgrounds assess a surcharge; a few exercise *pet restrictions,* which means they decide on an individual basis, perhaps based on the pet's breed or size. When in doubt, telephone ahead and ask.

Although a few campgrounds have fenced dog runs where pets can frolic off the leash, almost all require *dogs to be on leashes* in the campground at all times. Owners also are required to *clean up after their pets at all times.* Some campgrounds even provide dispensers of cleanup plastic bags at the dog runs and receptacles for the used bags on site. Otherwise, carry your own cleanup bags and dispose of them properly.

Dogs *never* should be left alone in an RV at the campground or tied up outside the RV while the owners are away. Never leave the pet in the RV for more than 10 or 20 minutes in mild weather when running an errand, and don't shut them up at all when temperatures are hot.

The following tips can help you and Fido have an enjoyable RV trip:

- ✔ **Feed pets at night.** Feed pets after you're finished driving for the day, especially if they're susceptible to motion sickness.

✔ **Give pets water only during the day.** Give your pets bottled water, which you need to introduce at home in advance of the trip. As is true with humans, we suggest using bottled water because mineral content in water changes from one campground to the next. A contented tummy is something that you want to have with a traveling pet.

✔ **Bring familiar toys and bedding for the pet.** Like security blankets, objects from home can comfort your pet on the road.

✔ **Help your pet become accustomed to the RV.** If you have access to the RV in advance of the trip, spend some time in it with the pet.

✔ **Keep the cat's litter box in the shower or tub.** Encase the litter box inside a 30-gallon plastic trash bag. Put the bottom of the box in the trash bag, dump a 10-pound bag of cat box filler inside the box, and snap on the litter box cover. You may also want to carry a folding cat cage so your pet can enjoy the outdoors at the campground.

✔ **Carry a couple of small washable throw rugs.** Putting a small rug over the RV carpeting can protect it from little cat or dog feet.

Debate continues as to whether pets are safer when kept in or out of a kennel crate while in a moving RV. Defenders of the crate (many of them professional dog handlers who travel to and from shows in RVs) say the pet and the driver are safer with the animal confined while the vehicle is in motion. On the other hand, people who favor freeing-up a pet during the ride claim that it enables the animal to better protect itself from injury.

A good online resource for information about traveling with your pet is www.petswelcome.com, which dispenses medical tips and lists the names of animal-friendly lodgings and campgrounds, kennels, and veterinarians.

RVing for the Disabled

Recreational vehicles, especially motorhomes, can be made as accessible and comfortable for the physically challenged — especially those in wheelchairs — as any home. Mechanical seat lifts, either installed at the factory or retrofitted into existing units, can be added to motorhomes for people who have trouble climbing steps. Wider doors, raised toilets, roll-in showers, roll-under sinks, lower kitchen counters and cabinets, and a permanent place to lock in the wheelchair while the RV is in motion all are special options that can be installed at the factory or added later on.

More campgrounds now offer handicap-accessible campsites with wide level-paved sites to accommodate wheelchairs, walkers, or electric scooters. They also improved access to public toilets and showers by installing ramps and handrails.

Not only can wheelchair travelers adjust well to RVs, but many other handicapped travelers — from those on dialysis to people requiring a constant supply of oxygen — also find much more comfort and security in a specially equipped motorhome than they do in an automobile, plane, or train.

RVIA (Recreation Vehicle Industry Association; ☎ **703-620-6003**) publishes a directory with information about RV accessibility for handicapped travelers. Another valuable resource is the **Society for Accessible Travel and Hospitality** (☎ **212-447-7284;** www.sath.org), which offers a wealth of travel resources for people with all types of disabilities and informed recommendations on destinations, access guides, and companion services. Annual membership fees are $45 for adults and $30 for seniors and students.

For information on RVing with other disabled travelers, see the listings for **Good Sam Club** and **Handicapped Travel Club** under "RV clubs," later in this chapter.

RVing for Seniors

For anybody who has ever been in a campground, the title "RVing for Seniors" is redundant, because it appears that seniors obviously make up at least half of the RVing public. But for anyone nearing retirement age who's thinking about taking up RVing for the first time, we say, "Go for it!"

We've heard stories through the years about couples who worked years saving for their retirement, planning to buy an RV and travel full time, only to have one of the pair fall ill and die. In a surprising number of cases, the surviving spouse went ahead with the plans — often against the advice of other family members — and not only managed but thrived.

Some smaller, residential-style RV parks advertise as "for seniors only" or "for over 55." Seniors who want to avoid children (except visiting grandchildren) for a long stay can count on peace and quiet in these places. But as transient RVers, moving every few days, we enjoy staying in campgrounds with mixed ages, couples, and families with children.

Senior discounts on attractions and activities are getting more common all the time; always ask about senior discounts. We've even found supermarkets in the Sunbelt that give senior discounts on grocery or wine purchases on designated days.

The **U.S. National Park Service** (NPS) offers a **Golden Age Passport** that gives seniors ages 62 and older lifetime entrance to national parks in the U.S. for a one-time processing fee of $10. These passports can be purchased at any NPS facility that charges an entrance fee. Besides free entry, the passport also comes with a 50% discount on federal-use fees charged for camping, swimming, parking, boat launching, and tours. For more information, click onto www.nps.gov/fees_passes.htm or call ☎ **888-467-2757.**

AARP (formerly the American Association of Retired Persons), 601 E St. NW, Washington, DC 20049 (☎ **800-424-3410** or 202-434-2277; www. aarp.org), offers members travel information and a wide range of discounts and benefits, including *AARP: The Magazine* and a monthly newsletter. Anyone older than 50 can join.

For information on educational RV trips with other seniors, see the listing for **RV Elderhostel** under "RV clubs" later in this chapter.

Joining an RV Club

Although every campground is a place to find new friends when you stay more than a day or two, many travelers want to find and stay in touch with others who share the same interests. Joining an RV travel club enables travelers to do just that. The sociability of this type of travel attracts some, particularly singles who may otherwise feel like wallflowers in a campground full of couples. Others find comfort in traveling to new places in organized groups, particularly if the destination is a foreign country, such as Mexico, where the language and customs may be unfamiliar.

Caravan tours and rallies

RVers who prefer to travel or camp with a group can join up with any number of like-minded people for a paid vacation tour in their own rigs rather than a tour bus. These *caravans* are the RV equivalent of a group tour with structured itineraries, sightseeing, communal meals, and many group social functions. RVers can also attend *rallies,* friendly get-togethers with other owners of the same brand of RV.

Popular caravan destinations include Mexico, Alaska, and New England at autumn foliage time. To find out about caravan and club tours, read general monthly RV publications such as *Trailer Life* and *MotorHome,* available through subscription or from most magazine racks; *Highways* (for Good Sam Club members); or other club or RV manufacturing company publications. For details about these publications, see the Appendix. Some popular caravan groups include:

- **Creative World Rallies and Caravans:** 4005 Toulouse St., New Orleans, LA 70119 (☎ **800-REC-VEES** (800-732-8337), 504-486-7259; www.creativeworldtravel.com).

- **Fantasy Caravans:** 103 W. Tomchi Ave., Suite C, Gunnison, CO 81230 (☎ **800-952-8496**; www.fantasyrvtours.com).

- **Good Sam Club:** 2575 Vista del Mar Dr., Ventura, CA 93001 (☎ 800-234-3450; www.goodsamclub.com).

- **Woodall's World of Travel:** P.O. Box 6852, Englewood, CO 80155-6852 (☎ 800-346-7572).

RV clubs

Many types of RV clubs offer membership to everyone from people who drive certain brand-name RVs or manufacturers (you automatically get mail about these if you buy a new RV from a manufacturer that has a club or association) to associations such as Good Sam that also sell RV services and promote membership campgrounds. Within Good Sam, you find subdivision clubs for families with children, retired military, singles, ham radio operators, and so on.

The following are some of the specialized RV clubs and associations that aren't affiliated with manufacturers.

- **Baby Boomers:** For RV enthusiasts born between 1940 and 1960. P.O. Box 23, Stoneham, CO 80754.

- **Family Motor Coach Association:** Members number around 170,000 families, each with its own ID number. The group provides a handsome monthly magazine and other benefits, including insurance. Costs are $35 for a family, including initiation fee and first-year dues. 8291 Clough Pike, Cincinnati, OH 45244; ☎ 800-543-3622 or 873-474-3622; www.fmca.com.

- **Good Sam Club:** A broad-range club with insurance, campground affiliates, financing, and other services. Members number nearly a million, and the club also has special-interest chapters for hobbyists, computer aficionados, singles, the deaf, and others. C/O Susan Bray, 2575 Vista Del Mar Dr., Ventura, CA 93001-3920; ☎ 800-234-3450; www.goodsamclub.com.

- **Handicapped Travel Club:** For disabled individuals who enjoy traveling and camping; also welcomes the nonhandicapped. For membership requirements, send a self-addressed, stamped, long-form envelope with first-class postage to 12555 Lantern Rd., Fishers, IN 46038; ☎ 317-849-8019.

- **Loners on Wheels:** Loners on Wheels is a club for single RVers, numbering around 3,000 widowed, divorced, or never-married members. P.O. Box 1060-WB, Cape Girardeau, MO 63702; for sample newsletter call ☎ 888-569-4478; www.lonersonwheels.com.

- **RV Elderhostel:** Offers study groups for RV owners at universities or on the road in caravans along a historic route. 11 Avenue de Lafayette, Boston, MA 02111; ☎ 877-426-8056, 617-426-7788; www.elderhostel.org.

Part II
Ironing Out the Details

The 5th Wave   By Rich Tennant

"Well, it would have said, 'Happy Birthday, Doug' if you'd driven slower around those curves. But since you didn't, you'll have to settle for, 'Hippy Buttday, Dong'."

In this part . . .

Okay, you did your research, climbed in and out of
vehicles at RV shows until your knees ached, made a
deal to rent or buy the type you like best for your upcoming vacation, and worked out a budget. Now comes the
good part — getting used to your RV. In these chapters, we
give you some tips on driving your rig, furnishing it just
the way you like, stocking your pantry with your favorite
foods, hanging up cool clothes in your closet, picking out
the best campsites, and keeping your RV clean and tidy,
because nothing is worse than a small, messy, moving
vehicle!

Chapter 6

Dealing with Your RV

· ·

In This Chapter

▶ Maneuvering a big rig through bad weather and more

▶ Finding out what extra gadgets can come in handy

▶ Dealing with electrical hookups

▶ Turning that RV into home sweet home

▶ Securing your RV when you're not using it

· ·

A lthough an RV can seem like a delightful new toy for grown-ups, as a road vehicle and substitute house, owning a rig brings certain responsibilities. Check out the cautions, tips, and handling hints in this chapter to make your maiden voyage safe and comfy.

Driving Your RV

Driving an RV isn't difficult, but the experience is different from handling the family car. No special license or driver training is required. However, before hitting the road, you'll want to know a few basics and brush up on your road etiquette.

Learning the basics

Wherever you rent or buy your RV, someone will go over all the details with you, from driving the rig to hooking it up. Don't nod along, pretending that you know what he's talking about. If something isn't clear, **ask questions** until you understand.

If you're a novice RV driver, or even an experienced one, getting accustomed to a different model or type may mean a round of **practice driving** in a large empty parking lot. After you get into the driver's seat and adjust your mirrors, ask someone to walk slowly around the entire vehicle so you find the locations of your blind spots. Many modern motorhomes have rearview back-up TV cameras mounted on the rear of the rig with a monitor on the dash. They help considerably when the time comes to back up.

The increased length and width of an RV makes turning more awkward, but making this adjustment is easy. You have to **make wider turns.** When turning right, for example, keep your vehicle closer to the left than you would with your car, and drive farther into the intersection before turning the steering wheel to the right. When turning left, make comparable adjustments: Keep your vehicle closer to the right and turn when you get farther than usual into the intersection.

Always **signal your intention** to turn or change lanes well ahead of time, so drivers behind you have plenty of warning. Your vehicle isn't as agile as the ones around you.

When backing up into a campsite or getting out of a tight situation at a gas station, you want someone outside and behind you, **giving you hand signals** or, better still, **giving you directions via a walkie-talkie.**

On the road, **check your position** often in the rearview mirrors, side or center mirrors, or the back-up camera. Always be aware of the relationship of your vehicle with the painted lines marking traffic lanes or the edges of the roadway.

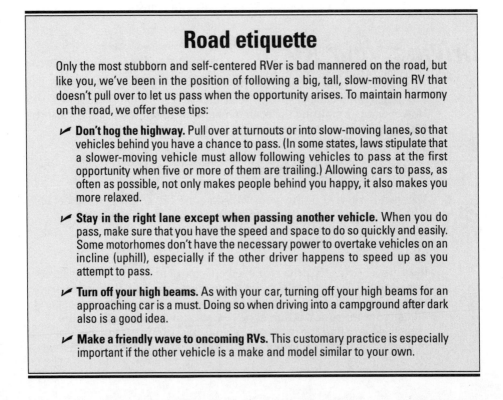

Road etiquette

Only the most stubborn and self-centered RVer is bad mannered on the road, but like you, we've been in the position of following a big, tall, slow-moving RV that doesn't pull over to let us pass when the opportunity arises. To maintain harmony on the road, we offer these tips:

- ✔ **Don't hog the highway.** Pull over at turnouts or into slow-moving lanes, so that vehicles behind you have a chance to pass. (In some states, laws stipulate that a slower-moving vehicle must allow following vehicles to pass at the first opportunity when five or more of them are trailing.) Allowing cars to pass, as often as possible, not only makes people behind you happy, it also makes you more relaxed.

- ✔ **Stay in the right lane except when passing another vehicle.** When you do pass, make sure that you have the speed and space to do so quickly and easily. Some motorhomes don't have the necessary power to overtake vehicles on an incline (uphill), especially if the other driver happens to speed up as you attempt to pass.

- ✔ **Turn off your high beams.** As with your car, turning off your high beams for an approaching car is a must. Doing so when driving into a campground after dark also is a good idea.

- ✔ **Make a friendly wave to oncoming RVs.** This customary practice is especially important if the other vehicle is a make and model similar to your own.

Wind speed is one special consideration to bear in mind when driving an RV. The large, flat surfaces of a trailer or motorhome can rock or sway when hit flat-sided with a heavy wind. Be aware that you'll feel gusts of wind when heavy trucks pass you at high speeds.

The biggest chore is mental. **Take it easy** on the road, **slow down,** and **allow more room** to change lanes or stop.

Going beyond the basics: Our tips

Having logged more than 100,000 miles in RVs, we consider ourselves experts on the subject. We went beyond the basics years ago. What follows are just a few of the driving tips we picked up along the way:

- ✔ **Buckle your seat belt.** When the vehicle is in motion, everyone inside needs to be in a seat with the seat belt fastened. Wait until the RV is safely parked before getting up and walking around, fetching a cold drink from the refrigerator, going to the bathroom, or cooking something on the stove.

- ✔ **Drive with headlights on in the daytime.** This safety measure makes your vehicle visible in marginal light and from a greater distance, especially on long, straight expanses of highway. More and more states require the use of headlights during the daytime, and we favor making this practice mandatory throughout the country.

- ✔ **Memorize your RV's height, weight, and girth.** You need to know quickly whether your vehicle fits the parameters when you see a sign ahead warning of a bridge with a five-ton limit or a tunnel with 10 feet of clearance.

- ✔ **Watch for cautionary road signs.** Everyone in the RV, not just the driver, needs to keep a look out, especially for signs denoting a tunnel ahead and giving its maximum clearance.

- ✔ **Take action if you don't see cautionary road signs.** Sometimes on streets in a town or city, you don't get ample warning of low-clearance tunnels or bridges. We were driving through Clarksdale, Mississippi, looking for the Delta Blues Museum and not paying much attention to other signage when suddenly the road dipped down to go under a railroad track. The pilot stopped the vehicle on the incline and the copilot got out to make an assessment. No, our RV wouldn't clear the underpass. So the copilot went into the roadway and directed traffic out of the way to enable the pilot to back the RV to the last intersection. Fortunately, motorists in Clarksdale were very polite (and more than a little amused); one helpful citizen gave us directions to the museum that avoided the in-town railroad track.

- ✔ **Slip on a pair of yellow sunglasses** (sold in ski shops as ski goggles) to combat glare, fog, snow, or oncoming headlights when driving after dark. You can also clip a pair over your regular glasses.

✔ **Scan the road ahead with binoculars.** In advance of changing lanes in heavy traffic, the copilot can use binoculars to check out the road signs ahead. Binoculars are especially useful when trying to determine whether interstate entry/exit ramps require you to be in the right or left lanes. They also help the copilot read signs at intersections.

✔ **Avoid driving at night.** We prefer early morning starts and stopping for the day by mid-afternoon. This enables us to hit the road before most vehicles and see what there is to see. After all, why drive along the spectacular California coast, for example, if you can't see it?

✔ **Drive defensively.** Other drivers don't seem to realize that motorhomes are like big tractor-trailer rigs; they can't stop on a dime. So drive a safe distance from the vehicle in front of you in case you need to slow down or stop unexpectedly. Many other drivers also make the erroneous assumption that RV drivers are elderly slowpokes, when most of us drive at the prevailing speed limit with the rest of the traffic. So we're always half-expecting a driver to pull out of a side road in front of us, and we're rarely disappointed on that account. One rule to follow: If you see a red pickup truck waiting at a side road to pull into traffic, you can count on it pulling out in front of your RV.

Controlling your speed

Although exceeding the speed limit never is laudable, doing so can also be extremely inconvenient for residents of California, Alaska, Hawaii, Montana, Oregon, Michigan, and Wisconsin — states that aren't signatories to the Non-Resident Violators Compact — when traveling out of state. What that means is that drivers with license plates from these seven states are subject to having their driver's licenses confiscated and being required to go to the nearest office of a judge, sheriff, or justice of the peace to appear before an officer, post bond, and/or pay a fine. If the necessary official isn't available, the individual may be jailed until a court appearance can be arranged, which may be several hours later.

Saving Money on Fuel

Fuel conservation is important for all RVers. Cutting down on the amount of gas you use helps not only your budget but also the environment. What follows are tips for conserving gas and finding the best fuel prices:

✔ **Consider staying longer in one location.** Because we're so happy and comfortable in our new, larger motorhome, we find ourselves staying longer in each place than we used to. Doing so cuts fuel costs by reducing the average number of miles driven per day.

Interestingly enough, we get almost the same gas mileage in our 36-foot motorhome as we did with our old 27-footer.

✔ **Forget the tow-along and walk or bike.** We still don't tow a car — another fuel savings — but instead enjoy a walk of a mile or two to the market, a museum, or a restaurant. Other RVers carry bicycles for short trips from the campground.

✔ **Mind and maintain the speed limit.** Experts say observing the speed limit saves fuel because fuel economy decreases at higher speeds. Cruise control, for those vehicles that have this feature, also contributes to fuel savings, because you maintain a constant speed. Being light-footed with the gas pedal rather than applying too much throttle also saves gas.

✔ **Keep your air filter clean.** Make sure your air filter is checked and replaced often. U.S. Department of Energy studies claim that a dirty air filter can raise the consumption of fuel as much as 10%. Keeping your engine tuned and not carrying any extraneous weight also help, the study points out.

✔ **Take advantage of gas competition.** We carry binoculars to check out posted gas prices along an interstate exit or in the outskirts of a town. Always go for the cheaper price, even when doing so requires turning around.

✔ **Pay with cash when you can.** Sometimes the lowest prices on gas are cash only. If you prefer using a credit card, watch for stations where prices are the same. If nothing is posted, ask before filling your tank.

Detecting Gas and Smoke

Remember that you're driving a vehicle that contains a **propane tank.** The propane tank simplifies your daily life by enabling heating and refrigeration to take place while your RV isn't hooked up to a campsite's power source; however, it also complicates your life because it's flammable. Some experts recommend driving with the propane tank turned off. Many long, highway bridges and tunnels require the tank to be turned off before entering. You must always turn off the tank before pulling into a service station to fill up with gas.

Propane gas-leak detectors that warn you of a propane leak with an alarm are mandatory in RVs. Modern RVs come equipped with them. If you hear the signal, get out of the RV, turn off the propane valve at the tank (reached from an outside door) and leave the RV open to let the gas escape.

Occasionally, your gas-leak detector may go off when you're cooking garlic in an open pan because the odor is similar to the odorant that's added to propane to make leak detection easier. If that happens, turn off the burner, remove the pan of garlic, turn off the detector, turn the burner back on, and finish cooking the dish, but be sure to reactivate the detector after you're done cooking.

Install a mandatory **smoke detector** in your RV, if you don't already have one. Always check the gas-leak and smoke detectors installed in your RV to make sure their batteries are fresh.

Carbon monoxide detectors also are mandatory in RVs. You want to inspect your RV regularly to make sure the floor, sidewalls, doors, and windows have no holes or openings through which toxic fumes can enter the vehicle while you're driving. If you find any, seal them up with silicone adhesive or make repairs before driving again.

Never run the **generator** while you're sleeping, and always open one of the roof vents when using the generator. In roadside rest areas, don't park for long periods in the vicinity of any tractor-trailers running their motors (to keep its refrigeration operating). The carbon monoxide can seep into your RV. *Note:* A generator won't operate when the gas level falls below one-quarter tank.

Equipping Your RV

Although an RV usually comes fully furnished and ready to go from the manufacturer, you'll probably want to pick up a few practical tools and gadgets. You can usually find these items at camping supply stores or even, sometimes, at the small convenience stores at campgrounds.

Marching into a specialty store and buying only what's on the shopping list is difficult for novices and experts. As you browse through the shelves, murmuring, "Gee, look at that!" or "I didn't know there was a gadget like this," you start dropping other items into your shopping cart that you suddenly realized you must have. For suggestions about optional essentials, see Chapter 7; for kitchen items, see Chapter 8.

Picking up a **basic tool kit** and an inexpensive **auto tool kit** is a practical way to start. Although we leave major repairs to experienced mechanics, numerous small jobs can be done easily with the right tools.

Most RVs arrive with a short sewer hose and sometimes (but not always) a water hose. The first thing you'll notice the first time you hook up is that both hoses are too short to be really useful in many campgrounds, so the next items on your shopping list are new longer sewer and water hoses. Look for a **15- to 20-foot sewer hose** with clamp and coupling devices that enable you to secure it quickly to the campground's sewer connection. You want a **25- to 50-foot plastic garden hose,** preferably one for drinking water (rubber hoses leave a taste in the water). Also helpful are a **quick-connect appliance** that enables you to make quick, snap-on watertight connections with the campsite water connection and a **water pressure regulator** to keep the water pressure balanced between the campground water supply and your RV.

If you have a big new motorhome with plenty of air conditioning, your ideal electrical hookup is 50 amps, but many older campgrounds may offer nothing higher than 30 amps or, in some state parks, a maximum of 20 amps. You have a clue right away at the campsite if your plug doesn't fit the receptacle in the electrical box. What you want are adapters that convert **50-amp to 30-amp service,** and **30-amp to 20-amp service.** To use a 20-amp outlet with your 50-amp system, you plug the 50- to 30-amp connector into your main electric shore line, plug the 30-to-20 connector into the 50-to-30 connector, and then plug everything into the 20-amp outlet or look for a 50-amp to 20-amp connector. For issues to keep in mind when dealing with amperages, see the next section, "Monitoring Electrical Hookups."

At the campsite, you want your RV to be level for sleeping comfort and for keeping the refrigerator level — a definite must. Although many new motorhomes come equipped with **automatic hydraulic levelers** installed under the body, older RVs may require the use of **manual levelers,** which can be anything from a couple of pieces of board for each tire to a commercially produced wood or plastic device. Make sure to evaluate a leveler carefully before buying it. Some of the plastic ones may not hold the weight of your RV; some stack-up versions are hard to maneuver the vehicle across. A **spirit level** (those little things with moving bubbles inside) laid on a countertop inside the RV lets you see how level the RV is at the campsite.

For TV lovers, a **50-foot length of antenna cable** with male connectors on each end keeps everyone happy when the campground offers cable TV hookup.

In your cabinets, **shelf liner** in a ridged pattern helps keep items from sliding while the vehicle is moving; match the color to your countertop or woodtone, if you wish. **Tension rods** of various lengths also are useful for installing like bars across your refrigerator or cabinet shelves to keep the items contained within. We find **Bubble Wrap,** an item we usually get free in shipping boxes, a godsend when packing up glassware and dishes (see Chapter 7).

Finally, two all-purpose items are a **heavy-duty extension cord** for outdoor use and **duct tape,** the wide silver-backed tape (called *gaffer's tape* in the film industry) that can hold just about anything together until you can get to a repair shop. On our first RV trip, we carelessly left a roof vent open when picnicking near a Colorado lake during a heavy wind. We even wondered about a white plastic object that we saw cartwheeling down the hill . . . until a rain shower came up and rain started coming in. A hasty retrieval of the plastic vent cover, a trip up the back ladder to the roof of the RV, and most of a roll of duct tape repaired the damage and kept out the rain.

Monitoring Electrical Hookups

Many older campgrounds, especially in state parks, may have 20- or 30-amp electrical hookups when your ideal electrical hookup is 50 amps. Plus, modern RVs have three-prong plugs requiring adapters for older two-prong sockets. (See the previous section, "Equipping Your RV" for info on adapters.) You can use the lower amperage so long as you remember not to run the air conditioner, microwave, and TV set at the same time. As new larger RVs with more and more electrical appliances and conveniences come on the market, the requirements for additional amperage raises the limits up to 50 amps. Consequently, many RV campgrounds have modified a number of sites to handle this greater need.

The total amperage of all electrical units that you're using in your RV shouldn't exceed the amperage limitation of your campground hookup. Amperage limitations vary from one campground hookup to another and are offered at 15, 20, 30, or 50 amps. We include specific limitations in the campground listings in this book. Manufacturers note amperages used by their appliances, such as TVs, refrigerators, microwaves, or air conditioners. Make a list of these amperages and refer to it when in doubt.

If you do exceed the hookup amperage limitation, the power goes off. The power going off usually isn't a huge problem if you're in a campground that's equipped with circuit breakers, but some older campgrounds may still use fuses and resetting them can be difficult.

Make turning off one appliance before you turn on another your routine to keep from going over the limit. We find that simply turning off the electric water heater often solves the problem, because it uses an abundance of power. Small appliances, such as toaster ovens, also draw much more power than you'd expect.

Preparing for Winter Camping

Our first winter camping trip was strictly an accident. Our desert trip included a swing north to the Grand Canyon, where we experienced an early snowfall. After a cheerful ranger pointed out a site that still had water connections along with electricity, we dutifully hooked up for the night and woke the next morning to find that our hose had turned into a 25-foot long Popsicle. That explains our first rule in the following list:

✔ **Avoid the big freeze.** Don't connect your water hose to an outdoor faucet overnight when temperatures are expected to fall below freezing. Instead, use water from the RV's supply and refill when necessary. Don't forget to set your furnace thermostat inside to a low temperature, usually around 60° F, to keep onboard water pipes from freezing and add antifreeze to holding tanks to keep drains from freezing.

✔ **Keep charged up.** Watch your battery strength. Batteries discharge quicker as temperatures drop.

✔ **Don't get buried.** Avoid parking under trees because branches can give way under the weight of ice or snow overnight and don't let snow accumulate on the refrigerator's exhaust area — some exhaust units are located on the side of the RV, some on the roof with a protective cover that may be blanketed in heavy snow.

✔ **Heat things up a bit.** If you're spending time in a very cold climate, you may want to add thermostat-controlled heaters to the freshwater and holding tanks; RV supply companies sell them.

✔ **Use the right blend of liquid propane (LP).** Liquefied petroleum gas is used for heating, cooking, and refrigeration in RVs. Exhibiting different characteristics in different temperatures, the liquid is specifically blended for the climate. If you're heading for the snow country from the desert, you should ask the LP dealer if you need to empty your tank and refill it with LP specifically blended for cold weather.

✔ **Handle snow with care.** If you're going into snowy or icy weather, carry chains or have snow tires for your tow car or motorized RV. And drive with extreme care. Even an experienced RVer finds handling a motorhome or towing a trailer much trickier in snow and ice. *Note:* A heavy motorhome can be difficult to stop on an icy surface.

For recommendations on storing an RV in a cold climate, see the "Storing Your RV" section later in this chapter.

Furnishing Your RV

Manufacturers furnish the average Type-A or Type-C motorhome at the factory with these built-in features: a kitchen counter and cabinets; a cooktop; a refrigerator/freezer; a dinette or free-standing table and chairs; a sofa or easy chair; a double or queen-size bed (twins are available on special order); wardrobe and drawer storage; a bathroom with toilet, sink, and shower; air conditioning; a heating unit; a TV; and a microwave. The driver and front passenger seats (pilot and copilot seats) can swivel around to face into the living area, adding two more comfortable seats to the arrangement.

Depending on the vehicle size and the manufacturer, the RV may also contain a swivel and/or reclining chair, an oven, a microwave/convection oven, a second TV in the bedroom, a shallow tub with shower head above, a washer-dryer combination, an icemaker in the refrigerator, a pull-out pantry with wire or wooden shelving, desk/dressing table combination in the bedroom, and a pull-up table adjacent to the sofa or swivel chair. Some manufacturers add a folding coffee table that stores in its own heavy bag and goes into place when the living room slideout is opened, adding more living space. Travel trailers and fifth-wheels contain all these items except the driver and navigator chairs. In many cases, these units have more living space and storage areas.

The clever design of RV interiors incorporates more furnishings than you'd imagine in such small spaces, so all you need to add are decorations. We like to add fresh flowers and pots of herbs for color, small rugs on top of carpeting or wood floors, large covered baskets for both decoration and storage in the kitchen/dining area, and additional cushions for color and comfort on the sofa and the bed. In built-in niches around the cabinets, we added wooden carvings picked up in our travels and anchored down with putty that can be purchased at RV supply stores. Books and magazines brighten up a tabletop, but you want to remember to stow them and plants and cut flowers safely before hitting the road.

Cleaning Your RV

We find keeping the RV as clean as possible day by day while we're on the road is easier than going through the equivalent of spring cleaning every week or two.

Outside the vehicle

Although car owners are accustomed to wielding a hose around in the driveway or in one of the little wash-it-yourself bays at a car wash, cleaning the outside of a motorhome by yourself is akin to bathing an elephant; you can't do it in your driveway or the average carwash even if you wanted to. Even a coin-operated carwash with an extra-large bay is far from satisfactory for us. We run out of quarters or patience long before the job is done. And most campgrounds don't allow you to wash the vehicle at the campsite.

Washing

For a big-time RV wash, which you want to do after it's been in storage or slogged through some dusty terrain, look for a truck wash. You're most likely to find them along interstate highways adjacent to truck stops. Simply get in line behind the trucks (if you're lucky, two or three bays may be working on a busy day) and ease your way into the wash bay where an energetic team with hoses cleans your RV — soaping, rinsing, wiping, and waxing (optional) until your home on wheels is sparkling. For this service, which takes 15 to 30 minutes after you get into the bay, expect to pay from $30 to $45. You want to be sure that all the windows and roof vents are closed tightly before you pull into the washing bay. While the truck wash cleans the outside, you can also put in some of your own elbow grease into cleaning some of the inside — washing mirrors or polishing the woodwork and cabinetry.

Dusting and debugging

To cut down on the costly full-vehicle wash jobs, we found that purchasing a dry dusting mop at the local supermarket cuts down the number of washings tremendously. Each evening after hooking up and settling in, do a quick once-over the exterior with the dry mop and get the day's dust and grime off before overnight dew cakes it. And don't forget the windshield and the vehicle's front end, which need a good scrubbing with a wet brush or windshield scrubber to remove the bugs that have accumulated during the day's drive. Putting the job off until morning lets them solidify into something like cement and doubles your job of cleaning.

Waxing

Regardless of whether it's a motorhome, travel trailer, or fifth-wheel, waxing a large RV is a major job and costly if done professionally. Many campground and RV supply stores, such as Camping World, have a number of waxes and protective materials that do the job. The work is up to you. We try to spread the joy around — doing the front of the vehicle one day, half the driver's side a few days later, the rest of the driver's side more days later, and so on until after a couple of weeks the vehicle has been completely covered, and you're not a physical wreck. But no matter how you approach the job, it's one that needs to be done regularly to save the finish of your exterior. Waxing is much cheaper than a new paint job.

Inside the vehicle

Keeping the interior clean is a matter of tidying up daily. Regular tasks, such as cleaning the windows and mirrors, can be done when you stop to fill up with gas; a 50-plus gallon tank takes 10 or 15 minutes to fill.

- **Woodwork:** Spray-and-polish wood cleaner repels dust and does a good job of keeping the cabinets and wood furniture looking and smelling clean.

- **Upholstery:** Even with modern fabrics that appear comparable to home interiors, RV upholstery is usually tough and hard to stain. We find spot-cleaning with a spray rug and upholstery cleaner that comes with a brush attachment does the job well.

- ✔ **Glass:** Windows and mirrors simply need a spray-and-wipe glass cleaner and a paper towel to be spotless and shiny again in no time.

- ✔ **Floors:** A small portable vacuum cleaner that can run without being plugged in when it's charged up is handy for quick cleaning or even heavy-duty cleaning in an area as compact as an RV.

   Spot-cleaning spills on the carpeting rarely is a problem because most carpeting in motorhomes is stain-resistant. We put a washable rug over high-traffic areas, such as the residential entrance, in front of the sink, beside the bed, and between the sofa and easy chair when the slideout is open.

- ✔ **Kitchen:** Wiping up kitchen spills when they happen helps keep the galley clean. We usually clean out the refrigerator when we bring the RV back home from a week or weekend away, or we clean it once a week when we're on the road for a long time. We give the sink a quick wipe-over every evening after doing the dinner dishes.

Holding tanks

Most RVs have two holding tanks — one for *gray water,* the water from the kitchen and bathroom sinks and shower; and one for *black water,* the waste from the toilet. Ongoing maintenance of these tanks requires the use of a liquid or powder, made especially for RV tanks, that deodorizes and dissolves of solids. RV manufacturers recommend using biodegradable toilet paper, which breaks up more readily in the tank.

When hooked up to the sewage drain in a campground, keep the black water tank outlet closed while the gray water outlet can remain open. When the time comes to empty the tanks, close the gray water tank outlet to allow water to build up in the tank, and then empty the black water tank first. Flush it out at the end with water poured in the toilet. (We store an empty one-gallon plastic water jug for this job.) When you're finished, close off the black water valve. Next, run about a gallon of fresh water into the gray tank from the kitchen or bathroom faucets and then open the gray water valve. This flushes out the hose as the gray water tank empties. Close the valve, unhook the hose, and flush out the hose again before storing. Wear disposable rubber gloves when handling the sewage hoses and draining the tanks.

Storing Your RV

Because we live in a city condominium, finding an RV storage area is a fact of life for us. Many of our friends in the suburbs face parking restrictions for their RVs, too. A smaller unit, such as a folding camping trailer or truck camper, can be stored in most garages, and a camper van can usually be kept in the driveway because it closely resembles a family car. But motorhomes and trailers often need to be stored somewhere away from the residence. Our **storage fee** averages **$65 a month** for a 36-foot motorhome. We go out and check the battery and crank up the motor at least monthly, and take the rig out at least every three months or so.

When storing the vehicle, do the following:

- ✔ Clean and defrost the refrigerator. Leave the door open to prevent mildew and put an open box of baking soda inside to keep odors out.

- ✔ Disconnect all electrical devices to prevent draining the batteries.

- ✔ Empty the holding tanks but leave a bit of water with deodorizer in the tanks to keep the seals moist. If the seals dry, they may crack and leak and have to be replaced.

- ✔ Close the propane tank valve.

- ✔ Draw all the shades and close the windshield curtain to keep the interior cooler when your RV's parked in the sun.

- ✔ Lock all doors and outside compartments.

- ✔ Fill the battery to the top with distilled water, if you're going to store it for a long time.

Putting an RV in storage in a cold climate, you need to drain all the water tanks and add nontoxic antifreeze, and drain and replenish the cooling system with water and antifreeze.

Chapter 7

Packing It In

● ●

In This Chapter

▶ Balancing the load

▶ Shopping for optional essentials

▶ Packing your paraphernalia

▶ Carrying cool clothes for all occasions

● ●

T he biggest difference between owning and renting an RV is that owners can pack their RVs once — and never unpack. But seriously, happy campers, this chapter tells you how to put some thought and organization into the chore of packing.

Beginning RVers may want to write a checklist to follow when packing and preparing the vehicle or setting up and breaking down camp. Some veterans suggest laminating the list and then checking off the items in grease pencil or erasable felt pen so that the list can be wiped clean and used again. For a packing list that you can use now, see the Cheat Sheet at the beginning of this book.

Stepping on the Scales

Before you load everything but the kitchen sink, you need to know the following important information. The manufacturer of every RV stipulates a maximum weight allowance called a **Gross Vehicle Weight Rating** (GVWR) that indicates the maximum weight that the vehicle's chassis can carry. You can check the weight of your loaded RV at a public scale. Look in the Yellow Pages, or ask local moving van and storage companies or recycling centers if you can use their scales for a fee. Get a reading for each wheel and, for a trailer, the *tongue weight,* which is the weight the trailer coupling puts on the tow hitch.

To determine whether your vehicle is overloaded, take the total weight and subtract your **Unloaded Vehicle Rate,** which is the weight of the RV before the weights of the water in the tanks, the people in the seats, the awnings, the generator, the air conditioners, and so on, are added. The manufacturer also stipulates the Unloaded Vehicle Rate. If the amount exceeds the GVWR, then your RV is overloaded. Overloading the vehicle not only means your driving costs are higher but also that you may also seriously damage the vehicle.

An **unbalanced load** also can cause damage. You want to distribute the weight as evenly as possible on both sides of the vehicle. Heavier items are best placed above or in front of the rear axle rather than behind it. Note, however, that your holding tanks often are located behind the rear axle. Heavy items stored behind the rear axle can cause the front of the vehicle to lift or the rear end to drag when you turn into service stations or other ramped roadways.

Stocking the Optional Essentials

In the old days of tent camping, you were a real dummy if you forgot to bring matches and a can opener. Today, a basic checklist can be as long as the one on the Cheat Sheet at the beginning of this book. For info on equipping your RV with the must-haves — sewer hose, water hose, electric adapters, and more — see Chapter 6. For details on what to put in the kitchen, see Chapter 8.

A big difference exists between what you have to carry and what you want to carry, but some of the optionals have become essentials to us.

Binoculars are important for helping you see a great distance ahead on the road to determine whether you need to be in the right or left lane for a turn or to access or exit the interstate, to figure out which service station on the exit road has the lowest gas prices, and to read the highway signs ahead when you're looking for an address.

A folding, artificial grass **cloth or mat** large enough to go under the picnic table and around the entrance to the RV helps keep sand and dirt from being tracked in. It also makes a dirt or sand campsite seem more hospitable.

Folding **outdoor chairs** are a must, because some campgrounds provide no outside table or furniture. We also carry small **folding tables,** so we can have snacks, drinks, or lunch outside even without a picnic table.

We always take some sort of grill along for outdoor cooking. Although some private campgrounds and many public parks provide grills, they're often so rusty and dirty that you won't want to put food directly on them. You can, however, carry a wire grill that looks like a popcorn popper with a sliding wire top to keep the food inside. We find that carrying a portable grill is easier. We started with one of the cheap charcoal grills that you can buy in most supermarkets or hardware stores and then graduated to a propane-fired portable grill with a lid that sets atop a folding base. Neither the charcoal grill nor the propane-fired grill requires an electric hookup. Now we also carry a new electric grill (which uses the same base) with lid, because the grill cook thinks it's easier to clean up afterward.

In the kitchen, a burner igniter, which sparks to light the propane stove burners, is easier and cleaner to use than matches. You may not need one, however, if your RV has an igniting device built into the cooktop.

Because picnic tables provided in most campgrounds have seen plenty of wear and tear and may be dusty and pocked with bird droppings, we carry a small **whisk broom** to brush the table and seats, and a **plastic tablecloth** held down with **clamps** and **plastic bench covers** with tie-ons to secure them. These items are found in camping supply stores.

Because we work on the road, our **office supplies** always are packed in the drawers near the bedroom desk and in small plastic stacking bins that fit under the kneehole of the desk. We always make sure to have Post-it notes, envelopes in several sizes, pens, pencils, staples, high-lighters, and paper — everything we have in our home office but in smaller quantities.

We like to take **games and puzzles** along for lazy days in camp. Our chess set and Scrabble board are travel editions, meaning they're smaller and store more easily than the standard issue. The Scrabble game has little indents to hold each letter in place on the board so that bumping or jarring doesn't upset the game. With the chess set, however, we bought a travel set with a durable folding wooden board that stores the pieces inside, but then we exchanged the lightweight pieces that came with the game for heavier-than-normal pieces so they stay in place if we're playing outdoors on a windy day.

Jigsaw puzzles are a favorite pastime, and after we finish one, we usu-ally donate it to the game room of whatever campground we're occupy-ing at the time. Occasionally the time to move on comes before a puzzle is finished, or we start putting it together outside on the picnic table but don't finish before dark. That's when puzzle caddies or felt cloths come in handy; you can fold up the puzzle carefully with all the pieces inside, store it, and unfold it somewhere else later on.

When traveling with children and/or pets, be sure to pack all their **favorite playthings** and **security blankets** — these items are rarely stored in the RV. For more about traveling with children and pets, see Chapter 5.

Stowing Your Gear

Ask yourself two questions about each piece of gear before you stow it: Where will I use it most? How weatherproof is it? With older RVs, no matter how well-built, seams are not solidly sealed, so that driving winds in sandy terrain, splashing from deep puddles, or torrential rain-storms can force dirt or water inside a storage bin. This problem usu-ally doesn't occur with new RVs.

RVs have much more storage space than you might imagine. Bins accessed only from the outside carry items that you use outdoors, while items stored inside need to be put as close to their point of use as possible. Sometimes adjustments must be made if you carry more of one item and less of another. Because we may have more food items on hand than the galley storage allows, for example, we may store extra canned goods in some otherwise impractical long narrow drawers in the bedside night tables or put bottles or dry goods in a plastic con-tainer on the floor of the closet.

Outside the RV

We keep our folding camping chairs, grills, and outdoor plastic table-cloths in the outdoor bin closest to the entry door of the RV. As this is where we keep the folding outdoor table and outdoor electrical con-nections, we also store the electric single burner that we use for out-door cooking here.

Seldom-used items, such as Christmas decorations, ladders, and skis, are stored in the bins underneath the living room slideout, storage areas that we can't easily access when we're on the road.

Inside the RV

Both motorhomes that we've owned have had beds that you can raise up to reveal a large storage area underneath, along with various tubes, ducts, and built-in equipment. We use this area to store lightweight, bulky items, such as extra bedding, backpacks, and a small roll-aboard suitcase, in case we need to travel by air or train in the midst of a long RV journey. In a camping store, we recently discovered a canvas shoe bag that fits neatly on the foot of the bed frame, concealed by the bed-spread overhang and holding four or five pairs of shoes in individual compartments, freeing up closet floor space.

Most RVs provide hanging closets that may be shirt-length or full-length or some of each. If your closets have only shirt-length hanging space, you have to double long items over the hanger to keep them from wrinkling at the bottom. If you want to figure out how many clothes your wardrobe can handle, measure the length of the pole, then measure your closet pole at home and count how many garments are hanging in that space.

An ode to Bubble Wrap

Mel Brooks, in the classic comic routine "The 2000-Year-Old Man," lauded plastic wrap as the greatest invention of the past two millenniums, but we'd have to say Bubble Wrap is a close second, at least in the wonderful world of RV cupboards.

Preferring heavy ceramic plates — bistro or restaurant grade — that can withstand microwave cooking, we confess to a bias against paper and plastic plates. We also refuse to sip wine from plastic stemware. But stacking dishes and glasses in an RV cupboard without some protection to keep them from chipping or breaking if you hit a rough stretch of highway is unrealistic. That's where Bubble Wrap comes into the picture.

The cylinder-shaped Bubble Wrap containers that come around bottles in airport duty-free shops make great sleeves for mugs and glasses, while the flat sheets that come in packing boxes are easy to slide between plates or pots and pans to protect them. You can also buy commercially produced plastic foam sleeves for glasses and pan and plate protectors in camping supply stores, such as the Camping World chain.

Alternately nesting baskets and metal bowls also keeps down the clatter from the cupboards. And lining the bottoms of drawers and cupboards with waffle-patterned rubber matting, available by the yard at hardware stores, RV dealers, and camping stores, makes a nonskid surface for dishes.

We store fragile items, such as tulip-shaped champagne glasses, in their original boxes and use other boxes or shaped Styrofoam packing protectors that come around appliances to wedge them firmly in the cupboard. Whenever possible, we use real dishes and utensils and cloth napkins that are recycled instead of disposable paper and plastic products. If we have guests for dinner, we like to surprise them with a dinner party comparable to one we'd have at home, including china, crystal, linens, and candles, when they're otherwise expecting paper plates and hot dogs on a stick.

If you plan to carry many clothes on your closet pole, reinforcing it before packing is a good idea. Some poles are lightweight and collapse easily. We bought a sturdy wooden dowel that's the length of the closet and covered it with ribbed plastic hose, the kind that's used for vacuum cleaner hoses. The ridges keep the hangers from sliding back and forth.

For tips on how to pack glassware and china, see the sidebar "An ode to Bubble Wrap," in this chapter.

Selecting the Right Kind of Wardrobe

One big advantage to having an RV is that you can always have your basic wardrobe packed and ready to go in the drawers and closets of the unit. Like most RVers, we always have a wardrobe stowed in our motorhome that can cover any situation we may encounter on the road, from an impromptu dinner in a fine restaurant to an outfit for cold-weather camping or white-water rafting.

Except on the largest motorhomes and fifth-wheels, wardrobe and drawer space is fairly limited, so you want to confine your permanent carry-along wardrobe to carefully selected basics and add seasonal or special apparel whenever the journey requires it.

We concentrate on basic clothing that's machine washable, stretchable with elastic waists, comfortable but loose fitting, and in styles and colors that harmonize with the other items in the closet. For cold-weather camping, even in parts of the California desert in winter, a set of **long silk underwear** is invaluable to wear under sweatshirts and pants. A **loose cotton gauze or linen shirt** and a pair of **shorts** always are on hand for unusually hot weather, such as the heat wave we encountered in New England last summer.

A spare pair of **hiking or jogging shoes** is handy to have, along with a comfortable pair of **slippers** to wear in the evenings after outside chores are finished. We each take one pair of slightly worn but acceptable **dress-up shoes,** and one **business or evening outfit** in case of an important appointment en route. Anyone planning to use the public showers in the campground also needs to take a pair of **rubber shower shoes.**

Several changes of **underwear, socks, pajamas,** and a **bathrobe** are folded and tucked into nightstand drawers beside the bed. We even carry spare bottles of **prescription medication** and a full supply of **toiletries,** so we can slip away on the spur of the moment yet still have everything we need aboard the RV.

Knit clothes that can be folded and stacked rather than put on a hanger take up less room and don't need ironing. We often take travel- or sample-size toiletries and stow them at home in a special RV box that's ready to be taken along on the next trip.

On our initial six-week journey, we took far too many clothes, forgetting that many campgrounds have coin laundries and that items of clothing can be worn more than once. *Remember:* At a campground, nobody pays much attention to what anyone wears anyhow.

Chapter 8

Eating on the Road

· ·

In This Chapter

▶ Setting up a galley

▶ Browsing around for the best local products

▶ Trying out our quick and easy recipes

· ·

*O*ne of our favorite things about being on the road in an RV is the access to great food. We have our choice of fresh fruits and vegetables from farm stands and farmers markets. Some of what we eat we pick ourselves, saving even more money. We also carry lists of all the great takeout places along the way, and with our own stove and refrigerator, we can pick up whatever we want to go and reheat it whenever we're ready to eat it.

Stocking Your Kitchen

Because we both enjoy cooking for ourselves, after so many years of dining out — we wrote food and travel articles for *Bon Appetit* magazine for more than ten years — our permanent equipment includes a food processor, spice rack, and pots of **fresh herbs.**

A large, stainless steel **stockpot** that doubles as a spaghetti pot is the biggest item in our cookware collection. Accompanying the pot are several small French enameled cast-iron **skillets** and **pans**, a nonstick **sauté pan** with lid, a well-seasoned cast-iron **frying pan,** several microwave-safe Pyrex **measuring cups and dishes,** a small whistling **teakettle** and an earthenware **teapot** that always travels in an old-fashioned, padded tea cozy. For coffee drinkers, most RV manufacturers offer the option of a built-in electric **coffeepot** that fits into a cabinet near the sink.

We also recently added a **pressure cooker,** which cuts down cooking time, thereby saving propane. In hot summer weather or to keep cooking odors outside when we have a hookup at the campground, we plug a single electric burner **hotplate** into the outlet near the counter of the outdoor entertainment center, if we're cooking something like Southern fried chicken, boiled shrimp, or a long-simmering stew, again saving on the propane consumption. A **slow cooker** that plugs into this outlet or inside the RV lets dinner cook while the family takes a hike or goes for a swim.

For eating, we have a set of sturdy French bistro **plates** and **soup bowls,** glass **wine glasses,** and two oversized ceramic **mugs** that fit nicely into the beverage-carrier on the cockpit dash. (See Chapter 7 for tips on packing breakables with Bubble Wrap.) New **dish towels** double as place mats and/or napkins and then become dish towels after a few washings. Preferring to recycle, we try to avoid using disposable paper products.

A large wooden **cutting board,** padded with a rubberized mat on the bottom, doubles as a cooktop cover when we're traveling; the board keeps the burners from rattling and has a slideout drawer that stores four sharp knives safely. We store the **food processor, electric can opener,** and utensils such as **tongs,** a **funnel,** and a long-handled **cooking fork** in overhead cabinets or in drawers under the cooktop.

On nonskid matting, the same color as our countertop (you can buy it in hardware stores, camping supply stores, and home-building emporiums), we put the **spice rack,** a jar of **coarse salt, paper towels** on a wooden spindle, and vacuum-topped **canisters** to keep dry items, such as cereals, chips, and snacks, crisp.

At one time or another, we've taken optional appliances, such as a **toaster oven** (indispensable if you don't have a regular oven and handy if you dislike the bending it takes to light the regular oven), a **sorbet maker** (you need a freezer that can be set extra low to use it), and a **bread maker** (as handy and easy to use on the road as at home).

We enjoy the surprise on the faces of dinner guests who arrive at the campground expecting a meal of hot dogs and hamburgers and end up with a hearty soup or stew, homemade bread, and homemade ice cream.

Eating Takeout Food

We enjoy stopping for takeout food or patronizing campground restaurants or cookouts when we've had a long day of driving and sightseeing. That way someone else prepares the meal, and we can wear casual clothes (or even a robe and slippers), and watch TV or listen to CDs while we eat, and the cleanup is minimal.

Another advantage of takeout is that you can enjoy sampling the food of a famous restaurant or cafe, even if it isn't mealtime or if you ate only an hour before. Just get the food to go — as many different dishes as you want to taste — and put it in the refrigerator for a later meal.

We often find, particularly in the South and Midwest where portions are huge, that a single takeout meal often is enough for both of us, especially when we add a fresh salad that we make in the RV.

Whenever we face a long day of driving, we find that getting takeout lunches saves plenty of time over eating in a restaurant or even preparing our own lunches in the vehicle (and dirties fewer dishes). We especially enjoy takeouts, such as clam chowder in Oregon and in Maine, that are satisfying on a cold day and ready in the time it takes the server to dish them up.

Shopping for Food

In each of the drives we describe in this book, you find a section called **"Stocking the Pantry,"** which suggests everything from local supermarket chains to cheese factories and bakeries as sources from which to purchase foods.

 Checking out the day-old baked goods and bagged surplus fruits and vegetables in a supermarket, we keep our budget firmly in mind especially when we're on a long trip. A few other tips to keep in mind:

- ✔ **Buy local produce.** Shopping roadside stands and farmers markets not only nets the freshest and cheapest local produce but also gives you a chance to chat with the locals and perhaps pick up tips on interesting things to see and do in the area.

- ✔ **Watch for pick-your-own farms in season.** In Chapter 18, we give you a list of pick-your-own fresh berry places in Minnesota, but you can find lists of these farms in free brochures available in state tourist information and welcome centers shortly after you cross the state lines on major highways.

- ✔ **Clip coupons locally.** Pick up handout newspapers or brochures (often available as you enter a local supermarket) or read the local daily to find coupon discounts on groceries. Watch for the "use before" date at the top. We also carry national coupons from home to use when we need something on the road.

- ✔ **Take food from home.** When we're leaving on a trip, we always take the fresh food and open jars of condiments, such as mayonnaise and mustard, from our home refrigerator rather than buying new ones on the road.

Cooking across the U.S.A.

An RV galley has less space than many kitchens (but bigger than the one we used to have in our New York apartment), so we worked out a bunch of simple, quick recipes that taste good, don't dirty many dishes, and take less than 30 minutes. Each recipe uses a locally available product from one of the drives in Chapters 11 through 24. All recipes serve four unless otherwise noted.

Katharine Hepburn's Brownies

Gourmet magazine published this easy recipe about 10 years ago, and it's an appropriate salute to New England and Chapter 11.

Preheat oven to 325 degrees. Butter an 8-inch-square baking pan; then put in about **1 tablespoon flour** and knock each side of the pan against the counter to make the flour cover the pan in a light dusting. Knock out any extra flour and discard. In a small heavy saucepan, melt **1 stick of butter** and **2 squares of unsweetened chocolate;** then remove from heat. Beat in **1 cup sugar, 2 eggs,** and ½ **teaspoon vanilla** until well mixed. Stir in ¼ **cup flour** and ¼ **teaspoon salt.** If desired, add **1 cup chopped walnuts** at this point. Pour into the prepared pan and bake at 325 degrees for about 40 minutes.

Mac and Cheese

For many the ultimate comfort food, this quick casserole uses some of the New York cheddar you find on your drive in Chapter 12.

Preheat oven to 350 degrees and butter two small ovenproof baking dishes. Bring a large pot of water to boil over high heat and cook **1 cup elbow macaroni, penne, or rigatoni** until a piece of it pulled from the water with a long fork or spoon is tender to your taste. (*Al dente,* slightly firm, is considered perfect.) Drain the pasta and put in a bowl with ½ **cup half-and-half** and **1 cup grated cheddar.** Season with a **dash of Tabasco, 1 teaspoon of salt,** and some **freshly ground pepper** and sprinkle with **2 tablespoons freshly grated Parmesan.** Spoon into the small buttered dishes and bake for 10 to 15 minutes until brown and bubbling.

Fried Green Tomatoes

Uncommonly delicious and easy to make, this southern treat uses tomatoes that haven't ripened yet; you can find them at produce stands in season throughout the Blue Ridge Mountains drive in Chapter 13.

Put a heavy-bottom frying pan on the stove and add **2 tablespoons oil, butter, or (tastiest of all) leftover bacon fat.** Slice **3 green tomatoes** in ½ inch thick slices, dip each slice into **cornmeal** seasoned with **salt, pepper, cumin,** and **chili powder,** and then fry it in the hot fat over medium heat about 3 minutes on each side. Serve hot.

Peel-and-Eat Shrimp

You find very inexpensive fresh shrimp in the shell on the Gulf Coast drive in Chapter 14.

Allow **1 pound of shrimp** in the shell for two people. In a large pot, pour **16 ounces of beer** per pound of shrimp (you can substitute water for some or all of the beer if you want), add a **small onion** cut into fourths,

1 clove garlic chopped, **juice of half a lemon, 8 peppercorns,** and **1 bay leaf.** Bring to a boil, cover, lower heat, and simmer 5 minutes. Raise heat to high, uncover pan, and add shrimp. When liquid boils again, stir shrimp, reduce heat, cover pan loosely, so it won't boil over, and simmer about 3 minutes or until the shrimp turn pinky orange. It takes longer if the shrimp are big. Remove from heat, drain shrimp, and serve in soup bowls with cocktail sauce and melted butter for dipping. For a full meal, make a quick coleslaw out of **1 packaged coleslaw mix** dressed with **mayonnaise** and a **dash of vinegar** to taste, and warm a loaf of **French, Italian, or sourdough bread.**

Chocolate Peanut Butter Cookies

Peanut butter reminds us of the Deep South where peanuts were first grown in the United States; that fits the Natchez Trace drive in Chapter 15.

From a **roll of refrigerated cookie dough** (sugar cookies or chocolate chip are good), scoop out a tablespoonful of dough, roll it into a ball and fit one into each cup of a minimuffin tin. Place in a 350-degree oven and cook until puffed and lightly browned, about 6 minutes. While the cookie balls are in the oven, unwrap **6 to 12 Reese's bite-size peanut butter cups,** one for every cookie ball, *being sure to remove the crimped brown paper on the bottom of each candy.* When the cookies are done, take them from the oven and immediately push one of the peanut butter cups, crimped side down, into each cookie and let them set in the pan until the cookie part is firm and the chocolate is melting, about 5 or 10 minutes. Then remove the cookies from the pan, using a table knife if necessary to loosen them, and let them cool on a rack or plate.

Texas Hill Country Chili Cheese Dip

Ro-Tel tomatoes, canned in Texas, are a snap to find in supermarkets throughout the Texas Hill Country (Chapter 16).

Open a **10-ounce can of Ro-Tel tomatoes with chilies** (note that they come in several degrees of hotness and with lime and other seasonings added to some) and dump the whole thing in a small, heavy saucepan. Add a **6-ounce package of grated cheddar or Monterey Jack cheese** and sprinkle **2 tablespoons of flour** over the top. Heat at medium temperature on a stovetop burner and stir frequently until the cheese melts and the mixture starts bubbling. Pour into a serving dish and serve hot with a big bowl of **tortilla chips** on the side. If the cheese dip starts to congeal as it cools, pop it into the microwave for a minute or two to reheat it. If you have leftovers, store them in the refrigerator and reheat later in the microwave.

Fresh Corn Pudding

When you tire of fresh corn on the cob, make this easy recipe during your drive through the farmlands of Ohio in Chapter 17.

Preheat oven to 350 degrees, and butter a shallow casserole or ovenproof dish. Take **4 to 6 ears of corn,** shuck and wash them, and stand them upright on a large cutting board. Using a large knife and cutting downward from the top of the ear to the bottom, cut off the fresh kernels. Put the kernels of corn in a bowl along with any milky juice that you can scrape from the cobs. You need 2 cups of corn kernels with juice. In another bowl, beat together **3 eggs, 1 cup heavy (or whipping) cream, and ⅓ cup milk.** Stir in **1 teaspoon salt, 1 tablespoon sugar,** and the corn. Pour this mixture into the buttered dish and bake for about 1 hour or until a knife inserted in the center comes out clean.

Garlic Mashed Potatoes

Yukon Gold potatoes were developed in northern climates like Minnesota, which we feature in Chapter 18.

Wash **4 large Yukon Gold potatoes,** cut each into four pieces, put in a large saucepan, and cover with cold water. Add **4 unpeeled garlic cloves** and cook until potatoes are tender, about 20 minutes. Using a potato masher or ricer, drain and mash the potatoes and garlic. Add **½ cup milk, ¼ cup olive oil, 1 teaspoon salt,** and **pepper** to taste and whip with masher or spoon until smooth. Serve immediately.

Fast Apple Tarts

You can pick your own apples at a local orchard or buy some from a roadside stand in Arkansas or Missouri in the autumn as you're driving the route in Chapter 19.

Preheat the oven or toaster oven to 400 degrees. On a floured board or piece of waxed paper, roll out **one thawed piece of puff pastry** (½ pound) from a one-pound box of frozen puff pastry until it's ⅛ inch thick. (Pepperidge Farm is the easiest brand to find in the supermarket freezer.) Cut it into four squares and transfer to baking sheet. Peel **one green or yellow apple,** such as Granny Smith or Golden Delicious, cut it in half lengthwise, then in quarters, and remove the core and seeds. Slice each quarter into very thin slices and overlap them slightly on top of the pastry. Mix **2 tablespoons sugar** with ¼ **teaspoon cinnamon** and sprinkle over the apples, and then dot with **butter,** using about 2 tablespoons altogether. Bake 25 minutes and serve plain or with **vanilla ice cream.**

Lentil Soup

Most of the dried lentils in the United States come from the northwestern mountains of Washington, Idaho, and western Montana. This dish is great for a cool day in Buffalo Bill country (Chapter 20).

In a large heavy soup pot, heat **3 tablespoons of olive oil** and fry a **medium onion,** chopped, over low heat until it softens, about 2 to 3 minutes. Add

3 **medium carrots** peeled and chopped and **2 stalks of celery** chopped, and cook, stirring, about 5 minutes longer. Add **1 cup dried lentils** and stir in the pan for about a minute. Raise the heat to medium high, add **5 cups chicken broth or water,** bring to a boil, and then reduce heat. Cover pan partially and simmer for about 45 to 50 minutes, or until the lentils are tender. Add more liquid while it is cooking if necessary. Garnish with **chopped onions or croutons** and serve hot.

Posole (Chicken and Hominy Stew)

This dish is a variation on a classic stew from New Mexico (Chapter 21).

Pour the contents of a **1-quart carton or can of chicken broth** into a large soup pot and turn the burner to medium or medium-high. While the soup is heating, chop up **1 pound of boneless, skinless chicken thighs** into bite-size pieces and add them to the soup when it starts to bubble. Reduce the heat to low and stir in **1 teaspoon salt, 1 teaspoon dried oregano, 2 teaspoons cumin powder,** and **1 tablespoon (or more, if you like spicy foods) of ground red chili or chili powder.** Let it simmer for about 10 minutes. Open **2 16-ounce cans of hominy,** either white or golden or one of each. Drain the hominy and put it into the soup, stirring so that it mixes in nicely. Continue to simmer another 10 minutes or longer if you need to do something else in the meantime (like preparing the garnishes). Serve it in soup bowls with little dishes of garnishes to sprinkle on top. Choose several or use all of the following: **fresh limes** cut into wedges, chopped fresh **cilantro,** diced **ripe avocado, tortilla chips,** sliced raw **radishes,** thinly sliced raw **cabbage (either red or white) or lettuce (iceberg or romaine works best),** grated **cheddar cheese,** and chopped **green onions.**

Easy Salmon in White Wine

You can use any fresh fish steaks or fillets you find on the Oregon coast in this dish; see the names of fish dealers in Chapter 22.

Butter a glass pie plate or microwave-proof casserole dish (nonmetal) and put **2 salmon steaks or 1 salmon fillet** (about 12–16 ounces) in the dish. Put **2 tablespoons of dry white wine (or water)** over it, put little **dots of butter,** one tablespoon or so altogether, on top of the salmon, and put on a little **fresh chopped parsley** (if you have it), along with a sprinkle of **salt** and **pepper.** Cover the dish with microwavable plastic wrap or its own lid and cook 5 minutes at high with the microwave turntable running. If you don't have a turntable, then open the microwave once every minute to turn the salmon around a quarter turn, and then turn the microwave back on and continue. Do this three times while it's cooking. When the 5 minutes is up, take the dish, still covered, from the microwave and let it rest on a heatproof surface for another 3 minutes before uncovering it. Serve at once.

Quick Enchiladas

Southern California may not have invented enchiladas, but it embraces them warmly. Here's a quick-and-easy version for the drive in Chapter 23.

Oil or butter an oven-proof casserole about 8 inches square. Preheat the oven or toaster oven to 375 degrees. Open a **package of corn tortillas** and remove them one at a time and cook them briefly (about 10 seconds) on each side over medium-high heat in a small frying pan with **2 table-spoons of vegetable oil.** As you remove each tortilla, put a **stick of natural (not processed) cheese (cheddar, Monterey jack, or pepper cheese)**, one inch thick and 5 to 6 inches long, in the middle of the tor-tilla. Roll up the tortilla and fit it into the greased pan. Repeat this until you use as many tortillas as you need, allowing two to three enchiladas for each person. Then open a **10-ounce can of enchilada sauce** and pour it over the top of the stuffed tortillas, making sure that you get them all covered. Cook in oven about 25 to 30 minutes, until sauce is bubbling. Serve at once.

Route 66 Breakfast Casserole

This dish is made the night before and put in the refrigerator, so all you do in the morning is bake it and eat it. Try it one morning before you get your kicks on Route 66 (Chapter 24).

Butter a 7 by 11 inch ovenproof casserole and line the bottom with **6 slices of buttered bread.** Sprinkle with **2½ cups grated cheddar or Monterey Jack cheese** (from a package if you wish) and **1 cup chopped ham** if you have some on hand. If not, leave it out. Beat **6 eggs** in a large bowl, then add ½ **teaspoon salt,** a **sprinkle of pepper,** and a **dash each of Tabasco and Worcestershire sauce.** Beat in **2 cups of milk.** Then care-fully pour the mixture over the bread and cheese in the casserole, cover it with plastic wrap, and refrigerate it overnight. In the morning, preheat the oven to 350 degrees, unwrap the casserole, and bake it 45 minutes or until eggs are set and casserole is beginning to brown on top. Remove from oven and let stand for 10 minutes before serving.

Chapter 9

Sleeping on the Road

· ·

In This Chapter

▶ Comprehending our campground criteria

▶ Considering private versus public campgrounds

▶ Picking the right spot to camp

▶ Maneuvering your RV like a pro

▶ Being thrifty at a campground

· ·

*O*kay, take a deep breath. Get ready to check into a campground and spend your first night out on the road. If you're worried about whether you can handle it, don't fret for a minute. For reassurance, check out the road diary from the original RV dummies in Chapter 1. Then plow ahead in this chapter, which tells you everything that you need to know.

For definitions of the campground lingo used in this chapter, see the Appendix.

Understanding Our Campground Recommendations

In each driving chapter of this book, we give you two campground lists — **our favorite campgrounds** and **runner-up campgrounds.** The campgrounds that are among our favorites may not rate as highly in a campground guide as some of the runners-up and certainly may not always be as posh. We prefer campgrounds with a quiet ambience and natural surroundings to fancier campgrounds that offer organized activities, such as square dancing and pancake breakfasts, swimming pools, and whirlpool spas.

Every camper has different priorities. Sometimes location is the most important aspect, for example, when you want to be positioned to be first in line the next morning for a famous museum or attraction and therefore want to be as close as possible to that place. At other times, you want to get away for a few days and hear nothing but birdsong, and you can care less whether the proprietors are fixing a pancake breakfast the next morning. At still other times, you may want a miniature golf course, a heated spa, and some square dancing on Saturday nights.

Whereas the campsites listed as our favorite campgrounds may be long on scenery and space but short on resort amenities or even campsite connections for electricity, water, and sewage, some of the runner-up campgrounds may be much more elegant and highly rated. You find some of each type campground in the driving chapters later in this book.

To help you narrow down your campground choices, use the **Choosing Your Campground** worksheet at the back of this book.

Using Campground Directories

Although we're frequently at odds with campground ratings, we find the big campground directories invaluable when traveling, particularly when we're making one-night stands and need to find a place to stop just long enough to eat dinner and sleep. Being able to call ahead for reservations also is helpful, so having a cellphone comes in handy. (See Chapter 10.)

Careful reading of a campground entry also can tell you the site width (important if you have an awning or slideout), what electrical power you can expect, whether pull-throughs are available, whether you can cool off under shade trees, whether the campground is open year-round or only seasonally; and whether a dump station is on the premises. For tips on using directories to select a site, see the sidebar "Choosing a site unseen" later in this chapter.

Directories also tell you whether a campground is privately owned or public. Calling ahead for reservations and specific information at private campgrounds is easy because charts and computer records of empty and occupied sites are kept up to date. In public campgrounds, rangers may be too busy to tell you anything beyond whether the campground is full yet. Even if it isn't full, don't expect them to hold a site until you arrive, because most public campgrounds don't accept reservations. Campers obtain sites on a first-come, first-served basis.

For a list of recommended campground directories, see the Appendix.

Choosing a site unseen

If you're picking out a campsite sight unseen from one of the voluminous park directories, here are some tips we've found useful through the years:

✔ Remember that ratings reflect the extras a campground offers, from playgrounds to clubhouses to cafes on the premises. If these amenities aren't important to you, pay more attention to the size, especially the width, of the sites and whether grass and trees are mentioned. New ratings reflect access to Internet and phone jacks at the campsite.

✔ Campgrounds with playgrounds, swimming pools, lakes, fishing, and game rooms attract families with children. If you want to avoid families, look for simpler surroundings.

✔ If you're a light sleeper, study the directions to the park from the interstate carefully. "Convenient" or "EZ-on-and-off" can be code words for "beside the Interstate." Some RV parks are what we call *three-point campgrounds* — near enough to hear the interstate trucks, planes taking off and landing at the airport, and postmidnight freight trains that sound loud whistles at rail crossings.

✔ Read between the lines. If a park has a large number of sites but only a few are available, it usually means that plenty of year-round residents commute to daily jobs, destroying some of the vacation atmosphere.

Comparing Private and Public Campgrounds

Privately owned campgrounds are convenient, offer full hookups, take advance reservations, and always have staff on duty during business hours. On the down side, they sometimes offer narrow sites as close as 15 to 20 feet apart and are set up in a parking lot configuration, which usually gives you a level setup and well-located hookups but no grass or shade.

We prefer finding private campgrounds that are members of a large national group, such as **KOA** or **Good Sam** because they're required to meet certain standards of upkeep to retain their membership and because they play host to traveling vacationers rather than full-time residents. See the "Saving Money on Campgrounds" section later in this chapter for information about becoming a member with these chains to obtain discounts.

Another kind of privately owned campground offers sites that are individually owned, but like time-share condos, they can be rented out when owners don't need them. These campgrounds may ban certain types of motorhomes or trailers; they all ban tents.

When you buy a membership in a time-share campground, you join a network of campgrounds where you can stay for only a couple of dollars a night. Although this deal may sound like a good one, the membership fees usually are between $2,500 and $5,000 (plus an annual maintenance fee), so you need to compute how many nights you plan to spend in campgrounds during the next few years at an average of $20 or so a night. The fee may equal 500 or more nights, which is perhaps more than you think you can use. You also may want to consider whether that membership chain has enough campgrounds to keep you happy for those 500 nights, and whether they're even located where you want to stay.

Some private campground owners go to plenty of trouble to create attractive campsites with terraces, privacy plantings, and extras from level concrete pads to small personal storage sheds on each site. An outstanding example of lavish camping is the superdeluxe site at **Buffalo KOA** in Buffalo, Wyoming (see Chapter 20). Campers who opt for the $75-per-night price get a private hot tub, fenced site with gazebo, patio table, built-in propane barbecue grill, glass and wrought iron patio table with chairs, planters full of bright petunias, and an abundance of trees and shrubs.

But in general terms, if you're looking for scenery and privacy, you often find much prettier and larger campsites at the **public campgrounds** in national forests or state parks, and even in some (but not all) national parks. What you won't always find are hookups or the ability to make reservations.

Among our favorite public campgrounds is **City of Rocks State Park** in southern New Mexico (see Chapter 21), where gigantic boulders surround sites that are far from each other and provide privacy. In Arkansas' **Jacksonport State Park** (see Chapter 19), the sites are near a river and are wide and grassy with mature shade trees. Oregon's **Sunset Bay State Park** is on the ocean with beachcombing, hiking trails, and a colorful lighthouse nearby (see Chapter 22). All three of these state parks also provide hookups.

Some of the most crowded campgrounds in the United States are in national parks — Yellowstone, for example. During peak season, you may want to stay in a private campground near a popular national park rather than in the park itself.

Choosing a Site

When we first started RVing, we wanted only perfect sites, secluded from other campers, surrounded by shade trees, preferably at the end of a row facing a view. The site had to be level — you'd be surprised how few sites outside paved parking lot campgrounds are really level — with a nice picnic table and fire pit or barbecue. These characteristics still are ideals to aspire to, but we had to get real. If we were the last RV to pull into the only campground with a vacancy sign at Mount Rushmore National Memorial at twilight on the Fourth of July weekend, we took what was left and learned to like it.

When site selection is abundant, we have a long list of preferences, all beginning with *L*.

✔ **Large:** The site must be big enough to park (and drive through or back in) our 36-foot motorhome and still have space for slideouts, chairs, table, and charcoal grill.

✔ **Latitude:** The width of a site becomes more important now that so many RVs of all types offer one or more *slideouts* (portions of the living and/or bedroom walls open up to expand the interior). Some older campgrounds can't handle slideouts and say so in their directory listings. Others have room for the slideout but no leftover space for you to use as a recreational area.

Any campsite less than 15 feet wide limits comfortable use of the site for durations longer than overnight.

✔ **Length:** The umbilical cords from the vehicle to the electric, water, and sewer connections must reach comfortably.

✔ **Level:** Whenever you don't have a big new RV with hydraulic jacks that level automatically, you have to do plenty of running back and forth inside and outside the vehicle to check *spirit levels* (those little things with moving bubbles inside); sometimes you have to wedge wooden blocks under the tires until that pesky little bubble hits the center. (What happens if your RV isn't level? Something dire and expensive befalls the refrigerator's hardware.)

✔ **Location:** We want to be away from the highway and campground entrance and not too near the swimming pool, bath facilities, office, laundry, garbage dumpster, playground, or dog-walking area.

✔ **Look out:** Watch for potentially noisy neighbors, any low-hanging branches or wires that can damage roof air conditioners or TV antennas, or wet or marshy ground that can mire you down if it rains all night. In addition, check the location of trees that can block opening slideouts or awnings, or interfere with reception if you have a satellite TV.

A campsite may or may not contain a picnic table, grill, or *fire ring* (a fire pit encircled by rocks) — all critical amenities for tent campers but luxuries for RVers, who already have a table, chairs, and cooktop inside their vehicle.

If you're going to stay in one campground for a while, look for an end site with hookups on the left side of the site. That means your door, folding chairs, and picnic table can face open space, perhaps even a view, rather than the RV next door and its hookups.

If you have no choice but to make your rig the meat in an RV sandwich, consider this: Unlike tent camping, where campers spend all their waking hours outdoors, RVs, especially motorhomes and trailers, enable you to go indoors for privacy. Even when you're parked only a foot or two away from the neighboring RV, you can close your curtains, draw the shades around your windshield, turn on some soft music, and you're totally alone.

Parking Your Rig

To choose the spot to put the RV overnight requires looking for the most level area and lining up the hookups in your vehicle with their connections on the site. If you have a back-in site, ask your copilot (if you have one) to get out and help back you in. If you have a pull-through, pull into the center of the site. In either case, make sure to leave room for the opening of slideouts and awnings. Your exact position depends on your hookups, however, which are accessible from the left rear of the vehicle. The electrical connection is usually a metal box mounted on a small post, with the water connection on the same post or nearby, and the sewer connection somewhere in the general vicinity. You may have to get out of the vehicle to pinpoint the sewer connection because it's usually a small hole in the ground covered with a white plastic cap that may or may not have a cemented area around it.

Occasionally, in older campgrounds, you may find side-by-side connections where two campsites share the same basic connections, with two water faucets, two electrical connections, and two sewer holes in the same area. Because all RVs hook up from their left rear, this means you and the neighboring RV would park facing opposite directions.

After you're in the position that you want, level the vehicle by using your built-in hydraulic system or blocks under the tires to achieve a level state. This is essential not only for your comfort and convenience but for proper functioning of your refrigerator.

Hooking Up

First-time RVers may have some fears about the process of hooking up when coming into a campground, but after a few times, you settle into a routine like this: Park and level your vehicle. (See the preceding section, "Parking Your Rig," for more on this.) Next comes the hooking up. You want a pair of work gloves and, for the sewer connections, disposable rubber gloves.

1. The first thing you want to do is **plug in your electrical shore cord** to the campground outlet, which is in the metal box affixed to a post and usually located at the left rear of the site. (Your RV's *shore cord* is the external electrical cord that connects the vehicle

to a campground electrical hookup.) Inside the box, you may have several connector choices, which can range from 20- to 50-amp.

Most outlets have an off/on switch that needs to be turned to the *off* position before plugging or unplugging your line. Turning the switch off prevents a surge that can knock out a circuit breaker in the vehicle. If your shore cord fits into one of the outlets, you won't need to use an adapter. If the shore cord doesn't fit, then you need the proper adapter for your unit. (See Chapter 6 for info on adapters.) You'll soon learn to recognize the amperage of an outlet on sight.

2. After you're plugged in properly, **turn on the switch** to the campground outlet. A good check to see whether you have electrical service is the timer light on your microwave, which lights up, perhaps even starts blinking a series of "8s," if you have electricity.

3. If you have an automatic switchover from propane to electric on your refrigerator (which most RVs do), **check the dials** on the refrigerator door to make sure it has switched from LP to AC. Now your electricity is connected and should be working properly.

4. Now **connect your RV's water hose,** which is connected to your water intake, to the campground faucet. Using a water pressure regulator (see Chapter 6) attached at one end of the hose is wise because many campgrounds have strong water pressure.

5. Next comes the part most novice RVers dread, although it's as simple as the other two connections. **Connect your sewer hose** to your drain outlet and to the campground sewer pipe. We suggest that you drain any fluid stored in the tanks when you hook up rather than the next morning when you're in a hurry to get rolling. (If you stay several days, you drain the sewer tank both when hooking up and when unhooking.) Drain the black water tank first, close off that valve (they're labeled), and then open the gray water tank valve. This helps flush the hose while emptying the tank. You can leave this valve open while camping, but you shouldn't leave the black water valve open because solids that settle in the tank are hard to clean out later. For our tips on emptying the holding tanks, see Chapter 6.

6. You're finished. **Relax** with a cold soda, beer, or martini.

Campground etiquette

In the popular RVing magazines, a large proportion of the letters deal with other campers who failed to show what the letter writer believes is proper etiquette in a campground. Bad behavior ranges from failing to clean up after your pet to running your generator after hours. To prevent **you** from becoming the subject of one of these letters, here are ten good rules to follow:

(continued)

(continued)

✔ **No claim jumping.** Anything marking a campsite, from a jug of water on a picnic table to a folding chair set out in the parking space, means that site is occupied, and the campers are temporarily away in their car or RV. You may not set the marker aside and move into the site.

✔ **Mind your fellow campers' personal space.** Teach your kids never to take a shortcut across an occupied campsite, but to use the road or established pathways to get where they're going. No one wants to watch a parade of kids and a dog troop through his site.

✔ **Keep your pets from roaming.** Never let your dog roam free in a campground. Rules require that pets always be on a leash and exercised in a designated pet area.

✔ **Avoid using your generator whenever possible, even within designated generator-use hours, to keep from disturbing other campers with the noise and fumes.** If using electrical appliances, such as microwaves and TV sets, is that important, go camping in a private campground with hookups, where you won't ever need a generator.

✔ **Avoid loud and prolonged engine revving in the early morning and late evening hours.** Fumes from your engine can easily go into the open windows of a nearby RV, and the noise can wake someone who planned to sleep in.

✔ **Don't play radios or TVs loudly at any time in a campground.** Many of your fellow campers are there to enjoy the peace and quiet. If they were rap music fans or anxious about what was happening next on TV's *Friends,* they would've stayed in town.

✔ **Never ever dump wastewater from holding tanks, even gray water, on the ground.** Although some old-timers claim it's good for the grass, wastewater may contain fecal matter from diapers or virulent salmonella bacteria if raw chicken has been rinsed in the sink. This material can be transferred to anyone touching or stepping on contaminated ground. Gray water, like black water, belongs only in a dump station.

✔ **Do not cut trees for firewood.** Most campgrounds sell firewood at special stands or the camp store. Even picking up or chopping dead wood is forbidden in many parks.

✔ **Watch what you throw in the fire.** Never leave aluminum foil, aluminum cans, bottles, or filter-tipped cigarette butts in a campground fire ring or grill. They do not burn but remain as litter. And never crush out cigarettes on the ground without picking up the butts and putting them in the garbage.

✔ **Don't leave porch or entry lights on all night in camp.** The lights may shine in someone else's bedroom window.

Sleeping by the Side of the Road: A Good Idea?

Although more than half the states permit some overnight parking in highway rest areas except where posted, we wouldn't consider parking our RV overnight in a rest area, shopping mall parking lot, truck stop, or by the side of the road unless in an emergency, because so many violent incidents occur in these areas. Some of our friends frequently do, however, and consider us money-wasting wimps for insisting on overnighting at a secure private or public campground.

We're constantly amazed at how many owners of expensive motorhomes take the risk of sleeping free in a parking lot or by the side of the road when the cost of their vehicle advertises how much in cash, credit cards, and expensive electronics may be inside. All this to save a few bucks? Campground fees are a modest investment in security and peace of mind. Besides, unlike RVers, the poor truckers with whom you share the road have few options when they need to take a rest. Why take up their space?

Saving Money on Campgrounds

RV camping is a bargain, particularly if you compare the costs to staying in hotels. However, even with campground fees averaging $20 a night, the costs can add up on long trips. What follows are our tips for minding the bottom line. For more tips on creating a budget, see Chapter 4.

- ✔ **Never pay for more park than you can use.** Posh playgrounds with swimming pool, spas, tennis courts, and miniature golf are usually pricier than the simple, mom-and-pop campground, which may be all you need for an overnight stay. If you have to pay per hookup, take the electric and water and forgo the sewer unless you really need it.

- ✔ **Watch out for campground surcharges,** such as extra fees for running your air conditioner or hooking up to cable TV, a surcharge for 50-amp electricity, or "extra person" charges for more than two people when you're traveling with your kids. Some of the campgrounds that accept pets may also levy a fee on Fido's head.

- ✔ **Join membership clubs** that offer a discount to member campgrounds, such as **KOA** (☎ 406-248-7444; www.koa.com) and **Good Sam** (☎ 800-234-3450; www.goodsamclub.com). For a membership fee between $10 and $15, you get about 10% off on campground fees. KOA offers the discount whether you pay for your site by cash or credit card; Good Sam usually grants the discount only if you pay cash. In most cases, you can join at the campground when you register.

- ✔ **Take advantage of age.** If you're older than 62 and apply for a free **Golden Age Passport** with proof of age at a national park visitor center, your vehicle enters the park, national monument, recreation area, or wildlife refuge **free,** and you get a **50% discount** on overnight camping areas administered by the federal government. See Chapter 5 for more details on this pass.

- ✔ **Look for free campgrounds.** County, city, and national forest campgrounds range from free to considerably less expensive than most privately owned campgrounds, although they don't often offer the luxury of hookups.

✔ **Stay longer than a week** and you can negotiate discounts, usually from 10% to 20% or even more, depending on the season and length of stay.

✔ **Consider volunteering as a campground host** if you're interested in staying a long time in one area. You can camp free and may pick up a bit of pocket change in exchange for performing specified duties on the premises. (See the next section for details.)

Being Campground Hosts

Energetic retirees and full-timers on a budget can camp free and some-times pick up a little extra income by becoming campground hosts. You find hosts in many campgrounds, both public and privately owned; they double as troubleshooters when the office is closed or the rangers are off duty. They're usually camped in a conspicuous spot near the entrance with a sign indicating that they're your hosts.

In theory, being a campground host is a great idea — you live in your RV in a lovely campground with free hookups, maybe even with your choice of sites. In practice, however, veterans of the job seem to either love it or hate it. Some mutter darkly of being treated like migrant labor, while others describe the experience as a highlight of their lives. Much depends on how thoroughly you check out the campground and its management ahead of time and how realistic you are about doing hard and sometimes unpleasant chores, such as cleaning toilets and showers or telling noisy campers to turn down their radios.

If you already have a **specific campground** in mind, contact them with a resume that includes personal and business references; you may also be asked for a recent photo. Many campgrounds prefer a couple to a single host, or require a single person to work 30 to 40 hours a week as compared to the 15 or 20 hours a couple would work.

If you want to volunteer in a **national park or forest service camp-ground,** contact the National Forest Service or the National Parks Service. (See the Appendix for addresses.)

Good Sam Club members can apply through that organization to work as hosts in Good Sam member campgrounds, which require a 60-day minimum stay. In contacting Good Sam, tell them the size and type of your RV; the first, second, and third choice of the states where you'd like to be; and the months you're available for work. (See Chapter 5 for contact information.)

If you get a positive response, before making a commitment, ask the campground manager for references so you can interview people who previously worked for them.

Chapter 10

Tying Up Loose Ends

. . . .

. . . .

So you're ready to hit the road in your RV. Do you need to know anything else? You definitely need maps and RV insurance. You may or may not opt to carry a cellphone, cable or satellite TV connections, a firearm, or a computer — details on all of these follow.

Mapping the Way

We love maps. We pore over them the way fashion plates devour every page of *Vogue* or motorcycle nuts glue themselves to the latest *Cycle World*. Every United States map we own shows somewhere we've been or plan to visit some day.

When we were young, back in the days before you filled your own gas tanks and washed your own windshield, your friendly service station owner not only filled your tank, checked your oil, and cleaned your windshield, but also gave you a free state map. You still can find maps in service stations today, but you have to pay for them.

The best places to get **free road maps** these days are at tourist information welcome centers as you enter different states. The offices usually are located on main highways or interstates. If state maps aren't prominently displayed on the counter or in racks, ask someone behind the desk for one. Besides official state road maps, these centers display rack after rack of local, regional, and city maps, some of them pinpointing landmarks and major attractions.

We always carry at least one U.S. road atlas, choosing from the many bound collections containing all 50 U.S. states. Although most maps look the same on the surface, each has certain features that are useful to RV travelers.

- ✔ *American Automobile Association (AAA) Truck and RV Road Atlas* features regulatory information for big vehicles for each state, state fuel tax rates, low clearance highways, route size and weight restrictions, and 1,900 truck stop listings. (☎ **877-AAA-BOOK** (877-222-2665); www.aaa.com).

- ✔ *Good Sam Club Road Atlas* has dots on its state maps designating the locations of Good Sam campgrounds and repair facilities. 2575 Vista del Mar Dr., Ventura, CA 93001 (☎ **800-234-3450**; www.goodsamclub.com).

- ✔ *National Geographic, The American Road Atlas & Travel Planner* highlights scenic attractions. One version comes with a convenient spiral binding so the pages lie flat when you're using them. P.O. Box 98198, Washington, DC 20090 (☎ **888-255-5647**; www.nationalgeographic.com).

- ✔ *Rand McNally Road Atlas* is updated annually with each issue containing some 4,500 changes, so we find ourselves buying the new edition every year. Rand McNally also issues a large-scale road atlas that we particularly like because the larger print is much easier to read in a moving vehicle. PO Box 654, Skokie, IL 60676 (☎ **800-333-0136**; www.randmcnally.com).

Real road techies may also want to invest in a global positioning system (GPS) receiver and high-tech navigation software, which promises that you won't get lost — at least you won't most of the time. These tech toys to us take all the fun out of reading a map, but gadget fans may enjoy them. A few good dealers who have units designated for RVs include:

- ✔ **Garmin International:** 1200 E. 151st St., Olathe, Kansas 66062 (☎ **800-800-1020**; www.garmin.com).

- ✔ **Magellan Corporation:** 960 Overland Court, San Dimas, CA 91773 (☎ **800-669-4477**; www.magellangps.com).

- ✔ **Weems & Plath:** 222 Severn Ave., Annapolis, MD 21403 (☎ **800-638-0428**; www.weems-plath.com).

Staying Connected on the Road

If you're one of those people who likes to know what's happening all the time, you don't have to lose touch on the road. With cable and satellite TV, cellular phones, and Internet connections, you can continue to watch your favorite shows, call your friends, and even conduct business.

Cable TV

Many private RV parks offer cable TV connections as an option, sometimes with a dollar or two added to the nightly fee. If you don't have a built-in exterior cable connection, you can use a length of coaxial cable hooked to the campground connection at one end, and then route it through a window to your RV's TV set. Carrying your own cable is best, though, because campgrounds rarely provide them. Don't forget to turn off the switch to your roof antenna. (Look for a little red light by the switch that tells you when it's on.) Having a male and female connector is wise because campground cable connections often vary.

Satellite TV

Newer models of RVs now have satellite dishes mounted to the roofs of the vehicles with internal wiring that leads to a control box that's usually installed near the TV set. Software for whatever program system you use usually is included with the package. The two major systems are DISH Network and DIRECTV. One disadvantage of the mounted dish is that in many campgrounds trees always seem to be directly in the path of the satellite signal, thus requiring you to move the vehicle to make a connection. Mention whether you have such a system when checking in so the registrar can assign you a tree-free site, if one's available.

We carry a portable dish on a tripod using a secondary control box from our home. Doing so means we don't have to have a separate account for the RV. The dish can be set down almost anywhere — on the ground or on a picnic table, in front, beside, or behind the RV — making it much more versatile than a fixed dish atop the RV.

Fixed or portable, satellite dishes are particularly advantageous when you travel in rural areas with little or no local TV reception or when you plan to stay in one area for several days.

Remember, your dish programming is set on your home time, so as you move to other time zones, programs will air according to your television schedule at home. West Coast travelers RVing on the East Coast, for example, find that their 8 p.m. programs can't be seen until 11 p.m.

Cellular phones

We always carry a cellular phone with us, but it provides almost as much frustration as assistance. The places we like to drive and camp frequently are, if not always, in borderline or no-service areas. Our previous cellphone featured a roaming system that theoretically could forward our calls to almost anywhere in the U.S. and Canada that we happened to be. Our editors have been able to reach us in the wilds of British Columbia or when we're driving down an interstate in West

Texas, but they can't seem to get through to us when we're on a two-day outing in a park in San Diego or Santa Barbara counties, only a hoot and a holler from our Los Angeles base.

We find cellphones most helpful for dialing ahead for campground reservations or for returning business calls we've picked up from our home answering machine when campground or highway pay phones are too noisy. And we're certainly happy to have one in case of an emergency.

If you're happy with your present cellphone service, then stay with it. Otherwise, if you plan an RV vacation, find out in advance what kind of service you can expect on the road and at your destination. Sometimes the technology leaves much to be desired, with voices fading in and out when you're in fringe reception areas. Some pricing plans include long distance and roaming charges throughout the U.S. for a flat fee for a certain number of minutes. Check out all available systems and prices before deciding on one for your RV vacation.

If you're reluctant to invest in a cellular phone, be aware that most private campgrounds and many public campgrounds have a pay phone on the premises.

Computer online services

Online RV bulletin boards on computer services, such as AOL, enable RV enthusiasts or wannabe RVers to exchange dialogue, offer helpful hints, and discuss the pros and cons of the various vehicle brands. So logging on to one of the RV sites is fun and helpful before your trip.

While on the road, you may want to access your e-mail. Most campgrounds offer e-mail access, sometimes free, through a phone jack in the main office, store, laundry room, or recreation room. They obviously offer access only to a local or toll-free number for retrieving your e-mail, so it's a good idea to find out the numbers you need to use to access your Internet service provider at the places you're planning to stay. (In this book, campgrounds listed with e-mail access are designated as having "dataports.")

 Preparing your e-mail ahead of time — before you access the modem and go online — can save plenty of money. You save even more by downloading your incoming e-mail and disconnecting from the phone jack before reading your messages.

Some upscale campgrounds now have phone connections at the campsites (designated as "phone jacks" in the listings of this book) for those newer motorhomes that have phone lines built into the wiring system. This feature enables you to send and retrieve e-mail from your RV.

Buying RV Insurance

We were pleasantly surprised to find that our RV insurance was very affordable, even in costly Southern California. Safe driving records, a shorter use period during the year, and slightly older drivers (on average) mean less risk for the insurer. Before buying, check with your own automobile insurance carrier and the following specialized RV insurance carriers.

- ✔ **AARP Insurance:** ☎ 800-541-3717; www.aarp.com.

- ✔ **Foremost Insurance Company:** ☎ 800-545-8608; www.foremost. com.

- ✔ **Good Sam Club's National General:** ☎ 800-234-3450; www.good samclub.com.

- ✔ **RV Alliance America:** ☎ 800-521-2942; www.rvalliance america.com.

Securing towing insurance in case of a breakdown is a good idea; in many cases, AAA (American Automobile Association) members can extend that company's towing coverage to their RVs.

If you're renting an RV, the rental company usually carries basic insurance on the vehicle covering bodily injury, property damage, uninsured motorist, no-fault, and fire and theft. The renter may be liable for a deductible on collision and comprehensive. Check it out before taking out the vehicle. You may want to pay an additional sum for Vacation Interruption Protection in the event of a vehicle breakdown; the rental agencies usually can provide this coverage.

Staying Safe and Secure on the Road

Staying overnight in a parking lot or truck stop instead of a legitimate campground or public park just to save a few dollars is false economy. Your RV, especially if it's big and shiny, advertises your net worth to anyone with thievery on the brain. If you're stranded, it's dark, and all the campgrounds are full, then that's a different situation, but we see RVers staying free in Wal-Mart or Camping World lots with their folding chairs and sometimes even their charcoal grills out, having a full camping experience instead of simply parking overnight and leaving when morning comes.

Campgrounds, on the other hand, generally are safe, but not the way they used to be. Back when we were tent campers, we departed on hikes leaving all our worldly goods protected only by the tent zipper. These days, we lock our RV even when we're just going to the campground store or laundry for a while. Not everyone in campgrounds these days is on vacation. Some are unemployed people looking for work or part of a transient population permanently on the move.

Privately owned RV parks probably are safer in the long run than public campgrounds that aren't sufficiently staffed to keep a constant eye on things. Reports of stolen folding chairs or bicycles are becoming more common. We even left our sewer hose with its expandable drain stand and water hose hooked up at one California campsite, guarded by a red "Campsite Occupied" sign, while we went away for a few hours in our motorhome; we returned to find the hose, the drain stand, and even the sewer host had been taken. But the "Campsite Occupied" sign still was there.

In the long run, we recommend using the same precautions in a campground that you normally would at home, that is, if you're an urban dweller. If you live in what you believe is a safe neighborhood, however, then pretend you're in New York or Los Angeles.

Carrying a Gun

If you want to start a lively argument around a campground, try this as an opener. We personally never would carry a firearm of any sort in our motorhome, but then we'd never have one at home, either. Although many frequent and full-timing RVers agree, just as many others disagree, sometimes vociferously.

One RVer we know is a retired policeman who says the purpose of a gun is to kill, and if you're not prepared to kill, you need to reconsider taking a gun along. If you insist on carrying one, he says, you must take professional training in how and when to use it, and more important, when not to use it.

Entering Mexico with a firearm of any sort can land an RV owner in jail — and has, in several documented cases. Canada also prohibits you from entering the country with guns of any sort. Don't take a chance. The days of RVs simply being waved through border crossings are gone.

Despite our feelings that our motorhome is indeed our home, the law in many states considers the RV a motor vehicle when moving and a home only when parked in camp. Therefore, when in transit, any firearms you're carrying must be unloaded with the bullets stored separately from the weapon.

Firearms are prohibited in many state parks.

If we did choose to carry a firearm, we'd make it a point to keep abreast of each state's regulations, because they can differ radically the moment you cross a state line.

Part III
Exploring the East

In this part . . .

This part guides you through five drives in the eastern United States. Take the drive in Chapter 11, and find yourself at the seashore eating more lobster at cheaper prices than you ever believed possible. Select the drive through western New York in Chapter 12, and you'll be reminded of why you love Lucy, where Jell-O came from, and why baseball is a uniquely American sport. Choose the drive in Chapter 13 to cruise a scenic and historic road through the Blue Ridge Mountains, where dogwood blooms and autumn leaves turn vivid crimson and gold. Dig your toes into sugary white sand along the balmy coast of the Gulf of Mexico in Chapter 14, or visit historical sites from the Civil War to the life of Elvis in Chapter 15.

Chapter 11

The Coast of Maine: Lobster Land

● ●

In This Chapter

▶ Traveling the rocky coast of Maine

▶ Feasting on fresh lobster

▶ Finding fantastic factory outlets

▶ Hiking and biking through Acadia National Park

▶ Discovering Andrew Wyeth's world

● ●

The rocky coast of Maine evolved through the centuries from a now-submerged mountain range — a sheet of ice scoured and then flooded the mountains, with only the peaks remaining above the ice-melt. Somes Sound, which bisects the lower half of Mount Desert Island in Acadia National Park, is the only true *fjord* (a narrow sea inlet bordered on both sides by steep cliffs) on the east coast.

The mystique of the craggy shore and pounding waves, the sharp peeps of shore birds and the clanging of a bell buoy, stalwart lighthouses puncturing lingering fog, the tangy saltwater scent, weathered buildings, and peeling lobster pots — all lend color, sound, taste, touch, and smell to the experience that is Maine.

For us, Maine offers a blend of scenic and culinary sensations — the vivid orange-red hue of a freshly boiled lobster; the creamy white-on-white blend of Maine potatoes, cream, clams, and fatty bacon in a chowder; and the puckery, purple, sweet-sour crunch of a handful of wild blueberries.

Getting There

Kittery, on the Maine/New Hampshire border at I-95, is one hour north of Boston. Our drive follows U.S. 1, parallel to I-95, 72 miles to **Brunswick,** and then turns east away from I-95 to follow the Maine coastline through **Bath** to **Rockland, Camden, Belfast, Bucksport,** and **Ellsworth.** It then drops south to **Bar Harbor** and **Mount Desert Island** by following SR 3

The Coast of Maine

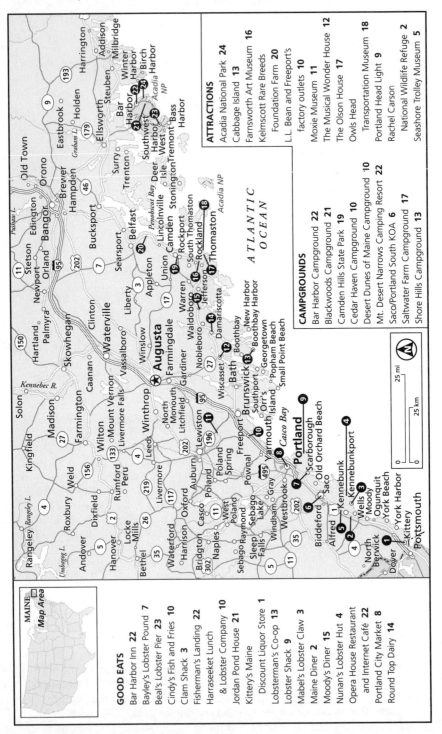

ATTRACTIONS

Acadia National Park **24**
Cabbage Island **13**
Farnscott Art Museum **16**
Kelmscott Rare Breeds
  Foundation Farm **20**
L.L. Bean and Freeport's
  factory outlets **10**
Moxie Museum **11**
The Musical Wonder House **12**
The Olson House **17**
Owls Head
  Transportation Museum **18**
Portland Head Light **9**
Rachel Carson
  National Wildlife Refuge **2**
Seashore Trolley Museum **5**

CAMPGROUNDS

Bar Harbor Campground **22**
Blackwoods Campground **21**
Camden Hills State Park **19**
Cedar Haven Campground **10**
Desert Dunes of Maine Campground **10**
Mt. Desert Narrows Camping Resort **22**
Saco/Portland South KOA **6**
Saltwater Farm Campground **17**
Shore Hills Campground **13**

MAINE □
Map Area

GOOD EATS

Bar Harbor Inn **22**
Bayley's Lobster Pound **7**
Beal's Lobster Pier **23**
Cindy's Fish and Fries **10**
Clam Shack **3**
Fisherman's Landing **22**
Harraseeket Lunch
  & Lobster Company **10**
Jordan Pond House **21**
Kittery's Maine
  Discount Liquor Store **1**
Lobsterman's Co-op **13**
Lobster Shack **9**
Mabel's Lobster Claw **3**
Maine Diner **2**
Moody's Diner **15**
Nunan's Lobster Hut **4**
Opera House Restaurant
  and Internet Café **22**
Portland City Market **8**
Round Top Dairy **14**

for 10 miles, taking the bridge across Mount Desert Narrows to the junction with SR 102, and then turning east on SR 3 another 6 miles into Bar Harbor. The distance is approximately 225 miles. For the route, see "The Coast of Maine" map in this chapter.

If you encounter traffic snarls on U.S. 1, you can use the parallel I-95, a much faster interstate route. Note, however, that between York Village at Exit 1 and Portland at Exit 15, I-95 is also called the Maine Turnpike, and a toll is charged. RV tolls vary, depending on the number of axles on the vehicle and the mood of the toll-taker, who may, if you're lucky, elect to charge RVs the same rate as cars. Otherwise, you usually pay 50% to 100% more.

Roads around popular beach resorts such as Scarborough, Old Orchard Beach, and Saco often are jammed with slow-moving traffic, but you'll find the going easier as you get farther north.

Planning Ahead

The **best time** to visit Maine is also the most crowded because everyone enjoys the warm summer months and colorful fall season. **May,** which is too early for the summer folk and the black flies, can be a good alternative, as can **late August and September,** which see a lessening of tourists and insect life. Unfortunately, after schools and colleges open in September, many small-town New England establishments close down for the winter because the minimum-wage crowd goes back to school and only a few other workers remain.

You need to make **campground reservations** well in advance (think March or April, if you're visiting in summer) for the more popular RV parks, especially those in national or state parks, and particularly if you're driving a large motorhome (some New England campgrounds are short on long sites) or planning a lengthy stay in any one campground. Most of the campgrounds along this drive were built back in the 1940s and 1950s, the days of tents and tiny trailers, the little two-wheel tow-alongs we think of as Minnie Mouse trailers. Our big, wide-body motorhome with two slideouts fits into them like Mama Cass trying to squeeze into Calista Flockhart's dress. But we found out early on that it's worth the effort. Just make reservations as far ahead as possible and emphasize your vehicle's needs so you can guarantee a workable space. And if you can remember to ask for a pull-through, plus a 30- or 50-amp hookup, you'll be able to reserve a campsite that fits you like a glove. (If you don't know what "pull-through" and "hookup" mean, see the Appendix in the back of this book.)

When **packing,** taking along an umbrella and raincoat, hiking boots, hot-weather gear, such as shorts and T-shirts, and cool-weather gear, such as slacks and sweaters or sweatshirts, is a good idea. **Maine coastal weather changes frequently,** sometimes several times a day.

Fortunately, with an RV, you're carrying your own closet and dressing room with you, so you can easily change when the weather does.

Although the distance covered isn't great, you need to allow **10 to 14 days** for a leisurely visit with time for enjoying camping and seeking out *lobster pounds* (a casual live lobster market with on-site cooking and takeout service and/or picnic tables) and little antiques shops. If you want to spend more time in New England, you can add on **Cape Cod** or a venture north into Canada's maritime provinces of **New Brunswick, Nova Scotia,** and **Prince Edward Island.** See our book, *Frommer's Exploring America by RV,* 3rd Edition (Wiley, Inc.).

Stocking the Pantry

If you want to restock on wine or other alcoholic items for your holiday at prices much lower than Manhattan or Boston, **Kittery's Maine Discount Liquor Store** at Exit 1 on 1-95 for northbound traffic is open daily except Thanksgiving, Christmas, and New Year's.

An essential shopping stop for us in Kittery is the downtown **Portland City Market** where we stock up on fresh, harvested-in-Maine products from seafood, such as Damariscotta's Maine Belon oysters, to farmhouse cheeses and three different varieties of local potatoes. Ready-to-eat foods also are on sale. (See "Good eats" later in this chapter.)

Driving the Coast of Maine

The crown jewel of New England is the rocky, windswept coast of Maine, and we never tire of traveling its winding, scenic roads and searching out its hidden treasures. For RVers, New England is an exhilarating blend of incredible scenery, exciting shopping, and delectable dining that counters the sobering prospect of easing a big motorhome or trailer into the typical local campsite. Sticking to U.S. 1 or its interstate parallel, I-95, is no problem for even the most inexperienced RV driver. Our driving tour begins in **Kittery,** the first town in Maine after crossing the border from New Hampshire.

The three Yorks — **York Village, York Harbor,** and **York Beach** — often are crowded with summer visitors on a budget who gravitate to the small motels and rooming houses that give this area its old-fashioned aura. A bit more classic is **Ogunquit,** the next town north, with its well-trod Marginal Way seaside walk, art galleries, and lofty allusions to painters such as Edward Hopper.

Environmentalists and birders need to visit the **Rachel Carson National Wildlife Refuge** north of Wells to grow acquainted with the salt-marsh wilderness. (See "More cool things to see and do" later in this chapter.)

Continue north on SR 9 past the wildlife refuge to **Kennebunkport,** the summer home to former president George Bush and his wife Barbara, a fashionable destination worth a thoughtful pause. The senior Bushes are known to dine amid the kitschy clutter at **Mabel's Lobster Claw** in Kennebunkport, but the supercasual **Nunan's Lobster Hut** at Cape Porpoise is a hit with almost everybody (See "Good eats.") The world's largest collection of streetcars, some 250 of them, is gathered at the **Seashore Trolley Museum.** On view is one of New Orleans' streetcars named Desire. (See "More cool things to see and do.")

Continuing north on U.S. 1, you come to **Saco, Biddeford,** and **Old Orchard Beach.** The last is where you're likely to hear more French than English spoken on the beaches and in the amusement parks. Ever since 1853, when the Grand Trunk Railroad ran between Montreal and Old Orchard Beach, thousands of French Canadians have flocked to the 7 miles of sandy beach lined with modestly priced lodgings and restaurants. This is the closest thing to Coney Island or the Jersey shore that you'll find in Maine.

Traveling a few miles farther north on U.S. 1 brings you to **Portland,** one of America's great small cities, colorful, accessible, and fairly easy to navigate with an RV.

One of our favorite detours from Portland is a drive around Cape Elizabeth to **Portland Head Light,** Maine's oldest lighthouse. (See "Must-see attractions," later in this chapter.)

 But even a bright coastal light fades next to America's most appealing shopping mall, the town of **Freeport.** The center of town is the mailorder giant **L.L. Bean,** open 24/7, surrounded by some **200 factory-outlet retailers** with every brand name you can think of from Coach to Nike. (See "Must-see attractions.")

 Freeport always is full of shoppers, but don't let that deter you from stopping to snap up some bargains. The L.L. Bean Factory Outlet store, site of the best bargains in town, is next to the special free RV parking area, which in turn, is just steps away from all the factory outlets. Although you aren't permitted to stay overnight there, the town nevertheless has several campgrounds. (See "Sleeping and Eating on the Road" later in this chapter.)

One of the great lobster pounds is also in Freeport, at **Harraseeket Lunch & Lobster Company.** (See "Good eats.")

Wiscasset calls itself the prettiest village in Maine, and nobody yet has arm-wrestled it down on that claim. Many buildings in town are on the National Register of Historic Places; one of them, **The Musical Wonder House,** an 1852 sea captain's house at 18 High Street, displays and plays a collection of 19th-century music boxes, gramophones, pump organs, crank organs, player pianos, and mechanical musical birds. (See "More cool things to see and do.")

Damariscotta: Round Top Dairy

If your sweet tooth acts up as you're dawdling along U.S. 1 between **Wiscasset** and **Nobleboro,** take the Business U.S. 1 loop off the main highway so you can pause in **Damariscotta** at **Round Top Dairy,** a family ice cream shop. Choose from among more flavors than you can imagine in a pretty, little cafe decorated with 1940s and 1950s pictures of 4-H kids with prize-winning cows.

Two miles east of Wiscasset, you can take a 12-mile detour south on SR 27 to **Boothbay Harbor,** a colorful fishing, lobstering, and boat-building town. From the harbor, you can take a day cruise on the *Argo* to Cabbage Island for the traditional **Cabbage Island Clambake.** (See "More cool things to see and do.")

In **Waldoboro** on U.S. 1, **Moody's Diner** is the quintessential Maine diner, opened first in 1927 as a three-cabin campground and outhouse for hunters and fishermen. In 1935, the diner joined the scene and quickly built a lasting reputation for huge breakfasts at budget prices. (See "Good eats.") We cheated on our midmorning repast here, politely forking up the rather bland corned beef hash and eggs, and then gobbling down a slice of fantastic chocolate cream pie for dessert.

For art buffs, **Rockland** is the equivalent of hitting the jackpot on a $1 Vegas slot. All available on one easy ticket, the **Farnsworth Art Museum** complex salutes three generations of the Wyeth family and other great artists who lived in or worked in this part of Maine, with its legendary light and mystique. Clustered in town you'll find the furnished, Victorian Farnsworth Homestead; the striking, contemporary, six-level, art museum (most of it underground); and the new Wyeth Center, austerely installed in a former church. (See "Must-see attractions.")

A few miles away outside the farm community of **Cushing** is the evocative **Olson House,** the remote farm with its unpainted house and barn that's in the background of *Christina's World,* Andrew Wyeth's masterpiece. Wyeth spent more than 20 years painting in and around the Olson House, and today, visitors can match a room or view with a print of a Wyeth work displayed on-site in the otherwise unfurnished house. (See "Must-see attractions.")

A short detour south from Rockland takes you to the **Owls Head Transportation Museum,** a dandy if sometimes-noisy place on weekends when aficionados crank up pre-1930s planes, steam farm vehicles, and antique automobiles, and take a ride. (See "More cool things to see and do.")

Rockport and **Camden,** where the mountains meet the water, are picturesque enough to eat up multiple rolls of color film, but you need to find a parking spot big enough for your RV before you can settle down to shoot. Several public parking lots are adjacent to the Rockland Harbor Trail, a 4-mile footpath that winds through the historic waterfront. In Camden, look for street parking along Elm Street (U.S. 1) on the hill above the waterfront area.

Off U.S. 1 between **Lincolnville** and **Belfast, Kelmscott Rare Breeds Foundation Farm,** a working farm of rare livestock breeds — sheep, Shire horses, and Gloucestershire Old Spots pigs — offers a diversion for pet lovers or families with children in tow. The shoppers among you can hurry to its shop to buy items made from wool shorn from the sheep on the premises. (See "More cool things to see and do.")

On your way into Bar Harbor, you may want to stop at the **Acadia Information Center** (☎ 800-358-8550) on SR 3 just after you cross the bridge to pick up armloads of maps and brochures about the area and some information about **Acadia National Park.** The center is open daily from 10 a.m. to 6 p.m. between mid-May and mid-October.

We suggest lingering several days in **Bar Harbor** to browse in the colorful and whimsical town shops along Main Street, Cottage Street, and Mount Desert Street around the Village Green, and to spend some time exploring nearby Acadia National Park. If time is short, spend most of the day in the park and hit the shops that evening after dinner; most shops are open until 9 p.m. in summer. Seasonal shops open in early to mid-May and close down by the end of October.

Don't count on being able to park a trailer or large motorhome anywhere in downtown Bar Harbor. A designated lot is on the edge of town at the south end of Main Street, but your wisest choice if you have a large RV or are towing an RV is to leave the unit at the campground and use a car or utilize the free shuttle-bus service offered in the summer months.

Must-see attractions

Acadia National Park

Although you can cram the scenic wonders of Acadia National Park into one day's drive, you'll be rewarded if you allow some extra time.

For a one-day visit, drive scenic **Park Loop Road,** which makes a 27-mile circle out of Bar Harbor from SR 3 south of town, with all the attractions pointed out by signage. If you start by heading south on the loop toward the **Wild Gardens** and **Sand Beach,** you can cover the sometimes traffic-clogged one-way stretch from **Otter Cliffs** to **Seal Harbor** earlier in the day, take a lunch or tea break at **Jordan Pond** (see "Good eats" later in this chapter), and climax the day with the drive up **Cadillac Mountain.** At 1,530 feet, it's the highest mountain on the Atlantic coast of North America.

If you have another day to spend in Acadia National Park, consider taking a bike ride along some of the 45 miles of **carriage roads** between Hulls Cove Visitor Center and Jordan Pond, where motor traffic is forbidden. John D. Rockefeller, who hated automobiles, commissioned these gravel roads for horse-drawn vehicles, walkers, and bicyclists.

Or you may opt for a hike up **Acadia Mountain.** A moderate, 2-mile, round-trip trail through pines and birch trees sets out from the Acadia Mountain parking area 3 miles south of Somesville on SR 102. (To get there from Bar Harbor, drive west on SR 233, which turns into SR 198 at Somesville.) Then afterward, treat yourself to a lobster lunch at **Beal's Lobster House** in Southwest Harbor (see "Good eats").

Find the best detailed information and maps for Acadia at the **Hull's Cove Visitor Center** (☎ 207-288-3338) on SR 3 north of Bar Harbor. The center is open daily mid-April through the end of October from 8 a.m. to 4:30 p.m. and to 6 p.m. in July and August.

Although Park Loop Road, one of the park's most popular attractions, generally is accessible for RVs, we suggest that you consider leaving your RV in the campground, especially if you're driving a large motorhome or towing a trailer, because parking space is limited in many park turnouts. Likewise, if you have an unusually tall RV, note that the SR 3 bridge underpass on Park Loop Road near Blackwoods **does not clear vehicles higher than 11 feet, 8 inches** and that the Stanley Brook park entrance from the southeast **does not permit vehicles higher than 10 feet, 4 inches.**

You can avoid knocking off your TV antenna by traveling the route in your own or a rental car, by bicycle (rentals are available from **Acadia Bike and Coastal Kayak Tours,** 48 Cottage St., ☎ 800-526-8615 outside Maine or 207-288-9605, or **Bar Harbor Bicycle Shop,** 141 Cottage St., ☎ 207-288-3886), or by local shuttle bus (**Island Explorer,** ☎ 207-667-5796), which makes frequent circuits between campgrounds, town, and designated points in the national park during the summer. The shuttle buses are equipped with bicycle racks.

The park's main entrance is on SR 3 at Hulls Cove.

Farnsworth Art Museum
Rockland

When the Farnsworth family's sole remaining member, an eccentric and reclusive maiden lady, died in 1935 at the age of 96, executors were astonished to find that she left a sizeable estate, along with directions to preserve the home and create an art museum. Today, the complex consists of the Farnsworth Homestead, Farnsworth Art Museum, the Wyeth Center, and a teaching center in Rockland and the Olson House in Cushing.

The **Farnsworth Homestead** is a well-preserved mid-19th-century home with many of its original furnishings.

The seven galleries of the **Farnsworth Art Museum** (most of the floors in this contemporary building are underground) showcase not only the Wyeths — grandfather, N.C., son, Andrew, and grandson, Jamie — but also American artists from Gilbert Stuart and Thomas Eakins to Winslow Homer and Childe Hassam and Rockland-born sculptor Louise Nevelson.

The **Wyeth Center** is housed in a converted church stripped down to bare wood floors and movable sailcloth dividers framed in mahogany. The ground floor displays book illustrations from patriarch N.C. Wyeth, who lamented much of his life that his work wasn't appreciated as fine art, and the upper gallery is dedicated to Jamie Wyeth, a strikingly original artist in his own right, best-known for his portraits of John F. Kennedy and Andy Warhol.

356 Main St. (which also is U.S. 1), downtown Rockland. ☎ 207-596-6457. www. farnsworthmuseum.org, www.wyethcenter.com. RV parking: Museum parking lots (some enclosed and too low for large vehicles) and street parking in the area. Admission: $9 adults, $8 seniors, $5 students older than 18 with valid ID, free ages 17 and younger; add $2 to also visit Olson House (see listing later in this section). Open: Farnsworth Homestead, guided or self-guided tours daily Memorial Day to Columbus Day 10 a.m.–5 p.m.; Farnsworth Art Museum and Wyeth Center, daily Memorial Day to Columbus Day 9 a.m.–5 p.m.; rest of the year Tues–Sun 10 a.m.–5 p.m. Allow a half-day.

L.L. Bean and Freeport's factory outlets
Freeport

The L.L. Bean dynasty has been around since 1911, when Leon Leonwood Bean sold 100 pairs of leather-and-rubber hunting boots and had 90 pairs returned because the boot fell apart from faulty stitching. He returned the money to the buyers, corrected the problems in construction, and went into the mail-order sporting goods business backed by a retail store that was kept open 24 hours a day, 365 days a year. Today, the company he founded stocks more than 12,000 different items, and the main retail store at 95 Main St. (☎ **800-341-4341**) still is open for business 24/7.

But L.L. Bean no longer is alone in the pretty little town of Freeport. Now, some 200 other name brands vie with Bean in an easy-to-stroll village atmosphere. Our favorite bargain spot is **L.L. Bean's Factory Discount Store** (☎ **800-341-4341**), across Main Street from the parent store and around the corner on Depot Street.

On U.S. 1, 16 miles north of Portland. Free visitor guide available by calling ☎ 800-865-1994 or logging on to www.freeportusa.com. RV parking: Free lot located one block south of Main Street at Depot Street; overnight parking not permitted. Allow a half to full day, depending on your stamina and your pocketbook.

The Olson House
Hathorne Point near Cushing

In 1948, Andrew Wyeth painted *Christina's World* in tempera, depicting a young Christina Olson, wearing her favorite pink dress and dragging her crippled body up the hill to the family home, where she lived with her brother Alvaro. Wyeth, who spent his summers in Cushing, continued to devote many hours to the Olson farm, painting images of the house and the views from its windows, even after Christina and Alvaro had died — he on Christmas Eve 1967 and she a month later. Both are buried in the small family graveyard by the sea, only a short distance in back of the spot where Christina is depicted in the painting.

Today, the house and farm are preserved and tended by the Farnsworth Art Museum, and to visit it on a foggy autumn day, as we did, is to summon up the ghosts of the past in an incredibly moving setting.

Hathorne Point Road. (Take Wadsworth River Road from the center of Thomaston, turning east by the Maine Prison Showroom — which sells crafts turned out by inmates of the state system — then follow the road 6.2 miles to Pleasant Point Road, turn left and follow it 1.5 miles to Hathorne Point Road, which you then follow 1.9 miles to its end, where the Olson House is found on the left. The signage is good all along the route after you make the turn in Thomaston.) ☎ *207-596-6457.* www.wyethcenter.com. *RV parking: Park along the shoulder of the roadway rather than in the small lot behind the house if you're driving a large motorhome or towing a trailer. Admission (self-guided tours): $4 adults, free ages 17 and younger. Open: Daily Memorial Day to Columbus Day 11 a.m.–4 p.m. Allow 1 hour.*

Portland Head Light
Cape Elizabeth

The historic Portland Head Light, commissioned by George Washington in 1790, built of "rubblestone set in lime" and finished in 1791, is the oldest of Maine's Lighthouses. Still in service and virtually unchanged from its beginning, the lighthouse is part of Fort Williams, a military outpost for coastal defense. In the former lighthouse keeper's quarters, a small museum chronicles the history of the lighthouse along with anecdotal local details.

1000 Shore Rd., Fort Williams (From I-295 in downtown Portland, take SR 77 south and shortly after crossing the bridge, turn east on Cottage Road, which becomes Shore Road. Follow signs.) ☎ *207-799-2661. RV parking: Designated parking area. Admission: $2 adults, $1 ages 6–18. Open: Weekends early Apr to May 30 10 a.m.–4 p.m.; daily May 31 to Labor Day 10 a.m.–4 p.m. Allow 1–2 hours.*

More cool things to see and do

The family friendly coast of Maine offers a number of things to see and do. During your drive, you'll run across many examples, particularly commercial attractions that may not be included in the list that follows:

✔ **Have a clambake.** The **Cabbage Island Clambake** on Cabbage Island is a traditional lobster-and-clam supper served in summer at lunch and dinner. You board the *Argo* at Pier 6 in Boothbay Harbor, cruise over to the island, and feast on local lobster, clams, corn on the cob, and boiled potatoes.

Pier 6, Boothbay Harbor (12 miles south of Wiscasset on SR 27). ☎ **207-633-7200.** RV parking: Street parking. Admission: $41.95 per person for cruise and clambake, daily from June to mid-September; reservations required; no credit cards.

✔ **Play Dr. Doolittle.** The **Kelmscott Rare Breeds Foundation Farm** is a nonprofit working farm dedicated to conserving rare breeds of livestock, everything from cuddly, curly-haired Cotswold sheep to endangered Gloucestershire Old Spots pigs and Nigerian dwarf goats. More than 200 animals representing ten rare breeds are on the premises, and visitors can "adopt" one of the animals by helping to pay for its feed and care. Wagon rides with Pete the Shire horse, and Border collie trials of the kind that you saw in the movie *Babe* may be on the calendar of events. A **woolen shop** at the farm sells a line of classic English wool blankets, scarves, duvets, and hats.

RR 2, Box 365, Lincolnville. (Drive 6 miles southwest of Belfast via SR 52, then west on Van Cycle [Farm Road 90].) ☎ **800-545-9363** or 207-763-4088. www.kelmscott.org. RV parking: Large parking area. Admission: $5 adults, $3 ages 4–15. Open: May–Oct Tues–Sun 10 a.m.–5 p.m., Nov–Apr Tues–Sun 10 a.m.–3 p.m. Closed Monday. Allow 1–2 hours depending on your age.

✔ **Acquire some Moxie.** We met the Moxie Man, Frank Anicetti II, in his **Moxie Museum** at the **Moxie Bottling Company** and corner store, still selling America's oldest soft drink. Moxie, made from gentian root, started as a "nerve medicine" in 1884, but gathered fame in the 1920s when its name entered the dictionary as a synonym for "nerve, courage, and energy." Anicetti ships Moxie by the case across the entire U.S., and welcomes in-person visits from fans such as mystery novelist Stephen King, who on our visit, had signed the Moxie guest book four signatures above ours. Besides Moxie in bottles and cans, Anicetti sells Moxie T-shirts and other memorabilia and souvenirs in his free museum/store.

Located in downtown Lisbon Falls, on Main Street, which also is SR 196, where it crosses SR 125. SR 196 is the Lisbon Falls exit off I-95 at Brunswick. ☎ **207-353-8173.** RV parking: Street parking. Admission: Free. Open: Daily 9 a.m.–5 p.m. Allow half an hour unless you're thirsty.

✔ **Wind down.** A wonderful collection of music boxes, player grand pianos, and talking machines can be seen in **The Musical Wonder House,** which offers three tours: a standard 35-minute tour, an extended 75-minute tour, and a deluxe 3-hour version that tours the entire mansion (the last one requires a prior reservation and a minimum of two people).

18 High St., Wiscasset. ☎ 207-882-7163. www.musicalwonder house.com. RV parking: Street parking. Admission: standard tour $10 adults, $9 seniors and ages 17 and younger; extended tour $18 adults, $17.50 seniors and ages 17 and younger; deluxe tour $30 per person (no discount rates). Open: Mid-May to mid-Oct daily 10 a.m.–5 p.m.

✔ **Ride a Stanley Steamer.** This museum isn't one of those boring ones where you walk past the exhibits. At **Owls Head Transportation Museum,** you get to see machines in action and maybe even ride on one if you visit on summer weekends. From the Red Baron's World War I Fokker Triplane to Clara Bow's Rolls Royce and a hissing Stanley Steamer steam automobile, the exhibits still are in working order. Call ahead to see what's going to be cranked up when you're in the vicinity.

Located 2 miles south of Rockland, on SR 73 at the Knox County Airport; signage is plentiful. ☎ 207-594-4418. www.ohtm.org. RV parking: Large parking lot. Admission: $7 adults, $6 seniors, $5 ages 12 and younger. Open: Apr–Oct daily 10 a.m.–5 p.m., Nov–Mar daily 10 a.m.–4 p.m.; closed major holidays. Allow 1–2 hours depending on your interest and available activities.

✔ **Take a walk on the wild side.** Environmentalists and birders need to visit the **Rachel Carson National Wildlife Refuge** to walk a self-guided 1-mile nature trail through a pine forest and along the Little River out to a salt marsh. Pick up the map at the resident manager's office near the entrance. You'll find the trail head by the refuge headquarters north of Wells.

On SR 9 north of Wells, 7 miles east of U.S. 1. RV parking: Designated parking areas, may be crowded in summer and fall. Admission: Free. Open: Daily year-round sunrise to sunset. Allow 1 hour.

✔ **Hop a trolley.** The **Seashore Trolley Museum** was founded back in 1939 with a single $150 acquisition, a red open-sided car from Maine's Biddeford-Saco Line. Today, the museum houses the world's largest collection of rolling cars, some 225 of them, in an exhibit hall or spread around an old railroad right-of-way with overhead wires that power the still-working relics. Visitors ride one of the trolleys to the exhibit barn, where they can admire a San Francisco cable car from 1910, an ornate 1906 Manchester and Nashua Street Railway car from New Hampshire, and examples from Glasgow, Rome, Montreal, and Budapest.

125 Log Cabin Rd., north of Kennebunkport. (Drive 3.5 miles north of Kennebunkport via North Street, which becomes Log Cabin Road.) ☎ 207-967-2800. RV parking: Adjacent to the museum. Admission: $7.50 adults, $5.50 seniors, $5 ages 6–16, 5 and younger free ($20 maximum per family). Open: Daily May to mid-Oct, noon to 5 p.m.; July–Aug 10 a.m.–5 p.m. Allow 1–2 hours.

Weekend wonder

Urban residents of the northeast seeking a getaway can squeeze the highlights of this tour into a three-day weekend, but must bear in mind that round-trip, the journey totals 450 miles from the Maine–New Hampshire border to Bar Harbor and back. The drive between Portland and Bar Harbor takes 3½ to 4 hours with no stops. For details on the sights listed below, check out the "Must-see attractions," earlier in this chapter. For campgrounds and restaurants, see the next section, "Sleeping and Eating on the Road."

You can spend the first night at a campground on Maine's southern coast around **Saco** or **Biddeford,** drive through Portland to Freeport Saturday morning, allowing a couple of hours of shopping at **L.L. Bean and the factory outlets,** and then drive on to Rockland for a quick afternoon tour of the **Farnsworth Art Museum.** If you're a Wyeth fan, give priority to the renovated church that houses the Wyeth Center; if you want to see a variety of artists, go first to the museum itself; and if you adore furnished Victorian houses, make your major stop the Farnsworth Homestead.

Get to **Bar Harbor** in the late afternoon and stay in a campground that provides shuttle service into town so you can have a leisurely stroll through the shops and enjoy a **lobster dinner** before returning to your RV for the night. Check out early and spend the morning driving the Park Loop Drive in **Acadia National Park** as long as your RV can clear an underpass that's **11 feet 8 inches high.** If it's a clear day, drive to the summit of Cadillac Mountain, but if it's foggy, you won't find a view, so don't bother tackling the very curvy road. Return to U.S. 1 from Bar Harbor, take Alternate U.S. 1 to **Bangor,** and return south via the fast I-95.

Sleeping and Eating on the Road

Along U.S. 1 between Kittery and Bar Harbor, you find no dearth of campgrounds — nearly three dozen — and plenty of casual eating spots; Maine virtually invented the roadside diner. You can make reservations at most private campgrounds and some, but not all, public ones in state and national parks; having reservations in July and August is a good idea. If you're visiting in May or September, you can rely on serendipity to find a place.

All campgrounds listed below are open year-round and have public flush toilets, showers, and sanitary dump stations unless designated otherwise. Toll-free numbers, where listed, are for reservations only. See Chapter 9 for how we choose our favorite campgrounds.

Our favorite campgrounds

Bar Harbor Campground
$$$ **Bar Harbor**

Contrary to its peers, this privately-owned RV park accepts no reservations and lets campers select their own sites rather than assigning them. This gives all procrastinators and serendipity fans a chance to find a campsite in midsummer without planning ahead. The campground has both pull-through and back-in sites, some with grass and shade.

RFD 1, Box 1125, Bar Harbor, ME 04609. (From the junction of SR 3 and SR 102, follow SR 3 for 5 miles south, campground is on the left.) ☎ 207-288-5185. www.bar harborcamping.com. *Total of 300 sites; 165 with water and 20-, 30-, and 50-amp electric; of the 165, 60 full hookups, 75 pull-throughs. Dataport, laundry, pay showers. Rates: $22–$28 per site. No credit cards. Open: Late May to early Oct.*

Blackwoods Campground
$$ **Acadia National Park**

Located in the scenic heart of Acadia National Park, Blackwoods prefers advance reservations for its 45 RV sites (no hookups) and stipulates **no slideouts and a 35-foot maximum vehicle length.** The reservations office begins accepting requests in the first week of February for the summer months. Most of the heavily wooded sites in the campground are for tents, and the hardier backwoods aficionados may snub RVers as softies.

But if you're willing to forgo your TV, microwave, and air conditioner, you can enjoy a genuine camping experience by day and sleep in a comfortable bed by night. Your refrigerator, heater, and water heater run off your propane supply, and if you want to stay for the maximum 14-day limit, you can fill up your freshwater tanks and empty your holding tanks when necessary without leaving the campground. The 20-foot-wide sites are back-ins only.

From Bar Harbor at the junction of SR 3 and SR 233, follow SR 3 south 5 miles to the campground. ☎ 207-288-3338. Total of 45 RV sites with water (seasonally); no hookups. Rates: $18 per site. DISC, MC, V. Open: Year-round but water turned off Dec to mid-April.

Desert Dunes of Maine Campground
$$–$$$ **Freeport**

Located beside the commercial tourist attraction Desert of Maine, 40 acres of unlikely sand dunes operated as a billboard-type roadside phenomenon, the Desert Dunes provides shuttle service to downtown Freeport, freeing RVers from having to unhook or move their rigs during a stay. Both wooded and open sites are available. Kids like exploring the dunes and looking for "precious stones" sprinkled in the sand for them to find.

95 Desert Rd., Freeport, ME 04032. (Exit 19 from I-95 on Desert Road, then west 2 miles.) ☎ *207-865-6962.* www.desertofmaine.com. *Total of 40 sites with water and 20- and 30-amp electric, 14 full hookups. Dataport, pool, laundry. Rates: $19–$30 per site. DISC, MC, V. Open: Early May to mid-Oct.*

Saco/Portland South KOA
$$$$ **Saco**

Comfortable and centrally located, this campground offers big, wooded sites and many pull-throughs, a short drive to several excellent lobster pounds and plenty of food and snack opportunities when you don't feel like cooking. A snack bar serves nightly desserts, including blueberry pie, and pancake and waffle breakfasts. A lobster cruise and other New England tours leave from the campground; the management is friendly and efficient.

814 A Portland Rd., Saco, ME 04072. (Exit 5 from the Maine Turnpike, then east on I-95 to Exit 2B for U.S. 1, and drive north 1.5 miles; campground is on the left.) ☎ *800-KOA-1886 (562-1886) or 207-282-0502. Total of 88 sites with water and 20- and 30-amp electric, 42 full hookups. Pool, laundry. Rates: $32–$40 per site. MC, V. Open: Early May to early Sept.*

Shore Hills Campground
$$$–$$$$ **Boothbay**

Only 3½ miles from Boothbay Harbor, this Good Sam resort has swimming and canoeing with picnic tables and fireplaces. You can leave your rig at the campsite and take the campground shuttle to Boothbay Harbor. Both pull-throughs and back-ins are a good 30 to 32 feet wide and 60 to 70 feet long.

553T Eiscasset Rd., SR 27, Boothbay, ME 04537. (From junction of U. S. 1 and SR 27, go south 7.5 miles on SR 27 to the campground on the right.) ☎ *207-633-4782.* www.shorehills.com. *Total of 135 sites with water and 30- and 50-amp electric, 91 full hookups, 24 pull-throughs. Laundry, swimming, and canoeing in Cross River, saltwater fishing with tackle for rent. Rates: $26–$32 per site. DISC, MC, V. Open: Apr 15–Oct 15.*

Runner-up campgrounds

Camden Hills State Park
$$ **Camden** The Mount Battie Auto Road with its sweeping view that inspired Edna St. Vincent Millay is part of this 5,500-acre park with 25 miles of hiking trails. Most sites are shaded, and all are back-ins. *U.S. 1,*

Camden, ME 04841 (2 miles north of Camden on U.S. 1). ☎ *207-236-3109 in summer, 207-236-0849 in winter. Total of 112 sites, no hookups. Handicap access, pay showers, public phone. Rates: $15–$20 per site. DISC, MC, V. Open: Mid-May to mid-Oct. 14-day maximum stay.*

Cedar Haven Campground

$$$–$$$$ Freeport   A bit closer to town but inland, this Good Sam member campground offers three narrow pull-throughs. You're better off in one of the wide back-in sites. *39 Baker Rd., Freeport, ME 04032. (From I-95 Exit 20, take SR 125 north to Baker Road, then go northeast 0.3 miles; the campground is on the left.)* ☎ *800-454-3403 or 207-865-6254.* www.campmaine.com/cedarhaven. *Total of 60 sites with water and 30-amp electric, 6 full hookups. CATV (some sites), dataport, pool, laundry, mobile sewer service. Rates: $26–$34 per site. DISC, MC, V. Open: May 1–Nov 1.*

Mount Desert Narrows Camping Resort

$$$$–$$$$$ Bar Harbor   This resort-style RV campground offers live entertainment, a playground, a video arcade, canoe rentals, wide pull-throughs, and shuttle bus service into Bar Harbor. Prices for oceanfront sites go up to $60 a night, but you can sleep in the woods and walk to the sea for a twenty and some change. *1219-T SR 3, Bar Harbor, ME 04609. (From the junction of SR 3 and SR 102, follow SR 3 for 1.5 miles southeast to campground entrance on the left.)* ☎ *207-288-4782.* www.barharborcampgrounds.com. *Total of 189 sites with water and 30- and 50-amp electric, 66 full hookups, 75 pull-throughs. ATM, CATV, dataport, pool, laundry, mobile sewer service, and phone service on-site. Rates: $38–$60 per site. DISC, MC, V. Open: mid-April to late Oct.*

Saltwater Farm Campground

$$$–$$$$ Thomaston   Conveniently located near the Olson House at Cushing and the Farnsworth Art Museum in Rockland, this family run campground provides wide, deep sites. *PO Box 165, Thomaston, ME 04861. (From U.S. 1 in Thomaston by the Maine State Prison Craft Store, turn south on Wadsworth Street and travel 1.5 miles; campground is on the left.)* ☎ *207-354-6735. Total of 35 sites with water and 20- and 30-amp electric, 25 full hookups. Dataport, pool. Rates: $28–$32 per site. DISC, MC, V. Open: May 15–Oct 15.*

Good eats

Because we're carrying our own kitchen, we usually opt for casual eateries rather than fancy restaurants, and often order takeout, so we control the time and place we eat.

Lobster central

The best reason to travel through Maine in an RV is that you can buy fresh lobster every day to eat in, take out, or cook later, even on a budget, because of an establishment called the **lobster pound.** Every town has at least one of these simple spots where the owner usually sends his own fishing boats to haul the lobsters home every day and then dumps them in a huge vat of seawater. This container isn't one of those wimpy lobster tanks that you see in fancy urban restaurants. Those tropical fish aquariums contain a couple of desultory, over-the-hill crustaceans languidly waving what's left of a claw. A lobster pound is a repository of spunky, fighting specimens that a lobster wrangler must wrestle to get on the scales and into a pot of boiling water.

You pay by the pound (around $10) to get your **whole lobster** cooked to order; a 1¼ or 1½ pounder makes a generous portion for one average eater and takes about 20 minutes to cook. (If you want to buy a live lobster and cook it later yourself, ask the lobster wrangler for his recipe.) The server usually includes a dish of hot melted butter and sometimes a package of crackers or potato chips. Everything else on the menu — fried potatoes, onion rings, chowder, steamed clams, and corn on the cob — is extra.

If an entire lobster seems too much to handle, order a **lobster roll,** which is hot or cold chunks of lobster mixed with melted butter (the hot) or mayonnaise and chopped celery (the cold) and heaped into a buttered, toasted hot dog bun sliced open across the top rather than the side. Plan to pay around $5.95 to $8.95 for these.

What follows are some of our favorite spots for whole lobster or lobster rolls. Many are open seasonally only (May–Sept) and may not follow a regular schedule.

- **Bayley's Lobster Pound:** Pine Point, Scarborough (☎ **800-932-6456** from outside Maine or 207-883-4571), off U.S. 1 at the end of SR 9. Bayley's is the place to go if you want to ship live Maine lobsters to a very dear friend. (They have to be dear because the prices are high — not for the lobster but the air freight.) Open daily 9 a.m. to 7 p.m. in summer.

- **Beal's Lobster Pier:** Clark Point Road, Southwest Harbor (☎ **207-244-3202**). One of the greats, Beal's serves softshell lobster and steamer clams at the end of a wooden pier with picnic tables. Sides of steamed corn, onion rings, and even jug wine can be purchased at a subsidiary next door to the open-air picnic tables. Be prepared to shoo away the local gulls, who'll land near your table, hungrily eying *your* lobster. Open daily year-round from 7 a.m. to 8 p.m.

- **Cindy's Fish and Fries:** Four miles south of Freeport on U.S. 1 (no telephone). This is a lobster-roll mecca. Cindy's doting parents — the eponymous entrepreneur is away at college — serve their creations from a food wagon with a takeout window. The lobster rolls can be ordered in sandwich form or as a lobster roll basket with fries and coleslaw; the latter is neater to handle. You can eat at the picnic tables on the site or in your RV. Homemade lemonade is also a Cindy's special. Open daily in summer for lunch only.

✔ **Clam Shack:** On Dock Square by the bridge in Kennebunkport (☎ 207-967-3321). The Clam Shack excels in both fried clams and lobster rolls. (Who says you can't order both?) Year-round, the place opens daily around 11 a.m. and closes around 9 p.m., but staff isn't always punctual. *Note:* The navigator needs to hop out of the RV to place the order while the driver moves along and comes back later; no space is available to park in the vicinity.

✔ **Fisherman's Landing:** 35 West St., Bar Harbor, on the waterfront near the town pier (☎ 207-288-4632). This spot is operated by a family with its own boats. Order a side of their delicious fried onion rings and take your meal outside to one of the picnic tables in the patio or up the steps on top of the adjacent building. If the weather is cold, foggy, or drizzly, you can eat at additional tables inside, where a bar sells beer, wine, and soft drinks. Open daily in summer from 11:30 a.m. to 8 p.m.

✔ **Harraseeket Lunch & Lobster Company:** South Freeport Harbor (☎ 207-865-3535). Swing by here for a quick picker-upper. Just don't try to go down the narrow road leading to the pier in a large RV; the locals have passed an ordinance against it. Park up on the main road (South Freeport Road) and walk the quarter-mile down to the restaurant. If you don't want to order the lobster from the pound in back, you can line up at the lunch counter (which opens at 11 a.m. daily) and order anything from lobster rolls to clam-burgers and homemade Whoopie Pies (two cylinders of devil's food cake sandwiched with marshmallow cream and dipped in chocolate). If you want beer or wine, bring your own. Open daily May 1 through October 15 from 11 a.m to 8 p.m.

✔ **Lobster Shack:** 225 Two Lights Rd., Cape Elizabeth (☎ 207-799-1677). Located at Two Lights lighthouse since the 1920s, the Lobster Shack sits atop a rocky plateau with plenty of picnic tables and a view. The venerable, family-run eatery serves home-made clam chowder, boiled lobster dinners, lobster rolls, fried clams, and even burgers and hot dogs. Open daily April to mid-October from 11 a.m. to 8 p.m.

✔ **Lobsterman's Co-op:** Atlantic Avenue (near the aquarium), Boothbay Harbor, ME (☎ 207-633-4900). Here you find a wooden pier with outdoor picnic tables and a choice of hard-shell or soft-shell lobster (defined on a hand-printed sign as "SOFT SHELL = LESS MEAT, SWEETER TASTE"). Open for lunch and dinner from mid-May to Columbus Day, 11:30 a.m. to 8:30 p.m.

✔ **Mabel's Lobster Claw:** 124 Ocean Ave., Kennebunkport (☎ 207-967-2562). Mabel's wins the presidential endorsement of George Sr. and wife Barbara Bush. You can order a whole boiled lobster, a baked stuffed lobster, a lobster roll dressed with mayonnaise and garnished with lettuce, and (as if you needed a few more calories) peanut butter ice cream pie with hot fudge topping. Open daily in summer from 11:30 a.m. to 3 p.m. and 5 to 9 p.m.

✔ **Maine Diner:** On U.S. 1 at 2265 Post Road in Wells (☎ **207-646-4441**). The diner serves the absolute best hot lobster roll slathered in melted butter. Their famous lobster pie also is memorable. Open daily year-round from 7 a.m. to 10 p.m., except major holidays.

✔ **Nunan's Lobster Hut:** 11 Mills Rd., Cape Porpoise (☎ **207-967-4362**), 3 miles northeast of Kennebunkport on SR 9. The hut is famous for steaming its lobsters in a small amount of water rather than a large amount. They throw in a bag of potato chips and a hard roll with butter, and also sell homemade apple and blueberry pie. They take no reservations or credit cards. Open every evening from 5 p.m. to 9 p.m.

More than lobster: Markets and meals

While Maine is mainly about lobster in our book, you can also track down goodies from chowders to popovers.

✔ **Bar Harbor Inn:** On Newport Drive in Bar Harbor, adjacent to the municipal pier (☎ **207-288-3351**). At this classic inn, you can get a really great (albeit expensive) hamburger at lunch time in the **Reading Room** or outside on **Gatsby's Terrace,** which has a front-row waterfront view.

✔ **Jordan Pond House:** In Acadia National Park on Park Loop Road, north of Seal Harbor (☎ **207-276-3316**). Despite the line during peak season, you'll want to queue up for a teatime feast of hot popovers, homemade jams and ice creams, cookies, and pastries. They also serve lunch and dinner, but teatime on the lawn, weather permitting, is tops. Open early May to late October, 11:30 a.m. to 8 p.m.

✔ **Moody's Diner:** U.S. 1 in Waldoboro (☎ **207-832-7785**). Breakfasts are the big attraction. Open from 4:30 a.m. to 10:30 p.m. weekdays, until 11:30 p.m. Fridays and Saturdays.

✔ **Opera House Restaurant and Internet Café:** 27 Cottage St., Bar Harbor (☎ **207-288-3509**). Serve yourself tea, coffee, and home-made breakfast pastries before or after pursuing your e-mail. Open in summer from 7 a.m. to 11 p.m.

✔ **Portland City Market:** On Cumberland Avenue between Preble and Elm Streets, Portland (☎ **207-228-2001**). At this good food-shopping stop, vendors purvey the best of Maine foods from farm-house butter and cheeses to organic fruits and vegetables to local seafood and four or five different varieties of Maine potatoes. Visit on weekends when plenty of street parking is available. Open Monday through Saturday from 9 a.m. to 7 p.m., and Sundays from 10 a.m. to 5 p.m.

Fast Facts

Area Code
The area code is **207**.

Emergency
Call ☎ **911**.

Hospitals
Hospitals along the route include Penobscot Bay Medical Center, Rockport (☎ 207-596-8000), and Mount Desert Island Hospital, 10 Wayman Ln., Bar Harbor (☎ 207-288-5081).

Information
Helpful sources include the Maine Office of Tourism, 59 Statehouse Station, Augusta, ME 04333-0059 (☎ 888-624-6345 or 207-287-5711; www.visitmaine.com or www.maine.com), and Acadia Information Center (☎ 207-667-8550; www.acadiainfo.com).

Laws
All RV passengers must wear seat belts. The maximum speed limit on interstate highways is 65 mph. Speed limits in urban areas are lower.

Pharmacies
Most towns have a Rite-Aid drugstore, which contains a pharmacy.

Post Office
The U.S. Post Office in Bar Harbor is located at 55 Cottage St. (☎ 207-288-3122).

Road and Weather Conditions
For weather and construction information, in Maine, New Hampshire, and Vermont call ☎ 511.

Taxes
Maine charges a 7% tax on meals and lodging. The state gasoline tax is 20¢ a gallon.

Time Zone
Maine follows eastern standard time.

Chapter 12

Western New York: Cooperstown to Niagara Falls

In This Chapter

▶ Pointing out the Finger Lakes

▶ Misting up at Niagara Falls

▶ Batting a thousand at Cooperstown

▶ Laughing with Lucy and Desi

▶ Jiggling at the Jell-O Museum

From the thundering cascade of Niagara Falls, the cliché honeymoon destination for the first half of the 20th century, to the serene Finger Lakes, flanked by vineyard-covered slopes, Western New York has some awesome scenery to lure the vacationer.

We like the quirky aspects of the area — the Lucy and Desi Museum in Jamestown, the squeaky cheese curds for sale at the cheese factories around Cuba and Dewittville, the Original American Kazoo Company in Eden, and the Jell-O Gallery museum in LeRoy.

The roads are good, the campgrounds spacious and appealing, the road food tasty and imaginative, and the natives friendly, so come on out to Western New York for a unique journey through a big slice of Americana.

Getting There

We start our drive in **Cooperstown,** 225 miles northwest of New York City, and zigzag north, south, and west from there, ending up some 500-plus miles later at **Niagara Falls** on the Canadian border. (For the route, see the "Western New York" map in this chapter.) From Cooperstown, we head north via SR 80 to **Ilion** and **Herkimer,** then west to **Utica** and **Rome** for the historic **Erie Canal Village,** and then west to **Syracuse** via I-90 or the slower, more scenic back road, SR 5.

Western New York

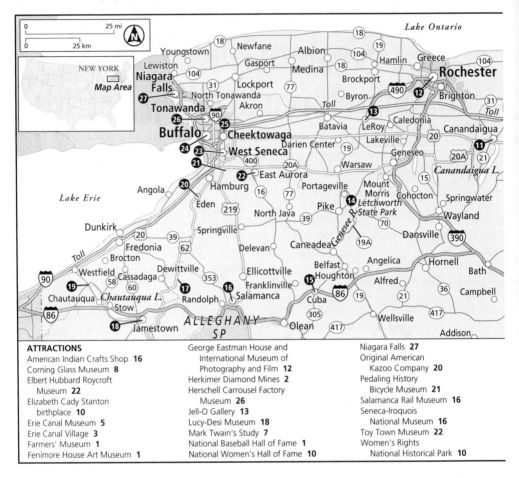

ATTRACTIONS		
American Indian Crafts Shop **16**	George Eastman House and	Niagara Falls **27**
Corning Glass Museum **8**	International Museum of	Original American
Elbert Hubbard Roycroft	Photography and Film **12**	Kazoo Company **20**
Museum **22**	Herkimer Diamond Mines **2**	Pedaling History
Elizabeth Cady Stanton	Herschell Carrousel Factory	Bicycle Museum **21**
birthplace **10**	Museum **26**	Salamanca Rail Museum **16**
Erie Canal Museum **5**	Jell-O Gallery **13**	Seneca-Iroquois
Erie Canal Village **3**	Lucy-Desi Museum **18**	National Museum **16**
Farmers' Museum **1**	Mark Twain's Study **7**	Toy Town Museum **22**
Fenimore House Art Museum **1**	National Baseball Hall of Fame **1**	Women's Rights
	National Women's Hall of Fame **10**	National Historical Park **10**

From Syracuse, we follow SR 175 to **Skaneateles,** then take U.S. 20 to the junction with SR 89, which follows the western shore of **Cayuga Lake** to **Ithaca,** and then continue southwest on SR 13 to **Elmira.** From there, the jog over to **Corning** on I-86 is a short one. Back up into the Finger Lakes, we follow the western shore of **Seneca Lake** on SR 14 north to **Geneva,** and then head west to **Rochester** on I-90.

From Rochester, we swing south again to I-86, following I-490 to SR 19, and then 19A from Letchworth State Park, cutting off on SR 305 from **Belfast** to **Cuba.** Follow I-86 west to **Jamestown,** and then drive along Lake Chautauqua to the town of **Chautauqua.** Follow SR 58 to **Cassadaga,** then jog over to I-90 and drive northeast to Exit 57, take U.S. 62 to U.S. 20A, and drive east to **East Aurora.** From that point, follow SR 400 into **Buffalo,** and then north to **Niagara Falls** on I-190. The total drive is **725 miles.**

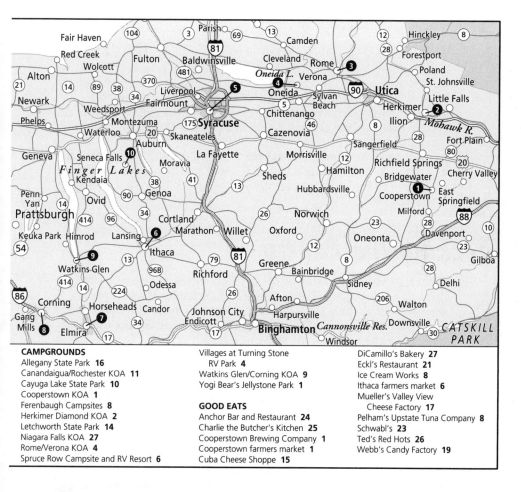

CAMPGROUNDS
Allegany State Park **16**
Canandaigua/Rochester KOA **11**
Cayuga Lake State Park **10**
Cooperstown KOA **1**
Ferenbaugh Campsites **8**
Herkimer Diamond KOA **2**
Letchworth State Park **14**
Niagara Falls KOA **27**
Rome/Verona KOA **4**
Spruce Row Campsite and RV Resort **6**

Villages at Turning Stone
   RV Park **4**
Watkins Glen/Corning KOA **9**
Yogi Bear's Jellystone Park **1**

GOOD EATS
Anchor Bar and Restaurant **24**
Charlie the Butcher's Kitchen **25**
Cooperstown Brewing Company **1**
Cooperstown farmers market **1**
Cuba Cheese Shoppe **15**

DiCamillo's Bakery **27**
Eckl's Restaurant **21**
Ice Cream Works **8**
Ithaca farmers market **6**
Mueller's Valley View
   Cheese Factory **17**
Pelham's Upstate Tuna Company **8**
Schwabl's **23**
Ted's Red Hots **26**
Webb's Candy Factory **19**

Major citywide construction has been going on in Buffalo for several years, and may not be complete when you're there. Allow extra time for getting around this town.

Planning Ahead

Any time of year **when it isn't snowing** or freezing is a good time to visit Western New York. Some recent years have seen Buffalo get record snowfalls, so cross out the winter months for a visit. The best times for this drive are **late spring and early autumn,** with summer a close second, only because campgrounds are busier when families with children are on the road during school holidays.

You need to make **campground reservations** in advance whenever possible during the peak season, Memorial Day to Labor Day. Niagara Falls KOA almost always is busy.

When **packing,** take along a range of clothing weights because you may face anything from very warm and humid summer temperatures to a sudden cool, rainy day when you'll want a jacket or sweater. Clean T-shirts and shorts with sandals or jogging shoes are acceptable summer tourist garb throughout Western New York, although we'd suggest dressing up one notch if you're in a city like Buffalo or Syracuse.

Allow a week or more for this drive, especially if you want to spend much time in the National Baseball Hall of Fame in Cooperstown (fans are known to stay three or four days to see everything) or sightseeing at Niagara Falls.

Stocking the Pantry

You won't have any problems finding food stores and restaurants throughout this region. We've found **Top's Friendly Markets** to be a very good local chain throughout Western New York. The **Hannaford's** chain also sells high-quality products; we found one in Herkimer, and others in locales around the state.

DiCamillo's Bakery with several locations in the Niagara Falls area is a good place to stock up on breads and cookies, especially biscotti, and the **Cuba Cheese Shoppe** in Cuba carries 100 varieties of imported and domestic cheeses, some of which they make themselves. (For details on both, see "Good eats" later in this chapter.)

Farmers markets flourish all summer through the region. We particularly recommend the Saturday morning market in **Ithaca** with a full range of fruits, vegetables, meats, cheeses, and cut flowers. **Cooperstown** also has a Saturday morning market in summer.

Driving through Western New York

In south-central New York, we start in **Cooperstown,** which is named for its founder, who was the father of author James Fenimore Cooper. A good all-American starting point for this drive, the town includes the **National Baseball Hall of Fame,** Cooper memorabilia and a fine art collection in the **Fenimore House Art Museum,** and **Farmers' Museum** with costumed living history characters demonstrating crafts and farm work in 1845. (See "Must-see attractions" and "More cool things to see and do" later in this chapter.)

Pretty, tree-shaded Cooperstown has **limited parking** even for automobiles, not to mention large RVs and trailers, so we'd recommend parking in one of the free lots on the edge of town (signs direct you to them) and using the trolley service to shuttle back and forth to all the major attractions.

From Cooperstown, we head north on SR 80 along the shores of Otsego Lake, which Cooper called "Glimmerglass" in his stories, and past Hyde Hall in Glimmerglass State Park, the ancestral home of the Coopers.

Turn west on U.S. 20 and then go north on SR 28 across the Mohawk River to **Herkimer.** If it's time to stop for the night, drive 7 miles north, continuing on SR 28, to the **Herkimer Diamond KOA** (see "Our favorite campgrounds") and the **Herkimer Diamond Mines** (see "More cool things to see and do"). Not really diamonds, these naturally faceted quartz crystals are nice to display as mineral samples; prospecting season runs from April through mid-November.

From Herkimer, follow SR 5 south to **Rome,** and then take SR 69 to SRs 46 and 49, leading to the **Erie Canal Village,** a living history museum near the spot where the first shovelful of earth was turned for the original canal. The village is a reconstruction of a 19th-century canal village created by moving 15 historic buildings here from other places in the region. Costumed animators recreate the 1840s. (See "Must-see attractions.")

Seneca Falls: Feminist tour stop

In the same way that Memorial Day began in nearby Waterloo as a holiday honoring the dead from the Civil War, the town of Seneca Falls devoted its energies to the rights and achievements of women. **Elizabeth Cady Stanton,** a housewife and mother of seven, organized and led the first women's rights convention there in 1848.

So many powerful females are associated with this area — in Seneca Falls, Stanton and **Amelia Jenks Bloomer,** who invented and paraded in the divided full skirt named for her; in Auburn, **Harriet Tubman,** a major force on the Underground Railroad; and in Rochester, suffragist **Susan B. Anthony** — that a serious feminist must pause for a look. Highlights in Seneca Falls include **Stanton's birthplace,** 32 Washington St. (☎ 315-568-2991; open 9 a.m.–5 p.m.); the **National Women's Hall of Fame,** 76 Fall St. (☎ 315-568-8060; open 9 a.m.–5 p.m.), honoring outstanding women from the arts, athletics, science, government, and philanthropy; and the **Women's Rights National Historical Park** at 136 Fall St. (☎ 315-568-2991), the restored home of Stanton and the site of the first convention.

Return to I-90 and continue west to **Syracuse,** where you can visit the **Erie Canal Museum** if you enjoyed the Erie Canal Village (see "More cool things to see and do"). Then take SR 174 and SR 175 to **Skaneateles,** (pronounced sken-e-*at*-tel-les and nicknamed "Skinny Atlas"), a pretty little town full of boutiques, flowers, and cafes. From Skaneateles, drive west on U.S. 20 through Auburn to the north end of **Cayuga Lake** and turn south on SR 89 and follow the lakeside road, lined with wineries, south to **Ithaca.**

Ithaca, notable as the home of both **Cornell University** and **Ithaca College,** is one of many New York State towns named for classical cities. Built on some steep hills, the city is a challenge for RV drivers; if you want to look around, park in one of the large open lots downtown near the river around Buffalo Street, where the lake cruises take off, and explore on foot.

Head out of town on SR 13, driving southwest to **Elmira,** home of **Mark Twain's study,** now ensconced on the campus of **Elmira College** (see "Must-see attractions"). From Elmira, continue west on I-86 to **Corning,** home of the famous **Corning Glass Museum** (see "Must-see attractions"). If it's snack time, try the 1880s ice cream parlor at **Ice Cream Works** on West Market Street for some imaginative flavors including wine ice cream.

From Corning, take scenic SR 414 north to **Watkins Glen** and drive the west shore of **Seneca Lake** north to **Geneva** and **Seneca Falls.**

From Seneca Falls, the short drive west on I-90 takes you to **Rochester,** where shutterbugs may want to visit George Eastman's former home, now the **George Eastman House and International Museum of Photography and Film** (see "Must-see attractions"). Suffragette Susan B. Anthony and abolitionist leader Frederick Douglass also were born and buried in Rochester.

Salamanca secrets

Salamanca is believed to be the largest American city in the midst of an Indian reservation, in this case the Allegany Indian Reservation. Two interesting museums in town are the fine **Seneca-Iroquois National Museum,** 794–814 Broad St. (☎ 716-945-1738; open 9 a.m.–5 p.m.), which combines history with contemporary arts and crafts, and the **Salamanca Rail Museum,** 170 Main St. (☎ 716-945-3133; open Mon–Sat 10 a.m.–5 p.m., Sun 1–5 p.m.), where a 1912 passenger depot, now used for exhibition space, marks the spot where three major railroad lines once converged. In the same block with the Seneca-Iroquois National Museum is the **American Indian Crafts Shop,** 719 Broad St. (☎ 716-945-1225).

From here we head south again, striking out first on I-490 to SR 19, and then SR 19A south to **Belfast,** where we turn west on SR 305 to **Cuba.** Cuba is home to the **Cuba Cheese Shoppe** (see "Good eats").

The drive west along I-86 or surface SR 417 between **Olean** and **Salamanca** takes us past Allegany State Park, a 65,000-acre park with plenty of hiking trails and four different campgrounds with a total of 316 sites. (See "Our favorite campgrounds.")

From Salamanca, take I-86 over to **Jamestown** at the east end of Lake Chautauqua. Native daughter Lucille Ball is remembered in the **Lucy-Desi Museum** here. (See "Must-see attractions" for details.)

Some of the Ohio Amish resettled in this part of New York in 1949 in and around the town of **Conewango Valley,** 5 miles farther north on U.S. 62. **Mueller's Valley View Cheese Factory** (see "Good eats") offers free samples of locally made cheese along with other Amish cheeses from Ohio.

At the west end of Lake Chautauqua on SR 394 is **Mayville,** where **Webb's Candy Factory** offers free tours and samples of goat-milk fudge, a local delicacy. Don't worry if you don't think you'd like it; they also make several other types of candy. (See "Good eats.")

From Mayville, SR 58 travels north to New York's spiritualism centers, **Cassadaga** and **Lily Dale,** where assemblies delve into mysterious matters for ten weeks every summer. From Lily Dale, take SR 60 to **Fredonia,** home of a splendidly restored 1891 Opera House, but it bears no sign of the Marx Brothers, who borrowed the town's name for their film *Duck Soup.*

From Fredonia, take I-90 to Exit 57A to **Eden.** (See the "Do you kazoo?" sidebar in this chapter.) And then, from Eden, drive north about 10 miles on U.S. 62 to the junction of U.S. 20 Alternate, where you turn east to go to **East Aurora,** one of the most beguiling little towns in the state. Interesting to students of architecture and furnishings is the **Elbert Hubbard Roycroft Museum,** the American arm of the Arts and Crafts movement of the early days of the 20th century. (See "More cool things to see and do.")

On the way to Aurora, if bicycles are an interest, pause in Orchard Park for the **Pedaling History Bicycle Museum,** displaying 300 bikes including a replica of the 1817 Irish Mail four-wheel velocipede, the first ever made, some late 19th-century "boneshakers," and many historic accessories. (See "More cool things to see and do.")

Kids usually like the **Toy Town Museum** in East Aurora, which has a big collection of antique toys, including many from the local Fisher-Price plant. (See "More cool things to see and do.")

Do you kazoo?

In Eden, off I-90's Exit 57A, about halfway between **Fredonia** and **Buffalo** (follow the signs from the exit 4 miles east to the town of Eden), you find the **Original American Kazoo Company,** the only remaining factory in the world still producing the metal kazoo at 8703 S. Main St. (☎ **716-992-3960;** open Tues–Sat 10 a.m.–5 p.m., Sun noon to 5 p.m.; closed holidays). Visitors get a free look around the 1916 facility (or a free guided tour if they call ahead for an appointment).

State road 400 is the quickest way into **Buffalo** and is the way to go if you want to taste what we consider the best roast beef sandwich in America — the **beef on weck** at **Schwabl's** in **West Seneca.** (See "Good eats.")

Still on the subject of food, Buffalo was the birthplace of world-famous "buffalo wings," a snack so popular it has created its own humor. ("What do you do with the rest of the buffalo?") To taste the original, we visited the **Anchor Bar and Restaurant** in a fairly grungy neighborhood near downtown where owner Teressa Bellissimo is credited with inventing the spicy treat in 1964. Do as we did — go by in the daytime and get the wings to go. The bar is a dark neighborhood joint lit inside primarily by neon beer signs night and day. (See "Good eats.")

In **North Tonawanda,** north of Buffalo on SR 265/384, is the **Herschel Carrousel Factory Museum,** with its own historic carrousel; a ride is included in the basic fare. (See "Must-see attractions.") On the way to or from the museum, plan a detour to Sheridan Road (SR 324) in **Tonawanda** to **Ted's Red Hots,** one of America's great hot dog emporiums. (See "Good eats.")

Buffalo is only 25 miles from **Niagara Falls.** We like to camp on Grand Island, a big island in the middle of the Niagara River near the falls. The KOA there can arrange rentals and tours to the falls, so you can leave your RV plugged in and strike out on your own. (See "Must-see attractions.")

Must-see attractions

Corning Glass Museum
Corning

The striking exhibit hall displays fine contemporary glass art, including several examples by Dale Chihuly. The Glass Sculpture Gallery, Hot Glass Show, the Corning Museum of Glass, The Studio, Steuben Factory, the

Windows Gallery, the Glass Innovation Center, and the Glass Shops offer a primer on everything that you ever wanted to know about art glass from glassblowing to its 3,500 years of history.

151 Centerway. ☎ 800-732-6845, 607-974-8271. www.corningglasscenter. com. *RV parking: Designated lot. Admission: $12 adults, $6 ages 6–17, $36 family. Open: Daily Sept–June 9 a.m.–5 p.m., July–Aug 9 a.m.–8 p.m. Closed Thanksgiving, Christmas, and New Year's Day. Allow 2 hours, more if you want to browse through the shops.*

Erie Canal Village
Rome

The Erie Canal, constructed between 1817 and 1825, opened up Western New York and the Great Lakes to settlement and trade. Near where the first shovelful of earth was turned for the original canal is a reconstruction of a 19th-century village with 15 historic buildings that were moved there from around the area. A horse-drawn packet boat takes visitors for a ride along the canal, craftspeople work in the village and sell their wares, and several museums and a movie highlight historic features and artifacts. The lively history lessons make most kids forget that they're learning something. The oddest exhibit is the so-called Cardiff Giant, a 10-foot figure dug up in 1869 on a local farm and believed to have been a petrified prehistoric man. It turned out to be a hoax, but P.T. Barnum took "the giant" on tour with his sideshow anyhow.

5789 New London Rd. (Take Exit 32 or 33 from I-90, and follow signs on SRs 46 and 49.) ☎ 888-374-3226, 315-337-3999. www.eriecanalvillage.net. *RV parking: Plenty of space in the big open lot. Boat ride: $5. Admission to village: $5 adults, $4 seniors, $3 ages 17 and younger. Combination boat ride, village, and movie ticket: $11 adults, $10 seniors, and $8.50 17 and younger. Open: Memorial Day weekend to Labor Day, Wed–Sat 10 a.m.–5 p.m., Sun noon to 5 p.m. Allow a half-day.*

George Eastman House and International Museum of Photography and Film
Rochester

Bank clerk George Eastman worked for years to turn photography into a more portable art, and by 1888, he had his first Kodak on the market. Soon afterward, he gained control of the celluloid coating process that made film. His elegant mansion has been restored to his day with many of the original furnishings, and modern galleries showcase masterworks of photography and motion pictures. A collection of some 6,000 still cameras and a library of 42,000 books and manuscripts about film and photography also are open to the public by appointment.

900 East Ave. (which is also SR 96). ☎ 585-271-3361. www.eastman.org. *RV parking: Designated lot. Admission: $8 adults, $6 seniors, $5 students, $3 ages 5–12. Open: Tues–Sat 10 a.m.–5 p.m., Sun 1–5 p.m. Closed major holidays. Allow 2–3 hours.*

Herschell Carrousel Factory Museum
North Tonawanda

This grand old factory turned museum focuses on carrousels, including how they were made and who made them. A self-guiding brochure takes you through the various work areas in the factory and describes what went on in each. A beautiful collection of carrousel horses plus a working 1916 Allan Herschell carrousel are on the premises. Both you and the kids get a free ride with each admission.

180 Thompson St. (off Oliver Street which is SR 429). ☎ *716-693-1885.* www. carrouselmuseum.org/location.html. *RV parking: Some parking in lot behind museum, otherwise street parking in residential neighborhood. Admission, including carrousel ride: $4 adults, $3 seniors, $2 ages 2–12. Open: July–Aug daily 11 a.m.–5 p.m.; Apr–June and Sept–Dec Wed–Sun 1–5 p.m. Closed Jan–Mar. Allow 2–3 hours.*

Lucy-Desi Museum
Jamestown

Lucille Ball of *I Love Lucy* fame was born in Jamestown in 1911, and this museum was dedicated to her and her husband and straight man Desi Arnaz in the summer of 1996. TV and movie clips, interactive displays, collections of artifacts and clothing, even a complete replica of Lucy's bedroom/study with original furniture is on hand. A gift shop sells souvenirs and memorabilia.

212 Pine St. ☎ *716-484-0800.* www.lucy-desi.com. *RV parking: Street parking. Admission: $5 adults, $2.50 seniors and ages 17 and younger, $15 family. Open: May 15–Oct 15 Mon–Sat 10 a.m.–5:30 p.m., Sun 1–5 p.m. Oct 16–May 14 Sat 10 a.m.– 5:30 p.m., Sun 1–5 p.m. Allow 2 hours.*

Mark Twain's Study
Elmira

A glass-windowed octagon built in 1874 to resemble a riverboat pilot house was created for Twain's use as a writing study when he visited his wife's sister's Quarry Farm outside Elmira. Inside, he wrote some or all of his most famous works, including *The Adventures of Tom Sawyer* and *The Adventures of Huckleberry Finn.* In 1952, the study was donated and moved to Elmira College. (Previously, the Langdon family resisted all efforts from Henry Ford to buy the study for his Dearborn, Michigan, museum.) Memorabilia, period furniture, and photographs are on display.

1 Park Place, Elmira College. ☎ *607-734-3128.* www.elmira.edu/academics/ ar_marktwain.shtml. *RV parking: Street or designated lot. $6 adults, $5 seniors, $4 children 6–12, 5 and younger free. Open: Mid-June to Labor Day, Mon–Sat 9 a.m.–5 p.m., Sun noon to 5 p.m.; the rest of the year by appointment only. Allow 1 hour.*

National Baseball Hall of Fame
Cooperstown

This destination is one of America's favorite family summer vacations. Many stay in the area several days to cover everything. The legendary "Doubleday baseball" on display is believed to have been the ball used in 1839 when Albert Doubleday invented baseball in Elihi Phinney's cow pasture one afternoon — if, in fact, that ever happened, which some experts doubt. More authentic artifacts also are on hand, from Jackie Robinson's warm-up jacket to Joe DiMaggio's locker, Ty Cobb's sliding pads to Yogi Berra's glove, and bats used for record-breaking home runs by Babe Ruth, Roger Maris, Mickey Mantle, Hank Aaron, and Mark McGwire. The original game, called "town ball," involved anywhere from 20 to 40 people, and is reenacted occasionally at the **Farmers' Museum.** (See "More cool things to see and do" later in this chapter.)

25 Main St. ☎ **888-425-5633**, *607-547-7200.* www.baseballhalloffame.org. *RV parking: Very limited in town; leave large RVs in designated parking areas on the edges of town and use shuttle transportation to the museum. Admission: $9.50 adults, $4 ages 7–12. Combination ticket with Fenimore House Art Museum and Farmers' Museum: $22 adults, $9.50 ages 7–12. Open: Daily May–Sept 9 a.m.–9 p.m., Oct–Apr 9 a.m.–5 p.m. Closed Thanksgiving, Christmas, January 1 and 8. Allow 3 hours to 3 days.*

Niagara Falls
Niagara Falls, New York and Canada

You can view the awesome trio of waterfalls — American Falls and Bridal Veil Falls on the American side and Horseshoe Falls on the Canadian side — on foot, in a boat, from an observation deck, and from vantage points in two countries. A first-time visitor, especially during peak season when many of the 12 million annual visitors are milling about, needs to take a guided tour and put up with being herded along rather than standing in long lines. You also need to consider carefully just how wet you're willing to get in pursuit of a great photo of the falls. Although virtually all the tours provide plastic raincoats, you're still going to get splashed.

If you're staying in one of the nearby campgrounds, such as the Niagara Falls KOA, you can book a bus sightseeing tour that picks you up at the campground. The most praised vantage point (and arguably one of the wettest) is from the deck of the *Maid of the Mist* **boats** that cruise directly in front of the three falls. (*Maid of the Mist* has its own parking lot accessed by Prospect Street.) If you're on foot, the guided **Cave of the Winds tour** begins with an elevator ride from Goat Island down to the base of Bridal Veil Falls and a stroll across a wooden walkway to within 25 feet of the falls.

If you want to do it on your own, allow even more time and try to leave your RV back at the campground. Niagara Reservation State Park, south of town off the Robert Moses Parkway, provides a close-up of American Falls. Goat Island, with two big parking lots, is accessed from 1st Street by the Niagara Rapids Bridge (also called Goat Island Bridge).

From Table Rock House on the Canadian side, reached by Niagara Parkway 1 mile south of Rainbow Bridge, three tunnels open up to good vistas of the falls. To cross the border into Canada, you need a **passport or photo ID and birth certificate.**

For more detailed information about the various ways of seeing Niagara Falls, contact Niagara Falls Convention and Visitors Bureau, 310 Fourth St. (☎ 800-421-5223, 716-285-2400; www.nfcvb.com*).*

More cool things to see and do

Whether an attraction belongs in the "Must-see" or "More cool things" category is often a tossup. The following are some mainstream and off-beat places to go in Western New York — you may find that some of these qualify as "Must-sees" on your trip:

- ✔ **Live in style.** East Aurora became the home of the Roycroft design style, strongly influenced and represented by designer Gustaf Stickley and his Mission furniture. Perhaps the most stunning display of this design at work is the elegant **Roycroft Inn** at 40 South Grove St., but the **Elbert Hubbard Roycroft Museum** displays many examples from the American wing of the Arts and Crafts movement from the turn of the 20th century.

  363 Oakwood Ave., East Aurora. ☎ 716-652-4735. RV parking: Street parking. Admission: Free, donation requested. Open: June 1–Oct 15, usually Wed, Sat, and Sun 2–4 p.m.; call for exact hours.

- ✔ **Sing "Oh, the Ear-eye-eee was a'risin'."** A National Historic Landmark, the **Erie Canal Museum** is in the last of the weighlock buildings that once served as weigh stations along the canal. You can see crew quarters inside a replica canal boat, and find out about immigration along the canal during the 19th century.

  318 Erie Blvd. East, Syracuse. ☎ 315-471-0593. RV parking: Designated lot or street parking. Admission: Free, donation requested. Open: Tues–Sun year-round 10 a.m.–3 p.m. Allow 2 hours.

- ✔ **Revisit the good old days.** Visitors may get an occasional chance to see a game of "town ball," a 20- to 40-man game with a soft ball and a flat bat that preceded modern baseball. Call ahead for ball-game dates.

  SR 80, Lake Road, Cooperstown. ☎ 607-547-1450. www.nysha.org/about/index.htm. RV parking: Designated off-road lot. Admission: $9 adults, $8 seniors, $4 ages 7–12. Combination ticket with Fenimore House Art Museum: $14.50 adults, $6.50 children.

Combination ticket with Fenimore House Art Museum and Baseball Hall of Fame: $22 adults, $9.50 ages 7–12. Open: Jun–Sept daily 9 a.m.–5 p.m., Apr–May and Oct–Nov Tues–Sun 10 a.m.– 4 p.m., Dec Fri–Sun 10 a.m.–4 p.m. Closed Jan–Mar. Allow 3 hours.

✔ **Follow Leatherstocking trails.** A fine collection of American art and examples of folk art from the permanent collection of the **Fenimore House Art Museum** fill the former home of author James Fenimore Cooper.

SR 80, Lake Road, Cooperstown. ☎ **607-547-1400.** www.nysha. org/about/index.htm. RV parking: Designated lot. Admission: $9 adults, $8 seniors, $4 ages 7–12. Combination ticket with Farmers' Museum: $14.50 adults, $6.50 children. Combination ticket with Farmers' Museum and Baseball Hall of Fame: $22 adults, $9.50 ages 7–12. Open: Jun–Sept daily 9 a.m.– 5 p.m., April–May and Oct–Nov Tues–Sun 10 a.m.–4 p.m., Dec Fri–Sun 10 a.m.–4 p.m. Closed Jan–Mar, Thanksgiving, and Christmas. Allow 2 hours.

✔ **Glitter, NY style.** All that glitters around the **Herkimer Diamond Mines** is more likely to be doubly-terminated quartz crystals than diamonds, but beginners can keep what they dig, and lazy campers can buy samples from a gift shop on the premises. Digging equipment is available on-site.

At Herkimer Diamond KOA (see "Our favorite campgrounds" later in this chapter), 5661 SR 5, Herkimer. ☎ **800-562-0897,** 315-891-7355. www.herkimerdiamond.com. RV parking: Plenty of space. Admission: $7.50 adults, $6.50 ages 7–12. $1 discount for campground residents. Open: Apr–Nov 15, weather permitting. Allow 2–3 hours.

✔ **Follow the Jell-O brick road.** The brick walkway leads to the **Jell-O Gallery** in LeRoy, New York, where a local carpenter named Pearle Wait invented this amazing dessert. His wife May named it Jell-O, taking her inspiration from a local coffee substitute named Grain-O, but the pair couldn't seem to market it successfully (that was in the days before comedian Bill Cosby), so they sold the rights to Grain-O mogul Orator F. Woodward for $450. This museum lovingly recreates the product's history, including original advertising art, Jell-O jokes, and interactive displays.

LeRoy House and Jell-O Gallery, 23 E. Main St., LeRoy. ☎ **585-768-7433.** RV parking: Street parking is advisable because of the small parking lot; it's in a residential area. Admission: $3 adults, $1.50 ages 6–11. Open: Memorial Day to Labor Day, Mon–Sat 10 a.m.– 4 p.m., Sun 1–4 p.m. Allow 1–2 hours.

✔ **Pedal into history.** The world's largest bicycle museum with more than 300 historic vehicles is the **Pedaling History Bicycle Museum** in Orchard Park, south of Buffalo. Find history, nostalgia, technology, and a gift shop.

3943 Buffalo Rd., SR 240/277, Orchard Park. ☎ **716-662-3853.** RV parking: Large parking lot. Admission: $6 adults, $5.50 seniors,

$3.75 ages 17 and younger, $17.50 family. Open: Daily Mon–Sat 11 a.m.–5p.m., Sun 1:30–5 p.m. Closed Tues–Thurs Jan 15–Apr 1. Allow 2 hours.

✔ **Toys R them.** Rare, one-of-a-kind Fisher-Price toys manufactured in East Aurora as early as 1930 are the focus of the antique plaything collections at **Toy Town Museum.** Tin windup toys, hand-carved carrousels, turn-of-the-century dollhouses, marionettes, and a fully stocked gift shop with famous label American and European toys highlight this unique museum.

636 Girard Ave., East Aurora. ☎ **716-687-5151.** www.toytownusa. com. RV parking: Street parking. Admission: Free, donations suggested. Open: Mon–Sat 10 a.m.–4 p.m. Closed Sunday. Allow 2 hours.

Weekend wonders

This zigzag drive through Western New York can be simplified and stripped down to basic components if you start in **Cooperstown,** spend half a day at the National Baseball Hall of Fame, then follow SR 28 to I-90, head west to **Rome** and pause at the Erie Canal Village for a couple of hours, and then on to **Syracuse.** Pause for a tip of the hat to the feminist cause at West Seneca, take a quick photo of Seneca Lake, and shuffle off to **Buffalo,** allowing a half-day to see Niagara Falls.

Sleeping and Eating on the Road

Western New York has plenty of private and public campgrounds, plus New York's excellent state parks, so you won't need to worry about where to sleep. **Campground reservations** are a good idea in July and August anywhere around Cooperstown, Niagara Falls, and state parks that accept reservations. If you're traveling in spring or fall, you shouldn't have a problem finding room anywhere without reservations except during a major annual event, such as an auto race at Watkins Glen or the New York State Fair in Syracuse.

All campgrounds listed below are open year-round and have public flush toilets, showers, and sanitary dump stations unless designated otherwise. Toll-free numbers, where listed, are for reservations only. See Chapter 9 for how we choose our favorite campgrounds.

Our favorite campgrounds

Allegany State Park
$$ **Salamanca**

This sprawling, wooded 65,000-acre site is the largest state park in New York, with two major RV camping areas that provide 20-amp electric hookups but no water hookups — fill your freshwater tank before arriving. Hiking, boating, swimming, and mountain biking are among the available activities. Reserving space ahead of time during the peak summer season is a good idea.

2373 ASP, SR 1, Suite 3, Salamanca, NY 14779. (From I-86, Southern Tier Expressway, take Exits 19 and 20 for Red House; take Exit 18 for Quaker.) ☎ *716-354-9121.* **Red House campground:** *Total of 68 sites with 20-amp electric, no water.* **Quaker campground:** *Total of 95 sites with 20-amp electric, no water. Handicap access, laundry. Rates: $19 per site. No credit cards. 14-day maximum stay.*

Ferenbaugh Campsites
$$$–$$$$ Corning

Wide, deep sites, plus a fishing pond and miniature golf course, make this a good campground for the whole family. It's also the closest camping area to Corning Glass Center.

4121 SR 414, Corning, NY 14830. (From I-86, Exit 46 junction, go north for 5.2 miles on SR 414 to campground on the left.) ☎ *607-962-6193. Total of 128 sites with water and 30- and 50-amp electric, 30 full hookups, 50 pull-throughs. CATV, dataport, laundry, pool. Rates: $21–$33 per site. AE, DISC, MC, V. Open: Apr 15–Oct 15.*

Herkimer Diamond KOA
$$$–$$$$ Herkimer

Making this park appealing are fairly big grass campsites in a large open meadow and the adjacent West Canada Creek, which offers fishing and boating. But the big draw is the "diamond" mines, designated dig sites where you and the kids can shovel up sparkling quartz crystals to keep. Digging tools are available at the site.

5661 SR 5, Herkimer, NY 13350. (From junction of I-90 and SR 28, Exit 30, go north 8 miles on SR 28 to campground on the right.) ☎ *800-562-0897, 315-891-7355. www. koa.com. Total of 85 sites with water and 30- and 50-amp electric, 45 full hookups, 30 pull-throughs. Cable, dataport, laundry, pool, Rates: $28–$36 per site. AE, DISC, MC, V. Open: Apr 1–Nov 1.*

Letchworth State Park
$$ Castile

"The Grand Canyon of the east" is a scenic state park with white-water rafting, hot air balloon rides, hiking, swimming, and hunting and fishing (licenses required for both). Horseback riding can also be arranged. Sites are fairly large, with 20-amp electrical hookups but no water hookups. Plan to arrive with freshwater tanks filled.

1 Letchworth State Park, Castile, NY 14427. (From SR 36 and SR 39 junction, go south 2 miles on 36 to park entrance and follow signs to campground 5.5 miles on the left.) ☎ *585-493-3600. www.nysparks.state.ny.us/parks. Total of 270 sites with*

20-amp electric, no water. Handicap access, laundry, 2 pools. Rates: $19 per site. Camping area open mid-May to mid-Oct.

Niagara Falls KOA

$$$–$$$$ Grand Island

On an island in the Niagara River near Niagara Falls, this campground is very popular in July and August, so make reservations. The park is well-kept with pavement and grass, and a fishing pond. Car rentals and tours can be booked at the office.

2570 Grand Island Blvd., Grand Island, NY 14072. (From Buffalo, go north on I-190 to Exit 18A and go north 2.2 miles on Grand Island Blvd. to campground on the left.) ☎ *800-562-0787, 716-773-7583.* www.koa.com. *Total of 362 sites with water and 30- and 50-amp electric, 168 full hookups, 10 pull-throughs. Dataport, laundry, pool. Rates: $30–$39 per site. DISC, MC, V. Open: Apr 1–Oct 31.*

Spruce Row Campsite & RV Resort

$$$ Ithaca

Mature spruce trees that add privacy and shade fill Spruce Row, a pleasant, family-run campground on a quiet country road outside Ithaca. Sites are good-sized. A fishing pond and large swimming pool with a sand/concrete beach are on the premises.

2271 Kraft Rd., Ithaca, NY 14850. (From SR 13 and SR 96 junction, go north 7 miles on 96 to Jacksonville Road, then north 0.4 mile to Kraft Road and east 1 mile to campground on the right.) ☎ *607-387-9225. Total of 135 sites with water and 20- and 30-amp electric, 32 full hookups, 45 pull-throughs. Dataport, laundry, pool. Rates: $25–$28 per site. DISC, MC, V. Open: May 1–Oct 11.*

Yogi Bear's Jellystone Park

$$$–$$$$$ Cooperstown

This highly-rated Good Sam park provides a 35-acre lake for fishing with no license required and offers rowboats, paddle boats, miniature golf, and plenty of themed family activities.

111 E. Turtle Lake Rd., Garrattsville, NY 13342. (From SR 51 and CR 16 junction, go north 0.75 mile on 51 to CR 17, then west 1 mile to East Turtle Road and the campground on the left.) ☎ *800-231-1907, 607-965-8265.* www.cooperstownjellystone.com. *Total of 168 sites with water and 30-amp electric, 39 full hookups, 5 pull-throughs. Dataport, laundry. Rates: $30–$44 per site. MC, V. Open: May 1–Sept 30.*

Runner-up campgrounds

Canandaigua/Rochester KOA

$$$$ Farmington   Near the head of Canandaigua Lake, this KOA campground provides a pond and a large swimming pool and is only 20 minutes from the George Eastman House in Rochester. Sites are fairly wide, with big rig capability, but many have side-by-side hookups. *5374 Farmington Townline Rd., Farmington, NY 14425. (From I-90, Exit 44, go south 4 miles on SR 332 to Farmington Road, and then go left 1 mile to campground on the left.)* ☎ **800-562-0533**, 585-398-3582. www.koa.com. *Total of 90 sites with 20-, 30-, and 50-amp electric; 34 full hookups; 36 pull-throughs. Dataport, laundry, pool. Rates: $32–$37 per site. AE, DISC, MC, V. Open: Apr 1–Nov 1.*

Cayuga Lake State Park

$$ Seneca Falls   RVers find electrical hookups at 36 of the sites but not water hookups, so arrive with the freshwater tank already filled. Sites also are quite narrow; most of them are better adapted for tents. Fishing, boating, and swimming are available on Lake Cayuga. *2678 Lower Lake Rd., Seneca Falls, NY 13148. (From I-90 and SR 414 junction, Exit 41, go south 0.25 mile on 414 to SR 318, then east 7 miles to SR 5 and south 5 miles on SR 5 to SR 89, then south 4 miles to the campground on the left.)* ☎ **315-568-5163**. www.nysparks. state.ny.us/parks. *Total of 36 sites with 30-amp electric, no water. Handicap access. Rates: $19 per site. Open: May 4–Oct 26. 14-day maximum stay.*

Cooperstown KOA

$$$–$$$$ Cooperstown   We like this open, well-kept campground with grassy sites and plenty of spacious pull-throughs. Although getting there is a bit of a drive from Cooperstown, it makes a good overnight destination on your way to or from the National Baseball Hall of Fame. *PO Box 786, Cooperstown, NY 13326. (From SR 28 and I-90 [exit 30] go south to 28 to U.S. 20, then east 6 miles to McShane Road and north 1 mile to Ostrander Road, and then west 0.3 mile to campground on the right.)* ☎ **800-562-3402**, 315-858-0236. www.koa.com. *Total of 51 sites with water and 30-amp electric, 27 full hookups, 59 pull-throughs. Laundry, pool. Rates: $29–$35 per site. AE, DISC, MC, V. Open: Apr 15–Oct 15.*

Rome/Verona KOA

$$$ Verona   Near the Erie Canal Village, this KOA campground offers extralong sites for anyone towing a trailer or big car. Sites are grass and gravel, mostly shaded. Walkers can take advantage of the hiking trail. Movies and bingo are scheduled during July and August, and a casino is only 5 miles away. *6591 Blackmans Cor Rd., Verona, NY 13478. (From I-90, Exit 33, go east 3.5 miles on Rt. 365, and then left on Blackmans Cor Road north 1.5 miles to campground.)* ☎ **800-562-7218**, 315-336-7318. www.koa.com. *Total of 93 sites with water and 20- and 30-amp electric, 38 full hookups, 29 pull-throughs. Dataport, laundry, pool. Rates: $28 per site. Open: Apr 28–Oct 20.*

Villages at Turning Stone RV Park

$$$$ Verona   This posh Good Sam park has resort features, big paved sites that measure 50 feet by 60 feet, and free shuttle service to the nearby casino and golf courses. Kids like the video arcade, and parents can relax in the heated pool and spa. The campground also has a fishing and boating pond with rentals. *From I-90, Exit 33, go west 1 mile on SR 365 to* the campground on the right. ☎ *800-771-7711.* www.turning-stone.com. *Total of 175 full hookups with 30- and 50-amp electric, 50 pull-throughs. CATV, handicap access, pool/spa, laundry. Rates: $37 per site. DISC, MC, V. Open May 1–Oct 31.*

Watkins Glen/Corning KOA

$$$$ **Watkins Glen** With a good central location in the Finger Lakes region, this KOA puts you only 5 miles from the gorge at Watkins Glen and near the Corning Glass Center and many of the regional wineries. Book well ahead and expect to pay a premium surcharge for NASCAR and other racing weeks throughout the summer months. The campground has a fishing and boating pond with rentals. *Box 228, Watkins Glen, NY 14891. (From I-86, Exit 45, on Rt. 414, 15 miles north of Corning or 5 miles south of Watkins Glen.)* ☎ *800-562-7430,* 607-535-7404 www.koa.com. *Total of 92 sites with water and 20- and 30-amp electric, 47 full hookups, 35 pull-throughs. CATV, dataport, laundry, pool. Rates: $32–$35 per site. AE, DISC, MC, V. Open Apr 20–Nov 1.*

Good eats

Whether you're in the mood for dining or snacking, Western New York has the spot for you. When you prefer to eat in your home on wheels, see details on area markets in "Stocking the Pantry," earlier in this chapter.

The full-meal deal

Around Western New York, almost anything can be breaded or batter dipped and deep-fried as a meal or snack. Local favorites both in and out of the fryer include such treats as **grape pie** (you'll find it around Naples in the Finger Lakes); **white hots** (mild) and **red hots** (spicy) in the frankfurter category; and Buffalo's **beef on weck** (see Schwabl's in the list that follows), **Buffalo wings,** and **chicken lips** (breaded and fried cubes of chicken breast — see Anchor Bar in the following list).

- ✔ **Anchor Bar and Restaurant:** 1047 Main St., Buffalo (☎ **716-886-8920**). According to a duly notarized proclamation from the mayor of the city in 1977, this restaurant was the birthplace of spicy buffalo wings in 1964. The late Teressa and Frank Bellissimo, proprietors, created them as a late-night snack for friends of their son, who dropped by the restaurant one busy Friday night. Other claimants say the wings already were a local staple but that Teressa added the celery stalks and blue cheese dressing. Sauce choices range from plain to mild, medium, medium-hot, hot, or suicidal. Open Monday through Saturday from 11 a.m. to 11 p.m., and Sundays from noon to 11 p.m.

- ✔ **Charlie the Butcher's Kitchen:** 1065 Wehrle Dr. at Cayuga, Williamsville (☎ **716-633-8330**). This small, casual lunch counter near the Buffalo airport specializes in *beef on weck,* a sandwich with thinly sliced roast beef stacked in a *kummelweck,* a Kaiser roll topped with coarse salt and caraway seeds. Open Monday through Saturday from 10 a.m. to 10 p.m., and Sundays from 11 a.m. to 9 p.m.

✔ **Eckl's Restaurant:** 4936 Ellicott Rd., Orchard Park (☎ 716-662-2262). Another classic eatery featuring the beef on weck sandwich, Eckl's garnishes their version with hot, freshly ground horseradish. This stop can be handy for an early dinner if you're visiting the Pedaling History Bicycle Museum in Orchard Park, because it's closed at lunchtime but opens at 4:30 in the afternoon. Open daily from 4:30 to 10 p.m.

✔ **Pelham's Upstate Tuna Company:** 73 E. Market St., Corning (☎ 607-936-8862). Grill your own fresh fish steak (swordfish, salmon, or tuna) at your table or let the chef do it for you. Pelham's is located right in the middle of historic Market Street with its charming shops and cafes; reservations are suggested. Open Monday through Saturday from 5 to 9 p.m.; closed Sunday.

✔ **Schwabl's:** 789 Center Rd., West Seneca (☎ 716-674-9821). This place makes the greatest roast beef sandwich on earth. The superlative beef on weck boasts tender slices of rare round roast placed on a kummelweck moistened with a bit of pan juices and a dab of horseradish. A civilized old-fashioned bar at the entrance serves classic Manhattans and martinis. There's no use asking for takeout here; the proprietors won't risk letting the sandwich wait beyond its perfect moment. Open Monday through Saturday from 11 a.m. to 10:30 p.m., and Sunday from 1 to 8:30 p.m.

✔ **Ted's Red Hots:** 2312 Sheridan Dr., Tonawanda (☎ 716-834-6287); they have eight other locations. Order regular or foot-long hot dogs cooked before your eyes on a charcoal grill until they're dark brown, sizzling, and smoky. Add your choice of toppings — order the hot sauce. Don't walk out without a side of their shatteringly crisp onion rings, crunchy on the outside and chewy sweet inside. The local drink of choice is loganberry juice. Open daily from 10:30 a.m. to 11 p.m.

Nibbles along the way

Western New York produces plenty of cheese, mostly cheddar types, and does a lively business in fresh cheese curds, which around Salamanca may also be batter dipped and deep-fried as a snack.

✔ **Cooperstown Brewing Company:** River Street, Milford (☎ 607-286-9330). This English-style microbrewery produces Old Slugger, among other popular varieties. Tours are available year-round daily at 11 a.m., 2 p.m., 3 p.m., and 4 p.m., plus free samples in the tasting room.

✔ **Cuba Cheese Shop:** 53 Gesee St., Cuba (☎ 800-543-4938, 585-968-3949). The shop carries more than a hundred varieties of imported and domestic cheeses, including some made on the premises. Fresh cheese curds are a big seller; taste a free sample if you don't buy a bag. Open Monday through Friday from 9 a.m. to 6 p.m., and Saturday and Sundays from 9 a.m. to 5 p.m.

- ✔ **DiCamillo's Bakery:** 811 Linwood Ave., Niagara Falls (☎ **800-634-4363**, 716-282-2341). Decamillo's has been turning out great Italian breads, including flat bread and biscotti for more than 80 years, and the retail outlets (several are in Niagara Falls) pride themselves on displays and packaging in addition to the goodies inside. Open daily from 6 a.m. to 7 p.m.

- ✔ **Mueller's Valley View Cheese Factory:** SR 62, Conewango Valley (☎ **716-296-5821**). Some 40 varieties of Amish cheese are made here. Products from other Amish cheese factories in New York and Ohio also are for sale. Open from 8:30 a.m. to 5 p.m.; closed Sunday.

- ✔ **Webb's Candy Factory:** Route 394, Mayville (☎ **716-753-1381**). Goat-milk fudge started it all, but today, this candy factory turns out many candies cooked in old-fashioned copper kettles. Free tours take place between 10 a.m. and 4 p.m. weekdays year-round. Open daily from 9 a.m. to 9 p.m.

Fast Facts

Area Code
The following area codes are in effect in this part of New York State: **315, 585, 607,** and **716.**

Emergency
Call ☎ **911.**

Hospitals
Along the route, major hospitals are located in Syracuse, Rochester, and Buffalo, among other places.

Information
For tourism information, call ☎ 800-CALL-NYS (225-5697) or go online to www.iloveny.com.

Laws
In New York, seat belts must be worn in the front seat. The maximum speed limit on interstates and controlled access roads is 65 mph. Speed limits in urban areas are lower.

Road and Weather Conditions
For road and weather advisories, call New York State Thruway (☎ 800-847-8929) or go online to www.dot.state.ny.us.

Taxes
Sales tax is 4%; local taxes can add up to an additional 3.95%. The state gas tax is 32.35¢ a gallon.

Time Zone
New York follows eastern standard time.

Chapter 13

Blue Ridge Mountains: Skyline Drive and Blue Ridge Parkway

. . . .

In This Chapter

▶ Cruising the crest of the mountains

▶ Looking for down-home crafts

▶ Pigging out on country ham

▶ Scoping out the Smokies

. . . .

*T*he Blue Ridge Mountains once were America's Western frontier, and the fiercely independent Scots-Irish settlers who built isolated homesteads with logs and mud chinking were pioneers of the same mold as those who later set out from here in covered wagons to cross the plains to Oregon. The men split dead chestnut into rails, calling the zigzag fence patterns "snake," or "buck," or "post and rail." The women made quilts from clothing scraps and named them Double Wedding Ring and Flower Garden and Crazy Quilt.

Skyline Drive and the Blue Ridge Parkway are the essence of the southern mountains. They meander easily through time and space to touch a mountain homestead or a stretch of wilderness unchanged since the days of Daniel Boone. Back roads and byways seem to beckon around every curve. (And plenty of curves are on these routes.)

Skyline Drive mileposts are numbered from north to south, beginning with 0.6 at **Front Royal's** fee entrance station to 105 at **Rockfish Gap** and the entrance to the **Blue Ridge Parkway,** which begins numbering its mileposts north to south at 0 again, ending with mile 469 where the parkway intersects U.S. 441 in **Cherokee** at the entrance to the **Great Smoky Mountains National Park.** Although frequent turnouts are situated all along the way, not all are long enough for a motorhome or a vehicle towing a trailer.

Expect sometimes long and slow-moving lines of traffic during spring blossom, late summer, and autumn foliage seasons. Many of the facilities along the route are closed during winter. Plan early morning starts, when the air usually is clearest, and then stop in early afternoon to set up camp and take a hike.

Getting There

This north-to-south journey begins just south of the Washington/ Baltimore urban area in **Front Royal, Virginia,** at the beginning of the Skyline Drive in **Shenandoah National Park** (see the "Blue Ridge Mountains" map in this chapter for the route). The drive follows Skyline Drive to the place where it merges with **Blue Ridge Parkway** and then continues along the parkway through Virginia and North Carolina, all the way to the **Great Smoky Mountains National Park.** For convenience — in case you want to fly in and rent an RV for the drive — we've made the southern terminus **Knoxville, Tennessee.** The distance of the drive, without detours into adjacent towns, is **643 miles.**

The smooth, two-lane roads of Skyline Drive, Blue Ridge Parkway, and the Newfound Gap Road across the Great Smoky Mountains National Park are closed to commercial vehicles. ***Note:*** Posted speed limits are strictly enforced. The maximum limit on the Blue Ridge Parkway is 45 mph.

Planning Ahead

All seasons are beautiful on these drives, but winter can bring heavy fogs, even light snow or a glaze of ice on the roadway, so you need to plan to travel in spring, fall, or summer.

In **spring,** flame azalea, pink rhododendron, and mountain laurel decorate the roadsides, beginning some time in March, with some color lingering through the summer.

In **summer,** shade trees that follow the roadway provide a cool escape from the lowlands heat; if you don't believe us, take a few minutes to drive off the parkways and down into a nearby town. The parkway, even on the warmest days, is a good ten degrees cooler than the valleys.

Autumn is magnificent. The route becomes a spectacle of crimson-leafed black gums and sourwoods, maples and dogwoods, birch and buckeye, orange sassafras, and purple sumac.

Fog can occur during any season in the mountains. When you run into heavy fog on Skyline Drive or the Blue Ridge Parkway, try to exit and drive to a lower elevation out of the fog. After you're on lower ground, take a break and do some shopping or sightseeing, or drive in your intended direction parallel to the parkway. With no guardrails and the narrow two-lane roads, maneuvering an RV, especially towing a trailer, can be tricky. And if you're driving slowly, you may become a hazard to other drivers, who may not see you in the fog until they're right on your rear bumper.

Because this region, especially the Great Smoky Mountains, is one of the most visited in the United States, you need to make **campground reservations** wherever possible between Memorial Day and Labor Day. Even spring and autumn weekends are busy in the Shenandoah and Great Smoky Mountains National Parks.

You want to **pack** a variety of clothing weights, even in summer. The mountains can get cool and rainy any time of year, and you'll want a jacket or sweater. Always take rain gear; we've experienced drenching thunderstorms in the Smokies. Hiking boots are preferable to jogging shoes on mountain trails, but take both along. (That's another advantage of RVing; you have plenty of room for everything, and your clothes are already hanging in the closet.)

Plan to **spend at least a week** or two weeks if time permits, and try to get in some hiking, biking, golf, or fishing.

Stocking the Pantry

While on the parkways and in the park, you have little opportunity to buy food supplies. Campground stores carry undersized and over-priced bottles, cans, and jars of food if you run out of something at the last minute, so you definitely want to do your major shopping off the route in towns and cities.

If you're stocking up before getting on Skyline Drive in Northern Virginia, and it's a Friday or Saturday, consider a short 10-mile detour to **Middletown,** where "the world's smallest potato chip factory" turns out crunchy **Route 11** and **Yukon Gold potato chips** that are sold only in the region. The factory welcomes visitors Fridays and Saturdays. The rest of the time you have to search for the chips out in grocery stores in Northern Virginia. (See "Good eats" later in this chapter.)

In **Galax, Virginia,** near the Virginia/North Carolina border, a large **Wal-Mart** has a full supply of groceries, fresh meats, and produce about 10 miles off the Blue Ridge Parkway on U.S. 58/221 (take U.S. 52 west from the parkway to Hillsville, and then head south on U.S. 58/221 to Galax). Closer still is a certified **Virginia farmers market** in Hillsville open daily except Sundays spring through fall. A **North Carolina farmers market** is near Asheville. Both markets carry country ham, other smoked meats, and home baked breads and sweets. (See "Good eats.")

1

Blue Ridge Mountains

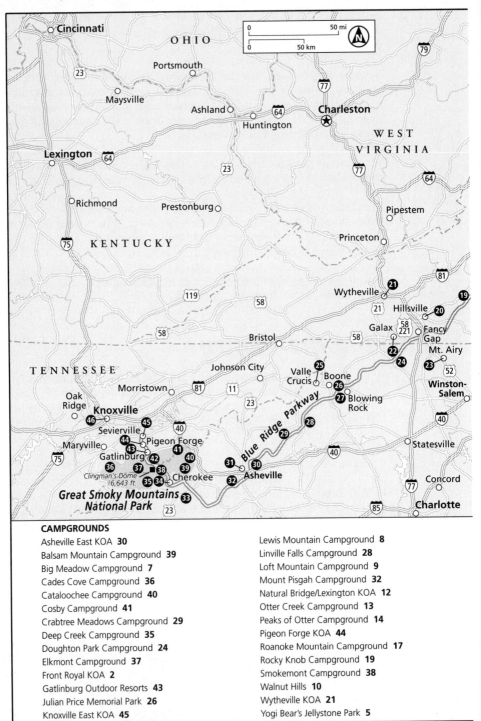

CAMPGROUNDS

Asheville East KOA **30**
Balsam Mountain Campground **39**
Big Meadow Campground **7**
Cades Cove Campground **36**
Cataloochee Campground **40**
Cosby Campground **41**
Crabtree Meadows Campground **29**
Deep Creek Campground **35**
Doughton Park Campground **24**
Elkmont Campground **37**
Front Royal KOA **2**
Gatlinburg Outdoor Resorts **43**
Julian Price Memorial Park **26**
Knoxville East KOA **45**

Lewis Mountain Campground **8**
Linville Falls Campground **28**
Loft Mountain Campground **9**
Mount Pisgah Campground **32**
Natural Bridge/Lexington KOA **12**
Otter Creek Campground **13**
Peaks of Otter Campground **14**
Pigeon Forge KOA **44**
Roanoke Mountain Campground **17**
Rocky Knob Campground **19**
Smokemont Campground **38**
Walnut Hills **10**
Wytheville KOA **21**
Yogi Bear's Jellystone Park **5**

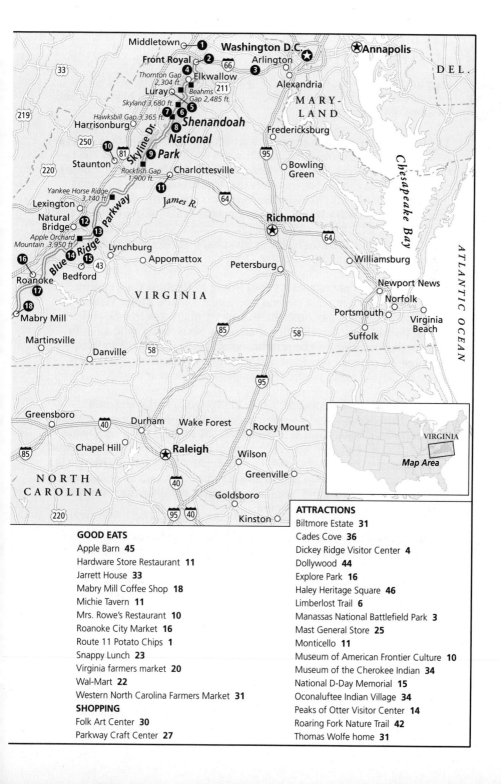

GOOD EATS

Apple Barn **45**

Hardware Store Restaurant **11**

Jarrett House **33**

Mabry Mill Coffee Shop **18**

Michie Tavern **11**

Mrs. Rowe's Restaurant **10**

Roanoke City Market **16**

Route 11 Potato Chips **1**

Snappy Lunch **23**

Virginia farmers market **20**

Wal-Mart **22**

Western North Carolina Farmers Market **31**

SHOPPING

Folk Art Center **30**

Parkway Craft Center **27**

ATTRACTIONS

Biltmore Estate **31**

Cades Cove **36**

Dickey Ridge Visitor Center **4**

Dollywood **44**

Explore Park **16**

Haley Heritage Square **46**

Limberlost Trail **6**

Manassas National Battlefield Park **3**

Mast General Store **25**

Monticello **11**

Museum of American Frontier Culture **10**

Museum of the Cherokee Indian **34**

National D-Day Memorial **15**

Oconaluftee Indian Village **34**

Peaks of Otter Visitor Center **14**

Roaring Fork Nature Trail **42**

Thomas Wolfe home **31**

Driving on Skyline Drive and Blue Ridge Parkway

TIP

Stop at the first visitor center on Skyline Drive and on Blue Ridge Parkway to pick up free mile-by-mile folders that list the highlights and facilities along the routes.

The beginning of **Skyline Drive** in Shenandoah National Park is only an hour away from the Washington/Baltimore area; zoom west on I-66 to Exit 6 to Front Royal, Virginia, where Skyline Drive begins only 2 miles south of I-66. Skyline Drive parallels the Appalachian Trail, a famous hiking and riding trail that wends along the crest of the mountains more than 2,000 miles from Maine to Georgia. It also skirts many of the Civil War battlefields, including **Manassas National Battlefield Park** (see "Must-see attractions" later in this chapter), 40 miles east of Front Royal and the beginning of Skyline Drive.

The first 28 miles of the route, **Front Royal** to **Beahms Gap,** climbs more than 1,000 feet, past several overlooks. **Dickey Ridge Visitor Center** at mile 4.6 is a good place to pick up maps, postcards, and books. Pocket-size identification guides for birds, trees, wild animals, and wildflowers also can be purchased at the center. At **Elkwallow,** milepost 24, you can buy food, ice, gasoline, and souvenirs between May and October, and picnic in a designated area year-round.

At **Thornton Gap,** milepost 31.5, U.S. 211 to Luray and Warrenton crosses the parkway, and a restaurant and gift shop are open in season. At milepost 41.7, **Skyland,** at 3,680 feet, is the highest point on Skyline Drive. It features a lodge with dining room and gift shop. The **Limberlost Trail** at milepost 43 is accessible to wheelchairs but some assistance is needed. This 1.3-mile loop makes an easy circle through an abandoned orchard and a grove of old hemlocks. You may see deer, and even wild turkeys, through much of this area.

From **Hawksbill Gap** at milepost 45.6 to **Big Meadows** at 51.9, you see low stone fences along the parkway and can camp at **Big Meadows Campground** (reservations are usually required). Two other camp-grounds, **Lewis Mountain** at milepost 57.5 and **Loft Mountain** at milepost 79.5, don't accept reservations. Loft Mountain is our favorite of the three. (See the "Shenandoah National Park campgrounds" sidebar in this chapter.)

At **Rockfish Gap,** milepost 105.4, Skyline Drive runs right into **Blue Ridge Parkway,** where milepost numbers revert to 0.

Twelve miles west of the parkway via I-64 is **Staunton** (pronounced *stan-*ton), birthplace of Woodrow Wilson and home of the **Museum of American Frontier Culture,** an excellent living history park that explores the origins of the Shenandoah Valley's first settlers, who came from farms in England, Germany, and Ireland, and how they adapted architectural and farming methods to the new world. (See "Must-see attractions.")

Travel 30 miles east of Rockfish Gap and you come to **Charlottesville,** home of the University of Virginia and Thomas Jefferson's **Monticello,** the magnificent (but not grandiose) home that he designed and built for himself. His gardens are also on display. An avid vegetable gardener, Jefferson introduced eggplant to the United States, so you probably either love him or hate him. (See "Must see attractions.")

At mealtime around Charlottesville, the historic **Michie** (pronounced *mik*-e) **Tavern** is famous for its fried chicken and biscuits, black-eyed peas and cornbread; unfortunately, it's also popular with bus tours, so you may want to drive right on past if the parking lot's full of buses, and head instead to **Hardware Store Restaurant** for a gourmet sandwich. Both restaurants also serve local Virginia wines. Thomas Jefferson, a noted wine lover, cultivated some of the earliest wine grapes in this area of Virginia. (See "Good eats.")

You get an instant introduction on the **Blue Ridge Parkway** to the scenery and the type of uphill and downhill climbing and curves that you must negotiate. The road climbs dramatically from 1,900-foot Rockfish Gap past Wintergreen Ski Resort to **Yankee Horse Ridge** at 3,140 feet. Then it starts downhill again to the **James River** — at 649 feet, it's the lowest elevation on the parkway. Then you go up again only 12 miles to the highest elevation on the Virginia stretch of parkway — **Apple Orchard Mountain** at 3,950 feet. The name comes from the shapes into which the sharp winter wind has twisted the northern red oaks, making them resemble apple trees.

The **Peaks of Otter Visitor Center,** milepost 85.6, features a lodge with a restaurant that's open year-round, a seasonal store, gift shop, and service station. Just past the center, at mile 86, SR 43 turns east to **Bedford,** the location of the **National D-Day Memorial**. (See "More cool things to see and do" later in this chapter.)

The junction of SR 43 with U.S. 220 at mile 121.4 leads to the city of **Roanoke,** the largest urban area along the parkway. The short detour to see the **Roanoke City Market,** a historic farmers market still vending fresh produce and baked goods, is worthwhile (see "Good eats"), and so is **Virginia's Explore Park,** a living history museum open during the summer with crafts demonstrations and special events. (See "More cool things to see and do.")

Mabry Mill at mile 176.1 is a must-visit for the colorful old mill that still grinds corn into cornmeal and the adjacent **Mabry Mill Coffee Shop** that serves pancakes made out of the cornmeal with its wonderful country ham and eggs breakfasts. (See "Good eats.")

At **Fancy Gap,** mile 199.5, the parkway intersects U.S. 52. A 14-mile detour south takes you into the town of **Mount Airy, North Carolina,** birthplace of TV's Andy Griffith and said to be the real-life prototype of Mayberry RFD. (One of this book's authors also grew up in Mount Airy but sees no resemblance whatsoever between her hometown and the bucolic community of Mayberry. But hey, it brings in the tourists. Before Andy Griffith, the town's main claim to fame was the world's largest open-air granite quarry.) The fried pork chop sandwich at the **Snappy Lunch** (see "Good eats"), often referred to on the TV series, is worth the detour.

At mile 291.9, the parkway intersects U.S. 221 to **Boone** and **Blowing Rock.** Eight miles west of Boone is the great-granddaddy of country stores in the tiny hamlet of **Valle Crucis** — the original **Mast General Store,** opened in 1883. (See "Must-see attractions.")

The flower-filled community of **Blowing Rock** was a big tourist attraction at the end of the 19th century for its Blowing Rock, an outthrust ledge of stone with updrafts of wind that return lightweight objects like a handkerchief dropped over the edge of the gorge. The rock even has its own lovers' legend. Today's more sophisticated travelers tend to bypass it in favor of the natural scenery of the region.

Back on the parkway at milepost 292.7 is the fine **Parkway Craft Center,** just the place to pick up a handcrafted rocking chair, homemade quilt, or distinctive hand-thrown pottery. (See "Shopping along the Way," later in this chapter.)

In **Asheville,** native son Thomas Wolfe's childhood home, the fictional Dixieland boarding house he portrayed in *Look Homeward, Angel* can be visited. Fire damaged the interior several years ago and interior reconstruction still is underway. (See "More cool things to see and do.") Writer F. Scott Fitzgerald also is associated with Asheville, because his wife Zelda spent the last years of her life in a hospital near there.

The most visited attraction in Asheville, however, is the palatial **Biltmore Estate** (see "Must-see attractions"), the largest private home in the United States, now a museum. Commissioned by George W. Vanderbilt in 1895, the 250-room mansion may be familiar to moviegoers who've seen the 1979 Peter Sellers film *Being There* or the 1994 Macaulay Culkin flick *Richie Rich.*

At milepost 469, **Cherokee, North Carolina,** is near the entrance to the Great Smoky Mountains National Park. Skip the touristy side of town, particularly the "Indian chiefs" who stand outside curio stands in feathered headdresses borrowed from the Great Plains tribes, waiting to pose for a $5 souvenir photo. Instead, discover the history of the Cherokee and their arts and crafts at the **Museum of the Cherokee Indian** and the **Oconaluftee Indian Village.** (See "More cool things to see and do.")

Choose one of several ways to see **Great Smoky Mountains National Park** — the quick tourist drive-through from **Cherokee** to **Gatlinburg** across Newfound Gap Road, with the option of a side trip up to Clingman's Dome, the highest point in the park; a slower version of the same route with side driving, biking, or hiking trips to **Cades Cove** and the Roaring Fork Nature Trail; or an in-depth camping stay. (See "Must-see attractions.")

The nearest city on the Tennessee side of the park is **Knoxville,** where a 13-foot bronze statue in Haley Heritage Square (in Morningside Park) honors native son Alex Haley, author of *Roots.*

Must-see attractions

Biltmore Estate
Asheville, North Carolina

As resplendent as any Loire Valley chateau, the massive 250-room Biltmore mansion and its gardens, crafts shops, and winery give a full picture of how the other half once lived. The Vanderbilts were American royalty, and with the help of architect Richard Morris Hunt and landscape designer Frederick Law Olmstead (who also designed New York's Central Park), created their own kingdom in the mountains of Western North Carolina in the late 1800s. Today, for a price, anyone can tour this splendid estate.

Exit the Blue Ridge Parkway at U.S. 25 north exit and follow the signs 4 miles to the estate. ☎ 800-411-3807. www.biltmore.com. *RV parking: Designated lots. Admission: $36 ages 16 and older, $18 ages 6–15, free 5 and younger for self-guided tour of house and grounds; rooftop and backstage tour extra. Open: Jan–Mar daily 9 a.m.–5 p.m., Apr–Dec daily 8:30 a.m.–5 p.m. Closed Thanksgiving and Christmas. Allow a half-day to a full day.*

Cades Cove
Great Smoky Mountains National Park, North Carolina and Tennessee

An auto or bicycle tour to Cades Cove (an isolated mid-19th-century mountain community) down an 11-mile, one-way, loop road off Newfound Gap Road is a must for any visitor to the Great Smokies. The road is flat and easy enough for even older kids to bicycle and is closed to auto traffic on Wednesday and Saturday mornings until 10 a.m. to allow bikers full access to the roadway. You can rent bicycles at Cades Cove Campground store for riding around the valley. The loop road is closed sundown to sunrise. Passing isn't allowed along the roadway, so if you're an impatient driver, plan an early morning start for your trip.

25 miles west of Newfound Gap Road via Little River Road and Laurel Creek Road. ☎ 865-436-1200. RV parking: Some turnouts along the roadway are large enough for RVs. Admission: Free. Cades Cove Road is open sunrise to sunset; closed to automobiles Wed and Sat mornings until 10 a.m.

Manassas National Battlefield Park
Manassas, Virginia

Known as Bull Run to the Union forces and Manassas to Confederates, this famous Civil War Battlefield was the scene of two southern victories in the early days of the war, cementing the reputation of General Stonewall Jackson as a strategist and hero. A visit to the 4,500-acre park includes an audio-visual presentation of the battles, an electric map tracing the fighting, and guides for auto tours through the battle sites.

6511 Sudley Rd. ☎ 703-361-1339. RV parking: Designated area at the visitor's center. Admission: $3 adults, free ages 17 and younger. Open: Daily 8:30 a.m.–5 p.m. Allow 3 hours or longer.

Mast General Store
Valle Crucis, North Carolina

A genuine piece of Americana, this country store has been in operation since 1883, and some of the stock looks as if it's been there since then. Once known for selling everything "from cradles to coffins," the store still sells penny candies from a giant candy barrel, 5¢ cups of coffee from a pot-bellied stove, and denims, bandannas, and tractor caps.

SR 194. ☎ 828-963-6511. www.mastgeneralstore.com. *RV parking: Street parking. Admission: Free. Open: Summer Mon–Sat 7 a.m.–6:30 p.m., Sun 1–6 p.m.; shorter hours in winter. Allow 2 hours.*

Monticello
Charlottesville, Virginia

This gracious home of our third president, Thomas Jefferson, along with its original furnishings, his gardens, and his grave tells a great deal about the man and the statesman. The house is elegant but on a human scale, designed by Jefferson himself, who hated the 18th-century brick buildings of Williamsburg. Lewis and Clark brought back the moose and deer antlers in the entry hall from their expedition. Always a generous host, Jefferson was $100,000 in debt, a sum equivalent to a million dollars today, when he died.

3 miles southeast of town on U.S. 53. ☎ 434-984-9844. RV parking: Designated lot. Admission: $11 adults, $6 ages 6–18. Open: Mar–Oct daily 8 a.m.–5 p.m., Nov–Feb 9 a.m.–4:30 p.m. Closed Christmas. Allow 3 hours.

Museum of American Frontier Culture
Staunton, Virginia

Scenic Skyline Drive and Blue Ridge Parkway take you past typical mountain farmhouses, but where did the settlers of this region come from? The Museum of American Frontier Culture presents exhibits of Old-World farmsteads from England, Ireland, and Germany — the origins of the area's settlers — to demonstrate their influence on American farms. Heirloom plants and rare breeds of farm animals are on display alongside costumed inhabitants who work the farms and talk with today's visitors. Kids enjoy the hands-on experience with farm animals.

From intersection of I-81 and I-64, take Exit 222 from I-81, following SR 250 west ½ mile to the museum entrance. ☎ 540-332-7850. www.frontiermuseum.org. *RV parking: Designated lot. Admission: $10 adults, $9.50 senior, $8 student 13–18 with ID, $6 ages 6–12. Open: Late Mar to Nov 30 daily 9 a.m.–5 p.m., Dec 1 to early Mar daily 10 a.m.–4 p.m. Closed Thanksgiving, Christmas, and New Year's Day. Allow 2½ hours for guided visit, 3 hours for self-guided visit.*

More cool things to see and do

The Blue Ridge Mountains offer numerous activities from walking through the Oconaluftee Indian Village to the exciting rides at Dollywood.

✔ **Go home again.** Novelist Thomas Wolfe wrote about his childhood in **Asheville** in *Look Homeward, Angel,* not troubling to disguise the details much. For many years, he was snubbed or ignored by his hometown, but today, the family home (his mother's boardinghouse) is open as a memorial. Artifacts from the house, which is under repair from a fire, temporarily are on display in an adjacent visitor center. The home is scheduled to reopen in the spring of 2004.

52 N. Market St., Asheville, North Carolina. ☎ **828-253-8304.** RV parking: Street parking. Admission: $1 adults, 50¢ students. Open: Nov–Mar Tues–Sat 10 a.m.–4 p.m., Sun 1–4 p.m; Apr–Oct Mon–Sat 9 a.m.–5 p.m., Sun 1–5 p.m. Allow 2 hours.

✔ **Hooray for Dollywood!** Pigeon Forge, Tennessee, once a tiny village of farmers and potters, has been turned into Disneyland Southeast by native daughter Dolly Parton. Despite the ticky-tacky town, the **Dollywood** theme park offers some appealing features, including an 1885 Dentzel carrousel with hand-carved animals, a train pulled by an old steam locomotive, and fun rides for the kids.

Don't plan on driving by for a look-see; the road funnels the traffic directly into the parking lot, and getting back out the entrance in an RV can be tricky.

Dollywood, Pigeon Forge, Tennessee. ☎ 865-428-9488. www.dollywood.com. RV parking: Designated lot. Admission: $40 ages 12–59, $37 ages 60 and older, $30 ages 4–11. Open: Daily 9 a.m.– 6 p.m., until 10 p.m. in July. Closed Tues and Thurs in fall. Allow half-day to full day.

✔ **Live history.** Virginia's **Explore Park** is a living history museum with an early American settlement, Colonial encampment, and Native American village.

Milepost 115, Blue Ridge Parkway, Roanoke, Virginia. ☎ 800-842-9163, 540-427-1800. www.explorepark.org. RV parking: Designated area. Admission: $8 adults, $6 seniors, $4 ages 3–11. Open: May–Oct Wed–Sat 10 a.m.–5 p.m., Sun 12–5 p.m. Allow a half-day.

✔ **Visit the first Americans.** The **Museum of the Cherokee Indian** uses everything from "hear phones" to holographic images to tell the story of this civilized tribe which occupied these hills for 10,000 years until forced out on the Trail of Tears march to Oklahoma.

U.S. 441 and Drama Rd., Cherokee, North Carolina. ☎ 828-497-3481. RV parking: Designated area. Admission: $8 adults, $5 ages 6–13. Open: Daily 9 a.m.–7 p.m., Sun 9 a.m.–5 p.m. Allow 2 hours.

✔ **Splash toward victory.** The **National D-Day Memorial** commemorates the Allied troops who landed on the Normandy beaches June 6, 1944, in an unprecedented military action under the command of General Dwight D. Eisenhower.

Off I-81 and Blue Ridge Parkway at intersection of SR 460 Bypass and SR 122, Bedford, Virginia. ☎ 800-351-DDAY (351-3329), 540-586-DDAY (586-3329). www.dday.org. RV parking: Street parking in vicinity. Admission: Free. Open: Sun–Thurs 10 a.m.–7 p.m., Fri–Sat 10 a.m.–9 p.m. Allow 30 minutes.

✔ **Travel to the 1750s.** The **Oconaluftee Indian Village** re-creates community life in the 18th century in this authentic replica of a village populated by craftsmen who demonstrate basket and bead-work typical of the Cherokees.

U.S. 441 and Drama Rd., Cherokee, North Carolina. ☎ 828-497-2111, 828-497-2315. www.oconalufteevillage.com. RV parking: Designated area. Admission: $13 adults, $6 ages 6–12. Open: May 15–Oct 25 daily 9 a.m.–5:30 p.m. Allow 2–3 hours.

Weekend wonder

For a shorter version of these routes, **choose one drive,** depending on where you want to be based. You can travel Skyline Drive and see the Shenandoah National Park easily over a weekend from the Washington area. Anywhere in Western Virginia and Western North Carolina allows access to the Blue Ridge Parkway for a weekend of road touring. One thing that makes the Great Smoky Mountains National Park the most visited of all is its location within a day's drive of more than half of all Americans.

Sleeping and Eating on the Road

As you can see from the following sections, plenty of campsites are close to the mountain drives in this chapter. Almost every exit from Blue Ridge Parkway and Skyline Drive can lead to a private RV park where, even in peak season, you should be able to find an overnight campsite with hookups.

A few lodges and restaurants serving food are spaced along Skyline Drive and Blue Ridge Parkway, but again, most exits lead a few miles into small towns where you can find a fast-food outlet, restaurant, or grocery store. Produce stands and farmers markets sell fresh peaches, corn, and tomatoes in season, so keep your pantry stocked.

All campgrounds listed below are open year-round and have public flush toilets, showers, and sanitary dump stations unless designated otherwise. Toll-free numbers, where listed, are for reservations only. See Chapter 9 for more information on how we select our favorite campgrounds.

Our favorite campgrounds

Front Royal KOA

$$$$ **Front Royal, Virginia**

This scenic mountain resort is a good starting point for the drive and a handy base camp for Washington, D.C., and the Shenandoah Valley. Numerous activities are available for kids, including a 350-foot waterslide (fee), a playground, a pond with freshwater fishing and rental tackle, and a basketball court. You can also take tours to D.C. and get discount tickets to the Skyline Caverns nearby.

PO Box 274, Front Royal, VA 22630. (From I-66 Exit 6 or 13, go 2 miles south of Front Royal on U.S. 340, entrance is 0.8 mile past Skyline Caverns.) ☎ *800-562-9114, 540-635-2741.* www.koa.com. *Total of 100 sites with water and 20- and 30-amp electric, 42 full hookups, 34 pull-throughs. Dataport, handicap access, laundry, pool/spa. Rates: $33–$39 per site. DISC, MC, V, Open: Mar 15–Nov 1.*

Gatlinburg Outdoor Resorts

$$$–$$$$ **Gatlinburg, Tennessee**

This upscale condo RV park has some spaces available for overnights. Sites are paved with patios; most are shaded. Although all the sites are back-ins, they're wide and large enough for big-rigs. The park has a fishing pond.

From junction of U.S. 441 and U.S. 321 north/SR 73 east, go east 11 miles on U.S. 321 to the campground on the left. ☎ *865-436-5861. Total of 70 full hookups with 20- and 30-amp electric, no pull-throughs. CATV, laundry, pool. Rates: $30–$35 per site. MC, V.*

Knoxville East KOA

$$$ **East of Knoxville, Tennessee**

Some sites are shaded, and all are comfortably large. A restaurant serves breakfast and dinner in summer season, and the country setting with views of the Smokies is only 12 miles from the attractions at Pigeon Forge.

Blue Ridge Parkway campgrounds

The nine campgrounds along the Blue Ridge Parkway, open May through October, offer facilities such as gift, book, or craft shops; gas stations; hiking trails; and ranger talks. Not all campgrounds have all facilities. Camping sites can handle RVs up to 30-feet long. Each campground has a dump station but no hookups for water or electricity. Restroom facilities and drinking water are provided, but showers and laundry facilities are nonexistent. Each campsite has a table and fireplace and handicap access. Rates are $12 per site. A 14-day stay is the maximum, and reservations are not accepted.

- ✔ **Crabtree Meadows Campground** (milepost 339.5): Total of 97 sites, 10 pull-throughs. Paved, mostly shaded. ☎ 828-765-5444.

- ✔ **Doughton Park Campground** (milepost 231.1): Total of 26 sites. Narrow back-ins. No slideouts, gasoline, or food. ☎ 910-372-8568.

- ✔ **Julian Price Memorial Park** (milepost 297.1): Total of 68 sites, 30 pull-throughs. Paved, mostly shaded, narrow sites, handicap access, fishing and boat rentals on Price Lake. No store, gasoline, or food. ☎ 828-963-5911.

- ✔ **Linville Falls Campground** (milepost 316.4): Total of 70 sites, 5 pull-throughs. Paved, some shaded, fishing access on Linville River. No gasoline or food. ☎ 828-765-7818.

- ✔ **Mount Pisgah Campground** (milepost 408.6): Total of 137 sites, 13 pull-throughs. Paved, patios, mostly shaded. ☎ 828-648-2644.

- ✔ **Otter Creek Campground** (milepost 60.9): Total of 25 sites. Paved, narrow back-ins, some shaded. No gasoline. ☎ 434-299-5496.

- ✔ **Peaks of Otter Campground** (milepost 86.0): Total of 59 sites, 25 pull-throughs. Paved and shaded sites, freshwater fishing in Abbott Lake. ☎ 540-586-4357.

- ✔ **Roanoke Mountain Campground** (milepost 120.4): Total of 30 sites, 6 pull-throughs. Paved, some shaded. No gasoline or food. ☎ 540-982-9242.

- ✔ **Rocky Knob Campground** (milepost 169.0): Total of 25 sites, 3 pull-throughs. Paved, some shaded, fishing. No slideouts or gasoline. ☎ 540-745-9660.

241 KOA Drive, Kodak, TN 37764. (From I-40 Exit 407, go east 0.25 mile on Dumplin Valley Road to campground entrance.) ☎ ***800-562-8693,*** *865-933-6393.* www.koa. com. *Total of 121 sites with water and 30- and 50-amp electric, 58 full hookups, 51 pull-throughs. CATV, dataport, laundry, pool, restaurant in season. Rates: $27–$29 per site. AE, DISC, MC, V.*

Yogi Bear's Jellystone Park

$$$$ Luray, Virginia

This Good Sam park is the answer to a kid's query, "What'll we do?" Activities include a 400-foot waterslide, fishing pond (and tackle), paddle boats, miniature golf, and the usual pool and playground. And it's only five minutes away from the entrance to Shenandoah National Park and Luray Caverns. Sites are large enough for big rigs.

From junction of I-81 and U.S. 211 (Exit 264), go west 5 miles on U.S. 211 to the campground on the left. ☎ ***800-420-6679.*** www.campluray.com. *Total of 142 sites with water and 30- and 50-amp electric, 83 full hookups, 67 pull-throughs. Laundry, pool. Rates: $32–$37 per site. AE, DISC, MC, V.*

Runner-up campgrounds

Asheville East KOA

$$$ Swannanoa, North Carolina   This mountain country setting offers shady sites and a pond with trout fishing, boating, swimming, and bike rentals. The Biltmore House in Ashville is only 12 miles away. *Box 485, Swannanoa, NC 28778. (From I-40 Exit 59, go north 1 block to traffic light, turn right on U.S. 70 and go 2 miles to campground on the left.)* ☎ ***800-562-5907,*** *828-686-3121.* www.koa.com. *Total of 200 sites with water and 30- and 50-amp electric, 100 full hookups, 20 pull-throughs. CATV, dataport, laundry, pool. Rates: $27–$30 per site. DISC, MC, V.*

Natural Bridge/Lexington KOA

$$$ Natural Bridge, Virginia   This campground, located in a wooded section of the Shenandoah Valley, lies between Natural Bridge and Lexington. A restaurant operates on the premises year-round. *Box 148, Natural Bridge, VA 24578. (From southbound I-81 Exit 1808, go straight beyond the stop sign on Kildeer Lane to the campground. If coming northbound on I-81, take Exit 180, go left on U.S. 11 under I-81, and turn left at the gas station onto Kildeer Lane.)* ☎ ***800-562-8514,*** *540-291-2770.* www.koa.com. *Total of 87 sites with water and 20- and 30-amp electric, 23 full hookups, 62 pull-throughs. Dataport, laundry, pool. Rates: $23–$27 per site. DISC, MC, V.*

Great Smokies National Park campgrounds

Ten developed campgrounds are in Great Smokies National Park, but not all are suitable for large RVs because of the access roads. Those listed below are the most suitable for RVs. Campers with smaller vehicles can check out the other campgrounds listed on the map that you receive as you enter the park. Park campgrounds have no hookups, but they do provide fireplaces, tables, restrooms, and water. Some sites are suitable only for tent camping. Stays are limited to 7 days between May 15 and October 31, 14 days the rest of the year. During the summer period, making reservations is wise at Cades Cove, Elkmont, and Smokemont campgrounds by calling ☎ 800-365-CAMP (365-2267). See the map in this chapter for locations.

- ✔ **Balsam Mountain Campground:** Total of 46 sites, 30-foot length limit. Rates: $10 per site, no reservations. Open late May to October.

- ✔ **Cades Cove Campground:** Total of 161 sites. Paved, some shaded, back-ins, can handle up to 35-foot RVs, dump station. Rates: $15. Open year-round.

- ✔ **Cataloochee Campground:** Total of 27 sites. Dirt, back-ins can handle up to 31-foot RVs. No slideouts. Stream nearby. Rates: $10 per site, no reservations. Open Mar 15–Nov 15.

- ✔ **Cosby Campground:** Total of 175 sites. Some shaded, back-ins only, 25-feet maximum length. No slideouts. Rates: $14 per site, no reservations. Open Mid-March to early November.

- ✔ **Deep Creek Campground:** Total of 35 sites. Paved, mostly shaded, narrow, back-ins, dump station, stream. Rates: $12, no reservations. Open early April through October.

- ✔ **Elkmont Campground:** Total of 220 sites. Gravel, some shaded, back-ins, can handle up to 32-foot RVs. No slideouts. Rates: $15. Open mid-March to late November.

- ✔ **Smokemont Campground:** Total of 140 sites, 45 pull-throughs. Paved, shaded, narrow, handicap access, dump station, and fishing and swimming in Oconaluftee River. No slideouts. Rates: $15 per site. Open year-round.

Pigeon Forge KOA

$$$$ **Pigeon Forge, Tennessee** This KOA offers a great location for families who want to visit Dollywood and revel in the gaudy tourist traps of Pigeon Forge. It's just off the main street and has trolley shuttle service to town and the park. Wide, mostly shaded sites are pavement and gravel. *PO Box 310, Pigeon Forge, TN 37868. (In Pigeon Forge, turn east off U.S. 441 at Dollywood Lane. Go across the river, past the traffic light, and the campground is*

one block on the left.) ☎ **800-562-776**, *865-453-7903.* www.koa.com. *Total of 181 sites with water and 30- and 50-amp electric, 106 full hookups, 74 pull-throughs. CATV, dataport, laundry, pool/spa. Rates: $32–$38 per site. MC, V.*

Walnut Hills

$$$$ **Staunton, Virginia** Conveniently situated near the Museum of American Frontier Culture, this open, grassy campground has big sites, some shaded, and features a stocked fishing pond that's also good for swimming. Activities include hay wagon rides and Saturday night music and dancing. *484 Walnut Hills Rd., Staunton, VA 24401. (From I-81 and Rt. 654, go 0.7 mile on 654 to U.S. 11, and then south 1.5 miles to SR 655 and east 1 mile to the campground.)* ☎ **800-699-2568**, *276-337-3920.* www.walnuthillscampground. com. *Total of 90 sites with water and 30- and 50-amp electric, 58 full hookups, 29 pull-throughs. Dataport, laundry, pool, SATV. Rates: $31–$37 per site. MC, V. Open May 1–Nov 15.*

Wytheville KOA

$$$–$$$$ **Wytheville, Virginia** In addition to the usual pool and playground, this family oriented campground offers indoor batting cages, miniature golf, hiking, horseback riding, canoe and kayak trips, archery, live entertaiment, and a farm zoo. Sites are fairly large, and most can handle big rigs. *231 KOA Rd., Wytheville, VA 24382. (From I-81 Exit 77, go 0.3 west on south frontage road to SR 758, then 0.3 mile south to SR 776, and west 0.2 mile to the campground.)* ☎ **800-562-3380**, *540-228-2601.* www.koa.com. *Total of 91 sites with water and 30- and 50-amp electric, 28 full hookups, 67 pull-throughs. Dataport, laundry, pool, SATV. Rates: $25–$40 per site. AE, DISC, MC, V.*

Shenandoah National Park campgrounds

These three campgrounds along Skyline Drive in Shenandoah National Park operate May through October, with facilities, such as gift, book, and craft shops, and restaurants, gas stations, and hiking trails. Sites are available for RVs but no hookups. Drinking water, restrooms with flush toilets, pay showers, and a laundry are available. Dump stations exist for RVs. Some sites are paved and have handicap access. The maximum stay is 14 days.

✔ **Big Meadows Campground** (milepost 51.3): Total of 227 sites, 32 pull-throughs. Some paved, some gravel, stream for fishing. ☎ **540-999-3231,** reservations required. Rates: $17 per site. DISC, MC, V.

✔ **Lewis Mountain Campground** (milepost 57.5): Total of 31 sites, 3 pull-throughs. Paved, mostly shaded. ☎ **540-999-3500.** Rates $14, no reservations.

✔ **Loft Mountain Campground** (milepost 79.5): Total of 221 sites, 140 pull-throughs. Paved, some shaded. ☎ **540-999-3500.** Rates $14, no reservations.

Good eats

Although all the classic southern dishes from fried chicken to collard greens and black-eyed peas abound throughout the region, the culinary theme that ties together the mountains of Virginia, North Carolina, and Tennessee is country ham. If your only previous acquaintance with ham is the supermarket kind or the spiral-cut, honey-baked ham on a Super-Bowl Sunday or New Year's buffet, this mahogany-colored, chewy, often salty meat may surprise you. Pioneers who settled in these mountains preserved meats without refrigeration, and the best way of holding hams for a year or two was to rub down the fresh meat with a mixture of salt, sugar, and perhaps saltpeter, and then cover it for four to six weeks in a bed of salt. The ham then was hung in a smokehouse to be infused with hickory smoke for several months.

In addition to other specialties, many of the home-style restaurants in the following list offer country ham.

- **Apple Barn:** 230 Apple Valley Rd., off U.S. 441, Sevierville, Tennessee (☎ **800-421-4606** or 865-453-9319). What began as a barn where cider was made from the orchard's apples has turned into a complex of food production, visible to visitors. Apples are turned into cider, butter, pies, dumplings, doughnuts, wines, and candies; if you want more, a restaurant and grill are on the premises and so are a country ham store and a crafts shop selling baskets and birdhouses. Open daily from 9 a.m. to 7 p.m.

- **Hardware Store Restaurant:** East Main and Water Streets, Charlottesville, Virginia (☎ **434-977-4344**). Stop by for authentic turn-of-the-century decor, light and large meals, and gourmet sandwiches to go. Park on the Water Street side. Open Monday through Saturday from 11 a.m. to 9 p.m.

- **Jarrett House:** 100 Haywood St., Dillsboro, North Carolina (☎ **800-972-5623** or 828-586-0265). One of our all-time favorite restaurants is this family-style dining room in a small town inn with its front porch lined with rocking chairs. Budget-priced family-style meals may include country ham, fried chicken, hot biscuits, fried apple slices, and the specialty dessert, a rich and creamy vinegar pie. Open daily from 11:30 a.m. to 2:30 p.m. and from 4 to 7:30 p.m.

- **Mabry Mill Coffee Shop:** Blue Ridge Parkway milepost 176, near Meadows of Dan, Virgina (☎ **276-952-2947**). Cornmeal and buckwheat pancakes cooked from the stone-ground grains from the mill next door accompany rainbow trout, country ham, eggs, and homemade biscuits served all day long. You can also buy grains at the mill or in the coffee shop. The coffee shop is open late April through October, daily from 8 a.m. to 6 p.m. Be prepared to stand in line.

- **Michie Tavern:** 683 Thomas Jefferson Parkway, SR 53, Charlottesville, Virginia (☎ **434-977-1234**). This historic tavern (pronounced *mik*-e) serves traditional southern lunches at moderate prices and, unfortunately, all too often to bus tours. Offerings include fried chicken, black-eyed peas, stewed tomatoes, and local Virginia wines. Open daily from 11:30 a.m. to 3 p.m.

✓ **Mrs. Rowe's Restaurant:** I-81 at Exit 222, Staunton, Virginia (☎ 540-886-1833). A favorite country kitchen, Mrs. Rowe's is conveniently located just off I-81 (easy-on easy-off as the signs say) and as good a filling station as you find around here. Hearty breakfasts star country ham, pancakes, muffins, and sticky buns, and lunches and dinners always offer hot biscuits, macaroni and cheese, homemade applesauce, real mashed potatoes, skillet-fried chicken, country ham, corn pudding, and that nostalgic southern favorite, banana pudding. Open daily from 7 a.m. to 8 p.m.

✓ **Roanoke City Market:** Bounded by Norfolk Avenue, Williamson Road, Church Avenue, and Jefferson Street in downtown Roanoke, Virginia. This historic city market, selling produce and crafts, is the pride of this rapidly growing city beside the Blue Ridge Parkway. The location is in the center of an area filled with cafes and restaurants, boutiques and antique stores. Shops and restaurant hours vary; restaurants are open into the evening.

✓ **Route 11 Potato Chips:** 7815 Main St., Middletown, Virginia (☎ 540-869-0104). You can usually visit the plant on Fridays and Saturdays (call ahead to double-check) to see the potato chips turned out by this, the smallest potato chip factory in the country. Otherwise, check area grocery stores and cafes for the Route 11 or Yukon Gold chips.

✓ **Snappy Lunch:** 125 N. Main St., Mount Airy, North Carolina (☎ 336-786-4931). Stop here for breakfast or lunch. The must-order is the fried pork chop sandwich, a crunchy, tender, juicy pork chop dipped in batter and grilled. We like it with lettuce, tomato, and mayonnaise, but it also comes with cole slaw and a thick homemade chili sauce. Open Monday through Wednesday and Friday from 5:45 a.m. to 1:45 p.m., Thursday and Saturday from 5:45 a.m. to 1:15 p.m.

✓ **Western North Carolina Farmers Market:** 570 Brevard Rd., on SR 191 between I-26 and I-40, Asheville, North Carolina (☎ 828-253-1691). The retail division of this market sells fresh local fruits and vegetables, breads and baked goods, mountain crafts, ham, honey, and plants and shrubs. Open daily year-round from 8 a.m. and 6 p.m.

Shopping along the Way

One of the great pleasures of touring the southern mountains is finding high-quality crafts still made in the age-old traditions, elegantly crafted, although not inexpensive.

✔ **Folk Art Center:** Milepost 382, Blue Ridge Parkway near Asheville, North Carolina (☎ 828-298-7928). The Southern Highland Craft Guild has been promoting the crafts of this region for more than 60 years. Craft demonstrations are presented at the center from April through October, and juried shows are scheduled throughout the year. Pottery, quilts, rocking chairs, baskets, handcrafted children's toys, weavings — the finest works of skilled craftsmen are on display; most are for sale. Open daily from 9 a.m. to 6 p.m.

✔ **Parkway Craft Center:** At Moses Cone Manor, milepost 294, Blue Ridge Parkway near Blowing Rock, North Carolina (☎ 828-295-7938). Like the Folk Art Center, this place displays and sells premium examples of genuine mountain crafts. Open April through October daily 9 a.m. to 6 p.m. Closed major holidays.

Fast Facts

Area Code

The following area codes are in effect in the Blue Ridge Mountains: **828** in North Carolina; **423** and **865** in Tennessee; and **434, 504,** and **804** in Virginia.

Emergency

Call ☎ **911** in all states. Mobile phone users can touch *47 in North Carolina and *847 in Tennessee.

Hospitals

Major hospitals along the route are located in Roanoke, Virginia, and Asheville, North Carolina.

Information

For North Carolina, go online to www.ncgov.com or www.visitnc.com, or call Blue Ridge Parkway (☎ 828-298-0398) or Great Smokies (☎ 423-436-1200). For Tennessee, contact the Department of Tourist Development (☎ 615-741-8299; www.state.tn.us). For Virginia, go online to www.stateva.us or www.virginia.org, or contact Travel Guide (☎ 800-742-3935) or Blue Ridge Parkway (☎ 704-271-4779).

Laws

Those riding in the front seats must wear seat belts in North Carolina, Tennessee, and Virginia; those 16 and younger anywhere in the vehicle also must wear seat belts in North Carolina. The maximum speed limit on interstate highways in North Carolina and Tennessee is 70 mph; the maximum speed limit in Virginia is 65 mph. Speed limits in urban areas are lower in all three states.

Road and Weather Conditions

Sources include ☎ 919-733-2520 or www.ncdot.org for North Carolina; ☎ 800-858-6349 (road construction), ☎ 800-342-3258 (weather conditions), or www.tdot.state.tn.us for Tennessee; and ☎ 800-367-ROAD (roadway assistance) for Virginia.

Taxes

North Carolina state sales tax is 4.5%; local taxes can raise rates to 6.55%. Tennessee state sales tax is 6%; local taxes can raise rates to 8.35%. Virginia state sales tax is 3.5%; local taxes can raise rates to 4.5%.

State gas taxes are 24.2¢ a gallon in North Carolina, 20¢ a gallon in Tennessee, and 17.5¢ a gallon in Virginia.

Time Zone

North Carolina, Eastern Tennessee, and Virginia follow eastern standard time.

Chapter 14

The Gulf Coast: Tallahassee to New Orleans

- -

In This Chapter

▶ Strolling in sugar-soft sand

▶ Grilling fresh shrimp on the barbie

▶ Riding a glass-bottomed boat over the Black Lagoon

▶ Soaring with the Blue Angels

- -

Sugary white sand beaches, scrumptious shrimp, antebellum gardens scarlet and pink with azaleas, and oak trees dripping Spanish moss mark the Gulf Coast. This sunny vacation strip of land runs from **Tallahassee** across **Florida's Panhandle,** along the **gulf shores of Alabama and Mississippi,** and straight into the partying town of **New Orleans.**

In the little-known Florida Panhandle, where Mickey Mouse never paraded and Cuban coffee is unheard-of, you meet old-timers who call themselves "crackers" after the sound of a bullwhip wielded by their ancestors to drive teams of oxen at lumber camps. They relish smoked mullet and swamp cabbage, and mix, sometimes reluctantly, with the hotshot jet pilots of Pensacola Naval Air Station and the chic residents of Seaside, the Panhandle equivalent of The Hamptons. Florida writer Marjorie Kinnan Rawlings (author of *The Yearling*) described her cracker neighbors as people who made do, lived off the land, never put on airs, and wore their southern heritage with pride.

The fashionable coast between Apalachicola and Pensacola always boasts the top-ranked beaches in America, according to Dr. Stephen Leatherman, known as "Dr. Beach," a coastal geologist who puts out the listings of the nation's best. After a few years of his listings, the area's tourist offices began to call it "the emerald coast." An older, less tourist-conscious nickname for the region is "the Redneck Riviera."

Alabama and Mississippi serve up all the lush romance of their Gulf Coast in an economical 150 miles or so, with oceanside golf courses, Vegas-style casinos, and RV parks and campgrounds so close to the beach you're lulled to sleep by the waves. A few more minutes on the road, and you're in New Orleans, the Big Easy, where you can let the good times roll.

Getting There

Tallahassee, located in the center of northern Florida on I-10, is the starting point for this drive. (See the route on "The Gulf Coast" map in this chapter.) We drive south on U.S. 319 for a few miles, then turn off on SR 363 to the historic town of **St. Mark's,** then continue west on U.S. 98 and 319 to **Panacea** and **Carrabelle** on the Gulf of Mexico. **St. George Island** and **St. Joseph's Peninsula,** each with state park campgrounds, take us on a detour off U.S. 98 around Apalachicola, and then we continue along the Gulf Coast past Mexico Beach into **Panama City.**

Between Panama City and **Pensacola** lie the most fashionable stretches of Florida's Emerald Coast. From Pensacola, we make a detour down to the **Gulf Islands National Seashore,** follow SR 292 (the Gulf Beach Highway) into Alabama, where it becomes SR 182, to **Gulf Shores.** A circle around **Mobile Bay** highlights Alabama's Gulf Coast attractions, and then we follow U.S. 90 (or the faster I-10, which runs parallel) past **Pascagoula, Biloxi,** and **Gulfport,** and then continue on I-10 into **New Orleans.** The full distance of the drive is approximately **610 miles.**

Planning Ahead

This Gulf of Mexico coastal **drive can be made any time of year.** Beach-lovers should opt for summer, when the water is bathtub-warm (85 degrees) for swimming, but the air temperatures are too high for hiking and exploring. Flower fanciers love the route in early-to-late spring when the azaleas and camellias are blooming everywhere, and days are mild and sunny. In early fall, the weather still is warm enough for sunning and swimming (the Gulf of Mexico water averages 75 degrees in March and November), and in winter the weather is mild, encouraging beachcombing, bird-watching, and exploring small towns for antiques and local color.

Making **campground reservations** for RV camping is a good idea during summer, spring break, and around holidays, although you should be able to find a good spot without reservations in winter and during weekdays in early spring and late fall. Along our driving route between Tallahassee and New Orleans are some 36 communities with RV camping.

Pack swimming apparel and light cotton clothes for spring, summer, and fall, and add a light jacket or sweater for most winter days. Dress is casual everywhere along the coast, so don't plan on bringing jackets and ties, fancy dresses and high heels, unless you're taking some time off from the RV to stay in one of the expensive coastal resort hotels.

Always carry sunglasses, a sun hat, and sunblock. Having insect repellent is a good idea; veterans of the mosquito wars recommend buying
the most effective local repellent.

 Take along rain gear because this coast gets wind and rain periodically
throughout the year, especially in fall's hurricane season. Stay tuned to
weather forecasts from July to November, and if a bad blow is expected,
head inland with your RV.

Allow three to seven days for this drive, depending on how much beach
time you want to include. If you want to spend more time in the area, you
can easily add on the Natchez Trace Drive (see Chapter 15). The distance between New Orleans, where this drive ends, and Natchez, where
the Natchez Trace Drive begins, is only 176 miles.

Stocking the Pantry

With plenty of fresh fish and shellfish available along the route, roadside
produce stands open all year, and small supermarkets from **Winn-Dixie,
Piggly Wiggly, Kroger, IGA,** and other regional chains, you needn't
worry about running short of food. You may even encounter roadside
stands selling boiled peanuts, a much-loved delicacy in southern Georgia
and northern Florida that we've never developed a taste for; you need
to try them, however, if you think you'd like soggy, lukewarm peanuts.

Some of our favorite shopping spots along the way include

- **Bradley's Country Store** in Tallahassee for homemade sausages,
  cracklings (crisp fried pork rinds), and grits.

- Pensacola's **Joe Patti Seafoods** with every imaginable kind of
  fresh fish and shellfish, plus sauces and accompaniments.

- **Burris Farm Market,** open all year in Loxley, Alabama, with fruits,
  vegetables, and homemade breads for sale.

- **Sweet Home Farm** in Elberta, Alabama, for wonderful homemade
  cheeses produced from the farm's own cows. (See "Good eats"
  later in this chapter for information on all these spots.)

Driving the Gulf Coast

Tallahassee is a surprise for anyone familiar with Miami, Fort Lauderdale,
and even Orlando because it's a romantic southern city — not a tropical Florida resort. It was chosen as the capital of Florida in 1823 because
back then when Miami was still a swamp, it was equally distant from
the two most important cities in the state, Pensacola and St. Augustine.
Magnolia trees and azaleas surround the graceful old capitol building,
erected in the 1840s.

The Gulf Coast

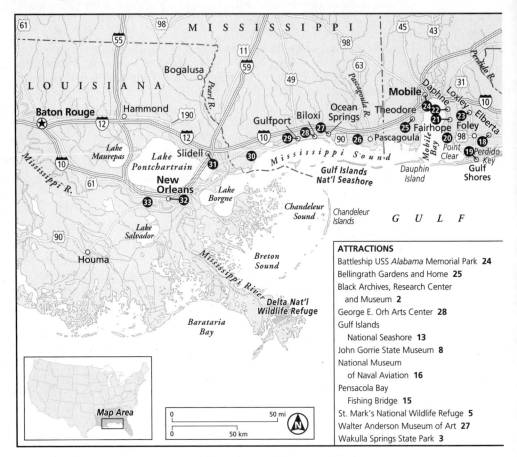

ATTRACTIONS

Battleship USS *Alabama* Memorial Park **24**

Bellingrath Gardens and Home **25**

Black Archives, Research Center
  and Museum **2**

George E. Orh Arts Center **28**

Gulf Islands
  National Seashore **13**

John Gorrie State Museum **8**

National Museum
  of Naval Aviation **16**

Pensacola Bay
  Fishing Bridge **15**

St. Mark's National Wildlife Refuge **5**

Walter Anderson Museum of Art **27**

Wakulla Springs State Park **3**

Perhaps the most unusual museum in the city, even the state, is the
Black Archives Research Center and Museum on the campus of
Florida A & M University in Tallahassee. This group of 5,000 artifacts
from slave days and the post–Civil War period is one of the nation's
largest groups of African American artifacts. (See "More cool things
to see and do" later in this chapter.)

From Tallahassee, we drive south, leaving town on U.S. 319 and almost
immediately turning off on SR 363 to **Wakulla Springs State Park,** where
the classic 1954 monster film *Creature from the Black Lagoon* was shot
in the deep, still waters of the springs. (See "More cool things to see
and do.") The old-fashioned **Wakulla Springs Lodge** serves regional
dishes including breakfast with biscuits, gravy, and grits, and luncheon
fried chicken with sawdust pie for dessert. (See "Good eats" later in
this chapter.)

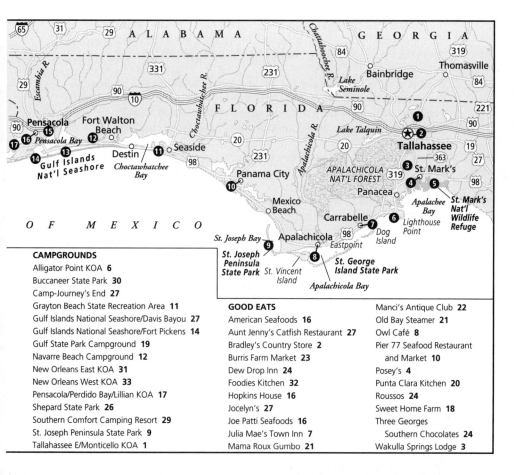

CAMPGROUNDS
Alligator Point KOA **6**
Buccaneer State Park **30**
Camp-Journey's End **27**
Grayton Beach State Recreation Area **11**
Gulf Islands National Seashore/Davis Bayou **27**
Gulf Islands National Seashore/Fort Pickens **14**
Gulf State Park Campground **19**
Navarre Beach Campground **12**
New Orleans East KOA **31**
New Orleans West KOA **33**
Pensacola/Perdido Bay/Lillian KOA **17**
Shepard State Park **26**
Southern Comfort Camping Resort **29**
St. Joseph Peninsula State Park **9**
Tallahassee E/Monticello KOA **1**

GOOD EATS
American Seafoods **16**
Aunt Jenny's Catfish Restaurant **27**
Bradley's Country Store **2**
Burris Farm Market **23**
Dew Drop Inn **24**
Foodies Kitchen **32**
Hopkins House **16**
Jocelyn's **27**
Joe Patti Seafoods **16**
Julia Mae's Town Inn **7**
Mama Roux Gumbo **21**

Manci's Antique Club **22**
Old Bay Steamer **21**
Owl Café **8**
Pier 77 Seafood Restaurant
  and Market **10**
Posey's **4**
Punta Clara Kitchen **20**
Roussos **24**
Sweet Home Farm **18**
Three Georges
  Southern Chocolates **24**
Wakulla Springs Lodge **3**

Five miles farther south on 363 is **St. Mark's,** notable today for the excellent **National Wildlife Refuge,** some historic remains from 17th-century Spanish explorers, and a down-home roadhouse called **Posey's,** where everybody gathers on weekends for beer, smoked mullet, and live rockabilly music. (See "More cool things to see and do" and "Good eats," respectively.)

From St. Mark's, we turn west again on U.S. 98 and follow it to **Panacea** and **Carrabelle.** From here, side road CR 370, sets off for **Alligator Point,** a remote peninsula jutting out in the bay where you find a quiet KOA campground. (See "Our favorite campgrounds" later in this chapter.)

At **Eastpoint,** 6 miles east of Apalachicola, County Highway 300 and a toll bridge lead across the bay to **St. George Island** and its state park.

Follow U.S. 98 on to **Apalachicola,** famous around the world for its oysters. But don't ignore the local grouper, blue crab, and clam chowder at places such as the **Owl Café.** (See "Good eats.") The **John Gorrie State Museum** here salutes the inventor of ice cubes, refrigeration, and air conditioning. (See "More cool things to see and do.")

West of Apalachicola, take CR 30, and then CR 30E to the **St. Joseph Peninsula State Park,** one of Dr. Beach's prime picks, named Best Beach in 2002. The park makes a great spot for beach camping. (See "Runner-up campgrounds" section later in this chapter.)

Return to U.S. 98 and continue west, driving past the almost empty stretches of perfect sand at **Mexico Beach,** and then on into **Panama City,** the capital of the "Redneck Riviera." If you should happen to be driving through here any time during college Easter vacation, often called "spring break," *don't stop, don't pause, and don't linger.* The beaches belong to the kids, and it isn't a pretty sight.

After you're safely past Panama City Beach, however, you can slow down again. Don't miss taking the back road off U.S. 98 through **Seaside** (a marked left turn just past Point Washington) to get a quick look at the award-winning architecture of the beach houses, but don't attempt to stop; streets are narrow, traffic is heavy, and parking is unavailable anywhere for RVs. If you're a movie fan, you may recognize the town from the 1998 *The Truman Show,* which was filmed, in part, in Seaside. If you're a shopper, you're in better luck — the big modern malls that line the highway from Panama City to Pensacola, especially around Destin and Fort Walton Beach, have big parking lots that can handle your vehicle.

Grayton Beach State Recreation Area, named Best Beach by Dr. Beach back in the '90s, allows RV camping in designated campgrounds. (See "Runner-up campgrounds.")

When you're enjoying the beaches of the Gulf Coast, especially during hurricane season between June and October, always look at the flags that denote water conditions. *Blue* means calm water safe for swimming, *yellow* means take care, and *red* means don't go in the water or get out at once.

The **Gulf Islands National Seashore** extends 150 miles from Destin to Gulfport, Mississippi. Established in 1971, the park protects the barrier islands along this coast, many of them undeveloped and unreachable. (See "Must-see attractions" later in this chapter.) Only two campgrounds suitable for RVs are available in the national seashore: **Fort Pickens** near Pensacola, Florida, and **Davis Bayou** near Ocean Springs, Mississippi. (See "Our favorite campgrounds" for both.)

Pensacola is a charming surprise of a city with a lovely old historic district downtown, the Navy's ace flying team the Blue Angels, and the world's longest fishing pier (also considered a great place to spot

UFOs). In a soaring glass tower, the **National Museum of Naval Aviation** displays A-4 Skyhawks in formation as if the Blue Angels were flying them, along with flight simulator, cockpit trainers, and IMAX theater. (See "Must-see attractions.") The city also has **Joe Patti Seafoods,** the biggest and best fresh indoor seafood market we've ever seen, and a down-home, family style restaurant called **Hopkins House.** (See "Good eats" for both food spots.)

After you've explored the city of Pensacola, we suggest that you drive south to see more of the Gulf Islands National Seashore; take SR 292 to **Perdido Key** and across into Alabama, where it becomes SR 182 to Gulf Shores. If you're in a hurry, you can take U.S. 98 across Perdido Bay into Alabama.

Eatin' and antiquin', Mobile-style

Mobile, 300 years old in 2002, was the French capital of America before there was a New Orleans, and the city logo proudly shows off a historic home, the battleship USS Alabama, an azalea in full bloom, and a shrimp. What does it all mean? The historic home is to remind you that Mobile offers tours of antebellum houses. The battleship, open daily for tours in **Battleship USS *Alabama* Memorial Park,** is a World War II veteran. The azalea stands for world-famous **Bellingrath Gardens and Home,** a glorious splash of seasonal flowers all year-round. And if the shrimp makes you think of Forrest Gump, you won't be surprised to discover that its author Winston Groom has a home just outside Mobile. (See "Must-see attractions" in this chapter for info on the battleship and gardens.)

RVers seeking other gratification in the area need to make the scenic drive on U.S. 98 and 98A along the eastern shore of Mobile Bay. En route, you can visit the Bloody Mary capital of the Eastern Shore, as **Manci's Antique Club** (1715 Main St.; ☎ 251-626-9917) in downtown Daphne calls itself, to see the largest collection of Jim Beam decanters outside the distillery's own.

Fairhope is lined with antique shops and art galleries, and punctuated with a long pier jutting out into the bay. The notable **Old Bay Steamer** serves the region's famous Royal Red shrimp. (See "Good eats" in this chapter for details.)

Point Clear is home to the Grand Hotel, now a Marriott and the latest in a line of classic southern resorts built on this spot, and to the **Punta Clara Kitchen,** where homemade candies abound. (See "Good eats.")

On the western side of the bay, SR 193 leads to **Bellingrath Gardens and Home** and beyond to **Dauphin Island** and **Fort Gaines,** where you can look across to **Fort Morgan,** the Civil War fortress barricaded with a string of underwater mines across the channel that inspired Admiral David Farragut's famous command, "Damn the torpedoes — full speed ahead!"

In Mobile, on the northwestern edge of the city on Old Shell Road, a super snack-time stop, the **Dew Drop Inn,** has been serving up great hot dogs since 1927. (See "Good eats.")

New Orleans: Easing into the Big Easy

Generally speaking, New Orleans is one of the friendliest cities on earth — that is, to everybody except RVers. It's not that the good folks of Louisiana don't welcome us; they do. But their roads, even the interstates, are bumpy and rough, causing our pots and pans to rattle as we bounce through.

Equally troubling are the confusing roadway markings for the interstate, expressway, and surface street system, which can catapult an innocent RVer into the traffic-clogged French Quarter or the Superdome before you can say, "Laissez les bon temps roulez!" ("Let the good times roll," a traditional Cajun partying cry.)

So instead of driving into the heart of New Orleans in your RV, select an RV park, preferably one that has frequent shuttle service to and from downtown if you don't have your own car, park and secure your living quarters, and then set out to have footloose fun in a city that never sleeps.

We like the **Gulf State Park** at Gulf Shores, Alabama, for beachfront camping and plenty of shrimp sellers. (See "Our favorite campgrounds".)

From Gulf Shores, food shoppers will want to drive north on SR 59 to **Foley** and detour east to **Elberta** to visit **Sweet Home Farm** cheese shop. (See "Good eats.") The one-mile road to the farm is unpaved but fairly smooth. If it's been raining recently, however, you shouldn't drive down this road in a large RV because the red mud can be slippery. Another favorite local food shop is **Burris Farm Market** in **Loxley,** open daily year-round with seasonal produce, boiled peanuts, homemade breads, and ice cream. (See "Good eats.") From Loxley, drive north to I-10 and make the quick 15-minute drive into **Mobile.**

From Mobile, it takes only 20 minutes or so to get into Mississippi via I-10. Where Alabama's Gulf Coast consists of quiet towns and fishing villages on dead-end roads, Mississippi's stretch of coastline is four-lane U.S. 90 brightened by intervals of glitz.

From the moment you cross the causeway from **Ocean Springs** to **Biloxi,** the casinos — a dozen of them — pop up like glittering psychedelic mushrooms. (So you won't be taken as a Yankee, pronounce the town "bu-*lux*-ee," not "bill-*lox*-ee.")

This new Las Vegas of the Deep South revives a sagging economy left bereft by a lag in local shipbuilding. The good news is Mississippi has 31 RV parks on or near the water on the Gulf Coast, all with hookups. (See "Our favorite campgrounds" and "Runner-up campgrounds.")

From **Gulfport,** following U.S. 90, it's 34 miles to the Louisiana border; just before you get to the border, you pass **Buccaneer State Park** (see

"Runner-up campgrounds"). If you're in a hurry to get to the Big Easy, New Orleans, take I-10.

Must-see attractions

Battleship USS Alabama Memorial Park
Mobile, Alabama

The decommissioned World War II battleship that carried a crew of 2,500 is on display, along with the submarine USS *Drum*, a B-52 aircraft, cannons, tanks, armored personnel carriers, and helicopters. Kids love to climb all over the military hardware and explore the hidden corners of the ship, which is Alabama's most popular tourist attraction.

Battleship Parkway, Mobile Bay. (Exit marked from I-10.) ☎ *251-433-2703. RV parking: Large parking area. Admission: $10 adults. Open: Oct–Mar 8 a.m.–4 p.m.; Apr–Sept 8 a.m.–6 p.m. Allow 2–3 hours.*

Bellingrath Gardens and Home
Theodore, Alabama (south of Mobile)

Six themed formal gardens are strung together with a series of bridges, walkways, pools, and streams to create one of the most appealing floral displays in the world. In spring, 250,000 azaleas blaze with color, in summer everything comes up roses, in autumn chrysanthemums bloom by the thousands, and winter's poinsettias and camellias glow in the semitropical landscape. The 15-room Bellingrath family home (he was the first Coca-Cola bottler in the Mobile area) houses collections of antique china and glass, including 200 pieces of Edward Marshall Boehm porcelain. A cafe is also on the estate.

12401 Bellingrath Gardens Rd. (From Mobile, take Exit 22 off I-10 and travel south on SR 163, Dauphin Island Parkway, to SR 193, which continues to the gardens; signage is frequent.) ☎ *800-247-8420, 251-973-2365.* www.bellingrath.org. *RV parking: Large designated parking areas. Admission: $9 adults gardens only, $16.50 gardens and house; $8.10 seniors gardens only, $15.75 gardens and house; $6 ages 5–12 gardens only, $11 gardens and house; 4 and younger free. Open daily 8 a.m.–5 p.m. Closed Christmas. Allow 2 hours for the gardens only, 3 hours for gardens and house.*

Gulf Islands National Seashore
Florida and Mississippi

Extending 150 miles from Destin, Florida, to Gulfport, Mississippi, the Gulf Islands National Seashore is divided into 11 sections, six of them in Florida, and five of them in Mississippi. Miles of uncrowded beaches famous for acres of soft white sand and sea oats attract day visitors and overnight campers in modest numbers. Two campgrounds, Florida's Fort Pickens and Mississippi's Davis Bayou (see "Our favorite campgrounds," later in this chapter) are available on a first-come, first-served basis. Much of the parkland consists of offshore islands reachable only by boat. Areas accessible by motor vehicles offer hiking trails, bike paths, and nature trails.

Headquarters: 1801 Gulf Breeze Parkway, Gulf Breeze, FL 32561, or 3500 Park Rd., Ocean Springs, MS 39564. ☎ *850-934-2600 (FL), 228-875-9057 (MS).* www.nps. gov/guis. *RV parking: Designated off-road areas. Admission: Free except Fort Pickens and Perdido Key, $8 for 7-day permit. Open: Year-round.*

National Museum of Naval Aviation
Pensacola, Florida

Climb into a cockpit trainer, observe a flight simulator in action, see A-4 Skyhawks like those flown by the Blue Angels, learn the history of flying from wooden planes to the Skylab module, and see big-screen aviation films with a pilot's point of view in the adjoining IMAX theatre.

1750 Radford Blvd., Naval Air Station. ☎ *850-452-3604.* www.naval-air.org. *RV parking: Designated lot. Admission: Free. Open: Daily 9 a.m.–5 p.m. Closed major holidays. Allow 3 hours (real buffs spend a whole day).*

Walter Anderson Museum of Art
Ocean Springs, Mississippi

This museum displays the astonishing works of an eccentric loner named Walter Anderson. A master artist who painted plants, animals, and people of the Gulf Coast, he sometimes isolated himself in primitive conditions on an uninhabited barrier island for months at a time. After his death in 1965, his family went into the small cottage he used as a studio to find the "little room," every inch of its floor, walls, and ceilings covered with paintings of plants, animals, and an allegorical figure thought to represent the Mississippi River. The little room, his paintings and murals, and ceramic pieces from the family's Shearwater Pottery collection are on display here.

510 Washington Ave. ☎ *228-872-3164.* www.walterandersonmuseum.org. *RV parking: Use street parking because the museum lot is small. Admission: $6 adults, $5 seniors and students, $3 ages 6–12, 5 and younger free. Allow 2 hours.*

More cool things to see and do

Fascinating attractions fill the Gulf Coast. A few more of our favorites follow, although you'll no doubt make your own discoveries.

✔ **Explore black history.** With 5,000 items and 500,000 documents, one of the most extensive collections of African American artifacts in the United States, the **Black Archives, Research Center and Museum** at Florida A & M University in Tallahassee displays everything from slave-era implements and old non-PC Aunt Jemima pancake packages to the first ironing board, built in 1872 by a servant named Sarah Boone who got tired of ironing on the floor and propped a board up on legs. A hands-on Underground Railroad exhibit fascinates the kids.

Carnegie Center, Gamble St., Tallahassee, Florida. ☎ **850-599-3020.** RV parking: Designated guest parking area or street parking. Admission: Free. Open: Mon–Fri 9 a.m.–5 p.m. Closed holidays. Allow 2 hours.

✔ **Meet the mad potter of Biloxi. George E. Orh Arts Center** commemorates the mad potter of Biloxi, who had a genius for self-promotion, with 130 pots of his creation.

George E. Orh St., Biloxi, Mississippi. ☎ **228-374-5547.** RV parking: Street parking. Admission: Free. Open daily 9 a.m.–6 p.m. Allow 1 hour.

✔ **Invent the ice cube.** In 1851, Dr. John Gorrie invented a machine to cool down the rooms of malaria patients, but when it kept clogging its pipes with ice cubes, he realized he was on to something and invented ice cubes, ice making, and air conditioning. The machine in the **John Gorrie State Museum** is a replica; the original is in the Smithsonian.

46 Sixth St., Apalachicola, Florida. ☎ **850-653-9347.** RV parking: Street parking. Admission: $1 for ages 6 and older, ages 5 and younger free. Open: Thurs–Mon 9 a.m.–5 p.m. Allow 1 hour.

✔ **Hook a grouper, spot a UFO. Pensacola Bay Fishing Bridge** is not only the world's longest fishing pier — the 3-mile pier was part of the old highway bridge — but it also is the source of many UFO spotting reports through the years. (The fact that it's near Pensacola Naval Air Station is, of course, immaterial.) Fishing gear and bait is available for rent on-site at the Bridge Store.

1750 Bayfront Parkway, Pensacola, Florida. ☎ **850-444-9811.** www.fishthebridge.com. RV parking: Designated lot in the vicinity or roadside parking where permitted. Admission: Free. Open: Mon–Thurs daybreak–11 p.m., Fri–Sun 24 hours.

✔ **Look out for alligators!** Bike, hike, and canoe numerous trails and streams in **St. Mark's National Wildlife Refuge** bordering Florida's Apalachee Bay. An excellent visitor center has maps and advice.

U.S. Fish & Wildlife Service, P.O. Box 68, St. Mark's, Florida 32355. Refuge entrance south of Newport on SR 59. ☎ **850-925-6121.** RV parking: Designated lots at visitor center or trailheads. Admission: Free. Open: Daylight hours.

✔ **Trail Tarzan.** Many of the early Tarzan movies with Johnny Weismuller and Maureen O'Sullivan were filmed at **Wakulla Springs State Park** in Florida, and so was the 1954 horror classic *The Creature from the Black Lagoon.* The clear, almost bottomless springs and the lush jungle foliage make this a popular family vacation area. Take a glass-bottom boat ride across the springs.

550 Wakulla Park Dr., Wakulla Springs Lodge, Florida. ☎ **850-922-3632.** RV parking: Designated parking areas in the park and at the lodge. Admission: $3.25 per vehicle. Open: Daily year-round; lodge open for overnight guests.

Weekend wonder

If you want to take a shorter version of this Gulf Coast drive, make the drive from **Tallahassee** southwest to **Apalachicola,** and then continue west along the Emerald Coast to **Pensacola,** pausing at whatever beach and campground strike your fancy. The distance between Tallahassee and Pensacola on the route outlined earlier in this chapter is 310 miles. To return from Pensacola to Tallahassee quickly (with a refrigerator stocked with fresh seafood) take I-10 east back to Tallahassee. This loop drive is 505 miles.

Sleeping and Eating on the Road

The Gulf of Mexico is a favorite destination for RVers, whether family vacationers, snowbirds, or full-timers, and plenty of RV parks, state parks, and recreation areas with camping line the way. Supermarkets, country stores, restaurants, cafes, and national fast food outlets also thickly dot the route.

All campgrounds listed below are open year-round and have public flush toilets, showers, and sanitary dump stations unless designated otherwise. Toll-free numbers, where listed, are for reservations only. See Chapter 9 for more information on how to choose your favorite campgrounds.

Our favorite campgrounds

Alligator Point KOA
$$$$ Alligator Point, Florida

Located down a dead-end side road on the Gulf of Mexico, Alligator Point looks like the place to get away from it all — but of course, you're carrying everything with you that you really want. At the campground, you find salt- and freshwater fishing, shrimping, and dolphin watching, and boat and surf bike rentals.

1320 Alligator Dr., Alligator Point, FL 32346. (On U.S. 98 go 5 miles west from Panacea, and then 5 miles south on CR 370 to campground.) ☎ ***800-562-0848,** 850-349-2525.* www.koa.com. *Total of 99 sites with 30- and 50-amp electric, all full hookups, 32 pull-throughs. CATV, dataport, laundry, pool. Rates: $35 per site. DISC, MC, V.*

Gulf Islands National Seashore/Davis Bayou
$$ Ocean Springs, Mississippi

Davis Bayou, the Mississippi campground inside Gulf Islands National Seashore, is much smaller than its Florida equivalent at Fort Pickens, and the paved, back-in sites are narrower. Sites are open on a first-come, first-served basis. It's on the ocean side of U.S. 90 near a golf course and a shopping mall.

3500 Park Rd., Ocean Springs, MS 39565. (From Biloxi, go east 5 miles on U.S. 90 to the campground on the right.) ☎ ***228-875-9057.** Total of 52 sites with water and 30-amp electric, no full hookups, no pull-throughs. Rates: $14–$16 per site. DISC, MC, V. No reservations.*

Gulf Islands National Seashore/Fort Pickens
$$ Gulf Islands National Seashore, Florida

Fort Pickens, the larger of the two campgrounds in the Gulf Islands National Seashore has moderately large back-in sites, and charges a park entrance fee in addition to the camping fee. On the gulf, it offers saltwater fishing and swimming, and paved patios, some of them shaded. If you're traveling with pets, check ahead; some restrictions may be in effect. In the past, pets have been allowed in the campground on a six-foot leash but not on the beach.

From junction of U.S. 98 and Hwy. 399, go southwest 1 mile on 399 to Fort Pickens Rd., and then west 5 miles to campground on the right. ☎ ***800-365-CAMP,** 850-934-2621. Total of 200 sites with water and 30- and 50-amp electric, no full hookups, no pull-throughs. Laundry. Rates: $15–$20 per site. DISC, MC, V. 14-day maximum stay.*

Gulf State Park Campground
$$–$$$$ Gulf Shores, Alabama

Despite its large size, this state park is one of the best in the country for RVers, with big pull-through and back-in sites, plenty of grass, some shade, and some side-by-side hookups. There's a 2.5-mile beach of powdery white sand, a long fishing pier, boating, a nature trail to hike, and a resort hotel with all-you-can-eat buffets if you don't feel like cooking. Reserving ahead of time in spring and summer is a good idea.

From junction of SR 59 and SR 182, go east 2.1 miles on SR 182 to CR 2, north 0.5 mile to park on the right. ☎ ***251-948-7275.** Total of 468 sites with water and 30-amp* *electric, 210 full hookups, 41 pull-throughs. Handicap access, laundry. Rates: $11–$34 per site. DISC, MC, V.*

New Orleans East KOA

$$$ **Slidell, Louisiana**

If you take our advice in this chapter's sidebar "New Orleans: Easing into the Big Easy," you'll settle in here or at the New Orleans West KOA, because at both you can happily leave your RV behind while you take a shuttle to the French Quarter. This park, 30 minutes from New Orleans, offers new facilities and a rural, shady setting. Amenities include freshwater fishing, car rentals, and swamp tours — a kid favorite.

56009 SR 433, Slidell, LA 70461. (Off I-10, Exit 263, go southeast 0.9 mile on SR 433 to campground on the right.) ☎ ***800-562-2128***, *985-643-3850.* www.koa.com. *Total of 109 sites with water and 30- and 50-amp electric, 100 full hookups, 96 pull-throughs. Dataport, handicap access, laundry, pool. Rates: $28 per site. DISC, MC, V.*

New Orleans West KOA

$$$$ **River Ridge, Louisiana**

We've stayed here numerous times and always enjoyed the well-kept surroundings and friendly management. Besides the daily shuttle bus, a city bus that goes into downtown New Orleans stops at the campground entrance. Car rentals also are available at the campground. Sites are large, mostly shady back-ins. The location is about 15 minutes from the casino and the French Quarter.

11129 Jefferson Hwy., River Ridge, LA 70123 (From junction of I-10 and SR 49, Exit 223A, go south 3 miles on SR 49, and then 0.75 mile east on SR 48 to campground on left.) ☎ ***800-562-5110***, *504-467-1792.* www.koa.com. *Total of 97 sites with 30-and 50-amp electric, all full hookups, no pull-throughs. CATV, dataport, handicap access, laundry, pool. Rates: $32 per site. AE, DISC, MC, V.*

Pensacola/Perdido Bay/Lillian KOA

$$$ **Lillian, Alabama**

Just across Perdido Bay from Pensacola, Florida, this quiet rural campground is a short walk uphill from a swimming beach and fishing pier on the premises. If you want to stay a while — and the long shady sites are appealing, and so are the Saturday night ice cream socials — you get every third night free.

33951 Spinaker, Lillian, AL 36549. (From junction of U.S. 98 and CR 99, go south 1.3 miles to campground on the left.) ☎ ***800-562-3471***, *251-961-1717.* www.koa.com. *Total of 104 sites with water and 30- and 50-amp electric, 58 full hookups, 94 pull-throughs. CATV, dataport, pool/spa, laundry. Rates: $25 per site. DISC, MC, V.*

Runner-up campgrounds

Buccaneer State Park

$$ Waveland, Mississippi   Large campsites make this state park a comfortable stopover, even though you have to back in to hook up. The location is right on the Gulf with swimming and saltwater fishing. *From junction of U.S. 90 and SR 603, go south 1.2 miles on 603 to Central Ave., then west 9.7 miles to Coleman, then south 0.4 mile to Beach Blvd., and west 2.7 miles and follow the signs to the campground on the right.* ☎ *228-467-3822. Total of 149 sites with water and 30- and 50-amp electric, 80 full hookups, no pull-throughs. Handicap access, laundry. Rates: $14 per site. MC, V. 14-day maximum stay.*

Camp-Journey's End

$$$ Ocean Springs, Mississippi   This Good Sam park is near traffic but still a few miles away from the bustling casino strip. The sites are large and shady, and fishing and boating are available on the Fort Bayou River. *7501 SR 57, Ocean Springs, MS 39565 (0.4 mile north of I-10 on SR 57 on the left).* ☎ *888-288-8449, 228-875-2100. Total of 110 sites with water and 30-amp electric, 72 full hookups, 32 pull-throughs. CATV, dataport, laundry, pool. Rates: $30 per site. AE, DISC, MC, V.*

Grayton Beach State Recreation Area

$–$$ Grayton Beach, Florida   The recreation area, with its beautiful beach, provides saltwater fishing, swimming, and boating. Campsites are comfortably sized; some are shaded. *From junction of U.S. 98 and CR C283, go south 1 mile on CR 283 to SR 30A, and then east 0.6 mile to campground on the right.* ☎ *850-231-4210. Total of 37 sites with water and 30-amp electric, no full hookups, no pull-throughs. Rates: $8–$18 per site. DISC, MC, V.*

Navarre Beach Campground

$$$$ Navarre, Florida   Large grassy sites, most of them shaded and some of them waterfront, make this Good Sam park a nice spot for fresh-water and saltwater fishing and swimming. A boat dock is on the Santa Rosa Sound. *9201 Navarre Parkway, U.S. 98, Navarre, FL 32566. (From junction of SR 87 and U.S. 98, go east 2 miles on 98 to campground on the right.)* ☎ *888-639-2188, 850-939-2188.* www.navarrebeachcampground.com. *Total of 148 sites with water and 30- and 50-amp electric, all full hookups, 60 pull-throughs. CATV, dataport, handicap access, laundry, pool. Rates: $31 per site. MC, V.*

Shepard State Park

$$ Gautier, Mississippi   If the bayou is better by you than the Gulf of Mexico, you'll like this state park in an inland location on Lamotte Bayou, with freshwater fishing and boating. *From junction of U.S. 90 and Ladnier Road, go south 2 miles on Ladnier to Graveline Road, and then east 1.2 miles to the campground on the left.* ☎ *228-497-2244. Total of 28 sites with water and 30- and 50-amp electric, no full hookups, 2 pull-throughs. Dataport. Rates: $13 per site. No credit cards. 14-day maximum stay.*

Southern Comfort Camping Resort

$$$ **Biloxi, Mississippi** Big trees festooned with Spanish moss provide shade at this venerable RV park across the road from the beach and not far from clubs and casinos. Sites are fairly wide, most of them back-ins, and the management is friendly. We do, however, remember some train noises in the night. *1766 Beach Blvd., Biloxi, MS 39531. (Across from the beach on U.S. 90.)* ☎ *877-302-1700, 228-432-1700. Total of 118 sites with water and 30- and 50-amp electric, 84 full hookups, 56 pull-throughs. CATV, dataport, laundry, pool. Rates: $23 per site. MC, V.*

St. Joseph Peninsula State Park

$$ **Port St. Joe, Florida** Dr. Beach selected this state park as the most beautiful beach in the United States in 2002. The remote park provides sandy beaches, boardwalks for exploring, even alligators inhabiting ponds near the campground entrance. Sites are fairly narrow, with side-by-side hookups, but most are large enough for big RVs. *From town, go east 2 miles on U.S. 98 to CR 30, then south 10 miles to Cape San Blas Road, and then north 11 miles to the campground.* ☎ *850-227-1327. Total of 118 sites with water and 30-amp electric, 96 full hookups, 2 pull-throughs. Handicap access. Rates: $19 per site. AE, DISC, MC, V. 14-day maximum stay.*

Tallahassee E/Monticello KOA

$$$ **Monticello, Florida** This KOA makes a handy overnight stop at the beginning of the drive. Day canoe trips, horseback riding, and fresh-water fishing (in Lake Catherine) are available. Sites are large, some shaded. *Route 5, Box 5160, Monticello, FL 32344. (From Junction of I-10 and U.S. 19, Exit 33, go south 0.5 mile on 19 to CR 158B, then west 2 miles to CR 259, north 0.5 mile to access road, and east 0.25 mile to campground.)* ☎ *800-562-3890, 850-997-3890.* www.koa.com. *Total of 47 sites with water and 30- and 50-amp electric, 24 full hook-ups, 33 pull-throughs. Dataport, laundry, pool. Rates: $26 per site. DISC, MC, V.*

Good eats

Southern cooking has a well-deserved reputation around the world, and the Gulf Coast provides the best examples anywhere. In this section, you can find perhaps more than you ever wanted to know about fresh shrimp, great home-style, all-you-can-eat cafes and restaurants. And the prices are great!

Seafood markets

Delectable fresh shrimp in the big, bigger, and biggest giant size are for sale all along the Gulf Coast at prices that are unbelievably cheap to urbanites from the northeast and the west coast. The finest local shrimp are called Royal Red; ask for them by name. For our tips on how to prepare them, see this chapter's sidebar "Put another shrimp on the barbie." Although several good seafood sellers are along the route, what follows is a list of our favorites.

Put another shrimp on the barbie

Although you can buy boiled, fried, or grilled shrimp in every little restaurant and takeout along the route, the most delicious are those that you buy fresh and cook for yourself. It only takes a few minutes until they turn red and are ready. What follows are our favorite ways to serve 'em up.

✔ **Steam them** in their shells in boiling salted water or beer with a little bit of local "shrimp boil" seasoning (bay leaves and dried herbs).

✔ **Grill them** in the shell on your barbecue grill.

✔ **Peel them** and string them on skewers to lay over the coals.

✔ To turn out instant **shrimp scampi,** as some restaurants call them, peel them and cook them quickly in a frying pan with a little butter or olive oil and chopped garlic and herbs.

✔ Peel them, leaving the tail part of the shell for a handle. Dip them in flour that's been salted and peppered, then in a beaten egg with a little water, and finally in dry breadcrumbs. (The Japanese panko crumbs are best; you can find them in Asian food sections of supermarkets.) Then **deep-fry them** in a half-inch of hot oil a few minutes on each side — yummy!

✔ **American Seafoods:** 528 South B St., Pensacola, Florida (☎ 850-432-4133). Open Monday through Saturday from 7 a.m. to 6 p.m.

✔ **Joe Patti Seafoods:** 524 South B St., Pensacola, Florida (☎ 850-432-3315; www.joepattis.com). Open daily from 7 a.m. to 7 p.m.

✔ **Pier 77 Seafood Restaurant and Market:** 3016 Thomas Dr., Panama City, Florida (☎ 850-235-3080). Stop here for super-jumbo shrimp and frozen clam strips. Open Tuesday through Saturday from 5 p.m. to 11 p.m.

More markets

Our two favorite markets specialize in produce, bread, and cheese. For suggestions on where you can purchase other basics, see "Stocking the Pantry," earlier in this chapter.

✔ **Burris Farm Market:** SR 59, Loxley, Alabama (☎ 251-964-6464). Stock up here on fresh fruits and vegetables and homemade breads. Open daily from 8 a.m. to 6 p.m.

✔ **Sweet Home Farm:** 27107 Shoen Rd., Elberta, Alabama (☎ 251-986-5663). The farm owners make sophisticated European-style cheeses from milk produced by their own herd of purebred Guernseys. All cheeses are aged at least 60 days; tastes of each are offered in the shop. Offerings include a semisoft cheese called Elberta that melts well; a Bama Jack similar to California's

Monterey Jack; Gouda; Montabella, a creamy Italian-style cheese; feta; Swiss; Romano; blue; Asiago, and flavored cheeses. Open Wednesday through Saturday from 10 a.m. to 5 p.m

Snacks and full-meal deals

Along the Gulf of Mexico, you find not only great seafood but also other tasty treats.

✔ **Aunt Jenny's Catfish Restaurant:** 1217 Washington Ave., Ocean Springs, Mississippi (☎ 228-875-9201). Obviously, fried catfish fillets — all you can eat — are the main meal here, along with fried okra, fried green tomatoes, and turnip greens. Open Monday through Thursday from 5 p.m. to 9 p.m., Friday and Saturday until 9:30 p.m., and Sunday from 11:30 a.m. to 8 p.m.

✔ **Bradley's Country Store:** 10655 Centerville Rd., Tallahassee, Florida (☎ 850-893-1647). Homemade smoked sausages and special sausage biscuits hot off the griddle are the attractions at this store with a lunch counter. Open Monday through Friday from 8 a.m. to 5 p.m., and Saturday from 8 a.m. to 6 p.m.

✔ **Dew Drop Inn:** 1808 Old Shell Rd., Mobile, Alabama (☎ 251-473-7872). Stop here for hot dogs with chili, sauerkraut, mustard, ketchup, and pickles, or the cheeseburgers that singer Jimmy Buffett, a Mobile native, raves about. Open Monday through Saturday from 11 a.m. to 8 p.m.

✔ **Foodies Kitchen:** 720 Veterans Blvd., Metairie, Louisiana (☎ 504-837-9695). (Veterans Blvd. runs parallel to I-610 to the north, from Exits 225 to 230.) The kitchens at Commander's Palace, one of New Orleans's finest restaurants, prepare everything from gumbo to jambalaya for takeout at Foodies. Open Monday through Friday from 10 a.m. to 9 p.m., and Saturday through Sunday from 8 a.m. to 9 p.m.

✔ **Hopkins House:** 900 N. Spring St., Pensacola, Florida (☎ 850-438-3979). All you can eat served family style; no reservations, just wait in line. Offerings include famous fried chicken, corn biscuits, and great Southern-style vegetables. Breakfast is less than $5; lunch and dinner are less than $8. Open Tuesday through Sunday from 7 to 9:30 a.m. and from 11:15 a.m. to 2 p.m., and Tuesday through Friday from 5 to 7:30 p.m.

✔ **Jocelyn's:** U.S. 90, Ocean Springs, Mississippi (☎ 228-875-1925). In a pretty pink house by the side of the highway, Jocelyn's serves elegant dinners of seafoods, such as pompano, and homemade pies of pecan, peanut butter, or banana split flavors. Cash only. Open Tuesday through Saturday from 5 to 10 p.m.

✔ **Julia Mae's Town Inn:** U.S. 98, Carrabelle, Florida (☎ 850-697-3791). Stop by for great grouper burgers and fried seafood plates overflowing with goodies. On Sundays, the lines are long; after lunch, people leave carrying big Styrofoam doggie bags. Open daily from 11 a.m. to 9 p.m.

✔ **Mama Roux Gumbo:** 2 S. Church St., Fairhope, Alabama (☎ 251-928-4100). This takeout stand sells gumbo with saltines on the side, beer, and soft drinks. Open Monday through Saturday from 11 a.m. to 11 p.m.

✔ **Old Bay Steamer:** 195 S. Section St., Fairhope, Alabama (☎ 251-928-5714). Local oysters and Royal Red shrimp are among the seafood specialties, which you can enjoy indoors or on the patio. Open Monday through Saturday from 11 a.m. to 10 p.m.

✔ **Owl Café:** 15 Avenue D, Apalachicola, Florida (☎ 850-653-9888). A favorite with the locals, the Owl serves excellent clam chowder, real crab cakes, and great fried grouper. Open Monday through Saturday from 11 a.m. to 3 p.m. and from 5:30 to 10 p.m.

✔ **Posey's:** 55 Riverside Dr., St. Mark's, Florida (☎ 850-925-6172). The hush puppy was invented here, so they claim, and they serve "topless oysters." On Sundays, people come from miles around to this funky hangout to chew on rich-and-famous smoked mullet between healthy swallows from longneck beer bottles. Live music starts in the late afternoon. Open Monday through Wednesday from 11 a.m. to 3 p.m.; Thursday until 9 p.m.; Friday, Saturday, and Sunday until 11 p.m.

✔ **Punta Clara Kitchen:** U.S. 98, Point Clear, Alabama (☎ 251-928-8477). A candy and gift shop in an 1897 gingerbread house delights young visitors and sells pecan butter crunch, bourbon balls, and buckeyes (peanut butter centers hand-dipped in chocolate). Open Monday through Saturday from 9 a.m. to 5 p.m., Sunday from 12:30 to 5 p.m.

✔ **Roussos:** 166 S. Royal St., Mobile, Alabama (☎ 251-433-3322). Like many southern port cities, Mobile has a long history of Greek restaurateurs. With 30 years of tradition behind it, Roussos, in a brick warehouse downtown, serves a crab salad called a West Indies salad, fried crab claws, gumbo, Greek salad, and a richly succulent fried chicken. Open Monday through Saturday from 11 a.m. to 10 p.m.

✔ **Three Georges Southern Chocolates:** 226 Dauphin St., Mobile, Alabama (☎ 251-433-6725). Three Greek friends, all named George, established this confectionary in 1917, and their descendents still are turning out hand-dipped chocolates and distinctive handmade southern sweets, such as divinity, pralines, and heavenly hash. Open Monday through Saturday from 9 a.m. to 5 p.m.

✔ **Wakulla Springs Lodge:** 550 Wakulla Park Dr., Wakulla Springs, Florida (☎ 850-224-5950). Breakfasts are big, with biscuits, grits, ham, and eggs; lunch and dinner go from fried chicken to sawdust pie, a rich custard pie topped with toasted coconut. The dining room is open daily from 11:30 a.m. to 2 p.m. for lunch and from 6 to 8 p.m. for dinner.

Fast Facts

Area Code

Area codes along this drive include **251** for Alabama, **850** for Florida, **504** for Louisiana, and **228** for Mississippi.

Emergency

Call ☎ **911** in all states.

Hospitals

Major hospitals along the route are in Tallahassee, Mobile, Biloxi, and New Orleans.

Information

Helpful sources in the individual states include: Alabama Bureau of Tourism & Travel (☎ 800-ALABAMA (252-2262); www.touralabama.org); Visit Florida (☎ 888-7-FLA-USA (735-2872); www.flausa.com); Louisiana Office of Tourism (☎ 800-227-4386; www.louisianatravel.com); and Mississippi Division of Tourism (☎ 800-WARMEST (800-927-6378); www.visitmississippi.org).

Laws

In Alabama, Florida, Louisiana, and Mississippi, riders in the front seats must wear seat belts. The maximum speed limit on interstate highways in Alabama, Florida, Louisiana, and Mississippi is 70 mph. Speed limits in urban areas are lower.

Road and Weather Conditions

Call the following for road and weather advisories: in Alabama (☎ 334-242-4128); in Florida, Department of Transportation (☎ 888-558-1518); in Mississippi, Highway Patrol (☎ 601-987-1211). In Louisiana, mobile phone users can touch *577 for State Police assistance.

Taxes

Alabama state sales tax is 4%; local taxes can raise it to 7.45%. Florida state sales tax is 6%; local taxes can raise it to 6.5%. Louisiana state sales tax is 4%; local taxes can raise it to 8.35%. Mississippi state sales tax is a flat 7%.

State gasoline taxes are as follows: Alabama 18¢/gallon; Florida 13.9¢/gallon; Louisiana 20¢/gallon; and Mississippi 18¢/gallon.

Time Zone

Eastern Florida is on eastern standard time. Western Florida from Apalachicola, Alabama, Mississippi, and Louisiana are on central standard time.

Chapter 15

The Natchez Trace: Natchez, MS, to Nashville, TN

. . . .

In This Chapter

▶ Walking the original trace

▶ Sampling deep-fried dill pickles

▶ Tracking down Elvis

▶ Playing sports announcer

. . . .

Consider leaving the clogged arteries of crowded interstates behind to enter a shaded, curved, rural highway that doesn't allow commercial traffic or speeding — 50 mph is the limit. Along the way, you find campgrounds, craft shops, picnic tables, and nature trails to explore, including a boardwalk through an eerie swamp with lime-green water and sunken trees.

In spring and summer, the route is green with thick, lush grass and plenty of hardwood trees, with occasional glimpses of small farms and villages through the foliage. The highway is easy and undulating but not wide. Most but not all overlook turnoffs, however, are spacious enough for large motorhomes or vehicles pulling trailers.

The Natchez Trace meanders nearly 500 miles from a point northeast of **Natchez, Mississippi,** to a point southwest of **Nashville, Tennessee,** passing the places where TV megastar Oprah Winfrey, rock idol Elvis Presley, and blues musician W.C. Handy were born, and where Meriwether Lewis of Lewis and Clark fame died under mysterious circumstances.

Following an 8,000-year-old Indian trail, the *trace* — an old-fashioned term for a path or roadway — was turned into a scenic highway drive in the 1930s. The route preserves some 300 segments of the old trace that was commissioned in 1806 by Thomas Jefferson. And don't worry about the speed limit — it's so peaceful and scenic along the way that you won't even be tempted to rev up the RV.

Getting There

Our Natchez Trace drive begins in **Natchez** and goes north to **Nashville,** but it's just as simple to begin in Nashville and drive south to Natchez. (For the route, see "The Natchez Trace" map in this chapter.) If you're driving from Nashville to Natchez and have extra time, check out the Gulf Coast drive between New Orleans and Tallahassee in Chapter 14.

The trace is unfinished at a couple of spots. It begins 8 miles northeast of Natchez, so you travel on U.S. 60 from Natchez to the marked beginning. Again near Jackson, you need to leave the parkway at the junction of I-20, follow I-20 to I-220 north, and then continue on I-55 to Exit 105, which reconnects you to the parkway.

Similar to the Skyline Drive and Blue Ridge Parkway drive described in Chapter 13, the Natchez Trace has well-marked entrances and exits that take you onto commercial highways and in and out of towns and villages. And the trace has numbered mileposts that double as addresses for sites along the route. The route begins at milepost 8 near Natchez, and finishes past milepost 440 near Nashville.

At the end of the parkway, you exit by a recently completed dramatic bridge past milepost 440 that swoops you down onto Route 100 about 10 miles west of Nashville. The total drive runs around **500 miles.**

Planning Ahead

Although the parkway is comfortable to drive year-round, the best times are in **early spring and fall** when the weather is mild, the flowers are in bloom, and the pilgrimage tours through antebellum homes are on the agenda. (See "More cool things to see and do," later in this chapter.) Winter usually is mild but can be rainy and sometimes chilly; summers are hot.

You don't need **campground reservations** for any of the places in this chapter except for Ratliff Ferry and the Ross Barnett Reservoir campgrounds in summer. You also need reservations for the Opryland KOA, Nashville, in June when Fan Fair, a gathering of country music fans from around the world, takes place. (See "Our favorite campgrounds" later in this chapter.)

Allow three to seven days for the drive.

Stocking the Pantry

You won't find food outlets, restaurants, or stores along the Natchez Trace, but this itinerary frequently detours off the trace through a

The Natchez Trace

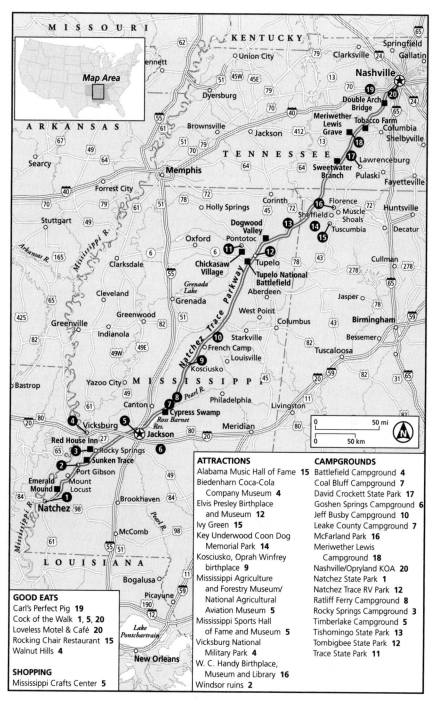

ATTRACTIONS
Alabama Music Hall of Fame **15**
Biedenharn Coca-Cola
  Company Museum **4**
Elvis Presley Birthplace
  and Museum **12**
Ivy Green **15**
Key Underwood Coon Dog
  Memorial Park **14**
Kosciusko, Oprah Winfrey
  birthplace **9**
Mississippi Agriculture
  and Forestry Museum/
  National Agricultural
  Aviation Museum **5**
Mississippi Sports Hall
  of Fame and Museum **5**
Vicksburg National
  Military Park **4**
W. C. Handy Birthplace,
  Museum and Library **16**
Windsor ruins **2**

CAMPGROUNDS
Battlefield Campground **4**
Coal Bluff Campground **7**
David Crockett State Park **17**
Goshen Springs Campground **6**
Jeff Busby Campground **10**
Leake County Campground **7**
McFarland Park **16**
Meriwether Lewis
  Campground **18**
Nashville/Opryland KOA **20**
Natchez State Park **1**
Natchez Trace RV Park **12**
Ratliff Ferry Campground **8**
Rocky Springs Campground **3**
Timberlake Campground **5**
Tishomingo State Park **13**
Tombigbee State Park **12**
Trace State Park **11**

GOOD EATS
Carl's Perfect Pig **19**
Cock of the Walk **1, 5, 20**
Loveless Motel & Café **20**
Rocking Chair Restaurant **15**
Walnut Hills **4**

SHOPPING
Mississippi Crafts Center **5**

number of towns and villages. The major southern supermarket chains include **Winn-Dixie, Kroger, Piggily Wiggily,** and **IGA,** the Independent Grocers Association.

Keep your eyes open as you pass through small towns in the South during spring, summer, and fall; vegetable and fruit growers often put out produce stands in their farmyards or even on their front lawns during harvest time. The prices always are very low.

Driving the Natchez Trace

The Natchez Trace Parkway, like the Blue Ridge Parkway and Skyline Drive described in Chapter 13, is a federally designated scenic drive along a two-lane highway with a **50 mph speed limit** where no commercial traffic is permitted. Frequent turnouts are indicated with half-mile warning signs shaped like **arrowheads** that tell you whether the spot ahead is of historic interest, a trailhead, or a segment of the original roadway.

Plan on spending a day or two exploring the Natchez area before you set out on the trace itself. Historic homes are open all year with hoop-skirted hostesses to show you around.

When you're ready to hit the road, drive northeast from Natchez on U.S. 60 about 8 miles to the designated entrance of the **Natchez Trace.** Just before the entrance to the parkway, stop at the Mississippi Welcome Center and pick up an official Natchez Trace map and guide, handy materials to keep with you. Almost immediately after entering the park, you come to the spot where a **section of the original trace** can be seen; look for the arrowhead-shaped sign. At mile 10.3 is **Emerald Mound,** the second largest Indian mound in the United States. The ancestors of the Natchez tribe built the mound around A.D. 1400. It covers some eight acres; you can walk to the top if you want.

At mile 15.5, you come to **Mount Locust,** a restored historical house that served as a "stand" or overnight stop for travelers along the trace. Jefferson had encouraged innkeepers to open these primitive lodging establishments to care for travelers; more than 20 were in operation by 1820, when the trace was at its peak.

Exit on U.S. 61 near mile 37 to drive a short loop detour into **Port Gibson.** General Ulysses S. Grant reportedly said this town was "too pretty to burn" and so Port Gibson survived the Civil War intact and was the first town in Mississippi to be designated a National Historic District. What strikes visitors initially today is the huge golden hand atop the 1859 First Presbyterian Church at Walnut and Church Streets, the index finger pointing heavenward. Southwest of town are the haunting **ruins of Windsor,** the largest antebellum house ever built in Mississippi, used in a memorable scene with Alec Baldwin in *Ghosts of Mississippi.* (See "More cool things to see and do.")

Jefferson's road: A 19th-century trade, mail, and military route

In 1806, Thomas Jefferson ordered a roadway "12 feet in width and passable for a wagon" to be built along the trade routes originally used by flatboat men returning upriver from delivering their furs, tobacco, pork, and farm products in Natchez and New Orleans.

Although traveling downriver was easy, the Kaintucks, as they were called, were unable to row or pole upstream against the current. After selling their goods, and maybe their rafts too, they had to walk or ride horseback to return home. The traders had little enough remaining from their profits after the gamblers, cutthroats, and prostitutes of Natchez-Under-the-Hill had finished with them, but the toughest part of the trip was yet to come — to protect themselves and their money from the highwaymen who lurked along the trace. Jefferson was thinking not only about the traders but also the postal service riders who would use the roadway to deliver mail and the military troops who might need the wide clear pathway for wagons and cannons.

Ladies and gentlemen of fashion, circuit-riding preachers, frontier prostitutes, pioneer families, medicine peddlers, and flatboat men — everybody used the Natchez Trace. A despondent Meriwether Lewis died mysteriously along the trail in 1809, and in 1815, a triumphant Major General Andrew Jackson, better known as "Old Hickory," marched his Tennessee militia along the trace back from the Battle of New Orleans.

But in 1812, the first steamboat arrived in Natchez, and by 1820, the boats dominated the rivers. Eventually, except for a brief period during the Civil War, the little-used Natchez Trace reverted to woods again. Only in the 1930s, under the administration of Franklin D. Roosevelt, did restoration of the trace begin; today's road closely follows the contours of the original.

Back on the Natchez Trace at mile 41.5 is the **Sunken Trace** section, a five-minute walk along a deeply eroded section of the original trace. A designated parking turnout is nearby. In the right light, this is one of the spookiest parts of the trace.

At mile 54.8, you come to **Rocky Springs ghost town,** formerly a thriving metropolis with a population of 2,616. Take a short uphill trail from the upper parking area to the site of the notorious **Red House Inn,** where highwaymen sized up travelers and then robbed them later. The town fell into decline during the Civil War, when first the war, then the boll weevil, yellow fever, and soil erosion wiped it out. A campground without hookups (see "Runner-up campgrounds" later in this chapter for more on Rocky Springs Campground) and a foot trail are located along a section of the old road.

Around milepost 67 is the exit to **Vicksburg,** SR 27. You can also go to Vicksburg from Port Gibson at milepost 37, but you'd miss the points of interest on the parkway.

The Civil War seems to be the main preoccupation of Vicksburg, with the **Vicksburg National Military Park** on its northern boundary. Comparable to Gettysburg in scope, Vicksburg is known not only for its fine old houses but also for the bravery and endurance of its citizens during a 47-day siege in 1863, when General Grant's troops bombarded the city almost constantly. As if to add insult to injury, the Mississippi River itself abandoned Vicksburg in 1876, changing its route to cut across the neck of land that Grant had worked so hard to take. Years later, the waters of the Yazoo River were diverted into the Mississippi's old channel so Vicksburg could have its harbor back.

Vicksburg is famous for two beverages. It was the first city to bottle Coca-Cola; the **Biedenharn Coca-Cola Company Museum** displays replicas of the original bottling equipment and still sells 5¢ bottles of Coke. (See "More cool things to see and do.") And the mint julep was invented in Vicksburg.

A family-style restaurant in Vicksburg called **Walnut Hills** is the epitome of Southern home cooking with help-yourself bowls and platters filled with fried chicken, pork chops, a dozen vegetables, salads, corn muffins, biscuits, and iced tea. (See "Good eats.")

Back on the Natchez Trace, the drive is interrupted just past milepost 90 on the outskirts of **Jackson.** To return immediately to the trace, follow the parkway detour signage along I-20 to I-220, then to I-55, rejoining the trace at milepost 102.

If you have a few hours, however, spend some time in Jackson, the state capital. The expansive and excellent **Mississippi Agriculture and Forestry Museum** — much more interesting than it sounds for adults and children — features a 1920s town with costumed inhabitants and craftsmen (and hand-pumped gas for 15¢ a gallon), a crop-dusting museum, and an entire working farm that was moved here from southern Mississippi. (See "Must-see attractions.")

The **Mississippi Sports Hall of Fame and Museum** (see "Must-see attractions") also is in Jackson, sharing the same big parking lot. Here you can broadcast play-by-play action from a replica press booth that's stocked with videos of outstanding game highlights; walk through a museum salute to Dizzy Dean, Mississippi's own baseball great; stroll into a locker room housing uniforms and equipment used by sports heroes; and try your skills in golf, baseball, soccer, or football.

When you reenter the parkway at milepost 101.5, look for the sign for the **Mississippi Crafts Center**, a marvelous collection of hand-woven Choctaw baskets, pottery, weavings, jewelry, books, and carved wooden toys, to mention only a few of the treasures. (See "Shopping along the Way," later in this chapter.)

At 105.6, a road from a turnoff to the **Ross Barnett Reservoir** follows the Pearl River and parallels the parkway for 8 miles, accessing four campgrounds with hookups. (See "Runner-up campgrounds.")

One of the prettiest spots along the route is a **tupelo and bald cypress swamp** at milepost 122 with board walkways leading across yellow-green, algae-covered water so smooth it looks like a chartreuse mirror that you could walk on. The nature trail takes about 20 minutes to walk: first across the swamp, then along the other side through the woods, and back across the swamp on a second walkway.

When you drive past **Kosciusko** (pronounced koz-e-*esk*-ko) at milepost 159.7, take a moment to remember that this is where TV diva **Oprah Winfrey** was born January 29, 1954. Liberty Presbyterian Church has a sign outside pointing out that "she said her first piece here," in other words, made her first public appearance. (See "More cool things to see and do.")

French Camp at milepost 180.7 comes to life every fall when its time to demonstrate the making of sorghum molasses from sugar cane. The parkway's only bed and breakfast is here, along with a crafts shop, exhibits, and a lunch cafe.

One mile east of milepost 259.7 is **Tupelo National Battlefield,** site of a major Civil War battle in 1864. On this site, Union General A.J. Smith trapped Confederate General Nathan Bedford Forrest, famous for quick strikes and tough fights. General William Tecumseh Sherman ordered Smith to "follow Forrest to his death."

Louisiana Purchase: The deal of the century

In the annals of real estate coups, few can match the 1803 Louisiana Purchase, ordered by Thomas Jefferson and negotiated by future president James Monroe. Three years earlier, Napoleon had traded with Spain, swapping the Italian kingdom of Parma, home of Parmesan cheese, for the territory of Louisiana — in those days it stretched from the west banks of Mississippi River westward to the Rocky Mountains and from Canada in the north to the Gulf of Mexico in the south.

Monroe paid Napoleon around $15 million, or 4¢ an acre. Ironically, all Jefferson had wanted was to regain the port of New Orleans and the land along the Mississippi so Americans could continue to use the river for trade.

Turn off the Natchez Trace on SR 6 for the Tupelo Battlefield and for the **Elvis Presley Birthplace and Museum** in downtown **Tupelo.** The rock icon was born in a simple two-room house that his father built; sometimes a relative or friend of Elvis is on hand to share personal memories. (See "Must-see attractions.") **Tombigbee State Park** with RV camping is just east of Tupelo. (See "Our favorite campgrounds.")

Return to the parkway by the same route you took to go off into Tupelo, so you don't miss any of the highlights.

A **Chickasaw village site** at mile 261.8 presents exhibits on Indian life, and a nature trail displays plants that were used in daily life for foods and medicine. The park headquarters at **Tupelo Visitor Center,** mile 266, also offers a 20-minute nature walk showing forest regrowth. At milepost 269.4, a short walk along the old trace leads to the graves of 13 unknown Confederate soldiers. A nature trail at 275.2 into **Dogwood Valley** takes about 15 minutes to explore a grove of dogwood trees.

Tishomingo State Park at milepost 302.8, shortly before the parkway crosses from Mississippi into Alabama, offers camping, swimming, canoeing, and picnicking. (See "Our favorite campgrounds.") At milepost 310, the parkway crosses into **Alabama.**

Although the parkway traverses only a 38-mile corner of northwestern Alabama on its way north, this little stretch of land is full of fascinating discoveries. Just past milepost 320, turn east on U.S. 72 to **Tuscumbia,** which, with its nearby sister towns of **Sheffield, Muscle Shoals,** and **Florence,** offers a great place to eat down-home Southern cooking and four not-to-be-missed attractions.

Plan to spend a day in lively northwestern Alabama, where attractions include:

- ✔ **Ivy Green,** birthplace of **Helen Keller,** immortalized in the play and film *The Miracle Worker.* Here you find the world's most famous backyard pump where she learned the word "Water!" (See "More cool things to see and do.")

- ✔ **Alabama Music Hall of Fame,** a splendid museum saluting Alabamians from Jimmie Rodgers and Tammy Wynette to Nat King Cole and Jimmy Buffett. (See "Must-see attractions.")

- ✔ **W.C. Handy Birthplace, Museum, and Library,** celebrating the blues composer and musician who wrote "St. Louis Blues," "Memphis Blues," and other classics. (See "More cool things to see and do.")

- ✔ **Key Underwood Coon Dog Memorial Park,** the only cemetery in the world dedicated solely to coon hounds, dating from 1937. (See "More cool things to see and do.")

> ⌕ **Rocking Chair Restaurant** where staff serves meat specials, such
> as roast turkey, fried chicken, or pork roast, accompanied by your
> choice of any three vegetables from the lengthy menu, and hot
> biscuits and cornbread, all for around $5 or $6. (See "Good eats.")

At milepost 341.8, the parkway crosses the border from Alabama into
Tennessee. Another section of the sunken trace is open for walking at
milepost 350.5, and a nature trail along **Sweetwater Branch** crosses a
section of brilliant wildflowers in spring and early summer. The walk
takes 20 minutes.

You find the **grave of Meriwether Lewis** of Lewis and Clark fame at
milepost 385.9, along with a campground, picnic area, ranger station,
restrooms, and a reconstruction of the log inn called Grinder's Stand,
where Lewis died. The famous explorer, only 35 years old, was on his
way back to Washington, D.C., on government business when he died
mysteriously here on the night of October 11, 1809, of gunshot wounds
in an incident that history never has decided whether it was suicide or
murder.

At milepost 401.4 is a **tobacco farm** with a barn and field on exhibit,
and a 2-mile drive along the old trace.

The Natchez Trace ends with a dramatic soaring **double-arch bridge** at
SR 100 some 10 miles southwest of **Nashville.**

Must-see attractions

Alabama Music Hall of Fame
Tuscumbia, Alabama

From the first touring motorhome used by the band Alabama to artifacts
from jazz innovator Sun Ra, this modern, interactive museum salutes the
great musicians who were born in or lived in Alabama. The list includes
Hank Williams, Nat King Cole, Jimmie Rodgers, Jimmy Buffett, Tammy
Wynette, Emmylou Harris, Big Mama Willie Mae Thornton, Odetta,
Martha Reeves, Bobby Goldsboro, Dinah Washington, Lionel Richie, Toni
Tennille, and Wilson Pickett.

The museum was built here instead of in a major Alabama city because
nearby Muscle Shoals in the 1960s and 1970s housed popular recording
studios where Percy Sledge recorded the rhythm-and-blues classic
"When A Man Loves A Woman," Aretha Franklin cut early soul records,
and a young Duane Allman was a studio guitarist. Listening on individual
earphones, kids of all ages groove to original music tracks performed by
artists spanning decades.

U.S. 72 West. ☎ *800-239-2643, 256-381-4417.* www.alamhof.org. *RV parking: Large parking lot. Admission: $6 adults, $5 seniors and students, $3 ages 12 and younger. Open: Mon–Sat 9 a.m.–5 p.m., Sun 1–5 p.m. Closed major holidays. Allow 2–3 hours.*

Elvis Presley Birthplace and Museum
Tupelo, Mississippi

This little two-room cottage was built by Elvis's father Vernon, who borrowed $180 and had the house finished in time for the birth of Elvis Aron and his stillborn twin brother Jesse Garon. They were evicted two years later when they couldn't repay the loan. Besides the birthplace, you can see a small memorial chapel and pick up the map for a **local driving tour** that takes you past other Elvis shrines, such as the local Tupelo Hardware, where his mother bought him his first guitar for $12.98. Some Tupelo relatives say Elvis really wanted a BB rifle instead.

306 Elvis Presley Dr. (Exit U.S. 78 at Elvis Presley Drive and follow the signs.) ☎ *662-841-1245.* www.tupelo.net/welcome.html?main-elvis.html. *RV parking: Small parking lot, adequate street parking. Admission: A combination house and museum ticket is $7.50 adults, $3.50 ages 17 and younger. Open: Mon–Sat 9 a.m.–5 p.m., Sun 1–5 p.m. Closed Thanksgiving and Christmas. Allow 1–2 hours.*

Mississippi Agriculture and Forestry Museum
Jackson, Mississippi

Far more fun than it sounds, this sprawling complex includes a 1920s rural Mississippi town, complete with craftsmen and shopkeepers; a working farm (moved here in its entirety from southern Mississippi) that includes several Mississippi mules, a breed famous for its stubbornness. Kids enjoy wandering about the area and experiencing "the olden days" and then ending up at a general store that sells cold soft drinks and a staple of southern snack fare, the Moon Pie.

Inside the main building is a well-arranged historical museum, and around the complex in separate buildings are the Mississippi Crafts Guild display area and shop, the museum cafe, and the National Agricultural Aviation Museum and Hall of Fame, saluting crop-dusters. All these can be entered on the same ticket. The adjacent Mississippi Sports Hall of Fame and Museum (see next listing) requires a separate admission ticket.

1150 Lakeland Dr. (Take Exit 98B from I-55.) ☎ *800-844-8681, 601-713-3365. RV parking: Large parking lot. Admission: $4 adults, $3 seniors, $2 ages 6–12, 50¢ ages 5 and younger. Open: Memorial Day to Labor Day Mon–Sat 9 a.m.–5 p.m., Sun 1–5 p.m.; rest of the year Mon–Sat 9 a.m.–5 p.m. Closed major holidays. Allow 3 hours.*

Mississippi Sports Hall of Fame and Museum
Jackson, Mississippi

This museum salutes sports heroes of Mississippi and automatically makes every fan, young and old, who enters a hero, too. With interactive machines, visitors can play golf, check the speed and impact of their baseball pitch, or take penalty kicks against a soccer goalie. A "press box" mockup lets wannabe sports announcers call the play-by-play for a game, and the locker room displays uniforms and equipment that famous players have used. A special second-floor museum salutes Mississippi baseball great **Dizzy Dean,** and touch-screen kiosks let visitors look up archival sports information and interviews.

1152 Lakeland Dr. (Take Exit 98B or 98C off I-55 to Cool Papa Bell Drive.) ☎ **800-280-FAME,** *601-982-8264.* www.msfame.com. *RV parking: Large parking lot adjacent. Admission: $5 adults, $3.50 seniors and children. Open: Mon–Sat 10 a.m.–4 p.m., Sun 1:30–4:30 p.m. Allow 3 hours.*

Vicksburg National Military Park
Vicksburg, Mississippi

The battlefield commemorates one of the most decisive battles of the Civil War. General Ulysses S. Grant and 50,000 men held the city under siege for 47 days. The national cemetery contains the graves of some 17,000 Union soldiers. A 16-mile auto tour around the park passes markers, monuments, and recreated breastworks. In the museum, you can see the gunboat *Cairo* pulled up from the Yazoo River 100 years after it sank in 1862.

3201 Clay St. ☎ **601-636-0583.** www.nps.gov/vick. *RV parking: Visitor lot at center, turnouts along Park Road. Admission: $5 per motor vehicle. Open: Park daily dawn to dusk, visitor center daily 8 a.m.–5 p.m.*

More cool things to see and do

Culturally rich and sometimes quirky attractions line the Natchez Trace from antebellum ruins to a coon dog cemetery and the hometown of a well-known TV diva.

✔ **Swig down a cheap Coca-Cola.** You can see the original bottling machinery from the world's first Coca-Cola bottling plant, used from 1894 to 1924 in Vicksburg at **Biedenharn Coca-Cola Company Museum** and buy a bottled Coke for a nickel.

1107 Washington St., Vicksburg, Mississippi. ☎ 601-638-6514. RV parking: Street parking. Admission: $2.25 adults, $1.75 ages 6–12. Open: Mon–Sat 9 a.m.–5 p.m., Sun 1:30–4:30 p.m. Allow 1 hour.

✔ **Meet Helen Keller. Ivy Green,** the birthplace and childhood home of Helen Keller, a lecturer and essayist who lost her sight and hearing in infancy, has been restored to the way it looked during her childhood. A production of *The Miracle Worker,* depicting how she overcame her handicaps, is presented here every summer. In the backyard is the famous water pump where the child first made the connection with language.

300 W. North Commons, Tuscumbia, Alabama. (From U.S. 72, follow Woodmount Drive to Commons.) ☎ **256-383-4066.** RV parking: Large parking lot and street parking. Admission: $6 adults. Open: Daily 8:30 a.m.–4 p.m. Allow 2 hours.

✔ **Howl with the hounds. Key Underwood Coon Dog Memorial Park** is the only cemetery in the world dedicated to the raccoon-hunting hound. More than 160 champions are buried here, some with elaborately carved granite tombstones such as that of Doctor Doom, listing his awards. Others have simple wooden markers with handwritten sentiments like, "He wasn't the best coon dog there ever was, but he was the best I ever had."

From Tuscumbia, Alabama, take U.S. 72 west for 7 miles, then turn left on CR 247 for about 12 miles, and then turn right at sign and follow signs to park. Plenty of parking space, always open, no telephone. Admission: Free. For information, call Tuscumbia Tourism Bureau ☎ **800-344-0783** or 256-383-0783. Allow at least 30 minutes.

✔ **Tune into a TV diva.** The little town named **Kosciusko** (pronounced koz-e-*esk*-ko), named for a Polish general in the American Revolutionary war, was the birthplace and early childhood home of **Oprah Winfrey,** and a road named for her goes past her first church, her family cemetery, and the site of her birthplace.

Kosciusko Tourist Promotion Council, P.O. Box 696, Kosciusko, Mississippi. ☎ **601-289-2981.** www.kosciuskotourism.com. RV parking: Street parking. Admission: Free. Open: Roadway always open. Allow 1 hour.

✔ **Sing the blues and all that jazz.** Florence, Alabama, is home of the **W.C. Handy Birthplace, Museum and Library.** The blues genius, a trained musician with his own brass band, wrote a campaign song for Memphis political boss Edward R. Crump that introduced jazz breaks into a composed piece for the first time. Retitled "Memphis Blues," it's the first composition recognized as jazz.

620 W. College St., Florence, Alabama. (Downtown Florence just off U.S. 72.) ☎ **256-760-6434.** RV parking: Street parking. Admission: $2 adults, 50¢ ages 17 and younger. Open: Tues–Sat 10 a.m.–4 p.m. Allow 2 hours.

✔ **Revisit *Gone with the Wind.*** The 23 Corinthian columns are all that's left of a formerly grand Greek Revival mansion, now the **Windsor ruins.** The mansion still evokes the ghost of the antebellum South. It survived the Civil War but succumbed to a fire in 1890 caused by a cigarette, a newly fashionable way to use tobacco at that time.

Rodney Road, Port Gibson, Mississippi. (Take U.S. 61 south from Port Gibson, turn right on SR 552 and follow the signs.) RV parking: Plenty of open area at the site, but a short, narrow dirt road with bushes leads to it. Admission: Free. Open: Dawn to dusk. Allow 30 minutes; photographers may want more time.

Weekend wonder

The easiest way to make a shorter version of the Natchez Trace drive is simply to **drive the 444-mile trace,** overnighting at one of the campgrounds along the way, without turning off to see the attractions in Port Gibson, Vicksburg, Jackson, and Nashville, or the state of Alabama.

Sleeping and Eating on the Road

The Natchez Trace provides plentiful overnight camping all along the route, either directly on the parkway or a few miles off on a side road. Few public campgrounds accept reservations, so if you're making the trip during a busy season, such as spring, plan to stop earlier in the day than usual to be sure that you'll have an overnight spot, or reserve a day or two in advance at privately owned campgrounds near the parkway.

The same convenience isn't true for eating on the road, so you'll be happy to have a stocked refrigerator and operating kitchen. Even where a town is near the parkway, that doesn't mean any special eating treats await; some of the small communities in Mississippi, for instance, don't have even the most common fast-food places. A grocery store or small-town drugstore may be the only place to find something already prepared for lunch. To help you find tasty food to eat in or take out, we guide you to some simple, homey places in the "Good eats" section, later in this chapter.

All campgrounds listed below are open year-round and have public flush toilets, showers, and sanitary dump stations unless designated otherwise. Toll-free numbers, where listed, are for reservations only. The only campground with RV hookups is at Ratliff Ferry. See Chapter 9 for more information on how we select our favorite campgrounds.

Our favorite campgrounds

Battlefield Kampground
$$ Vicksburg, Mississippi

Located within walking distance of the Vicksburg National Military Park, this campground provides free narrated cassette tours of the park. Sites are fairly large, with concrete pads.

4407 I-20 N. Frontage Rd., Vicksburg, MS 39183 (From junction of I-20 and Clay St., Exit 4B, go north 0.5 mile to Frontage Road, then east 0.5 mile to the campground on the left.) ☎ *601-636-2025. Total of 65 sites with water and 30-amp electric, 33 full hookups, 28 pull-throughs. CATV, dataport, laundry. Rates: $15–$19 per site. MC, V.*

David Crockett State Park

$$ **Lawrenceburg, Tennessee**

Davy Crockett lived in this area, and his cabin and a museum are open free of charge in town. At the 987-acre park, you find a water-powered gristmill and an interpretive center that reveals Crockett's interest in water-powered machinery. Sites are paved but fairly narrow, and some hookups are side by side.

From junction of U.S. 45 and U.S. 64, go west 1.5 miles on 64 to the campground on the right. ☎ *931-762-9408. Total of 107 sites with water and 30-amp electric, no full hookups, no pull-throughs. Handicap access, pool. Rates: $17 per site. DISC, MC, V. No reservations.*

Nashville/Opryland KOA

$$$$–$$$$$ **Nashville, Tennessee**

We've been staying in this well-run, conveniently located park for years. A concierge arranges tickets and transportation for shows and events, and a coordinator offers daily tours — you won't miss a thing. Another bonus is free, live entertainment in the park's own theater from May to October. A branch of Cock of the Walk catfish restaurant is next door, and within walking distance are additional eateries, the Opryland Hotel, and other Opryland area attractions. Playgrounds, pool, and entertainment give kids plenty to do.

2626 Music Valley Dr., Nashville, TN 37214. (From junction of I-65 and Briley Parkway, take Exit 90B southbound or Exit 90 northbound, go south 4.5 miles on Briley to McGavock Park, then west 0.2 mile to Music Valley Drive and north 2 miles to campground on the left.) ☎ *800-562-7789, 615-889-0286.* www.koa.com. *Total of 402 sites with water and 30- and 50-amp electric, 291 full hookups, 125 pull-throughs. Dataport, handicap access, laundry, pool. Rates: $35–$42 per site. AE, DISC, MC, V.*

Tishomingo State Park

$$ **Tishomingo, Mississipppi**

The CCC (Civilian Conservation Corps) built this park in the 1930s, using rock quarried on-site. Over Bear Creek, note the swinging bridge, which dates from those days. Sites are paved and mostly shaded. Haynes Lake provides freshwater fishing and boating; ramp, dock, and boat rentals are available. A fishing license is required; the state tourism board can tell you how to get one. (See "Fast Facts" at the end of this chapter for the board's contact info.)

From junction of Natchez Trace Parkway and SR 25, go north 0.5 mile on 25 to park road (CR 90) then east 1.6 miles to campground. ☎ 662-438-6914. Total of 62 sites with water and 30- and 50-amp electric, no full hookups, no pull-throughs. Rates: $13 per site. MC, V. 14-day maximum stay.

Tombigbee State Park
$$ Tupelo, Mississipppi

At this state park, you're near the Elvis birthplace and the famous battlefield if you want to go sightseeing. The campground provides medium-size paved sites with patios, some with shade, and freshwater fishing, boating, ramp, dock, and boat rentals on Lake Lee.

From Natchez Trace, take SR 6 to Veterans Boulevard, then drive southeast 3.3 miles to park access road, and follow signs east 2.8 miles to campground on the right. ☎ 662-842-7669. Total of 20 sites with water and 20- and 30-amp electric, 6 full hookups, no pull-throughs. Rates: $14 per site. MC, V.

Trace State Park
$$ Pontotoc, Mississipppi

Large sites, most of them shaded and paved, are conveniently near Tupelo and the Natchez Trace. Freshwater fishing, boating, boat ramp, dock, and boat rentals are available for would-be sailors. Elvis fans can drive into Tupelo instead and look at The Birthplace.

From the Natchez Trace, take SR 6 west of Tupelo, drive 7.8 miles southwest to Faulkner Road, then northwest 2.1 miles to campground on the left. ☎ 662-489-2958. Total of 52 sites with water and 30- and 50-amp electric, no full hookups, 3 pull-throughs. Rates $13 per site. MC, V.

Runner-up campgrounds

McFarland Park
$ Florence, Alabama   A public park with large sites and paved patios on the Tennessee River, McFarland provides freshwater fishing, boating, boat ramp, and dock. The area is subject to flooding in heavy rains, so check before arriving if they've had recent rainstorms. *From junction of U.S. 43 and SR 20, go west 0.2 mile on SR 20 to the campground on the left. ☎ 256-740-8817. Total of 38 paved sites with water and 30-amp electric, no full hookups, 12 pull-throughs. Rates $1–$6 per site. MC, V.*

Natchez State Park
$$ Natchez, Mississipppi   Reservations are suggested in summer for this park with its popular, stocked fishing lake. A fishing license is required. (See "Fast Facts" for the number of the state tourism board, which can tell you how to get this license.) Paved RV sites with patios

are fairly wide, many of them shaded. *From north junction of U.S. 61/U.S. 98, and U.S.84, go north 5.1 miles on 61 to Stanton Road, and then east 0.3 mile to Wickliff and 0.3 mile to campground on the left.* ☎ *601-442-2658. Total of 50 sites with water and 30- and 50-amp electric, 6 full hookups, 2 pull-throughs. Rates: $13 per site. MC, V.*

Natchez Trace RV Park

$$ Tupelo, Mississipppi   This Good Sam Park can handle big rigs, and sites throughout are comfortably wide. Amenities include a pond with freshwater fishing and tackle for rent. *189 CR 506, Shannon, MS 38868. (From junction Natchez Trace Parkway and SR 6, go southwest 8.5 miles on the Parkway to CR 506 between mileposts 251 and 252, then east 400 feet to the campground on the right.)* ☎ *662-767-8609. Total of 22 sites with water and 30- and 50-amp electric, 10 full hookups, 15 pull-throughs. Dataport, laundry. Rates: $20 per site. No credit cards.*

Natchez Trace Parkway National Park Campgrounds: Jeff Busby, Meriwether Lewis, and Rocky Springs

$ Along the Natchez Trace   These national park campgrounds are free, operate on a first-come, first-served basis, and have a 15-day maximum stay. None have hookups, and sites are mostly shaded. Flush toilets are available but not showers. *To get to each location, follow signs from the milepost. For information on all three, call* ☎ *800-305-7417 or go online to* www.nps.gov/natr. *Jeff Busby Campground, milepost 183.1; total of 18 sites, all pull-throughs, all paved. Meriwether Lewis Campground, milepost 385.9; total of 32 sites, some pull-throughs. Rocky Springs Campground, milepost 54.8; total of 22 sites, 12 pull-throughs.*

Ratliff Ferry Campground

$$ Ratliff Ferry, Mississipppi   This is the only campground right on the parkway with hookups, but don't expect anything fancy. Besides freshwater fishing and boating, you find only the basics — a grassy spot to back into, an outlet for your electrical connections, and a hookup for your water hose. Your neighbor will be very nearby. *From the junction of Natchez Trace Parkway and Ratliff Ferry Road. (Exit milepost 123.5; go southeast 0.5 mile on Ratliff to the campground.)* ☎ *601-859-1810. Total of 16 sites with water and 30-amp electric, no full hookups, 7 pull-throughs. Dataport. Rates: $15 per site. AE, DISC, MC, V.*

Ross Barnett Reservoir: Coal Bluff, Goshen Springs, Leake County, Timberlake

$$ Greater Jackson, Mississippi   The Ross Barnett Reservoir has four campgrounds around its perimeter; we suggest making reservations for weekends. All offer hookups, all are back-ins with no pull throughs, and all provide access to freshwater fishing. *Rates are $20 per site. MC, V. Coal Bluff, Ludlow, Mississippi (take Coal Bluff Road north off SR 25 for 10.3 miles, then turn west on Riverbend Road for 1.5 miles;* ☎ *601-654-7726), total of 39 sites with* water and 30- and 50-amp electric, 11 with full hookups, no pull throughs. **Goshen Springs,** Brandon, Mississippi (take Natchez Trace exit SR 43, 3 miles to campground; ☎ **601-829-2751**), total of 33 full hookups with 30- and 50-amp electric, no pull throughs; laundry. **Leake County,** Ludlow, Mississippi (from SR 25, take Utah Road exit to campground; ☎ **601-654-9359**), total of 28 full hookups with 30- and 50-amp electric, no pull throughs. **Timberlake,** Jackson, Mississippi (from junction of I-55 and Lakeland Drive [also SR 25], go east on Lakeland to Old Fanin Road, and then north 3.7 miles to the campground on the left; ☎ **601-992-9100**), total of 108 sites with 30- and 50-amp electric, all full hookups, no pull-throughs; dataport, laundry.

Good eats

You find plenty of vegetables in this part of the world, but don't expect them to be cooked al dente. Southern vegetables are cooked until very well done as a rule and made tastier by the addition of outside seasonings, often butter, bacon fat, pot juices, even sugar. You mustn't expect to find fresh herbs and olive oil or a judicious sprinkle of balsamic vinegar, but if you're willing to be open-minded, you may find some unfamiliar side dishes that please you. Take a chance and order fried green tomatoes, corn pudding, collard or turnip greens, yams, hominy, black-eyed peas or field peas, okra, squash, lima beans, or green beans, often called snap beans, cooked in water with a little chopped bacon or bacon fat until tender and succulent.

You can always find a wedge of lemon to squeeze over everything because lemon is an essential accessory in this land of iced tea. By the way, iced tea usually comes sweetened here; if you don't want sugar, ask for unsweetened tea. When ordering tea at breakfast, be sure to specify *hot* tea, or you'll get iced tea. Don't ask for a "soda"; carbonated drinks are called "pop" or "soda pop" in the South.

Hot breads, usually biscuits and/or cornbread, are the general rule as well. By the way, unlike the cornbread and corn muffins in other parts of the United States, southern cornbread rarely has sugar added. You won't find hot breads at barbecue joints; there, multiple slices of soft white bread straight from the grocery-store package come as a side dish.

Servings are large in this part of the country; we find that one takeout meal often is enough for both of us. If it seems skimpy when we open the Styrofoam box, we add a homemade green salad or a dessert.

The following restaurants and food suppliers are some of our own favorites for regional cooking at moderate prices. Many may require cash rather than credit cards. Most don't serve beer or wine with meals; even when dining out in fancy restaurants, many Southerners drink iced tea, colas, hot coffee, or even a cocktail with their meals. For information on buying the basics, see "Stocking the Pantry," earlier in this chapter.

Southern cooking, state by state

In northwestern **Alabama,** breakfasts can be feasts with grits, ham, biscuits, sausage, eggs, and gravy. Fried chicken stars at lunch and dinner (the former sometimes called "dinner" and the latter "supper" in the rural South), and you may run across dessert curiosities, such as Coca-Cola cake and mile-high meringue pies.

Mississippi cuisine is high on fried catfish — hardly unusual because the state turns out 70% of all the catfish farmed in the United States. In fact, the catfish capital of the world is **Belzoni,** a few miles west of the Natchez Trace. Fried fish of all sorts usually are served with hush puppies, which are deep-fried balls of cornbread seasoned with onions, and hot tamales. The hot tamales are a mystery; nobody is sure where they originated, but most Mississippi restaurants, especially in the delta, serve them as appetizers or side dishes. Rolled in parchment paper rather than cornhusks and ordered by the half-dozen or dozen, Mississippi hot tamales are smaller and spicier than the Mexican version.

Down-home **Tennessee** restaurants around Nashville serve what they call meat-and-three, meaning your choice of a main dish of meat and three side vegetables. Country ham on a southern menu, especially in Tennessee, describes a smoked or dry-cured ham that spends weeks in a bed of salt and turns out as a salty, densely textured, and intensely flavored meat that can be sliced and fried for breakfast or boiled whole and then baked and served cold in paper-thin slices. And don't miss Nashville's famous **Goo Goo Cluster** candy bars with peanuts, chocolate, marshmallow, and caramel.

✔ **Carl's Perfect Pig:** U.S. 70, White Bluff, Tennessee (☎ 615-797-4020). A pretty, pink barbecue joint by the side of the road serves pulled or chopped sandwiches from pork shoulders that have been slow-cooked on a bed of hickory coals for 24 hours and then steeped in a vinegar sauce overnight. Open Wednesday and Thursday 10:30 a.m. to 5:45 p.m., Friday and Saturday until 7 p.m., Sunday until 2:30 p.m.

✔ **Cock of the Walk:** 2624 Music Valley Dr., Nashville, Tennessee. (☎ 615-889-1930). An easy stroll from the Opryland KOA campground, this popular and casual eatery provides sit-down and takeout service, and the latter, with its own order window, is much quicker. The fried catfish is delectable, and so are the fried shrimp and a sampler dinner that adds fried chicken. Side dishes include fried dill pickles (don't laugh till you taste them), fried onions, and a cooking pot of beans or greens. Cocktails, beer, and wine als are served. Two locations are in Mississippi: 200 N. Broadway, Natchez

(☎ 601-446-8920), and Madison Landing, Ridgeland (☎ 601-856-5500). All locations are open Monday through Thursday from 5 a.m. to 9 p.m., Friday and Saturday from 5 a.m. to 10 p.m., and Sunday from 11 a.m. to 9 p.m.

✔ **Loveless Motel & Cafe:** 8400 SR 100, Nashville, Tennessee, about 10 miles southwest of town (☎ 615-646-9700). A motel by the side of the road with a neon sign that says "Loveless" in pink and green serves the world's best breakfasts — country ham, grits, gravy, eggs, homemade biscuits, and homemade jams and jellies. Lunches and dinners are great, too, with meals built around country ham or fried chicken. (Get one of each and trade tastes.) The same generous servings of hot biscuits, butter, and homemade jams come with every meal, and they sell jars of the jam to go. Open Sunday through Thursday from 8 a.m. to 8 p.m., and Friday and Saturday until 9 p.m.

✔ **Rocking Chair Restaurant:** U.S. 72 West, Tuscumbia, Alabama (☎ 256-381-6105). The Sunday lunch turkey special here came with mashed potatoes and green beans, while a four-vegetable plate came crowded with black-eyed peas, candied yams, white beans with ham, fried okra, and hot biscuits and cornbread. The whole thing cost around $10. Open Monday through Thursday from 10:30 a.m to 9 p.m., and Friday through Sunday from 7 a.m. to 9 p.m.

✔ **Walnut Hills:** 1214 Adams St., Vicksburg, Mississipppi (☎ 601-638-4910). We covered this restaurant for *Bon Appetit* magazine and will never forget the help-yourself bowls and platters heaped with southern fried chicken, ribs, smothered pork chops, stuffed peppers with Creole sauce, rice and gravy, green beans with potatoes, lima beans, fresh-field peas, yellow squash with onions, glazed carrots, coleslaw, corn muffins, iced tea, and blueberry cobbler. The cooks were amused when we asked for such "everyday" recipes. Open Sunday through Friday from 11 a.m. to 8:30 p.m.

Shopping along the Way

Mississippi Crafts Center, 1150 Lakeland Dr., Natchez Trace Parkway, Jackson, Mississippi (☎ 601-981-0019; www.mscraftsmensguild.org), sells handicrafts created by local artists and craftsmen, including weavers from the local Choctaw and Chickasaw people. Items are attractively arranged in this little unpainted mountain cottage. Standouts include quilt-work handbags, pottery, Choctaw baskets, and books about the region. Prices range from affordable to expensive. The center is open Monday through Friday from 9 a.m. to 5 p.m.

Fast Facts

Area Code

The following area codes are in effect along the Natchez Trace: in Alabama, **251**; in Tennessee, **931, 615,** and **256**; in Mississippi, **601** and **662**.

Emergency

Call ☎ **911**. Mobile phone users can touch ***847** in Tennessee.

Hospitals

Major hospitals along the route are in Vicksburg and Jackson, Mississippi, and Nashville, Tennessee.

Information

Helpful sources in the individual states include: Alabama Bureau of Tourism & Travel (☎ 800-ALABAMA (800-252-2262); www.touralabama.org); Mississippi Division of Tourism (☎ 800-WARMEST (800-927-6378); www.visitmississippi.org); and in Tennessee, the Department of Tourist Development (☎ 615-741-8299; www.state.tn.us).

For information on fishing licences in Mississippi, call ☎ 800-5GO-HUNT (800-546-4868) or 601-362-9212.

Laws

In Alabama, Mississippi, and Tennessee, riders in the front seats must wear seat belts. The maximum speed limit on interstate highways in Alabama, Mississippi, and Tennessee is 70 mph. Speed limits in urban areas are lower.

Road and Weather Conditions

Contact numbers include ☎ 334-242-4128 in Alabama; ☎ 601-987-1211 for the Highway Patrol in Mississippi; and ☎ 800-858-6349 for road construction and ☎ 800-342-3258 for weather conditions in Tennessee.

Taxes

Alabama state sales tax is 4%; local taxes can raise it to 7.45%. Mississippi state sales tax is 7%. Tennessee state sales tax is 6%; local taxes can raise rates to 8.35%.

State gasoline taxes are as follows: Alabama, 18¢/gallon; Mississippi, 18¢/gallon; and Tennessee, 20¢/gallon.

Time Zone

Alabama, Mississippi, and western Tennessee are on central standard time.

Part IV
Discovering Mid-America

The 5th Wave   By Rich Tennant

"Yes, you can have the house tonight. But keep it under 60 miles per hour, and have it back by 10:00."

In this part . . .

Whether you're headed back home or hitting the country's midsection for the first time, you'll find Mid-America full of surprises. Among the many discoveries you can make, we show you where to kick back with tasty Texas Hill Country barbecue (Chapter 16), to see the Wright stuff and talk to dead presidents in Ohio (Chapter 17), to paddle through the Land of Lakes or fish in northern Minnesota (Chapter 18), or to dig for diamonds or tune in to toe-tapping music in Branson and the Ozarks (Chapter 19).

Chapter 16

Texas Hill Country: Bluebonnets and Barbecue

● ●

In This Chapter

▶ Strutting with some barbecue

▶ Lucking into Luckenbach

▶ Learning the ABCs of LBJ

▶ Going wild for wildflowers

● ●

*T*he heart of Texas is hardscrabble country, pink and gray granite and creamy white limestone, longhorn cattle ranges, and flood-washed gullies. But the tough terrain has a soft, loving heart. As the singing cowboy said, the stars at night are big and bright, and the sage is like perfume. In a good springtime, the hills are blanketed with intensely beautiful wildflowers — bluebonnets, scarlet Indian paint-brush, buttercups, and poppies as thick as those that put Judy Garland to sleep in *The Wizard of Oz*.

The Texas Hill Country is full of surprises — zany San Antonio where every day brings another chance for a celebration; barbecue a billion times tastier than those boring racks of chain-restaurant ribs coated with thick, sweet, red sauce from a bottle; Austin with its rock-and-roll and country music ties to such artists as Janis Joplin and Lyle Lovett; laid-back Luckenbach where Willie Nelson sometimes hangs out; cool jazz spots along San Antonio's River Walk; and German Fredericksburg with bratwurst and beer gardens.

Texas also is probably the most RV-friendly state, with plenty of camp-grounds, including state parks with hookups, great bargain-priced take-out food, and well-paved back roads. What are you waiting for? Yee-haw! Let's hit the road!

Getting There

San Antonio is an excellent starting point for a circle tour of Texas Hill Country. (See "Texas Hill Country" map in this chapter for the route.) From here, you drive northeast 30 miles on I-35 to **New Braunfels,** a prominent community first settled by Germans, then strike out on back roads east to **Luling** and **Lockhart,** center of barbecue country, and then north to the colorful old town of **Bastrop** and the hot sausage capital of **Elgin.** From here, you head north to **Taylor** for more barbecue, then west again to the Texas capital of **Austin,** and then due west to **Johnson City** and **Fredericksburg** on U.S. 290. Go north to **Llano** on SR 16, a scenic back road, then west to **Mason** through bluebonnet fields on SR 29, turn southwest to **Junction,** and make a fast loop back into San Antonio on I-10 through **Kerrville.** The entire route covers around **400 miles** plus a few side road detours.

Planning Ahead

The absolute best time to go is in **spring** when the wildflowers are at their peak. That can be any time from the end of March through April and into early May, depending on winter rainfall and spring weather. Call the Texas Wild Flower Hotline at ☎ **800-452-9292** to get information on the best times and areas for maximum bloom.

But you can enjoy an RV vacation in the Texas Hill Country **all year round.** Winter usually is mild, summers are warm to hot but not sweltering, and fall is almost perfect, except the wildflowers are not at their peak.

When bluebonnets are in bloom, any Texan with a motor vehicle heads for the hill country for a leisurely drive along the best wildflower routes, especially on Saturdays and Sundays. RVers need to plan to drive the scenic routes on weekdays, and then spend weekends in and around the cities of San Antonio and Austin when all the urban dwellers have gone to the country.

If you know your exact dates and itineraries for the Texas Hill Country, especially in spring wildflower season, you need to make **campground reservations** for the private RV campgrounds.

You want to **pack** light, all-cotton clothes for summer in Texas, along with some safari-type long pants and long-sleeved jackets for hikes in the wild year-round. Spring brings frequent rain showers, so be prepared with umbrellas and raincoats. Winter can be chilly on overcast days; bring a jacket or heavy sweater and plan to layer your clothing.

Allow a week for a leisurely drive around the hill country; add more time if you want to spend more than a day or so each in San Antonio and Austin.

Texas Hill Country

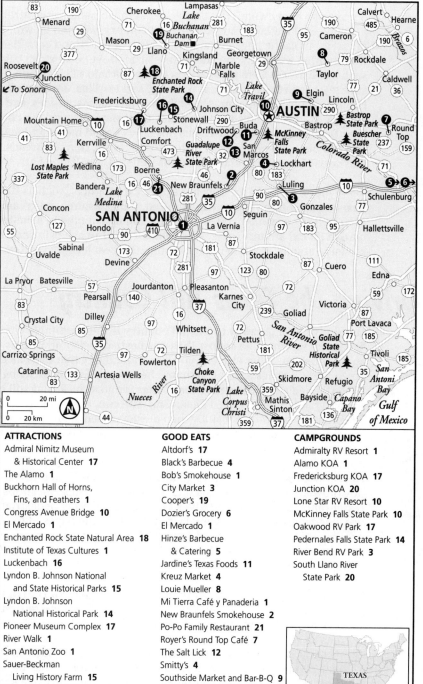

ATTRACTIONS

Admiral Nimitz Museum
& Historical Center **17**
The Alamo **1**
Buckhorn Hall of Horns,
Fins, and Feathers **1**
Congress Avenue Bridge **10**
El Mercado **1**
Enchanted Rock State Natural Area **18**
Institute of Texas Cultures **1**
Luckenbach **16**
Lyndon B. Johnson National
and State Historical Parks **15**
Lyndon B. Johnson
National Historical Park **14**
Pioneer Museum Complex **17**
River Walk **1**
San Antonio Zoo **1**
Sauer-Beckman
Living History Farm **15**
Witte Museum of History
and Science **1**

GOOD EATS

Altdorf's **17**
Black's Barbecue **4**
Bob's Smokehouse **1**
City Market **3**
Cooper's **19**
Dozier's Grocery **6**
El Mercado **1**
Hinze's Barbecue
& Catering **5**
Jardine's Texas Foods **11**
Kreuz Market **4**
Louie Mueller **8**
Mi Tierra Café y Panadería **1**
New Braunfels Smokehouse **2**
Po-Po Family Restaurant **21**
Royer's Round Top Café **7**
The Salt Lick **12**
Smitty's **4**
Southside Market and Bar-B-Q **9**
Threadgill's **10**
Wimberley Pie Company **13**

CAMPGROUNDS

Admiralty RV Resort **1**
Alamo KOA **1**
Fredericksburg KOA **17**
Junction KOA **20**
Lone Star RV Resort **10**
McKinney Falls State Park **10**
Oakwood RV Park **17**
Pedernales Falls State Park **14**
River Bend RV Park **3**
South Llano River
State Park **20**

TEXAS

Map Area

Stocking the Pantry

Because so many wonderful barbecue establishments with extralarge portions are located throughout the hill country, we wind up with plenty of extras in plastic bags in the refrigerator. Under "Good eats," later in this chapter, we offer some ideas for using leftovers. Mexican bakers, such as **Mi Tierra Café y Panaderia** in San Antonio's El Mercado (market square), sell breads, breakfast pastries, and tortillas. **Jardine's Texas Foods** in Buda, south of Austin, sells gourmet salsas, sauces, and seasonings at lower prices than the fancy food shops around the country. **New Braunfels Smokehouse** sells not only cooked meats and meals but also has a full-service deli with smoked meats, German breads, and mustards. For details on these establishments, see "Good Eats."

Keep your eyes open for only-in-Texas food products, such as **Bob's Texas-style potato chips,** manufactured in Brookshire, and creamy **Blue Bell ice cream,** made in Brenham and distributed in a limited market in and around Texas. Also look for **local peaches** in season at roadside stands around Fredericksburg, the peach capital of Texas.

Driving the Texas Hill Country

One convenient gateway to the hill country is the hospitable city of **San Antonio,** where no sooner than one fiesta or celebration ends than another begins. What else can you say about a city that dyes its river green for St. Patrick's Day, celebrates New Year's Eve by breaking confetti-filled eggshells called *cascarones* for good luck, and still has a big party in late April called **Fiesta San Antonio,** created in the late 19th century to honor a visit by then-president Benjamin Harrison? Everyone was having such a great time few noticed that the guest of honor failed to show up.

San Antonio is full of places to go and things to see. Don't miss the old downtown market square called **El Mercado** with Mexican shops and restaurants; the enchanting **River Walk,** a meandering pedestrian walkway lined with restaurants and jazz clubs along the banks of the San Antonio River; the **Institute of Texas Cultures** (not an oxymoron); and, of course, you remember **The Alamo.** (See "Must-see attractions," later in this chapter, for details on all these spots.)

You may also enjoy the **San Antonio Zoo,** the **Buckhorn Hall of Horns, Fins, and Feathers** in the Buckhorn Saloon, and the **Witte Museum of History and Science,** where you can step into an exhibit and punch buttons to see, hear, and smell the world the way animals do. (For all these attractions, see "More cool things to see and do," later in this chapter.) You may want to divide the San Antonio city attractions into two sections: some to see before you set off on your RV drive and some to catch when you come back.

From San Antonio, drive northeast on I-35 to **New Braunfels.** Regardless of whether it's time to eat, you need to stop at **New Braunfels Smokehouse** for some smoked meats and sausages. (See "Good eats.") If you visit in November, plan to attend the ten-day annual Wurstfest to celebrate local sausages. From New Braunfels, drive southeast on SR 46 to connect with I-10, and then travel east to **Luling,** home of the annual Watermelon Thump and Watermelon Seed Spitting Festival in late June. Luling is home to the **City Market** barbecue spot, more gentrified than most from the outside but authentic on the inside. (See "Good eats.")

From Luling, **Lockhart** and three more magical barbecue takeouts are a short 13 miles north on U.S. 183. (We warned you that you'd have leftovers.) **Kreuz Market,** founded in 1900, always was the leader here, with **Black's Barbecue,** founded in 1932, playing Avis to Kreuz's Hertz. Not long ago a split in the Schmidt family that owns Kreuz resulted in a third establishment called **Smitty's** in the original Kreuz Market building; the original Kreuz is now in a new location in Lockhart. (See "Good eats" for details on all three.)

Next, you're going to head northeast on SR 21 bound for **Bastrop,** an old city (1832) that predates the birth of Texas statehood. A casual stroll along Main Street takes you past a 19th-century drugstore called **Lock's** with an ice cream parlor and lunch counter. Drive north on SR 95 another 18 miles to **Elgin** (pronounced with a hard "g" as in "good"), home of the world's most delicious hot links. Don't groan; just walk up to the counter at **Southside Market and Bar-B-Q** and buy a pound of grilled links. (See "Good eats.") While they're hot, take a bite of one with the saltine crackers that accompany them, and store the rest in the refrigerator to reheat later. (On our first visit, it was 9 a.m., and we'd had nothing for nourishment but some hot tea from the Thermos. The fragrance from the sausages filled the RV, and we tore into the package while we still were in the parking lot. The taste was incredible, smoky and a bit spicy but full-flavored and rich, leaving us craving more.) You need to restrain yourself, however, because you still have one more world-class barbecue joint to hit before Austin.

Louie Mueller's in **Taylor,** 15 miles north of Elgin on SR 95, is our candidate for the best barbecue in Texas, but some days the place runs out around noon. Then they just clean up and close up for the day. Besides the delicious taste, there's a good reason for the sellout — Mueller's opens early to feed local railroad workers, whose favorite breakfast is a good plate of barbecue. (See "Good eats.")

Well fortified for the rest of the drive, continue west to **Austin** on U.S. 290, another 18 miles or so. Besides being home to the University of Texas, a thriving arts center, and the "live music capital of the world," with 25 years of producing *Austin City Limits* for PBS, this sophisticated city has a variety of good restaurants and plenty of metropolitan parks with hiking, rock-climbing, and biking.

Bluebonnets in bloom

The first time you see a field of **bluebonnets** (*Lupinus texensis*), you probably won't believe your eyes. This isn't a cute little cluster or a photogenic patch, but a blue carpet of thousands and thousands of bluebonnets in every direction. Up close, they bear a strong resemblance to a California wildflower called lupine (*Lupinus subcarnosus*), but because this is Texas and they're the state flower, bluebonnets they are.

In a good spring, you witness one floral spectacular after another, each seemingly more magnificent than the one before. Sometimes splashy **red Indian paintbrush** kicks in; at other times, you see **lavender verbena**; sometimes, what the Texans call **yellow buttercups** appear, looking very much like black-eyed Susans. Herds of Texas longhorns lying lazily about among the flowers treat the lavishness of the displays offhandedly.

You see bluebonnets from a spot between West Texas and central Texas, somewhere around **Sonora** and **Junction,** east to the hill country around Austin and almost to the Louisiana border. Some good wildflower spotting areas are along U.S. 377 from Junction on I-10 east to **Mason,** and then east along SR 29 to **Llano.** In the same vicinity, the Highland Lakes Bluebonnet Trail meanders a back road from Austin north along FM ("farm-to-market" road) 1431 past man-made lakes and small wineries, through the little towns of **Marble Falls, Burnet, Buchanan Dam, Kingsland,** and **Llano.** Some stretches are narrow, so if you're driving or towing a large RV, check on road conditions locally.

In Austin, take a **horse-and-buggy tour** around town and check out the largest state capitol in the nation, Old Pecan Street restaurant row, and the **Mexican freetail bats** that live under the Congress Avenue Bridge. (See "More cool things to see and do" for info on buggy tours and bats.)

From Austin, drive south on I-35 to **Buda** to pick up some Texas sauces and seasonings from **Jardine's Texas Foods** (you get a free bottle of Texas Champagne Sauce for stopping by), and then zigzag west on FM 967 to **Driftwood,** where you find **The Salt Lick,** another barbecue discovery. Continue north from Driftwood on SR 12 to join U.S. 290 at Dripping Springs, and then turn west to **Johnson City.** (See "Good eats" for info on Jardine's Texas Foods and The Salt Lick.)

The famous **Pedernales River,** where Lady Bird and Lyndon Johnson used to play host to huge barbecues on their ranch, lends its name to a state park with camping — **Pedernales Falls State Park.** (See "Our favorite campgrounds," later in this chapter.) In **Johnson City,** named for the late president's ancestors, is one division of the **Lyndon B. Johnson National Historical Park,** where a visitor center and his boyhood home are open to the public. To visit the second division (**Lyndon B. Johnson National and State Historical Parks**), drive another 14 miles west to **Stonewall** for a bus tour from the visitor center through the LBJ Ranch, the only way to see the property. (See "Must-see attractions" for both park divisions.)

To follow or precede the 90-minute bus tour, depending on bus availability, take a walking tour through the **Sauer-Beckman Living History Farm** that includes a good look at some grazing longhorn cattle. (See "Must-see attractions.")

Another 15 miles west from Stonewall on U.S. 290 brings you to **Fredericksburg,** home of the outstanding **Admiral Nimitz Museum & Historical Center** (see "Must-see attractions"), a dulcimer factory, a brew pub, an herb farm, wineries, a working wildflower seed farm (the nation's largest), and the **Pioneer Museum Complex** (see "More cool things to see and do").

Luckenbach is an eccentric little town that's famous around the world thanks to a song about it by Waylon Jennings and Willie Nelson. The beer-drinking, guitar-picking community that roars in on weekends often slumbers during the week, leaving the town empty and quiet. A writer compared Luckenbach to Brigadoon — "You're almost afraid to go back because it might not be there again." (See "More cool things to see and do.")

From Fredericksburg, especially in spring when the bluebonnets are blooming, take a scenic drive 38 miles north to **Llano** via SR 16, pausing to sample the famous barbecue at **Cooper's** outdoor pit. (See "Good eats.") The drive west to **Mason** on SR 29 is another outstanding wildflower area in good years. From Mason, head west on U.S. 377 to Junction and an easy return south to San Antonio on I-35. En route, the little town of **Comfort,** 2 miles off Exit 523, is famous for its antiques shops and laid-back little restaurants.

Must-see attractions

Admiral Nimitz Museum & Historical Center
Fredericksburg

This monument to a famous World War II admiral is much more than military history; the Nimitz family was among the early German settlers in the area, and the museum is housed in the restored **Nimitz Steamboat Hotel,** owned by the family and birthplace of the admiral. Film clips, interactive exhibits, and major displays indoors and out make this museum a fascinating trip through time.

304 E. Main St. ☎ 830-997-4379. RV parking: Look for space on side streets around the museum. Admission: $5 adults, $3 students, free 5 and younger. Open: Daily, gardens 8 a.m.–4:45 p.m., museum 10 a.m.–5 p.m. Allow 3 hours.

Deep in the *herz* (heart) of Texas

In the overpopulated old country, Prussian nobility recruited German immigrants, the first major nonnative settlers in this part of Texas, to settle the New World. Thousands landed on the Gulf Coast between 1845 and 1847; those who survived the sea journey and the diseases of the new land settled in the areas around what is now Fredericksburg. The Germans started farms in the outlying terrain, but because they came into Fredericksburg on Saturdays to do their shopping and wanted to stay over for church on Sunday morning, they built "Sunday houses" from local limestone, tacking on an extra bedroom or two as the family grew and then adding outdoor stairways and a room or two on top when necessary. Today, the Sunday houses are in great demand as retirement homes and bed-and-breakfasts.

The early German settlers also brought sausage and beer making to the region. Today, their descendants speak a long-forgotten German, and most have never been to their homeland. Still, they happily grill sausages, drink beer, and celebrate an annual Oktoberfest with just as much gusto as their European ancestors.

The Alamo
San Antonio

If all you remember about the Alamo comes from the John Wayne movie of the same name, filmed on a special set constructed way down on the Rio Grande near the Mexican border, you may be startled to see the real thing hunkered down in the middle of downtown San Antonio. A high-rise hotel and office buildings dwarf the Franciscan mission that was the site of that bloody battle between Mexicans and Texans in 1836. The adjacent museum relates the story. In front of the Alamo, note the cenotaph, which lists the men who died in the battle. The facade of the chapel is one of the most photographed spots in the nation.

300 Alamo Square. ☎ 210-225-1391. www.thealamo.org. *RV parking: Some nearby public parking lots can handle RVs. Admission: Free. Open: Mon–Sat 9 a.m.–5:30 p.m.; Sun 10 a.m.–5:30 p.m. Closed Christmas Eve and Christmas Day; limited hours Mar 6 (the anniversary of the fall of the Alamo). Allow 3 hours.*

El Mercado
San Antonio

A commercial Mexican-theme market, El Mercado is fun for strolling, but better for eating a hearty, inexpensive Tex-Mex meal in one of the outdoor cafes, which make good spots for margarita-sipping and music-listening, too. (See "Good eats" for our favorite restaurants.) You can also shop here for typical Texas and Mexican souvenirs.

Downtown at Santa Rosa and West Commerce Streets. ☎ 800-THE-ALAMO (800-843-2526), 210-207-6700 (San Antonio Convention & Visitors Bureau;

www.sanantoniocvb.com). *RV parking: In a parking lot located under the I-35 freeway overpass one block west of El Mercado on Dolorosa Street. Admission: Free. Shops open daily Sept–May 10 a.m.–6 p.m., June–Aug until 8 p.m. Closed Thanksgiving, Christmas, New Year's Day, and Easter, but some restaurants may be open. Allow 1 hour for looking around; add more for a meal or margarita stop.*

Institute of Texas Cultures
San Antonio

This museum really comes to life on weekdays during the school term when busloads of children from across the state attentively listen to museum docents explaining the history and traditions of some 25 ethnic groups that settled Texas. Meanwhile, a fiddler plays "Irish Washerwoman" and talks about early Irish settlers in one area, while in another, a man near a chuckwagon discusses trail cooking: "They ate this same meal, beans and biscuits and meat, every single day for breakfast, lunch, and dinner."

Hemis Fair Park, 801 S. Bowie St. ☎ *210-458-2300. RV parking: Large parking lots in the area; watch for RV- and bus-parking signs. Admission: $6.50 adults, $4 seniors, $3 ages 3–12. Open Tues–Sat 9 a.m.–5 p.m., Sun noon to 5 p.m. Allow 3–4 hours.*

Lyndon B. Johnson National Historical Park
Johnson City

The boyhood home of the 36th president reflects his early life and comfortable, if sometimes accident-prone, childhood. Gain insights at the **visitor center** and then walk down into the **Johnson Settlement** where his grandparents and other relatives lived.

On U.S. 290 just outside of Johnson City. ☎ *830-868-7128, ext.231 or 244. RV parking: Street parking in the area. Admission: Free. Open: Daily, visitor center 8:45 a.m.–5:00 p.m., Johnson Settlement 9:00 a.m. to sunset. Closed Thanksgiving, Christmas, and New Year's Day. Allow 3 hours.*

Lyndon B. Johnson National and State Historical Parks
Stonewall

The larger part of the divided national park is in Stonewall, 14 miles west of Johnson City and 16 miles east of Fredericksburg. Go first to the **visitor center,** where you can take an air-conditioned tour bus through the famous LBJ Ranch, the late president's pride and joy. (This tour is the only way visitors can enter the ranch itself.) Depending on the bus schedule (tours last 90 minutes), take a walk through the **Sauer-Beckmann Living History Farm** adjacent to the visitor center before or after the ranch tour, but do take it in. You see a herd of longhorns, and at the farm, women in long cotton dresses and sunbonnets boiling wash in a big iron pot outdoors, clabbering milk to make cottage cheese, churning butter, and preserving ham and bacon. (They also cook lunch here for the park rangers.)

Located on U.S. 290 just east of Stonewall. ☎ *830-868-7128, ext 231 or 244. RV parking: Large parking lot adjacent to visitor center. Admission: Free except for bus tours ($3 ages 7 and older). Open: Daily, visitor center 8 a.m.–5 p.m., Sauer-Beckmann Living History Farm 8 a.m.–4:30 p.m., LBJ Ranch bus tours 10 a.m.–4 p.m. Closed Thanksgiving, Christmas, and New Years.*

River Walk
San Antonio

An already delightful city multiplied the fun back in 1939 by creating River Walk, a meandering walkway one level below the downtown streets along the San Antonio River. River Walk is the city's beating heart, the pulse of its party mood. The sidewalk wends its sun-dappled way through downtown, a few stairsteps below traffic in a pedestrian-scaled world of sidewalk cafes, paddleboats, sightseeing barges, and morning-through-midnight street life. In one trip, you may walk by musicians playing Dixieland and Cajun music and by an Irish tenor singing "Danny Boy." Don't leave San Antonio without taking a stroll here day or night!

Entrance access from city streets including South Alamo, Lojoya, Presa, Navarro, St. Mary's, Market, Commerce, and Crockett. RV parking: Large parking lots are located at Commerce Street near the Convention Center and at the Southwest Craft Center, 300 Augusta St., near Navarro. You may also park your RV in the lot near El Mercado, and then walk the six or so blocks along Commerce or Dolorosa Street to River Walk. Walkway always open; restaurants and bars operate late morning until late evening; shop hours vary.

More cool things to see and do

Attractions from nature's Enchanted Rock to a fine collection of circus artifacts and miniatures fill the Texas Hill Country. The San Antonio Zoo is world famous for its breeding in captivity program, and the Buckhorn Hall of Horns, Fins, and Feathers always is good for a surprise or two.

- ✔ **Go batty in Austin.** Summer evenings at sunset is the best time to see the **bats of Congress Avenue Bridge,** the nation's largest urban colony of bats. They fly out from under the bridge in search of their evening meals, 20,000 pounds of mosquitoes and other pesky insects. This colony of Mexican freetail bats is in residence from late March until the end of October. Watch from the bridge. Allow 5 to 15 minutes for their exit after they start.

- ✔ **Fish got to swim, birds got to fly.** Located in a century-old saloon, the zany **Buckhorn Hall of Horns, Fins, and Feathers** has 4,000 exhibits, including Ol' Tex, a stuffed longhorn with an 8-foot, 9-inch spread on his horns. Gunfighters face off at high noon on weekends, and an arcade and gift shop offer chances to spend even more money.

318 E. Houston St., San Antonio. ☎ **210-247-4000.** www.buckhorn museum.com. RV parking: Small parking lot adjacent, also street parking in the area. Admission: $9 adults, $8 seniors, $6.50 ages 17 and younger. Open: Daily 10 a.m.–5 p.m. Allow 1–2 hours.

✔ **Like a rock.** Rock climbing, hiking, and picnicking are great at **Enchanted Rock State Natural Area,** but unfortunately, the rest of the world already has discovered it, so restrictions are plentiful. During heavy use periods, the park closes for the day when a maximum number of visitors is reached. Don't even think of visiting on weekends, holidays, or during spring break. Local tribes venerated the rock, a National Natural Landmark.

18 miles north of Fredericksburg, off FM 965. ☎ **915-247-3903.** RV parking: A large lot below the office. Admission: $5 ages 13 and older. Open: Daily 8 a.m.–10 p.m., office closes at 9 p.m. No RV overnighting. Allow a half to full day, if you're able to get in.

✔ **Giddyap! Did you bring the champagne?** The most romantic way to see Austin, Texas, is to book a **horse-drawn carriage** for a tour around downtown.

Call Austin Carriage Service (☎ **512-243-0044**) or Die Gelbe Rose (☎ **512-477-8824**) for prices, schedules, and reservations.

✔ **This Bud's for Hondo.** The late Hondo Crouch, Texas writer and all-round character, purchased the tiny town of **Luckenbach,** which was made famous in a song by Willie Nelson and Waylon Jennings. It's busiest on Sunday afternoons, when many people show up with guitars and drink longneck bottles of Shiner Bock beer to live out the song's lyric, ". . . in Luckenbach, Texas, ain't nobody feelin' no pain."

Don't count on signage to help you find it; the signs are torn down almost as quickly as they're put up. From Fredericksburg, drive east on U.S. 290 for 6 miles, turn south on FM 1376 and continue another 4 miles, and then take the second left where the sign (if it's there) says Luckenbach Road.

✔ **A Sunday kind of house.** The local historical society created the **Pioneer Museum Complex,** a replica of old Fredericksburg, with an 8-room furnished home and store from 1849, a wine cellar and brewery, barn, blacksmith shop, Sunday house, log cabin, and fire museum with period equipment.

309 W. Main St., Fredericksburg. ☎ **830-997-2835.** RV parking: Street parking. Admission: $4. Open: Mon–Sat 10 a.m.–5 p.m., Sun 1–5 p.m. Allow 2 hours.

✔ **It's a jungle out there.** One of the best zoos in America, the **San Antonio Zoo** is notable for its success with breeding in captivity and its sanctuaries for endangered species, such as snow leopards, whooping cranes, and white rhinos. The wide expanse of open exhibits gives kids a chance to run and see a variety of exotic animals.

3903 N. St. Mary's at Brackenridge Park, San Antonio. ☎ **210-734-7183.** RV parking: Parking lot at zoo under U.S. 281. Admission: $8 adults, $4 seniors and ages 3–11. Open: Daily 9 a.m.–5 p.m., June–Aug until 6 p.m. Allow half a day.

✔ **Climb a tree.** With hands-on exhibits for all ages, the **Witte Museum of History and Science** presents dioramas and exhibits about Texas flora and fauna. The two-level H-E-B Science Treehouse by the river even has binoculars for wildlife viewing.

3801 Broadway, San Antonio. ☎ **210-357-1900.** RV parking: Across the street in the back lot of the IHOP. Admission: $5.95 adults, $4.95 ages 11–17, $3.95 ages 4–11; free Tues 3 p.m.–9 p.m. Open: Mon–Sat 10 a.m.–5 p.m., Sun noon to 5 p.m. Allow 2–3 hours.

Weekend wonder

If you're going to be in the area and want to make a quick trip around the Texas Hill Country in a couple of days, you can do so if you cut out a couple of small towns and barbecue joints. Begin in **San Antonio** as the main driving tour does, take a quick look at the Alamo and River Walk, and then head north to **New Braunfels** for a stop at the Smokehouse for some smoked meats. From there, strike out on CR 12 north to its junction with CR 697, turn east to **Driftwood,** and stop at The Salt Lick for a barbecue lunch or dinner. Continue north to rejoin U.S. 290 at **Dripping Springs,** then turn west to **Johnson City,** pausing for the Lyndon B. Johnson National and State Parks there and in nearby Stonewall. Drive into **Fredericksburg,** look at the Admiral Nimitz Museum, have a German meal or snack, and then follow U.S. 87 to rejoin I-35 at **Comfort.** You can pause here for a little antiquing, if time allows; then follow I-35 back into San Antonio.

Sleeping and Eating on the Road

Texas is an RV-friendly state, so you find plenty of privately owned and state-owned campgrounds, all with hookups. As for good eats, they're inescapable in this land of barbecue and Mexican restaurants. Because the Texans themselves are big-time RVers, you want to make **campground reservations** whenever convenient, especially in the spring on weekends when the bluebonnets are blooming. During the heat of summer, campgrounds are less crowded than in the spring — spring break is very busy — or fall when the summer weather cools down. In the middle of the summer, Texas is hot, topping 100 degrees Fahrenheit on occasion. In the winter, weather is mild, and campgrounds aren't crowded.

All campgrounds listed in this chapter are open year-round and have public flush toilets, showers, and sanitary dump stations unless designated otherwise. Toll-free numbers, where listed, are for reservations only. See Chapter 9 for information on how we select our favorite campgrounds.

Our favorite campgrounds

Fredericksburg KOA

$$$ **Fredericksburg**

At a junction in the road not far from Luckenbach, this comfortable campground is convenient to both the attractions of Fredericksburg and the LBJ Ranch and parks.

5681 U.S. 290 E, Fredericksburg, TX 78624. (5 miles east of Fredericksburg at the junction of U.S. 290 and FM 1376, on the right.) ☎ ***800-562-0796****, 830-997-4796.* www.koa.com. *Total of 98 sites with water and 30- and 50-amp electric, 78 full hookups, 58 pull-throughs. Dataport, food service, handicap access, laundry, pool, SATV. Rates: $25–$30 per site. MC, V.*

Junction KOA

$$$ **Junction**

Located on the Llano River, this quiet, pleasantly rural campground offers good deer and bird-watching and freshwater fishing with tackle for rent. A restaurant and golf course are nearby.

2145 N. Main St., Junction, TX 76849. (Take Exit 456 from I-10 and drive south half mile to campground on right.) ☎ ***800-562-7506****, 915-446-3138.* www.koa.com. *Total of 52 sites with water and 30- and 50-amp electric, 39 full hookups, 50 pull-throughs. CATV, dataport, laundry, pool. Rates: $25–$29 per site. DISC, MC, V.*

Lone Star RV Resort

$$$–$$$$ **Austin**

Conveniently close to Austin, this Good Sam RV park has back-in sites on terraced levels with shade trees and larger pull-through sites on top of the hill with less shade. Car rentals are available.

7009 S. I-35, Austin, TX 78744. (Take Exit 227 southbound or Exit 228 northbound from I-35, travel north on east frontage road to campground on right.) ☎ ***800-284-0206****, 512-444-6322.* www.austinlonestar.com. *Total of 153 sites with water and 30- and 50-amp electric, 145 full hookups, 68 pull-throughs. CATV, dataport, laundry, pool/hot tub. Rates: $30–$45 per site. AE, DISC, MC, V.*

Oakwood RV Park

$$–$$$ **Fredericksburg**

Sites in this recently built campground are shaded but narrow. Many activities are available for the whole family, including golf, shuffleboard, horseshoes, and croquet. Each site has a concrete patio, picnic table, and barbecue grill.

78 FM 2093, Fredericksburg, TX 78624. (From the junction of U.S. 290 and SR 16S, drive 2 miles south on SR 16S, also known as Airport Road and as FM 2093; campground is on the right.) ☎ *800-366-9396, 830-997-9817. Total of 132 sites with water and 30- and 50-amp electric, 118 full hookups, 30 pull-throughs. CATV, dataport, laundry, phone jacks, pool, spa. Rates: $20–$25 per site. MC, V.*

Pedernales Falls State Park
$$ **Johnson City**

Swimming, tubing, hiking, and freshwater fishing are available on the Pedernales River. Sites are wide with some shaded back-ins.

From U.S. 281/290 in town, take FM 2766 east 9.2 miles; the park is on the left. ☎ *830-868-7304. Total of 66 sites with water and 30-amp electric. Rates: $22 per site. DISC, MC, V.*

Runner-up campgrounds

Admiralty RV Resort
$$$–$$$$ **San Antonio** Sites aren't particularly wide at this Good Sam membership campground, but all have paved patios. You can catch a city bus from here to the Alamo, downtown, and River Walk or rent a car through the campground office. The campground also offers a free shuttle to nearby Sea World. *1485 N. Ellison Dr., San Antonio, TX 78251. (From I-410, take Exit 9A and drive northwest on SR 151 for 1.3 miles to Potranco Road, then drive west 1.4 miles to Ellison Drive and north 0.7 miles to campground on left.)* ☎ *210-647-7878. Total of 240 sites with 30- and 50-amp electric, all full hookups, 120 pull-throughs. CATV, dataport, laundry, phone jacks, pool, spa. Rates: $28–$32 per site. DISC, MC, V.*

Alamo KOA
$$$ **San Antonio** Sites are narrow, although mostly shaded, in this campground, offering freshwater fishing on Salado Creek, which flows past. City bus service is available to the Alamo, downtown, and River Walk. Ice cream socials and Texas barbecues are offered on occasion. *602 Gembler Rd., San Antonio, TX 78219. (From Exit 580 on I-10, go north on W.W. White Road to Gembler, and then west 1 mile to campground on left.)* ☎ *800-562-7783, 210-224-9296. www.koa.com. Total of 261 sites with water and 30- and 50-amp electric, 145 full hookups, 200 pull-throughs. Dataport, laundry, pool, spa. Rates: $27–$30 per site. MC, V.*

McKinney Falls State Park
$$ **Austin** Sites are wide with paved patios, and some are shaded in this handsome state park on the southwest edge of Austin. Freshwater

fishing and swimming are available in Onion Creek. *From I-35, take Exit 230 B east on Ben White Road 0.4 mile to Burleson Road, drive 2.7 miles to McKinney Falls Parkway, and turn southwest and drive for 1.8 miles to campground on right.* ☎ *512-243-1643. Total of 84 sites with water and 30- and 50-amp electric, no full hookups, 27 pull-throughs. Rates: $14 per site. DISC, MC, V. 14-day maximum.*

River Bend RV Park

$$ **Luling**   This new family run RV park fills a 20-acre riverside site with fishing docks, access for canoes and boats on San Marcos river, and a nearby 9-hole municipal golf course. *1881 SR 80, Luling, TX 78648. (From I-10, take Exit 628 on SR 80 and drive ¼ mile to campground on right.)* ☎ *830-875-9548. Total of 36 sites with water and 30-amp electric, no full hookups, 24 pull-throughs. Dataport, handicap access, phone jacks. Rates: $20 per site. DISC, MC, V.*

South Llano River State Park

$$ **Junction**   Large sites and great bird-watching make this park special. Springtime is good for spotting wild deer, wild turkey, rabbits, hummingbirds, and songbirds. The South Llano River runs through the park. *From I-10, Exit 456, turn south on U.S. 377 and drive 5.2 miles to Park Road 73; drive northeast 1.8 miles to campground on right.* ☎ *915-446-3994. Total of 54 sites with water and 20- and 30-amp electric, no full hookups, no pull-throughs. Rates: $15 per site. DISC, MC, V.*

Good eats

Regional cooking, takeouts, rural family restaurants on a side road with long lines of patrons waiting for Sunday dinner in the midday — all these are signs of good eats establishments. Because the Texas Hill Country is about barbecue, we begin there, and then tell you about some equally ethnic places from Tex-Mex to German.

Barbecue joints

Texans like beef, so the pride of a *pit boss* (barbecue chef) is almost always slow-cooked cuts of beef, most often from the brisket or shoulder. Cooking fuel depends on local supply, with mesquite dominant in the hill country and pecan wood as you move east. Sometimes, it seems that everybody in Central Texas has a barbecue establishment, rusty tin-sided contraptions by the side of the road with crude hand-painted signs faded by time. Most don't keep regular hours, but if smoke is coming out and you can smell the meat, it's open.

The best barbecue joints in Texas are casual places where the clients line up to order their food, and then eat it wherever it's convenient — at a nearby table, an outdoor picnic table, or back in their RV. We have several rules about barbecue places:

- Never stop at a barbecue joint that advertises along the freeway with a string of billboards.

- Be wary of proprietors who sell their own bottled barbecue sauce; they may be putting more effort in the bottling than the barbecuing.

- Never try to impose your own tastes in barbecue on the proprietor; the reason he's famous is because he makes it *his* way.

- Never patronize a barbecue joint that has its own Web site.

- Watch out for fancy decorations, such as tablecloths and silverware, or numerous side dishes; they just add clutter and confusion and take the attention away from the meat.

- Don't add any sauce or additional seasoning before tasting the barbecue. The best Texas barbecue speaks for itself, and stands up to a taste test without any sauce or seasoning.

- Always know what you want to order before you get in line; never stand dumbfounded and ask the server what's good today — the mark of a rank amateur.

Street parking for RVs or empty lot parking is generally easy to find near most barbecue vendors, because they're in small towns or, in the case of Bob's Smokehouse in San Antonio, a residential/industrial area. Some, notably Smitty's and Southside Market, have their own parking lots with plenty of room for RVs.

The following list includes some of our favorite Texas Hill Country barbecue vendors.

- **Black's Barbecue:** 215 N. Main St., Lockhart (☎ 512-398-2712). Despite a display of tacky roadside signs such as, "Black's is open 8 days a week," this barbecue turns out a wonderful smoked pork loin, tasty enough when it's hot but delectable cold the next day on sandwiches spread with *chipotle* (smoked chile) flavored mayonnaise. Don't bother with Black's rather bland serve-yourself sauce. Open daily 10 a.m. to 8 p.m.

- **Bob's Smokehouse:** 3306 Roland Ave., San Antonio (☎ 210-333-9611). Take Exit 578 from I-10 and drive south on Roland Avenue. An unpainted building in southeast San Antonio is covered with slogans from Bob ("Bob Knows: Bar-B-Q Must Come Off A Pit, Not From Under Red Lights") but has no large sign to identify that this is Bob's Smokehouse. Ribs (pork, beef, and lamb) and brisket top the takeout orders, with double sauce on the side. Open daily 11 a.m. to 7 p.m. except Mondays, Fridays and Saturdays until 9 p.m.

- **City Market:** 633 E. Davis St., Luling (☎ 830-875-9019). Business types in suits line up at lunchtime for briskets, ribs, and sausages; it looks gentrified from the outside but is the real thing inside. Open Monday through Saturday from 7 a.m. to 6 p.m.

✔ **Cooper's:** 604 W. Young St., Llano (☎ **915-247-5713**). All the cooking is done outdoors under a big roof. Brisket, sausages, chuck and club steak are cooked on mesquite; weekends, you can also get *cabrito* (kid goat) and thick pork chops. Open Sunday through Thursday from 10 a.m. to 8 p.m., Friday and Saturday from 10 a.m. to 9 p.m.

✔ **Dozier's Grocery:** 8222 FM 359, Fulshear (☎ **281-346-1411**). Take Exit 720 from I-10 and drive 12 miles south on SR 36 to CR 1093, and then turn east 5 miles to Fulshear. A bit to the east of hill country proper, this rural store dishes up pecan-smoked brisket and sausages and a hearty barbecue sauce. Dozier's also has a sales rack of **Bob's Texas-Style Potato Chips,** made in nearby Brookshire and distributed locally only. Open Tuesday through Sunday from 10 a.m. to 7 p.m.

✔ **Hinze's Barbeque & Catering:** 2101 SR 36 S., Sealy (☎ **979-885-7808**). Take Exit 720 from I-10 and drive 1 mile north to Sealy. Pecan wood cooks the barbecued beef brisket and side dishes of pinto beans, okra gumbo, and onion-bacon potatoes, served cafeteria-style. (We know that we said no side dishes, but Hinze's is an exception.) Open daily from 10:30 a.m. to 9 p.m.

✔ **Kreuz Market:** 619 N. Colorado St., Lockhart (☎ **512-398-2361**). Our favorite ambience is gone now that Kreuz (pronounced *kritz*) has left their ancient, no-frills location and reopened in a new building with character, but the flavor of the beef is as good as ever. You buy here by the pound, not the sandwich. Open Monday through Saturday from 9 a.m. to 6 p.m.

✔ **Louie Mueller:** 206 W. Second St., Taylor (☎ **512-352-6206**). This venerated establishment is the only business still existing in an ancient block marked by vacant buildings, broken sidewalks, and years of neglect. Open the creaking screen door, and inside, several neon beer signs provide just enough light to see the quiet, dark room, smoky from decades of wood fires. Barbecued brisket doesn't get any better than this; order the thin, peppery, oniony sauce (one customer mistook it for onion soup until he tasted it) on the side. Open Monday through Saturday from 10 a.m. to 6 p.m. or until barbecue is sold out, usually early to mid-afternoon.

✔ **The Salt Lick:** 18001 FM 1826, Driftwood (☎ **512-858-4959**). Driftwood is 20 miles southwest of Austin on FM 1826 between FM 967 and FM 150. An old stone ranch house way out in the boonies, open since 1969, The Salt Lick is an institution. Open pit–barbecued brisket, ribs, and sausage, served with potato salad, cole slaw, beans, pickles, onions, and bread make up the family style meal, but you also can order à la carte. Bring your own beer in your RV refrigerator. Open daily from 11 a.m. to 10 p.m.

✔ **Smitty's:** 208 S. Commerce St., Lockhart (☎ **512-398-9344**). Formerly Kreuz Market, the place has the genuine reek of authenticity and decades of barbecued meats. You enter from the dirt parking lot into a hot, dark back room with four or five workers who fork up the meats you order, slap them down on a big wood slab, and slice them, wrapping everything in pink butcher paper. Both the brisket and the beef shoulder roast are charred crunchy and black on the outside, juicy and tender on the inside. Serious eaters don't douse them with sauce. Open daily from 9 a.m. to 6 p.m.

✔ **Southside Market and Bar-B-Q:** 1212 SR 290, Elgin (☎ 512-285-3407). The sausages, called Elgin Hot Guts and served with cellophane-wrapped saltine crackers, are fantastic, but they also sell brisket, mutton ribs, barbecue sandwiches, and have a well-stocked meat market on one side and a Blue Bell ice-cream-cone bar on another. Open Monday through Thursday from 8 a.m. to 8 p.m., Friday and Saturday from 8 a.m. to 10 p.m., and Sunday from 9 a.m. to 7 p.m.

Beyond barbecue: Old-timey good eats

Texas is full of good eats. Try these hill country places.

✔ **Altdorf's:** 301 W. Main St., Fredericksburg (☎ 830-997-7865). This homey German *biergarten* and dining room serves German dinners indoors and out in the beer garden, along with Texas chow, such as charbroiled ribeye steaks, tacos, and enchiladas. Try a sausage dinner, such as bratwurst, knockwurst, or bockwurst, or a meat specialty, such as wiener schnitzel, sauerbraten, or *rindsrouladen*, a rolled slice of beef stuffed with pickles, onion, and mustard. Open daily except Tuesdays from 11 a.m. to 9 p.m., and Sundays from 11 a.m. to 4 p.m.

✔ **El Mercado:** Market Square, 514 W. Commerce St., San Antonio. This historic Mexican market began in the days of the "chili queens" when local women served a spicy meat-and-beans concoction called "chili con carne" at night, first from stalls set up around the Alamo and later from this marketplace, and local farmers sold produce during the day. Today, you can sample anything from Blue Bell ice-cream cones to pecan pralines, sip margaritas and listen to strolling mariachi bands who take requests (and expect a tip), and shop for Southwestern art, dried herbs, Kahlua, embroidered peasant blouses, and big sombreros. Open seven days a week.

✔ **Jardine's Texas Foods:** Jardine Ranch, Buda (☎ 512-295-4600). From I-35, Exit 221, take loop 4 to Buda, and then go 1.1 miles and turn right at the sign. Although selling its products to many high-priced gourmet food dealers, Jardine's has the best, cheapest, and freshest food available. You can buy everything from their unique Texas Champagne Cayenne Pepper Sauce to peach salsa and gift boxes of goodies for chili-heads. Open Monday through Friday from 9 a.m. to 4 p.m. Closed on weekends.

Ways to use leftover barbecue

Never let those leftovers go to waste. Try one of the following four ways to create new meals the second time around.

✔ Gently reheat the meat in the sauce for sandwiches or a main dish — it doesn't get easier than this.

✔ Sauté chopped bits of the brisket with chopped cooked potatoes and raw onions into a smoky Texas version of corned beef hash.

✔ Reheat and slice leftover hot links to impale with a toothpick for cocktail snacks.

✔ Thinly slice beef brisket, adding minced hot peppers and shredded lettuce and a dressing to serve as a Texas-Thai beef salad.

✔ **Mi Tierra Café y Panaderia:** In El Mercado (see listing earlier in this section) (☎ 210-225-1262). On a first-come, first-served basis, this cafe and bakery seats local families on holidays, paging, "Rodriguez, party of 20; Martinez, party of 14." Wend your way past the bakery and settle into one of the tables by the mural-filled wall, and, if you're lucky, on the menu will be the world's best *carne machaca,* beef braised in broth until the liquid evaporates and the meat browns, then cooled and shredded and recooked in oil or lard with garlic, onions, and chiles, then served for breakfast with eggs, refried beans, tortillas, and salsa. In the pastry shop, you can buy crisp hot *churros* (grooved sticks of fried pastry), *bunuelos* (thin fried pastries sprinkled with cinnamon and sugar), and *ricardos* (a custard-filled pastry sprinkled with pecans and named for the chef who invented it). Open 24 hours a day year-round.

✔ **New Braunfels Smokehouse:** Corner of SR. 46 and I-35, Exit 189, New Braunfels (☎ 830-625-2416). Since 1946, this friendly German restaurant and smokehouse has served sandwiches of smoked ham or turkey, beef barbecue, bratwurst, pastrami, and every imaginable combination, as well as chicken and dumplings, a huge smoked sausage platter, ribs and brisket, and breakfast tacos with smoked ham or sausage. Open daily from 7:30 a.m. to 9:30 p.m.

✔ **Po-Po Family Restaurant:** 435 NE I-10 Access Road, Boerne (☎ 830-537-4194). In the colorful little town of Boerne (pronounced *burn*-e), this rustic rock roadhouse with the neon "Eats" sign out front has been around since 1929, variously as a dance hall, skating rink, machine shop, and chicken hatchery. Today, it's a locally popular restaurant known for fried catfish, fried frog legs, fried shrimp, and mesquite-smoked ribs, but fried chicken is the favorite, using Ma Burgon's Original Recipe. Open Tuesday through Sunday from 11 a.m. to 10 p.m.

✔ **Royer's Round Top Café:** On the square in Round Top (☎ 979-249-3611). Deceptively down home with a chic urban clientele, Royer's specializes in grilled quail, pasta, fresh fish, and home-made desserts. You can also buy a big jar of vinegar-marinated peppers to take out that lasts forever; you just keep adding new vinegar when the stock gets low. Use it as a sauce on its own or to perk up salad dressings. Open Wednesday from 5:30 to 9:30 p.m., Thursday through Saturday from 11 a.m. to 9 p.m., and Sunday from noon to 7 p.m.

✔ **Threadgill's:** 6416 N. Lamar, Austin (☎ 512-451-5440). Since 1933, Threadgill's has fueled the folks in Austin — first as a service station and then as a restaurant tucked into the existing service-station facade. Two things put Threadgill's on the map: Janis Joplin sang here when she was starting her career, and they make the best chicken-fried steak in the world. Open Tuesday through Saturday from 10 a.m. to 11 p.m., Sundays from 11 a.m. to 9 p.m.

✔ **Wimberley Pie Company:** On SR 12, Wymberley (☎ 512-847-9462). Wimberley's sells wonderful homemade pies whole or by the slice, in such delicious flavors as buttermilk (try it, you'll love it!), coconut custard, pecan, lemon chess, key lime, peanut butter, and all the more familiar fruits and custards, as well as killer cheesecakes. Open Wednesday and Thursday from noon to 5:30 p.m., Friday from 9:30 a.m. to 5:30 p.m., Saturday from 10 a.m. to 5 p.m., and Sunday from noon to 4 p.m.

Fast Facts

Area Code

The area codes are **512** and **830**.

Emergency

Call ☎ **911.** For emergency assistance on the road, call Texas Motorists (☎ **800-525-5555**).

Hospitals

Major hospitals along the route are in Austin and San Antonio.

Information

To contact Texas's Department of Tourism, call ☎ 800-888-8TEX (800-888-8839) or go online to www.traveltex.com. For brochures, call ☎ 800-452-9292.

Laws

In Texas, riders in the front seats must wear seat belts; violators pay steep fines. The maximum speed limit on interstate highways is 70 mph. Speed limits in urban areas are lower.

Road and Weather Conditions

Call ☎ 800-452-9292.

Taxes

Texas has a 7.25% sales tax; some local taxes may raise it to 7.8%. The state gaso-line tax is 20¢ a gallon.

Time Zone

Texas is on central standard time.

Chapter 17

The Heart of Ohio: A Circle Around Circleville

. . . .

In This Chapter

▶ Shopping for antiques and Amish crafts

▶ Rockin' 'n' rollin' in Cleveland's great rock museum

▶ Checking out Cincinnati chili

▶ Seeing the Wright stuff

. . . .

Get down and get real — the Buckeye state is the heart of America. "Why, oh why, oh why, oh why did I ever leave Ohio?" sang the unhappy-in-New-York heroine of the Broadway musical *Wonderful Town,* written by Leonard Bernstein, Betty Comden, and Adolph Green. The roads of Ohio are lined with history — eight presidents lived here — and strewn with calories — Skyline chili parlors in exotic Cincinnati and homemade pies from just about everywhere. And can you think of any place cooler than the Rock and Roll Hall of Fame and Museum in Cleveland, designed by world-class architect I.M. Pei?

A fascinating blend of the urban, industrial, and rural, Ohio gave birth to the Wright brothers, Thomas Edison, astronauts Neil Armstrong and John Glenn, and the rubber tire industry, but on the quiet back roads around Millersburg, the world's largest Amish community still tends huge family farms without using electricity or the internal combustion engine. Native Americans left their marks on the land in the form of mounds; the most famous is shaped like a serpent, and some diligent Swiss kitsch fans built the world's largest cuckoo clock at Alpine Alpa in Wilmot.

Getting There

Our circle drive around the heart of Ohio begins in **Dayton,** swings east to **Springfield** along I-70, then south to **Yellow Springs** and **Xenia** on U.S. 68. (See "The Heart of Ohio" map in this chapter.) From Xenia, we take U.S. 42 through **Waynesville** and **Lebanon** south to **Cincinnati.** We

The Heart of Ohio

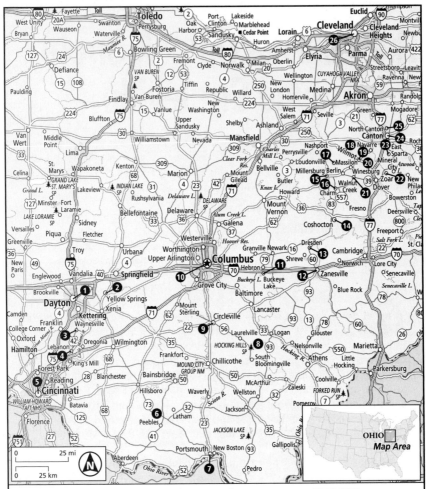

ATTRACTIONS
Alpine Alpa **19**
Amish country **15**
Carillon Historical Park **1**
Dayton Aviation Heritage
National Historic Park **1**
Dunbar House State Memorial **1**
German village **10**
Hoover Historical Center **25**
Huffman Prairie Flying Field **1**
James Thurber House **10**
Lehman's Hardware **17, 18**
Longaberger Basket Factory **13**
McKinley Museum
and National Memorial **23**
Museum Center
at Union Terminal **5**
National Road Museum **12**
Ohio Village **10**
Old Man's Cave **8**
Portsmouth Floodwall Murals **7**

Rock and Roll Hall of Fame
and Museum **26**
Roscoe Village **14**
Serpent Mound State Memorial **6**
Ted Lewis museum **9**
Topiary Garden **10**
United State Air Force Museum **1**
Wright Brothers Memorial **1**
Wright Cycle Company Shop **1**
Zane Grey Museum **12**
Zoar State Memorial **22**

CAMPGROUNDS
Bear Creek Resort Ranch KOA **23**
Buckeye Lake KOA **11**
Dayton Tall Timbers Resort KOA **1**
Hocking Hills State Park **8**
John Bryan State Park **2**
Lake Park Campground **14**
Wolfie's Kamping **12**
Zanesville KOA **12**

GOOD EATS
Camp Washington Chili **5**
Coblentz
Chocolate Company **21**
Der Dutchman **21**
Golden Lamb Inn **4**
Guggisberg
Cheese Company **16**
Harry London
Chocolate Factory **25**
Mrs. Yoder's Kitchen **17**
Ohio Sauerkraut Festival **3**
Schmidt's Restaurant
and Sausage Haus **10**
Skyline Chili **5**
Young's Jersey Dairy **2**

SHOPPING
The Basket Factory Outlet **20**
Lebanon antiques **4**
Waynesville antiques **3**

follow the broad Ohio River along winding, scenic U.S. 52 to **Aberdeen,** and then detour north on scenic SR 41 and SR 73 to see the Serpent Mound. Afterward, SR 73 takes us south again to **Portsmouth** on the river.

From Portsmouth, travel east on U.S. 52 to SR 93 and turn north to **Jackson,** where we make a short detour east into the scenic Hocking Hills via SR 93 to SR 56, then return on 56 driving northwest to **Circleville.** From there, we take U.S. 23 north to **Columbus,** the state capital.

From Columbus, we drive east on I-70 to **Zanesville** and **Norwich** along parts of the old National Road, then return to go north on SR 79 near **Hebron** to **Newark.** Then we go east on SR 16 to SR 60 and south 3 miles to **Dresden,** home of the world's largest basket factory, and then return to SR 16 turning east to **Coshocton.** From there, we drive north on SR 83 to **Millersburg** and the beginning of the Amish country. Take U.S. 62 east, detouring south on SR 557 to **Charm,** then return to U.S. 62 and continue through **Berlin** to **Winesburg** and **Wilmot;** turn southeast on U.S. 250 for 3 miles to SR 212 and follow it eastward to **Zoar.**

From Zoar, you can take I-77, the fast route north to Cleveland, pausing if you'd like to at intervals of interest around **Canton** and **Akron.** The distance is approximately **725 miles.**

Planning Ahead

Summer months are the prime season in Ohio, but that's also when Midwestern families take their camping and vacation trips, so you may consider visiting in **late spring or early fall.** We last drove this route in May, when rain threatens some days but temperatures are mild. **Late September** and **early October** are practically perfect but can be crowded in the Amish country because the harvest season is the most popular time to visit; April through June is less crowded there. Freak weather conditions called "the lake effect" can hit in **winter,** especially snow and ice storms along Lake Erie. We once spent a week in January in Cleveland during a blizzard and do not recommend it.

Be cautious about **Midwestern weather.** In spring's tornado season, local TV stations usually run a tornado alert information strip along the bottom of the screen by county name, so always find out the name of the county where you're camping and the names of those nearby or where you're headed next. While you're in the campground, if an alarm sounds, leave your RV and make your way to the designated shelter, which is often a recreation hall or even a storm cellar where you need to remain until the alert is over. You may also run into heavy driving rain so powerful that you must pull over to the side of the road at the first opportunity and wait for it to subside.

Campground reservations shouldn't be necessary in most of the RV parks recommended in this chapter, but you need to reserve ahead for big holiday weekends, such as Memorial Day, Independence Day, and Labor Day.

Pack a variety of clothing weights and options because weather can change suddenly. Out in the country in hot weather, anything clean and decent is acceptable, such as lightweight cotton shorts, shirts, and T-shirts, but always have a sweater or jacket handy if it cools off. Take an umbrella and moderate rain gear. If you want to walk around a large town or city, go into a nice restaurant, or attend a church service, pack long pants for men and dressy cotton slacks, skirt, or dress for women.

Allow a **week to 10 days** for this leisurely drive around the back roads of Ohio, more if you're a dedicated antiques shopper or museum-goer.

Stocking the Pantry

Ohio is chockablock with cafes, grocery stores, farm markets, and chain supermarkets, such as **Kroger,** so you'll have no problem stocking edibles. The Amish country is a great place to pick up locally made cheeses, especially Baby Swiss from **Guggisberg Cheese Company** in the hamlet of Charm. (See "Good eats" later in this chapter.)

In season, you see farmers markets in many towns, roadside produce stands, even small-town growers selling tomatoes and corn in their front yards with a help-yourself table, honor system cash box, and hand-lettered sign.

Driving the Ohio Heartland

On back roads, drive slowly and exercise caution because you may round a turn and run up behind a large, slow-moving tractor, a horse-drawn Amish carriage, or even a herd of cattle crossing the road and headed for the barn. Country roads in the Midwest also are famous for making sudden right or left turns at a property boundary where a farmer didn't want his land bisected for the sake of a straight road.

The drive begins in **Dayton,** home to the Wright stuff — the **Dayton Aviation Heritage National Historic Park** with four locations commemorating the Wright brothers and their part in the history of flight: the **Wright Cycle Company Shop,** the **Dunbar House State Memorial,** the **Carillon Historical Park** (where the 1905 Wright Flyer III is on display), and the **Huffman Prairie Flying Field,** home of the first permanent flying school. (See "Must-see attractions," later in this chapter.) The Wright Brothers Memorial is out on the edge of town on a hill overlooking Wright-Patterson Air Force Base, which also is the location for the

United States Air Force Museum, the largest museum of its kind in the world, displaying more than 300 airplanes in its gigantic hangars. (See "Must-see attractions.")

From the U.S. Air Force Museum, we drive northeast on SR 4 to I-70, then east a few miles to Exit 52 and turn south on U.S. 68 to **Yellow Springs** and **Xenia.** The pretty town of Yellow Springs, home of Antioch College and **Young's Jersey Dairy** (see "Good eats"), is at the junction of U.S. 68 and SR 343. Hikers find good trails in the nearby John Bryan State Park and the Glen Helen Nature Preserve.

From Xenia, U.S. 42 continues south to **Waynesville** and **Lebanon,** 10 miles apart but almost always spoken of in tandem as the antiques capitals of Ohio, with some 250 shops between them (see "Shopping along the Way" later in this chapter) and the renowned **Golden Lamb Inn** for a lunch break (see "Good eats").

Waynesville, at the junction of U.S. 42 and SR 73, also is home to the **Ohio Sauerkraut Festival** every October, where you can sample sauerkraut candy and sauerkraut pizza, among other offbeat offerings. (See "Good eats.")

Cincinnati is another 34 miles down U.S. 42. Mark Twain used to say he wanted to be in Cincinnati when the world ended because it was always 20 years behind the times, but today, the city that was called Porkopolis (because it led the pork-packing industry in volume) has laid on the charm with a refurbished riverfront. The splendid **Museum Center at Union Terminal** would make Twain change his tune. (See "Must-see attractions.") The city's unique **Cincinnati chili,** sold at numerous Skyline Chili franchises, is an acquired taste. (See "Good eats.")

From Cincinnati, head south on U.S. 52 for a scenic drive along the Ohio River as far as **Aberdeen** (60 miles), then turn northeast on SR 41 to **Locust Grove,** and then northwest on SR 73 to the **Serpent Mound State Memorial,** one of America's most distinctive archeological features. (See "Must-see attractions.")

Return to the river road by following SR 73 southeast to where it joins SR 104, and then continue south 8 miles into **Portsmouth.** This colorful town is where the late cowboy star Roy Rogers was born Leonard Slye in 1911. The walls along the town's riverfront are covered with the **Portsmouth Floodwall Murals** depicting each era of the city's history. (See "Must-see attractions," later in this chapter.)

From Portsmouth, continue east on U.S. 52 along the Ohio River to SR 93 and follow that north to Jackson. Then turn north on SR 93 and west on SR 56 into the Hocking Hills. Numerous campgrounds, caves, waterfalls, and hiking areas color this rugged, scenic section of Ohio, particularly around the area known as **Old Man's Cave** off SR 56 (look for signs), named for Richard Rowe, who lived in and is buried in the cave.

From **Hocking Hills State Park,** return to SR 56 and continue west to **Circleville,** where a small museum is dedicated to jazz and pop singer **Ted Lewis** (see "More cool things to see and do").

From Circleville, continue north on U.S. 23 to **Columbus,** Ohio's capital and a city that has several quirky attractions, including humorist **James Thurber House;** the **Topiary Garden,** which replicates the figures from Georges Seurat's classic painting *A Sunday Afternoon on the Island of La Grand Jatte* in clipped boxwood topiary; and a **German village** with an October beer festival and good German restaurants. (See "More cool things to see and do" for the house and garden and "Good eats" for the village.)

From Columbus, drive 56 miles east on I-70 to **Zanesville,** where the delightful **National Road Museum** and **Zane Grey Museum** are 10 miles east at Exit 164 at the same location. U.S. 40, which parallels I-70 at this point, was the first attempt at building a national road when people still traveled by horseback and oxcart. Detailed dioramas depicting the road at different stages of travel history fill the museum. (See "Must-see attractions.")

Retrace your steps through Zanesville on U.S. 40 or I-70, Exit 129, and turn north on SR 79 to a 25-mile strip of highway, SR 16, between **Newark** and **Dresden,** home of the **Longaberger Basket Factory,** which offers a fascinating tour but no factory outlet shopping (except for one style of basket). The most interesting part of this empire is the Newark-based company headquarters, a seven-story, basket-shaped building — the world's largest basket. (See "Must-see attractions.")

From Dresden, continue north 3 miles on SR 60 to its junction with SR 16, and then turn northeast on 16 to **Coshocton** and historic **Roscoe Village,** a restored canal town where crafts shops turn out beautiful handmade pottery, furniture, baskets, and weavings — and everything is for sale. (See "Must-see attractions.")

SR 83 leads north from Coshocton to the Holmes County **Amish country** around **Millersburg.** If you have time, set aside a day or two to explore. (See "Must-see Attractions.) In nearby **Mount Hope** and **Kidron,** the worthwhile stops include **Lehman's Hardware** with a full range of non-electrical appliances from hand-cranked wringer washing machines to wood-burning stoves. (See "More cool things to see and do.")

From Millersburg, if time permits, take a detour down SR 557 to **Charm,** a town as delightful as its name. Just past Millersburg on 557, you find **Guggisberg Cheese Company,** selling 40 different types of cheese including its own famous Baby Swiss. (See "Good eats.")

From the Millersburg area, drive east on U.S. 62 to **Berlin** (pronounced *Burr*-lin) and **Walnut Creek.** North of Walnut Creek on SR 515 at U.S. 62 is the town of **Winesburg,** which gave its name to a book of short stories by native son Sherwood Anderson. The real model for Winesburg, however, was probably Clyde, 20 miles southwest of Sandusky, where Anderson grew up.

Wilmot, 5 miles northeast of Winesburg on U.S. 62, boasts that it's home to the world's largest cuckoo clock at a restaurant/tourist attraction called **Alpine Alpa.** (See "More cool things to see and do.")

From Wilmot, drive east on U.S. 250 to **Strasberg,** home of **The Basket Factory Outlet** (see "Shopping along the Way"), then cut across SR 21 to SR 212, and drive to Zoar.

Zoar, a communal town founded in 1817 by a group of German separatists, is now the **Zoar State Memorial,** one of our favorite places in Ohio — perhaps because we visited it early on a Monday morning when nobody was around. On Mondays and Tuesdays, the historic buildings are closed to the public; costumed interpreters occupy them the rest of the week. Frankly, we enjoyed the peace and quiet and having the whole town to ourselves, but you may want to stop by when the buildings are open. (See "Must-see attractions.")

Leave Zoar by driving west on SR 212, following the signs to I-77, which you take north through **Canton** and **Akron** to **Cleveland.** In Canton, the **McKinley Museum,** next door to the tomb of this third American president to be assassinated, has animated figures of the president and his wife, who "chat" with visitors about life in Canton and the White House. (See "More cool things to see and do.")

North Canton is the home of the **Hoover Historical Center,** not another presidential home but rather the home of William Henry Hoover, founder of the vacuum cleaner company of the same name. (See "More cool things to see and do.")

And the **Harry London Chocolate Factory** also is in North Canton, just off I-77's Exit 113, with free factory tours (by reservation) and great prices on fresh-from-the-factory chocolates. (See "Good eats.")

From here, we continue north on I-77 to its junction with I-90 on the Cleveland lakefront, home of the striking **Rock and Roll Hall of Fame and Museum.** (See "Must-see attractions.") The drive ends in Cleveland.

Must-see attractions

Amish Country
Centered around Millersburg

Ohio's Amish country offers enough attractions to fill a week of sightseeing. Pick up one of the free Amish country maps (found in most shops and restaurants) that carry ads for shops, restaurants, and sightseeing.

For the best part of the journey, however, strike out along the back roads to glimpse farm families at work — men plowing the fields, women hanging out washing, and children on the way to school.

SR 77 between Berlin and Mount Hope is a colorful back road lined with big farms and horse-drawn Amish buggies going to and from town.

Dayton Aviation Heritage National Historic Park
Dayton

This four-part museum complex spread around the city salutes the Wright brothers and their contemporary and friend, African American poet Paul Laurence Dunbar. From 1895 to 1897, the brothers operated the **Wright Cycle Company shop,** which has been restored and furnished with period bicycles and machinery. The **Dunbar House State Memorial** is the home poet Dunbar bought for his mother when his work was published successfully. Exhibits include a bicycle that the Wright brothers gave him. **Carillon Historical Park** houses the *Wright Flyer III*, the first craft capable of controlled flight. The **Huffman Prairie Flying Field** was where the Wright brothers tested their planes and was home to the first permanent flying school.

The **Wright Brothers Memorial** is in northeastern Dayton on SR 444 overlooking Wright-Patterson Air Force Base.

Wright Cycle Company: 22 S. Williams St. ☎ 937-225-7705. Admission: Free. Open: Summer daily 8:30 a.m.–5 p.m., winter closed Mon and Tues. Dunbar House State Memorial: 219 Paul Laurence Dunbar St. ☎ 937-224-7061. Admission: $3 adults, $1.25 ages 6–12. Open: Nov to Memorial Day, weekdays (call for appointment); Memorial Day to Labor Day, Wed–Sat 9:30 a.m.–4:30 p.m. and Sun 12:30–4:30 p.m.; Labor Day to Oct, weekends only (call for appointment). Carillon Historical Park: 2001 S. Patterson Blvd. ☎ 937-293-2841. Admission: $5 adults, $4 seniors and ages 4–17. Open: Tue–Sat 9:30 a.m.–5 p.m., Sun noon to 5 p.m. Huffman Prairie Flying Field: Accessed through gate 12A at Wright-Patterson AFB off SR 444. ☎ 937-257-5535. Admission: Free. Open: Dawn to dusk. Allow 1 hour for each of the museums, 15 minutes for the memorial.

Longaberger Basket Factory
Dresden

This factory tour of the world's largest basket-making plant is extremely well-organized but without the free sample or discount prices of a factory store at the end. Only one basket, the $30 "tour model," can be bought at the plant. Otherwise, these finely handcrafted baskets must be purchased through home party sales like Tupperware. The huge plant covers 6½ acres but has no assembly line. Instead, the 2,200 basket weavers turn out their own baskets from start to finish and then sign each of them on the bottom. If you don't like regimentation, don't take this tour, because it's totally structured from start to finish; free spirits can't wander around on their own. East of the plant, also on SR 16, is the new **Longaberger Homestead,** a collection of replicas of period family homes and workshops, with retail shops and restaurants occupying various "rooms." In Newark, also on SR 16, the **company headquarters** is a seven-story building shaped like a giant basket.

5563 Raider Rd., which is also SR 16. ☎ 800-966-0374. RV parking: Huge parking lots, transfers by shuttle bus. Admission: Free. Open: Daily Mon–Fri 8:30 a.m.–2 p.m., Sat 10 a.m.–2 p.m. Closed major holidays. Tours leave every 15 minutes. Allow 1 hour for plant tour plus a half-hour for video and museum.

Museum Center at Union Terminal
Cincinnati

In a magnificently restored 1933 Art Deco railway station, the city has built three excellent museums, the **Cincinnati History Museum,** the **Museum of Natural History,** and the **hands-on Children's Museum.** You can walk through the Ice Age, explore a limestone cavern inhabited by live bats, and step onto a vintage steamboat from the Cincinnati landing. Because sightseeing can make you hungry, you also find a food court that includes a Skyline Chili branch.

1301 Western Ave. ☎ 800-733-2077, 513-287-7000. RV parking: Parking garage with height limits; try street parking or take public transportation to the museums. Admission: $6.75 adults, $5.75 seniors (Mon only), $4.75 ages 3–17. Open: Mon–Sat 9 a.m.–5 p.m., Sun 11 a.m.–6 p.m., holidays 9 a.m.–5 p.m. Closed Thanksgiving and Christmas. Allow 3–4 hours.

National Road Museum/Zane Grey Museum
Zanesville

Three for the price of one, this museum contains the road museum, a salute to native son Zane Grey, and a display of art glass made in the area. Road warriors love the dioramas depicting the various stages of the National Road from 1811 to the present day. You can follow the progress of travelers from early inns to early campers with tents and tin lizzies, and then a panorama with a trolley, a biplane, and Model Ts. Conestoga wagons are displayed with toll-road signs and other vintage vehicles. Another room houses a full-size replica of the studio used by Zanesville-born Western writer Zane Grey.

8550 E. Pike, Norwich, OH. (From Zanesville, go east 9 miles on I-70 and take Exit 164; follow signs to museum.) ☎ 800-752-2602, 740-872-3143. RV parking: Large open lot capable of handling big rigs. Admission: $6 adults, $5.50 seniors, $2 ages 6–12. Open: May–Sept Mon–Sat 9:30 a.m.–5 p.m., Sun noon to 5 p.m.; Mar–Apr and Oct–Nov Wed–Sat 9:30 a.m.–5:30 p.m., Sun noon to 5 p.m. Closed Dec–Feb and holidays. Allow 2 hours.

Portsmouth Floodwall Murals
Portsmouth

The pretty little river town of Portsmouth is where cowboy star Roy Rogers was born and cruise boats sailing the Ohio River frequently call. The waterfront is lined with huge murals depicting an awesome panorama of town history from the prehistoric days to the present. Yes, Roy Rogers and his horse Trigger are in one of the murals, but our favorite is an evening depiction of the town during the days of World War II, with a movie house, vintage cars, and soldiers in uniform. Some evocative shops in the Boneyfiddle Historic District also are appealing.

The murals line Front Street in downtown Portsmouth. ☎ *740-353-7647. (Portsmouth Convention & Visitors Bureau). RV parking: Street parking. Admission: Free. Open: Always. Allow 1 hour.*

Rock and Roll Hall of Fame and Museum
Cleveland

Cleveland's great rock museum, designed by I.M. Pei with a glass pyramid reminiscent of the same architect's entrance to the Louvre in Paris, is a great place to spend a day. Some of the most important exhibits are underground in the Ahmet M. Ertegun Exhibition Hall, a large, darkish area housing all sorts of displays and interactive exhibits, such as "One Hit Wonders" saluting now-forgotten artists who had one big hit and then vanished from view. On life-size mannequins are John Lennon's collarless Beatles jacket, Alice Cooper's bondage outfit, David Bowie's exaggerated 1970s fashions, Michael Jackson's sequined glove, Leadbelly's 12-string guitar, Jim Morrison's Cub Scout uniform — you get the idea.

Original rock 'n' rollers are happy to discover that the museum has a discounted senior rate because many of them are eligible for membership in AARP, the American Association of Retired Persons.

To get to the museum, follow the signage from I-90. ☎ *888-764-ROCK (888-764-7625). www.rockhall.com. RV parking: This is a big problem because the parking garage at the museum has a height limit that prohibits most RVs; point your RV to the right toward Burke Lakefront Municipal Airport. When you reach the intersection facing the museum, look for a spot in the airport parking lot, a block from the museum. Admission: $18 adults, $14 seniors, $11 ages 9–11, free 8 and younger. Open: Tues and Thurs–Sun 10 a.m.–5:30 p.m., Wed 10 a.m.–9 p.m. Allow half to a full day.*

Roscoe Village
Coshocton

An 1850s restored living history village along the Ohio and Erie Canal, Roscoe Village is a sort of mini-Williamsburg. Craftsmen demonstrate weaving, pottery making, and broom making in the shops along the main street, while a horse-drawn canal boat takes visitors through a restored section of the historic canal. Seasonal celebrations are scheduled frequently from May's Dulcimer Days to October's Apple Butter Stirrin' Festival.

381 Hill St. ☎ 800-877-1830, 740-622-9310. RV parking: Designated parking area at site. Admission: Free; tours $10.95 adults, $5.50 ages 5–12. Open: Daily 10 a.m.– 5 p.m., tours 11 a.m. and 2:30 p.m. Allow 3–4 hours.

Serpent Mound State Memorial
Peebles

Striking and unforgettable in its photographs in magazines, such as *National Geographic*, in person, the sinuous, grass-covered Serpent Mound is a bit of a bust. Unless you're in a low-flying aircraft, you don't get the gorgeous view depicted in most photographs. You can climb to the top of the visitor viewing tower, but you still don't get a full overview. The Adena people constructed the 1,348-foot-long earthwork sometime between 800 B.C. and A.D. 44. A pathway enables you to explore the perimeter of the mound, and an excellent museum discusses theories of how and why the mound was built. Our favorite theory was put forth by the Reverend Loudon West of Pleasant Hill, Ohio, who said that God built it to identify Adams County as the Garden of Eden.

3850 SR 73. ☎ 937-587-2796. RV parking: Plenty of space in designated lots, but a fee applies (cars $6, motorhomes $8). Admission: Free. Open: Memorial Day to Labor Day daily, park and museum 9:30 a.m.–5 p.m.; Apr to Memorial Day and Labor Day to Oct weekends only, park 10 a.m.–7 p.m., museum 10 a.m.–5 p.m. Allow 1 hour.

United States Air Force Museum
Dayton

Wear comfortable shoes if you plan to see all of this museum — it's the world's largest of its kind, filling 10 acres and displaying more than 300 aircraft inside and outside. From balloons to the B-1 bomber, from the plane that dropped the atomic bomb on Nagasaki in 1945 to the plane that took President Kennedy's body from Dallas to Washington in 1963, air history is here. The museum also has an IMAX theater that offers two films alternating hourly.

Wright-Patterson Air Force Base, 5 miles northeast of Dayton off SR 4. ☎ 937-255-3284. RV parking: Huge parking areas with designated areas. Admission: Free, IMAX theater extra $6 adults, $5.50 seniors, $4.50 students, $3 ages 3–7. Open: Daily 9 a.m.–5 p.m., IMAX films on the hour beginning at 11 a.m. Closed major holidays. Allow 3 hours.

Zoar State Memorial
Zoar

In 1817, German separatists from the Kingdom of Wurttermburg founded this communal town of Zoar. Named for Lot's biblical town of refuge, Zoar flourished as one of America's most successful Christian communal societies until the society disbanded in 1898. Men *and women* had voting power on the town board, and they produced their own food and operated blast furnaces, a blacksmith shop, a tin shop, a garden and greenhouse, and a wagon shop. They sold what they didn't need and had a million dollars in assets by 1852. Today, many of the town's buildings are staffed with costumed interpreters except on Mondays and Tuesdays and from November through March, but visitors are free to walk around the exteriors of all the public buildings at any time.

Zoar is off I-77, Exit 93, accessible by SR 212. ☎ *330-874-3211. RV parking: Street parking or designated lots off the main route. Admission: $6 adults, $5.50 seniors, $2 ages 6–12. Open: Building interiors, Memorial Day to Labor Day Wed–Sat 9:30 a.m.– 5 p.m., Sun noon to 5 p.m.; Apr–May and Sept–Oct weekends only.*

More cool things to see and do

Ohio's roadside attractions run the gamut from the world's largest cuckoo clock to the birthplace of humorist James Thurber. You can have fun and/or get informed at several spots along the way.

✔ **Spot the real big bird.** Put a quarter in the turnstile and climb the wooden stairs to the rooftop of **Alpine Alpa** to see the world's largest cuckoo clock. How big is it? 23 feet 6 inches by 24 feet by 13 feet 6 inches. When the clock strikes, a wooden band plays and wooden dancers with braids twirl around. Near the clock is a gnome garden with Snow White, her seven dwarfs, and many other small painted plaster people. Downstairs is a restaurant, a cheese factory, a deli with German food products, and a gift shop selling souvenirs, such as cuckoo clocks and musical beer steins.

1504 U.S. 62, Wilmot. ☎ **330-359-5454.** RV parking: Large parking lot. Admission: 25¢. Open: Daily 9 a.m.–8 p.m. Closed major holidays. Allow 1 hour.

✔ **Sprechen-sie Ohioan?** The **German village** in Columbus is one of Ohio's best-loved destinations. Saved from demolition in the 1950s, the 19th-century neighborhood is home to microbreweries, restaurants, antiques shops, and art galleries, and its brick streets are inviting to stroll.

Visitors Information Center, 588 S. Third St., Columbus. ☎ **614-221-8888.** RV parking: Street parking. Stay as long as you like.

✔ **Clean up your act.** Contrary to what you may think, **Hoover Historical Center** is not about a president but rather is about the founder of the famous vacuum cleaner company. When invented, the vacuum was considered a miracle because "it beats as it sweeps as it cleans." "To Hoover" came to mean both the cleaner and the cleaning action in many parts of the English-speaking world. This museum contains seven decades of cleaning history (including an early "portable" that weighed 100 pounds) plus a gift shop.

2225 Easton St. NW, North Canton. ☎ **330-499-0287.** RV parking: Small lot, street parking. Admission: Free. Open: Tues–Sun 1–5 p.m. Tours at 2, 3, and 4 p.m. Closed major holidays. Allow 1 hour.

✔ **Grind your own grist. Lehman's Hardware,** a tradition in Ohio's Amish country, is a treasure trove of nonelectrical appliances from hand-cranked wringer washing machines to wood-burning cookstoves, all brand new. Butter churns, stone crockery, hand-cranked grist mills (to make coarse meal out of dried corn), carpenter's adzes, solid oak furniture, handmade quilts, washboards, and apple peelers are only a small part of the collection.

Two locations near each other: SR 77 in **Mount Hope** (☎ **330-674-7474**) and One Lehman Circle in **Kidron** (☎ **330-857-5757**). RV parking: Lots large enough for Amish horse-and-buggies. Admission: Free. Open: Mon–Sat 7 a.m.–5:30 p.m.; Kidron also until 8 p.m. Thurs; Mount Hope also until 8 p.m. Fri and until 5 p.m. Sat. Allow 1 hour or more.

✔ **Chat with dead presidents.** The **McKinley Museum and National Memorial** honors the 25th president, who was assassinated in 1901. The animated figures of McKinley and his wife occupy the museum and talk about their life in the White House. The memorial is reached by a flight of 108 terraced stairs that fitness buffs often climb on the run.

800 McKinley Monument Dr. NW, Canton. ☎ **330-455-7043.** RV parking: Designated lot. Admission: $7 adults, $6 seniors, $5 ages 3–18. Open: Mon–Sat 9 a.m.–5 p.m., Sun noon to 5 p.m. Allow 2 hours.

✔ **Meet woolly mammoths. Ohio Village** recreates an Ohio town in the 1860s with costumed interpreters and craftsmen, keeping kids and adults interested in the past. In the Historical Center, you can meet woolly mammoths and hear some hair-raising ghost stories too.

1982 Velma Ave. (at I-71 and 17th Avenue), Columbus. ☎ **800-OLD-OHIO** (800-653-6446), 614-297-2300. RV parking: Designated lot. Admission: $6 adults, $5 seniors, $2 ages 6–12. Open: Tues–Sat 9 a.m.–5 p.m., Sun noon to 5 p.m. Allow 2 hours.

✔ **Is everybody happy?** That was the signature phrase for Jazz Age entertainer **Ted Lewis** from Circleville, who is remembered in his hometown with a pleasant little museum showcasing his battered top hat and clarinet, along with the sheet music for his hits "Me and My Shadow" and "When My Baby Smiles at Me."

133 W. Main St., Circleville. ☎ **740-477-3630**, 740-474-3231. RV parking: Street parking. Admission: Free. Open: Fri–Sat 1–5 p.m., other times by appointment. Allow 1 hour.

✔ **Chuckle with a humorist.** A unicorn stands in the garden across from the **James Thurber House,** birthplace of the eccentric and beloved humorist whose drawings graced the pages of *The New Yorker* for so many years. James Thurber was famous for drawing unicorns, clocks, bossy wives, and mournful dogs, and the house in Columbus is where "the ghost got in" in one of his famous stories. There's also a fine bookstore.

77 Jefferson Ave., Columbus. ☎ **614-464-1032.** RV parking: Street parking. Admission: Free. Open: Daily noon to 4 p.m., plus for author appearances. Call ahead. Allow a half-hour to an hour.

✔ **Step into a painting.** Sundays in the park with George come alive in Columbus's **Topiary Garden,** a replica in pruned shrubbery of Georges Seurat's painting *A Sunday Afternoon on the Island of La Grand Jatte* (which inspired the Stephen Sondheim musical *Sundays in the Park with George*) has 50 topiary people, 8 boats, 3 dogs, a monkey, and a real pond to represent the Seine.

Old Deaf School Park, corner of East Town Street and Washington Avenue, downtown Columbus. ☎ **614-645-0197.** Admission: Free. Open: Always.

Weekend wonders

You can't cover Ohio in one weekend, so concentrate on the section that interests you most. For crafts collectors and folks with hearty appetites, the Amish country fills the bill nicely. Start and end your trip in Columbus, driving north to Millersburg and Berlin and overnighting in that area.

Scenery, hiking, and camping fans need to drive along the Ohio River from Cincinnati and then go up into the Hocking Hills, where campgrounds abound.

One of our favorite weekend combinations for Ohio sightseeing — that pleases the whole family — is to start in Dayton, seeing all the airplane history, then driving south through the antiques capitals of Waynesville and Lebanon for a little shopping, pausing for a meal at the famous old Golden Lamb Inn, and then driving into Cincinnati for the trio of great museums at the Museum Center at Union Terminal.

Sleeping and Eating on the Road

Ohio has plenty of campgrounds, both private and public, but you need to make reservations for long holiday weekends and during the peak summer season. Having a reservation for a seasonal festival also is a good idea because Buckeyes enjoy RV camping in conjunction with special events.

On the food side, you find many cafes, including supper clubs, where you can have a late meal. Restaurant meals are generous in the Midwest, so if you stop to pick up a meal to go and don't want leftovers, you often can buy one to share with one another (in your motorhome, of course, not in the restaurant).

All campgrounds listed in this section are open year-round and have public flush toilets, showers, and sanitary dump stations unless designated otherwise. Toll-free numbers, where listed, are for reservations only. See Chapter 9 for more information on how we choose our favorite campgrounds.

Our favorite campgrounds

Buckeye Lake KOA
$$$$ **Buckeye Lake**

Big Bands used to play at the lakeside pavilion on Buckeye Lake in the good old days. This KOA campground isn't far from the lake shore but is convenient to all the attractions in Columbus. Big rig sites offer 50-amp electrical connections, the management is friendly, and the swimming pool is heated.

PO Box 972, Buckeye Lake, OH 43008. (From I-70, Exit 129A, go south on SR 79 1.5 miles to campground on the right.) ☎ *800-562-0792, 740-928-0706.* www.koa.com. *Total of 141 sites with water and 30- and 50-amp electric, 80 full hookups, 66 pull-throughs. CATV, dataport, laundry, pool. Rates: $40 per site. DISC, MC, V. Open: Apr 2–Oct 31.*

Dayton Tall Timbers Resort KOA
$$$$$ **Brookville**

Convenient to the Air Force Museum and the Wright Brothers memorials, this campground offers dataports at the campsites, a big swimming pool, a pond, and a golf course nearby. Food service also is available in this resort-style campground.

7796 Wellbaum Rd., Brookville, OH 45309. (From junction of I-70 and SR 49, go north 0.5 mile on 49 to Pleasant Plan Road, then west 0.6 mile to Wellbaum Road, and south 0.2 mile to campground on the left.) ☎ *800-562-3317, 937-833-3888.* www.koa.com. *Total of 201 sites with water and 30- and 50-amp electric, 108 full hookups, 83 pull-throughs. Dataport, laundry, pool. Rates: $44 per site. MC, V. Open: Apr 1–Nov 1.*

Hocking Hills State Park
$$$ **Logan**

This scenic park is 12 miles south of town on SR 664 with paved sites, some shaded but all fairly narrow. Big rigs must be stingy using their electric appliances and air conditioning because the hookups are a scanty 20 amps. Scenery and hiking in the area, combined with a lake for swimming and fishing, make up for the inconvenience of giving up the microwave.

From Logan, go south 12 miles on SR 664 to the campground on the left. ☎ *740-85-6165. Total of 159 sites with 20-amp electric, no water or sewer hookup, no pull-throughs. Laundry, pool. Rates: $21 per site. DISC, MC, V. 14-day maximum stay.*

Runner-up campgrounds

Bear Creek Resort Ranch KOA

$$$–$$$$ **East Sparta**   Dataports, fishing (with tackle for rent), horseback riding, and miniature golf are among the extras offered by this campground, which is convenient to the Canton and North Canton areas. Sites are fairly narrow but gravel-padded with some shade. *3232 Downing SW, East Sparta, OH 44626. (From junction of I-70 and Zoar Bolivar Road, Exit 93, go west 1 mile to CR 102, then north 3 miles to Haut Street, and east 1 mile to the campground on the right.)* ☎ *800-562-3903, 330-484-3901.* www.koa.com. *Total of 78 sites with water and 30- and 50-amp electric, 48 full hookups, 51 pull-throughs. Dataport, laundry, pool. Rates: $25–$36 per site. DISC, MC, V.*

John Bryan State Park

$ **Yellow Springs**   This lovely state park centered around the Clifton Gorge and Glen Helen nature areas has hiking trails but no hookups or flush toilets. Campsites are not outlined, but camping vehicles are required to park at least 16 feet apart. Large RVs should avoid the lower picnic area because of limited turn-around space. River fishing is available. *From junction of SR 343 and SR 370, go south 1 mile on 370 to the park on the left.* ☎ *937-767-1274. Total of 100 sites, 10 with 30- and 50-amp hookups, no pull-throughs. Rates: $17 per site. No credit cards.*

Lake Park Campground

$$ **Coshocton**   Narrow back-in sites with only electrical hookups don't diminish the popularity of this campground near Roscoe Village when the Dulcimer Days Festival takes place in May. You need to reserve well in advance for a campsite during the festival. The sites are grassy and shaded, and the lake offers swimming and fishing. *From junction of U.S. 36 and SR 83, go north 0.5 miles on 83 to the campground on the left.* ☎ *740-622-7528. Total of 60 sites with 30-amp electric, no water or sewer hookups, no pull-throughs. Rates: $20 per site. No credit cards. Open Apr–Nov.*

Wolfie's Kamping

$$ **Zanesville**   This Good Sam campground offers big sites, all with gravel pads and some with shade, and is conveniently located near the National Roads/Zane Grey Museum. *101 Buckeye Dr., Zanesville, OH 43701. (From I-70, Exit 155, go north 0.2 mile on SR 146 to SR 666, then north 1.2 miles to Buckeye Drive, and east 0.3 mile to campground on the left.)* ☎ *740-454-0925. Total of 50 sites with water and 30- and 50-amp electric, 35 full hookups, 18 pull-throughs. Dataport, laundry. Rates: $15–$20 per site. No credit cards.*

Zanesville KOA

$$$ **Zanesville**   Site length limits of 35 feet restrict really big rigs from this campground, and at 18 feet across, they're also quite narrow. But a fishing pond with tackle and boats for rent, its proximity to the National Road/Zane Grey Museum, and plenty of shade trees are pluses. *2850 S. Pleasant Grove Rd., Zanesville, OH 43701. (From junction of I-70 and SR 93, Exit 157, go south 0.2 mile to U.S. 40, then west 0.1 mile to Pleasant Grove Road, and south 0.75 mile to campground on the right.)* ☎ ***800-562-3390,** 740-452-5025.* www.koa. com. *Total of 91 sites with water and 20- and 30-amp electric, 40 full hookups, 25 pull-throughs. Laundry, pond. Rates: $23–$29 per site. AE, DISC, MC, V. Open: Apr 1–Nov 1.*

Good eats

Travelers in the Buckeye State can eat around the clock, choosing from snacks, really solid meals with enormous servings, and sweets for between meals or afterward.

Meals of chili, sauerkraut, and Amish cooking

Prices are modest, portions are large, and cooking is hearty in many of our recommended typically Ohioan restaurants, unpretentious eateries that win the balloting in Ohio magazine polls under headings, such as "best restaurant values" and "favorite neighborhood restaurants."

✔ **Camp Washington Chili:** Corner of Hopple and Colerain, Exit 3 off I-75, Cincinnati (☎ **513-541-0061**). This restaurant probably is the most colorful purveyor of Cincinnati's famous chili, an acquired taste to any chili-head who has come to love Southwestern chili. Greek Americans created the Cincinnati version — a mild, soupy chili seasoned with cinnamon and allspice, poured over a plate of spaghetti, and sprinkled with cheese. That's "three-way" chili. Add some chopped onions and it's "four way" chili; if you ladle beans over the top, it's "five way." Don't say we didn't warn you. Open Monday through Saturday for 24 hours, and closed Sunday.

✔ **Der Dutchman:** 4967 Walnut St., Walnut Creek (☎ **330-893-2981**); 10911 SR 212 NE in Bolivar, Ohio (☎ **330-874-1041**); and five other Ohio locations (www.derdutchman.com). Der Dutchman is an Amish eatery with its own bakery and family style dinners. Broasted chicken, roast beef, country cured ham, Swiss steak, plenty of mashed potatoes and noodles, a salad bar, and "pies made from scratch" highlight the offerings. Open Monday through Saturday from 7 a.m. to 8 p.m.

✔ **Golden Lamb Inn:** 27 S. Broadway, Lebanon (☎ **513-932-5065**). This venerable inn usually wins the vote as Ohio's favorite restaurant in *Ohio* magazine. Since 1803, the Golden Lamb has hosted Charles Dickens, Mark Twain, and ten American presidents, plus assorted ghosts. While Dickens complained loudly about the inn not serving spirits, you can order a bottle of wine today to enjoy with the meltingly tender lamb shanks, fried chicken, and fruit cobblers at lunch or dinner. Open daily from 11 a.m. to 3 p.m. and from 5 to 8 p.m.

✔ **Mrs. Yoder's Kitchen:** SR 241, Mount Hope (☎330-674-0922). At this Amish restaurant, family style dinners are priced by the number of main dishes you order; up to three is permitted. "All you can eat here" is emphasized on the menu; carry-out from the family style meal is not permitted. Instead, if you want take-out, order from the regular menu, which is structured around one main dish, two side dishes, and bread, all under $8. Look for special local dishes, such as wedding steak (ground beef with mushroom sauce), cracker pudding (a dessert based on crackers), and date nut cake with caramel sauce. Open Monday through Saturday from 7 a.m. to 8 p.m.

✔ **Ohio Sauerkraut Festival:** Old Main Street, Waynesville (☎ 513-897-8855). Held the second weekend in October, the festival draws more than 200,000 visitors with its live music, crafts sales, and most of all, traditional pork-and-sauerkraut dinners, cabbage rolls, hot dogs with sauerkraut, sauerkraut candies, and sauerkraut pizza.

✔ **Schmidt's Restaurant and Sausage Haus:** 240 Kossuth St., Columbus (☎ 614-444-6808). At this restaurant in the colorful German village section of town, look for bratwurst, wiener schnitzel, pork and sauerkraut, red cabbage, German potato salad, and the house special dessert, a jumbo cream puff. Open daily from 11 a.m. to 10 p.m.

✔ **Skyline Chili:** ☎ 513-874-1188 (Corporate office). This big local chain has some 60 locations around Cincinnati, including one in the food court in the Museum Center at Union Terminal. Skyline often wins the title for the best version of the local chili, seasoned with cinnamon and allspice. Oyster crackers are served on the side, and Buckeyes enjoy it with a glass of buttermilk. (See Camp Washington Chili earlier in this section for a complete description of the dish.) Open Monday through Friday from 9 a.m. to 5 p.m.

Snacks of chocolate, cheese, and ice cream

Ohio has its priorities straight: Along our drive are several havens for lovers of chocolate and dairy treats.

✔ **Coblentz Chocolate Company:** 4917 SR 515 at SR 39 in Walnut Creek (☎ 800-338-9341, 330-893-2995). In a charming Victorian house in the heart of Amish country, Coblentz displays its home-made candies in wood-and-glass cases. Open in summer daily from 9 a.m. to 6 p.m., and the rest of the year until 5 p.m.

✔ **Guggisberg Cheese Company:** SR 557, Charm (☎ **330-893-2500**). You can't miss this place in the tiny town of Charm. Just look for the big Swiss chalet with stainless steel towers and a cuckoo clock tower. Sample the cheeses; buy a whole Baby Swiss to go, along with other picnic-makings from the deli. Open Monday through Saturday from 8 a.m to 6 p.m., and Sundays from 11 a.m. to 4 p.m.

✔ **Harry London Chocolate Factory:** 5353 Lauby Rd. (right off I-77 Exit 113), North Canton (☎ **800-321-0444**, 330-494-0833). The factory offers tours ($3 adults and $2 ages 6–18) and chocolate shopping at a flat per-pound rate, even if you wander around the huge store and buy "one of those and two of these." Open Monday through Saturday from 8 a.m. to 6 p.m., and Sunday from noon to 5 p.m.

✔ **Young's Jersey Dairy:** SR 68, 2 miles north of Yellow Springs in Hustead (☎ **937-325-0629**). Young's does quadruple duty as a bakery, soda fountain, sandwich shop, and ice-cream store. Extra thick shakes include the calf shake with two scoops of ice cream, a cow shake with four, or a bull shake with five scoops. Really hungry visitors order the King Kong sundae for dessert. Open daily from 6 a.m. to 10 p.m.

Shopping along the Way

Ohio, home of the world's largest Amish community, has potters, basket makers, weavers, quilt makers, and artists of all sorts. Outside the Amish area, craftsmen staff historic villages and sell goods at every special event. (Refer to "Good eats" for more on the Ohio Sauerkraut Festival.) Antiques also are a main attraction at many events.

The Basket Factory Outlet, 11052 SR 21 NW, Strasburg (☎ **800-327-7016**), considerably smaller than you may expect from its name, is jam-packed with baskets from all around the world, hanging from the ceiling, triple-stacked on the floor, and crowding the open shelves. Prices are very modest, especially for the Asian imports. Open Tuesday through Saturday from 9 a.m. to 5 p.m.

Ohio boasts two antiques centers. **Lebanon,** on U.S. 42 at the junction of SR 63, about 33 miles north of Cincinnati, has much history — Charles Dickens slept here — along with some 70 antiques shops and boutiques in its downtown area, along with Ohio's oldest inn, the Golden Lamb Inn. (See "Good eats.") **Waynesville,** at the junction of U.S. 42 and SR 73, about halfway between Dayton and Cincinnati, has trademarked the title of Antiques Capital of the Midwest for its 35-plus antiques shops, along with art galleries, specialty shops, and boutiques.

Fast Facts

Area Code

The following area codes are in effect in Ohio: **216, 234, 330, 380, 419, 440, 513, 614, 740** and **937**.

Emergency

Call ☎ **911**.

Hospitals

Major hospitals along the route are located in Akron, Canton, Dayton, Cincinnati, Columbus, and Cleveland.

Information

Go online to www.ohiotourism.com or call ☎ 800-BUCKEYE (800-282-5393).

Laws

In Ohio, seat belts must be worn in the front seats. The maximum speed limit on interstates and controlled access roads is 65 mph. Speed limits in urban areas are lower.

Road and Weather Conditions

Sources include the Ohio Transportation Information System online at www.dot. state.oh.us/, or the Ohio Highway Patrol by phone, ☎ **877-7-PATROL** (877-772-8765) in Ohio. In Ohio or adjacent states, call ☎ 888-264-7623 for road conditions.

Taxes

Sales tax is 5.75% to 7% depending on the county. The state gasoline tax is 22¢ a gallon.

Time Zone

Ohio is on eastern standard time.

Chapter 18

Northern Minnesota: Paul Bunyan Country

• •

In This Chapter

▶ Picking your own fresh berries

▶ Jumping across the Mississippi

▶ Perching in Paul Bunyan's palm

▶ Hanging out at the Mall of America

• •

S ome unique American icons came out of Minnesota — entertainer Judy Garland, folk/rock musician Bob Dylan, the Greyhound bus, the Mississippi River, and the giant logger Paul Bunyan, so big when he was born that it took five storks to deliver him. According to legend, his footprints and those of his companion Babe the Blue Ox filled with water and became the state's ten thousand lakes. If you have trouble picturing Paul Bunyan, just think of wrestling star and Minnesota politician Jesse Ventura for a comparable larger-than-life image.

We like Minnesota for its down-to-earth qualities, and picture small towns in winter on frozen lakes populated by the characters in the film *Grumpy Old Men* with Jack Lemmon and Walter Matthau. For less hardy individuals, however, Minnesota is best seen in spring, summer, and fall, when the weather is mild and the lakes have all thawed. Fishing, canoeing, hiking, biking, and — lest we forget — shopping in the biggest mall in the United States, Bloomington's Mall of America, complete the experience.

Northern Minnesota

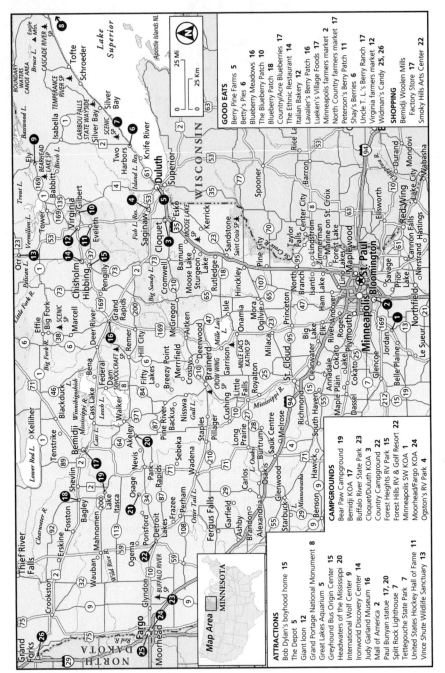

GOOD EATS
Berry Pine Farms **5**
Betty's Pies **6**
Blueberry Meadows **16**
The Blueberry Patch **10**
Blueberry Patch **18**
Country/Acre Blueberries **17**
The Ethnic Restaurant **14**
Italian Bakery **12**
Lavalier's Berry Patch **16**
Lueken's Village Foods **17**
Minneapolis farmers market **2**
North Country farmers market **17**
Peterson's Berry Patch **11**
Shay's Berries **6**
Uncle T. L.'s Berry Ranch **17**
Virginia farmers market **12**
Widman's Candy **25, 26**

SHOPPING
Bemidji Woolen Mills
  Factory Store **17**
Smoky Hills Arts Center **22**

CAMPGROUNDS
Bear Paw Campground **19**
Bemidji KOA **17**
Buffalo River State Park **23**
Cloquet/Duluth KOA **3**
Country Campground **22**
Forest Hills RV Park **15**
Forest Hills RV & Golf Resort **22**
Minneapolis SW KOA **1**
Moorhead/Fargo KOA **24**
Ogston's RV Park **4**

ATTRACTIONS
Bob Dylan's boyhood home **15**
The Depot **5**
Giant loon **12**
Grand Portage National Monument **8**
Great Lakes Aquarium **5**
Greyhound Bus Origin Center **15**
Headwaters of the Mississippi **20**
International Wolf Center **9**
Ironworld Discovery Center **14**
Judy Garland Museum **16**
Mall of America **2**
Paul Bunyan statue **17, 20**
Split Rock Lighthouse **7**
Tettegouche State Park **7**
United States Hockey Hall of Fame **11**
Vince Shute Wildlife Sanctuary **13**

Meeting Paul Bunyan

We fell in love with Minnesota at first because of the hilarious tales of St. Olaf that actress Betty White told on TV's *Golden Girls.* Other fans probably found the state through Garrison Keillor's thoughtful and amusing Lake Woebegon stories on National Public Radio. We suspect that not too many travelers these days are drawn to Minnesota because of something as old as the Paul Bunyan yarns.

For those who don't know about Paul Bunyan, he was a giant logger with a blue ox named Babe, remembered in statues rising all around north central Minnesota. The unlikely stories of his strength and endurance originated in the logging camps of the North Woods. A public relations man named William Laughead, who worked for the Red River Lumber Company, gave the tales a spin when he issued a series of illustrated booklets from 1914 to 1934 that glorified the Paul Bunyan myth. The folk hero first got on the map in a big way in 1937 when the town of Bemidji erected the first known statues of the logger and his ox.

Some of the tales about Paul say that he was born in Maine, where the rocking of his cradle toppled four acres of timber. When he and Babe set out for the North Country, they left a trail of lake-size footprints behind them.

Getting There

We begin in **Duluth** at the southern end of Lake Superior, and drive north via U.S. 53 to the town of **Virginia,** the beginning of the great Mesabi Iron Range. (See the map of "Northern Minnesota" in this chapter for the route.) We then turn west on U.S. 169 to **Grand Rapids,** continue west on U.S. 2 to **Bemidji,** and drive south to Mississippi Headwaters at **Itasca State Park** by following U.S. 2 west to **Shevlin,** and then turning south on SR 2 to **Lake Itasca.** From there, the route turns east through Paul Bunyan National Forest to the junction with SR 64, which we follow south to **Akeley.** From Akeley, we turn west again, following SR 34 some 56 miles to the junction of U.S. 10, then follow U.S. 10 west to **Moorhead,** Minnesota, and just across the Red River to **Fargo,** North Dakota. The distance is approximately **357 miles.**

One optional detour visits the gigantic Mall of America in **Bloomington,** a suburb south of Minneapolis, adding 157 miles each way from Duluth. A second detour follows **North Shore Drive** (SR 61) along Lake Superior from Duluth to the Canadian border; the return, alas, is along the same route, but when you're halfway back to Duluth, you can cut off on SR 1 south of Little Marais and head northwest to Ely, and then follow SR 1/ U.S.169 southwest to Virginia and join the longer drive. The North Shore Drive covers 264 miles.

Planning Ahead

Spring and **fall** temperatures are mild and comfortable, and **summer** temperatures, although humid because of all the surface water in this state of 12,000 lakes, rarely rise above the 80s. **Fall** foliage in the North Woods, a nickname for northern Minnesota, attracts sightseers, who also take advantage of pick-your-own apples in orchards where the harvest coincides with the autumn leaves color season.

Northern Minnesota is never really swamped with visitors, so **campground reservations** are only needed for the most popular parks on holiday weekends. Even in peak summer season, RVers can find campground sites somewhere in the area.

When **packing,** consider layered clothing to cover weather extremes from hot, sticky summer on the lake to a sudden chill or early snowfall. Also bring along heavy-duty hiking boots, serious rain gear, and a strong sunblock. Fishing gear, boats, and white-water rafting outfits can usually be rented on-site.

Allow a leisurely **week for the drive.** Add a day for the Mall of America, perhaps more time if you want to linger there, and two days for the North Shore Drive along Lake Superior.

Stocking the Pantry

When you find a good supermarket, stock up on basic supplies because the North Woods doesn't have an endless supply of goodies. In summer, towns and cities have farmers markets with local growers bringing in fresh-picked produce for sale, and pick-your-own fruits and vegetables are available in season as well. **Minneapolis has a daily farmers market** every morning from 6 a.m. to 1 p.m. between late April and late December; take Exit 230 from I-94 and follow the signs for three blocks to the market. You find not only seasonal produce grown in Minnesota but also fish, meat, flowers, and baked goods.

In Bemidji, **Lueken's Village Foods,** 1171 Paul Bunyan Dr. NW, carries a good supply of foods, and the **North Country farmers market** sets up in the Pamida store's parking lot on Paul Bunyan Drive on Tuesdays and Thursdays between 9 a.m. and 3 p.m. in season. The **Virginia farmers market** is open Tuesday and Friday afternoons from July to early September in the Armory parking lot on 8½ Street South.

If you're a skillful fisherman, you may be able to hook enough finny friends for at least one meal a day until you tire of seafood.

The North Shore Drive

SR 61 strikes out north from Duluth along the shore of Lake Superior, traveling 168 miles to Grand Portage at the Canadian border, where you can catch ferries in season (May to October) to Isle Royale National Park. The drive is especially attractive in the early autumn when the leaves begin changing colors. Some half-dozen state parks with campgrounds are well spaced along the route.

Highlights along the way include **Split Rock Lighthouse,** the highest waterfall in Minnesota in **Tettegouche State Park** near Little Marais; and **Grand Portage National Monument,** a re-created fur trading post 5 miles south of the Canadian border.

About 30 miles north of Duluth, in the town of Two Harbors right on the highway is **Betty's Pies,** open only in summer but worth a stop. If it's too crowded to sit down, get a pie (or at least a couple of slices) to go. (See "Good eats" later in this chapter.)

Rather than take the entire route north and then double back to Duluth, you can turn around at Grand Portage and continue south as far as Little Marais, where you can turn inland and drive northwest on SR 1 to Ely, home of the **International Wolf Center,** and then continue southwest to pick up the longer drive at Virginia. (See "More cool things to see and do" later in this chapter.)

Driving the Paul Bunyan Trail

Although this route through the land of Paul Bunyan sets out from Duluth and ends in Fargo, we allow enough slack for dedicated shoppers to start their journey in Bloomington, a southern suburb of Minneapolis/St. Paul that is home to the country's largest shopping mall, **Mall of America.** (See "Must-see attractions" later in this chapter.)

We also suggest that sightseers with a couple of extra days begin the trip by following the **North Shore Drive** (SR 61) along Lake Superior from Duluth to the Canadian border. (See this chapter's "The North Shore Drive" sidebar.)

Our basic route starts in Duluth, or more properly in the town of **Cloquet,** the location of a comfortable campground. (See "Runner-up campgrounds" later in this chapter.) On the northeast end of Cloquet at the junction of SRs 45 and 33, you find an unexpected landmark — the only gas station that world-famous architect Frank Lloyd Wright ever designed. Today, an undistinguished yellow and green structure with a hint of Googie Moderne style, it's still pumping gas. From here, we follow SR 33 to U.S. 53 all the way to the Mesabi Iron Range near **Virginia,** Minnesota.

Minnesota's great **Mesabi Iron Range,** which stretches across a vast area of the state north of Virginia and Chisholm, attracted miners from all around the world around the turn of the 20th century. Most of the miners were Finnish, but they came from 43 different areas, including the Balkans, Scandinavia, Italy, Greece, Ireland, Germany, Belgium, Slovenia, Russia, Wales, and Cornwall. The Cornish brought along their hot meat-filled pies called *pasties* (pronounced *pass*-teas), which you still find today in small cafes and bakeries around the region. Polkas, Polish sausages, accordion music, and a rich nut pastry called *potica* (pronounced po-*teet*-sah) were some of the other souvenirs the miners left behind, changing the cultural face of Minnesota's north country.

Just south of Virginia in the little town of **Eveleth,** is the **United States Hockey Hall of Fame,** commemorating the first U.S. game, which was played in Eveleth back in 1903. (See "More cool things to see and do" later in this chapter.)

Virginia also is the best jumping-off point for animal fans to venture north to observe and photograph wild black bears and wolves in their natural habitats. You find wolves at the **International Wolf Center** in **Ely,** 52 miles northeast of Virginia on SR 169, and black bears at the **Vince Shute Wildlife Sanctuary** in **Orr,** 46 miles northwest of Virginia on U.S. 53. (See "More cool things to see and do.") If you want to visit them both, an 11-mile shortcut on SR 1, a paved road, cuts off some miles between Angora on U.S. 53 and Tower on SR 169.

From Virginia, follow U.S. 169 west to **Chisholm,** where the wonderful **Ironworld Discovery Center** tells you everything that you ever wanted to know (and then some) about iron mining and details the cultures of those miners who flocked here from so many different places. Children also find a park, special playground, and Pellet Pete's miniature golf course. Make sure to notice the huge statue saluting iron ore miners, just across from the Ironworld entrance. (See "Must-see attractions.")

The town of **Hibbing,** 6 miles south of Chisholm on U.S. 169, gave America two symbols that may have led many to escape the ordinary and run away from home. The Greyhound Bus Company originated here in 1914 with a single bus, a Hupmobile that carried miners from Hibbing to Alice. The **Greyhound Bus Origin Center** displays one of the early vehicles along with many other historic Greyhounds. In 1941, singer **Bob Dylan** was born in Hibbing as Robert Allen Zimmerman; you can drive past his boyhood home. (See "More cool things to see and do" for info on both sights.)

About 30 miles farther down the road in **Grand Rapids,** another even more famous singer born in 1922 was christened Frances Ethel Milne Gumm. She would one day be known as **Judy Garland.** Several small museums here today remember Baby Gumm and her family with photographs and personal memories. (See "Must-see attractions.")

From Grand Rapids, it's a straight 54-mile shot on U.S. 2 through scenic lake country — past Leech Lake, Winnibigoshish, and Cass Lake — to **Bemidji**. Keep your eyes open for wild rice sellers because this area produces Minnesota's hand-harvested real wild rice (as opposed to commercially harvested paddy-grown wild rice). **Eighteen-foot Paul Bunyan and Babe statues** decorate the shore of pretty Bemidji Lake near the town's visitor center.

Nearby **Itasca State Park** contains the area generally accepted as the headwaters of the Mississippi. Every self-important geographer and explorer who managed to find his way to the general area thought he was the only one who had found the correct headwaters and should have the local lakes named after himself. (See "Must-see attractions.")

From Lake Itasca, the Paul Bunyan route swings east on SR 200, and then just before the town of LaPorte, it turns south on SR 64 to **Akeley,** where we turn west on SR 34. In Akeley, right by the side of SR 34, is a gigantic **statue of Paul Bunyan,** one arm lowered with hand open to allow anyone to sit comfortably in his palm. The local museum, open only between Memorial Day and Labor Day, is adjacent to the statue, but fortunately for fans of photo ops, the statue always is open.

Continue on SR 34 about 28 miles west to Osage. Just 1.5 miles west of town is the **Smoky Hills Arts Center,** a group of artisans that usually includes painters, potters, blacksmiths, glassblowers, and woodcarvers with studios and shops in the Smoky Hills National Forest beside the road and reached by a boardwalk. Open only Memorial Day to Labor Day, the center charges a modest entrance fee.

The drive follows SR 34 into Detroit Lakes, and then turns west on U.S. 10 to **Moorhead,** the westernmost town in this part of Minnesota, directly across the Red River from Fargo, North Dakota.

Must-see attractions

The Depot
Duluth

This renovated 1892 railway station is nicknamed "the Ellis Island of Minnesota" because of the numbers of immigrants who arrived here by train at the turn of the 20th century. Today, the bustling depot has been turned into a museum and entertainment complex with steam locomotives and their wooden coaches filling the **Lake Superior Railway Museum** framed by a life-size reproduction of downtown Duluth in 1910. You also find galleries operated by the **Duluth Art Institute,** the **St. Louis County Historical Society,** and the **Duluth Children's Museum.** One low-price ticket accesses the lot, and two museum stores sell collectibles and books. The **Duluth Playhouse** also is on the premises, and so are other performing arts companies.

506 W Michigan St. ☎ 888-733-5833 (recorded info), 218-727-8025. www.duluth
depot.org. *RV parking: Designated area or street parking. Admission: $8 adults,
$4.50 ages 3–12. Open: Memorial Day to Labor Day daily 9:30 a.m.–6 p.m.; rest of
the year Mon–Sat 10 a.m.–5 p.m., Sun 1–5 p.m. Allow 3 hours.*

Great Lakes Aquarium
Duluth

The only all freshwater aquarium in the United States gives visitors a look
at what's in Lake Superior, including some 70 species of fish from the
Great Lakes, including a giant lake sturgeon in the Isle Royale tank. Thirty
interactive exhibits plus exhibits from other freshwater lakes and rivers
of the world are on display, including a current show of animals and fish
from Africa's Lake Victoria.

353 Harbor Dr. ☎ 218-740-FISH (218-740-3474). www.glaquarium.org. *RV parking: Designated lot or street parking. Admission: $10.95 adults, $8.45 seniors, $5.95
ages 3–11. Open: Fri–Wed 10 a.m.–6p.m., Thurs 10 a.m.–8 p.m. Allow 2 hours.*

Headwaters of the Mississippi
Itasca State Park, Lake Itasca

In 1832, a scholarly geographer named Henry Schoolcraft, after trekking
through the area with local Indians, decided the headwaters of the great
Mississippi lay in this lake in northern Minnesota. Although both local
Ojibwas and French trappers called it Elk Lake, he renamed it Itasca from
syllables in the Latin *veritas caput,* meaning "true head." What's fun here
for the visitor is to leap or tiptoe across the small trickling stream form-
ing the Mississippi via a log footbridge or a footpath of slippery rocks
placed in the water. A museum at the site details the evidence. A quarter-
mile walk along a wooded trail takes you to the headwaters.

*Take U.S. 2 west from Bemidji to its junction with SR 2 at Shevlin, turn south and
follow SR 2 to Lake Itasca, and then follow signage to Itasca State Park's east
entrance off U.S. 71. ☎ 218-266-2100. RV parking: Large designated parking lot.
Admission: Free. Open: Daily year-round. Allow 1–2 hours.*

Ironworld Discovery Center
Chisholm

We arrived at Ironworld on a September day dedicated to the
International Button Box Festival. It took only a moment to realize that a
button box actually is an accordion, and that this form of music didn't
fade with the death of TV's Lawrence Welk but rather is very much alive
and well in Minnesota. Music, storytelling, and polka dancing filled the
day along with plenty of snacks and dinners from **The Ethnic Restaurant.**
(See "Good eats.") You find a splendid museum on the history of the Iron
Range and the various ethnic groups that arrived in the New World to
work the mines. A small amusement park with a steam calliope carrousel

and Pellet Pete's miniature golf course entertains kids. Other attractions include a gem and mineral display, the Polka Hall of Fame, a vintage trolley ride to a reconstructed mining settlement called Glen Mine, early Scandinavian buildings, and a tribute museum to the CCC (Civilian Conservation Corps) camps of the 1930s, an organization that built many state and national parks facilities.

U.S. 169 W. ☎ *800-372-6437, 218-254-7959.* www.ironworld.com. *RV parking: Large designated lots adjacent to the center. Admission: $8 adults, $7 seniors, $6 ages 7–17. For special event days add $1. Open: Daily June to Labor Day, 9:30 a.m.–5 p.m. Allow half to a full day.*

Judy Garland Museum
Grand Rapids

Judy Garland was almost born in a trunk. In 1922, she arrived as the third daughter in a wannabe show business family — her dad Frank Gumm managed the local movie house and her mother Ethel played the piano to accompany the silent films. Garland started her career as Baby Gumm, tap dancing on the theater stage between features, and then graduated into the singing Gumm Sisters with her two older siblings. She changed her name to Judy Garland when she signed her first Hollywood contract. The downtown Central School, now called the **Itasca Heritage Center,** showcases **A Family Scrapbook** saluting Judy Garland, with replica costumes and ruby slippers, posters, photos, programs from local amateur theatrical productions directed by her mother, her father's golf clubs, and an abundance of family childhood photos. The center claims to have the world's largest collection of Garland memorabilia. The gift shop offers *Wizard of Oz* items, books, and videos.

Itasca Heritage Center (Central School), downtown at the junction of U.S. 169 and SR 2. ☎ *218-326-6431. RV parking: Street parking. Admission: $4 adults, $3 seniors, $2 ages 6–12. Open: Memorial Day to Labor Day, Mon–Sat 9:30 a.m.–5 p.m., Sun 11 a.m.–4 p.m.; rest of year closed Sun and major holidays. Allow 2 hours.*

Mall of America
Bloomington

Claiming to be the biggest shopping mall in the United States and the Midwest's largest entertainment complex, Mall of America offers the ultimate hanging-out-at-the-mall experience. Hundreds of brand name shops, dozens of theme restaurants, such as Rainforest Café, a roller coaster, aquarium, Knott's Camp Snoopy for kids, a LEGO center, sports bars, dance clubs, and a simulated motor speedway do their part to separate you from your money — but offer plenty of bang for the buck. You can walk around and ogle the attractions without spending a cent. Or you can shop 'til you drop.

I-494 and 24th Avenue. ☎ *952-858-8500 (Bloomington Convention & Visitors Bureau), 952-883-8600 (Camp Snoopy), 952-854-7700 (NASCAR Silicon Motor*

Speedway), 952-854-LIVE (854-5483) (America Live! Entertainment complex), 888-DIVE-TIME (888-348-3846) (UnderWater World). RV parking: Extremely large lots surround the mall. Admission: Free. Open: Mon–Sat 10 a.m.–9:30 p.m., Sun 11 a.m.–7 p.m. Closed Thanksgiving Day and Christmas Day.

More cool things to see and do

Minnesota is a great state for outdoor lovers with its countless lakes and forests. Animal fans can commune with wolves and bears in their natural habitats, fresh-food fanatics can pick their own fruits and vegetables in season for pennies, and trivia collectors find a treasure trove of oddities.

 ✔ **Like a rolling stone.** Singer **Bob Dylan's boyhood home** is in Hibbing, where he was born Robert Zimmerman in 1941 and attended the local high school, a fortresslike building erected by the area mine owners to entice workers to move to the area, so they could enlarge the mine in 1918. The home at 2425 Seventh Avenue South is privately owned, so you can *only drive by for a look;* do not attempt to visit.

 ✔ **Calling all loons.** A **giant loon** 20 feet long and 20 feet high floats on Silver Lake in the heart of Virginia; the big bird serves as the centerpiece to the Land of the Loon Festival, an arts and crafts festival that takes place over a weekend each June. ☎ 218-741-2717.

 ✔ **Leave the driving to them.** The **Greyhound Bus Origin Center** museum in Hibbing displays some beautiful examples of vintage buses, beginning with the 1914 Hupmobile, the company's first vehicle that was used to transport miners from Hibbing to nearby Alice. The 1956 Scenicruiser with its big windows and the very first Bookmobile also are on display.

 Hibbing Memorial Buildings, 23rd Street and Fifth Avenue East, Hibbing. ☎ 218-263-5814. RV parking: Street parking. Admission: $3 adults, $2 ages 17 and younger, $8 for a family. Open: Mid-May to mid-Sept, Mon–Sat 9 a.m.–5 p.m.; rest of year call for appointment, ☎ 218-262-3895 or 218-262-4166. Allow 1 hour.

 ✔ **Howl at the moon.** The **International Wolf Center** in Ely not only tells the story of timber wolves through exhibits and displays but also has a pack of wolves in residence in a natural habitat area. A viewing theater enables visitors to watch wild wolves going about their daily routines, including feeding on roadkill deer (not a sight for the young or the squeamish). Scheduled night strolls near the center let you howl with the wolves. Intensive weekend programs are available.

 96 SR 169 (east of town), Ely. ☎ 800-ELY-WOLF (800-359-9653), 218-365-4695. www.wolf.org. RV parking: Designated lot. Admission: $7 adults, $6 seniors, $3.25 ages 6–12, special weekend programs at

various prices. Open: May–Sept daily 9 a.m.–7 p.m., Oct–Apr weekends only. Wolf demonstrations at 11 a.m., and 2, 4, and 6 p.m. Allow a minimum of 2 hours.

✔ **Go for the goal.** Eveleth is entitled to be hockey's mecca because the first ice hockey game in the United States was played in this town in 1903. The **United States Hockey Hall of Fame** salutes the stars, tells the history of the game, even has a Zamboni display and a mock shooting rink with an electronic goalie for you to try to score against. The world's largest hockey stick, 107 feet long and weighing more than three tons, is on display with its own giant rubber puck.

U.S. 53 and Hat Trick Avenue, Eveleth. ☎ **800-443-7825**, 218-744-5167. www.ushockeyhall.com. RV parking: Designated lot or street parking. Admission: $8 adults, $7 seniors, $6 ages 13–17, $4 ages 6–12. Open: May–Nov Mon–Sat 9 a.m.–5 p.m., Sun 10 a.m.– 3 p.m.; Dec–Apr Thurs–Sat 9 a.m.–5 p.m. Closed major holidays. Allow 1–3 hours, depending on how big a fan you are.

✔ **Bear in mind.** The **Vince Shute Wildlife Sanctuary** shelters some 60 black bears (in addition to other native wildlife) in a 360-acre property. From a viewing platform, visitors can get close enough to photograph the bears without disturbing their habitat.

Orr. ☎ **218-757-0172.** www.orrmn.com. RV parking: A parking lot large enough for RVs is nearby with a free shuttle to the sanctuary. Call the Orr Chamber of Commerce at ☎ 800-357-9255 for information about the area. Admission: Free/donation suggested. Open: May to early Oct, Tues–Sun 5 p.m. to dusk. Allow 1 hour.

Weekend wonder

Instead of traveling the entire Paul Bunyan route, you can opt for one of three short road trips in northern Minnesota. First, the **North Shore Drive** from Duluth along Lake Superior offers some great sightseeing, good camping, and easy driving except for sometimes bumper-to-bumper conditions in peak season. Our second suggestion is a **round-trip from Duluth up SR 53 to Virginia** and the Iron Range, with a half-day spent at Ironworld, then heading west across U.S. 169 to Grand Rapids, and returning to Duluth on U.S. 2. A third possibility is to take **U.S. 2 from Duluth west to Bemidji,** visit Paul Bunyan and Babe the Blue Ox in both Bemidji and **Akeley,** cover the **Mississippi headwaters,** and then return to Duluth on SR 200 and U.S. 2.

Sleeping and Eating on the Road

You'll have no trouble finding a place to camp because northern Minnesota is chockablock with private campgrounds and state parks at a ratio of one or more per lake in some areas. Still, if areas seem crowded with campers as you travel through them, you can call ahead and make a reservation for your next overnight.

All campgrounds in this chapter have public flush toilets, showers, and sanitary dump stations unless designated otherwise. Toll-free numbers, where listed, are for reservations only. See Chapter 9 for how we choose our favorite campgrounds.

Our favorite campgrounds

Bear Paw Campground
$$ Itasca State Park, Lake Itasca

This park combines history, sightseeing, and camping, and some sites are open year-round. An 11-mile Wilderness Drive meanders through the park, and a number of short hiking trails suitable for children lead to individual points of interest. The lakeside location comes with swimming, boating, and fishing, as well as boat and tackle rentals. Make reservations if you plan to stay in July or August.

From SR 200 and U.S. 71, follow state park signs to park, campground is off Wilderness Drive. ☎ *218-266-22129. Total of 35 sites with water and 20- and 30-amp electric, no full hookups, no pull-throughs. Rates: $15–$18 per site. MC, V. 15-day maximum stay.*

Bemidji KOA
$$$ Bemidji

The owners of this quiet, shaded, rural campground love their trees and take good care of their park. You find plenty of level pull-throughs, although RVers with slideouts will need to maneuver around trees at some sites. Summer weekend activities include hot dog roasts, movies, and bike rentals. The location isn't far from the headwaters of the Mississippi, casinos, amusement parks, and shopping.

5707 U.S. 2, Bemidji, MN 56601. (2 miles west of Bemidji, north side of U.S. 2 between mileposts 109 and 110.) ☎ *800-562-1742, 218-751-1792.* www.koa.com. *Total of 75 sites with water and 20- and 30-amp electric, 30 full hookups, 60 pull-throughs. CATV, dataport, laundry. Rates: $30 per site. MC, V. Open: May 1–Oct 15.*

Forest Hills RV & Golf Resort
$$$ Detroit Lakes

As the name implies, campers get a resort atmosphere and two golf courses: an 18-hole championship golf course and an 18-hole miniature golf course. Other bonuses include a large indoor pool and hot tub. Sites are large, measuring 45 feet wide by 60 feet long.

From junction of U.S. 59 and U.S. 10, go west 3.3 miles on U.S. 10 to campground on the left. ☎ *800-482-3441. Total of 150 sites with 30- and 50-amp electric, all full hookups, 9 pull-throughs. Dataport, laundry, golf course, pool/spa. Rates: $26 per site. MC, V. Open: May 1–Oct 1.*

Minneapolis SW KOA

$$$–$$$$ **Jordan**

Conveniently located near Mall of America, this resort-style RV park has a heated indoor pool, miniature golf, volleyball, and horseshoes. Golf and horseback riding are nearby. Also a member of Good Sam, the park provides wide sites, some with side-by-side hookups. Site surfaces are gravel and grass with some patios and some shade. Big rigs are welcome.

3315 W 166th St., Jordan, MN 55352. (From Junction of U.S. 169 and SR 41, go south 4 miles on U.S. 169 to campground on the left.) ☎ *800-562-6317, 952-492-6440.* www.koa.com. *Total of 93 sites with water and 30- and 50-amp electric, 33 full hookups, 50 pull-throughs. Dataport, laundry, phone jacks, pool. Rates: $28–$33 per site. DISC, MC, V. Open: Apr 1–Oct 16.*

Ogston's RV Park

$$$ **Saginaw**

Ten miles northwest of Duluth, this campground provides large sites, 40 feet wide by 100 feet long. The park has a pond with freshwater fishing, swimming, and boating.

6189 Old Highway 53 (U.S. 53), Saginaw, MN 55779. (From junction of SR 194 and U.S. 53, go north 4.7 miles on U.S. 53 to CR 15, then north 0.1 mile on CR 15 to Miller Trund Road, and east 0.5 mile to campground on the left.) ☎ *218-729-9528. Total of 64 sites with 30- and 50-amp electric, all full hookups, 21 pull-throughs. Laundry. Rates: $23 per site. MC, V. Open: May 1–Oct 1.*

Runner-up campgrounds

Buffalo River State Park

$$ **Glyndon**   Just off U.S. 10 a few miles east of Moorhead, this state park is on the Buffalo River, which offers swimming and fishing. Some of the narrow, gravel sites are shaded, and all provide water and electric hookups. In season, a naturalist program is provided. *From juncton of U.S. 10 and SR 9, go east 1.5 miles on U.S. 10 to state park on the right, follow signs to campground.* ☎ *218-498-2124. Total of 35 sites with water and 20- and 50-amp electric, no full hookups, no pull-throughs. Rates: $12–$15 per site. DISC, MC, V. 14-day maximum stay.*

Cloquet/Duluth KOA

$$$–$$$$ **Cloquet**   We like this well-kept campground, which makes a good base for Duluth attractions and the North Shore Drive along Lake

Superior. The only drawback, at least when we stayed there, were train noises at night. Some side-by-side hookups. *1479 Old Carlton Rd., Cloquet, MN 55720. (From I-35 Exit 239, follow blue camping signs; from U.S. 2, go south on SR 33 to Washington, turn left to 14th Street, and then right 3 miles to campground.)* ☎ *800-562-9506, 218-879-5726.* www.koa.com. *Total of 51 sites with water and 20- and 30-amp electric, 5 full hookups, 26 pull-throughs. Dataport, laundry, pool/spa. Rates: $26–$32 per site. DISC, MC, V. Open: May 1–Oct 15.*

Country Campground

$$ **Detroit Lakes** This Good Sam park offers wide grass sites 40 by 60 feet, paddleboats to explore Glawe Lake, fishing and other boat rentals. A fenced playground keeps the kids safe, and two different amusement parks are within a short distance. *From junction of U.S. 10 and U.S. 59, go south 2.2 miles on U.S. 59 to CR 22, then south 0.5 mile to West Lake Drive, and east 1.2 miles to 260th Avenue, and then south 0.8 mile to the campground on the left.* ☎ *218-847-9621.* www.lakesnet.net/ccdl. *Total of 30 sites with 30-amp electric, all full hookups, 14 pull-throughs. Dataport. Rates: $18 per site. MC, V.*

Forest Heights RV Park

$$ **Hibbing** In the heart of the Iron Range, this campground provides grass sites, some of them shaded, most fairly narrow. The location is convenient for the Ironworld Discovery Center and the Greyhound Bus Origin Center museum. *2240 E 25th St., Hibbing, MN 55746. (From junction of U.S. 169 and SR 37, go north 1.3 miles on 169 to 25th Street, and then east 1 mile to campground on the right.)* ☎ *218-263-5782. Total of 44 sites with 20-, 30-, and 50-amp electric, all full hookups, 20 pull-throughs. Dataport, laundry. Rates: $16–$18 per site. MC, V. Open: May 1–Oct 15.*

Moorhead/Fargo KOA

$$$ **Moorhead** Just across the Red River from Fargo, North Dakota, this KOA offers wide sites, and mostly side-by-side hookups. Golf and shopping area nearby. *4396 28th Ave. S., Moorhead, MN 56560. (From junction of I-94 and SR 52, go north 1 block on SR 52 to CR 14, and then east 1 mile to campground on left.)* ☎ *800-562-0271, 218-233-0671.* www.koa.com. *Total of 85 sites with water and 30- and 50-amp electric, 16 full hookups, a few pull-throughs. CATV, dataport, laundry, pool. Rates: $24–$29 per site. AE, DISC, MC, V. Open: May 1–Oct 15.*

Good eats

Treats to look for in Minnesota include wild rice (especially the hand-picked wild version as opposed to the paddy-grown wild rice), fresh walleye pike, the Yugoslav nut pastry called potica, fresh-picked berries in season (see the sidebar "Picking your own fresh berries"), Cornish pasties, Gouda and cheddar farm cheeses, Harelson apples, and smoked fish from Lake Superior. For information on grocery stores and farmers markets, see "Stocking the Pantry" earlier in this chapter.

Picking your own fresh berries

The whole family can have fun picking fresh berries in season or even ordering ahead to get already picked berries. In northern Minnesota, strawberries peak in June and July and raspberries and blueberries in July and August. We eat our fill of fresh berries, and then freeze them or make jams and jellies in our RV kitchen to take home. The following list names a few berry growers along the Paul Bunyan drive, although you may spot others. The berry growers ask that you call ahead, whether you're looking to pick your own berries or buy fresh-picked ones. They can give you the hours and directions to their farms.

- **Berry Pine Farms,** Duluth (☎ 218-721-3250), offers prepicked or pick-your-own strawberries; containers are provided. Children are welcome. Homemade jams and jellies also are for sale.

- **Blueberry Meadows,** Grand Rapids (☎ 218-326-0671), has four varieties of pick-your-own blueberries. Open late July through Labor Day.

- **Blueberry Patch,** Bagley (☎ 218-785-2332), offers pick-your-own blueberries, usually beginning the last week of July. Call after July 20 for opening date.

- **The Blueberry Patch,** Gilbert (☎ 218-865-4100), asks that visitors bring their own containers for blueberries; strawberry containers provided. Supervised children are welcome. Open daily Monday through Saturday from 9 a.m. to 8 p.m. Hand-harvested wild rice also is for sale.

- **Country/Acre Blueberries,** Bemidji (☎ 218-751-0193), offers two varieties of organically grown blueberries available in July and August.

- **Lavalier's Berry Patch,** Grand Rapids (☎ 218-327-9199), has strawberries and blueberries to pick yourself or have picked for you.

- **Peterson's Berry Farm,** Eveleth (☎ 218-744-5759), offers strawberries, Saskatoons (Juneberries), raspberries, and blueberries; free picking containers provided. Open late June through August.

- **Shay's Berries,** Two Harbors (☎ 218-834-5221), has pick-your-own organic blueberries. Prepicked raspberries, and organic herbs and vegetables, such as basil, leeks, and tomatoes, are for sale.

- **Uncle T.L.'s Berry Ranch,** Bemidji (☎ 218-751-0830), has pick-your-own hours for blueberries, raspberries, and currants. Asparagus is for sale in May and June.

- **Betty's Pies:** 215 SR 61 East, Two Harbors (☎ 218-834-3367). Betty's sells just what the name implies, plenty of homemade pies, plus sandwiches, salads, and soups, and the occasional slab of walleye pike. Pies range from custard to fresh blueberry, a dozen different flavors a day, plus homemade cookies and cakes. Open daily from 7 a.m. to 7 p.m.

- **The Ethnic Restaurant:** In the Ironworld Discovery Center, U.S. 169 W, Chisholm (☎ 800-372-6437, 218-254-7959). On designated days and special events weekends, the restaurant serves a $10 ethnic buffet that may include roast lamb, *sarmas* (stuffed cabbage), *porketta* (thinly sliced, highly-seasoned roast pork), Swedish meatballs, and potica. If the buffet isn't open during your visit, or if you want something simpler, look for the open-air snack bar that vends porketta in a potato roll, gyros, sarmas, pasties, bratwurst with sauerkraut, Polish sausage, and "pickle on a stick." Open daily from 11 a.m. to 2 p.m.

✔ **Italian Bakery:** 205 S First St., Virginia (☎ **218-741-3464**). This bakery is the home of a Yugoslav dessert called potica (pronounced po-*teet*-sah), a dense, multi-layered pastry filled with finely chopped walnuts in butter and cream. Sold in loaves of 1 or 1½ pounds, potica keeps wonderfully well in the refrigerator and freezes well. If you want a quick dessert, warm a slice in the microwave and top it with a scoop of ice cream. The biscotti also are delicious. Open Monday through Friday from 5 a.m. to 5 p.m. and Saturday from 6 a.m. to 3 p.m.

✔ **Widman's Candy Shop:** 4325 13th St. SW, Fargo, North Dakota (☎ **800-688-8351**), and 106 S Third St., Grand Forks, North Dakota (☎ **701-775-3480**). Widman's heads our North Dakota list because we're addicted to the crunchy, salty-sweet, chocolate-dipped potato chips they call Chippers. The ruffled potato chips are made from local Red River Valley potatoes, and then dipped into a thick dark chocolate. On the shelf, you also find cow pies, chocolate covered marshmallow and caramel, far more elegant than the name implies, and "hot air," a buttery honeycomb candy covered with chocolate. Open Monday through Saturday from 9:30 a.m. to 7 p.m.

Shopping along the Way

If shopping is your passion, plan to detour your RV to the **Mall of America** in Bloomington. (See "Must-see attractions.")

In the Smoky Hills National Forest, beside SR 34 west of Osage and reached by a boardwalk, is the **Smoky Hills Arts Center,** a group of artisans with studios and shops.

The **Bemidji Woolen Mills Factory Store,** 301 Irvine Ave., Bemidji (☎ **218-751-5166**), sells woolen goods produced on-site since 1920, along with other selected American brand names — sweaters, casual and dress wool slacks for men and women, and outerwear. Shop hours are Monday through Saturday from 8 a.m. to 5 p.m. and Sundays from 10 a.m. to 5 p.m.

Fast Facts

Area Codes

The following area codes are in effect in Minnesota: **218, 320, 507, 612, 630, 651,** and **952.**

Emergency

Call ☎ **911.** Call ☎ **651-282-6871** for the State Patrol.

Hospitals

Major hospitals along the route are in Duluth, Grand Rapids, and Minneapolis.

Information

Contact the Department of Tourism online at www.exploreminnesota.com or call ☎ 800-657-3700 or 651-296-5029.

Laws

RV riders in the front seats and children 4 and younger anywhere in the vehicle must wear seat belts. The maximum speed limit on interstate highways is 70 mph. The limit in urban areas is lower.

Road and Weather Conditions

Call ☎ 800-542-0220.

Taxes

Minnesota sales tax is 6.5%; local taxes may raise this figure. The state gas tax is 20¢ a gallon.

Time Zone

Minnesota is on central standard time.

Chapter 19

The Ozarks and Branson: Hot Springs to Springfield

. . . .

In This Chapter

▶ Driving through the Ozarks

▶ Toe-tapping to real mountain music

▶ Canoeing the Buffalo National River

▶ Frying some catfish and hush puppies

. . . .

*F*or all their craggy remoteness, the **Arkansas Ozarks,** among America's oldest mountains, are only about 2,300 feet high. "Our mountains ain't high," goes the saying, "but our valleys sure are deep."

The Ozarks are the heart of American folk crafts and music, preserved primarily because the area has been remote and poor for almost a century. During the Depression of the 1930s, many of the hill people gravitated to industrial cities of the North to make a living, leaving parts of the Ozarks to revert to wilderness. In the 1950s, when so much of the South was tearing down Victorian buildings to put up modern facades, lovely-but-declining old towns, such as **Hot Springs** and **Eureka Springs,** made do with what they had because they couldn't afford modernization.

In the 1960s, a little-known lakeside Missouri town called **Branson** pioneered live country music shows. By the 1980s, major music stars flocked to Branson to build their own theaters, and the town soon grew into the second most-visited tourist site in the United States, outnumbered only by Orlando, Florida.

Getting There

A rambling loop drive from **Hot Springs, Arkansas,** heads north on SR 7 to **Harrison,** and then west via U.S. 412, north via SR 23, and west again via SR 12 to **War Eagle, Rogers,** and, via SR 112 north to **Bentonville.** From there, we follow U.S. 62 to the picturesque Victorian town of

The Ozarks and Branson

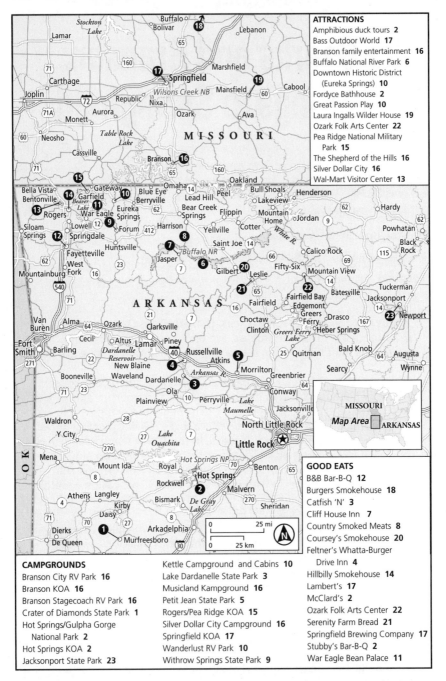

ATTRACTIONS
Amphibious duck tours **2**
Bass Outdoor World **17**
Branson family entertainment **16**
Buffalo National River Park **6**
Downtown Historic District
   (Eureka Springs) **10**
Fordyce Bathhouse **2**
Great Passion Play **10**
Laura Ingalls Wilder House **19**
Ozark Folk Arts Center **22**
Pea Ridge National Military
   Park **15**
The Shepherd of the Hills **16**
Silver Dollar City **16**
Wal-Mart Visitor Center **13**

GOOD EATS
B&B Bar-B-Q **12**
Burgers Smokehouse **18**
Catfish 'N' **3**
Cliff House Inn **7**
Country Smoked Meats **8**
Coursey's Smokehouse **20**
Feltner's Whatta-Burger
   Drive Inn **4**
Hillbilly Smokehouse **14**
Lambert's **17**
McClard's **2**
Ozark Folk Arts Center **22**
Serenity Farm Bread **21**
Springfield Brewing Company **17**
Stubby's Bar-B-Q **2**
War Eagle Bean Palace **11**

CAMPGROUNDS
Branson City RV Park **16**
Branson KOA **16**
Branson Stagecoach RV Park **16**
Crater of Diamonds State Park **1**
Hot Springs/Gulpha Gorge
   National Park **2**
Hot Springs KOA **2**
Jacksonport State Park **23**

Kettle Campground and Cabins **10**
Lake Dardanelle State Park **3**
Musicland Kampground **16**
Petit Jean State Park **5**
Rogers/Pea Ridge KOA **15**
Silver Dollar City Campground **16**
Springfield KOA **17**
Wanderlust RV Park **10**
Withrow Springs State Park **9**

Eureka Springs and east to **Bear Creek Springs,** and then drive north to **Branson** and **Springfield, Missouri,** on U.S. 65.

Head back into Arkansas on U.S. 65, turning east at Leslie on SR 66 to **Mountain View,** home of the Ozark Folk Center, and scenic Jacksonport State Park with its spacious, appealing campground. A short jog south on U.S. 67 takes you into **Little Rock** to conclude the journey. The total distance driven is approximately **700 miles.** (See "The Ozarks and Branson" map in this chapter.)

Note that some of the most colorful roads through the Ozarks are also narrow, steep, and winding. If you and your RV aren't comfortable maneuvering the back roads, you can stick to main routes — taking the less curvy SR 9 or I-30 to Little Rock, and I-40 west to Fort Smith and U.S. 71 north to Bentonville. U.S. 62 from Eureka Springs to U.S. 65 at Bear Creek Springs also is easy to drive, and so is U.S. 65 north to Branson and Springfield. We've safely driven motorhomes from 27- to 36-feet long through the Ozarks on all the routes suggested in this driving tour.

The only real traffic jams in this area are on the streets of Branson, where you can spend more than an hour inching your way along SR 76 through the middle of town in high season. Locals tell of wives who hop out of the RV, go shopping, and return to the vehicle a block or two farther along. The best way to avoid this is to leave your RV at the campground and go into town via the local shuttle.

Planning Ahead

Branson bustles with activities and shows between **April and the end of October.** During the off-season, most of the theaters and campgrounds are closed. The Ozarks are beautiful in **spring** — when the dogwood trees, redbuds, lilacs, and May apples are blossoming and the weather is mild — and in **autumn** when fall temperatures turn leaves red and gold and good weather is likely through October. In **summer,** days can be awfully hot, and the heaviest traffic and campground use is in effect.

If you know when you want to go and where you want to stay, making **campground reservations** in Branson well ahead of time is a good idea. Making show reservations doesn't seem to be as important. Most RVers wait until they arrive at their campground, then make reservations and/or purchase tickets. Check the Branson Web site at www. bransonworld.com to see who's playing when.

Branson has some **35 live-music theaters,** including the new Roy Rogers/ Dale Evans Museum and Theater, that play daily matinee and evening shows; some also even offer breakfast shows. Don't expect a late night, however, because the last show usually starts at 8 p.m.

Dress is casual in this part of the world, so **pack** your jeans, shorts, T-shirts, and lightweight cottons if you're coming in summer. For spring and fall, add a sweater or jacket, some lightweight rain gear, and hiking boots. You can easily arrange mountain biking, canoeing, white-water rafting, hiking, fishing, and horseback riding when you're in the Ozarks, so bring along the gear for your favorite sport.

Allow **one to two weeks** for your Ozarks vacation, depending on how many sports activities you plan to schedule and how many shows you want to attend in Branson.

Stocking the Pantry

You need to stock up your pantry in Little Rock, Hot Springs, or Springfield, because most rural stores in the Ozarks are long on country ham, smoked bacon, homemade jams, and pepper relish, but short on everything else. Cooked and ready to eat in or take out, chicken, barbecue, and catfish are cheap and available almost everywhere.

If you want any alcoholic beverages in your pantry, stock up ahead of time because parts of Arkansas and Missouri are *dry,* meaning they have restricted sales or no sales of alcoholic beverages. Even in communities where sales are legal, Sundays may be completely dry. Some communities that do permit limited alcohol sales operate on a *private-club basis,* whereby you pay to become a member to access the bar.

Driving the Ozarks and Branson

Hot Springs, Arkansas, is home to the only urban national park in the United States, a fact that mystifies many foreign visitors who arrive expecting to see another Yellowstone or Yosemite. Known nowadays as the town where former President Bill Clinton grew up, Hot Springs once was the most fashionable watering hole in the Midwest. The notorious gangster Al Capone loved to soak in the hot springs and booked the entire fourth floor of the Arlington Hotel when he came to take in the waters. Baseball great Babe Ruth was another frequent visitor. Until the 1960s, gambling flourished in Hot Springs. Elegant old hotels and bathhouses, such as the **Fordyce Bathhouse,** which has been renovated to serve as a visitor center for the national park, line Central Avenue. (See "Must-see attractions," later in this chapter.) You can also board *amphibious ducks* — World War II landing craft converted to tourist transportation — and bop around Lake Hamilton over land and water. (See "More cool things to see and do," later in this chapter.) When it's time to eat, make a beeline for **McClard's** famous barbecue restaurant. (See "Good eats," later in this chapter.)

Parking space in downtown Hot Springs is limited for RVs, so you're better off leaving the motorhome or trailer at an RV campground and heading into town in a smaller vehicle. Town parking lots are across Central Avenue from Bathhouse Row along Bath and Exchange streets and opposite the Arlington Hotel on Central Avenue, which is also SR 7. *Note: Vehicles longer than 30 feet are not permitted* to drive up Hot Springs Mountain Drive.

Some 65 miles south of Hot Springs via U.S. 70 and SR 27 is **Crater of Diamonds State Park,** America's only publicly accessible diamond mine, where you not only can dig for the elusive gems for a modest fee, but you also get to keep any diamonds that you unearth. (See "Our favorite campgrounds," later in this chapter.)

The **most scenic mountain drive** from Hot Springs north to Harrison is the 160-mile stretch of SR 7, a winding two-lane highway that meanders past Lake Ouchita State Park, the Ouchita Mountains (which can be dazzling in autumn), Nimrod Dam and Lake, and **Lake Dardanelle State Park** (see "Our favorite campgrounds"). Along the way, you have plenty of opportunities to shop for country ham, handmade quilts, and tacky "hillbilly" souvenirs.

An even more rugged stretch of mountains lies ahead in the **Ozark National Forest.** If you want a relaxing change of pace from the demanding road, take I-40 west from **Russellville to Fort Smith,** then head north on I-540 to **Bentonville,** and pick up the original tour.

North of Dardanelle, SR 7 winds its way up through the Ozark National Forest past hillbilly trading posts and pretty mountain villages, such as **Pelsor,** home of Hankins Country Store, dating from 1922, and **Cowell.**

The Buffalo River, the only major stream in Arkansas without a dam, courses its way for 125 miles through the Ozarks between Buffalo City and Boxley. Along this route you find the **Buffalo National River Park,** a favorite destination for canoeing. SR 7 crosses the river park at **Pruitt.** You can rent gear at several outfitters along the river. (See "More cool things to see and do.")

From **Harrison,** a major junction and gateway to Branson, Missouri, our drive turns west to **War Eagle,** off SR 12 near Rogers. The War Eagle Mill, a working gristmill, and the **War Eagle Bean Palace** sell and serve stone-ground grits, cornbread, pancakes, and waffles. (See "Good eats.") A few miles west is **Bentonville,** where Sam and Mary Walton opened their first five- and ten-cent store in 1945. Enshrined on the main square in town, the original store, now a museum and visitor center, was the modest beginning of the Wal-Mart empire. (See "More cool things to see and do" for the **Wal-Mart Visitor Center.)**

From Bentonville, SR 72 leads northeast to Pea Ridge, site of the **Pea Ridge National Military Park** and one of the Civil War's most unusual battles. (See "More cool things to see and do.")

Continuing east on U.S. 62 from Pea Ridge, SR 23 leads to **Eureka Springs,** probably the most charming town in the Ozarks. Block after block of Victorian houses are listed on the National Register of Historic Places. Hillsides are so steep that some houses can be entered on the first floor on one street and on the fifth floor on the next street uphill.

This jewel of a town delighted even as tough a character as Carry Nation, fiery opponent of alcohol, who settled here in 1908, naming her home Hatchet Hall after her favorite saloon-smashing tool. The town has continued to attract fundamentalists and the religious right, and major tourist attractions today include the long-running *Great Passion Play* (see "More cool things to see and do"); the Anita Bryant Theater, where the former orange-juice spokeswoman appears on stage in her live musical autobiography; and a trio of attractions — a 70-foot concrete statue of Christ that can be seen over the treetops, a Bible museum, and a Christ Only Art Gallery with some 500 portraits of Jesus.

Our route continues east along U.S. 62 to its junction with U.S. 65 and then turns north to **Branson.** This little town that nobody ever heard of a few years ago now claims to be "the country music capital of the universe," in case a few banjo-strumming Martians try to horn in on the act. Today, it claims to attract more visitors every year than Yellowstone, Grand Canyon, or Washington, D.C., and comes in second only to Orlando, Florida, as America's most-visited locale.

For the kids, **Silver Dollar City** is a classic 40-year-old theme park. For the sentimental, an outdoor evening drama called *The Shepherd of the Hills* is based on a book popular back in 1907. Strictly G-rated, the play, written in mountain dialect, features a large cast, horse-drawn wagons, and a burning cabin. (See "More cool things to see and do" for details on the park and play.)

From Branson, **Springfield** is only 40 miles north via U.S. 65. Springfield boasts not only the **Bass Outdoor World** (also called Bass Pro Shop), one of Missouri's major tourist attractions, but also offbeat **Lambert's,** a restaurant known as "the home of the throwed roll." (See "Must-see attractions" and "Good eats," respectively.)

Fans of the *Little House on the Prairie* books and long-running TV series may want to drive the 35 miles east from Springfield on U.S. 60 to **Mansfield,** where the **Laura Ingalls Wilder House** has been turned into a museum. Author Wilder wrote the popular series here. (See "More cool things to see and do.")

The route returns to Arkansas and the Ozarks via U.S. 65 to **Harrison** and southeast across Buffalo National River Park at **Silver Hill.** We like to pause in the pleasant little town of **Leslie** for some delectable baked goods from **Serenity Farm Bread.** (See "Good eats.")

From Leslie, cut across SR 66 to **Mountain View** and the **Ozark Folk Arts Center.** (See "Must-see attractions.") Folk musician Jimmy Driftwood probably best described the music at the center. When asked the difference between the folk music at the Ozark Folk Arts Center and the hillbilly and country music shows staged elsewhere in Arkansas, Jimmy said, "We don't allow counterfeit cornpone around here," referring to the cornbread made in the area. The cultural traditions of the mountain regions — the music, dancing, handicrafts, foods, and folkways — are cherished and preserved at the center.

From Mountain View, follow scenic SR 14 east to **Jacksonport State Park.** (See "Our favorite campgrounds.") From Jacksonport, you can easily swing south along U.S. 67 to **Little Rock** and the end of the tour.

Must-see attractions

Bass Outdoor World
Springfield, Missouri

This vast sporting goods store and museum offers everything that you can imagine from hunting and fishing licenses to fly-tying demonstrations and deer-processing books, such as *Field Dressing and Skinning.* Four-story waterfalls flow inside the store, surrounded by craggy rock cliffs and mounted masterpieces of taxidermy (goats and bears, in particular). You can test your new rifle, too, at the indoor shooting range. On the second floor is a museum of the outdoors, a barbershop, and a macho all-day eatery called Hemingway's with a 30,000-gallon aquarium stocked with sharks.

1935 S. Campbell at Sunshine, which is also U.S. 60 and SR 13. ☎ *800-227-7776 General information, 417-887-7334 store.* www.basspro.com. *RV parking: Huge parking lot with plenty of room. Admission: Store is free, museum $5.50 adults, $4.50 seniors, $2.50 ages 17 and younger, $14.50 family. Open: Museum Mon–Sat 8 a.m.– 8 p.m., Sun 9 a.m.–5 p.m.; store Mon–Sat 7 a.m.–10 p.m., Sun 9 a.m.–6 p.m. Allow 2–3 hours.*

Branson family entertainment
Branson, Missouri

With some 35 live music theaters, the rapidly growing entertainment center of Branson claims more theater seats than Broadway, as much musical excitement as Nashville, and a wholesome atmosphere for the whole family. The stars, many with their own theaters, range from aging pop singers, such as Andy Williams and Bobby ("Blue Velvet") Vinton, to Texas honky-tonk musician Mickey Gilley, violin virtuoso Shoji Tabuchi, Russian comic Yakov Smirnoff, country singer and comedienne Barbara Fairchild, Las Vegas headliner Wayne Newton, stars of the Lawrence Welk TV show, the Roy Rogers/Dale Evans Museum and Theater, and the Osmond Brothers. Throw in a few spectacles — Dixie Stampede horse show with racing ostriches, pianist Frederick Antonio with two grand pianos and 40,000 gallons of swirling water fountains, and *The Promise,* a dramatization of the story of Jesus including live animals and award-winning special effects — and you can see how they please the crowds and the kids.

Branson is in southwestern Missouri on U.S. 65, 12 miles north of the Arkansas border. Branson Chamber of Commerce/Convention & Visitors Bureau, ☎ *800-214-3661.* www.explorebranson.com. *Most attractions closed Jan and Feb. Show tickets: adults $19–$36, children $10–$22, some free for ages 12 and younger. Show times: Some breakfast shows, afternoon matinees, most evening shows at 8 p.m.*

Downtown Historic District
Eureka Springs, Arkansas

The entire downtown area of Eureka Springs is on the National Register of Historic Places with colorful Victorian "painted ladies" lining the steep, narrow streets. Limestone walls built from native stone mark boundaries, and streets cross at peculiar angles, none making a perfect right angle. Some houses that appear to be single story with an entrance from one street turn out to have four more floors underneath when you get to the next block downhill. The Catholic church is entered through its belltower.

The town was founded to exploit its 63 healing hot springs with board-inghouses springing up to feed health-seekers. The arrival of the railroad in 1883 spurred the building of more than 50 plush hotels in the next three decades. Today, crafts shops, art galleries, superb inns, and several outstanding restaurants make Eureka Springs a romantic getaway for urban honeymooners with the largest and most upscale collection of bed-and-breakfasts in the state.

Don't attempt to drive your RV in Eureka Springs. Instead, leave the rig at the campground if you're staying in the area or park it in one of the open-air lots at the base of the town (before the main roads climb uphill), and use the town's open air trolleys for sightseeing.

Eureka Springs is in the northwestern corner of Arkansas on U.S. 62. ☎ *800-6EUREKA (800-638-7352). (Eureka Springs Tourist Center).* www.eurekasprings chamber.com. *RV parking: Scarce; use the Eureka Springs Trolley System (*☎ *479-253-9572) for a 1-hour guided tour or transport around town; $7.50 adults and children. Allow 2–3 hours.*

Fordyce Bathhouse
Hot Springs National Park, Arkansas

The Spanish Renaissance Fordyce Bathhouse, the most splendidly restored structure along the town's famous Bathhouse Row, doubles as the visitor center for the national park and a museum of thermal bathing history. Go in and get park information from the rangers on duty, and then look around. An 8,000-piece stained-glass skylight illuminates the De Soto Fountain with its art deco statue of an Indian maiden offering a bowl of spring water to explorer Hernando De Soto. In the 1915 gymnasium, a spartan fitness center displays punching bags, vaulting horses, and acrobatic rings.

369 Central Ave., Hot Springs. ☎ *501-624-3383, ext 640.* www.nps.gov/hosp. *Admission: Free. Open: Daily 9 a.m.–5 p.m. Allow 1 hour.*

Ozark Folk Arts Center
Mountain View, Arkansas

The first folk cultural center in the United States, this center was created in 1973 to preserve the music, dancing, handicrafts, and folkways of the Ozarks. Two dozen individual craftsmen work inside the center. Cloggers, many of whom are elderly and who banter among themselves before, during, and after performances, often dance to the tunes of musicians who play at frequent intervals throughout the day. All musical selections must precede 1937; percussion and electronic amplification is not permitted. The center offers special gospel music concerts on Sunday evenings. The folk center's restaurant serves honest Arkansas food (see "Good eats") and a snack bar vends barbecue sandwiches and fried peach and apple pies.

Folk Center Road, north of town off SRs 5, 9, and 14. ☎ *870-269-3851.* www.ozark folkcenter.com. *RV parking: Large lot at base of center, free tram uphill to center. Admission: Center $9 adults, $6 ages 6–12; music shows $9 adults, $6 ages 6–12; combination ticket $15.50 adults, $8.25 ages 6–12. Open: May–Oct; center daily 10 a.m.–5:30 p.m.; music shows Mon–Sat 7:30 p.m.–9:30 p.m. Allow a half to a full day.*

More cool things to see and do

The Ozarks is a haven of unique American innovations and creations that reflect earlier eras. Sometimes you may think that you not only entered another time zone but also another century.

- ✔ **Paddle away the day.** During winter and spring months, the Buffalo River reaches its peak flow for canoeists and rafters. The **Buffalo National River Park,** the first designated national river, is a natural stream that's unique in a state of multiple fishing streams and lakes created by the U.S. Corps of Engineers.

   Wild Bill's Outfitter, Buffalo Point, Junction of SR 14 and SR 268 #1, Yellville, Arkansas. ☎ **800-554-8657** or 870-449-6235. www.ozark-float.com. You can rent canoes, rafts, and kayaks at Wild Bill's. You find additional outfitters in Jasper where SR 7 crosses the park, in Ponca where SR 43 crosses the park, in Tyler Bend and Silver Hill where U.S. 65 crosses the park, and in Buffalo Point where SR 14 crosses.

- ✔ **Waddle with the ducks.** Amphibious **duck tours** are popular land-and-sea excursions undertaken in World War II landing craft that have been converted for tourist transport. The ducks lumber along the main roads in town and then head for Lake Hamilton to walk on the water with plenty of laughing and splashing by kids and adults alike.

In Hot Springs, Arkansas: **Ducks in the Park Tours,** 316 Central Ave. (☎ **501-624-3825**), and **National Park Duck Tours,** 418 Central Ave. (☎ **800-682-7044,** 501-321-2911). RV parking: Scarce in town; look for parking lots across from Bathhouse Row on Bath and Exchange streets. Admission: $12 adults, $11 seniors, $7 ages 3–12. Tours: 9 a.m.–7 p.m. Allow 3 hours.

✔ **Catch the Ozarks' own religious spectacle.** More than 6 million people have come to see the *Great Passion Play,* the story of the last week of the life of Jesus with a large cast and many special effects. The popular Eureka Springs production has a cast of 250 actors, 40 sheep, 12 horses, 5 donkeys, and 3 camels.

Statue Road off U.S. 62 East, Eureka Springs, Arkansas ☎ **800-882-7529,** 479-253-9200. www.greatpassionplay.com. RV parking: Designated lots. Admission: $23.25 adults, $11.75 ages 4–11. Open: Late Apr through Oct, Mon–Tues and Thurs–Sat, 8:30 p.m., 7:30 p.m. after Labor Day.

✔ **Visit the little house in the Ozarks.** The **Laura Ingalls Wilder House** in Mansfield, Missouri, was the author's home from 1894 until her death in 1957. She wrote all nine of her "Little House on the Prairie" books here. The house is preserved as she left it, and handwritten manuscripts of the books are on display.

3068 Highway A, 1 mile east of the town square, Mansfield, Missouri. ☎ **417-924-3626.** RV parking: Designated lot. Admission: $8 adults, $6 seniors, $4 students ages 6–18. Open: Daily Mar 1–Oct 31 9 a.m.–5 p.m., Sun 12:30–5:30 p.m. Allow 2 hours.

✔ **Flip for Missouri. Pea Ridge National Military Park** commemorates the 1862 battle that decided whether Missouri became a member of the Union or the Confederacy. The battle also was the first in the Civil War in which Native Americans — two regiments of Cherokees on the Confederate side under tbe command of Brigadier General Albert Pike — participated. Depending on which historian you read, on the second day, the Cherokee troops either stood aside and were not sent into the battle or, more likely, went home after the first day, seeing little real reason to fight again.

On U.S. 62, 2 miles west of Garfield and 10 miles northeast of Rogers, Arkansas. ☎ **479-451-8122.** www.nps.gov/peri. Admission: $2 adults, free ages 17 and younger. Open: Daily 8 a.m.–5 p.m. Closed major holidays. Allow 2 hours.

✔ **Count sheep.** *The Shepherd of the Hills* is a rustic, outdoor drama based on Harold Bell Wright's 1907 novel of the same name. (The book also was made into a 1941 film starring John Wayne, which bears little resemblance to the original.) With a cast of 75, a whole herd of sheep, and a roaring bonfire on stage, the play holds your attention, even in a 2,000-seat arena.

SR 76, Branson, Missouri, 2 miles west of the strip. ☎ 417-334-4191. RV parking: Designated lots. Admission: Dinner and show $37.32 adults, $20.24 ages 4–16, family $101.39. Open: Daily dinner 6 p.m.– 8 p.m., show 8:30 p.m.

✔ **Skip the cave and hit the midway.** The original theme park called **Silver Dollar City** grew up around Marvel Cave back in the 1960s, but today's visitors tend to skip the cave (the 500 steep steps leading down into it may be one reason) and visit the rides, shops, craftsmen venues, and country music groups that perform daily throughout the park. Kids love the waterslide, the roller coaster, and rides on the paddlewheeler *Branson Belle.*

Indian Point Rd, Branson, Missouri, 9 miles west on SR 76. ☎ **800-475-9370,** 417-338-2611. www.silverdollarcity.com. RV parking: Large designated lot. Admission: $39.21 adults, $37.09 seniors, $28.61 ages 17 and younger. Open: Mid-Apr to late Dec, daily 9:30 a.m.–7 p.m. Allow a half to a full day.

✔ **Witness the dawn of Wal-Mart.** In Bentonville, Arkansas, Sam and Mary Walton opened their first modest five- and ten-cent store in 1945. Today, the store is the **Wal-Mart Visitor Center,** a museum filled with 1950s and 1960s merchandise, 35 electronic historical displays, and Sam's original desk.

105 N Main St., on the Square, Bentonville, Arkansas. ☎ **479-273-1329.** RV parking: Street parking. Admission: Free. Open: Mar–Oct Tue–Sat 9 a.m.–5 p.m., closed Sunday and Monday. Allow 1 hour.

Weekend wonders

If you want to condense this scenic Ozarks drive and Branson entertainment holiday into a weekend, you can begin your drive in **Hot Springs,** Arkansas, follow SR 7 north through the Ozarks into **Harrison**, and on to **Branson,** Missouri. The drive itself is slightly less than **200 miles,** but may take all day on the narrow, curvy road.

An alternative route is to drive from **Little Rock** north on I-40 to U.S. 65, turn east at **Clinton** on SR 16 to **Mountain View** for a visit to the Ozark Folk Center, and then follow scenic SR 14 northwest across the Buffalo National River Park at Buffalo Point and on to **Yellville,** where you turn west on U.S. 62/U.S. 412 to join U.S. 65 for the short trip north to **Branson.** This shortened tour runs around **230 miles.**

Sleeping and Eating on the Road

Arkansas state parks are RV friendly. Most have hookups and all are in scenic areas. With 9,700 miles of streams and rivers and 6,000 acres of surface water, the state promises plenty of fishing, boating, floating, and canoeing in public and private campgrounds. For July and August and spring weekends, we recommend that you make campground reservations, especially around Branson and Eureka Springs.

All campgrounds in this section are open year-round and have public flush toilets, showers, and sanitary dump stations unless designated otherwise. Toll-free numbers, where listed, are for reservations only. See Chapter 9 for information on how we choose our favorite campgrounds.

Our favorite campgrounds

Branson KOA

$$$–$$$$ **Branson, Missouri**

Although you can't walk into town from here, free shuttle transportation to selected shops and shows is provided in season, and the quiet location on Lake Taneycomo offers a rewarding camping experience, with trout fishing, tackle, and boat rentals available. A free pancake breakfast also is served daily.

1025 Headwaters Rd., Branson, MO 65616. (From U.S. 65, go north 6 miles on SR 165.) ☎ *800-562-4177, 417-334-7450.* www.koa.com. *Total of 165 sites with water and 30- and 50-amp electric, 150 full hookups, 122 pull-throughs. Dataport, laundry, pool. Rates: $22–$35 per site. DISC, MC, V. Open: Mar 1–Dec 10.*

Crater of Diamonds State Park

$$ **Murfreesboro, Arkansas**

Few places in the world allow you to camp and dig up diamonds that you can keep. A 35-acre field, the eroded surface of an ancient diamond pipe and the only publicly accessible diamond mine in the United States, is plowed regularly to bring stones to the surface. Digging tools are for rent at the park, and the rangers help you with identification. If diamonds aren't your passion, you can go fishing in the Little Missouri River.

From Murfreesboro, take SR 301 southeast 2 miles to campground on the right. ☎ *870-285-3113. Total of 60 sites with water and 20- and 30-amp electric, no full hookups, no pull-throughs. Handicap access, laundry. Rates: $15. AE, DISC, MC, V. 14-day maximum stay.*

Jacksonport State Park

$$ **Jacksonport, Arkansas**

This charming park with an historic stern-wheeler and 1872 courthouse was a busy county seat and steamboat port until the arrival of the railroad. A quiet, peaceful campground today, the park offers big grassy sites on the White River with fishing and many mature shade trees.

From Jacksonport, go north on SR 69S 0.25 mile to park on the left. ☎ 870-523-2143. Total of 20 sites with water and 20- and 30-amp electric, no full hookups, no pull-throughs. Handicap access. Rates: $18 per site. DISC, MC, V. 14-day maximum stay.

Lake Dardanelle State Park

$$–$$$ **Russellville, Arkansas**

This handsome hilltop park by a lake with ducks and swans is divided into three different campgrounds with shade trees and picnic tables. On Lake Dardanelle, you can boat, fish, or water ski; the park's marina rents the necessary equipment.

From junction of I-40 and SR 7 (Exit 81), go south 1 block on SR 7 to SR 326, then west 5 miles to park on the right. ☎ 479-967-5516. Total of 65 sites with water and 20- and 30-amp electric, 14 hookups, 1 pull-through. Rates: $15–$22 per site. AE, DISC, MC, V. 14-day maximum stay.

Hot Springs KOA

$$$–$$$$ **Hot Springs, Arkansas**

The highest-rated RV park in the area, this campground has terraced sites with well-planned landscaping, so although individual spaces are not large, they do have a sense of privacy. Weekend pancake breakfasts are available.

838 McClendon Rd., Hot Springs, AR 71901. (Drive east of city 4 miles on U.S. 70 [Exit 4] and follow signs to campground on the left.) ☎ 800-562-5903, 501-624-5912. www.koa.com. Total of 73 sites with 30- and 50-amp electric, all full hookups, 15 pull-throughs. CATV, dataport, laundry, pool. Rates: $24–$32 per site. AE, DISC, MC, V.

Springfield KOA

$$–$$$$ **Springfield, Missouri**

This park, convenient to I-40 but far enough away that you don't hear the traffic noises, provides wide sites with many young trees and an adjacent 18-hole golf course with senior discounts.

5775 W. FM 140, Springfield, MO 65802. (From I-40, Exit 70, go south 0.1 mile on CR MM to FM 140, then east 1.1 mile to campground on the left.) ☎ 800-562-1228, 417-831-3645. www.koa.com. Total of 78 sites with water and 30- and 50-amp electric, 39 full hookups, 71 pull-throughs. Dataport, laundry, pool. Rates: $20–$34 per site. DISC, MC, V.

Runner-up campgrounds

Branson City RV Park

$$ **Branson, Missouri**   This big lakeside public park is within walking distance of the shopping areas and some of the Branson music shows.

Amenities include fishing and boating on Taneycomo Lake. *300 S. Boxcar Willie Dr., Branson, MO. (From the junction of U.S. 65B, drive east 0.2 miles on East Long Street to the park.)* ☎ *417-334-2915.* www.cityofbranson.org. *Total of 350 sites with water and 30- and 50-amp electric, 345 full hookups, 120 pull-throughs. CATV, dataport. Rates: $17–$20 per site. DISC, MC, V.*

Branson Stagecoach RV Park

$$$ **Branson, Missouri** This Good Sam park is out on the edge of town near the Showboat Branson Belle and Table Rock Dam. Sites are wide and extralong for big rigs. *5751 SR 165, Branson, MO 65616. (From SR 76, go south 3.2 miles on U.S. 65 to SR 165, then west 5 miles to campground on the right.)* ☎ *800-446-7110,* 417-335-8185. *Total of 50 sites with 30- and 50-amp electric, all full hookups, 33 pull-throughs. CATV, dataport, laundry, phone jacks, pool/spa. Rates: $24–$27 per site. DISC, MC, V.*

Hot Springs/Gulpha Gorge National Park

$ **Hot Springs, Arkansas** This Hot Springs National Park campground has flush toilets but no hookups or showers. Sites, most of them narrow, are available only on a first-come, first-served basis. *From U.S. 70 east of Hot Springs, go north 0.25 mile on U.S. 70B to campground on the left.* ☎ *501-624-3383. Total of 43 sites, no hookups, no pull-throughs. Rates: $10. No reservations. 14-day maximum stay.*

Kettle Campground and Cabins

$$ **Eureka Springs, Arkansas** The family that operates this well-shaded campground can book your tickets for the Great Passion Play, arrange your transportation, and feed you dinner in summer. *4119 E. Van Buren (U.S. 62), Eureka Springs, AR 72632. (From SR 23S, go east 2.25 miles on U.S. 62 to the campground on the left.)* ☎ *800-899-2267,* 479-253-9100. *Total of 50 sites with water and 30- and 50-amp electric, 30 full hookups, 9 pull-throughs. Dataport, laundry, pool. Rates: $21–$23 per site. DISC, MC, V.*

Musicland Kampground

$$–$$$$ **Branson, Missouri** Sites are fairly narrow but shaded in this Good Sam campground within walking distance of shows, restaurants, and attractions. Shuttle service and rental cars are available. *116 N. Gretna Rd., Branson, MO 65616. (From junction of U.S. 65 and SR 248, go west 3.8 miles on 248 to campground on the left.)* ☎ *888-248-9080.* www.musiclandkampground.com. *Total of 115 sites with water and 30- and 50-amp electric, 96 full hookups, 16 pull-throughs. CATV, dataport, laundry, pool. Rates: $17–$32 per site. MC, V.*

Petit Jean State Park

$$ **Morrilton, Arkansas** This state park offers such attractions as 95-foot Cedar Falls, pedal boating, fishing, hiking trails, and a rustic lodge. Winthrop Rockefeller's Museum of Automobiles is nearby. *From I-40, Exit 108, go south 9 miles on SR 9 to SR 154, then west 12 miles to the campground on the right.* ☎ *501-727-5441. Total of 127 sites with water and 20- and 30-amp electric, no*

full hookups, 38 pull-throughs. Handicap access, pool. Rates: $15–$18 per site. 14-day maximum stay.

Rogers/Pea Ridge KOA

$$–$$$ **Garfield, Arkansas** Only a mile south of Pea Ridge National Military Park, this campground has sites shaded by mature oak trees and is near Beaver Lake for fishing and boating. *P.O. Box 456, Rogers, AR 72757. (From U.S. 71, Exit 86, go northeast 11 miles on U.S. 62 to campground on left.)* ☎ *479-451-8566.* www.koa.com. *Total of 38 sites with water and 30- and 50-amp electric, 24 full hookups, 15 pull-throughs. Laundry, pool. Rates: $20–$22 per site. MC, V.*

Silver Dollar City Campground

$$–$$$ **Branson, Missouri** Adjacent to the amusement park, Silver Dollar City provides a swimming pool, waterslide, and three playgrounds for the kids, a fully stocked store, and fresh homemade doughnuts daily. *From U.S. 65, go west 8.3 miles on SR 76 to SR 265, and then south 0.5 mile to campground on right.* ☎ *800-477-5164,* 417-338-8189. *Total of 138 sites with water and 30- and 50-amp electric, 110 full hookups, 21 pull-throughs. CATV, dataport, laundry, pool. Rates: $19–$27 per site. AE, DISC, MC, V.*

Wanderlust RV Park

$$–$$$ **Eureka Springs, Arkansas** With a trolley stop and bus stop on the premises, Wanderlust makes a good choice for RVers who want to sightsee in town without navigating its narrow, winding, hilly streets. This park is the closest one to the Great Passion Play. *468 Passion Play Rd., Eureka Springs, AR 72632. (From SR 23S, go east 2 miles on U.S. 62 to Passion Play Road, then north 0.5 mile to the campground on the left.)* ☎ *800-253-7385,* 479-253-7385. *Total of 90 sites with water and 30- and 50-amp hookups, 87 full hookups, 52 pull-throughs. Dataport, laundry, pool. Rates: $20–$25 per site. MC, V.*

Withrow Springs State Park

$–$$ **Forum, Arkansas** Located in a wilderness area near the War Eagle River, this state park has a swimming pool, snack bar, and bathhouse, and features tennis, fishing, and boating (rentals available). *From SR 412, go north 5 miles on SR 23 to campground on the left.* ☎ *479-559-2593. Total of 17 sites with water and 20- and 30-amp electric, no full hookups, no pull-throughs. Pool. Rates: $8–$15 per site. 14-day maximum stay.*

Good eats

Penny-pinchers are delighted with the Ozarks, because prices, especially for restaurant meals, generally are much lower than in most other areas of the country. Big, family style, all-you-can-eat buffets dominate the scene in places such as Branson. Because we prefer to avoid these, our list of favorites doesn't include any, but you can find reasonably priced big buffets by asking locally.

Bringing home the bacon

Hickory-smoked, salt-cured country ham is an Ozarks specialty. This rich, salty ham lasts for months in a cool dark place, so you can buy one to take home and store it in the RV. What follows are some of our favorite spots to pick one up; all are open daily except Sunday.

Burgers Smokehouse, Highway 87 South, California, Missouri, 134 miles north of Springfield near Jefferson City (☎ 800-624-5426, 573-796-3134).

Country Smoked Meats, Highway 7 South, Dogpatch, Arkansas (☎ 888-743-1638; www.countrysmokedmeats.com).

Coursey's Smokehouse, SR 65 between Leslie and St. Joe, Arkansas (☎ 870-439-2503).

Hillbilly Smokehouse, 1801 S. Eighth St., Rogers, Arkansas, on SR 17B (☎ 800-759-9439, 479-636-1927).

Here are some of our favorite places to pick up some down-home cooking; most are open for lunch and early dinner but don't arrive fashionably late because they'll probably be closed.

- ✔ **B&B Bar-B-Q:** 230 S East St., Fayetteville, Arkansas (☎ 479-521-3663). The barbecue pit is fired with hickory, and the bread is homemade. You place your order using an orange telephone in your booth, and when the phone lights up, it means your food is ready. Beef and pork barbecue, batter-dipped fries, fried dill pickles, and fried peach or apple pies dusted with sugar make a generous if fat-laden meal. Don't worry, you can have tofu and sprouts tomorrow. Open daily from 11 a.m. to 8 p.m.

- ✔ **Catfish 'N':** 210 Dam Rd., on SR 7 near the Arkansas River Bridge in Dardanelle, Arkansas (☎ 479-229-3321). Catfish 'N' serves up award-winning fried catfish and hush puppies, French fries, coleslaw, and pickled peppers. On our to-go orders, one plate had four catfish fillets, the other five, plus at least half a dozen hush puppies apiece. You can also get fried or boiled shrimp, fried chicken, and hot fruit cobblers for dessert. Open Tuesday through Saturday from 4 p.m. to 9 p.m., and Sunday from 10 a.m. to 3 p.m.

- ✔ **Cliff House Inn:** SR 7, 5 miles south of Jasper, Arkansas (☎ 870-446-2292). This convenient spot with a great view of Arkansas' Grand Canyon from its balcony serves burgers, sandwiches, homemade pies, and main dishes from catfish and fried chicken to steak. Open daily from 8 a.m. to 3 p.m.

- ✔ **Feltner's Whatta-Burger Drive Inn:** 1410 N. Arkansas Rd., Russellville, Arkansas (☎ 479-968-1410). Feltner's cooks up the most famous hamburger in Arkansas, an award-winner for more than a decade. If you're hungry, order a *double double* — double meat and double cheese. And don't overlook the famous fries and shakes. Open daily from 10:30 a.m. to 10 p.m.

✔ **Lambert's:** 1800 W Hwy. J, off U.S. 65, Springfield, Missouri (☎ 417-581-ROLL [417-581-7655]). Despite its nickname, "The home of the throwed roll," you're not pelted with your dinner here, only certain parts of it. All you can eat is promised, and some of the meal, the fluffy, slightly sweet dinner rolls, for example, are tossed at you as the servers make their dining room rounds. Kids love the fun. Good main-dish selections include Lambert's crunchy fried chicken and the delicious ham and white beans with a side order of collard greens. Open daily from 10:30 a.m. to 9 p.m.

✔ **McClard's:** 530 Albert Pike, Hot Springs, Arkansas (☎ 501-624-9586). Bill Clinton, who cites this as a favorite hangout when he was growing up in Hot Springs, recalls in particular the "tamale spreads" — one or two tamales topped with corn chips, beans, chopped beef, cheese, and onions. Open Tuesday through Saturday from 11 a.m. to 8 p.m. No credit cards.

✔ **Ozark Folk Arts Center:** Mountain View, Arkansas, (☎ 870-269-3139). The rustic restaurant at the folk arts center serves fresh trout and catfish, country ham, and fried chicken. If you just want a small bite, the snack bar serves sandwiches and fried apple and peach pies throughout the day. Open May through October daily from 7 a.m. to 8 p.m.

✔ **Serenity Farm Bread:** One block east of U.S. 65, Leslie, Arkansas (☎ 870-447-2211). Dedicated baker David Lower bakes sourdough bread in the European style without artificial yeast or sugar, using only freshly milled flour from organically grown, stone-ground wheat, unrefined sea salt, and filtered water. Tasty loaves to treasure include French, whole wheat, rye, focaccia, and fruit-filled breakfast loaves. Open Monday through Friday from 9 a.m. to 5 p.m., Saturday from 9 a.m. to 4 p.m., and Sunday from 9 a.m. to 3 p.m.

✔ **Springfield Brewing Company:** 305 S. Market, Springfield, Missouri (☎ 417-832-TAPS). This nostalgic brew pub with a rooftop beer garden, live music at night, and a Sunday brunch buffet is only a few blocks from Bass Pro Shops Outdoor World. Open Monday through Saturday from 11 a.m. to midnight and Sunday from noon to midnight.

✔ **Stubby's Bar-B-Q:** 310 Park Ave., Hot Springs, Arkansas (☎ 501-624-1552). We found Stubby's because an adjacent dirt parking lot was the only place we could find to put our RV on a busy summer Saturday afternoon. Out of guilt, we picked up our dinner to go — smoky baked potatoes cooked in the barbecue pit; meaty ribs coated with a rich, dark sauce; and piquant coleslaw — and realized we'd made a find. Open Sunday through Thursday from 11 a.m. to 8 p.m., and Friday and Saturday from 11 a.m. to 9 p.m.

✔ **War Eagle Bean Palace:** SR 98 south of SR 12E between Eureka Springs and Rogers, Arkansas. (☎ **479-789-5343;** www.wareagle mill.com). From Eureka Springs, take SR 23 south to SR 12E and then turn south on SR 98 to the mill. A working, water-powered gristmill on the War Eagle River sells stone-ground grits, cornmeal, flour, waffle and pancake mix, hush puppy mix, and a popular fish-fry coating, all in pretty patterned cloth bags. In the Bean Palace, breakfasts include buckwheat waffles with sorghum, stone-ground grits with sausage, and biscuits and sausage gravy. Lunchtime brings old-fashioned baked beans and cornbread. Open March through December daily, with mill hours from 8:30 a.m. to 5 p.m., and restaurant hours from 8:30 a.m. to 4 p.m.; January through February weekends only.

Fast Facts

Area Code

The area codes are as follows: Arkansas, **479, 501,** and **870;** Missouri, **573** and **417.**

Emergency

Call ☎ **911** in both states. Other sources include the Arkansas State Police (☎ **501-618-8100**) and the Missouri Highway Patrol (☎ **573-751-3313**).

Hospitals

Major hospitals along the route are in Hot Springs, Branson, and Little Rock.

Information

Contact the Arkansas Department of Tourism (☎ 501-682-7777, or 800-NATURAL [800-628-8725] for a vacation planning kit; www.arkansas.com) or the Missouri Division of Tourism (☎ 573-751-4123, or 573-564-2551 for campground information; www.missouritourism.org).

Laws

In Arkansas and Missouri, riders in the front seats must wear seat belts. The maximum speed limit on interstate highways in both states is 70 mph. Speed limits in urban areas are lower.

Road and Weather Conditions

Contact the Arkansas State Highway and Transportation Department (☎ 800-245-1672 or 501-569-2374; www.ahtd.state.ar.us/roads.htm), or the Missouri Department of Transportation (☎ 888-Ask MoDot (888-275-6638) or 573-751-2551; www.modot.state.mo.us/local/d8/CurrRoad Con.html).

Taxes

Sales taxes are 4.625% (local taxes can add 2.125%) in Arkansas, and 4.225% (local taxes can add 2.325%) in Missouri. State gasoline taxes are 21.5¢ a gallon in Arkansas and 17¢ a gallon in Missouri.

Time Zone

Arkansas and Missouri are on central standard time.

Part V
Seeing the West

In this part . . .

Western scenery and RVs were made for each other. You need big windshields to take in the endless vistas, and you can sleep out in the wide-open spaces — not just look down on them from 20,000 feet.

Many adventures await you in the West. On our drive through Montana and Wyoming in Chapter 20, you can ride the trails, bite into a buffalo burger, follow Buffalo Bill across Yellowstone and through the Bighorn Mountains, and see where Custer made his big mistake. While cruising New Mexico in Chapter 21, you can buy a cool pair of cowboy boots, hear some classified X-files info at a UFO museum, and see where Billy the Kid made his last escape. In Chapter 22, you can discover the best spots for whale-watching, kite-flying, and camping among the dunes along the Oregon coast. In Chapter 23, we guide you to the best of California's central coast, pointing out where you can camp among migrating monarchs or take in glorious coastal views. If you yearn for the adventures of the Mother Road, we show you the best places to experience historic Route 66 in Chapter 24.

Chapter 20

Montana and Wyoming: Tracking Buffalo Bill

A famous collection of stories about **Montana** called *The Last Best Place,* issued in 1988 to mark a century of statehood, pretty much sums up the state for outsiders who want to be insiders. Everyone is discovering Montana from movie stars such as Mel Gibson to tycoons like Ted Turner, but plenty of room still exists for the rest of us. Wait until you see the Beartooth Highway between Red Lodge and Yellowstone; no less an expert than TV's RV maven, the late Charles Kuralt, once called it the most beautiful roadway in America.

The same is true of **Wyoming,** which calls itself "high, wide, and handsome." Marked off in a near-square by some civil servants and disdained by pioneers in covered wagons heading for Oregon, the state began as big ranches, many of them owned by Europeans. Even today, cattle outnumber people three to one.

What's so fantastic about Montana and Wyoming — **Big Sky Country** — is the emptiness, the openness, and the plenitude of landscape. Driving an RV, knowing that everything you need for comfort is with you and that the road ahead waits with open campsites, roadside trout fishing, and scenic surprises is as good as it gets in the 21st century.

Getting There

Setting out from **Billings, Montana,** and driving south on U.S. 212 to **Red Lodge,** our tour follows the curves of spectacular Beartooth Highway (named for a rocky outcropping at the summit shaped like a bear's tooth) across a pass with a 10,940-foot summit that drops into **Wyoming** and **Yellowstone National Park.** Next, we make a circle tour

Buffalo Bill Country

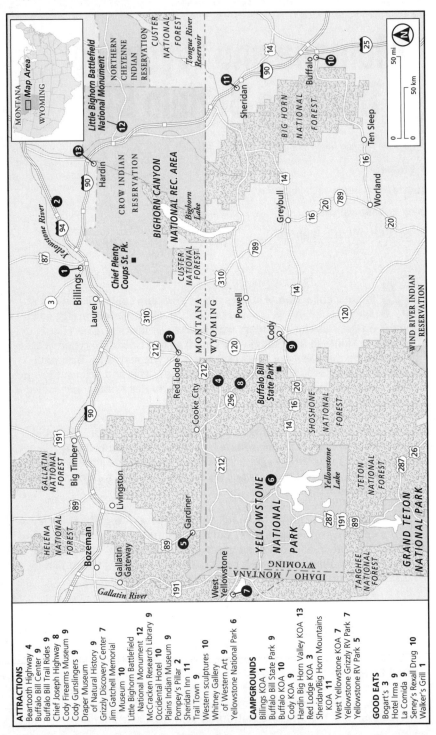

of Yellowstone highlights, then drive east along little-traveled Chief Joseph Highway into **Cody.** From Cody, we go east on U.S. 14 to **Greybull,** then travel south on U.S. 16 to **Worland,** and then east on U.S. 16 to **Buffalo** across the Powder River Pass. From Buffalo, we return to Billings by driving north on I-90 back into Montana and pausing at **Little Bighorn Battlefield National Monument.** The distance traveled is **772 miles.** (For the route, see the "Buffalo Bill Country" map in this chapter.) For a shorter loop that covers many of the highlights, see "Weekend wonder" later in this chapter.

Planning Ahead

The best time to take this drive is in **late spring, summer, or early fall.** In winter, snow closes many of the scenic highways, most of the entrances into Yellowstone, and most of the campgrounds. Early spring brings snowmelt and mud, and wildflowers don't start blooming until June. July and August usually offer the warmest weather, and always the biggest crowds, with sometimes-maddening traffic and no room to turn off at photo opportunities. Early fall, from Labor Day until early October, is probably the best time to visit because the weather usually is mild although days may be rainy.

You can figure any time during late spring, summer, or early fall to be crowded in Yellowstone, meaning you need to make **campground reservations** six months in advance for the immediate area of the park. Towns such as Billings, Buffalo, and even Red Lodge are not as busy.

 If you plan to drive the Yellowstone National Park loop (141 miles) on one long day of sightseeing, you probably don't need campground reservations. But if you want to spend more time in the park, make campground reservations at one of the five campgrounds in the park that accepts them (see sidebar "Camping in Yellowstone National Park" in this chapter) or in a commercial campground just outside the park in West Yellowstone or Gardiner. (See "Our favorite campgrounds" and "Runner-up campgrounds" later in this chapter.)

When you **pack,** keep in mind that Big Sky Country attire is casual, and you always need to include garb for all kinds of weather. Rain gear is essential, and so are hiking boots, jeans, jackets, and sweatshirts or sweaters. The days can get hot with temperatures around Little Bighorn Battlefield sometimes topping 100 degrees Fahrenheit in summer, but during that same week, you can drive over Beartooth Pass in below-freezing weather.

 Many of the roads in Yellowstone National Park are rough and bumpy because of winter freezes that buckle the pavement. Although road-work goes on constantly every summer, you may encounter gusts of dust (or mud, if it's been raining), traffic jams, and closed sections of roadway. You also run into frequent traffic jams around sightings of bear, buffalo, and elk. Allow twice as much time as you'd expect to negotiate Yellowstone's roads. You also find that many of the park's turnoffs that work well for travelers in automobiles don't allow enough space for motorhomes or vehicles towing trailers. Consider leaving your RV in a campground and taking your own or a rental car around the park for maximum efficiency.

In July and August, you may also consider skipping Yellowstone entirely and cutting 200 miles out of the total itinerary. Doing so enables you to spend more time in the wide-open spaces and less on bumpy, traffic-clogged roads and in RV campgrounds that sometimes resemble urban parking lots, only more crowded.

For the entire drive, including Yellowstone, allow **two weeks.**

Stocking the Pantry

Plan ahead for grocery shopping because supermarkets, like restaurants, are few and far between in the wild, wild West. **Billings,** the largest city on the drive, is a good place to stock up. The reliable **Safeway** supermarket chain can be found in many towns in Montana and Wyoming. **Buttrey Fresh Foods** also can be found in Cody, at 1526 Rumsey St., and in other communities.

Buffalo is a favorite Montana and Wyoming meat; it comes fresh or smoked in just about every form that you find beef — as steaks, ground meat, jerky, and sausages.

In Buffalo, Wyoming, **DJ's Thriftway** at 895 W. Fort St., also known as Highway 16, has an adequate selection of bakery, deli items, groceries, and liquors, and accepts all major credit cards. And most commercial campgrounds have a small store with a basic stock of supplies.

Driving Buffalo Bill's Montana and Wyoming

Before setting out from Billings, take a look around town and then head to a unique landmark, 28 miles east of town on I-94, called **Pompey's Pillar.** (See "More cool things to see and do," later in this chapter.) The Lewis and Clark expedition passed this spot in 1806, and William Clark paused to carve his name in this sandstone tower that later acquired other 19th-century graffiti left by fur trappers, missionaries, soldiers, and settlers on their way West.

From **Billings,** head west on I-90, which is also U.S. 212, driving 18 miles to Exit 434 at **Laurel,** and continue to follow U.S. 212 southwest to **Red**

Lodge. The pretty town of Red Lodge is a good place to take a rest break; from here to Yellowstone, the next 61 miles are difficult to drive but spectacular to see.

The **Beartooth Highway** (see "Must-see attractions," later in this chapter) is usually open from the end of May or beginning of June, when the snowmelt is sufficient for road crews to clear the road, until early to mid-October, when the snowfall begins again in earnest. The switchback twists and turns as it climbs out of Red Lodge at 5,555 feet to the summit of Beartooth Pass at 10,940 feet and then winds downhill again to Cooke City, elevation 7,651 feet, near the entrance to Yellowstone.

In **Cooke City,** the white-knuckled RVer can stop for a break or forge on to **Yellowstone National Park.** (See "Must-see attractions.") In Yellowstone, a figure-8 loop road enables you to see the major scenic highlights — from **Tower-Roosevelt** to **Mammoth Hot Springs,** south to **Old Faithful,** around **West Thumb** to **Fishing Bridge** and north again to **Tower Junction** — in a 141-mile circuit. If you already visited Yellowstone and don't relish the idea of crawling along in a July or August traffic jam, you can turn southeast on SR 296 to Cody, Wyoming, before you get to Cooke City. Doing so cuts about 200 miles off the route, allowing you more time for the uncrowded parts of Montana and Wyoming.

The **Chief Joseph Highway** (see "Must-see attractions"), SR 296, runs 46 miles between the Beartooth Highway and SR 120 into Cody. Although paving was completed several years ago, this wonderfully scenic roadway still is uncrowded, and numerous forest service campgrounds, some of them large enough for big RVs, are spread out along the way.

Cody is the city most associated with Buffalo Bill because it's where he spent some of his last years. The immense museum of Western history called the **Buffalo Bill Center** is the town's most outstanding sight. (See "Must-see attractions.")

From Cody, we drive 47 miles east on U.S. 14 to **Greybull,** and then drop south to **Worland** on U.S. 16, where a wood carving by Peter Toth called *Trail of the Whispering Giants* adorns the courthouse lawn. The Hungarian sculptor created 50 Native American–style carvings between 1972 and 1988, donating one to each state.

The route from Worland continues east, still on U.S. 16, to **Ten Sleep,** a town named for the way local tribes measured the distance between places by how many nights of sleep, along with days of riding, it took to travel between them.

From Ten Sleep, the next 69 miles takes you over the Powder River Pass to the town of **Buffalo,** named not for the bison who used to congregate in this area but for the town of Buffalo, New York. As the story goes, five settlers dropped names into a hat and the winner was a man from Buffalo. The town is worth a visit of several days if you have the time.

Buffalo Bill: An American myth

William F. Cody was born in a log cabin in Iowa, signed on as a bullwhacker driving teams of oxen for 50¢ a day when he was 11, and by age 14, was the youngest Pony Express rider ever hired. During the Civil War, too young to be a soldier, he volunteered as a scout, ranger, and messenger with the 7th Kansas Cavalry on the Union side. His nickname Buffalo Bill came in the late 1860s when he was hired to kill buffalo to feed workmen building the Kansas Pacific Railroad.

But Buffalo Bill turned out to be bigger than life, thanks to dime novelist Ned Buntline, who told impossibly heroic stories about him in cheap paperbacks during the 1870s and 1880s. Cody cashed in on the publicity and created a hugely successful touring show about the Old West with cowboys and Indians, roping and shooting, and stagecoach races around the ring.

The **Buffalo Bill Wild West Show** triumphantly toured America and Europe for 30 years at the end of the 19th century and the beginning of the 20th; Queen Victoria wrote in her diary that she loved it. (She saw it twice.) The show starred at times such diverse Western characters as crack shot **Annie Oakley, Buck Taylor ("King of the Cowboys")**, and **Chief Sitting Bull,** who was paid $50 a week and all of his favorite dish (oyster stew) that he could eat.

City fathers of a newly developing town near Yellowstone in western Wyoming persuaded Cody to head up their company because he was "the best-advertised man in the world." He agreed on the stipulation that they name the town after him. Cody built a luxury hotel in his namesake town and called it **Hotel Irma** after his daughter. He moved to Cody after the Wild West show folded in 1913. He died during a visit to his sister in Denver, where he was buried in 1917.

The **Buffalo KOA** (see "Our favorite campgrounds") has a *super-luxury site* that you can rent by the night with its own private hot tub, fenced patio, gazebo, and propane grill.

Take a walk along Main Street for a look at some charming antiques shops, small cafes, and a drugstore with an old-fashioned soda fountain. At the intersection of Main and Angus streets, notice the two wrought-iron **Western sculptures** commemorating the 1892 Johnson County War, a skirmish between big ranchers who wanted to keep the range open and small ranchers and farmers who wanted to fence their lands. One is called *Ridin' for the Brand,* the other *Living on the Edge.*

From Buffalo, drive north on I-25 to the junction with I-90 and continue to **Sheridan,** where Buffalo Bill owned and ran the **Sheridan Inn.** (See "More cool things to see and do" for more on the inn.)

From Sheridan, I-90 zips north back across the Montana border, where, in about 50 miles, you find **Little Bighorn Battlefield National Monument** (see "Must-see attractions"), commemorating a hot June day in 1876, when Sitting Bull and other great chiefs, joined by a force of some 1,500 Sioux and Cheyenne warriors, wiped out the 210 troopers of General George Custer in less than an hour while two other battalions of the U.S. Cavalry Seventh Regiment were on a distant ridge. From the battlefield, drive 50 miles back to Billings on I-90 to complete the tour.

Must-see attractions

Beartooth Highway
Red Lodge, Montana

To drive over the 10,947-foot Beartooth Pass is one of America's great thrill rides, especially for an RVer. Even the curves have names like "Mae West" and "Frozen Man." Have your cameras ready for once-in-a-lifetime views and be prepared for some roadside snow play.

In marginal weather and at the fringes of the late May to early October season, *check the road conditions* before setting out by calling the U.S. Forest Service office in Red Lodge (see below for number). After you hit the road, tackle the switchbacks with caution, especially when you're towing a vehicle. Most turnouts along the way are big enough for any RV, so if your courage fails, you can always turn around and go back. The alternate route to Yellowstone from Red Lodge is to return to I-90 and travel east to Livingston and then south on U.S. 89 to Gardiner and the north entrance to the park near Mammoth Hot Springs.

U.S. 212 between Red Lodge and the northeast entrance to Yellowstone National Park, a distance of 68 miles. ☎ *406-446-2103 for road conditions. Road open from late May or early June until early to mid-October, depending on local snow conditions. Driving time is 3 hours.*

Buffalo Bill Center
Cody, Wyoming

In the middle of Cody, five world-class museums are gathered together in one sprawling complex that many experts call "the Smithsonian of the West." The **Buffalo Bill Museum** is particularly lively with posters from his shows, family furniture, jewelry, and gifts that European royalty presented to him.

The **Plains Indian Museum** is magnificent with life-size figures in various ceremonial dress. Filling the exhibit areas are cradleboards, painted buffalo robes, medicine blankets, pipe bags for carrying ceremonial pipes, grizzly bear claw necklaces, and ceremonial dresses used in the religious Ghost Dances of the 1890s.

The **Whitney Gallery of Western Art,** named for New York sculptor Gertrude Vanderbilt Whitney, displays a replica studio of artist Frederic

Remington and the original studio of Western illustrator W.H.D. Koerner, along with major Western works. The auxiliary H. Peter and Jeannette Kriendler Gallery of Contemporary Western Art celebrates today's artists.

The **Cody Firearms Museum,** one of the world's largest and certainly the most detailed of its kind, includes an engraved gun that belonged to **Annie Oakley,** one of the stars of the Wild West show.

The brand-new **Draper Museum of Natural History** is an interactive walk-through of Yellowstone National Park's geology, including a path displaying slabs from different geologic ages and exhibits about current issues, such as the reintroduction of wolves into the environment.

The **McCracken Research Library** houses a collection of traditional cowboy songs and range ballads, and extensive archives of photographs, documents, films, books, and original manuscripts relating to the West.

720 Sheridan Ave. ☎ *307-587-4771.* www.bbhc.org. *RV parking: Designated lots adjacent to the center. Admission: $15 adults, $13 seniors, $6 students 18 and older with valid ID, $4 ages 6–17. Open: Daily Apr 10 a.m.–5 p.m., May 8 a.m.–8 p.m., June 1–mid-Sept 7 a.m.–8 p.m., Mid-Sept–Oct 31 8 a.m.–5 p.m.; Nov–Mar Tues–Sun 10 a.m.–3 p.m. Allow half to a full day for the full complex.*

Chief Joseph Highway
Cody, Wyoming

The Chief Joseph Highway, SR 296, was a longtime favorite of intrepid travelers who didn't mind the gravel roadway. But now this scenic route is completely paved, lightly traveled, and breathtakingly beautiful. Running 46 miles between the turnoff from Beartooth Highway (U.S. 212) to SR 120, 17 miles northwest of Cody, the Chief Joseph is named for the heroic Nez Perce chief who led his tribe through this area in 1877 while fleeing the U.S. Army. The route follows William Clark's Fork of the Yellowstone River for the first part of the journey and then turns into a corkscrew of switchbacks as it climbs to Wyoming's highest bridge, 8,060 feet, at Dead Indian Summit. This construction, finished in 1995, completed Wyoming's goal to pave all its state highways.

SR 296, between U.S. 212 (Beartooth Highway) and SR 120 (17 miles northwest of Cody), a distance of 46 miles. Road open year-round. Allow 2 hours.

Jim Gatchell Memorial Museum
Buffalo, Wyoming

With 15,000 artifacts arranged in two adjacent buildings, this small-town museum offers the real story of the Wyoming range wars and the Indian wars set out in miniature dioramas. Gatchell was a local druggist who collected historical artifacts from the day he opened his drugstore in 1900. Among the various collections are dolls, firearms, Crow and Cheyenne beaded deerskin garments, buffalo and horsehide winter coats, and home-made knives confiscated from prisoners in the Johnson County Jail.

10 Fort St. (at the corner of SR 16 and Main Street). ☎ **307-684-9331.** www.jim gatchell.com. *RV parking: Free city parking lot across from museum sometimes has space, otherwise use street parking. Admission: $4 adults, $2 ages 6–16. Open: Apr 10–Dec 24 daily 9 a.m.–5 p.m. Closed July 4. Allow 2 hours.*

Little Bighorn Battlefield National Monument
Crow Agency, Montana

The famous battle lasted less than an hour on June 25, 1876, when a force of some 5,000 Sioux and Cheyenne warriors under the leadership of Sitting Bull and other great chiefs wiped out Custer's troops while two other battalions of the Seventh Cavalry waited on a distant ridge for word to join Custer. The handsome, cocky Custer, underestimating the Plains Indian forces, had rashly decided to divide his 600 troops into thirds to create a pincers action and then attacked without waiting for the others.

From a small visitor center, you walk uphill to a fenced cemetery with tombstones that document the soldiers' names, insofar as they were known, and where the men were believed to have fallen. Although eye-witness accounts vary widely, estimates put the number of Indian casualties at 150.

Signs on the site caution visitors wandering around the battlefield to watch out for rattlesnakes.

Little Bighorn, 2 miles south of the town of Crow Agency, Montana, off I-90 at Exit 510, east on U.S. 212 to battlefield turnoff (marked). ☎ **406-638-2621.** *RV parking: Large lot at visitor center. Admission: $10 per passenger vehicle. Open: Daily spring and fall 8 a.m.–6 p.m., summer 8 a.m.–8 p.m., winter 8 a.m.–4:30 p.m. Allow 2 hours.*

Yellowstone National Park
Yellowstone National Park, Wyoming

Glorious, awe-inspiring, sometimes infuriating, Yellowstone National Park has more attractions to offer a visitor than almost any other park in the country, but sometimes, finding them is difficult. During the past decade, we visited almost every year in differing seasons, trying to determine the one that's best and having thrown up our hands in defeat. In July and August, the roads are so bad and so full of traffic — yes, RVs are among the worst culprits — that we want to turn around and head out, back to less-crowded highways and friendlier campgrounds. The big burns — entire hillsides of dead trees for miles and miles — are depressing to look at and slow to return to life. Early autumn may bring drizzly days without diminishing the crowds; springtime often is muddy, making the already-bad roads worse. And more than 3 million visitors a year keep passing through.

Yellowstone National Park

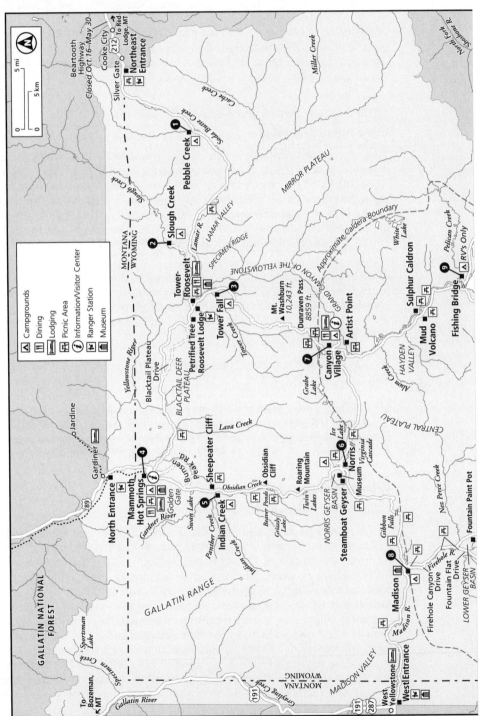

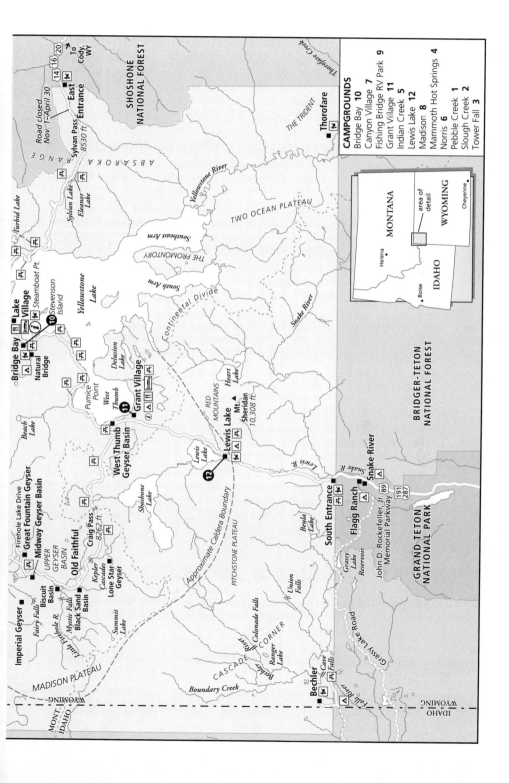

CAMPGROUNDS
Bridge Bay **10**
Canyon Village **7**
Fishing Bridge RV Park **9**
Grant Village **11**
Indian Creek **5**
Lewis Lake **12**
Madison **8**
Mammoth Hot Springs **4**
Norris **6**
Pebble Creek **1**
Slough Creek **2**
Tower Fall **3**

Since an earthquake threw off its rhythm a few years ago, **Old Faithful** has turned into Old Faithless, and you may have to wait anywhere from 50 to 100 minutes to catch the famous geyser act. You can do better, if time is limited, by driving through the geothermal areas keeping your eyes open for eruptions. **Steamboat**, in the **Norris Geyser Basin** at Norris, is the tallest geyser but rarely shows off for visitors. Nearby **Echinus** is more reliable, spouting off about once an hour. (For the locations of these attractions, see the "Yellowstone National Park" map in this chapter.)

Mammoth Hot Springs is the place to see technicolor terraces of colored limestone boiling up from the earth and numerous animals on cold days; large elk congregate around Mammoth where it's warm. **Grand Canyon of the Yellowstone** has plenty of RV parking at a large lot at the trailhead and a short walk to a dramatic viewpoint. **Lamar Valley** offers good, if distant, animal spotting for herds of buffalo; we've shot good close-ups during the fringe seasons at Sylvan Lake on the east entrance road and along the Firehole River at Lower Geyser Basin. Bears are a long shot; you may glimpse one along the highway, but sightings are much rarer than they used to be because rangers now discourage the furry free-loaders and those who feed them.

Never approach a wild animal on foot. Do not leave your vehicle when you see one. You can be maimed or killed. Be cautious in thermal areas. Never step off the designated walkways or boardwalks onto the fragile crust.

Northwestern corner of Wyoming with a few acres in the eastern edges of Idaho and Montana. ☎ *307-344-7381 for road information and general information,* ☎ *307-344-7311 for lodging, dining, and camping reservations.* www.travel yellowstone.com. *RV parking: Some designated RV parking in populated and commercial areas; 12 campgrounds with RV camping; some but not all turnouts along the roadways large enough for RVs. Admission: $20 a car, $10 for hikers and bicyclists, $15 for motorcyclists. Seniors with Golden Age Passports and disabled with Golden Access passports free. Open: Year-round. Road access all year from the north entrance, U.S. 89 at Gardiner, Montana; other park entrances open on seasonal basis, usually closed from Nov to May.*

More cool things to see and do

Montana and Wyoming are full of fascinating sights, activities, and out-door pursuits. See the following list for some of our favorites; you'll find many more on your driving tour.

✔ **Ride the trail. Buffalo Bill's Trail Rides** set out from the Cody KOA Campground (see "Runner-up campgrounds") daily in summer. Reservations are advised.

5561 Greybull Hwy., Cody, Wyoming. ☎ **307-587-2369,** 307-527-9959. Open: June–Sept. Allow half a day.

✔ **Shoot the gunslingers.** Bring a camera, because the photogenic **Cody Gunslingers** congregate and shoot it out every afternoon except Sundays at 6 p.m. in and around the Irma Hotel.

Irma Hotel, Sheridan and 12th streets, Cody, Wyoming. ☎ **307-587-4221.** Admission: Free. Shoot out: Memorial Day to Labor Day Mon–Sat 6 p.m. Allow 1 hour.

✔ **Greet a grizzly.** The closest you can safely get to a grizzly bear is at the **Grizzly Discovery Center.** Here, in a natural habitat, a non-profit center takes care of bad boy bears from Canada and Alaska, like Toby and Fred and Max and Lewie, and a resident wolf pack.

Grizzly Park near the west entrance to Yellowstone National Park in West Yellowstone, Montana. ☎ **800-257-2570,** 406-646-7001. RV parking: Designated lot. Admission: $8.50 adults, $4 ages 5–12. Open: Daily 8 a.m.–6:30 p.m. Allow 2 hours.

✔ **Shoot it out at high noon.** The first classic Western confrontation or "walk down" is in the pages of Owen Wister's novel *The Virginian* and is said to have been set in front of the **Occidental Hotel.** The renovated hotel initially was constructed of logs in 1878 and finished in 1880.

Occidental Hotel and Saloon, 10 Main St., Buffalo, Wyoming. ☎ **307-684-0451.** RV parking: Street parking or free city lot at the corner of Main and Fort streets. Admission: Free, drinks sold. The Virginian Restaurant (☎ **307-684-3976**) is open Mon–Sat noon to midnight, closed Sun. Allow 10 minutes for a visit to the hotel, longer for food and drink.

✔ **Do the touristy thing.** The big, loopy handwriting still is clear behind the framed section of the sandstone pillar: "W Clark, July 25, 1806." William Clark of Lewis and Clark fame couldn't resist leaving his name and the date of his visit carved on **Pompey's Pillar,** a 700-foot sandstone plug sticking up from the flats along the Yellowstone River east of Billings, Montana. A wooden staircase with handrails leads up 500 steps to the top of the pillar.

Pompeys Pillar National Historic Landmark, 28 miles east of Billings, Montana, on I-90 at Exit 23, follow the signs. ☎ **406-875-2233** (visitor center at monument). RV parking: Large lot by visitor center. Admission: Free. Open: Memorial Day weekend to Sept 30 daily. Allow 1 hour.

✔ **Set 'em up, Bill . . .** Established in 1893 and a National Historic Landmark, **Sheridan Inn** once was owned and run by Buffalo Bill, and still boasts the **Buffalo Bill Cody Saloon** with its original bar. Today, the many-dormered hotel takes no overnight guests but is open as a museum, restaurant, and gift shop.

Sheridan Inn, 858 Broadway, Sheridan, Wyoming. ☎ **307-674-5440,** 800-453-3650 (Sheridan Convention & Visitors Bureau). www.sheridaninn.com. RV parking: Street parking or designated lot. Restaurant (☎ **307-673-4700**) open 11 a.m.–7 p.m.

✔ **Brave Butch Cassidy.** Historic buildings from all across Wyoming are set up in **Trail Town** at the edge of Cody in a photogenic Western setting. Mountain man Jeremiah Johnson's grave is in the cemetery, and outlaw hideout cabins, such as the Sundance Kid's Mud Spring Cabin and Butch Cassidy's Hole in the Wall Gang Cabin, are fun to look into.

Trail Town,1831 Demaris Dr., Cody, Wyoming. ☎ 307-587-5302. www.nezperce.com/trltown.html. RV parking: Large lot. Admission: $6 adults, $5 seniors, $2 ages 6–12, free ages 5 and younger. Open: May–Oct daily 8 a.m.–7 p.m.

Weekend wonder

Buffalo Bill country is a little distant for a weekend stopover for most of us, but if you're in the vicinity in summer and have a yen to see the best part in a couple of days, plan a driving tour from **Billings** to **Red Lodge,** Montana, over the Beartooth Highway to the Chief Joseph Highway and into **Cody,** Wyoming. In Cody, spend all your spare time at the Buffalo Bill Center quintet of museums. Stay at the Cody KOA and you can take a trail ride right from the campground.

Sleeping and Eating on the Road

Montana and Wyoming are **RV-friendly states** with plenty of public and privately owned campgrounds; good, lightly traveled roads (except those in Yellowstone National Park); and wide-open spaces. Although state parks and national forest campgrounds don't usually offer RV hookups, the scenery is so great and the vistas so wide that staying a day or two is worth the hassle of not having a hookup.

All campgrounds listed in this chapter are open year-round and have public flush toilets, showers, and sanitary dump stations unless designated otherwise. Toll-free numbers, where listed, are for reservations only. For Yellowstone National Park campgrounds (except Fishing Bridge RV Park), see this chapter's sidebar "Camping in Yellowstone National Park." See Chapter 9 for details information on how we choose our favorite campgrounds.

Our favorite campgrounds

Billings KOA
$$$–$$$$$ **Billings, Montana**

The Billings KOA is the world's first KOA campground, and Montana and Wyoming still claim 37 KOAs between them. This grandaddy of them all offers shady sites, some with gravel but most with grass. You can choose a spot on the Yellowstone River with freshwater fishing, trees, grass, and long pull-throughs with patios. When you don't feel like cooking, you can buy breakfast and evening BBQ dinners at the campground in summer.

547 Garden Ave. Billings, MT 59101. (From I-90 at 27th Street, Exit 450, go east 200 yards to Garden Avenue, turn right and follow signs to second campground on the left.) ☎ *800-562-8546, 406-252-3104. Total of 100 sites with water and 30- and 50-amp electric, 51 full hookups, 85 pull-throughs. CATV, dataport, handicap access, laundry, pool/spa. Rates: $26–$55 per site. AE, DISC, MC, V. Open: Apr 15–Oct 15.*

Buffalo Bill State Park
$ Cody, Wyoming

Two campgrounds belong to Buffalo Bill State Park — the **North Shore Bay,** 9 miles west of Cody on U.S. 14/16/20, and **North Fork,** 14 miles west on the same highway. You find no hookups and narrow sites, but the areas are attractive, each offering fishing and boating, and you can't beat the price — $6 a night! Reservations are not accepted.

North Shore Bay, Buffalo Bill State Park, Cody, WY. (9 miles west of Cody on U.S. 14/16/20; campground is on the left.) ☎ *307-587-9227. Total of 35 sites, no hookups, 32 pull-throughs. Rates: $6 per site. No credit cards. Open: May–Sept. 14-day maximum stay.*

Buffalo KOA
$$–$$$$ Buffalo, Wyoming

This KOA has one ultradeluxe campsite with its own private hot tub, fenced patio with landscaping, gazebo, propane barbecue, glass and wrought-iron picnic table with four chairs, and a planter filled with bright petunias for $65 a night for two; you can reserve the site ahead of time. Other sites are much less elaborate and fairly narrow. You can also enjoy freshwater fishing, a fenced dog walk, kid-pleasing miniature golf, and blueberry pancake breakfasts with bacon and sausage in summer.

Box 189, Buffalo, WY 82834. (From junction of I-90 and U.S.16, Exit 58, go west 1 mile on U.S. 16 to campground on the left.) ☎ *800-562-5403, 307-684-5423.* www.koa. com. *Total of 63 sites with water and 30- and 50-amp electric, 39 full hookups, 37 pull-throughs. Dataport, laundry, pool/spa. Rates: $20–$38 per site. DISC, MC, V. Open: Apr 15–Sept 30.*

West Yellowstone KOA
$$$$–$$$$$ West Yellowstone, Montana

In a quiet location outside of town, this campground offers large sites with patios. Daily breakfasts and barbecues are available in summer when you don't feel like cooking. You can rent bikes, arrange tours, book horseback riding nearby, and go fishing. Big fancy motorhomes can fit comfortably in the 64 pull-throughs.

Yellowstone Park/West Entrance KOA, Box 348, West Yellowstone, MT 59758. (The park is 6 miles west of West Park entrance on U.S. 20.) ☎ ***800-562-7591***, *406-646-7606.* www.koa.com. *Total of 198 sites, 145 with water and 30- and 50-amp electric, 75 full hookups, 64 pull-throughs. Dataport, handicap access, indoor pool/spa, laundry. Rates: $31–$48 per site. DISC, MC, V. Open: May 22–Oct 1.*

Yellowstone Grizzly RV Park

$$$$ **West Yellowstone, Montana**

Conveniently located in town, Yellowstone Grizzly is a good choice for RVers who are towing or have rented a car and want to spend two or three days exploring Yellowstone National Park. Sites are wide with patios and gravel, and pull-throughs are a comfortable 70-feet long. As many as six people pay the same rate as two, making this a good choice for families. Shops and restaurants are just a walk away.

210 S Electric St., West Yellowstone, MT 59758. (From junction of U.S. 191 and Hwy. 20, go south 0.5 mile on 191/Canyon Street to Gray Wolf Avenue, and west 0.2 miles to entrance.) ☎ ***406-646-4466***. *Total of 152 sites with 30- and 50-amp electric, all full hookups, 64 pull-throughs. CATV, dataport, handicap access, laundry. Rates: $32–$38 per site, AE, DISC, MC, V. Open: May 1–Oct 21.*

Camping in Yellowstone National Park

Pay special attention if you want to book a campsite in Yellowstone National Park. Here's how it goes: Yellowstone has **12 campgrounds** suitable for RVs (depending on size). Five of them have sites that can be reserved in advance by contacting Xanterra Parks and Resorts (☎ **307-344-7311**). Of those five, only one has hookups — the **Fishing Bridge RV Park** with 333 parking-lot-type spaces for $33 a night. If you've come to experience the great outdoors with plenty of peace and quiet and birdsong, this campground may not be the place for you. And if your RV is soft-sided, like a folding camping trailer, or has any canvas on its body instead of metal, you won't be permitted to camp because this is *bear country.* But if you want a convenient and easy location in the park with a hookup, don't mind crowds, and know the date that you want to stay, then you need to make a reservation here well ahead of time. (See "Runner-up campgrounds.")

The other four campgrounds that can be reserved in advance, like Fishing Bridge, also are in heavily used areas. If you have a reservation date near the campgrounds' opening or closing dates, check again before your arrival to make sure that the facilities are open; bad weather can cause late openings or early closings. These campgrounds are usually just as crowded as Fishing Bridge but without the convenience of hookups. Generator use is limited. All sites are *back-ins* (meaning you have to back your rig into the site).

The campgrounds listed below charge $18 a night per site, have a 14-day limit, and accept credit cards (DISC, MC, V). For reservations, call ☎ **307-344-7311**.

✔ **Bridge Bay:** On Yellowstone Lake not far from Fishing Bridge. 425 narrow, paved campsites, marina. Open May to September.

✔ **Canyon Village:** In Canyon Village near the Grand Canyon of the Yellowstone. 280 narrow, grassy sites (no slideouts permitted). Open June to September.

✔ **Grant Village:** In Grant Village on Yellowstone Lake. 406 narrow, grassy sites. Open June to October.

✔ **Madison:** On the Madison River 14 miles from the west entrance. 292 paved, narrow (12-feet wide) campsites and no showers. Open May to November.

The park service operates seven other campgrounds in Yellowstone National Park that accept no reservations. Camping is on a first-come, first-served basis and limited to 14 days. Generator use is limited. Except for Mammoth Hot Springs, these campgrounds are in less-traveled areas of the park. *Note the vehicle size restrictions for each.*

✔ **Indian Creek:** On the Grand Loop Road about halfway between Mammoth Hot Springs and Norris Geyser Basin. 74 narrow paved sites, 12-feet wide, maximum length of 28 feet. $10 a night per site, cash only. Open June to September.

✔ **Lewis Lake:** In a wooded area near a lake 12 miles north of the park's south entrance on U.S. 89. 85 narrow paved sites, 12-feet wide, maximum length of 35 feet, no flush toilets, no showers. $10 a night per site, cash only. Open June to November.

✔ **Mammoth Hot Springs:** At Mammoth Hot Springs, 5 miles south of the park's north entrance at Gardiner, open year-round. 85 narrow grassy sites, 12-feet wide, maximum length of 35 feet, no showers. $12 a night per site, cash only. Open year-round.

✔ **Norris:** On Grand Loop at Norris Geyser Basin, 25 miles south of the park's north entrance at Gardiner. 60 paved narrow sites, some trees, 12-feet wide, maximum length of 28 feet, no showers. $12 a night per site, cash only. Open May to September.

✔ **Pebble Creek:** On the Lamar Valley Road 7 miles southwest of the park's northeast entrance at Cooke City. 36 narrow paved sites, 12-feet wide, maximum length of 30 feet, no flush toilets, no showers. $10 a night per site, cash only. Open June to September.

✔ **Slough Creek:** Off Lamar Valley Road near Tower Junction, access road is 2.5 miles of gravel. 29 narrow dirt sites, 12-feet wide, maximum length of 30 feet, no showers. $10 a night per site, cash only. Open May to November.

✔ **Tower Fall:** 2.5 miles south of Tower Junction on Grand Loop Road. 32 narrow dirt sites, 12-feet wide, maximum length of 25 feet, no flush toilets, no showers. $10 a night per site, cash only. Open May to September.

Runner-up campgrounds

Cody KOA

$$$–$$$$$ **Cody, Wyoming**   Out on the edge of town with narrow sites in a big open area, this KOA offers many extras, including free pancake

breakfasts daily, trail rides on horses, and a free shuttle to the rodeo, which operates throughout the summer. *5561 Graybill Hwy., Cody, WY 82414. (Drive 3.1 miles east of Cody on U.S. 20 to campground on the left.)* ☎ *800-562-8507, 307-587-2369.* www.koa.com. *Total of 123 sites with water and 20- and 30-amp electric, 63 full hookups, 50 pull-throughs. Dataport, laundry, pool/hot tub. Rates: $28–$41 per site. Open: May 1–Oct 1.*

Fishing Bridge RV Park

$$$$ **Yellowstone National Park, Wyoming** The only campground in Yellowstone National Park with hookups, this RV park is handy for travelers who want comfort and convenience and don't mind crowds. Because the campground is in bear country, only hard-sided vehicles are permitted. Sites are fairly narrow, but paved with small patio areas. Plan to reserve well ahead of time. *From Lake Junction, go east 1 mile on U.S.14/16/20. Campground is 0.5 mile past Fishing Bridge on the left.* ☎ *307-344-7311. Total of 333 sites with 20- and 30-amp electric, all full hookups, no pull-throughs. Laundry. Rates: $33 per site. AE, DISC, MC, V. Open: Mid-May to mid-Sept.*

Hardin Big Horn Valley KOA

$$–$$$ **Hardin, Montana** History fans who want to spend more time at Little Bighorn Battlefield find this campground handy. This KOA has fishing in the Big Horn River, a hot tub, and weekend barbecues in summer. Sites are gravel with mostly side-by-side hookups. *Rt. 1, Hardin, MT 59034. (From I-90, Exit 495, go north 1.5 miles on SR 47 to campground on the left.)* ☎ *800-562-1635, 406-665-1635. Total of 58 sites with water and 30- and 50-amp electric, 16 full hookups, 58 pull-throughs. Dataport, laundry, pool/spa, SATV. Rates: $15–$25 per site. DISC, MC, V. Open: Apr 1–Sept 30.*

Red Lodge KOA

$$–$$$ **Red Lodge, Montana** This rural campground with shade trees, a babbling brook, and grass sites makes a restful overnight stop before tackling the Beartooth Highway. You can go trout fishing in Rock Creek. Some hookups are side by side. *HC 50, Box 5340, Red Lodge, MT 59068. (Drive 4 miles north of Red Lodge on U.S. 212; 38 miles south of I-90.)* ☎ *800-562-7540, 406-446-2364. Total of 37 sites with water and 30- and 50-amp electric, 12 full hookups, 27 pull-throughs. Dataport, laundry, pool. Rates: $20–$26 per site. DISC, MC, V. Open: May 18–Sept 9.*

Sheridan/Big Horn Mountains KOA

$$$ **Sheridan, Wyoming** With easy-on, easy-off interstate access, this KOA makes a handy overnight stop. This rural, tree-shaded campground offers long pull-throughs, freshwater fishing, and miniature golf on the premises. *63 Decker Rd., Box 35 A, Sheridan, WY 82801. (From junction of I-90 and Main Street, Exit 20, go south 0.1 mile on Main to SR 338 (Decker Rd.), then north 0.5 mile to campground on right.)* ☎ *800-562-7621, 307-674-8766.* www.koa.com.

Total of 78 sites with water and 30- and 50-amp electric, 38 full hookups, 71 pull-throughs. Laundry, pool. Rates: $28 per site. AE, DISC, MC, V. Open: May 1–Oct 5.

Yellowstone RV Park

$$$–$$$$ **Gardiner, Montana** Although it lacks charm, this park is convenient if you want to spend several days exploring Yellowstone National Park from a base camp with hookups. The sites, although not wide, overlook the Yellowstone River. Take care entering the campground because of the moderate grade. *117 U.S. 89 S, P.O. Box 634, Gardiner, MT 59030. (From Roosevelt Arch at Yellowstone National Park boundary, go north 1.3 miles on U.S. 89 to campground on the left.)* ☎ *406-848-7496. Total of 46 sites with 30-amp electric, all full hookups, 13 pull-throughs. CATV, dataport, handicap access, laundry. Rates: $24–$31 per site. Good Sam and KOA discounts. No credit cards. Open: May1–Oct 31.*

Good eats

Cafes and restaurants in Montana and Wyoming are mainly in the plains, and primarily in towns and cities. Don't expect to find so much as a McDonald's out on the scenic highways. Be thankful that you're carrying your own kitchen with a stocked refrigerator.

Be sure to stock up on groceries and gasoline whenever you see a suitable and convenient spot. (See "Stocking the Pantry" for our recommended stops.)

- ✔ **Bogart's:** 11 S. Broadway, Red Lodge, Montana (☎ **406-446-1784**). RV parking: Street parking. Pizza, hamburgers, and Mexican food, along with boutique beer, bring a bigger-than-Bogart smile. A fan named the place after actor Humphrey Bogart, whose likeness adorns the place. Open daily from 11 a.m. to 9 p.m.

- ✔ **Hotel Irma:** 1192 Sheridan, Cody, Wyoming (☎ **800-745-4762**, 307-587-4221). RV parking: Designated parking in city lots off Sheridan on side streets. Stop for prime rib, served daily, or such lunch and dinner specials as mountain trout or buffalo burgers. Open daily from 6 a.m. to 9 p.m.

- ✔ **La Comida:** 1385 Sheridan, Cody, Wyoming (☎ **307-587-9556**). RV parking: Street parking, or in designated city lots off Sheridan on side streets. Slurp down margaritas and scarf down Mexican food indoors or outside on the streetside patio. Open daily from 11 a.m. to 9 p.m.

- ✔ **Seney's Rexall Drug:** 38 S. Main, Buffalo, Wyoming (☎ **307-684-2253**). RV parking: City lot at Main and Fort streets or street parking. An old fashioned soda fountain in this modern drugstore serves sodas, sundaes, and sandwiches. Open Monday through Saturday from 9 a.m. to 6 p.m.

✔ **Walker's Grill:** 301 N. 27th St., Billings, Montana. ☎ **406-245-9291**). RV parking: Designated lot or street parking. Open only for dinner, Walker's serves hot homemade bread, meatloaf with gravy and mashed potatoes, pizzas, burgers, and fries, and some trendy offerings, such as tapas and grilled lamb salad. Open Monday through Saturday from 5:30 a.m. to 10:30 p.m.

Fast Facts

Area Code

The area codes are ☎ **406** in Montana and ☎ **307** in Wyoming.

Emergency

Call ☎ **911** in both states.

Hospitals

Along the route, major hospitals are in Billings, Montana, and Cody and Sheridan, Wyoming.

Information

Sources include Travel Montana (☎ 800-847-4868; www.visitmt.com) and the Wyoming Department of Tourism (☎ 307-777-7777; www.wyomingtourism.org).

Laws

All RV occupants must wear seat belts in Montana and Wyoming. The maximum speed limit on interstates in Montana and Wyoming is 75 mph. Speed limits are lower in urban areas.

Road and Weather Conditions

In Montana, call ☎ 800-226-ROAD (800-226-7623) or the Highway Patrol at ☎ 406-444-7000. When in Wyoming, call ☎ 888-996-7623 or 307-772-0824; or hit #ROAD (#7623) on a mobile phone.

Taxes

Montana does not have sales tax. In Wyoming, sales tax is 4% but local taxes can raise it to 6%. State gasoline taxes are 27.75¢ a gallon in Montana and 14¢ a gallon in Wyoming.

Time Zone

Montana and Wyoming are on mountain standard time.

Chapter 21

New Mexico: Billy the Kid Meets E.T.

● ●

In This Chapter

▶ Tracking down Billy the Kid

▶ X-filing UFOs in Roswell

▶ Checking your chile capacity

▶ Shopping for cowboy boots

● ●

***L*and of Enchantment** is the longtime license plate slogan for New Mexico, and the magic is everywhere. Red rock canyons and mesas abut hazy blue hills, which in turn stand out against snowcapped peaks topping 10,000 feet. *Ristras,* strings of dried red chile peppers, hang from the eaves of adobe houses, and silver and turquoise jewelry twinkles from the windows of battered trading posts. Ancient cliff dwellings rest within sheltered rocky overhangs, Native Americans invoke the spirits of the past with traditional dances, and golden aspen leaves quiver in the first cold puffs of winter wind.

The first inhabitants arrived around 25,000 years ago. The Southwest is where, in the late 19th century, a slight, cocky Brooklyn-born boy nicknamed "the Kid," and later, **Billy the Kid,** entered legend, and here too, some believe that **aliens** from flying saucers crashed in the middle of the 20th century. A real bear cub that survived a Lincoln County forest fire in 1950 entered America's annals as **Smokey Bear,** the animated animal on everybody's black-and-white TV sets who growled, "Only *you* can prevent forest fires." Five years earlier, the **world's first nuclear test** at Trinity Site broke windows 120 miles away in Silver City, the town where Billy the Kid grew up.

Getting There

El Paso, Texas, makes an ideal jumping-off point for southern New Mexico. Our route follows the Rio Grande north, paralleling I-25 on rural roads that bisect pecan groves and chile fields to **Hatch,** some

New Mexico

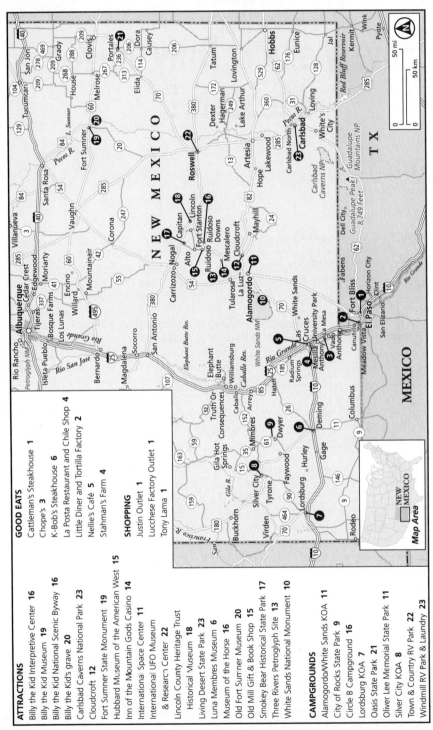

ATTRACTIONS
Billy the Kid Interpretive Center **16**
Billy the Kid Museum **19**
Billy the Kid National Scenic Byway **16**
Billy the Kid's grave **20**
Carlsbad Caverns National Park **23**
Cloudcroft **12**
Fort Sumner State Monument **19**
Hubbard Museum of the American West **15**
Inn of the Mountain Gods Casino **14**
International Space Center **11**
International UFO Museum
  & Research Center **22**
Lincoln County Heritage Trust
  Historical Museum **18**
Living Desert State Park **23**
Luna Membres Museum **6**
Museum of the Horse **16**
Old Fort Sumner Museum **20**
Old Mill Gift & Book Shop **15**
Smokey Bear Historical State Park **17**
Three Rivers Petroglyph Site **13**
White Sands National Monument **10**

CAMPGROUNDS
Alamogordo/White Sands KOA **11**
City of Rocks State Park **9**
Circle B Campground **16**
Lordsburg KOA **7**
Oasis State Park **21**
Oliver Lee Memorial State Park **11**
Silver City KOA **8**
Town & Courtry RV Park **22**
Windmill RV Park & Laundry **23**

GOOD EATS
Cattleman's Steakhouse **1**
Chope's **3**
K-Bob's Steakhouse **6**
La Posta Restaurant and Chile Shop **4**
Little Diner and Tortilla Factory **2**
Nellie's Café **5**
Stahman's Farm **4**

SHOPPING
Justin Outlet **1**
Luchese Factory Outlet **1**
Tony Lama **1**

65 miles away, and then turns west, following SR 26 and then U.S. 180 to **Silver City** another 100 miles. Return south on U.S. 180 to I-10, and drive east to **Las Cruces,** and then along I-70 past **White Sands National Monument** to **Alamogordo,** another 168 miles. Continue east to **Roswell** and then north to **Fort Sumner,** a total of 200 miles. Drive east on U.S. 60 to **Clovis,** and then south via I-70 back to Roswell, 168 miles total. Some 77 miles south are **Carlsbad Caverns,** and another 165 miles along U.S. 62 returns you to El Paso. The total drive is **943 miles.** (See the "New Mexico" map in this chapter for the route.) For a shorter loop that covers many of the highlights, see "Weekend wonder" later in this chapter.

Planning Ahead

Spring and fall are the best seasons to visit New Mexico. Winter brings snow to higher elevations like Silver City in the Southwest, although the deserts around Carlsbad in the southeast usually are mild. Summer heat sizzles the terrain surrounding Carlsbad Caverns, but the temperature below ground stays at 56 degrees Fahrenheit — a real treat. Even in winter, most days are sunny. The southern part of the state claims 300 days of sunshine a year. The mountains around Cloudcroft get 25 inches of rain a year, while the city of Las Cruces, less than 100 miles away, gets only 8 inches. Expect to see a torrential late afternoon thunderstorm or two in July and August, and *never* camp in a dry riverbed because of the potential danger from flash floods.

Although **campground reservations** are a good idea, they're not essential in many parts of southern New Mexico, especially after summer has gone. If you want to make reservations, you can do so at a commercial RV park near one of the major attractions. State parks, such as City of Rocks, don't accept reservations.

When **packing,** take along sweaters and jackets no matter when you visit because summer nights are cool even in the desert, and Carlsbad Caverns is a constant 56 degrees Fahrenheit. Winter days, even in ski resorts, are cold but usually dry and clear. Bring plenty of sunscreen because the rays can reach your skin instantly through the clear air.

Allow 7 to 14 days to drive this itinerary with time for hiking and exploring Carlsbad Caverns.

Stocking the Pantry

The first day of the drive from El Paso takes you past several notable tortilla factories and through the town of Hatch, famous for its chile products. We like the **Little Diner and Tortilla Factory** in Canutillo, Texas, north of El Paso, where you can take away both thick and thin homemade corn tortillas. Local and national supermarket chains in El Paso and throughout New Mexico usually stock both red and green versions of Hatch brand enchilada sauces, which come in various strengths from mild to *very hot.*

Driving Southern New Mexico

Leave **El Paso** on I-10 and take Exit 6 to SR 28, which wends past pecan orchards and chile fields. The same Rio Grande River that separates El Paso, Texas, from Juarez, Mexico, also irrigates the valley that carries its name. A dozen varieties of chiles are grown in and around Hatch, and harvested in early September, when the air is heavy with the smell of roasting peppers. Local farmers roast the chiles and freeze them, so they always have plenty for cooking.

The most famous chile restaurant in this part of the valley is **Chope's** in **La Mesa,** favored by the local chile growers for *chiles rellanos,* fresh green chiles filled with cheese, dipped in egg batter, and fried. The blue-corn version of tortillas, which used to be unique to New Mexico, also is served. (See "Good eats.") Look for produce stands selling local chiles, tomatoes, pecans, and melons in season.

Mesilla, the next town north from La Mesa on SR 28, is a must-stop destination, especially for first-time visitors to New Mexico who can see in one small town all the details — a plaza, a mission-style church, and an abundance of adobe shops and restaurants — that go into creating such superstar tourist meccas as Santa Fe and Taos.

From Mesilla, continue north to **Hatch;** between here and **Canutillo** to the south, farmers grow most of New Mexico's chiles. This state, where the chile is the official state vegetable, leads all the rest in production of the spicy pods. From Hatch, we turn southwest on SR 26, and then north on U.S. 180, to Silver City. (An alternative, if you're driving a small RV and/or the season is summer, when there's little chance of snow on the roadway, is to continue north on I-25 to **Caballo** and turn west on SR 152 at Exit 63 for a hilly, scenic, 86-mile drive into Silver City. This route doesn't repeat the drive along U.S. 180 between Silver City and Deming on the way out.)

Silver City commemorates the youthful Billy the Kid, born as Henry McCarty but later known as Henry Antrim (he took the surname of his mother's second husband after she died of tuberculosis). Her grave can be found at 21 Cypress Lane by the ninth tree from the entrance of the local cemetery on Memory Lane. A year later, the 15-year-old Kid had his first arrest for stealing clothes from a Chinese laundry. He was locked up but broke out of jail during the night by climbing up a chimney. He ran away to Arizona, severing his ties with Silver City forever.

The Trinity Site: Testing the first atomic bomb

Due north of the White Sands National Monument, on the White Sands Missile Range, about 50 miles as the crow flies, is the Trinity Site. This closely guarded area is where the world's first nuclear bomb was tested on July 16, 1945. A stone memorial stands at Ground Zero, where the force of the blast melted the dirt in the area into a strange green glassy substance called Trinitite.

The site is open to the public only two days a year, the first Saturdays of April and October, when tours are conducted from Alamogordo. Cars line up in single file with headlights on and proceed behind a military escort to Ground Zero. You also can visit the ranch house where the bomb was assembled. Some radiation remains at the site. For more information, call ☎ 505-437-6120.

One of our favorite state parks is **City of Rocks,** an eerie collection of gigantic boulders with campsites hidden in, around, between, and under the rocks. The nearby town of **Deming,** reached by following U.S. 180 to I-10, is home of the **Luna Membres Museum,** with a fine collection of distinctive local black-and-white Indian pottery. (See "More cool things to see and do" later in this chapter.)

From Deming, make the fast trip across I-10 to **Las Cruces,** where you join I-25 north and then turn off on U.S. 70 at Exit 6. About 50 miles up the road is the entrance to **White Sands National Monument,** the world's largest gypsum dunes field, an improbable 275 square miles of sugar-white sand as fine and soft as powder. (See "Must-see attractions," later in this chapter.)

Alamogordo with its **International Space Hall of Fame** is 10 miles or so up the road from White Sands National Monument. (See **International Space Center** under "Must-see attractions.") It's hard to imagine that more than a century ago, this infant town set out as a planned city to attract eastern socialites with plenty of money and culture. When that plan fizzled, Alamogordo — described by one local writer as "miles and miles of nothing but miles and miles" — slept until the 1941 attack on Pearl Harbor plunged America into war. Then all that emptiness was turned into a bombing and gunnery range, training British and American heavy bomber crews. Today, you find a missile range, space museum, and Air Force base.

Ski areas, lavish resorts, golf courses, racetracks, petroglyphs, and museums clustered within a triangle-shaped area north of Alamogordo could fill a month-long holiday almost any season of the year — if you're willing to zigzag back and forth to get there. **Cloudcroft,** as cool and romantic a four-seasons town as it sounds, is 19 miles northeast of Alamogordo on U.S. 82. (See "More cool things to see and do.")

Lincoln: The Lincoln County War

In 1878, the paths of five tough-minded men crossed, and their differences erupted into bloodshed. When the **Lincoln County War**, as locals called it, was over, many men were dead, and the reputation of one minor-league gunslinger grew into the icon of **Billy the Kid**. In 1877, the courthouse was the Murphy-Dolan Store, sole recipient of lucrative government supply contracts to provide beef and other supplies for nearby Fort Stanton and the Mescalero Apache Reservation to the south. Murphy was smarting under a charge of cattle rustling from a local land baron named Chisum when two newcomers, a Kansas lawyer named Alexander McSween and a young English adventurer named John Tunstall, opened a rival store down the street. Murphy figured Chisum had helped fund the new store.

Matters came to a head early in 1878 when Sheriff Brady dispatched a posse to take over Tunstall's ranch, claiming that the Englishman's partner McSween owed Murphy money. In the ensuing argument, Tunstall was shot and killed, and that might have ended the trouble then and there if Tunstall hadn't previously befriended and hired an 18-year-old cowboy calling himself William H. Bonney. Bonney — the new name taken by Henry Antrim, also known as Billy the Kid — swore to avenge his friend's death. The Murphy-Dolan team had Sheriff Brady and his deputies on its side. Billy the Kid and his "Regulators" had Dick Brewer, the newly appointed Lincoln County constable and former foreman for the Tunstall Ranch on its side. Brewer "deputized" Billy the Kid and some of his friends, and within days they had captured and shot two of Sheriff Brady's posse. On April 1, Billy and his Regulators crouched in ambush by the Tunstall Store as Brady and his deputies walked toward the Wortley Hotel. Shots rang out, Brady fell into the street, and the deputies ran for cover.

In mid-July, after a shootout at the Chisum Ranch, Billy and his men took refuge in the McSween home, next door to the Tunstall Store. The Murphy-Dolan faction surrounded the house and fired into it from a vantage point atop a small hill. At dusk on July 19, they set fire to the house. Billy the Kid and several others made a successful dash for freedom and escaped into the underbrush.

After 3 years on the loose, Billy the Kid was accused of the murder of Sheriff Brady (the Kid was the only member of either Lincoln County War faction ever to go to trial), captured by Sheriff Pat Garrett and brought to Mesilla for trial, found guilty, and sentenced to be hanged. He was removed to Lincoln County Jail but soon managed to escape by overpowering and shooting the two deputies guarding him. A friend of Billy's helped him to sever the chain holding his leg shackles and brought him a horse that belonged to the deputy clerk of the probate court. The Kid escaped and hid out in the Fort Sumner area at ranches belonging to several different Hispanic families. In July 1881, Sheriff Garrett caught and shot the Kid in a darkened bedroom of one of the houses.

Follow U.S. 54 north from Alamogordo for 30 miles to find **Three Rivers Petroglyph Site.** (See "More cool things to see and do.") On U.S. 70 east from **Tularosa,** you pass **Inn of the Mountain Gods,** a lavish resort and casino that Mescalero Apaches own and operate on their reservation. The parking lot is big enough for RVs, so you can stop and look around, and perhaps have lunch and a whirl in the casino. Continue east on U.S. 70 to **Ruidoso** and **Ruidoso Downs,** home of the world's richest quarter horse race with its summer-long racing season. The **Hubbard Museum of the American West** displays 10,000 items relating to the horse and to the breathtaking "Free Spirits at Noisy Water," a bigger-than-life outdoor display of eight horses sculpted by Dave McGary and poised as if frozen in mid-air against a New Mexico meadow. (See "More cool things to see and do.") Ruidoso also is a good starting point to drive the **Billy the Kid National Scenic Byway.** (See "Must-see attractions.")

Continue north to U.S. 380 — you can reach it via U.S. 54 north of Alamogordo and then east at **Carrizozo** — to find more Billy the Kid country, and Smokey Bear habitat. **Smokey Bear Historical State Park** in **Capitan** houses the grave of Smokey, a longtime favorite resident at Washington's National Zoo, and every camper's reminder to be sure to *put that campfire out* before you leave a campsite. (See "More cool things to see and do.") From Capitan, continue driving east for 12 miles on U.S. 380 to **Lincoln,** where you need to plan to spend some time exploring the area. Pick up a town map and guide at the **Lincoln County Heritage Trust Historical Museum.** (For details on Lincoln, see the listing Billy the Kid National Scenic Byway under "Must-see attractions" and the sidebar "Lincoln: The Lincoln County War.")

Some 50 miles east of Lincoln is the city of **Roswell,** forever on the map for an alleged UFO incident on or around July 4, 1947. Everything you ever wanted to know about flying saucers and extraterrestrials is on display in the **International UFO Museum & Research Center** in downtown Roswell. (See "Must-see attractions.")

Fifty-four miles up the road from Roswell is **Fort Sumner,** the last resting place of Billy the Kid. The gravesite is on SR 212 some 3 miles east of the present town of Fort Sumner. The tombstone was stolen twice, taken once to Texas for 26 years and once to California for 2 years, but it's now securely shackled at the site. Adjacent to the grave is the **Old Fort Sumner Museum.** The **Billy the Kid Museum** is near the junction of U.S. 60 and U.S. 84 in town. (See "More cool things to see and do" for info on all these Kid sights.)

Take U.S. 60/84 for 57 miles east to **Clovis,** where Buddy Holly recorded "That'll Be the Day," "Peggy Sue," and "Maybe Baby" at the Norman Petty Studio, and then continue south 19 miles on U.S. 70 to **Portales,** the Valencia peanut capital of the United States. Another 92 miles driving southwest on U.S. 70 returns you to Roswell.

From Roswell, drive south on U.S. 285 to **Carlsbad,** the site of **Carlsbad Caverns National Park,** one of the world's largest cave systems and the **Living Desert State Park,** a wonderful collection of Chihuahua Desert animals, plants, and reptiles. (See "Must-see attractions" for details on both parks.)

From Carlsbad, the quickest route back to **El Paso** is a 165-mile straight shot down U.S. 60/120 past Guadalupe Mountains National Park, dominated by 8,749-foot **Guadalupe Peak,** the tallest mountain in Texas.

Must-see attractions

Billy the Kid National Scenic Byway
Lincoln County, New Mexico

An official highway route leads along the Billy the Kid trail, starting from the new **Billy the Kid Interpretive Center** on U.S. 70 in **Ruidoso Downs,** and adjacent museum with its scaled-down walk-through version of the byway. The route seems guilty of lassoing and roping in items that have even the faintest of connections with the Western icon, so use your common sense to disconnect the tourist come-on from historic reality. (For example, Ruidoso Downs also boasts the Billy the Kid Casino with 300 electronic slot machines. Hel-lo?)

The **69-mile trail** (90 minutes driving time if you don't stop anywhere) goes west on U.S. 70 and north on SR 48 to Ruidoso, where the **Old Mill Gift & Book Shop** on Suddarth Drive claims to be a Billy the Kid Hideout. Actually, the Kid reputedly hid in a flour barrel here to escape armed pursuers, so naturally today, the shop sells souvenir bags of flour. From Ruidoso, SR 48 continues north to U.S. 380 and **Capitan** (Smokey Bear headquarters), dips south to **Fort Stanton** on SR 220, and then continues east along U.S. 380 to **Lincoln,** which is the key to the most historic part of the Kid's life, the Lincoln County War. (See this chapter's sidebar "Lincoln: The Lincoln County War.")

The whole town of Lincoln is a National Historic Landmark and a State Monument. Kids of all ages enjoy the Old West atmosphere. **A self-guided walking tour map** of the town is available at the Lincoln County Heritage Trust Historical Museum. Follow the trail from the museum to the Wortley Hotel, the old courthouse across the street, the Tunstall Store, the site of the Murphy-Dolan Store, and the site of the McSween House.

Billy the Kid Interpretive Center: U.S. 70 East (next door to Hubbard Museum of the American West), Ruidoso Downs. ☎ *505-378-5318. RV parking: Large lot adjacent to the center. Admission: Center is free but adjacent museum admission is $5 adults, $4 seniors, $2 ages 6–12. Open: Daily 10 a.m.–5 p.m. Closed major holidays. Allow 1 hour.*

Carlsbad Caverns National Park
Carlsbad, New Mexico

Even card-carrying claustrophobics won't mind going underground to tour the spacious caverns of Carlsbad, unless the elevator ride from the visitor center down 75 floors is too unnerving. The quick, self-guided tour takes an hour (including the elevator ride down and back) and covers a lit circular trail around a gigantic cavern, big enough to contain 14 football fields. Highlights include **Hall of Giants, Giant Dome, Lower Cave,** and **Top of the Cross** with its 255-foot ceiling. The **Bottomless Pit** gave us shivers, and so did a close encounter with a cluster of sleeping Mexican freetail bats. Most of the bats are far from the main tour routes with one exception: Visitors can gather every summer evening at **Bat Flight time** in an amphitheater at the mouth of the cave to watch the 300,000-member bat colony speed out at the rate of 5,000 bats a minute in search of their evening meal, three tons of insects. (Think of it this way — one less mosquito or fly to pester you.)

Wear low-heeled, nonskid walking shoes, and anticipate a walk of approximately 1 mile inside the Big Room. Take a sweater; even when the outside temperature climbs to 97 degrees Fahrenheit, the temperature inside the caverns always is 56 degrees.

Although kids love the caves, they can't run about freely; all visitors must stay on the pathways. The best tour for kids is the self-guided tour of the Big Room. Ranger-led tours are more informative, but kids may get anxious during these lectures.

3225 National Parks Hwy. (Drive southeast from Carlsbad 18 miles to Whites City and take SR 7 west into the park for 7 miles to the visitor center.) ☎ **888-900-CAVE** *(888-900-2283), 505-785-2232 for information,* **800-967-CAVE** *(800-967-2283) for reservations. RV parking: Designated area in large lot at the visitor center entrance. Admission: Big Room tour $6 adults, $3 children; additional fees for touring other areas of the caverns (see next paragraph); Bat Flight program free. Open: Visitor center daily year-round 8 a.m.–5 p.m., Big Room opens at 9 a.m., last tour at 2 p.m. for walking, 3:30 p.m. by elevator. Closed Christmas Day. Allow a half-day. No campgrounds in the park. No pets allowed in caverns but kennels available.*

Additional tours: **Natural Entrance Tour,** *self guided, 1 mile of walking, $6 adults, $3 ages 6–15;* **Kings Palace Tour,** *ranger led, 1½-hour tour of four caves, $8 adults, $4 ages 6–13, reservations required;* **Slaughter Canyon Cave,** *ranger-led, slip-and-slide tour of a cave without man-made walkways or added lighting, $15 adults, $7.50 ages 6–16, younger than 6 not admitted, reservations required. Tours available daily in summer, weekends only in winter.*

International Space Center
Alamogordo, New Mexico

You can't miss this gold-tinted, four-story glass tower as you drive south on U.S. 54. The distinctive building houses the **International Space Hall of Fame** with a simulated walk on Mars, an IMAX dome theater and planetarium, an Astronaut Memorial Garden, and a Shuttle Camp program for kids. Ham, the Astro Space Chimp, wearing his space suit, may still be in residence.

At the end of SR 2001. (Turn east off SR 54 on Indian Wells Road and follow the signs.) ☎ **877-333-6589**, *505-437-2840. RV parking lot. Admmission: $2.50 adults, $2.25 seniors, $2 ages 6–17; IMAX, $6 adults, $5.50 seniors and military, $4.50 ages 6–12. Open: Daily 9 a.m.–5 p.m. Allow 2 hours, more depending on how far out you are.*

International UFO Museum & Research Center
Roswell, New Mexico

The city of Roswell has a tongue-in-cheek attitude about its flying saucer fame. One city brochure is headlined, "Some of our most famous visitors . . . came from out of state."

The International UFO Museum & Research Center gets some 200,000 visitors a year from around the world to see displays about the Roswell incident in 1947 (see the sidebar "UFOs: The Roswell incident") and other purported UFO sightings in New Mexico and elsewhere. A large gift shop does a brisk sale in UFO souvenirs and T-shirts. In 1996, the state named the museum "Top Tourist Destination in New Mexico."

114 S. Main St. ☎ **505-625-9495**. www.iufomrc.com. *RV parking: Street parking; city streets are wide enough for RVs to park comfortably. Admission: Donation. Open: Daily 9 a.m.–5 p.m. Allow 2 hours.*

UFOs: The Roswell incident

The **International UFO Museum & Research Center** (see "Must-see attractions"), founded by key figures, who were in Roswell and close to the events of July 1947, has been open since 1991. Lt. Walter G. Haut, public relations director for Roswell Army Air Field in 1947, wrote the first narrative of the events, which appeared in the *Roswell Daily Record* of July 8, 1947. Glenn Dennis, an ambulance driver for the Ballard Funeral Home in Roswell, was at the army base hospital on the night of the alleged crash and was told by medical staff that at least five bodies of aliens had been recovered from the crash site and brought into the hospital. But within a week, all stories of the crash were denied, all informants and witnesses hushed, and nothing else was heard about it until 1978, when some writers started looking into the story again and published one of the early books about Roswell in 1980. Haut and Dennis felt a museum needed to be established in Roswell to give what information is available about the alleged crash, and while Haut is convinced that aliens have visited the earth, the museum simply presents the amassed information. (But we figure that if the museum or the city of Roswell ever took the position that space aliens couldn't possibly have dropped in back in 1947, their tourist revenue would drop off considerably.)

Although the details of the event often are confusing or conflicting, it seems irrefutable that *something* happened in Roswell in the summer of 1947.

Living Desert State Park
Carlsbad, New Mexico

The stars of the show at Living Desert are its birds and animals, all of them native to the Chihuahua Desert, most of them brought here because of injuries or illness and scheduled to be released back into the wild. Those too ill or too old to return, such as a Mexican gray wolf, stay on. The wolf spends most of his time napping atop a rocky ledge in the sun. The setting is a hilltop covered with native cacti and other plants. A well-manicured trail wends its way through the terrain — the design of the path brings surprises at every turn. Kids have a chance to see the animals in a natural environment. In the gift shop, you can buy small, native cactus plants in pots.

Skyline Drive off U.S. 285 north of Carlsbad, watch for signs. ☎ **505-887-5516**. *RV parking: Large paved lot in front of the museum. Admission: $4 adults, $2 ages 7–12. Open: Daily summer 8 a.m.–8 p.m. with last tour at 6:30 p.m., winter 9 a.m.–5 p.m. with last tour at 3:30. Allow at least 2 hours.*

White Sands National Monument
Alamogordo, New Mexico

Imagine the lure of 60-foot pure white gypsum sand dunes sparkling in the sunlight. When our son was 8 years old, he leaped from the car the moment that we slowed down, ran up the nearest dune, and slid down in the powdery sand, laughing all the way. For more serious visitors, all sorts of discoveries await, from the bleached, earless lizard whose species turned white for camouflage to the handful of plants tough enough to survive surrounded by the constantly shifting sands.

On nights during a full moon, park rangers or special guests present "howling at the moon" evenings.

The **Dunes Drive** goes 8 miles into the heart of the dunes, turns at a circle, and then comes back out the same way. A picnic area, boardwalk, and two hiking trails are reached from turnouts along the drive.

No one is allowed to drive across the dunes, but hiking is permitted. Be aware that you can get lost easily, especially if a windstorm produces whiteout. The powdery white sand blows easily and can penetrate your RV even when doors and windows are closed.

Photographers need to visit at times other than midday when the high sun flattens the terrain. Use a polarizer for best results.

15 miles southwest of Alamogordo on U.S. 70/82. ☎ **505-679-2599**. *RV parking: Parking lot at visitor center, frequent turnouts along Dunes Drive. Admission: $3 adults 17 and older, free ages 16 and younger. Open: Visitor center, daily summer 8 a.m.–7 p.m., winter 8 a.m.–5 p.m.; Dunes Drive, daily summer 6:30 a.m.–10 p.m.,* *winter 7 a.m. to sunset. Closed Christmas Day. $3 entrance fee. No campground in the park. (**Note:** Dunes Drive occasionally may be closed to private traffic when testing is taking place on the White Sands Missile Range.)*

More cool things to see and do

New Mexico is full of fascinating sights. What follows are more of our favorites. In addition to these, you may also want to try your luck at the **Inn of the Mountain Gods Casino** (☎ 877-277-5677 or 505-464-4100), east of Tularosa on U.S. 70.

✔ **See the Kid's grave.** If you have the time and inclination to make the long, arid drive up to **Billy the Kid's grave** in Fort Sumner, you may appreciate how long it took the outlaw to reach this destination on horseback. Take the time to poke around, although none of the local museums are world-class. The **Old Fort Sumner Museum** is adjacent to the gravesite and **Fort Sumner State Monument,** while the **Billy the Kid Museum** is in town in Fort Sumner near the junction of U.S. 60 and U.S. 84. His tombstone is now securely set inside a fenced site after being stolen twice.

Drive east on U.S. 60/84 3 miles from the town of Fort Sumner, New Mexico, to SR 212, and then turn south 4 miles to Fort Sumner State Monument. Chamber of Commerce ☎ 505-355-7705, Old Fort Sumner Museum ☎ 505-355-2942, Fort Sumner State Monument ☎505-355-2573, Billy the Kid Museum ☎ 505-355-2380. RV parking: Large lot at gravesite, adjacent to Old Sumner Museum; smaller lot at Billy the Kid Museum but streetside parking also available. Admission: $4 adults, $2 children 6–12. Allow 1 hour for the grave site and the museum and 1 or more hours for the museum in town.

✔ **Take a walk in the clouds.** The town of **Cloudcroft,** at an elevation of 9,200 feet and surrounded by 500,000 acres of Lincoln National Forest, makes a cool, pretty spot for a morning or afternoon pause if you tire of the hot valley climate. The Lodge, built in 1899, still welcomes visitors to its restaurant, and a ski slope, golf course, and quaint Western-style boutiques provide distraction.

Be aware that snow in winter may require tire chains in this area; check conditions before leaving the Alamogordo area.

From I-70, 2 miles north of Alamogordo, take U.S. 82 east 16 miles to Cloudcroft, New Mexico. ☎ 505-682-2733 (Chamber of Commerce) RV parking: On the street.

✔ **Appraise collectibles.** On the way to or from Silver City, you should pause at Deming's **Luna Membres Museum,** housed in a 1917 brick armory, to see some good examples of local black-and-white Mimbreno pottery, one of the most elegant tribal collectibles. The museum also is a starting point for a self-guided, historic walking tour of the town; pick up a map at the museum.

301 S. Silver St., Deming, New Mexico. ☎ **505-546-2382.** RV parking: On-street parking plentiful. Admission: By donation. Open: Mon–Sat 9 a.m.–4 p.m., Sun 1:30–4 p.m. Allow 1 hour, add an additional hour for the walking tour.

✔ **Horse around.** The nucleus of the **Hubbard Museum of the American West** is a much-loved 10,000-piece collection of horse artifacts collected by the late Anne C. Sterling, a New Jersey heiress and aficionado. But the best reason to go, even if you don't venture inside, is to see the magnificent sculptures of eight running horses in the outdoor monument.

U.S. 70 East, Ruidoso Downs, New Mexico (1 mile east of Ruidoso Downs Race Track). ☎ **505-378-4142.** RV parking: Nearby in a small lot or street parking. Admission: $6 adults; $5 seniors, military, and ages 5–17; monument only, $1. Open: Daily summer 9 a.m.–5 p.m. Allow 1 hour.

✔ **Drop the "The."** Repeat after me: There is no "the" in Smokey Bear. If you didn't know that, you'll discover it right away at **Smokey Bear Historical State Park.** In May, 1950, when firefighters found a badly singed bear cub clinging to a burnt pine tree near the town of Capitan, a cartoon Smokey Bear in a ranger costume had already been informing campers about the dangers of forest fires for five years. The young black bear was named Smokey, and when his burns healed, he was sent to the National Zoo in Washington, D.C., where he was a favorite of visitors. After Smokey died in 1976, he was returned to Capitan for burial.

118 Smokey Bear Blvd., Capitan, New Mexico. ☎ **505-354-2748.** RV Parking: Designated lot. Open: Daily 9 a.m.–5 p.m. Closed major holidays. Admission: $1 adults, 50¢ ages 7–12. Allow 2 hours.

✔ **Dig a petroglyph.** At **Three Rivers Petroglyph Site,** you can see some 500 *petroglyphs* (images that have been scratched, carved, or chiseled into a rock face). The pictures of people, animals, fish, and reptiles were carved by the Mogollon people between A.D. 900 and 1400. A path wends for a mile through the hilltop site.

From U.S. 54 about 30 miles north of Alamogordo, New Mexico, take SR 579 to the site, following the signs. ☎ **505-525-4300** (Bureau of Land Management offices). RV parking: Large lot at site. Admission: $2 per vehicle. Open: Daily sunrise to sunset. Allow 2 hours, more if you want to do additional hiking.

Weekend wonder

If time is short, you can eliminate parts of this journey to make an accelerated dash to the main attractions. Get an early start from **El Paso,** drive north on I-25 to **Las Cruces,** where U.S. 70 (Exit 8) turns east to **Alamogordo.** Pause to take the Dunes Drive through **White Sands National Monument,** and then continue along U.S. 70 to **Ruidoso**

Downs. The 69-mile **Billy the Kid National Scenic Byway** takes only an hour to cover; allow a second hour for a walking tour around Lincoln. If you have kids (or kids at heart) on board, pause at **Smokey Bear Historical State Park** in **Capitan.** And **Roswell's International UFO Museum & Research Center** is a must-stop. Then head south to **Carlsbad Caverns National Park,** allowing a minimum of an hour for a self-guided tour through the Big Room. Return to El Paso via U.S. 62/180. Without advance reservations, your best bets for campground overnight lodging is around Alamogordo and again around Roswell or Carlsbad.

Sleeping and Eating on the Road

More than 16 of the communities along our driving route have at least one RV campground, most of them several. You can eyeball the action early in the drive to figure out whether you need to make reservations for the remainder of the trip. If most campgrounds look full as you drive by in the afternoon, you may consider calling ahead for a spot. But usually, you'll have no problem finding lodgings except perhaps in the Carlsbad Caverns area in tourist season, which is summer, the Christmas holidays, and Presidents Weekend.

If you're traveling the route in summer, when temperatures can reach 90-plus degrees Fahrenheit at lower elevations, plan ahead for an electrical hookup capable of running your RV's air conditioning unit full blast. Never set up camp in dry streambeds because summer thunderstorms can cause flash floods.

All campgrounds listed in this chapter are open year-round and have public flush toilets, showers, and sanitary dump stations unless designated otherwise. Toll-free numbers, where listed, are for reservations only. See Chapter 9 for our criteria on choosing favorite campgrounds.

Our favorite campgrounds

Alamogordo/White Sands KOA

$$$ **Alamogordo, New Mexico**

Close to White Sands National Monument, the Space Center, and the Mescalero Apache Reservation, this tree-shaded campground with grass and privacy walls has narrow sites. The park is right in the edge of town, so if you don't want neighbors and urban surroundings, you may want to choose a different destination.

412 24th St., Alamogordo, NM 88310 (1½ blocks east of U.S. 54/70). ☎ 800-562-3992, 505-437-3003. www.koa.com. *A total of 65 sites with water and 20- and 30-amp electric, 57 with full hookups. CATV, dataport, laundry, pool. Rates: $26 per site. DISC, MC, V.*

Circle B Campground

$$–$$$ **Ruidoso Downs, New Mexico**

This large, modern RV park, a member of the Good Sam group, is conveniently near Hubbard Museum of the American West, the Billy the Kid Interpretive Center, Ruidoso Downs race track, and Billy the Kid Casino. Sites are narrow and some have side-by-side hookups, but the campground offers valet RV parking, RV parts, and on-site RV service — everything a beginner could want.

Box 1800, Ruidoso Downs, NM 88346. (From the junction of U.S. 70 and SR 48, go east 4 miles on U.S. 70 to campground on the right.) ☎ *505-378-4990. Total of 196 sites, 185 full hookups with 30- and 50-amp electric, 102 pull-throughs. Dataport, laundry, SATV. Rates: $20–$24 per site. DISC, MC, V.*

City of Rocks State Park

$–$$ **Deming, New Mexico**

One of our favorite campgrounds in the world is this field of house-size boulders where rocks surround sites that sit far apart. Arrive early to get a good site because reservations aren't accepted. Eighteen of the sites have electric hookups, so scope these out first. But even if you don't luck into a hookup, you'll still love this campground.

Follow U.S. 180 north from Deming 28 miles to SR 61, turn east for 5 miles. ☎ *505-536-2800. Total of 57 sites, 19 with water and 50-amp electric, 10 with full hookups. Handicap access. No sanitary dump station. Rates: $10–$18 per site. No credit cards. Reservations:* ☎ *877-664-7787.*

Silver City KOA

$$$ **Silver City, New Mexico**

Cooler in summer than the other campgrounds in the area, this park also offers such bonuses as copper mine tours, hiking trails, biking trail access in the vicinity, and an outdoor cafe in summer. The sites are narrow, but the park location, 4.9 miles east of town, is quiet.

11824 Hwy. 180 E, Silver City, NM 88061. ☎ *800-562-7623, 505-388-3351.* www.koa.com. *A total of 57 sites with water and 30- and 50-amp electric, 42 full hookups, 33 pull-throughs. Dataport, laundry, pool. Rates: $30 per site. AE, DISC, MC, V.*

Town & Country RV Park

$$–$$$ **Roswell, New Mexico**

We headed straight for this campground, a Good Sam member, after our visit to the International UFO Museum & Research Center because their brochure said, "Crash Here, They Did!" The park is a big, modern RV park with everything a snowbird could want for the whole winter, including big-rig sites with 50-amp hookups, 90-foot-long pull-throughs, new bathrooms, and instant local phone hookups.

331 W. Brasher Rd., Roswell, NM 88203. (From Second and Main streets, drive south on Main to Brasher Road, and go west 2 blocks.) ☎ **800-499-4364**, *505-624-1833.* www.roswell-usa.com/tandcrv. *A total of 131 sites with water and 30- and 50-amp electric, 71 full hookups, 32 pull-throughs. CATV, dataport, laundry, phone jacks, pool. Rates: $18–$25 per site. DISC, MC, V.*

Runner-up campgrounds

Lordsburg KOA

$$$ **Lordsburg, New Mexico**   In sight of the freeway behind a Shell service station, this campground is convenient for an overnight stop. All sites are pull-throughs, some with side-by-side hookups. *1501 Lead St., Lordsburg, NM 88045 (Exit 22 from I-10, follow the signs).* ☎ **800-562-5772**, *505-542-8003.* www.koa.com. *A total of 63 sites with water and 30- and 50-amp electric, 31 full hookups, all pull-throughs. CATV, laundry. Rates: $26 per site. DISC, MC, V.*

Oasis State Park

$–$$ **Portales, New Mexico**   This 194-acre state park is conveniently located between Clovis and Portales, with hiking and freshwater fishing. Sites are quite narrow, but most are shaded and some offer handicap access. *6 miles north of Portales on SR 467.* ☎ **505-356-5331.** *A total of 23 sites, 13 with water and 30- and 50-amp electric. Rate: $10–$15 per site. No credit cards. No reservations.*

Oliver Lee Memorial State Park

$$ **Alamogordo, New Mexico**   See some rare desert plants in this secluded park, a former Indian stronghold, with visitor center, hiking trails, and history exhibits. *409 Dog Canyon Rd., Alamogordo, NM 88310. (Drive 10 miles south of Alamogordo on U.S. 54, and then 5 miles east from roadside rest area.)* ☎ **505-437-8284.** *A total of 16 sites with water and 30-amp electric. Rates: $15 per site. No credit cards. No reservations.*

Windmill RV Park & Laundry

$$–$$$ **Carlsbad, New Mexico**   This Good Sam RV park, on the road south of Carlsbad toward the caverns, has wide spaces, several pull-throughs, and, obviously, a place to catch up on doing the laundry. The location also is convenient to Living Desert State Park. *3624 National Parks Hwy., Carlsbad, NM 88220. (From the junction of U.S. 62/180 and U.S. 285 south of Carlsbad, drive ¾ mile southwest on U.S. 62/180 to campground on the left.)* ☎ **888-349-7275**, *505-887-1387. A total of 61 sites with 30- and 50-amp electric, all full hook-ups, all pull-throughs. CATV, dataport, laundry, pool. Rate: $20–$25 per site. DISC, M, V.*

Good eats

Restaurants and snack bars may be many miles apart in the wilds of southern New Mexico, so you'll be glad that you're carrying your own kitchen — with a well-stocked refrigerator. At the same time, be aware that some of the small, scruffy-looking country kitchens that you encounter are treasured word-of-mouth secrets whispered from one chile-head to another.

The Hatch Chile

"You spell it chili, and I spell it chile . . . " but before we call the whole thing off, let's explain. In New Mexico, the spicy *capiscum* pod always is spelled "chile" and often the dishes made from it as well. Texans like the spelling "chili," just as Anglo-Indians often use "chilli." Hatch is the center of New Mexico chile-growing, and New Mexico leads the nation in total production. The official state vegetables are chiles and *frijoles* (beans, usually the pinto variety).

Chiles come in two colors, red and green. The red chile is simply a riper version of the green chile. Most New Mexican restaurants give you the choice of red or green chile stews, soups, and sauces. Always ask which is hotter, because it varies from pepper to pepper. The most commonly grown variety is the New Mexico long green, moderate on a chile heat scale that ranks jalapenos as moderately hot. Tiny serrano and habanero chiles rate much higher on the Scoville heat scale.

New Mexico chile is made primarily of fresh, frozen roasted, or canned chile peppers, while Texas *chili con carne* is meat (without beans) seasoned with dried chili.

Some like it hot: A glossary of New Mexico chile dishes

Burrito — A flour tortilla wrapped around beans and/or meat and chile; the breakfast version is made from eggs, cheese, potatoes, chorizo sausage or bacon, and red or green chiles.

Carne adovada — Pieces of pork marinated in red or green chiles and baked.

Carne asada — Strips of beef or pork grilled or roasted and served with red or green chiles.

Carnitas — Little pieces of beef or pork cut in strips and marinated in red or green chiles.

Chile con queso (*case*-o) — Melted cheese with red or green chiles served with corn chips as a dip.

Chile rellenos (re-*yay*-nos) — Whole green chiles stuffed with cheese, dipped in batter and fried.

Chimichanga — Deep-fried meat or bean burritos topped with chiles or salsa.

(continued)

(continued)

Enchiladas — Corn tortillas wrapped or stacked with various combinations of meat, cheese, beans, and chiles.

Flautas — Crisp rolled corn tortillas filled with meat and chiles.

Frito pie — The ultimate New Mexico fast food/junk food; a gloppy mixture of meat, cheese, chiles, and beans spooned over an opened package of Fritos corn chips in the original sack.

Green chile stew — Green chiles, meat, potatoes, and sometimes other vegetables served in a soup bowl.

Huevos rancheros (*whey*-vos ran-*cher*-os) — Corn tortillas topped with fried eggs, beans, cheese, and chiles.

Indian taco — A fried flour tortilla or puffy Navajo fry bread filled or topped with ground beef, cheese, beans, guacamole, sour cream, and red or green chiles.

Menudo (men-*you*-doe) — Soup made from tripe, onions, and chiles; considered the perfect hangover remedy in the Southwest and Mexico.

Pico de gallo (*peek*-o dee-*guy*-o) — Salsa made from coarsely chopped raw tomatoes, onions, cilantro, and chiles.

Posole (puh-*sol*-a) — A soup made from pork, hominy, Mexican oregano, and chiles.

Quesadillas (case-a-*dee*-yas) — Corn or flour tortillas sandwiched together with cheese and fried or baked.

Stuffed sopapillas (soap-a-*pee*-yahs) — Puffy fried pillows of dough stuffed with meat, cheese, beans, and chiles.

Tamale — Corn meal dough wrapped around spicy fillings of meat, cheese, or corn and steamed in dried cornhusks.

What follows are some good eats establishments in southern New Mexico and the adjacent area around El Paso, Texas.

✔ **Cattleman's Steakhouse:** 3045 S. Carlsbad Rd., Fabens, Texas (☎ 915-764-2283). The restaurant isn't hard to find after you get to Fabens, about 25 miles south of El Paso on I-10. Just take Exit 10 from I-10 and head north, following the signs. This dude ranch and steak restaurant serves great steaks; a display case shows the raw steaks in each size, so you can gauge your appetite. Reservations suggested. A huge parking lot by the restaurant can handle RVs. Open Monday through Friday from 4:30 to 10 p.m., Saturday from noon to 10 p.m., and Sunday from noon to 9 p.m.

✔ **Chope's:** SR 28, La Mesa, New Mexico (☎ 505-233-9976). Chope's is where the chile growers eat chiles rellenos, blue corn enchiladas, and green chile enchiladas. Park on the street. Open Tuesday through Saturday from 11:30 a.m. to 1:30 p.m. and from 6 to 8:30 p.m.

✔ **K-Bob's Steakhouse:** 316 E. Cedar St., Deming, New Mexico (☎ 505-546-8883). This popular eatery is locally famous for its chicken fried steak with baked potato for a low, low price. If you've eaten chicken fried steak before, you know it's a pounded cube steak dipped in industrial-strength batter and deep-fried, and you know whether you like it. If you never tried the dish before, this is a good, cheap place to order one for the first time. A parking lot and easy street parking are available. Open daily from 10:30 a.m. to 10 p.m.

✔ **La Posta Restaurant and Chile Shop:** 2410 Calle de San Albino, Mesilla, New Mexico (☎ 505-524-3524). At the chile shop, look for hot sauces, salsas, recipe books, canned chiles, and other accessories for chile cooking. In the restaurant, an American classic since 1939, large portions of tacos, enchiladas, chile con queso, and tostados are served at lunch and dinner. RV parking is on the street. Both restaurant and chile shop are open Tuesday through Sunday from 11 a.m. to 9 p.m.

✔ **Little Diner and Tortilla Factory:** 7209 Seventh St., Canutillo, Texas (☎ 915-877-2176). Crowds always are standing in line at this popular place that sells tortillas to go, and a full gamut of other New Mexico treats to eat in or take out. (This part of Texas unofficially is in New Mexico.) We like the deep-fried masa patties called *gorditas* filled with spicy red chile sauce and chunks of pork, but the local children were gobbling them down stuffed with ground beef, chopped lettuce, and tomatoes, sort of a **McGordita.** Large, adjacent parking lot has plenty of space for RVs. Open Thursday through Tuesday from 11 a.m. to 8 p.m.

✔ **Nellie's Café:** 1226 W. Hadley, Las Cruces, New Mexico (☎ 505-524-9982). Servings are enormous, and the atmosphere is relaxed at breakfast, lunch, and dinner. Order anything with chiles, even the chile cheeseburger, and don't skip the refried beans, even at breakfast. RV parking is available in large open lots nearby or on the street. Open daily from 8 a.m. to 4 p.m.

✔ **Stahman's Farm:** SR 28, 6 miles south of Mesilla, New Mexico (☎ 505-526-8974). The farm sells plenty of pecans shelled or unshelled, plus candies and other goodies made from the local nuts. Large parking lot offers space for RVs. Open Monday through Saturday from 9 a.m. to 6 p.m., and Sundays from 11 a.m. to 5 p.m.

Shopping along the Way

El Paso, Texas, is a great place to buy cowboy boots because so many brands are available in the factory outlet stores lining I-10 east of town. When buying ready-made boots, be sure the heel slips a little when you walk; when the sole gets more flexible, the slippage stops. If the heel doesn't slip when you first try it on, the boot is too tight and will give you blisters. The instep should be snug, the boot shank long enough to cover your arch fully, and the ball of your foot should fit into the widest part of the boot and not sit forward or back of it. Some stores worth a peek are

- ✔ **Justin Outlet,** 7100 Gateway East, I-10 at Hawkins (☎ **915-779-5465**).
- ✔ **Tony Lama,** 7156 Gateway East, just off I-10 (☎ **915-772-4327**).
- ✔ **Lucchese Factory Outlet,** 6601 Montana (☎ **915-778-8060**).

Fast Facts

Area Code

Area codes include **505** in New Mexico and **915** in El Paso, Texas.

Emergency

Call ☎ **911.**

Hospitals

Along the route, major hospitals are in El Paso, Roswell, and Carlsbad.

Information

Sources include New Mexico Tourism, 491 Old Sante Fe Trail, Santa Fe 87501 (☎ 800-733-6396; www.newmexico.org); and El Paso Covention and Visitors Bureau (☎ 800-3561-6024). For a New Mexico Vacation Guide, call ☎ 800-733-6396, ext. 0175.

New Mexico Campground Reservations (☎ **877-664-7787**)

Laws

All RV occupants must wear seat belts in New Mexico. The maximum speed limit on interstates is 75 mph. Speed limits are lower in urban areas.

Road and Weather Conditions

In New Mexico, call ☎ 800-432-4269.

Taxes

New Mexico has a motel and campground tax of 10%. State gasoline taxes are 17¢ a gallon.

Time Zone

New Mexico and El Paso follow mountain standard time.

Chapter 22

The Oregon Coast: California to Washington

. . . .

In This Chapter

▶ Beachcombing in world-class style

▶ Hiking in the Oregon dunes

▶ Riding the wind in the Kite Capital of the World

. . . .

*O*regon is not like any other state. Oregonians are overwhelmingly, genuinely — there's no other word for it — *nice*. Even today, you can find traces of those gentle eccentrics, who 150 years ago packed up pianos and plows, cousins and cows, and set out along the Oregon Trail. And for anyone who remembers or read about the 1960s, the latter-day hippies still live along the beaches or up in the hills above the Pacific.

If you look at a road map of Oregon — and you need to if you're making this drive — you can see that its major cities are lined up neatly in a vertical row along I-5 an hour or two inland, but each of them — **Portland, Salem,** and **Eugene** — has a corridor road leading to its own closest beach. The heaviest tourist developments — restaurants, shops, motels, dune-buggy rentals, and jet boat excursion companies — are clustered for a mile or two on either side of the place where the corridor reaches the sea. Get away from those access roads, and you find untrampled dunes, bleached driftwood, lonely beaches, and the wild surf of your dreams.

The coast is dotted lavishly with state parks that have RV hookups, overnight camping spots, and picnic tables. Although the water often is too cold for swimming for all but the hardiest, walking and beach-combing are world-class. Alert strollers may find Japanese fishing floats, bits of agate, and driftwood twisted into fantastic shapes. Kite flyers love the sea breezes, sand castle builders compete for the most grandiose constructions, and chowderheads can dig for Oregon razor clams and giant geoducks.

Getting There

U.S. 101 follows the Oregon coastline for almost all of its 365 miles, dipping inland occasionally but always returning to the sea. Even when the main route leaves the water, minor side roads cling to the coast. This drive begins in the south, at the **Oregon/California border,** and continues north to **Astoria,** the spot where Lewis and Clark spent the winter of 1805 to 1806. If you prefer, you can make the drive in the opposite direction by simply reversing the route directions. The entire route covers approximately **400 miles,** more if you take some of the side detours. (See "The Oregon Coast" map in this chapter.)

We added the Long Beach Peninsula in Washington State, just across the Columbia River from Astoria because many Oregon coast visitors consider the beach an extension of the coast drive. Official mileposts along the way on U.S. 101 begin with 0 at the Oregon/Washington border, in the middle of the Columbia River, and continue through mile 363 at the Oregon/California border. The Long Beach Peninsula extension adds another 40 or so miles.

Planning Ahead

While you can drive along the Oregon coast year-round, **summer is the best time.** Temperatures are warmer, and less rain falls. The winter weather in Oregon is a mixed bag. Here we quote the Oregon Tourism Commission itself: "You've heard the old joke that people in Oregon don't tan. They rust. Or if you wait outside for a bus, you'll grow moss on your north side. But lest you assume that it rains every day here in winter, let's set the record straight. Some days it snows."

Between **December and February,** the **gray whales** migrate south along the Oregon Coast from Alaska to their calving grounds in Baja, Mexico. Then they head north again, passing even closer to the coast with their baby whales nearby, in the months of **March, April, and May.** So winter and springtime are good for whale-watching. And fall offers many dry sunny days interspersed with days of drizzle.

Whenever you go to the Oregon Coast, be prepared for some rainy days. We use those days to settle in comfortably in our RV, reading, working puzzles, baking cookies or muffins to munch on down the road, or puttering around the campsite. Then when the sun comes out, we drop everything and head for the beach.

Expect crowds on summer weekends at the beaches, but the rest of the week, even in summer, long stretches of coastline can be empty. State parks are popular with Oregonians in the summer, so make **campground reservations** whenever possible during that season. The rest of the year, you may well have a campground entirely to yourself, the way we have on many occasions.

The Oregon Coast

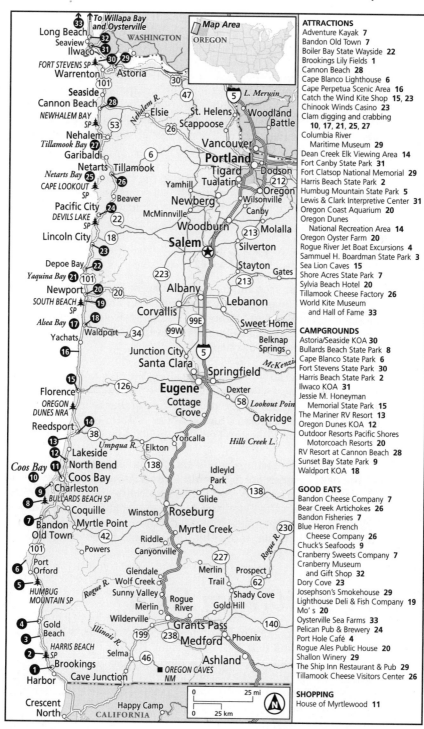

ATTRACTIONS
Adventure Kayak **7**
Bandon Old Town **7**
Boiler Bay State Wayside **22**
Brookings Lily Fields **1**
Cannon Beach **28**
Cape Blanco Lighthouse **6**
Cape Perpetua Scenic Area **16**
Catch the Wind Kite Shop **15, 23**
Chinook Winds Casino **23**
Clam digging and crabbing
 10, 17, 21, 25, 27
Columbia River
 Maritime Museum **29**
Dean Creek Elk Viewing Area **14**
Fort Canby State Park **31**
Fort Clatsop National Memorial **29**
Harris Beach State Park **2**
Humbug Mountain State Park **5**
Lewis & Clark Interpretive Center **31**
Oregon Coast Aquarium **20**
Oregon Dunes
 National Recreation Area **14**
Oregon Oyster Farm **20**
Rogue River Jet Boat Excursions **4**
Sammuel H. Boardman State Park **3**
Sea Lion Caves **15**
Shore Acres State Park **7**
Sylvia Beach Hotel **20**
Tillamook Cheese Factory **26**
World Kite Museum
 and Hall of Fame **33**

CAMPGROUNDS
Astoria/Seaside KOA **30**
Bullards Beach State Park **8**
Cape Blanco State Park **6**
Fort Stevens State Park **30**
Harris Beach State Park **2**
Ilwaco KOA **31**
Jessie M. Honeyman
 Memorial State Park **15**
The Mariner RV Resort **13**
Oregon Dunes KOA **12**
Outdoor Resorts Pacific Shores
 Motorcoach Resorts **20**
RV Resort at Cannon Beach **28**
Sunset Bay State Park **9**
Waldport KOA **18**

GOOD EATS
Bandon Cheese Company **7**
Bear Creek Artichokes **26**
Bandon Fisheries **7**
Blue Heron French
 Cheese Company **26**
Chuck's Seafoods **9**
Cranberry Sweets Company **7**
Cranberry Museum
 and Gift Shop **32**
Dory Cove **23**
Josephson's Smokehouse **29**
Lighthouse Deli & Fish Company **19**
Mo's **20**
Oysterville Sea Farms **33**
Pelican Pub & Brewery **24**
Port Hole Café **4**
Rogue Ales Public House **20**
Shallon Winery **29**
The Ship Inn Restaurant & Pub **29**
Tillamook Cheese Visitors Center **26**

SHOPPING
House of Myrtlewood **11**

Obviously, you want to **pack rain gear.** Even those two-piece yellow slicker suits can come in handy if you — like us — enjoy walking along the beach in the rain. Although coastal temperatures are comfortable to cool, even in summer, a short drive inland takes you into warmer weather, so take along some lightweight cotton clothing. Sweaters with silk turtlenecks underneath or sweatshirts and sweatpants make good Oregon RV travel clothes. Even in the best restaurants in Oregon, folks don't dress up much; we can't imagine a place where you'd need to wear a tie unless you're combining your RV vacation with a business trip. Take sturdy walking shoes, preferably hiking boots, with a spare pair in case one pair gets wet, and a pair of waterproof boots if you want to explore tidal pools.

Allow a week for a leisurely tour along the Oregon Coast, although you can drive the route straight through in a couple of days, something we don't recommend, because you'd miss some wonderful experiences.

Stocking the Pantry

Oregon manufactures some excellent **cheeses,** especially mild to sharp cheddars, which you can buy from the factory at **Tillamook** and the outlet store at **Bandon-by-the-Sea.** French-style soft cheeses also can be found in Tillamook at **Blue Heron French Cheese Company.** (See "Good eats" later in this chapter.)

Seafood is superlative everywhere along the coast. Watch for roadside fish markets. Local salmon smoked in the Northwestern style over alder wood or in Nova Scotia–lox style can be purchased at several producers, including **Josephson's Smokehouse** in Astoria, **Chuck's Seafoods** in Charleston, and **Bandon Fisheries** in Bandon. (See "Good eats.")

If you enjoy wine-tastings, you'll enjoy sampling **Oregon's wines.** Some of the best wineries are in **Yamhill County** around **McMinnville,** just inland from **Lincoln City** via SR 18. Pinot Noirs are especially outstanding; interestingly, the Pinot Noir grapes grow happily in the same region with hazelnuts, also called filberts. Follow Scenic Route 99W and SR 47 north of McMinnville, and within 15 to 20 miles, you come across some two dozen wineries.

Driving the Oregon Coast

The drive begins at mile 363 on the **Oregon/California border** on U.S. 101 in the **Banana Belt.** Yes, that's right, Banana Belt. It's called that because the weather is unusually mild because of a consistent weather pattern that produces the warmest average temperatures on the Oregon Coast. The **Brookings** area is where most of America's Easter lilies are grown, where an annual azalea festival takes place Memorial Day week-end at the end of May, and where retirees increasingly are flocking. Look for the lily fields along U.S. 101 south of Brookings.

At milepost 355.6 in **Harris Beach State Park** is an **Oregon Welcome Center,** where you can pick up maps and materials about the Oregon Coast. Look particularly for the free *Oregon Coast Mile-by-Mile Guide to Highway 101.* The center is closed in the winter months.

North of Brookings, **Samuel H. Boardman State Park** is spread along 12 miles of roadway with hiking trails striking off from a dozen way-sides where you can park the RV. (See "More cool things to see and do," later in this chapter.) Only 0.7 miles north of North Island View-point, **China Beach** is a favorite.

At **Gold Beach,** Oregon's famous **Rogue River** surges into the Pacific. Miners discovered gold on the beach in the mid-1800s, giving the town its name. **Jet boat tours** up the river leave from Gold Beach daily between May 1 and October 30 and travel variously 64, 80, and 104 miles up the river. (See "More cool things to see and do" for details on boat tours.)

Humbug Mountain State Park, just south of **Port Orford** at milepost 305.5, stands 1,730 feet above the beach, waiting for hikers to challenge its 3-mile loop trail (see "More cool things to see and do"). Port Orford, the oldest town site along the Oregon Coast, is blessedly free of so-called tourist attractions, but you can stroll around to see the boats dry-docked at the marina, an unusual arrangement. At low tide, you can walk over to the Battle Rock landmark at milepost 301, a good place for whale-watching. The **Cape Blanco Lighthouse** at milepost 296.6 north of Port Orford is open for tours in summer (see "More cool things to see and do"), and the **Cape Blanco State Park** has a campground with electrical hookups. (See "Runner-up campgrounds" later in this chapter.)

Bandon Old Town, or as they've begun calling it, Bandon-by-the-Sea, is one of our favorite coastal towns because if you come in off-season or early in the day, you can drive in, park in one of the designated RV parking lots or along the street, and just walk around and groove on the place. (See "Must-see attractions," later in this chapter). You'll find art galleries, a fishing plant with a retail outlet, a cheese store outlet with free samples, a candy company with free samples, and a fish-and-chips takeout. You can also rent a sea kayak from **Adventure Kayak** to travel the Coquille River. (See "More cool things to see and do.")

Just north of Bandon around milepost 283 lie Oregon's cranberry bogs, a big surprise to anyone from New England, who thought Massachusetts had an exclusive on the Thanksgiving berry. From Bandon, U.S. 101 turns inland for the 17 miles into the **Coos Bay** area. Take some time to drive the back road that passes a string of state parks on its way into

Charleston; to get to the back road, take a left turn on West Beaver Hill Road near milepost 236 about 8 miles north of Bandon. **Shore Acres State Park** has some of the most spectacular wave action along the coast; you can watch winter storms from an enclosed shelter in the park. You can also stop at several vantage points to look at sea lions. **Sunset Bay State Park** is a sheltered camping area with hookups. (See "Our favorite campgrounds," later in this chapter.)

Charleston is an off-the-beaten-path fishing community with a good fish market and oyster company, **Chuck's Seafoods,** on the west end of the bridge. (See "Good eats" for details.)

Coos Bay is the heart of Oregon's myrtlewood country. This prized hardwood grows only at this site and is used for making salad bowls and utensils, goblets, and even jewelry. Local factories, such as **House of Myrtlewood,** offer free tours. (See "Shopping along the Way" later in this chapter.)

North of North Bend, the **Oregon Dunes National Recreation Area** begins and continues through **Reedsport,** where the headquarters are located, 45 miles north to Florence. You find some trailheads with parking large enough for RVs, so you can stop and play in the sand. (See "Must-see attractions.")

From Reedsport, SR 38 turns inland 3.5 miles to the **Dean Creek Elk Viewing Area,** where you stand a good chance of getting a look at one of the 120 or so resident Roosevelt elk almost any time. On one autumn day, near sunset, we saw a dozen or more grazing quietly close to the roadway and viewing platform. (See "More cool things to see and do.")

Florence and **Lincoln City,** Kite Capital of the World, have branches of **Catch the Wind Kites Shops,** great places to pick up a kite if you have the urge to fly one on the beach. (See "More cool things to see and do.") Lincoln City claims that its winds are the world's best for kite flying because of its location halfway between the equator and the North Pole.

Florence also is home to the famous **Sea Lion Caves,** 12 miles north, one of the most interesting and certainly the smelliest of the Oregon Coast attractions. Instead of scrambling down the rocks to see the wild Stellar sea lions, you get into an elevator and ride 208 feet down to sea (or sea lion) level. The creatures spend most of the fall and winter months inside the gigantic caves and then move outside in spring and summer to breed and bear young. (See "Must-see attractions.")

At **Cape Perpetua Scenic Area,** stop to visit the Interpretive Center, with a Discovery Cove for kids; allow time to hike at least one of the three trails. The Giant Spruce Trail is 2 miles round-trip along a creek through tall trees; the Captain Cook Trail is a 1-mile trail down to the sea; and the Cape Perpetua Trail climbs the south face of the 803-foot cape itself. (See "More cool things to see and do.")

The next coastal town along the route is **Yachats,** pronounced *ya*-hots, known as "the gem of the Oregon Coast," and most popular, we suspect, with people who know how to pronounce it.

Newport is a favored destination for its splendid **Oregon Coast Aquarium** (see "Must-see attractions") and the **Sylvia Beach Hotel,** named for the Paris bookshop owner who befriended numerous authors in the 1920s. Each of its 20 rooms is decorated in the spirit of and named for a noted author from Edgar Allen Poe to Agatha Christie, Dr. Seuss to Ernest Hemingway. The rooms don't have TVs, radios, or phones, but books and games are everywhere. Smoking is prohibited.

While you're in the aquarium vicinity, if it's lunchtime, head south to the **Lighthouse Deli & Fish Company** for some of the best fish and chips on the Oregon Coast. Native Yaquina Bay oysters farmed in the beds of the bay were the expensive oysters so popular with miners who struck it rich during the California gold rush in 1849. Do a little digging on your own. The clam chowder champion in these parts is the original **Mo's.** (See "Good eats" for both restaurants. For info on doing a little clam digging on your own, see "More cool things to see and do.")

![TIP]

Depoe Bay is another good area for whale-watching and for spotting seals and sea lions, both members of the order *Pinnipedia*, meaning they have finlike feet or flippers. The harbor, one of the smallest in the world, is fascinating to watch as vessels maneuver the narrow channels between rocks. *Spouting horns,* rock formations that turn waves into plumes of water, line the town's sea wall. Gray whales come in so close, locals say, because they like to scratch their backs on the rocks. **Boiler Bay State Wayside** north of town is one of the best bird- and whale-watching spots in the area.

Lincoln City is one of the more commercial beach towns along the Oregon Coast, pioneering the area's first factory outlet center at milepost 115.6. RVs are welcome, if you're in the mood for a bit of shopping. To complete the un-Oregon atmosphere, the **Chinook Winds Casino,** belonging to the Siletz tribe, also is in Lincoln and promises coupons for cheap gas to winners. (See "More cool things to see and do.")

Detour off 101 and head east to Pacific City, have some fish and chips at the **Pelican Pub & Brewery,** and drive the curvy but beautiful **Three Cape Scenic Route** into Tillamook.

Tillamook always is one of our favorite stops along the Oregon Coast because of its delicious cheeses, but the **Tillamook Cheese Factory,** right on U.S. 101, also makes rich ice cream and sells other made-in-Oregon items. (See "Must-see attractions.") The **Blue Heron French Cheese Company** is right off 101 on a marked driveway and offers wine-tasting along with cheese-tasting. (See "Good eats.") Both spots have plenty of RV parking.

Cannon Beach is a popular resort community with a sandcastle competition and a kite-flying festival. Between April and October, you may
see tufted puffins around **Haystack Rock** at milepost 30.5.

Seaside, only 10 miles up the coast from Cannon Beach, was the
Oregon Coast's first resort; its amusement park dates from 1873. A
Ferris wheel remains, but formerly, the complex included a zoo, racetrack, and posh hotel. Members of the Lewis and Clark party ventured
to Seaside from their quarters at Fort Clatsop during the winter of
1805 to 1806 to boil sea water for salt to preserve meats for the long
journey home. (See Fort Clatsop National Memorial under "Must-see
attractions.")

Astoria can claim to be the oldest American city west of the Missouri
River, because John Jacob Astor founded it in 1811 as a fur-trading
port. The **Columbia River Maritime Museum,** one of the best of its
kind anywhere, has an interesting gift shop. (See "Must-see attractions.") Today, the town retains much of its charm, although feisty
locals like to display bumper stickers saying, "We Ain't Quaint."

From Astoria, we recommend driving north across the Columbia into
Washington State to explore the **Long Beach Peninsula,** which has a
magnificent long sandy beach on the ocean side and some of the best
oysters on the West Coast on the Willapa Bay side. Take U.S. 101 across
the bridge, then follow it west to **Ilwaco** and **Seaview,** then take SR 103
to the northern tip of the peninsula at **Oysterville.** Along the peninsula, you find the **World Kite Museum and Hall of Fame,** the only kite
museum in the United States, and the **Lewis & Clark Interpretive
Center** near Cape Disappointment. (See "More cool things to see and
do" for both attractions.) You also pass **Oysterville Sea Farms,** which
sells all sorts of homemade condiments (see "Good eats"). This extension to visit the peninsula adds 40 miles to the basic journey.

Must-see attractions

Bandon Old Town
Bandon-by-the-Sea, Oregon

The Old Town of Bandon isn't *that* old. In 1936, a fire destroyed the original town, which then was rebuilt along the mouth of the Coquille River.
Known as the "Storm Watching Capital of the World" and the "Cranberry
Capital of Oregon," this town is a great place to look for agates on the
beach, dig clams at Coquille Point, browse in the local art galleries, order
fish and chips to go, and munch on a super-large cone of local Umpqua
Dairy Co. ice cream. The fun here is making your own special discovery
while you stroll around. We suggest that you explore the area between
First and Second streets along Alabama, Baltimore, Chicago, Delaware,
Elmira, and Fillmore streets.

Milepost 270 on U.S. 101. ☎ *541-347-9616 (Chamber of Commerce). RV parking: Designated lots, plenty of street parking on weekdays. Admission: Free. Shops open daily 8:30 a.m.–5:30 p.m. Allow a half-day.*

Columbia River Maritime Museum
Astoria, Oregon

The museum recently was renovated and expanded with a large indoor and outdoor collection that includes the conning tower of a submarine, the reconstructed bridge of a U.S. Navy destroyer, displays of early fishing boats, lighthouses, fishing, navigation, and naval history. You can tour a floating lighthouse, the lightship *Columbia,* ponder the personal effects of passengers who went down in ships snagged on the disastrous reefs at the mouth of the Columbia River, and browse in the well-stocked museum store.

1792 Marine Dr. ☎ *503-325-2323.* www.crmm.org. *RV parking: Two large parking lots adjacent to museum, also street parking. Admission: $8 adults, $7 seniors, $4 ages 6–17. Open: Daily 9:30 a.m.–5 p.m. Closed Thanksgiving and Christmas. Allow 3 hours.*

Fort Clatsop National Memorial
Astoria, Oregon

This replica of the fort where the members of the Lewis and Clark expedition spent the winter of 1805 to 1806 turned out to be more accurate than even the historians suspected; in 1999, an anthropologist turned up a 148-year-old map showing that the site of the original was very close to where the copy was built. During the summer, buckskin-clad, fur-hatted expeditioners show visitors what day-to-day life was like for the Corps of Discovery. A fine gift shop carries books and videos about the Lewis and Clark expedition. Expansion plans for the bicentennial in 2005 may change the parking area and admission prices. Call for information.

92343 Fort Clatsop Rd. ☎ *503-861-2471. RV parking: Large parking lot capable of handling tour buses. Admission: $3 ages 17 and older, $5 for a family, free ages 16 and younger. Open: Daily 8 a.m.–5 p.m., mid-June through Labor Day until 6 p.m. Closed Christmas. Allow 3 hours.*

Oregon Coast Aquarium
Newport, Oregon

If children like this aquarium half as much as a couple of jaded adults that we know, they'll have a great day! You can see eye-to-eye with a tufted puffin in a walk-through aviary with special windows to let you see them "fly" underwater as they dive for fish. A glass tunnel through the water puts you in the ocean with sharks, sea lions, seals, sea otters, and a giant Pacific octopus. Oregon Coast Aquarium is where Keiko, star of the film *Free Willy,* was rehabilitated before returning to the wild.

2820 SE Ferry Slip Rd. ☎ *541-867-3474.* www.aquarium.org. *RV parking: Designated lots. Admission: $10.75 ages 14 and older, $9.50 seniors, $6.50 ages 4–13. Open: Daily summer 9 a.m.–6 p.m., winter 10 a.m.–5 p.m. Closed Christmas. Allow 3–4 hours. Rental wheelchairs available.*

Oregon Dunes National Recreation Area
Reedsport (headquarters), Oregon

Stretching 45 miles along the coast between North Bend and Florence, the Oregon dunes have access areas with off-road parking, some of it large enough for RVs and some of it not quite. If you can, eyeball entrances before entering to determine whether you can park and/or turn around. One good trail is the 2.5-mile Umpqua Dunes route, accessed from the trailhead 10.5 miles south of Reedsport near Lakeside. Or head for Oregon Dunes Overlook, 10 miles north of Reedsport on U.S. 101, where kids of all ages can run and roll in the sand.

855 U.S. 101. ☎ *541-271-3611. Reesport visitor center open daily 8 a.m.–4:30 p.m. Allow as much time as you can spare.*

Sea Lion Caves
Florence, Oregon

Wild Stellar sea lions, the largest of the sea lions, inhabit these caves or the rocks outside them year-round, spending fall and winter inside and spring and summer outside. Open since 1932, this commercial attraction is fascinating for anyone who hasn't been to a sea lion or seal rookery before. An elevator descends 208 feet down into the caves; you have to negotiate some stairs and ramps to get to the elevator. Take a sweater or jacket, camera and binoculars, and be prepared, especially in fall and winter, for plenty of noise and some really rank smells. If you prefer your sea lions cute and cuddly, don't venture farther than the gift shop where you can buy the stuffed kind. Most kids get a kick out of the elevator ride and the novelty of being in a cave, although they may complain about the smell.

91560 U.S. 101. ☎ *541-547-3111.* www.sealioncaves.com. *RV parking: Designated RV lot. Admission: $7 adults, $4.50 ages 6–15. Open: Daily summer 8 a.m.–7:30 p.m., winter 9 a.m.–3:30 p.m. Allow 1 hour.*

Tillamook Cheese Factory
Tillamook, Oregon

This factory tour with its free samples is Oregon's third most-popular tourist attraction. The attraction draws many people who have no idea how milk from cute black-and-white cows turns into mild or sharp cheddar cheese. The Tillamook County Creamery Association was founded back in 1918, and today's modern factory turns out 40 million pounds of cheese a year, plus ice cream, and other dairy products.

4175 U.S. 101. ☎ *503-842-4481. RV parking: Designated lots. Admission: Free. Open: Daily summer 8 a.m.–8 p.m., winter 8 a.m.–6 p.m. Closed major holidays. Allow 2 hours.*

More cool things to see and do

Oregon seems big as all outdoors with so much to do along its beaches that you can never get bored. In addition to the suggestions in the following list, you may want to check out **Cannon Beach** (☎ **503-436-2623** for the Chamber of Commerce; www.cannonbeach.org); **Chinook Winds Casino,** on the beach in Lincoln City (☎ **888-CHINOOK** (888-244-6665), www.chinookwindscasino.com); or **whale-watching** (☎ **541-563-2002**).

✔ **Kayak Coquille-style.** Go kayaking up the Coquille River past a wildlife refuge with a guide from **Adventure Kayak** for two to three hours in one-man or two-man kayak.

First Street, Bandon, Oregon. ☎ **541-347-3480.** RV parking: Large lot in town or street parking. Tour: $35 per adult or child. Open: Daily 9 a.m.–5 p.m. Allow 3 hours.

✔ **Go fly a kite. Catch the Wind Kite Shops** can fill the need when you have a sudden urge to run along an Oregon beach with a brightly colored kite. Prices range from $7.95 to $200.

Two Oregon locations: 266 SE U.S. 101, Lincoln City (☎ **541-994-9500**); Bay Street near the Siuslaw Bridge, Florence (☎ **541-997-9500**). Open: Daily 10 a.m.–5 p.m.

✔ **Dig in. Clam digging** and **crabbing** in Yaquina, Alsea, Coos, Tillamook, and Netarts bays doesn't require a license, just some basic skills and equipment. You can rent the equipment, and the vendor can probably clue you in to the technique. Get information booklets and approved locations from the Oregon Department of Fish and Wildlife. (See "Fast Facts" at the end of this chapter.)

✔ **Rack up an elk.** At **Dean Creek Elk Viewing Area** near Reedsport, you can sometimes get a good look at a Roosevelt elk or maybe a whole herd. The best times to go are early morning and late afternoon.

The viewing platform is 3.5 miles east of Reedsport, Oregon, on SR 38. RV parking: Off-road parking lot. Admision: Free. Open: Always.

✔ **Follow the trail.** The **Lewis & Clark Interpretive Center** overlooks the often-foggy mouth of the Columbia River, where a lighthouse towers above Cape Disappointment. Walk along a series of ramps that traces the expedition and then take a look at the lighthouse from the grounds of the center. If you climb quietly up the path from the parking lot to the center, you may see some of the deer that like to hang around the park picnic area.

Take the SR 100 loop from Ilwaco to **Fort Canby State Park**, Ilwaco, Washington. ☎ **306-642-3029.** RV parking: Limited to roadside parking at the foot of the stairs leading up to the center and lighthouse. Admission: Free. Open: Daily 10 a.m.–5 p.m. Allow 2 hours. A campground with hookups is located in the park.

✔ **Lighten up.** Cape Blanco was discovered in 1603 by a Spanish explorer, and its **lighthouse,** open for tours in summer, is on the westernmost point in Oregon.

In **Cape Blanco State Park**, milepost 296.6 on U.S. 101, north of Port Orford, Oregon. ☎ **800-551-6949.** RV parking: Designated lot. Admission: Donation requested. Open: Summer Thur–Mon 10 a.m.–3:30 p.m. Allow 1 hour.

✔ **Hike the coast.** The scenery is dramatic, the waves thundering, and the trails exciting. RV roadside parking may be limited at some lookouts and trailheads. Follow the trails; information is at each trailhead. Some good hiking areas: **Oregon Dunes National Recreation Area, Cape Perpetua Scenic Area, Samuel H. Boardman State Park, Humbug Mountain State Park,** and **Shore Acres State Park.**

Oregon Dunes, Reedsport (☎ **541-271-3611**); Cape Perpetua (☎ **541-547-3289**); and state parks information (☎ **800-551-6949**).

✔ **Cruise the bay.** Board the 49-passenger *Discovery* in Newport for tours of Yaquina Bay that may include visits to the **Oregon Oyster Farm,** an introduction to crabbing by friendly onboard naturalists, whale-watching in season, and a closeup of sea lions.

Marine Discovery Tours, Bay Blvd., Newport, Oregon. ☎ **800-903-2628.** www.marinediscovery.com. Call for times, tour types, prices, and reservations. Allow a half-day.

✔ **Up a roguish river. Rogue River Jet Boat Excursions** set out from Gold Beach, Oregon, and go up the river with stops to see and photograph wildlife. Trips vary from 64 to 108 miles, and reservations are suggested.

Jerry's Rogue River Jets (☎ **800-451-3645**); and **Rogue River Mail Boat Hydro-Jets** (☎ **800-458-3511**). Daily departures May 1–Oct 30. Call for times, rates, and reservations.

✔ **String yourself along.** The **World Kite Museum and Hall of Fame** is the only American museum dedicated exclusively to kites. The long smooth stretch of sandy beach on the peninsula offers optimum conditions for kite-flying.

On North Third east of Pacific Hwy., Long Beach, Washington. ☎ **360-642-4020.** www.worldkitemuseum.com. RV parking: Street parking. Admission: $4 adults, $3 seniors and children, $9 family. Open: June–Aug daily 11 a.m.–5 p.m., Sept–May weekdays only 11 a.m.–5 p.m.

Weekend wonder

Although driving the 360 or so miles of 101 along the Oregon Coast in one day is possible, no one in their right mind would do it. For a nice weekend along the northern coast, starting from Portland's main access route of U.S. 26, drive over to **Seaside** and **Cannon Beach,** then drive south through **Tillamook** to **Lincoln City,** and return to the **Portland** area by SR 18 through **McMinnville** and the **Oregon wine country.** To highlight the central coast for the weekend, start from **Eugene** and drive across SR 126 to **Florence,** then drive north as far as **Newport,** and return to I-5 via U.S. 20 to **Corvallis.** Then a short 45-mile drive down I-5 returns you to Eugene. For a weekend on the southern Oregon Coast, start from **Brookings** at the California border and drive north as far as **Florence** and then cross SR 126 to **Eugene.**

Sleeping and Eating on the Road

The Oregon Coast is thickly dotted with campgrounds, both state parks (19 of them with RV camping and hookups) and commercial parks (26 towns and communities along the coast have one or more RV parks). Although making reservations is a good idea at beachfront state parks in summer, especially on weekends, you should be able to find an empty spot almost anywhere during the rest of the year. An RV-friendly state, Oregon has 37 designated waste disposal or sanitary dump stations and a corresponding map/guide with access hours and locations. Many of the State Parks outshine their commercial counterparts in site size and separation. Call **Oregon State Parks (☎ 800-551-6949)** for a brochure or pick one up at any state welcome center.

 Oregon State Park Discovery Season, from October through April, offers RV campers a savings from $2 to $5 a night for renting a full hookup site at any state park.

All campgrounds in this chapter are open year-round and have public flush toilets, showers, and sanitary dump stations unless designated otherwise. Toll-free numbers are for reservations only unless noted otherwise. See Chapter 9 for our criteria on choosing our favorite campgrounds.

Our favorite campgrounds

Astoria/Seaside KOA

$$$$–$$$$$ **Warrenton, Oregon**

Convenient to Astoria and Fort Clatsop National Memorial, this KOA is at the mouth of the Columbia River a mile from the beach and offers free shuttle service in summer. Free pancake breakfasts are dished up on weekday mornings, and weekends bring special programs and activities. Fishing and clamming are good in the vicinity. Some of the paved sites are wide. If you need slideout space notify them when checking in. Most sites are shaded.

1100 NW Ridge Rd., Hammond, OR 97121. (From U.S. 101, go 3 miles south of Astoria, follow signs to Fort Stevens State Park; campground is opposite the entrance of the park.) ☎ *800-562-8506, 503-861-2606. Internet.* www.koa.com. *Total of 231 sites with water and 30- and 50-amp electric, 146 full hookups, 96 pull-throughs. Dataport, handicap access, laundry, indoor pool/spa, SATV. Rates: $33–$50 per site. DISC, MC, V.*

Bullards Beach State Park
$$$ Bandon, Oregon

North of Bandon near the Coquille River with freshwater fishing and boating available, Bullards Beach with 1,266 acres offers access for RVers, horseback campers, hikers, and bicycle campers, with an assortment of hookup sites, *yurts* (a circular domed tent with wood floor), and primitive and walk-in sites. The park's varied terrain includes a beach, forest, dunes, and a jetty and lighthouse.

From junction of U.S. 101 and SR 42S (north end of Bandon), go north 2.3 miles on U.S. 101, turn on MP-249 and drive 0.25 miles to the park on the left. ☎ *800-452-5687. Total of 192 sites with water and 20- and 30-amp electric, 92 full hookups, no pull-throughs. Some handicap access. Rates: $21 per site. MC, V. 10-day maximum stay.*

Fort Stevens State Park
$$–$$$ Warrenton, Oregon

The Union Army built a military installation on this site to protect the mouth of the Columbia River from Confederate attack. Although the Confederates never arrived, a Japanese submarine shelled the fort in 1942. Troops were ordered to hold their fire, and the worst damage occurred when a shell blew up the backstop of the baseball diamond. The campground's 170 RV hookup sites are wide, paved, well spaced and mostly shaded. If you're tired of sleeping in your RV, you can rent a yurt.

From U.S. 101 and Fort Stevens State Park Road, go northwest 4.6 miles to the park on the left. ☎ *800-452-5687. Total of 477 sites with water with 20- and 50-amp electric, 174 full hookups, 48 pull-throughs. Handicap access. Rates: $17–$21 per site.*

Jessie M. Honeyman Memorial State Park
$$–$$$ Florence, Oregon

Dedicated to the memory of one of the early advocates for a state park system in Oregon, this park and campground, smack-dab against some of the most magnificent sand dunes in the Oregon Dunes State Recreation Area, offers hiking trails, dune buggy activities (only in winter), and freshwater swimming, fishing, and boating. In May, rhododendrons burst out in splendid bloom. Some sites are large enough for the biggest motorhomes and sheltered from each other with lush landscaping. In addition to the number of RV hookup sites are tent sites and yurts for car campers.

U. S. 101, Florence, OR 97439. (Park is 3 miles south of Florence.) ☎ **541-997-3641.** www.oregonstateparks.org. *Total of 123 site with water and 30- and 50-amp electric, 44 full hookups, no pull-throughs. Handicap access. Rates: $18–$22 per site. MC, V.*

The Mariner RV Resort

$$$–$$$$ **Winchester Bay, Oregon**

This public marina and RV resort has many large sites, all paved with manicured grass plots, a bike path and hiking trail, and saltwater fishing. The location is convenient to the Oregon Dunes National Recreation Area and the colorful Umpqua Lighthouse. Sites are pull-ins that face the water. Two sites can hookup more than one vehicle.

From U.S. 101 and Salmon Harbor Drive, go southwest on Salmon Harbor Drive to campground on the right. ☎ **541-271-0287.** www.marinarvresort.com. *Total of 138 sites with 30- and 50-amp electric, all full hookups, 60 pull-throughs. CATV, dataport, handicap access, laundry. Rates: $21–$56 per site. MC, V.*

Oregon Dunes KOA

$$$–$$$$ **North Bend, Oregon**

Except for the frequent buzzing in and out of all-terrain vehicles on summer weekends, this park, close to the Oregon Dunes and just north of the town of North Bend, is pleasant. They rent ATVs and are one of the few RV parks with access to the Oregon Dunes National Recreation Area — thus, the ATVs. You can also book a dune tour from the campground in an antique military vehicle with somebody else driving. The beach, a lighthouse, a casino, and freshwater and ocean fishing are nearby. Several attractive wide sites are available.

68632 U.S. 101, North Bend, OR 97459. (Head 9 miles north of Coos Bay, and 19 miles south of Reedsport on U.S. 101.) ☎ **800-562-4236,** 541-756-4851. www.koa.com. *Total of 55 sites with 30- and 50-amp electric, all full hookups, 41 pull-throughs. Dataport, handicap access, laundry, SATV. Rates: $27–$39 per site. AE, DISC, MC, V.*

Sunset Bay State Park

$–$$ **Charleston, Oregon**

A great campground for walking the beach, exploring tidal pools, and watching winter storms, Sunset Bay is connected to Shore Acres and Cape Arago State Parks by a 4-mile hiking trail, part of the Oregon Coast Trail. Other diversions include saltwater fishing, swimming, boating, and horseback riding. Sites are wide and paved with some full hookups.

10965 Cape Arago Hwy., Coos Bay, OR 97420. (From junction of U.S. 101 and Charleston Harbor exit in Coos Bay, drive west 11.7 miles on Cape Arago Hwy. to the west end of the Charleston Bridge, MP-12; park is on the left.) ☎ **800-452-5687.** *Total of 63 sites with water and 30-amp electric, 29 full hookups, no pull-throughs. Handicap access. Rates: $16–$21 per site. MC, V. 10-day maximum stay.*

Runner-up campgrounds

Cape Blanco State Park

$$ **Port Orford, Oregon**   This state park has a gorgeous location near the Cape Blanco Lighthouse on the westernmost tip of Oregon with trails to the lighthouse and the beach. Amenities include freshwater fishing and a boat ramp. *From junction of U.S. 101 and Madrona Ave. at the north end of Port Orford, take Madrona north 3.7 miles to Cape Blanco Road, and then travel west 5 miles to the park on the right.* ☎ **541-332-6775.** *Total of 54 sites with water and 20-amp electric, no full hookups, no pull-throughs. Rates: $16–$18 per site. MC, V. No reservations.*

Harris Beach State Park

$$ **Brookings, Oregon**   Right on the ocean, Harris Beach State Park boasts the coast's warmest temperatures. Because the park's 155 campsites are on the state reservations system, you can book ahead. Sites are paved, some of them shaded, and saltwater fishing and swimming (for the hardy) are available. *From junction of U.S. 101 and north Bank Chetco Bridge, go north 2.2 miles on U.S. 101 to Harris Beach State Park Road on the left.* ☎ **800-452-5687.** *Total of 87 sites with water and 30-amp electric, 334 full hookups, no pull-throughs. Some handicap access. Rates: $15–$20 per site. MC, V. 10-day maximum stay.*

Ilwaco KOA

$$$ **Ilwaco, Oregon**   A grassy, open campground with pleasant owners, the Ilwaco KOA is at the base of Washington's Long Beach Peninsula, convenient to all the area attractions. The campground faces the Columbia River and is only 10 minutes from the ocean. *P.O. Box 549, Ilwaco, WA 98624. (From U.S. 101, turn south on Alt U.S. 101 at the traffic light and go 0.25 mile south to the campground.)* ☎ **800-562-3258,** *360-642-3292,* www.koa. com. *Total of 80 sites with water and 20- and 30-amp electric, 34 full hookups, 34 pull-throughs. CATV with full hookup sites, dataport, laundry. Rates: $22–$30 per site. MC, V.*

Outdoor Resorts Pacific Shores Motorcoach Resorts

$$$$–$$$$$ **Newport, Oregon**   This resort is the RV equivalent of a five-star hotel. The park is exclusively for motorhomes over 25 feet, and offers a large recreation hall with an indoor lap pool, a golf course, and food service. All sites have fire pits and picnic tables; some sites are shaded, but most are in the open, a boon given the cool weather along the coast. The beach is adjacent to the park. *6225 North Coast Hwy. 101,*

Newport, OR 97365. (From junction of U.S. 101 and U.S. 20, go 3 miles north on U.S. 101 to campground on the left.) ☎ **800-333-1583**, 541-265-3750. www. outdoor-resorts.com. Total of 252 sites with 30- and 50-amp electric, all full hookups, 100 pull-throughs. CATV, dataport, handicap access, laundry, and pool/spa. Rates: $35–$55 per site. MC, V.

RV Resort at Cannon Beach

$$$–$$$$ **Cannon Beach, Oregon**   A public resort park, this campground offers large back-in and pull-through sites, all of them paved and some shaded. The park is clean and handsomely situated. From junction of U.S. 101 and U.S. 26 (north of Cannon Beach), go south 4 miles on U.S. 101 to 2nd Cannon Beach exit, and east 200 feet to campground on the left. ☎ **800-847-2231**. Total of 100 sites with 30- and 50-amp electric, all full hookups, 1 pull-through. CATV, dataport, handicap access, laundry. Rates: $24–$36 per site. AE, DISC, MC, V.

Waldport KOA

$$–$$$ **Waldport, Oregon**   Some 14 miles from the Oregon Coast Aquarium or the beach, this newly expanded campground provides gravel sites, some shaded. Back-in sites are shorter but wider than the pull-throughs. Saltwater fishing on the Alsea River, kite flying, beachcombing, storm-watching, and seal- and whale-watching all are available nearby. P.O. Box 397, Waldport, OR 97394. (From junction of U. S. 101 and SR 34, go north 0.9 mile to Alsea Bay [MP-155] then southwest 0.2 mile to campground on the right.) ☎ **800-562-3443**, 541-563-2250. www.koa.com. Total of 72 sites with 30- and 50-amp electric, all full hookups, 10 pull-throughs. CATV, dataport, handicap access, laundry. Rates: $19–$30 per site. DISC, MC, V.

Good eats

Besides the usual fast-food outlets, coastal Oregon towns have many small diners and cafes, seafood sellers both wholesale and retail, cheese and candy makers, and various chowder houses, bakeries, and pie makers.

Full-meal deal

The Oregon Coast is lined with good eats from mom-and-pop diners to fish markets with real fishing boats tied up out back.

  ✔ **Dory Cove:** 5819 Logan Rd., Lindoln City, Oregon (☎ **541-994-5180**). Clam chowder, thick half-pound hamburgers with cheese and bacon on onion buns, and homemade pies — that says it all. Open daily from noon to 8 p.m.

  ✔ **Lighthouse Deli & Fish Company:** 3640 U.S. 101, South Beach, Oregon (☎ **541-867-6800**). Stop here for great fish and chips. Open daily from 8 a.m. to 8 p.m.

Cheese, please

Although Oregon **seafood, hazelnuts, wines, pears,** and **cranberries** may be famous, not many think of **cheese** as a major state food product. But Oregon is one cheesy state — in the best sense of the word — as the following list of coastal cheese producers proves. (California, eat your heart out!)

✔ **Tillamook Cheese Visitors Center:** 4175 U.S. 101, N. Tillamook, Oregon (☎ 503-815-1300). You can take a self-guided tour through this huge factory, which produces some 40 million pounds of cheese a year. Enticements include free samples of cheese and recipes, a deli, an ice cream bar selling Tillamook ice cream on freshly baked waffle cones, and a gift shop with Oregon food products and plenty of cow kitsch. Open daily from 8 a.m. to 6 p.m.

Tillamook Cheese Company became the big cheese in Oregon when it bought out the **Bandon Cheese Company.** The company produces cheese under the Bandon label using original recipes and is keeping the Bandon-by-the-Sea store open at 682 E Second St. in Bandon (☎ 503-347-2456, 800-548-8961 mail orders). In addition to free samples of all the cheddar flavors that they make, you can buy giant hand-dipped cones of rich Umpqua ice cream at the store. Open daily in summer from 8:30 a.m. to 5:30 p.m.

✔ **Blue Heron French Cheese Company:** U.S. 101, 1 mile north of Tillamook, Oregon (☎ 800-275-0639; www.blueheronoregon.com). French-style brie and Camembert cheeses are specialties, but the company also features a wine-tasting room, children's petting corral, deli, espresso bar, and gift shop. Open daily in summer from 8 a.m. to 8 p.m. and in winter from 9 a.m. to 5 p.m.

✔ **Mo's:** 622 SW Bay Blvd., Newport, Oregon (☎ 541-265-2979). Mo's serves its famous clam chowder in this original diner and several branches along the coast, but "NO MO TAKEOUT" as the old sign on the wall says: Sit down and eat your chowder! Open daily from 11 a.m. to 9 p.m. If the line's too long, check out Mo's Annex across the street.

✔ **Port Hole Café:** 29975 Harbor Way, Gold Beach, Oregon, 97444. (☎ 541-247-7411). Clam chowder, fresh seafood, chicken, steaks, and homemade pies. Open daily from 6 a.m. to 9 p.m. A fresh fish and seafood store is located next door.

✔ **The Ship Inn Restaurant & Pub:** 1 Second St., Astoria, Oregon (☎ 503-325-0033). Notable for English-style fish and chips, the Ship Inn also serves chowder, seafood main dishes, other English dishes, soups, and sandwiches. Open daily from 11:30 a.m. to 9 p.m.

Regional specialties

Other Northwest tastes run the gamut from artichokes (hurrah!) to lemon-meringue wine (boo!) to oysters (hurrah!) and more. In the following list, we tell you what to look for (and where to find it):

- **Artichokes.** Head to **Bear Creek Artichokes,** Tillamook, Oregon (☎ 503-398-5411), located 11 miles south of Tillamook on U.S. 101. Open daily from 10 a.m. to 5 p.m.

- **Boutique beer.** Check out **Rogue Ales Public House,** 748 SW Bay Blvd., Newport, Oregon (☎ 541-265-3188), which serves hand-crafted ales, lagers, stouts, porters, and bitters, along with fish and chips. Turn right at the north side of the bridge. Another option is **Pelican Pub & Brewery,** on the beach at 33180 Cape Kiwanda Dr., Pacific City, Oregon (☎ 503-965-7007; www.pelicanbrewery. com), pouring Doryman's Dark Ale and Tsunami Stout to accompany pub food. Outdoor dining available.

- **Cranberry candy.** Try **Cranberry Sweets Company,** First Street and Chicago, Bandon, Oregon (☎ 541-347-9475). Besides sampling cranberries, you get free tastes of dozens of other innovative sweets from lemon meringue pie candy to cheddar cheese fudge. Open daily from 9 a.m. to 5 p.m. Or stop at the **Cranberry Museum and Gift Shop,** Pioneer Road, Long Beach, Washington (☎ 360-642-5553), to try local cranberry products and tour the demonstration farm. Open April through December daily from 10 a.m. to 5 p.m.

- **Smoked salmon.** If you're feeling fishy, swing by **Bandon Fisheries,** 250 SW First St., Bandon, Oregon (☎ 541-347-2851), for fresh, frozen, and canned local seafood, including shrimp from April through September, Dungeness crab from December through July, and salmon from May through September. Open daily from 10 a.m. to 5:30 p.m. Or check out **Chuck's Seafoods,** west end of the bridge, Charleston, Oregon (☎ 541-888-5525), for fresh, smoked, and canned tuna, albacore, salmon, shrimp, and crab-meat. Open daily from 9 a.m. to 5:30 p.m. Or try **Josephson's Smokehouse,** 106 Marine Dr., Astoria, Oregon (☎ 503-325-2190), an elegant old-fashioned store with fine smoked salmon. Open daily from 9 a.m. to 5:30 p.m.

- **Weird wines.** Head to **Shallon Winery,** 1598 Duane St., Astoria, Oregon (☎ 503-325-5978; www.shallon.com). A little old wine-maker named Paul van der Veldt makes chocolate-orange wine, lemon-meringue pie wine, and cran au lait, among other flavors. Fortunately, he turns out only about 500 gallons a year. Open daily from noon to 6 p.m.

- **Willapa Bay oysters.** Stop at **Oysterville Sea Farms,** Oysterville, Washington (☎ 800-CRANBERRY (800-272-6237), 360-665-6585). Fresh oysters in the shell or shelled and in a jar, as well as smoked oysters, are for sale in this charming shingled cottage by the bay. To accompany them, try some Oysterville Victorian cake mixes, cranberry condiments, and fancy preserves, all available on the spot or by mail order. You can also pick up gifts with a local accent from Wholly Cow cereals to hand-printed T-shirts with Oysterville themes. Open daily from 10 a.m. to 5 p.m.

Shopping along the Way

If you're an outlet fan, you may want to run your rig to **Lincoln City,** where you find factory outlets at milepost 115.6. on U.S. 101.

For something unique to Oregon, look for products made from myrtle, a hardwood that grows only on the coast in the Coos Bay area. **House of Myrtlewood,** U.S. 101, South Coos Bay (☎ **800-255-5318**), offers a free factory tour, where you can watch myrtle logs turned into salad bowls, and see local craftsmen create everything from golf putters to trays and bowls. If you're bored with woodworking, the place also makes and serves fudge. Open daily from 9:30 a.m. to 5 p.m. but closed major holidays.

Fast Facts

Area Code

The area codes for Oregon are **503** and **541.**

Emergency

Call ☎ **911.**

Hospitals

Along the route, major hospitals are in Coos Bay, Florence, Reedsport, Seaside, and Astoria.

Information

Sources include Oregon Tourism Division, 775 Summer St. N.E., Salem, OR 97310 (☎ 800-547-7842); Oregon State Parks (☎ 800-551-6940 for information or 800-452-5687 for reservations; www.oregonstateparks.org); COCA (Central Oregon Coast Association (☎ 800-767-2064 or 541-265-2064; www.orcoast.com/coca); and Oregon Department of Fish and Wildlife, P.O. Box 59, Portland, OR 97207 (☎ 503-229-5403).

Laws

All RV occupants must wear seat belts in Oregon. The maximum speed limit on interstates is 65 mph. Speed limits are lower in urban areas.

Road and Weather Conditions

Call the Oregon Department of Transportation, ☎ 800-977-6368, available only in Oregon.

Taxes

Oregon has no sales tax. The state gasoline tax is 24¢ a gallon.

Time Zone

Oregon is on pacific standard time.

Chapter 23

California Central Coast: Malibu to Monterey

. . . .

In This Chapter

▶ Seeing the most spectacular coast on earth

▶ Standing amid a million Monarch butterflies

▶ Sampling Santa Maria barbecue

▶ Unearthing ancient movie sets in the sand dunes

. . . .

*T*he dramatic California coastline winds for 1,200 miles between **Crescent City** in the north to **San Diego** in the south, but the most scenic part is the central coast, the most beautiful place on earth. This drive takes you along a stretch of highway that we've been driving, singly and together, for more years than either of us is willing to admit.

The *real* California isn't found among the glittering boutiques of Beverly Hills, the false-front glamour of movie studio back lots, among San Francisco's hilly cable car routes, or Sausalito's chic waterfront. The real California turns green in winter rains when wildflowers embellish the hillsides and then turns golden under the summer sun. You're seeing the real California when you spot trail riders stirring up a cloud of dust on horseback; strawberries, lettuce, tomatoes, and peppers growing in long neat rows, moistened by the coastal fog; a solitary figure and two dogs walking a lonely, windswept beach; weathered adobe walls sheltering the relics of 18th-century Spanish friars; and vineyards covering the hillsides of what was a spreading *Californio rancho*.

Getting There

Set out from **Malibu,** only a few minutes north of **Santa Monica,** the pretty coastal city surrounded on three sides by Los Angeles and on the fourth by the Pacific Ocean. The drive follows SR 1 (California 1, CA 1), also called the **Pacific Coast Highway** (PCH, as locals call it), for 340 miles north to the **Monterey Peninsula,** which juts out into the Pacific about 100 miles south of San Francisco. PCH sometimes joins up with wider, faster **U.S. 101,** notably from the **Oxnard/Ventura** area to **Gaviota,** north of **Santa Barbara,** and then again from **Pismo Beach** to **San Luis Obispo,** but for much of the time, you and your RV are alone along the coastline. Along the way, you encounter surf pounding the roadway close enough to splash you and the cliffs of the curving roadway. You drive from Malibu along the central coast, past world-famous **Big Sur,** to the Monterey Peninsula, a distance of some **340 miles.** (See the "California Central Coast" map in this chapter for the route.)

Planning Ahead

The central coast makes a splendid destination **any season of the year,** although summer coastal fogs and winter rains can make driving diffi- cult, and rock and mudslides triggered by the winter rain may even close Pacific Coast Highway at intervals. Be prepared with sweaters and jackets if you visit in summer; cool dense fogs roll in during the night and hang on through the morning hours but usually burn off before midday. (Mark Twain remarked that the coldest winter he ever spent was summer in San Francisco.) Warm, sunny days often occur along the route in February or March. September and October also are often warm and clear — most summer visitors are gone by then.

You need **campground reservations** on weekends throughout the year; state parks often divide their sites into first-come, first-served sites and those reserved months ahead. The best commercial RV parks often are fully booked in summer and on holidays. In "Sleeping and Eating on the Road," later in this chapter, we suggest which of our favorite campgrounds need to be reserved ahead and which ones may have a spot at the last minute.

When **packing,** take along warm clothes, even in summer, sturdy hiking boots if you want to strike out along some of the coastal trails and beaches, binoculars, and plenty of film for your camera.

You can make the drive in two or three days, but you'll want more time to visit the area's must-see attractions. To really enjoy the coast and its beaches, plan to spend several days camping in at least one serendipi- tous area that sings to you. We spend as much as a month at our hide- away in Morro Bay and still hate to leave when our time is up. Allow **seven to ten days** for a perfect RV vacation.

Stocking the Pantry

This part of California's coast has plenty of supermarkets, wineries, and other food suppliers. If you want to do some wine-tasting and stocking up on vintages from the area, see Santa Barbara wineries under "More cool things to see and do," later in this chapter.

California Central Coast

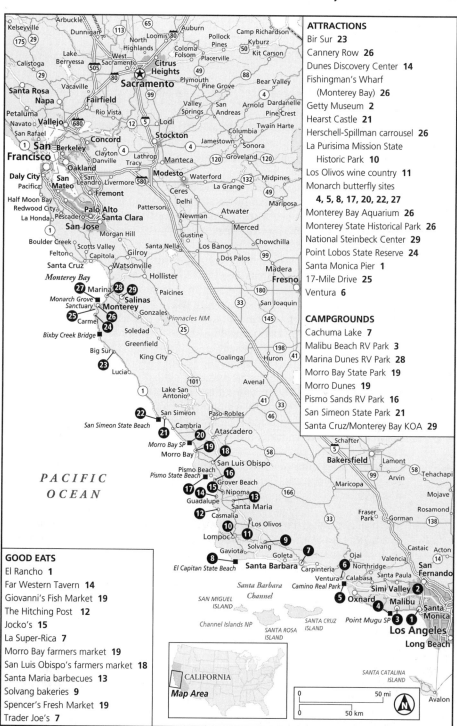

ATTRACTIONS
Bir Sur **23**
Cannery Row **26**
Dunes Discovery Center **14**
Fishingman's Wharf
  (Monterey Bay) **26**
Getty Museum **2**
Hearst Castle **21**
Herschell-Spillman carrousel **26**
La Purisima Mission State
  Historic Park **10**
Los Olivos wine country **11**
Monarch butterfly sites
  4, 5, 8, 17, 20, 22, 27
Monterey Bay Aquarium **26**
Monterey State Historical Park **26**
National Steinbeck Center **29**
Point Lobos State Reserve **24**
Santa Monica Pier **1**
17-Mile Drive **25**
Ventura **6**

CAMPGROUNDS
Cachuma Lake **7**
Malibu Beach RV Park **3**
Marina Dunes RV Park **28**
Morro Bay State Park **19**
Morro Dunes **19**
Pismo Sands RV Park **16**
San Simeon State Park **21**
Santa Cruz/Monterey Bay KOA **29**

GOOD EATS
El Rancho **1**
Far Western Tavern **14**
Giovanni's Fish Market **19**
The Hitching Post **12**
Jocko's **15**
La Super-Rica **7**
Morro Bay farmers market **19**
San Luis Obispo's farmers market **18**
Santa Maria barbecues **13**
Solvang bakeries **9**
Spencer's Fresh Market **19**
Trader Joe's **7**

One of our favorite food suppliers, the **Trader Joe's** chain, notable for budget-price wines and specialty food products, has a big market in Arroyo Grande on a hilltop beside U.S. 101. We also suggest shopping spots for tri-tip roast, the backbone of Santa Maria barbecue, in Morro Bay and Santa Maria. (See "Good eats.")

Driving California's Central Coast

We set out from scenic **Malibu Beach RV Park,** right in the middle of expensive, exclusive Malibu on a hilltop above Pacific Coast Highway. (See "Our favorite campgrounds," later in this chapter.) If you have access to a car (a car that you're towing or a rental vehicle), visit both the **Getty Museum** in Brentwood and **Santa Monica Pier** before heading north. You can also take public transportation to these sights. (For the Getty, see "Must-see attractions," and for the pier, see "More cool things to see and do," later in this chapter.)

For fans who grew up watching Raymond Burr as TV's **Perry Mason,** the coastal town of **Ventura** can claim to be the home of the famous lawyer/detective because this is where creator Erle Stanley Gardner lived and practiced law. Ventura's city hall, formerly the courthouse, was used to film parts of the long-running TV series. The city even offers an Erle Stanley Gardner walking tour. (See "More cool things to see and do.")

The drive from Malibu to **Santa Barbara** is 83 miles, so if you can time your arrival around the midday, stop for lunch at the world's most written-about taco stand, Julia Child's favorite, **La Super-Rica.** (See "Good eats.") Driving around the city of Santa Barbara in a large motorhome or towing a trailer is not recommended because you have to depend on street parking, and these streets aren't made for RVing. But sometimes you may find space in the residential neighborhood around the taco stand. The city of Santa Barbara offers a public transit service that visits many of the city's highlights.

North of Santa Barbara is a mostly undiscovered area of the central coast, ranging from the terminally cute Danish town of **Solvang** (from SR 1 or U.S. 101, go east on SR 246) to ranches owned by such divergent personalities as former President Ronald Reagan and rock star Michael Jackson. (For more on Solvang, see this chapter's sidebar "Solvang: A little bit of Denmark.")

North of Las Cruces, we suggest following SR 1 rather than U.S. 101. Two hundred years of history have barely left an imprint on this land. Rolling sandy hills covered with scrubby vegetation along the coast give way to rich valleys where market vegetables grow year-round and lush ranchos where Arabian horses breed. The dazzling flower fields in **Lompoc** bloom in rainbow colors much of the year and produce 85% of all the flower seeds for America's home gardeners.

Solvang: A little bit of Denmark

Depending on your own sugar capacity, not only for Danish pastries but also cuddly sweetness, you either love or hate Solvang, America's very own Danish community. Back in the 1960s, this was a Scandinavian settlement selling a few Danish souvenirs and celebrating a mid-September festival with *aebelskiver* (round apple pancakes cooked in a special pan) and sausage served for the few visitors who showed up. Today, Solvang is a burgeoning tourist attraction that fills the town with so many vehicles only the most intrepid RVer would attempt to join them, although the city of Solvang offers some edge-of-town RV parking.

Bakeries selling buttery pastries and cookies include **Danish Mill Bakery,** 1682 Copenhagen; **Mortensen's Danish Bakery,** 1588 Mission; **Olsen's Danish Village Bakery,** 1529 Mission; and **Solvang Bakery,** 1655 Copenhagen. Other local shops sell Danish china, chocolate candies, Danish costumes, leather-and-wood clogs, and European antiques.

The whole peninsula west of U.S. 101, except for **Vandenberg Air Force Base** where spacecraft land when the weather is bad in Florida, is a throwback to old California when the state still belonged to Mexico. In 1849, eager to claim the riches just discovered in the Sierra foothills inland, a group of gold miners drew a flag with a klutzy-looking bear on it and proclaimed the **Bear Flag Rebellion,** claiming California for the United States.

In the 18th century, Spanish friars created a string of 21 missions located a day's horseback ride apart. Today, most of them sit in the middle of urban areas where parking is difficult for RVs, and the ambience doesn't evoke the former mission days. An exception is our favorite mission, **La Purisima Concepcion,** 5 miles out of Lompoc, which remains in a rural setting. This mission is worth a special visit, particularly in summer, when the nearby flower fields of Lompoc are in full bloom. (See La Purisima Mission State Historic Park under "Must-see attractions.")

Great barbecued steaks (the world's best, say the proprietors) are cooked in tiny **Casmalia,** a few miles south of Vandenberg's main gate, at **The Hitching Post.** An offshoot of this eatery is now in **Buellton** just off U.S. 101 if you opt for the fast road instead of taking SR 1 through the area. (See "Good eats.")

Good food abounds in **Guadalupe,** a farming community along the coast with a whole string of good Mexican restaurants (choose any one of them), and the famous **Far Western Tavern,** an old California ranch-style steakhouse serving steaks barbecued over red oak with Santa Maria *pinquito* (little pink) beans and salsa. (See "Good eats.")

The mating game on the butterfly coast

The **monarch butterfly** (*Danaus plexippus*) is one of the most exotic but dependable winter visitors to the central coast, arriving in late October by the hundreds of thousands to more than 300 nesting sites within 2 miles of the ocean. Although the migration territory ranges from a golf course in San Leandro in the San Francisco Bay area southward to groves on the campus of the University of California at San Diego, the main sites are along the central coast.

Look for monarchs between mid-October and late February or early March at the following state parks and sanctuaries: **Monarch Grove Sanctuary,** Ridge Road near Lighthouse Avenue, Pacific Grove (☎ 888-746-6627); **San Simeon State Beach,** SR 1, 5 miles south of Hearst Castle (☎ 805-927-2068); **Morro Bay State Park,** State Park Road, off SR 1 south of Morro Bay (☎ 805-772-7234); **Pismo State Beach,** North Beach Campground, SR 1, 0.25 mile south of Pismo Beach (☎ 805-489-1869); **El Capitan State Beach,** U.S. 101, 17 miles west of Santa Barbara (☎ 805-968-1033); **Camino Real Park,** Dean Drive near Varsity Street, Ventura (☎ 800-333-2989); **Point Mugu State Park,** 9000 W. SR 1, Malibu (☎ 805-488-5223). Call ahead for directions and information.

Nipomo and **Oceano** are distinctive for 1920s connections. Nipomo, home of towering, shifting sand dunes that have doubled for the Sahara in many films, is now also an archeological dig unearthing (are you ready?) the remains of a gigantic movie set created by Cecil B. De Mille for his 1923 epic *The Ten Commandments.* Although the dig is closed, you can see some of the artifacts at the **Dunes Discovery Center,** north end of town. (See "More cool things to see and do.")

Pismo Beach, known since the 1930s as a one-liner joke delineating a rural California settlement and a retiree getaway, is, thankfully, much the same today. A topnotch RV snowbird winter retreat, Pismo Beach remains popular for its mild weather and the ease of getting around town. While the famous Pismo clams are more a memory than a fact today (none can be sold commercially), you can get tasty chowders made from imported eastern and northwestern clams or strike out to dig your own with a local clamming license available from the state fish and game authorities. (See "Fast Facts" at the end of this chapter.) The problem with the big clams (minimum legal size to keep is 4½ inches wide and there's a catch limit of ten) is that most have been eaten by California sea otters, those adorable little tool-smart critters who swim around in the Pacific carrying their own rocks for breaking shellfish against their chests.

At Pismo Beach, SR 1 rejoins U.S. 101 to take you as far as **San Luis Obispo,** home of California Polytechnic State University; the Mission of San Luis Obispo de Tolosa; a pair of vintage grocery stores, the 1884 Ah Louis Store and the 1874 Sinsheimer Brothers Store; and Bubble

Gum Alley, a bizarre ongoing work of art on Higuera Street between Garden and Broad Streets. This easygoing town, nicknamed SLO, also is the scene of a famous **Thursday night farmers market,** when vendors of Santa Maria barbecue and farmers selling fresh produce line closed-off blocks of Higuera Street. (See "Good eats" for details on the market.)

SLO is where SR 1 returns to the coast and the fishing town of **Morro Bay,** dominated by landmark Morro Rock, a 576-foot-high volcanic plug dome that may be 50 million years old. Peregrine falcons nest on the rock; great blue herons nest between January and June in a grove of eucalyptus trees by the estuary's wetlands; brown pelicans and raucous white gulls check out the fishing boats on the waterfront; and sandpipers leave their footprints on the wet sand of the beach as the tide washes in. RVers have two splendid hookup campground choices: **Morro Bay State Park** on the estuary and **Morro Dunes** by the sea, sheltered by grass-topped sand dunes. (See "Our favorite campgrounds" for both.) Morro Bay marks the jumping-off point for the Big Sur section of the drive. As you continue north on SR 1, you pass the little beach town of **Cayucos** with a handful of antiques shops and seafood restaurants on the pier. Next comes **Harmony,** population 18, as its roadside signage announces, (be alert or you can miss the whole town) and then precious **Cambria** with many antiques shops and scores of collectibles, chic restaurants, and a thin veneer of ever-so-quaint-ye-olde cuteness.

Just up SR 1 a piece from Cambria is **San Simeon,** coastal headquarters for "the ranch," as publishing tycoon William Randolph Hearst referred to his opulent 165-room hilltop castle built on the same spot where the family used to go camping. Allow most of a day if you want to visit the famous castle, because you must take one of several daily guided tours, the only option for getting through the gates. Film buffs immediately recognize San Simeon's connection with Orson Welles' masterpiece film *Citizen Kane;* "Rosebud" is all that's missing. (See "Must-see attractions.")

From San Simeon, SR 1 winds nearly 100 miles to the Monterey Peninsula, passing through legendary **Big Sur** on a white-knuckle highway. Don't miss stopping at a viewpoint to admire the delicate arches of **Bixby Creek Bridge,** spanning a 260-foot gorge against a backdrop of gently rounded treeless hills. After you cross over the bridge, the best views of this much-photographed 1932 concrete span are from the turnouts to the north.

Take your time driving along the Big Sur stretch of the coast, turning off frequently into the pullouts (those that are big enough to handle your rig) and getting out to stretch and photograph the spectacular scenery. However tempting some of the signs and driveways may be, before you enter, consider carefully whether you can turn your RV around and get back out. And be wary of traffic on this two-lane highway. The restaurant **Nepenthe,** the most famous eatery along the way, is noted for its ambrosiaburgers; expect a crowd on a sunny midday. Sometimes there isn't even space enough for a modest automobile to park in the restaurant's lot, let alone an RV. Opt for a space along the roadway.

Carmel, an artists' Mecca in the early years of the 20th century, has turned into a traffic-clogged bed-and-breakfast town of tearooms and upscale shops. Once admired as the home of photographer Ansel Adams, the town is best known these days for resident and former mayor Clint Eastwood, whose Hog's Breath Inn on Ocean Avenue was the focus for innumerable tourist cameras until he closed it down a few years ago. Today, he runs the Mission Ranch, a chic hotel filled with furniture that he designed himself, located south of town near the mission on Dolores Street. The hotel was converted from an 1850s ranch house that doubled as a New England estate in the 1959 tearjerker *A Summer Place.*

The **Monterey Peninsula** is John Steinbeck country. The author grew up in the area and wrote about it in such diverse books as *East of Eden* and *Cannery Row.* The **National Steinbeck Center** in **Salinas** joins such must-see peninsula attractions as the **Monterey Bay Aquarium, Point Lobos State Reserve, Cannery Row,** and **Fisherman's Wharf.** (See "Must-see attractions" and the sidebar "Monterey: Cannery Row and Fisherman's Wharf.")

The 17-Mile Drive, an expensive and much-touted *toll road* that swings past Pebble Beach, is restricted to cars and vans, so don't expect to drive your RV, whether a motorhome or a towable trailer, along the famous route. Locals park outside the entrance and walk or bicycle in to avoid the fee. Because the entrance is in a posh residential district, however, you won't be permitted to park an RV on-site. Leave the RV in the campground and use your tow car or rental car to navigate the narrow streets of the peninsula.

From Monterey, you can continue north on SR 1 to San Francisco or return to Los Angeles.

Must-see attractions

Getty Museum
Los Angeles

Allow most or all of a day to see this complex of galleries, gardens, gift stores, and restaurants. The gorgeously lit galleries display everything from Old Masters to Impressionists (Van Gogh's *Irises* is one acquisition), sculpture and decorative arts to photography (a major collection of Walker Evans' work), while the landscaped gardens invite strolling and contemplating a drop-dead view in all directions.

Travelers often are told, "You can't miss it," but if you head north on I-405 from I-10 toward U.S. 101, you really *can't* miss the Getty Center. First, you see a huge stone complex crowning the top of a hill to the west of I-405 as the highway climbs toward the crest at Mulholland Drive. Next you see signage labeled Getty Center and Getty Center Drive with arrows directing you to the parking garage. In a twist from the usual, the Getty charges for parking, but the museum itself is free.

1200 Getty Center Dr., off I-405 in Brentwood. ☎ **310-440-7300**. www.getty.edu. *RV parking: Parking ($5 for cars) is by reservation only on weekdays (not needed on weekends) in a parking garage not suitable for most RVs; park in the lot opposite the entrance or use a car or public transportation (MTA Bus #561 or Santa Monica Bus #14); a free shuttle bus operates from Constitution and Sepulveda boulevards in Westwood. Admission: Free. Open: Tues–Thurs and Sun 10 a.m.– 6 p.m., Fri–Sat 10 a.m.–9 p.m. Restaurant reservations* ☎ **310-440-6810**. *Allow a half to full day.*

Hearst Castle
San Simeon

Arranging these must-see sights in alphabetical order underscores the impact that captains of industry — J. Paul Getty in oil and international business and William Randolph Hearst in publishing — have had on California culture. Getty's museum was a long-planned gift to the people of California, while Hearst's castle was his own opulent hideaway until his death in 1951; the Hearst estate endowed the castle to the state of California, and it became a state park in 1958.

Although building went on from 1919 to 1947, Hearst Castle never was finished. Hearst intended eventually to add a bowling alley, a clock tower, an aviary, a croquet lawn, and a polo field. The rich and famous of the 1930s dined at the long refectory table set with priceless china and silver, along with paper napkins and condiments like catsup still in their original bottles. They were, after all, camping out at the ranch.

Allow time to visit the artifacts rescued from storage and on view in the reception exhibit hall and to see the 40-minute film, "Building the Dream" ($8 adults, $6 ages 17 and younger), and the huge tapestries in the lobby of the theater.

Hearst San Simeon State Historical Monument, 750 Hearst Castle Rd. (Off SR 1 at the town of San Simeon, about halfway between Los Angeles and San Francisco.) ☎ **800-444-4445**, *805-927-2020, for tour reservations.* www.hearstcastle.org. *RV Parking: Large lots at the visitor center, where all tours begin. Admission: daytime tours, $18 adults, $9 ages 17 and younger; evening tours, $24 adults, $12 ages 17 and younger. Open: Daily, day tours start at 8:20 a.m. with the last tour beginning at 3:20 p.m. Closed major holidays. Visitors have a choice of four different day tours, all of which require a half-mile walk and negotiating 200 to 500 stairs. Evening tours with docents in period costume are scheduled on selected spring and fall dates. Tours for visitors in wheelchairs need to be scheduled 10 days in advance by calling*

☎ *866-712-2286. Strollers, backpacks, camera bags, and flash photography are not permitted. Allow at least a half-day, more if you're at the back of the line.*

La Purisima Mission State Historic Park
Lompoc

Locals call the town *Lom*-poke, not *Lom*-pock, as comedian W. C. Fields pronounced it in his film *The Bank Dick,* shot on-site in 1940. The fully restored 1787 mission, now a state park, remains in a rural setting. Costumed guides, who carry on the original daily routines and demonstrate the crafts of the early 19th century, staff the site. The long, low adobe-and-wood mission buildings house chapels, a kitchen where candles are made by hand, a museum of artifacts and early photographs, Indian workshops, soldiers' barracks, and the small, simple cells where the friars slept. Allow at least two hours for the visit, more if you want to hike or go horseback riding (available on-site) on one of the 25 miles of trail around the mission.

The **flower fields** surrounding the mission start to bloom in June but are brightest in July and August. Take Ocean Avenue west from downtown and drive until you spot the first fields, and then zigzag back and forth between Ocean Avenue and Central Avenue on the connecting streets to enjoy a dazzling display of sweet peas, delphiniums, bachelor's buttons, marigolds, petunias, and zinnias. Also make sure to see Lompoc's **50 historical murals** painted on public and private buildings in the middle of town, especially the temperance-minded lady smashing a whiskey keg with an ax.

2295 Purisima Rd, Lompoc (3 miles northeast of town on SR 246 and Purisima Road, just off SR 1). ☎ *805-733-3713. RV parking: Large parking lot. Admission: $4 per family. Open: Daily 9 a.m.–5 p.m. Closed major holidays. Allow at least 2 hours.*

Monterey Bay Aquarium
Monterey

Design magic and some $50 million turned the last remaining sardine factory on Monterey's Cannery Row into one of the world's top aquariums. Inside is pure enchantment from the dramatic three-story kelp tank to a two-level sea otter habitat. Hands-on exhibits let you touch anemones and bat rays, and you even find a corner that runs period films from the sardine cannery days. Some 360,000 creatures are on-site, from jellyfish to sharks, and some giant whale models hanging overhead. The world's biggest window gives a look into the Outer Bay exhibit, a million-gallon, man-made ocean populated by tuna, sunfish, sea turtles, and other denizens of the deep.

886 Cannery Row. ☎ *831-648-4888.* www.montereybayaquarium.org. *RV parking: In nearby lots (look for signage). Admission: $17.95 adults, $15.95 seniors and ages 13–18, $8.95 disabled and ages 3–12. Open: Daily 10 a.m.–6 p.m. Closed Christmas. Allow a half-day (explore Monterey the rest of the day).*

National Steinbeck Center
Salinas

Although the inland city of Salinas is a few miles off our coastal route, the fantastic National Steinbeck Center, along with the surrounding pedestrian-friendly city center, makes this 16-mile detour more than worth the trip. The whole family will love exploring this hands-on museum.

Author John Steinbeck is familiar to RVers as a pioneer of the movement as detailed in his popular *Travels with Charley,* the story of his ramblings around America with his French poodle Charley in 1961 in a truck camper named Rocinante after Don Quixote's horse. From the thousands of readers who bought his book came many of today's RV aficionados. In the museum, you find the original Rocinante truck camper, along with walk-in galleries for each of his major books filled with touch, see, and smell exhibits. Film clips from movies made from Steinbeck books, including *Cannery Row, East of Eden, The Grapes of Wrath, Tortilla Flat, The Red Pony,* and *Of Mice and Men,* play in each area.

The newest part of the center takes a look at California agriculture from the human point of view, documenting personal history of farm workers in the Salinas Valley.

1 Main St. (directly off U.S. 101, 16 miles east of SR 1 via SR 68 from Monterey). ☎ *831-796-3833.* www.steinbeck.org. *RV parking: Use the railway station lot across the street or street parking. Admission: $10.95 adults, $8.95 seniors, $7.95 ages 13–17, $5.95 ages 6–12, 5 and younger free. Open: Daily 10 a.m.–5 p.m. Allow 2–3 hours.*

Point Lobos State Reserve
Carmel

You see the same twisted Monterey cypress trees and fog-misted headlands in Point Lobos as you do on the 17-Mile Drive, except that instead of driving through posh, old-money suburbs, you're traveling through natural coastal scenery. Go as early in the morning as possible so that you won't be tied up in a long row of cars that brake upon sightings of sea otters, sea lions, harbor seals, and seabirds. Explore 9 miles of hiking trails and 456 acres of reserve; carry binoculars to look for California gray whales offshore during migration seasons, which occur in mid-January (southbound) and in April and early May (northbound). No dogs are allowed ever, and *no vehicles longer than 20 feet are allowed during the summer season.* However, you can park along the highway and walk in.

SR 1 south of Carmel. ☎ *831-624-4909.* www.pointlobos.org. *Admission: $5 per vehicle, $1 for a map. Open: Daily 9 a.m.–5 p.m., limit of 150 vehicles at any one time. Allow anywhere from an hour to a half-day depending on your hiking plans.*

More cool things to see and do

Although the scenery is spectacular along every mile of this drive, you may want to check out these other cool activities. Don't overlook Monterey with its colorful attractions. (See the sidebar "Monterey: Cannery Row and Fisherman's Wharf.")

✔ **Uncover Egypt.** Movie fans who also are archeology buffs love the Nature Conservancy's **Dunes Discovery Center** in Guadalupe, which combines hands-on educational exhibits about the landscape and the creatures that inhabit the dunes with an ongoing excavation of a long-buried movie set depicting Egypt in the biblical era.

In 1923, on the Nipomo Dunes south of Guadalupe, Cecil B. DeMille constructed a movie set only slightly less ambitious than the Great Pyramids at Giza for *The Ten Commandments.* The production involved 1,600 laborers, 2,500 movie stars and extras (who slept in tents on adjacent sand dunes), and 110-foot walls flanked by 4 statues of Ramses II and 21 Sphinxes. At the end of shooting, he brought in a horse-drawn bulldozer and knocked down the set to keep a rival producer from coming in, shooting a cheap picture, and releasing it first. The constantly moving sands soon buried the set. Some 60 years later, a storm uncovered some of it, and a pair of documentarians rushed in to preserve and catalogue what they could. Now 16 years in the making, the dig is not yet complete. The center also offers docent-led hikes through the dunes that focus on the film, along with bird-watching, dune photography, and botanical and animal life. To visit on your own, drive west on the road by the cemetery to the parking lot right on the beach at Guadeloupe Dunes Preserve, or go three miles north of town and west three miles on Oso Flaco Lake Road to a parking lot ($4) and hike along a trail and a boardwalk over the lake to the dunes. Two miles round-trip.

1055 Guadalupe St. (also CA 1), Guadalupe. ☎ **805-343-2455.** www.dunescenter.org. RV Parking: Street parking. Admission: Free. Open: Tues–Sun 10a.m.–4:30 p.m. Allow 2–3 hours if you visit the dunes.

✔ **Wine-tasting 101.** Off U.S. 101 in and around the little town of **Los Olivos** lies a representative sampling of Santa Barbara County wineries, including Firestone, Fess Parker (yes, *that* Fess Parker in the Davy Crockett coonskin cap), Zaca Mesa, Foxen Vineyard, and Gainey Vineyard.

Call Santa Barbara County Vintner's Association at ☎ **800-218-0881** or log onto www.sbcountywines.com for a detailed map for all the county's wineries with tasting and tour times and types of wines produced.

Monterey: Cannery Row and Fisherman's Wharf

Cannery Row was, in the words of John Steinbeck, "a poem, a stink, a grating noise, a quality of light, a tone, a habit, a nostalgia, a dream." Today, the canneries are silent, the smell of the sardines long gone, and only the dream and nostalgia remain, along with a bustling commercial center aimed squarely at tourists.

The **Monterey Bay Aquarium** at 886 Cannery Row is a must-see, but as long as you're in the neighborhood and have some time, check out the rest of the attractions. If you know Steinbeck's novels set here — *Cannery Row* and *Tortilla Flat* — you can recognize the remaining landmarks — **Wing Chong Market,** called Lee Chong's Grocery in the books; **Ed Ricketts' Pacific Biological Laboratories,** named Western Biological in the books; and **Flora Wood's Lone Star Café,** the Bear Flag Restaurant in the books. A historic marker in **Cannery Row Memorial Park** memorializes the books' Chicken Walk and Palace Flophouse.

A 1905 **Herschell Spillman carrousel** whirls at 640 Wave St.; a playground named for Dennis the Menace, the comic strip character created by local resident Hank Ketchum, calls out to eager kids from Pearl Street. If you're in the mood, you can take advantage of Cannery Row's factory outlet shops, wine-tasting, fish restaurants, and tacky souvenir shops.

Monterey State Historical Park and **Fisherman's Wharf** jut out into the bay a few blocks east of Cannery Row but with much less spacious parking, so plan to park in the Cannery Row area. The wharf is lined with seafood takeout places similar to Fisherman's Wharf in San Francisco; one local specialty is clam chowder served in hollowed-out loaves of sourdough bread. Forget the overpriced abalone — a former staple of coastal California, the delectable shellfish has been overfished and most of it sold on the wharf today is frozen and imported. Instead, order the local *calamari* (squid), delicious when fried to a crunch and served with lemon wedges and tartar sauce.

Cannery Row, on the street named Cannery Row, is adjacent to Foam Street and Lighthouse Street in Monterey. A parking lot in the area (look for the signage) is large enough for RVs; leave your vehicle in the lot and walk the six or so blocks over to Fisherman's Wharf. For info online, go to www.canneryrow.com.

✔ **Pier into the past. Santa Monica Pier,** Ocean and Colorado avenues, was earmarked to be the port of Los Angeles, but through political machinations the area lost out to San Pedro at the turn of the 20th century. Undeterred, the city fathers created instead a broad sandy beach park and a playland pier, which was built between 1904 and 1921 and restored in the last decade. A 1916 carrousel, which starred in the film *The Sting,* a penny arcade, a Ferris wheel, bumper cars, games of chance, fortune tellers — all lend a Coney Island or Jersey Shore accent to this sunny pocket of southern California.

Contact Santa Monica Visitor Center at ☎ 310-393-7593. RV parking in designated lots.

✔ **Shadow Perry Mason.** The city of **Ventura** was home of **Erle Stanley Gardner,** a lawyer and prolific writer whose Perry Mason series began on-site in 1933. Today, you can take a walking tour past Gardner's several homes and law offices in town.

Ventura Visitors & Convention Bureau, 89 S. California St., Suite C, Ventura. ☎ **800-333-2989,** 805-648-2075. www.ventura-usa.com. RV parking: Street parking and some off-street lots available. Allow a couple of hours.

Weekend wonder

You can make a quick weekend run from **Los Angeles to Monterey** comfortably in one direction if you're bound for other areas, but don't try to make a round-trip. If you only have a weekend for a round-trip, try driving from **Los Angeles** as far as **Morro Bay,** overnighting on the bay and heading south again, or drive from **San Francisco** along the Big Sur coast as far as **Morro Bay** and return. You can catch the best of scenery, enjoy a seafood or Santa Maria barbecue meal, even take in a couple of hours of antiques shopping, but you won't have time for the major museums and the aquarium.

Sleeping and Eating on the Road

The Pacific Coast Highway (California 1 — SR 1) is chockablock with state park campgrounds where an RV can overnight (usually without hookups), if advance reservations have been made or the driver arrives early on a weekday when other campers are just checking out. Private campgrounds are more lenient; you can make a phone call and leave a credit card number to reserve an open site for as long as you want to stay. Altogether, some three dozen RV parks, including state and national forest campgrounds, are located along the coastal route. Note that the toll-free reservations numbers for the state parks listed below are for a central reservations system that may involve a long wait on hold and much punching in of numbers from your touchtone phone.

Food is plentiful, especially familiar fast food for nonfussy travelers. Road-food fans, however, may find the unique central coast eateries that serve Santa Maria barbecue far more interesting.

Because the coast drive is rewarding year-round, plan to make reservations for weekends whenever possible. On winter weekdays, you may find plenty of empty spots in some campgrounds, so you can rely on serendipity.

All campgrounds listed in this chapter are open year-round and have flush toilets, showers, and sanitary dump stations unless designated otherwise. Toll-free numbers, where listed, are for reservations only. See Chapter 9 for the criteria we use to select our favorite campgrounds.

Our favorite campgrounds

Malibu Beach RV Park

$$$–$$$$$ Malibu

If you ignore how near your next-door neighbor is parked and concentrate on the knockout view of the Pacific, you may like this close-to-LA campground, but be sure to *reserve ahead.* Going to the beach means walking downhill and crossing (very, very carefully) the SR 1. Other activities include sitting in the sun in a folding chair outside your RV with a pair of binoculars looking for passing whales and dolphins, or hiking in the Santa Monica Mountains. The park has only six pull-throughs, so you may have to back (very, very carefully) into your cliff-top site.

25801 SR 1, Malibu CA 90265. (Take SR 1 from Santa Monica north to Malibu Canyon Road and Pepperdine University, then continue west on SR 1 for 2 miles to campground uphill on the right.) ☎ *800-622-6052, 310-456-2532.* www.maliburv.com. *Total of 142 sites with water and 30-amp electric; 97 full hookups, 6 pull-throughs. Laundry. Rates: $26–$46 per site, lower in winter. AE, DISC, MC, V.*

Marina Dunes RV Park

$$$$–$$$$$ Marina

This well-landscaped campground is 8 miles north of Monterey on the ocean near a wild stretch of beach and dunes that are a short distance away via a sandy walkway. All sites are back-ins, not particularly wide but framed by foliage for privacy.

3330 Dunes Dr., Marina CA 93933. (Follow SR 1 for 6 miles north of Monterey, then exit on Reservation Road and drive west a half block to Dunes Drive; campground is on the right.) ☎ *831-384-6914. Total of 65 sites with water and 30- and 50-amp electric, 60 with full hookups. CATV, dataport, laundry. Rates: $38–$50 per site. MC, V.*

Morro Bay State Park

$$ Morro Bay

Located on the Morro Bay estuary rather than directly on the sea, this charming state park provides great bird-watching, scenic camping, and a pretty 1-mile walk into town. From fall through early spring, the park is full of wintering monarch butterflies that sleep in the numerous eucalyptus trees in the campground. An 18-hole public golf course is adjacent, so bring your clubs. Kayak and canoe rentals are available across the road. Sites are spacious; most of them shaded and landscaped for privacy, with picnic tables, wooden food lockers, and stone firepits/grills that look as if the Civilian Conservation Corps handmade them back in the 1930s. A number of campsites can be *reserved ahead.* Otherwise, it's first come, first served.

State Park Road, off SR 1 at South Bay Blvd. and west on State Park Road to campground on the right. ☎ ***805-772-7434,*** *reservations only* ☎ *800-444-7275. Total of 137 sites, 30 with water and 20- and 30-amp electric. Pay showers. Rates: $19 per site. No credit cards.*

Morro Dunes
$$–$$$ Morro Bay

This clean, well-run campground is right on the dunes by the sea in the fishing and tourist town of Morro Bay. Most campsites view Morro Rock and dramatic sunsets, and from the campground fence, the distance is 0.1 mile to the beach where shorebirds outnumber walkers. If you want to be close enough to hear the waves, ask for one of the back-in sites arranged like spokes of a wheel and designated with the letters A through G. If you like more space, book one of the pull-throughs at the back of the lot, still close to the beach but less noisy. *Call ahead for reservations* any time of year; this is one of the most popular campgrounds in California.

1700 Embarcadero, Morro Bay CA 93442. (Off SR 1 at SR 41 Atascadero exit, drive west 0.5 mile to campground on the left.) ☎ ***805-772-2722.*** www.morrodunes. com. *Total of 178 sites with water and 30-amp electric, 141 full hookups, 35 pull-throughs. CATV, dataport, laundry. Rates: $19–$27 per site. MC, V.*

Santa Cruz/Monterey Bay KOA
$$$$$ Watsonville

This well-kept family resort offers special summer events for children from Kids Olympics (a local event) and softball games to hot dog and s'mores cookouts — and year-round holiday observances, including free champagne breakfast and roses for Mother's Day, an Easter egg hunt, and a Thanksgiving dinner. Other amusements include miniature golf, a heated pool, and bike rentals. Sites are wide and the park is well landscaped. The ocean is less than a mile's walk away. In spring and early summer, Watsonville's strawberry fields are full of ripening fruit; autumn brings the grape crush at nearby wineries.

1186 San Andreas Rd., Watsonville CA 95076. (From SR 1 at 5 miles north of Watsonville, take San Andreas Road exit and drive west 3 miles to campground on the left.) ☎ ***800-562-7701,*** *831-722-0551.* www.koa.com. *Total of 230 sites with water and 30- and 50-amp electric, 151 full hookups, 5 pull-throughs. Dataport, handicap access, laundry, pool. Rates: $52–$57 per site. AE, DISC, MC, V.*

Runner-up campgrounds

Cachuma Lake

$$–$$$ **Santa Barbara**   This big county-run campground with plenty of trees is off the driving route but well worth the detour. The location is on a quiet hilltop above a sprawling lake where bald eagles nest and osprey soar. Park rangers offer morning boat rides to spot the local wildlife. *18 miles north of Santa Barbara on SR 154. (Take SR 154 exit from U.S. 101, drive 18 miles to campground on the right.)* ☎ *805-686-5054. Total of 140 sites with water and 30-amp electric, 93 full hookups, 14 pull-throughs. Rates: $16–$22 per site. DISC, MC, V. 14-day maximum stay. No reservations.*

Pismo Sands RV Park

$$$$ **Oceano**   A clean campground and an award-winning Good Sam member as the best medium-size RV park in California. Location is five minutes to the beach, three minutes to town. *2220 Cienaga St., Oceano, CA 93445. (On SR 1 about 0.8 mile north of Halcyon Road South junction.)* ☎ *800-404-7004.* www.pismosands.com. *Total of 133 sites with 30- and 50-amp electric, all full hookups, 84 pull-throughs. CATV, dataport, laundry, phone jack, pool, spa. Rates: $32–$40 per site. AE, DISC, MC, V.*

San Simeon State Park

$$ **San Simeon**   This beach state park is near the visitor center for the Hearst Castle and makes a convenient place to overnight before or after your tour. Hookups are unavailable at the 135 sites, and the maximum length RV allowed is 35 feet. Reserve ahead for weekends. *5 miles south of San Simeon on SR 1.* ☎ *805-927-2020, reservations only 800-444-7275. No hookups, no showers. Rates: $13 per site. No credit cards.*

Good eats

Although chic and expensive restaurants line this route, some of them get uptight when they see an RV drive up. We prefer friendly, down-home, takeout spots and concentrate on local and regional cooking.

Santa Maria barbecue

After decades as a cherished secret central coast cuisine, the **Santa Maria barbecue** has reached national prominence because former LA residents and knowledgeable barbecue fans now edit major foodie journals, such as *Gourmet* and *Saveur.* Some of the bolder critics call this barbecue the best in the world, but we quibble there, since a fine piece of Texas brisket or Owensboro, Kentucky, mutton also is supremely satisfying. However, nobody else but Santa Maria serves up unique side dishes of tiny, tasty *pinquito* beans, grown only in Santa Barbara County, and piquant salsa inherited from the *Californios.*

The Santa Maria style probably began more than a century ago with the hospitable *Californios,* Mexican ranch families who welcomed strangers with a giant outdoor barbecue. Later, communal cattle roundups meant cooperating local ranchers celebrated the end of the work by throwing hunks of beef on live oak (also called red oak) logs in a hand-dug pit and having a party. Then, in the 1950s, butchers in Santa Maria isolated the *tri-tip,* a bottom sirloin usually designated for stew; seasoned it liberally with salt, pepper, olive oil, garlic, and red wine vinegar; and tossed it on the grill.

Today, you find Santa Maria barbecue in a few places — in sit-down restaurants along the central coast (a list follows) or along Broadway in Santa Maria on Saturdays and Sundays between noon and 6 p.m. in any parking lot where you see the smoke rising from a portable barbecue. You can also hit the Thursday night street market in **San Luis Obispo** where vendors with portable cookers clog Hiquera Street and vend sandwiches or cooked barbecue by the pound. Or you can make them yourself by buying a tri-tip roast or other suitable cut of beef, sometimes already marinated, from a local market, such as **Spencer's Fresh Market** in Morro Bay or El Rancho in Santa Maria.

Besides *pinquito* beans and an often-bland salsa, other acceptable side dishes in a restaurant meal of Santa Maria barbecue include a relish dish of pickles, olives, carrot and celery sticks, shrimp cocktail, garlic bread, and baked potato. When you buy from the roadside stand, take whatever they're offering on the side.

The best central coast purveyors of Santa Maria-style barbecued beef are as follows:

- ✔ **Far Western Tavern:** 899 Guadalupe St. (also SR 1), Guadalupe (☎ 805-343-2251). The owners prefer to use "bulls-eye" (rib eye) steaks up to 20 ounces cut from their own cattle but also offer "cowboy cut" top sirloin cooked in the Santa Maria style with *pinquito* beans and salsa on the side, along with an optional appetizer of crisp mountain oysters (called *calf fries,* these are *not* oysters from the ocean, but rather a delicate part of a calf's anatomy) with dipping sauce. Open Monday through Saturday from 11 a.m. to 9 p.m., and Sunday from 9 a.m. to 9 p.m.

- ✔ **The Hitching Post:** 3325 Point Sal Rd., Casmalia; north of Vandenberg Air Force Base, take Black Road from SR 1 to Point Sal Road (☎ 805-937-6151). The Hitching Post has been around since 1952. The meat is cooked in an open pit in the middle of the room, and dinner (without beans) is served on red tablecloths. Open Monday through Saturday from 4:30 to 9:30 p.m. and Sundays from 4 to 9 p.m.

  A second location is at 406 E. SR 246, Buellton (☎ **805-688-0676**). This Hitching Post is a slightly fancier version of its Casmalia parent, offering steaks of ostrich, turkey, and quail, also cooked over live oak logs, along with the house appetizer, grilled artichokes with smoky, spicy chipotle mayonnaise flavored with smoked chiles. Open daily from 4 to 9:30 p.m.

✔ **Jocko's:** 125 N. Thompson St., Nipomo (☎ **805-929-3686**). Standing on the corner in Nipoma like a pool hall or burger joint, Jocko's is notable for Santa Maria barbecue. Open daily from 8 a.m. to 10 p.m.

Markets and meals

In addition to checking out **Trader Joe's** (see "Stocking the Pantry" earlier in this chapter), you may want to fill your fridge with fresh fish and produce from some of our other favorite spots. We also include options for when you want someone else to do the cooking. For information on picking up Danish treats, see the sidebar, "Solvang: A little bit of Denmark," earlier in this chapter.

✔ **Giovanni's Fish Market:** 1001 Front St., Morro Bay (☎ **805-772-2123**). This market has a live crab tank and cooker outside, a take-out window for fish and chips and other seafood goodies, and a full-fledged fish market inside, selling everything from cooked crab and shrimp to calamari salad and fresh-from-the-Pacific rock cod, halibut, and petrale sole. The cooked and cleaned cracked crab comes in its own Styrofoam box lined with a red-and-white checked plastic mini-tablecloth, ready to devour, if you wish, on the nearby picnic tables that overlook the fishing fleet. The store is open daily from 9 a.m. to 5 p.m., the kitchen daily from 11 a.m. to 6 p.m.

✔ **La Super-Rica:** 622 N. Milpas St. (use the Milpas turnoff from U.S. 101), Santa Barbara (☎ **805-963-4940**). This taco stand is America's most famous, thanks to a long-ago rave by food icon Julia Child. Instead of grabbing the plug and running with it to found a fast-food franchise, owner and chef Isodoro Gonzalez retained the same pleasant little restaurant that he built in 1980, kept cooking what Julia liked, and continued adding new daily specials. Today, diners still queue up to place an order, pay in advance, take a number, and sit in the casual cafe awaiting the delivery of their cooked-to-order food. Beer and soft drinks are available, the counter has homemade sauces and salsas in several varieties, and recommended dishes include the super-rica, a grilled tri-tip beef with a fresh poblano chile stuffed with cheese, flavorful pinto beans, vegetarian tamales, and a dynamite *posole* (hominy and pork stew with spicy side sauces and add-ons), and a special on weekends. Open daily from 11 a.m. to 9:30 p.m.

✔ **Morro Bay farmers market:** In the large parking lot of **Spencer's Fresh Market,** 2650 N. Main St., Morro Bay (no phone). You find fresh harvested fruits and vegetables plus local crafts and cut flowers. Inside Spencer's, you find a full selection of homemade European-style sausages, cheeses, and eggs from California Polytechnic farms in San Luis Obispo; dried *pinquito* beans; and marinated tri-tip roasts. The market takes place every Thursday afternoon from 3 to 5 p.m.

✔ **San Luis Obispo's farmers market:** Higuera Street downtown, San Luis Obispo (☎ **800-634-1414**, Convention and Visitors Bureau). You can chow down on hot Santa Maria barbecue sandwiches while you shop. The market area is banned to traffic, so look for a parking place on the street nearby. The market runs year-round every Thursday from 6:30 to 9 p.m.

Fast Facts

Area Codes

This chapter includes four area codes: **310** and **805** south of San Luis Obispo, **831** north of San Luis Obispo, and **415** in San Francisco.

Emergency

Call ☎ **911**.

Hospitals

Hospitals along the route include French Hospital Medical Center, 1911 Johnson Ave., San Luis Obispo (☎ 805-543-5353); and Arroyo Grande Community Hospital, 345 S. Halcyon Rd., Arroyo Grande (☎ 805-489-4261). Major hospitals also are in San Francisco.

Information

Helpful sources include California Office of Tourism, 5381 Lincoln Ave., Cypress, CA 90630 (☎ 714-252-1134: www.visitcalifornia.com); California State Parks reservations (☎ 800-444-7275; www.parks.ca.gov);

California Travel Parks Association (☎ 888-STAY-CTPA (888-782-9287); www.camp-california.com); and California Department of Fish and Game (☎ 916-227-2244; www.dfg.ca.gov).

Laws

All RV occupants must wear seat belts in California. The maximum speed limit on some interstates is 75 mph. Speed limits are lower in urban areas.

Road and Weather Conditions

Call ☎ 916-445-1534.

Taxes

Sales tax is 8.75%: Some local taxes may raise that rate. The state gas tax is 18¢ a gallon.

Time Zone

California follows pacific standard time.

Chapter 24

Route 66: OK to LA

*J*ohn Steinbeck called Route 66 "the mother road" in his classic
novel *The Grapes of Wrath.* But whether being traversed by the
book's dirt-poor Joad family in the 1930s, headed for California with all
their possessions tied to a broken-down truck, or the handsome hero-
adventurers Tod and Buz in their shiny yellow Corvette in the 1960s TV
series *Route 66,* this highway has sung its invitation to anyone with a
dream to hit the road.

Route 66 is the highway that authenticated the age of the automobile,
painting the image of footloose Americans as car travelers, proving
that the going can be as rewarding as the getting there, that life can be
lived on the road as fully as at home. To match the road, Americans
invented diners, tourist cabins, campgrounds, motels and motor courts
that enabled travelers to park their vehicles beside their doors, and
see billboard teasers in comic-book colors screaming out roadside
attractions from rattlesnakes to *Jackalopes* (imaginary fast-moving offspring of jackrabbits and antelopes). Car lovers even came up with
drive-in restaurants, drive-in movies, and even drive-in churches.

The original Route 66 ran "from Chicago to LA," as anyone who's heard
the 1946 Bobby Troup song of the same name knows, but our drive
travels only between Claremore, Oklahoma, and Los Angeles. Not all
the old roadway remains, so much of the time our route follows I-40,
which parallels and sometimes covers the original tracks of Route 66.

Getting There

Because Route 66 also was dedicated as the **Will Rogers Highway** in
1952 to honor the famous humorist, we begin in his hometown of
Claremore, Oklahoma, right on Route 66, and follow it all the way to

Route 66

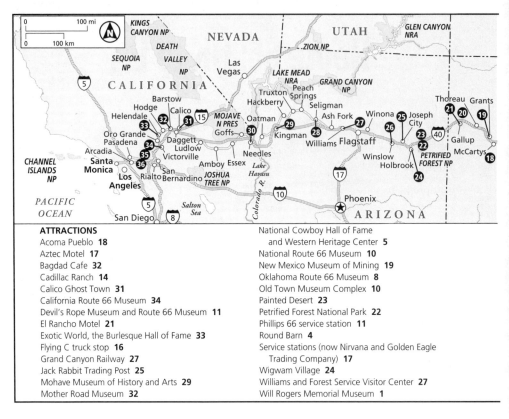

ATTRACTIONS

Acoma Pueblo **18**	National Cowboy Hall of Fame
Aztec Motel **17**	and Western Heritage Center **5**
Bagdad Cafe **32**	National Route 66 Museum **10**
Cadillac Ranch **14**	New Mexico Museum of Mining **19**
Calico Ghost Town **31**	Oklahoma Route 66 Museum **8**
California Route 66 Museum **34**	Old Town Museum Complex **10**
Devil's Rope Museum and Route 66 Museum **11**	Painted Desert **23**
El Rancho Motel **21**	Petrified Forest National Park **22**
Exotic World, the Burlesque Hall of Fame **33**	Phillips 66 service station **11**
Flying C truck stop **16**	Round Barn **4**
Grand Canyon Railway **27**	Service stations (now Nirvana and Golden Eagle
Jack Rabbit Trading Post **25**	Trading Company) **17**
Mohave Museum of History and Arts **29**	Wigwam Village **24**
Mother Road Museum **32**	Williams and Forest Service Visitor Center **27**
	Will Rogers Memorial Museum **1**

Santa Monica, California, where a plaque in Pacific Palisades, at the end of I-10 commemorates Rogers and the highway. Not far away is Will Rogers's beloved California ranch, now a state park and polo field.

Traveling from Claremore to **Tulsa** is only 20 miles on Route 66 and then 105 more to **Oklahoma City.** From the city, we follow a widened Route 66 out of town and through **El Reno** and then switch over to I-40, parts of which can be quite bumpy in this area. Business Route 40, which also is old 66, detours in the towns of **Weatherford, Clinton, Elk City,** and **Sayre** to enable us to drive segments of the original Route 66 (Oklahoma still has more original miles than any other state) interspersed with the faster I-40 all the way to the Texas border. In Texas, the route crosses the panhandle in the most direct line through **Amarillo** with more original Route 66 detours at **Shamrock, McLean, Alanreed, Groom, Vega,** and **Adrian.**

In New Mexico, the first major town is **Tucumcari,** followed by **Moriarity.** A few remnants of the old Route 66 remain in **Albuquerque,** so we detour through the Nob Hill section of town near the University of New Mexico, and then pick up a former stretch of Route 66 from **Laguna** to

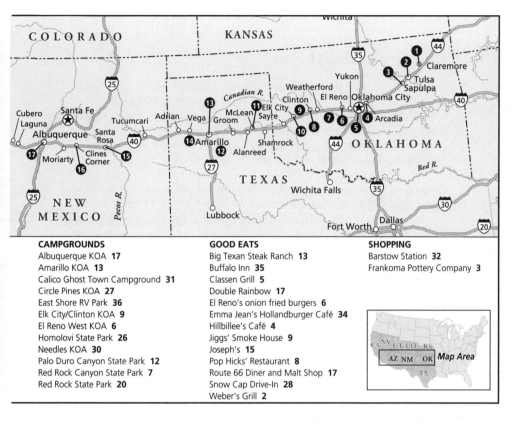

CAMPGROUNDS
Albuquerque KOA **17**
Amarillo KOA **13**
Calico Ghost Town Campground **31**
Circle Pines KOA **27**
East Shore RV Park **36**
Elk City/Clinton KOA **9**
El Reno West KOA **6**
Homolovi State Park **26**
Needles KOA **30**
Palo Duro Canyon State Park **12**
Red Rock Canyon State Park **7**
Red Rock State Park **20**

GOOD EATS
Big Texan Steak Ranch **13**
Buffalo Inn **35**
Classen Grill **5**
Double Rainbow **17**
El Reno's onion fried burgers **6**
Emma Jean's Hollandburger Café **34**
Hillbillee's Café **4**
Jiggs' Smoke House **9**
Joseph's **15**
Pop Hicks' Restaurant **8**
Route 66 Diner and Malt Shop **17**
Snow Cap Drive-In **28**
Weber's Grill **2**

SHOPPING
Barstow Station **32**
Frankoma Pottery Company **3**

Map Area

Cubero and between **McCartys** and **Thoreau.** The town of **Gallup** is filled with the spirit of Route 66 and makes a good place to camp overnight.

In **Arizona,** the **Petrified Forest** also retains Route 66 connections, and so do **Holbrook, Joseph City,** and **Winslow.** We rejoin I-40 to go on to **Flagstaff,** without forgetting **Winona,** as the silky voice of Nat King Cole reminded us in the song, but then get off the interstate to explore more old Route 66 roadway. One of the longest and smoothest stretches of Route 66 that's still around runs from **Ash Fork** to **Kingman** with another rewarding if narrower section from **Kingman** to **Oatman.**

In California, a turnoff at **Needles** travels north to **Goffs** and then south to **Essex** and **Amboy** before returning north to rejoin I-40 at **Ludlow.** We follow I-40 to **Barstow** and then rejoin old 66 from **Barstow** through **Hodge, Helendale,** and **Oro Grande** to **Victorville.** At Victorville, we pick up another interstate, I-15, down the long grade to **San Bernardino** and then, if in a hurry, take I-10 to the end of the road at **Santa Monica.** If you have time, poke along the 50 miles of Foothill Boulevard still numbered Route 66 between **San Bernardino** and **Pasadena.**

The basic distance is **1,453 miles;** some of the detours onto old Route 66 add more miles. (See "Route 66" map in this chapter.)

Planning Ahead

In general, this stretch of Route 66 can be traveled year-round, but in winter, snow sometimes falls in the upper elevations of New Mexico around Flagstaff. Conversely, summer can be quite hot along parts of the road in California, Arizona, and the Texas panhandle. Spring can bring gusty winds in the Texas panhandle and the California and Arizona deserts. Overall, **spring** and **fall** are the best times to travel Route 66.

Campground reservations aren't usually necessary unless you have your heart set on a particular park. We often decide in early to mid-afternoon how much farther we want to travel for the day, figure how far we'll get, and call ahead to a campground in that area to reserve a spot for that night.

When **packing,** take along hiking boots, rain gear, lightweight clothing for hot weather (even in winter), and warm clothing for cool days. Sunblock and sunglasses are essential in the bright desert sunlight of the Southwest. Take binoculars, camera, and film.

Allow at least 7 days but preferably 10 to 14 to make a leisurely tour along Route 66.

Driving Route 66

Because Route 66, the mother road, the Main Street of America, also is known as the Will Rogers Highway, our driving tour begins and ends with the famous cowboy humorist. A must-see in Claremore, Oklahoma, is the **Will Rogers Memorial Museum,** a large and well-displayed collection of personal possessions, mementos, costumes, artifacts, and many of Rogers's 70 films. (See "Must-see attractions" later in this chapter.)

Continue along Route 66, which parallels I-44, the Will Rogers Turnpike, through this part of Oklahoma.

In Tulsa, take I-44 or I-244 to the west side of town to rejoin Route 66 at Exit 220. This section of the old route is well maintained. Because the turnpike charges a toll and has limited access, you need to stay on Route 66 all the way to Oklahoma City, if you don't want to miss any of the old landmarks along the way.

In **Sapulpa,** the **Frankoma Pottery Company** still makes the classic Western-style dishes that it originally designed in 1933. (See "Shopping along the Way," later in this chapter.)

Arcadia's famous **Round Barn** has been restored and makes a good stop, both to admire the details of the roof from the inside and to pick up Route 66 postcards and signs. Across the road, **Hillbillies Café** serves breakfast, lunch, and dinner in a casual atmosphere with chicken fried steak and fried chicken local favorites. (See "Good eats.") Behind the cafe is a log cabin motor court turned offbeat bed-and-breakfast.

Oklahoma City is home to the **National Cowboy Hall of Fame and Western Heritage Center,** worth a good half-day minimum for cowboy fans who likes art or art aficionados who appreciate cowboys and Western movies. (See "Must-see attractions.") From the museum, follow I-44 west to Route 66 at Exit 123-B and continue west. You pass through **Yukon,** displaying on a water tower its pride in hometown hero Garth Brooks.

El Reno, the next town you pass, is the home of the **onion-fried burger,** where we spent the better part of two different visits sampling them at four different cafes. (See "Good eats.")

Clinton is a major stop, not only for its well-preserved strip of old 66, which goes right through town past some of the most famous landmarks of the mother road, but also for its fine **Oklahoma Route 66 Museum.** (See Route 66 Museums under "Must-see attractions.") On the east end of town is **Pop Hicks' Restaurant,** a Route 66 institution; if you want to hear some yarns and see some souvenirs, stop there. If you want to pick up some barbecue to go, pause at **Jiggs' Smoke House** just west of town for some barbecue sandwiches or home-smoked meats. (See "Good eats" for both restaurants.)

Elk City also boasts a **National Route 66 Museum** as part of its new **Old Town Museum Complex.** The lawns are decorated with painted metal kachina dolls and a textured metal buffalo, an opera house has cutout figures looking out of the upstairs windows, and a false-front Western town encourages even Pokemon kids to play cowboys again. (See Route 66 Museums under "Must-see attractions.")

In Texas, Route 66 zips you across the panhandle as slowly or as quickly as you want. You want to pause in tiny **McLean,** some 35 miles after you cross the border, for a look at the beautifully restored 1930s **Phillips 66 service station** on the west end of town. The **Devil's Rope Museum** on Route 66 at the corner of Kingsley shows examples of barbed wire and offers a small **Route 66 Museum.** (See Route 66 Museums under "Must-see attractions.")

The city of **Amarillo** is the Texas metropolis of Route 66, but the best-known landmark in town has been greeting the I-40 traveler for many miles with billboards advertising a free 72-ounce steak at the **Big Texan Steak Ranch.** (Catch onto the catch in "Good eats.")

What rhymes with Albuquerque?

In Albuquerque, you can leave I-40 and drive along Central Avenue to retrace old Route 66, but the eastern end has little to attract you unless used car dealerships and fast-food franchises make you nostalgic. The architectural scenery changes as you get to the Nob Hill area by the University of New Mexico. There you get a strong reminder of the 1930s and 1940s, especially the roadside service stations that were the lifeline of Route 66.

Look for the 1931 pueblo revival **Aztec Motel** at 3821 Central NE. See the two former service stations, too — a 1946 moderne-style station is now home to an East Indian restaurant called **Nirvana** at 3523 Central NE and a vintage Conoco now houses the **Golden Eagle Trading Company** at 3601 Central NE. Although the **Double Rainbow** at 3416 Central NE isn't from the 1930s, it does sell great coffees and desserts. Closer into town, appearing to be the real thing but actually reconstructed after a fire in 1995, is the **Route 66 Diner and Malt Shop** in a 1950s Phillips 66 gas station at 1405 Central NE (see "Good eats").

Just west of Amarillo, in plain sight from I-40 and accessible by a designated turn-off road, is the renowned **Cadillac Ranch,** erected in 1974. The ranch displays ten vintage Cadillacs dating from 1948 to 1964 buried grill-end first in the dirt with tail fins erect, all planted at the same angle as the Great Pyramid of Egypt. (See "More cool things to see and do," later in this chapter.)

The town of **Santa Rosa** also contains a number of Route 66 landmarks, including the notable Club Café, founded in 1935, closed in 1992, and still closed the last time we passed through, although the building was still standing. But **Joseph's,** dating back to 1956, still flourishes, selling some signature dishes from the Club Café, including sourdough biscuits. (See "Good eats.")

At **Clines Corners,** off Exit 218, is a **Flying C truck stop** dating back to 1934 that displays fake rattlesnakes, rubber tomahawks, and paintings on velvet collected since the 1920s. Neighboring **Moriarity** is the pinto bean capital of the world, offering a favorite local recipe of cookies made with mashed pinto beans and chocolate chips.

In Albuquerque, I-40 zips right through the middle of town, but if you want to take the time, Central Avenue crosses I-40 on historic Route 66, passing through scenic Old Town, filled with historic colonial buildings erected around a plaza, with restaurants and shops featuring New Mexican foods, arts, and crafts. After Albuquerque, the road skirts several Native American communities, including the Isleta lands, Laguna Pueblo and Mission at Laguna, and the wonderful **Acoma Pueblo** (see "Must-see attractions").

Grants is where a Navajo rancher named Paddy Martinez found uranium ore in 1950, triggering a latter-day, mini gold rush. Today, Grants is home to the **New Mexico Museum of Mining** with a re-created uranium mine in the basement.

Some 60 miles to the west, **Gallup** treasures its status as a Route 66 landmark city, showcasing the 1937 **El Rancho Hotel** at 1000 E. Route 66 — a hangout for Hollywood stars in the 1930s and 1940s.

Arizona, however, is where Route 66 reached the epitome of its 1930s image, lining its right of way with attractions. At Exit 311 from I-40, you're near the **Petrified Forest National Park and Painted Desert.** (See "Must-see attractions.")

Holbrook is home to the **Wigwam Village,** one of the only two remaining motels from a former national chain with cement teepees offered as sleeping units; the other is in Rialto, California, on Foothill Boulevard, which also is known as old Route 66. Nearby **Joseph City** still treasures the **Jack Rabbit Trading Post,** the subject of innumerable yellow billboards along Route 66.

Williams, 28 miles farther down I-40 from Flagstaff, is the gateway to the **Grand Canyon.** If you want to see the canyon without taking your RV there — you won't be permitted to drive it along the scenic Rim Road — consider hopping the **Grand Canyon Railway** in **Williams** for a one-day round-trip by train. (See "Must-see attractions.") You also find the **Williams and Forest Service Visitors Center** with a replica of an old roadside diner that's a memory bank for travelers along Route 66. (See Route 66 Museums under "Must-see attractions.")

From **Ash Fork** to **Kingman,** you want to drive the old route, which parallels I-40, making a point to pause at **Seligman,** pronounced *Slig*-man, where the zany Delgadillo brothers have been the driving force behind the Historic Route 66 Association of Arizona; Angel is the barber, Juan the proprietor of the **Snow Cap Drive-In** (see Good Eats"). The towns of **Truxton** and **Hackberry** still house landmark diners and gas stations. **Peach Springs** has resurrected some of the famous old Burma-Shave signs that lined roadways across the United States.

Kingman remembers native son Andy Devine, a comic sidekick for cowboy stars, in the **Mohave Museum of History and Arts.** (See "More cool things to see and do.") Near the museum is the turnoff on Historic Route 66 National Back Country Byway to **Oatman,** where wild burros walk the streets expecting handouts and a few colorful gift shops and cafes survive on mostly weekend tourist business. (See the sidebar "Kickin' back in Oatman" in this chapter.)

Needles may be familiar to comic-strip fans as the hometown of Snoopy's brother Spike in the Peanuts series; the strip's late creator **Charles Schulz** lived in Needles as a child.

WORTH THE SEARCH

Kickin' back in Oatman

Oatman, founded in 1906, produced $36 million in gold before the government decided in 1942 that gold was not essential to the war effort. Before the 1930s Depression years, Oatman had a population of 12,000; then it all but disappeared. Today, the resident numbers are growing again, but the town still is so small that wild burros roam the streets foraging for handouts from visitors.

Popular on the weekend RV circuit because of its nearness to **Laughlin, Nevada,** and **Lake Havasu City, Arizona,** Oatman hosts swap meets, antique shops, old saloons, and such silly annual events as the Labor Day weekend International Burro Biscuit Throwing Contest. (A clue: These biscuits aren't made from flour.)

The best time to go is on weekdays because weekend parking can get tight in town, especially for RVs. To get there: An evocative but narrow and winding part of the original Route 66 runs between Kingman and Oatman over the 3,652-foot Sitgreaves Pass. But the best route to and from Oatman, if you're driving or towing a large RV or if narrow, curvy roads make you nervous, is to stay on I-40 from Kingman to Topock on the Arizona/California border and drive north on SR 95 to the turnoff on historic Route 66 to Oatman. For information, contact the Oatman Chamber of Commerce (☎ 928-768-6222).

At **Daggett,** 12 miles west, you can take a short connecting side road to **Calico Ghost Town,** an old mining town and the location of two good RV parks. (See "Must-see attractions" and "Our favorite campgrounds," respectively, later in this chapter.)

A few miles further, movie buffs will want to pull off at **Newberry Springs** to see the location of the 1988 film, ***Bagdad Cafe.*** (See "More cool things to see and do.")

Barstow is endearing for its **Mother Road Museum** newly installed in the Casa del Desierto, the original Harvey House Hotel, now the bus and train depot. (See Route 66 Museums under "Must-see attractions.") The **Barstow Station** is so relentlessly touristy with its tacky souvenirs and fast-food restaurant housed in old railway cars that you mustn't miss it. (See "Shopping along the Way," later in this chapter.)

From Barstow, you can drive the original Route 66 roadway south to **Victorville** through **Helendale,** home of **Exotic World, the Burlesque Hall of Fame,** one of the desert's most popular attractions. (See "More cool things to see and do.")

The final stretch of Route 66 into **Los Angeles,** also called Foothill Boulevard, flies through **San Bernardino; Rialto,** where the Wigwam Motel sports teepee-shaped motel units; **Arcadia,** home of the lovely art deco Santa Anita racetrack; and **Pasadena**'s Colorado Boulevard where Old Pasadena has been turned into a row of inviting shops and restaurants. After you pass Pasadena, don't attempt to follow the twists and turns of old Route 66 in downtown Los Angeles; little, if any, remains of the color and ambience. From Pasadena, take the Pasadena Freeway (the 110) to the I-10 and follow that west to Santa Monica and the end of the trail.

Must-see attractions

Acoma Pueblo
Acoma, New Mexico

Called **Sky City,** this hilltop pueblo is said to be the oldest continuously inhabited community in the United States, dating back to A.D. 1250. Constructed atop a 367-foot sandstone mesa near Grants, the village is open to visitors daily year-round by guided tour only. A dozen families still are in residence, although most tribal members have settled in the valley below. Visitors can purchase Acoma pottery and bread loaves baked in the outdoor adobe ovens. Visitors are *not permitted* to enter the *kiva* (sacred chamber), and need to expect certain camera restrictions, including paying a fee for using cameras or sketch pads.

66 miles west of Albuquerque. (From I-40, take Exit 102 or Exit 96 and follow the signage to the visitor center.) ☎ *800-747-0181. RV parking: At the designated lot in the village below the Sky City. Admission: $10 adult, $9 seniors, $7 ages 6–17. Open: Daily summer 8 a.m–6 p.m. with the last tour starting at 5 p.m., winter 8 a.m.–4 p.m. with the last tour starting at 3 p.m. Closed Easter weekend, July 10–13, and the first or second weekend in Oct. No one can go beyond the parking lot in the village below the mesa without joining a tour. Allow 1–2 hours.*

Calico Ghost Town
Calico, California

Extremely popular with European and Japanese Old West aficionados, Calico isn't a built-for-tourists ghost town that some people expect but is rather a real silver-mining town that thrived from 1881 to 1907 with a population of 3,500. Walter Knott of Knott's Berry Farm fame, who had worked in the mines as a youth, restored and preserved the town, which is operated today by the San Bernadino County Park System. A modestly priced county RV park is adjacent to the town entrance; RVers camping on-site get free admission to the town. Original and reconstructed buildings, including a house made of glass bottles, sometimes serve as a backdrop for staged gunfights and other Western shenanigans on weekends and in summer.

Calico Exit from I-15 or I-40 east of Barstow. ☎ *760-254-2122.* www.calico town.com. *RV Parking: Large parking lots at entrance. Admission: $6 adults, $3 ages 6–15. Open: Daily 9 a.m.–5 p.m. Allow half-day or more.*

Grand Canyon Railway
Williams, Arizona

A steam train to the Grand Canyon leaves daily at 10 a.m. year-round from the restored 1908 train station in the town of Williams. Passengers ride the refurbished 1928 rail cars the 65 miles north to the canyon, have a few hours for sightseeing, and then return in late afternoon. The town has several nice campgrounds if you want to check in for the night. At the canyon, the train stops near El Tovar Hotel, where frequent shuttle departures set out to tour the South Rim.

Taking the train is a good idea because Grand Canyon National Park now prohibits private vehicles from the entire South Rim — a policy started in 2004. In summer, adequate parking space isn't always available in the lots at the entrance, especially for RVs.

Williams Depot is just off I-40 in Williams at 233 North Grand Canyon Blvd.; you can see the station from the highway. ☎ *800-843-8724. RV parking: Lot by station is big enough for any size RV. Tickets: Choose from five different classes of rail car, with prices ranging from $71.45 (coach) to $134.90 (first class) for adults, $27.35 (coach) to $90.80 (first class) for children. Departure: Train leaves Williams at 10 a.m., reaches Grand Canyon shortly after noon, boards to return at 3:30 p.m., and arrives back in Williams at 5:45 p.m. The train doesn't run when heavy snow covers the tracks. Reservations recommended. Allow a full day.*

National Cowboy Hall of Fame and Western Heritage Center
Oklahoma City, Oklahoma

Framed against the windows at the end of the massive entry hall that begins your tour, James Earle Fraser's white marble sculpture, *End of the Trail,* depicts an Indian warrior, his body slumped in exhaustion and defeat astride his horse, his lance drooping at the same angle as his horse's head. For Fraser, his subject represents the end of an era, the passing of the Old West. This excellent museum displays outstanding art and artifacts from the old and new West. Recently added or expanded galleries include the American Rodeo Gallery, Western Entertainment Gallery with movie posters and film and video clips, and Prosperity Junction, a life-size replica of an Old West town.

1700 N.E. 63rd St. (Take Exit 129 off I-44 west of the junction with I-35 and follow the signs.) ☎ *405-478-2250.* www.cowboyhalloffame.org. *RV parking: Designated area in front of the museum. Admission $8.50 adults, $7 seniors, $4 children 6–12, 5 and under free. Open: Daily 9 a.m.–5 p.m. Closed major holidays. Allow 2 hours or more.*

Petrified Forest National Park and Painted Desert
I-40 in northeastern Arizona

These two famous Route 66 landmarks lie across the highway from each other about 25 miles east of Holbrook. A loop road goes through both areas. Stop first at the visitor center near the entrance to the **Petrified Forest** to get a map and some idea of how this landscape was formed. In the time of the dinosaurs, 225 million years ago, a forest of trees fell into the water and gradually began to petrify, a process in which quartz replaces the organic cells of the trees.

Tempting as it may be, picking up any pieces of the petrified wood is *against the law* and bad luck, as letters on display in the Rainbow Forest Museum attest; people who picked up rocks returned them after having unsettling experiences. For those who want to acquire the wood legitimately, samples are for sale at the Crystal Forest Museum in the southern end of the area.

The **Painted Desert** is best seen early or late in the day when the sunlight hits at an angle that makes the colors brighter. If you wear polarized sunglasses and photograph the desert using a polarizing filter, you get more dramatic colors. The park doesn't have campgrounds.

From Exit 311 on I-40, the Petrified Forest is to the south and the Painted Desert is to the north. ☎ 928-524-6228. RV parking: At visitor center and at turnouts along the loop road. Admission: $10 per vehicle for 7-day pass. Open: Daily 8 a.m.–5 p.m., closed Christmas Day. Allow a half-day.

Route 66 Museums

All the following museums display artifacts, signs, and photographs of old Route 66 with varying degrees of sophistication. Our favorite is the **Oklahoma Route 66 Museum** in **Clinton,** Oklahoma, for its multigallery re-creation of the highway decade by decade, from a battered 1920s truck loaded down with family possessions to a painted hippie van of the 1960s. The new **Mother Road Museum,** housed in part of the old train station in Barstow, California, displays license plates, road signs, and a 1926 Dodge Touring Sedan that drove the highway when the trip was a real adventure. Barbed wire is the main focus of the **Devil's Rope Museum** in McLean, Texas, with the adjoining **Route 66 Museum,** all housed in a former bra factory. The **Williams and Forest Service Visitors Center** in Williams, Arizona, has a replica of an old diner with a diary for road pilgrims to enter their experiences on Route 66, and a video showing the highway's past.

California Route 66 Museum, 16825 D St. between Fifth and Sixth streets, Victorville, California. ☎ 760-951-0436. www.califrt66museum.org. *RV parking: Designated lot or street parking. Admission: By donation. Open: Thurs–Mon 10 a.m.–4 p.m. Allow 1 hour.*

Devil's Rope Museum and Route 66 Museum, Old Route 66 at Kingsley Street, McLean, Texas. ☎ 806-779-2225. RV parking: Street parking. Admission: By donation. Open: Tues–Sat 9 a.m to 5 p.m., Sun 1–4 p.m. Allow 1 hour.

Mother Road Museum, 681 N. First Ave., Barstow, California. ☎ 760-255-1890. RV parking: Designated lot or street parking. Admission: Free. Open: Fri–Sun 11 a.m.–4 p.m. Allow 1 hour.

National Route 66 Museum in the *Old Town Museum Complex,* Route 66 and Pioneer Road, Elk City, Oklahoma. ☎ *580-225-2207.* RV parking: Large lot at the complex. Admission: $5 adults, $4.50 seniors, $1 ages 6–16, 5 and under free. Open: Tues–Sat 9 a.m.–5 p.m., Sun 2–5 p.m. Closed major holidays. Allow 1 hour.

Oklahoma Route 66 Museum, 2229 Gary Blvd., Clinton, Oklahoma. ☎ *580-323-7866.* RV parking: Small lot at museum, street parking. Admission: $3 adults, $2.50 seniors, $1 ages 6–18. Audiotape for self-guided tour available. Open: May–Aug daily 9 a.m.–7 p.m.; Sept–Apr Tues–Sat 9 a.m.–5 p.m., Sun 1–5 p.m. Closed state holidays; call ahead. Allow 2 hours.

Williams and Forest Service Visitors Center, 200 W. Railroad Ave., Williams, Arizona. ☎ *928-635-4707.* RV parking: West side of the center. Admission: Free. Open: Daily 8 a.m.–5 p.m. Closed major holidays. Allow 1 hour.

Will Rogers Memorial Museum
Claremore, Oklahoma

This rather majestic memorial on a crest of hill with a view across the landscape is a museum devoted to the life and times of the famous humorist and film star and to his final resting place. A theater shows clips from some of his 70 films, radio sets play excerpts from his popular radio show, and a children's interactive center makes finding out about him fun. A gift shop also is on the premises.

1720 W. Will Rogers Blvd. ☎ *800-828-9643,* 918-341-0719. RV parking: Large open parking lot. Admission: free, donations requested. Open: Daily 8 a.m.–5 p.m., tours at 10 a.m. and 2 p.m. Allow 2 hours or more.

More cool things to see and do

Some of our favorite zany attractions line Route 66, the classic road to America's imagination. Where else can you see vintage Cadillacs buried front end–down to replicate Britain's Stonehenge or the Ghost Town of Calico with its own campground so you can return to the comfort of your RV after looking for the ghosts.

- ✔ **Burying the gas guzzlers.** At **Cadillac Ranch,** ten vintage tail-fin Cadillacs are buried front end–down in an open field on a ranch just west of Amarillo, Texas, causing the I-40 traffic to slow down and gape. To pull over, take the Hope Road exit that lets you pull off on a parking-permitted shoulder from where you can walk across some 500 yards of often-muddy field to get a closer look. Always open, always free. Allow 30 minutes if you stop.

- ✔ **Taking it off.** At **Exotic World, the Burlesque Hall of Fame,** former headliner Dixie Evans, known as the Marilyn Monroe of Burlesque, commemorates the days when disrobing seductively was a work of art for famous stars such as Lily St. Cyr, Tempest Starr, and Blaze

Storm. See Gypsy Rose Lee's cape, Jayne Mansfield's dressing room ottoman, and an urn with the ashes of Jennie Lee, who started this museum before her death from cancer. Every June, the museum hosts a Miss Exotic Universe Contest, but beware: Some of the audience members get rowdy.

29053 Wild Rd., Helendale, California. (From I-15 North, take SR 18, which is also historic Route 66, go north and turn left at Helendale Market and then right on Helendale Road, go 1 mile to Wild Road and turn right.) ☎ 760-243-5261. www.exoticworldusa.org. RV parking: Street parking. Admission: Free, donations accepted. Open: Daily 10 a.m.–5 p.m. Allow 1 hour.

✔ **Waking Andy Devine.** At the **Mohave Museum of History and Arts,** a casual, almost homemade museum, the city's favorite son is the main exhibit. He's the late film actor Andy Devine, who played comic sidekicks to various cowboy stars in countless B movies and various TV series, such as *Wild Bill Hickok.* Movie posters, a replica of his dressing room, and costumes he wore fill his part of the museum. Elsewhere, you find everything from World War II airplane nose art to displays of local turquoise jewelry. Route 66 souvenirs are for sale in the gift shop.

400 W. Beale St., Kingman, Arizona. ☎ 928-753-3195. RV parking: Designated lot or street parking. Admission: $3 adults, $2 seniors, free 12 and younger. Open: Mon–Fri 9 a.m.–5 p.m., Sat–Sun 1–5 p.m. Allow 1 hour or more.

✔ **Digging for uranium.** Go into a simulated uranium mine, check out local tribal regalia, and eyeball geology exhibits in the **New Mexico Museum of Mining,** the world's only museum of uranium mining.

100 Iron St., Grants, New Mexico. ☎ 800-748-2142, 505-287-4802. RV parking: Medium-size, off-street lot or street parking. Admission: $3 adults, $2 seniors and ages 7–18. Open: Mon–Sat 9 a.m.–4 p.m. Allow 2 hours.

✔ **Refueling at Bagdad Cafe.** The buses filled with French or German tourists pull up beside this undistiguished cafe on old Route 66 and pile out with cameras and remarks about how "It's just like the movie." They're talking about an obscure 1988 production called *Bagdad Cafe* staring, among others, Jack Palance. The movie didn't fare well in the United States, but it became a big hit in Europe with a cult following, hence the tourists yearning to have a Jack Palance burger or the Bagdad omelet. Along with the burgers, you may find such local characters as General Bob, who claims to have designed the Pentagon; Don, the mad hatter, who makes and sells knit hats; and River Bottom Dan, a waiter who lives in a trailer on a riverbed.

48548 Route 66, Newbury Springs (about 18 miles east of Barstow). ☎ 760-257-3101. Open: Daily 7 a.m.–8 p.m.

Sleeping and Eating on the Road

The original Route 66 pioneered roadside sleeping and eating, but many of the original establishments that sheltered early *tin-can campers,* as they were called, are boarded up, for sale, or long gone. Much of this journey parallels I-40, which is lined with RV parks and fast-food options all the way to the coast.

All campgrounds listed are open year-round and have public flush toilets, showers, and sanitary dump stations unless designated otherwise. Toll-free numbers, where listed, are for reservations only. See Chapter 9 for the way we choose our favorite campgrounds.

Our favorite campgrounds

Calico Ghost Town Campground
$$$ **Yermo, California**

Guests at this campground get free access to the colorful old ghost town of Calico. Although it's desert-hot on a summer midday, late afternoons bring glowing sunsets that fill the old town with golden light. Some reenactments of gunfights and other live shows take place, and shops and simple cafes line the main street. The weather is nice in winter unless a stiff wind is blowing from the desert; some weekends can be chockablock with tourists when a special event is scheduled, so *call ahead for reservations* whenever possible.

Ghost Town Road, Yermo, CA 92398. (Take Ghost Town Road exit from I-15 and drive 3.5 miles north to campground on the left.) ☎ ***760-254-2122.*** *Total of 46 sites with 30- and 50-amp electric, all full hookups, 23 pull-throughs. Rates: $22 per site. DISC, MC, V.*

Circle Pines KOA
$$$–$$$$ **Williams, Arizona**

Circle Pines manages to be away from the I-40 traffic noise and downtown Williams, but it offers convenient connections to everything from van tours to the Grand Canyon to free shuttle service to the railway station in Williams if you want to take the steam train there. Some extras include: an outdoor cafe serving breakfast and dinner, nightly movies in season, horse stables offering trail rides, heated indoor pool and two spas, country western entertainment in summer, and Budget rental cars available on-site. This KOA is also a Good Sam member.

1000 Circle Pines Rd., Williams, AZ 86046. (From I-40, take Exit 167, Circle Pines Road, and drive 0.75 mile to the campground on the left.) ☎ ***800-562-9379,*** *928-635-2626.* www.koa.com. *Total of 120 sites with water and 30- and 50-amp electric,*

80 full hookups, all pull-throughs. Dataport, laundry, pool, two spas. Rates: $24–$33 per site. AE, DISC, MC, V.

East Shore RV Park

$$$$ **San Dimas, California**

This spacious, Good Sam–member campground has hilltop sites that get summer breezes and lakeside sites that are in a valley with less circulating breezes. A number of mature shade trees surround the grass-paved sites. Our favorites are those beginning with the letter *B* on the bluff overlooking the Fairplex grounds and the local airport. Freshwater lake fishing is available.

1440 Camper View Rd., San Dimas, CA 91773. (From I-10, take Fairplex Drive exit and go north 0.5 mile, turn left on Via Verde, then right on Camper View Road; campground is at the end of the road.) ☎ 800-809-3778. Total of 201 sites with 30- and 50-amp electric, all full hookups, 13 pull-throughs. CATV, dataport, laundry, pools. Rates: $34 per site. DISC, MC, V.

El Reno West KOA

$$$ **El Reno, Oklahoma**

We love this campground because an Indian trading post with bargain-price moccasins and a live buffalo compound are on the premises. The location also is close to four restaurants making the famous onion-fried burgers (see "Good eats"). Other pluses are freshwater fishing, a pool, and snack bar. On the down side, sites are narrow, and some hookups are side by side.

Box 6, El Reno, OK 73036. (15 miles west of El Reno, take Exit 108 from I-40 and drive north on spur 281 some 300 feet to the Cherokee Trading Post, then turn right to the campground.) ☎ 800-562-5736, 405-884-2595. www.koa.com. Total of 73 sites with water and 30- and 50-amp electric, 31 full hookups, 37 pull-throughs. Dataport, laundry, pool. Rates: $22–$28 per site. DISC, MC, V.

Needles KOA

$$$ **Needles, California**

The only celebrity resident of Needles the world knows about is Spike, Snoopy's brother in the comic strip *Peanuts,* and, in all fairness, this campground looks sort of like Spike's cactus-filled terrain. The location is especially nice in winter when weather is mild and bird-watching is good. A seasonal cafe operates November through April, and pull-throughs are large and shady.

5400 National Old Trails Highway, Needles, CA 92363. (Take West Broadway exit from I-40 and turn left on National Old Trails Highway; campground is 1 mile down the road on the right.) ☎ 800-562-3407, 760-326-4207. www.koa.com. Total of 102 sites with water and 30-amp electric, 65 full hookups, 89 pull-throughs. Dataport, laundry, pool. Rates: $23–$26 per site. AE, DISC, MC, V.

Palo Duro Canyon State Park

$$ **Canyon, Texas**

If you zip rapidly across the Texas panhandle on I-40, you'll miss one of the most beautiful areas in the state, the spectacular Palo Duro Canyon, carved out of the red rock by the Red River. The canyon is 120 miles long, 1,000 feet deep, and as much as 20 miles wide. This campground in the canyon is reached via a downhill road that crosses some dry washes. Sites are comfortably wide at 40 feet, and each has its own individual look. Some offer access for handicapped campers.

Take I-27 16 miles south of Amarillo to SR 217, then drive east 10 miles to the park. ☎ *806-488-2227. Total of 63 sites with water and 30- and 50-amp electric, no full hookups, 7 pull-throughs. Rates: $18 per site. DISC, MC, V. 14-day maximum stay.*

Red Rock State Park

$$ **Church Rock, New Mexico**

This park east of Gallup is where the Inter Tribal Ceremonial, a gathering of Native American tribes, takes place every August; for details call the ITC (☎ **505-863-3896**). In summer, traditional tribal dances take place in the ampitheater on the premises, and a museum nearby displays kachina dolls, rugs, pottery, silver, and turquoise jewelry. The campground has 103 extrawide (50 by 55 feet) pull-throughs. The back-ins are narrower (30 by 40 feet) but still generous.

Box 10, Church Rock, NM 57311. (From Exit 26 on I-40 at SR 118, go east 3.5 miles on 118 to SR 566, and then travel north 0.5 mile to campground on the left.) ☎ *505-722-3839. Total of 135 sites with water and 30- and 50-amp electric, no full hookups, 103 pull-throughs. Rates: $15 per site. MC, V.*

Runner-up campgrounds

Albuquerque KOA

$$$$ **Albuquerque, New Mexico** On the eastern end of Albuquerque's commercial strip (fast foods and used cars) is this convenient and well-run campground with wide sites, including some extralarge ones for big rigs. Amenities include a pool and indoor hot tub. RV rentals are available. *12400 Skyline Rd., Albuquerque, NM 87123. (Take Exit 166 from I-40 south on Juan Tabo, drive 1 block to Skyline Road and turn left; campground is on the left.)* ☎ *800-562-7781, 505-276-2729.* www.koa.com. *Total of 157 sites with water and 30- and 50-amp electric, 101 full hookups, 100 pull-throughs. Dataport, laundry, pool. Rates: $34–$39 per site. AE, DISC, MC, V.*

Amarillo KOA

$$–$$$ **Amarillo, Texas** Sites are narrow with some side-by-side hookups, but this conveniently located park has a few extras, such as a

chuck-wagon menu (featuring the three B's — beef, beans, and biscuits) for delivery to campsites in season and shuttle service to nearby Palo Duro canyon for performances of the musical Texas. *1100 Folsom Rd., Amarillo, TX 79108. (Take Exit 75 from I-40 and travel north 2 miles to U.S. 60, then turn east 1 mile to Folsom Road, then travel south 0.3 mile to campground on the left.)* ☎ *800-562-3431, 806-335-1792.* www.koa.com. *Total of 96 sites with water and 30- and 50-amp electric; 69 hookups, 45 pull-throughs. CATV, dataport, laundry, phone jack, pool. Rates: $20–$25 per site. DISC, MC, V.*

Elk City/Clinton KOA

$$$ Canute, Oklahoma   This campground lies about halfway between two Route 66 museums, one in Clinton and the other in Elk City. Hot home-cooked dinners are available nightly in season, and all campers receive gasoline discount coupons. Mature trees shade the moderately wide sites. *P.O. Box 137, Canute, OK 73626. (Take Exit 50 off I-40 and travel north following the signs.)* ☎ *800-562-4149, 580-592-4409.* www.koa.com. *Total of 102 sites with water and 30- and 50-amp electric, 52 full hookups, 43 pull-throughs. CATV, dataport, laundry, pool. Rates: $27–$30 per site. AE, DISC, MC, V.*

Homolovi State Park

$$ Winslow, Arizona   The Homolovi Ruins are an archeological dig in the northern Arizona desert where ancestors of today's Hopi people lived around A.D. 1200. Archeological workshops are available. Hopi elders offer storytelling and traditional farming demonstrations, while park rangers lead bird-watching and wildlife-viewing trips. *From I-40 east of Winslow, take Exit 257 onto SR 87 and drive northeast 5 miles to park.* ☎ *928-289-4106. Total of 53 campsites with water and 20- and 30-amp electric. Water is available Apr–Oct only at the campsites, but showers and restrooms are open year-round. Rates: $19 with hookup, $12 without, per site. No credit cards. No reservations. Call ahead for availability of dig activity.*

Red Rock Canyon State Park

$$ Hinton, Oklahoma   After you maneuver the steep downhill entrance to the campground, you find fairly wide campsites, some with patios and trees. Freshwater fishing is available in a nearby stream. *Take Exit 101 from I-40 to SR 281, travel south 5 miles to campground on the left.* ☎ *405-542-6344. Total of 56 sites with water and 20- and 30-amp electric, 5 full hookups, 10 pull-throughs. Rates: $15–$18 per site. No credit cards. No reservations. 14-day maximum stay.*

Good eats

If it didn't actually invent the **hamburger,** Route 66 can certainly claim to have made it popular. You find some historical claims on the mother road — Harold and Rick Bilby, the owners of **Weber's Grill,** 3817 South Peoria, Tulsa, Oklahoma, said their great-grandfather was serving hamburgers in Indian Territory as early as 1891. They failed to say to whom.

The first time that we drove Route 66 cross-country in the 1950s, big, juicy hamburgers could be found everywhere, including in chains like A & W Root Beer where each franchise made burgers individually. The following list includes a few of the best spots along old Route 66 that still make old-fashioned burgers by hand. McDonald's fans need not apply.

- **Buffalo Inn:** 1814 W. Foothill Blvd., Upland, California (☎ 909-981-5515). Buffalo burgers are accompanied by buffalo chips (home-made potato chips) in this favorite college hangout for students at Claremont Colleges. Open daily from 11:30 a.m. to 11 p.m.

- **Classen Grill:** 5124 N. Classen Blvd., Oklahoma City, Oklahoma (☎ 405-842-0428). A choice of a dozen different toppings crown the charcoal-grilled burgers, and the breakfasts are notable, too. Open daily from 6 a.m. to 3 p.m.

- **El Reno's onion-fried burgers: Jobe's Drive-In,** 1220 Sunset Dr. (☎ 405-262-0194; open Mon–Sat 6 a.m.–8 p.m.); **Johnnie's Grill,** 301 S. Rock Island Ave. (☎ 405-262-4721; open Mon–Sat 6 a.m.–9 p.m., Sun 11 a.m.–8 p.m.); **Robert's Grill,** 300 S. Bickford Ave. (☎ 405-262-1262; open Mon–Sat 6 a.m.–9 p.m., Sun 11 a.m.–7 p.m.); and **Sid's Diner,** 300 S. Choctaw Ave. (☎ 405-262-7757; open Mon–Sat 7 a.m.–8:30 p.m.). In El Reno, Oklahoma, these four local eateries cook burgers on a grill together with thinly sliced onions, pressing them together as they cook so that the onion caramelizes, turning the burger and sizzling some more, then popping the whole business on a bun, and garnishing it with the chef's choice of trimmings that may include tomatoes, lettuce, mustard, mayonnaise, and/or sliced dill pickles. We confess being partial to Robert's because the diner itself is so tiny and colorful, and it was the first place that we sampled the onion-grilled burger.

- **Emma Jeans' Hollandburger Café:** 17143 D St., Victorville, California (☎ 760-243-9938). This old-time diner, right on old Route 66 in Victorville, serves up classic burgers from the short-order grill. Open Monday through Friday from 5 a.m. to 3 p.m. and Saturdays from 6 a.m. to 12:30 p.m.

- **Route 66 Diner and Malt Shop:** 1720 Central Ave. SW, Albuquerque, New Mexico (☎ 505-242-7866). Burgers are sharp and tasty with blue cheese and green chiles; order a malt to cool them down. Open daily from 10 a.m. to 6 p.m.

- **Snow Cap Drive-In:** Route 66, Seligman, Arizona (no phone listing). While Juan Degadillo's hamburgers are nothing to write home about, his sense of humor is great; don't miss this chance to chat with one of the founding fathers of the revitalized Route 66. Hours are erratic, but take a chance because even the exterior is worth a look.

Looking for something other than a hamburger? You're in luck — several options await. In addition to those in the list that follows, you may also want to check out **Pop Hicks' Restaurant,** 223 W. Gary, Clinton, Oklahoma.

- **Big Texan Steak Ranch:** 7701 I-40 East, Exit 75, Amarillo, Texas (☎ 806-372-6000). The billboards promise a free 72-ounce steak, but the catch is that you have to eat it all, including the side dishes — shrimp cocktail, baked potato, buttered roll, and green salad — in less than an hour or you pay $50 for it. Many are called but few can finish. Open daily from 6 a.m. to 10:30 p.m.

- **Hillbillee's Café:** 206 E. Highway 66, Arcadia, Oklahoma (☎ 405-396-8177). Across the road from the landmark **Round Barn,** Hillbillee's fries up some good chicken and locally popular chicken-fried steak and serves substantial breakfasts that rarely top $5. Open Monday through Thursday from 11 a.m to 9 p.m., Friday and Saturday from 8 a.m. to 10 p.m., and Sundays from 7 a.m. to 2 p.m.

- **Jiggs' Smoke House:** At the Parkersburg Road exit from I-40 between Clinton and Elk City, Oklahoma (no listed phone). This rustic little shack by the side of the road sells its own barbecued beef brisket chopped into sandwiches, along with homemade beef jerky, sausages, ham, and bacon from the butcher case. Open Monday through Saturday from 9 a.m. to 5 p.m. Closed Sunday.

- **Joseph's:** 865 Will Rogers Dr., Santa Rosa, New Mexico (☎ 505-472-3361). One of the old-time Route 66 stopovers, Joseph's still boasts an adjoining gift shop of tacky souvenirs, and a great breakfast menu that includes breakfast burritos and a spicy *carne adovado* (pork and red chiles) with eggs, refried beans, and flour tortillas. Open daily from 6 a.m. to 6 p.m.

Shopping along the Way

Although you'll come across numerous shops along Route 66, we want to point out these two.

- **Barstow Station:** East Main Street off I-15, east of Barstow, California (☎ 760-256-0812). Although we normally don't care for the architecture of McDonald's, we make an exception for this one created from vintage railroad cars and serving as the centerpiece of a sprawling tour bus stop and souvenir stand. Well, it's more like the mother of all souvenir stands with items piled on the floors, hanging from the ceiling, and stacked randomly all around on precarious shelves. Wonderfully tacky, the station's offerings range from life-size plaster of Paris howling coyotes to plastic cacti four feet tall, Marilyn Monroe cookie jars, plaster American eagles, and personalized mugs for every Tom, Dick, and Lupe who happens by. RV parking is in back of station where buses and trucks park. Open daily from 7 a.m. to 9 p.m.

- **Frankoma Pottery Company:** 2400 Frankoma Rd., Sapulpa, Oklahoma (☎ 918-224-5511). From the ridiculous to the sublime. We coveted the prairie green, wagon wheel–pattern pitchers because the first time we ever saw them, and finally, thanks to a factory visit, acquired an affordable version. Frankoma has manufactured Western-style pottery since 1933, and the factory in this suburb of Tulsa, has an adjoining museum and outlet store. The family owned company offers free plant tours and fantastic budget buys of factory seconds in another store behind the museum gift shop. RV parking is available in a lot adjacent to the factory. Open Monday through Saturday from 9 a.m. to 5 p.m., and Sundays from 1 to 5 p.m.

Fast Facts

Area Codes

The following area codes are in effect along Route 66: **928** in Arizona; **760, 909, 626, 213, 323, 310** in California; **405, 580, 918** in Oklahoma; **505** in New Mexico; and **806** in Texas.

Emergency

911 in all states. Mobile phone users can touch ***55** in Oklahoma, and call **800-525-5555** in Texas.

Hospitals

Major hospitals along the route are in Oklahoma City, Tulsa, Albuquerque, Gallup, Flagstaff, Barstow, San Bernardino, and Los Angeles.

Information

Sources include Arizona Office of Tourism (☎ 888-520-3434, www.arizonaguide.com); California Department of Tourism (☎ 800-GO-CALIF (800-462-2543); www.gocalif.ca.gov); New Mexico Department of Tourism (☎ 800-733-6396; www.newmexico.org); Oklahoma Tourism (☎ 800-652-6552); and Texas Department of Tourism (☎ 800-888-8839; www.traveltex.com).

Laws

Seat belts must be worn by those riding in the front seats in Arizona, Oklahoma, and Texas, and those riding anywhere in the vehicle in California and New Mexico. Children riding anywhere in a vehicle in Texas also must wear seat belts. The maximum speed limit on interstate highways in Arizona, New Mexico, and Oklahoma is 75 mph, and in California and Texas, 70 mph. In all states, speed limits are lower in urban areas.

Road Conditions

Call ☎ 888-411-ROAD (888-411-7623) in Arizona, ☎ 916-445-1534 in California, ☎ 800-432-4269 in New Mexico, ☎ 405-425-2385 in Oklahoma, and ☎ 800-452-9292 in Texas.

Taxes

Arizona sales tax is 5.6% (local taxes can raise it to 7.6%); gas tax is 18¢ a gallon. California sales tax is 8.25% (local taxes may be added); gas tax is 18¢ a gallon. New Mexico sales tax is 5% (local taxes can raise it to 5.95%); gas tax is 17¢ a gallon. Oklahoma sales tax is 4.5% (local taxes can raise it to 7.35%); gas tax is 17¢ a gallon. Texas sales tax is 7.25% (local taxes may be added); gas tax is 20¢ a gallon.

Time Zones

Oklahoma and Texas are on central standard time. New Mexico and Arizona are on mountain standard time, but Arizona doesn't have daylight savings time in the summer. California is on pacific standard time.

Part VI
The Part of Tens

The 5th Wave
By Rich Tennant

"Don't eat the Fig Newtons. Eat the chocolate chips. I'm using the Fig Newtons as wedges to keep things from rattling while we're on the road."

In this part . . .

*1*f you get as excited about RVing as we did when we started — and still are — you may want to add detours or even other drives to the 14 excursions in this book. In this part, we give additional sightseeing recommendations, from the enlightened to the hilarious, plus suggestions on ten great winter getaways for snowbirds seeking warm weather.

Chapter 25

Ten Great Snowbird Getaways

In This Chapter

▶ Crossing London Bridge to camp

▶ Setting up camp near the Walt Disney Resort

▶ Sleeping by the beach and more

*O*ne out of every ten RV owners — adding up to about 3 million — is a **snowbird,** who sets out every winter for warmer climates. Florida and Texas top the list of destinations, followed closely by California and Arizona.

Most snowbirds already are well traveled, and prefer to pick one campground and stay there for much of the season, venturing out in a tow automobile or truck for local sightseeing and shopping. The convenience of nearby shopping and restaurant facilities may outweigh scenery and recreation as considerations.

When you move into a campground for the season, you want to negotiate a lower price than the per-night price that you'd pay for staying a couple of days. Monthly rates vary from $250 to $500 or more, depending on the season, the site, the geographic location, the size of your vehicle, and the services that you require. Many campgrounds offer an additional discount if you stay longer than a month, and all rates are negotiable in privately owned campgrounds. Public campgrounds, such as state and national parks, impose a maximum-stay limit, usually around 14 days, which requires the camper to move out for several days, a week, or even longer before returning.

Snowbirds on a tight budget can apply to work as volunteer hosts in the campground in exchange for free camping and perhaps a little salary on the side for additional chores. See Chapter 9 for details.

The following locations are recommended only for winter stays; in most of them, summer temperatures reach three digits.

Lake Havasu City, Arizona

Just across the London Bridge (transported to this site brick by brick from England) from town, **Islander RV Resort** is set on a man-made island with 320 full hookup sites (up to 50-amp electric), some with waterfront locations on the Colorado River. The resort offers plenty to please RVing snowbirds — an adjacent 18-hole golf course, boat ramps, fish-cleaning stations, potluck suppers, bingo, dances, exercise classes, modem connections at your campsite, and an "English village" with pubs and half-timbered inns a mile away. Check ahead of time for pet restrictions. 751 Beachcomber Blvd. Weekly full hookup $204. ☎ 928-680-2000. www.islanderrvresort.com.

Borrego Springs, California

Not as fancy as the other snowbird hideaways, **Borrego Palm Canyon Campground** in Anza-Borrego Desert State Park is in the quiet country of central San Diego County. Amenities include 52 full hookups (30-amp electric), handicap access sites, and a visitor center with a book and map shop. The location at the edge of the colorful little town of Borrego Springs boasts hiking trails through the desert and fresh local grapefruit available for pennies. Be prepared to move in and out because of restrictions on length of stay. 200 Palm Canyon Drive (also SR 22), 2 miles west of town. ☎ 760-767-5311, reservations 800-444-7275. www.anzaborrego.statepark.org. Weekly full hookup $140.

Indio, California

Sociable and homier than some of the posh Palm Springs–area campgrounds, **Fiesta RV Park** has monthly arts and crafts shows around the big swimming pool and in the clubhouse; Sunday afternoon ice-cream socials; Friday night cookouts; organized golf outings to various courses in the area; a putting green; pancake breakfasts; seminars on health, anti-aging, RV maintenance; Wednesday afternoon massage service; and a billiards room. Restaurants and a small shopping mall are within walking distance, and some 200 paved sites provide full hookups and cable TV. The date festival and Bob Hope and Dinah Shore golf classics take place in the area in winter. The office accepts mail and telephone messages for campers, and offers a modem hookup for local service and long distance e-mail phone jack on a pay phone. 46–421 Madison St. ☎ 760-342-2345. www.fiestarvpark.com. Weekly full hookup $210.

Long Beach, California

Golden Shore RV Resort is within walking distance of public transportation to downtown shopping and restaurants, the beach, the Queen Mary, the Aquarium of the Pacific, and a lively Friday morning farmers market with fresh fruits and vegetables all winter long. With only 77 sites, all back-ins, the well-landscaped park is quiet and makes a good choice for independent people who don't want to be overwhelmed by a megaresort. You can take whale-watching tours during winter, all-day Catalina Island excursions, or meander the bike and beach path. A golf course is five minutes away; Disneyland and Knotts Berry Farm are a half-hour away. 101 Golden Shore. ☎ 800-668-3581, 562-435-4646. www.goldenshorerv.com. Weekly full hookup $260.

Long Key, Florida

Well-planned but compact, **Fiesta Key KOA Resort** offers some waterfront sites, a tent village, and 20 motel units. Swimming pool, hot tubs, bicycle and boat rentals, and a waterfront pub and seafood grill make this an appealing location halfway between Miami and Key West. As with other RV resorts in the Florida Keys, expect higher-than-average fees and some pet restrictions. Milepost 70 on U.S. 1. ☎ 800-562-7730. www.koa.com. Weekly full hookup $525.

Kissimmee, Florida

You can expect plenty of friends and family to visit during winter at **Tropical Palms Fun Resort,** a highly rated RV park bordering the Walt Disney World Resort. Bonuses include transportation to all the local theme parks and discount attraction tickets. Some 400 paved sites with full hookups have grass and shade, and the resort offers a central modem hookup, poolside cafe, heated pool for adults open 24 hours, kiddie pool, basketball and volleyball, and mobile sewer service. 2650 Holiday Trail. ☎ 800-64-PALMS (800-647-2567), 407-396-4595. www.tropicalpalmsrv.com. Weekly full hookup $203–$245.

River Ridge, Louisiana

New Orleans isn't always thought of as a snowbird getaway, but its mild winter climate and lively cultural scene is an attraction. The **New Orleans West KOA** runs a daily shuttle to and from the French Quarter and offers daily sightseeing tours of New Orleans and day and evening riverboat jazz cruises. Casinos are nearby and rental car pickup service is available at the campground. Located on the Mississippi less than a mile from the Rivertown Museum Center, this small, well-run park offers 94 full hookup sites in a grassy, tree-shaded, fenced area with city water and modem connections in the office. 11129 Jefferson Highway. ☎ 800-562-5110, 504-467-1792. www.koa.com. Weekly full hookup $217.

Donna, Texas

South Texas along the Rio Grande River between Brownsville and McAllen is lined with upscale RV parks, such as **Victoria Palms Resort** near Gulf coast beaches and Mexico. Victoria Palms offers more than 1,000 40-foot-wide pull-through and back-in sites with full hookups, its own restaurant and motel (handy if you have relatives or friends who want to visit), instant phone hookups at your site, free cable TV, barber shop, salon, card room, billiard room, arts and crafts programs, scenic area tours, an exercise room, live dance bands, a ballroom, heated pool, and two heated therapy pools. 602 North Victoria Rd. ☎ 800-551-5303, 956-464-7801. www.victoriapalms.com. Weekly full hookup $165.

Mission, Texas

Americana RV Resort in Mission is across the street from a new state park that affords quiet and scenic pleasure. In this over-55 resort are 154 hookups with water, 30- and 50-amp electric, and sewer connections. No pull-throughs, but the wide sites have patios and can handle big rigs. The park features two sections, with large trees and gravel sites in the older section and small trees and grass sites in the newer one. A new Spanish-style clubhouse resplendent in tile has a large recreation room with a kitchen that serves Saturday morning breakfast for the guests. 721 N. Bentsen Palm Dr. ☎ 956-581-1705. www.resort rvparks.com. Weekly full hookup $95–$135.

South Padre Island, Texas

With 190 full hook-up sites, each with its own modem connections and cable TV, **Destination South Padre Island RV Resort** on the Laguna Madre Bay boasts waterfront sites, bar, restaurant, boat dock, saltwater fishing, heated pool, and a spa. South Padre Island is a fully developed resort town adjacent to the commercially developed southern part of the national park. One Padre Boulevard, off Queen Isabella Causeway. ☎ 800-TO PADRE (800-867-2373), 956-761-5665. www.destination southpadre.com. Weekly full hookups $200–$250.

Chapter 26

The Ten Best Factory Tours

In This Chapter

▶ Sampling Ben & Jerry's new flavors

▶ Tasting a belly flop

▶ Watching how they make Winnebagos and more

Most RV travelers have a curiosity about everything, including how things are made. We always take notice of many other RVs in the big parking lots of manufacturers that offer tours. Another plus — most of the tours are free. This chapter includes the nine best factory tours in the United States, and one Web site that enables you to visit six more.

Ben & Jerry's Ice Cream

Tours of **Ben & Jerry's Ice Cream Factory** start every 10 to 30 minutes, depending on the season, and sign-up is on a first-come, first-served basis. Try to avoid visiting on Sundays and holidays when no ice cream is produced. The tour consists of a seven-minute "Moovie," a guided overview of the manufacturing process (no factory operation on weekends and holidays), free samples of the day, and finally, a shopping op in the scoop and gift shop. In summer, try to arrive before noon.

Waterbury, Vermont. (Take Exit 10 off I-89 and drive north on SR 100 for 1 mile to the entrance on the left.) ☎ **802-882-1260.** www.benjerry.com. RV parking: Designated lot. Admission: $3 adults, $2 seniors, free ages 12 and younger. Tours: Daily 10 a.m.–5 p.m., longer hours in summer. Closed New Year's Day, Thanksgiving, and Christmas. Allow at least 1 hour.

Cape Cod Potato Chips

The **Cape Cod Potato Chip Company** bagged only 200 packages a day in 1980. Today, the factory still uses the same kettle-cooking method to turn out 200,000 bags in the same amount of time. Watch the crispy, salty, kettle-cooked chips go through their production lines into six kettles filled with sizzling oil, after which you see chips drained, cooled, and packaged. You get a free package of your choice of chips at the end of the tour.

100 Breeds Hill Rd., Hyannis, Massachusetts (off SR 132 south near the airport). ☎ **508-775-3206.** www.capecodchips.com. RV parking: Large open lot behind factory. Admission: Free. Self-guided Tours: Year-round Mon–Fri 9 a.m.–5 p.m. Allow 1 hour.

Crayola Crayons

We'd like to say that you're watching the real Binney & Smith assembly line at the **Crayola Factory,** but this handsome, visitor-friendly facility is just a demonstration of how Crayola manufactures your favorite crayons. Built several years ago when the factory itself got swamped with curious visitors, this facility is designed especially for families and so are the hands-on coloring and crafts areas for kids. The presentations usually hold adults as spellbound as their offspring. Souvenirs can be purchased at the General Store gift shop and the big Crayola Store next door.

This attraction also is the home of the National Canal Museum, which offers a 40-minute canal boat ride at 9:30 a.m. and 2 p.m. (admission: $6 adults, $5.50 seniors, $4 children).

Two Rivers Landing, Centre Square, Easton, Pennsylvania. ☎ **610-515-8000.** www.crayola.com/factory. RV parking: Street parking. Admission: $9 adults and ages 3 and older, $8.50 seniors older than 65. Open: Tues–Sat 9:30 a.m.–5 p.m., Sun noon to 5 p.m. Allow 2 hours, more if you do the Canal Museum and boat ride.

Hallmark Greeting Cards

More a museum than a factory tour, the **Hallmark Visitors Center** showcases its famous cards with 14 exhibits, a keyhole walk-through leading to a gigantic artist's drawing board, and displays of company products.

Crown Center Complex, Kansas City, Missouri (1 mile south of downtown off Grand Avenue and 25th Street). ☎ **816-274-5672.** hallmarkvisitors center.com. RV parking: Street parking. Admission: Free. Tours: Mon–Fri 9 a.m.–5 p.m., Sat 9:30 a.m.–4:30 p.m. Closed holidays. Allow 2 hours.

Jelly Belly Jellybeans

The **Jelly Belly Candy Company** offers our hands-down favorite of all the factory tours in the United States. Here you can watch the candies being made on the assembly line and taste them at different stages, get free samples at the end of the tour, and buy low-price factory rejects called Belly Flops, which usually are two jellybeans that fused together during the process. Jelly Belly jelly beans are the favorites of knowledgeable candy lovers like former President Ronald Reagan, because the fillings are flavored in addition to the candy coatings on the outside. The tour also includes a collection of portraits of famous people, including Reagan, made from jellybeans. Guided tours set out frequently from the main desk.

2400 North Watney Way, Fairfield, California. (Take SR 12 exit from I-80 and follow the signs.) ☎ **707-428-2838.** www.jellybelly.com. RV parking: Huge lot. Admission: Free. 35-minute walking tours: Daily 9 a.m.–5 p.m. No production line on weekends, holidays, the last week of June and first week of July; a video shows the production line at these times. Allow 1 hour.

Louisville Slugger Baseball Bats

Fans of America's favorite pastime enjoy the **Louisville Slugger Museum.** First, walk through the museum that salutes famous sluggers, and then see the bat-making itself. Some 95% of the bats are machine made, but a few special orders still are hand-turned. A hot brand sizzles the mark, model number, and player's autograph into the wood.

800 W. Main St., Louisville, Kentucky. (Take Third Street exit from I-64 W, turn right on River Road, and turn left on Eighth Street and look for the world's tallest baseball bat.) ☎ **502-588-7228.** www.sluggermuseum.org. RV parking: Designated lot. Admission: $6 adults, $5 seniors, $3.50 ages 6–12. 90-minute tours: Mon–Sat 9 a.m.–5 p.m., last factory tour at 3:45 p.m. Allow 2 hours.

Sechler's Pickles

You discover that there's more to making pickles than you thought as you're guided around the huge vats that stand in the yard outside the family-owned **Sechler's Pickle Factory** where pickles may spend as long as a year marinating. Then you can watch cooking and processing, and finally the bottling. Different types of pickles are made on different days. Taste free samples and select pickles to purchase in the show room.

5686 SR 1, St. Joe, Indiana. ☎ **260-337-5461.** www.gourmetpickles.com. RV parking: Large lot outside factory. Admission: Free. Tours: Apr–Oct Mon–Fri 9–11 a.m. and 12:30–2 p.m. Closed Nov–Mar, weekends, and holidays. Allow 1 hour.

Tabasco Sauce

The world's most-famous hot sauce was invented on this family planta-
tion just after the Civil War and has been made on-site ever since.
Although the peppers come from around the world, the sauce is made
only here at the **McIlhenny Company** on Avery Island. You can watch
the sauce being bottled and the bottles labeled and packed into shipping
boxes. You get a miniature bottle of Tabasco and some recipes at the end
of the tour. The gift shop is full of cool souvenirs with the Tabasco logo.

Avery Island, Louisiana. (Take I-10 West from New Orleans to Exit 103A
and then U.S. 90 to New Iberia; exit at SR 14 and turn left, then turn
right on SR 329, and drive 6 miles to Avery Island, where you take a toll
road [.50¢, entry only] to the factory.) ☎ **337-365-8173.** RV parking:
Designated lot. Admission: Free. Tours: Mon–Sun 9 a.m.–4 p.m., last
tour 3:30 p.m. No production most Saturdays. Closed holidays and long
weekends. Allow 1 hour.

Virtual Factory Tours with Mr. Rogers

Here's a **group of factory tours** that you can take without leaving your
campsite — if you have a computer. You can see how people make
sneakers, wagons, plates, construction paper, crayons, and even fortune
cookies. Granted this site is designed for kids but even grownups can
learn a thing or two. Visit pbskids.org/rogers/R_house/picpic.htm
to join the late Fred Rogers from *Mr. Rogers' Neighborhood* as he nar-
rates information about each of the featured factories. You can explore
the factories via video, slides, or just narration depending on what kind
of software you have. Open year-round 24–7.

Winnebago Motorhomes

The **Winnebego Industries, Inc. Visitors Center** offers tours of the
world's largest production plant. You follow a catwalk around the plant
for a birds-eye view of the manufacturing processes, watching motorhomes move down assembly lines at 21 inches a minute. The dramatic
finish is when each unit is tested in a simulated rainstorm along a
pothole-studded roadway while standing still. You can buy logo caps
and jackets in the gift shop.

1316 S. Fourth St., Forest City, Iowa. (Take SR 9 exit off I-35 and then
turn south on SR 69 to Fourth Street). ☎ **641-585-6936.** RV parking:
Designated areas. Admission: Free. Tours: Apr–Oct Mon–Fri 9 a.m. and
1 p.m., Nov–mid-Dec 1 p.m. only. Closed mid-Dec to Mar 31, holidays,
and first week in July. Allow 2 hours.

Chapter 27

The Ten Zaniest Museums

In This Chapter

▶ Flushing out the history of plumbing

▶ Cutting the mustard in Wisconsin

▶ Discovering the truth about Spam and more

*W*e've been visiting zany museums for years. These off-the-wall attractions always get plenty of attention when we're traveling around the country talking about our RV travel books; now and then, we surprise local radio or TV interviewers by mentioning one in their own backyards that they've never heard of.

Fans of these zany spots may also want to take note of the **Moxie Museum** at the Moxie Bottling Company mentioned in Chapter 11, the **Lucy-Desi Museum** and the **Jell-O Gallery** in Chapter 12, the **Key Underwood Coon Dog Memorial Park** in Chapter 15, the **Judy Garland Museum** and the **Greyhound Bus Origin Center** in Chapter 18, the **International UFO Museum & Research Center** in Chapter 21, and **Exotic World, the Burlesque Hall of Fame** in Chapter 24.

American Sanitary Plumbing Museum

A collection of pipes, toilets, and lavatories attracts wannabe plumbers and appreciators of toilet humor. One item, perhaps an early dishwasher, is an electric sink with an agitator that washed dishes.

39 Piedmont St., Worcester, Massachusetts (off I-290 in the town center). ☎ **508-754-9453**. RV parking: Street parking. Admission: Free. Open: Jan–June and Sept–Dec Tues and Thurs 10 a.m.–2 p.m. Allow 30 minutes unless you're a plumber.

Colonel Harlan Sanders Cafe/Museum

The original Colonel Sanders Kentucky Fried Chicken Cafe has been turned into a museum but retains a branch of KFC on the premises. Colonel Sanders came up with his pressure cooker–fried chicken in 1940, and the world beat a path to his door until the highway system rerouted the main road. Then he took to the road himself to sell his cooking method to franchisees. (The museum is interesting, but the fried chicken that we sampled wasn't as good as at some other franchises.)

Corbin, Kentucky. (At junction of U.S. 25E and U.S. 25W, take Exit 29 from I-75 and drive south on 25E for 1 mile and then west on 25W for a half-mile.) ☎ **606-528-2163.** RV parking: Large lot. Admission: Free. Open: Daily 10 a.m.–10 p.m. Allow 1 hour.

James Dean Gallery

The gallery has moved from Main Street in James Dean's hometown of Fairmount, Indiana, to a new art-deco styled building with a 42-seat theater displaying film clips of Dean's brief career in Gas City, Indiana. On display are an expanded collection of photos and artifacts from the iconic actor who died in an automobile accident in 1955 at the age of 24 after making three notable films: *Giant, East of Eden,* and *Rebel Without A Cause.* You can also buy James Dean souvenirs, and the museum staff can direct you to the actor's grave on the edge of town in Fairmount.

Located at Exit 59 from I-69, Gas City, Indiana. ☎ **765-948-3326.** www. jamesdeangallery.com. RV parking: Large lot. Admission: $4.75 adults, free ages 10 and younger. Open: Daily 9 a.m.–7 p.m. Closed holidays. Allow 1 hour, longer if you want to watch video clips from his early TV performances.

John Dillinger Museum

Life-size wax mannequins and bullet-scarred automobiles fill what was the criminal courts building where Dillinger was arraigned. You can see the fake guns that he carved from wood or soap and blacked with shoe polish for some of his famous jail escapes, and discover that the famous "lady in red" who gave the FBI the signal as she left a movie house with the criminal actually was wearing orange.

7770 Corinne Dr., Hammond, Indiana (off I-80/94 at the Kennedy Avenue exit). ☎ **219-989-7770.** RV parking: Street parking. Admission: $4 adults, $3 seniors and ages 6–12. Open: Mon–Fri 8 a.m.–6 p.m., Sat–Sun 9 a.m.– 6 p.m. Allow 1 hour.

Miss Laura's Bordello

Claiming to be the only bordello listed on the National Register of Historic Places, Miss Laura's doubles as a museum and the visitor center for Fort Smith and was recently refurbished to look the way it did at the turn of the 20th century.

2 North B St., Fort Smith, Arkansas. ☎ **800-637-1477,** 479-783-8888. www.fortsmith.org. RV parking: Adjacent lot, street parking. Admission: Free. Open: Mon–Sat 9 a.m.–4 p.m., Sun 1–4 p.m. Allow 1 hour.

Mount Horeb Mustard Museum

This combination museum/shop stocks more than 2,500 kinds of mustard, which makes browsing the shelves an education in condiments. The owner, enthusiastic Barry Levenson, also publishes a newsletter, expounds on the history of mustard, quotes Shakespeare on mustard ("Good Master Mustardseed, I know your patience well"), and sells T-shirts and banners from his trademarked Mustard College, Poupon U.

100 West Main St., Mount Horeb, Wisconsin. ☎ **608-437-3986.** www.mustardweb.com. RV parking: Street parking. Admission: Free. Open: Daily 10 a.m.–5 p.m. Allow 1 hour, more if Barry is in residence.

Metropolis, Illinois

The only town in the United States named Metropolis decided to claim Superman as well and turn itself into a kind of living museum. The town put a nine-foot statue of the Man of Steel in its square, hired an actor to wear the costume, erected giant billboards, painted the hero on the water tower, and set up a phone booth where you can lift the receiver and get a message from Superman. You can also pick up a copy of the local newspaper, *The Daily Planet,* of course. A gift shop/museum on the square is named Super Museum. In the spring of 2001, the actor who plays Superman donned the costume and married his sweetheart by the statue in the square. (Her name wasn't Lois Lane, however.)

Metropolis, Illinois, is in the southern tip of Illinois on U.S. 45 about 12 miles northwest of Paducah, Kentucky, on the Ohio River. ☎ **800-949-5740** (Metropolis Chamber of Commerce).

National Freshwater Fishing Hall of Fame

Talk about Jonah! At this museum, you walk through a four-story giant muskie and stand in his open jaw, which is a balcony overlooking several other giant Fiberglas fish. Equally bizarre is a collection of several thousand fishhooks that doctors have retrieved from the flesh of fishermen; each case is carefully documented.

Hall of Fame Drive, Hayward, Wisconsin (near the junction of SR 63 and SR B). ☎ 715-634-4440. RV parking: Large designated lot. Admission: $5 adults, $3.50 ages 10–17, $2.50 ages 9 and younger. Open: Apr 15–Oct 30 daily 10 a.m.–4:30 p.m.

The Pest House Medical Museum

The morbid and medical-minded can visit this complex of three museums and a cemetery. In the 19th century, patients were quarantined in the **Pest House,** then, when they almost inevitably died, their bodies were buried in the **Old City Cemetery,** which dates from the Confederate era. Now a museum, the Pest House contains an 1860s hypodermic needle and an early chloroform mask, among other weird stuff; visitors look in the windows and listen to recordings. Also on-site are the **Victorian Mourning Museum** with wreaths and decorations made from the hair of the deceased, and the 1898 **C & O Station House.**

401 Taylor St., Lynchburg, Virginia (at Fourth and Taylor). ☎ 434-847-1465. www.gravegarden.org. RV parking: Street parking along the 1-mile loop road through the cemetery. Admission: Free. Open: Dawn to dusk. Allow 1 hour.

Shady Dell RV Park and Campground

This RV park is an outdoor museum of vintage Airstream trailers that rent by the night and are furnished with period furniture and cassettes from the Big Band era. You're welcome to drive up in your own RV and take a look. The campground also displays a terrific diner done up in 1930s style.

1 Douglas Rd., Bisbee, Arizona (just off U.S. 80 traffic circle 1.5 miles east of town). ☎ 520-432-3567.

Spam Museum

Spam stands for "spiced ham," a 64-year-old American icon and lunch-eon meat that made history in Army mess kitchens during World War II and is a daily staple in the menus of Hawaii. Interactive exhibits include a simulated production line that visitors can join, wearing rubber gloves and a hard hat; a game show about meat trivia; and a survey of Spam around the world.

1101 N. Main St., Austin, Minnesota (off I-90 via the Fourth Street exit). ☎ **800-588-7726.** www.hormel.com. RV parking: Designated lot. Admission: Free. Open: Mon–Sat 10 a.m.–5 p.m., Sun noon to 4 p.m. Closed holidays. Allow 1 hour or longer.

Appendix

Quick Concierge

Fast Facts

American Automobile Association (AAA)

For emergency road service, call ☎ 800-AAA-HELP (800-222-4357). To locate your nearest AAA office, log on to www.aaa.com.

ATM

Most banks and some campgrounds have ATMs. Cirrus (☎ 800-424-7787; www.mastercard.com) and Plus (☎ 800-843-7587; www.visa.com) are the two most popular networks in the U.S.

Credit Cards

Citicorp Visa's emergency number is ☎ 800-336-8472. American Express cardholders and traveler's check holders can call ☎ 800-221-7282. MasterCard holders can call ☎ 800-307-7309.

Emergencies

Call ☎ 911.

Hospitals

Look for the blue highway signs with a white "H" signifying an exit for a hospital with emergency services. For the locations of hospitals along the drives in this book, see the Fast Facts sections in Chapters 11 through 24.

Post Office

Most commercial campgrounds receive and send mail, sell stamps, and handle Federal Express and UPS pickups.

Road and Weather Conditions

Go online to www.fhwa.dot.gov/trafficinfo/index.htm for national weather and road advisories. For road and weather conditions along the drives in this book, see the Fast Facts sections in Chapters 11 through 24.

Taxes

The Federal tax on gasoline sales is 18.4¢ a gallon. For state gasoline taxes, see the Fast Facts sections in Chapters 11 through 24.

Toll-Free Numbers and Web Sites

RV associations

RVIA (Recreation Vehicle Industry Association)

☎ 703-620-6003

www.gorving.com or
www.gocampingamerica.com

RV rental agencies

Altman's Winnebago
Carson, California
☎ 310-518-6182
altmans.com/info/why_altmans.
cfm

Cruise America
Nationwide
☎ 800-327-7799
www.cruiseamerica.com

El Monte RV
Nationwide
☎ 888-337-2214
www.elmonte.com

Moturis Inc.
Nationwide
☎ 877-MOTURIS (877-668-8747)
www.moturis.com

Nolan's RV Center
Denver, Colorado
☎ 800-232-8989
www.nolans.com

Rent 'N' Roam RV Rentals
Shrewsbury, Massachusetts
☎ 800-842-1840
www.rentnroam.com

Road Bear International Motorhome
Agoura Hills, California
☎ 818-865-2925

Western Motor Coach
Lynnwood, Washington
☎ 800-800-1181
www.westernrv.com

U.S. agencies

National Forest Service
☎ 202-205-1680
www.fs.fed.us

National Parks Service
☎ 202-208-6843
www.nps.gov

U.S. Bureau of Land Management
☎ 202-452-5125
www.blm.gov

U.S. Department of Transportation
☎ 202-366-2981
www.fhwa.dot.gov

Where to Get More Information

Numerous online and published resources exist for the curious RVer. Many are listed here.

Helpful Web sites

www.campingworld.com: All kinds of supplies geared to the RV market.

www.gocampingamerica.com: From National Association of RV Parks and Campgrounds, camping information for more than 3,100 member properties.

www.gorving.com: A comprehensive source of RV information by the Go RVing Coalition, a nonprofit organization.

www.koa.com: Kampgrounds of America, operator of the KOA network of campgrounds.

www.rvamerica.com: An RV sales and industry information site sponsored by *RV News Magazine*.

www.rvda.org and www.rvra.org: How to buy and rent RVs.

www.rvia.org: A variety of information about manufactures, retail shows, and clubs.

www.rvtvdirect.com: Source for videotapes with helpful hints, budget ideas, and scenic tours.

www.rvusa.com: Find RV dealers, manufacturers, parts and accessory sources, rental units, and campgrounds.

Campground directories

Bureau of Land Management: 270 million acres of public land. Department of Interior–BLM, 1849 C St. NW, Room 5600, Washington, DC 20240. ☎ 202-452-5125. www.blm.gov. Free.

KOA: 615 campgrounds in the U.S., Canada, and Mexico. Kampgrounds of America Executive Offices, P.O. Box 30558, Billings, MT 59114-0558. ☎ 406-248-7444. www.koa.com. Free at campgrounds, $3 by mail.

National Forest Service: 4,000 campgrounds. U.S. Department of Agriculture Forest Service, Public Affairs Office, P.O. Box 96090, Washington, DC 20090-6090. ☎ 202-205-1680. www.fs.fed.us. Free.

National Park Camping Guide: 440 campgrounds. U.S. Government Printing Office, Superintendent of Documents, Washington, DC 20402-9325. www.gpo.gov. $4. Ask for stock #024-005-01080-7.

National Association of RV Park and Campgrounds: More than 3,000 RV parks and campgrounds. National ARVC, 113 Park Ave., Falls Church, VA 22046. ☎ 703-241-8801. www.gocampingamerica.com. Free.

National Wildlife Refuges: 488 refuges. U.S. Fish and Wildlife Services, Public Affairs Office, 1849 C St. NW, MS-5600/MIB, Washington, D.C., 20240. ☎ 202-452-5125. refuges.fws.gov. Free.

Trailer Life Campground/RV Park and Services Directory: Covers 12,500 campgrounds in the U.S., Canada, and Mexico. 2575 Vista del Mar Dr., Ventura, CA 93001. ☎ 800-234-3450. tldirectory.com. Available at bookstores, camping stores, or by writing. $20.

U.S. Army Corps of Engineers: 53,000 campsites near oceans, rivers, and lakes. U.S. Army Corps of Engineers, OCE Publications Depot, 2803 52nd Ave., Hyattsville, MD 20781-1102. ☎ **301- 394-0081.** www.usace.army.mil. Free.

Wheelers RV Resort & Campground Directory: Print Media Services, 1310 Jarvis Ave., Elk Grove Village, IL 60007. $12.95.

Woodall's Campground Directory: 2575 Vista Del Mar Dr., Ventura, CA 93001. ☎ **800-323-9076.** www.woodalls.com. $19.95.

Publications for campers and RV owners

Chevy Outdoors: 30400 Van Dyke Avenue, Warren, MI 48093.
☎ **810-574-9100.**

Coast to Coast: 64 Inverness Dr. East, Englewood, CO 80112.
☎ **800-368-5721.**

Highways: TL Enterprises, 2575 Vista Del Mar Dr., Ventura, CA 93001.
☎ **805-667-4100.**

Motorhome: TL Enterprises, 2575 Vista Del Mar Dr., Ventura, CA 93001.
☎ **805-667-4100.**

RV West: 3000 Northup Way, Suite 200, Bellevue, WA 98004.
☎ **800-700-6962.**

Trailer Life: TL Enterprises, 2575 Vista Del Mar Dr., Ventura, CA 93001.
☎ **805-667-4100.**

RV and Campground Lingo

In the same way that a potential home buyer must figure out the abbreviated language for real estate classified listings — *6 rms riv vu* (six rooms with river view), for instance — an RVer wants to know certain terms that are peculiar to owning and operating recreation vehicles. Some of the more common ones are as follows:

- ✔ **Auxiliary battery:** Extra battery to run 12-volt equipment.
- ✔ **Basement model:** An RV with large storage areas underneath a raised chassis.
- ✔ **Black water:** Wastewater from the toilet.
- ✔ **Boondock:** To camp without electrical or other hookups.

✔ **Cabover:** The part of a mini-motorhome (see Chapter 3 for RV types) that overlaps the top of the vehicle's cab, usually containing a sleeping area, storage unit, or entertainment center.

✔ **Camper shell:** Removable unit to fit in the bed of a pickup truck.

✔ **Curbside:** The side of the RV that's at the curb when parked.

✔ **Diesel pusher:** A motorhome with a rear diesel engine.

✔ **Dual electrical system:** An RV system in which lights and other electrical systems can run on 12-volt battery power, 110 AC electrical hookup, or gas generator.

✔ **Dump station:** Also called sanitary dump or disposal station; where an RV empties the *gray water* (wastewater from sinks and shower) and *black water* (wastewater from toilet) from its holding tanks.

✔ **Full hookup:** A campsite that provides connections for electricity, water, and sewage.

✔ **Generator:** Small engine fueled by gasoline or propane that produces 110-volt electricity that's built into many RVs but also available as a portable option.

✔ **Gray water:** Wastewater from the sinks and shower.

✔ **Hard-sided:** RV walls made of aluminum or other hard surface.

✔ **Hitch:** The fastening unit that joins a movable vehicle, such as a towable RV, to the vehicle that pulls it.

✔ **Holding tanks:** Tanks that retain *black water* (wastewater from toilet) and *gray water* (wastewater from sinks and shower) when the RV unit isn't connected to a sewer.

✔ **Hookups:** The land connections at a campsite for electricity, water, and sewage; sites that offer all three connections are called *full hookups,* sites that offer only one or two of three connections are called *partial hookups.*

✔ **Inverter:** A unit that changes 12-volt direct current to 110-volt alternating current to enable operation of computers, TV sets, and other electrical devices when an RV isn't hooked up to electricity.

✔ **Leveling:** Positioning the RV in camp so the rig is level, using ramps (also called levelers) placed under the wheels, built-in scissors jacks, or power-leveling jacks.

✔ **Overflow area:** That part of a campground that can handle late arrivals when all the regular sites are filled; the area usually is little more than a parking lot or open field.

✔ **Partial hookups:** Sites that offer one or two of the three land connections for electricity, water, and sewage.

✔ **Pop-up:** Foldout or raised additions to an RV that add height for standing room.

✔ **Propane or LPG:** Liquefied petroleum gas used for heating, cooking, and refrigeration in RVs.

✔ **Pull-through:** A campground site that enables the driver to pull the RV forward into the site for camping and then drive out of the site on the other end to leave without ever having to back up.

✔ **Self-contained:** An RV that needs no external connections to provide short-term cooking, bathing, and heating functions.

✔ **Shore cord:** The external electrical cord that connects the vehicle to a campground electrical hookup.

✔ **Slide-out:** A portion of the vehicle that slides open when the RV is parked to expand the living and/or bedroom area. If the RV is parked in a narrow area or there is a tree in the way and you can keep the slide-out closed or perhaps only open it part way.

✔ **Snowbird:** Resident of a cold climate who takes an RV and moves south to a warm climate for the winter.

✔ **Soft-sides:** Telescoping side panels on an RV that can be raised or lowered and usually are constructed of canvas or vinyl and mesh netting.

✔ **Solar panels:** Battery chargers that convert sunlight to direct current electricity.

✔ **Spirit level:** A device used for determining an even horizontal or vertical plane by centering a bubble in a slightly curved glass tube or tubes filled with alcohol or ether. Some RVs come with built-in levels.

✔ **Streetside:** The part of the vehicle on the street side when parked.

✔ **Telescoping:** Compacting from front to back and/or top to bottom to make the living unit smaller for towing and storage.

✔ **Three-way refrigerators:** An RV refrigerator/freezer that can operate on LP gas, electrical hookup, or gas generator.

✔ **Tow car:** A car towed by an RV to be used as transportation when the RV is parked in a campground.

✔ **Widebody:** Designs that stretch RVs from the traditional 96-inch width to 100 or 102 inches.

Making Dollars and Sense of It

Expense	Daily cost	x	Number of days	=	Total
RV rental					
Gasoline					
RV maintenance					
Tolls and parking					
RV and camping supplies					
Campgrounds					
Groceries					
Restaurants and takeout					
Attractions					
Activities					
Gift and souvenirs					
Entertainment					
Other					
Grand Total					

The Right Rig: Choosing Your RV

RV Rentals

When looking for the best RV rental contact several outlets and compare the following:

Cost per day_____ Number of free miles included_____
Cost of additional miles_____ Insurance costs_____
Drop-off charges_____
Furnishings provided_____ Package cost for additional furnishings_____
Number of beds_____ Instruction booklet provided?_____
Breakdown service provided?_____ Airport pickup provided?_____

Cost per day_____ Number of free miles included_____
Cost of additional miles_____ Insurance costs_____
Drop-off charges_____
Furnishings provided_____ Package cost for additional furnishings_____
Number of beds_____ Instruction booklet provided?_____
Breakdown service provided?_____ Airport pickup provided?_____

RV Purchases

When comparing RV prices, use the following checklist to organize your data:

Manufacturer_____ Type of vehicle_____
Model_____ Price_____
Accessories _____
_____
Furnishings options _____
_____
Financing_____

Manufacturer_____ Type of vehicle_____
Model_____ Price_____
Accessories _____
_____
Furnishings options _____
_____
Financing_____

Sweet Dreams: Choosing Your Campground

Make a list of the campgrounds where you'd like to stay and check with them directly or online for their quoted price. Remember prices may be quoted by the day, week or month.

Campground & page	Location	Internet	Tel. (local)	Tel. (Toll-free)	Quoted rate

Campground Checklist

Here's a checklist of things to inquire about when booking your campground, depending on your needs and preferences.

- ❏ Hookup facilities (full or partial; electric amperage available)
- ❏ Site size (width and length, pull-through, or back-in)
- ❏ Noise (Is the campground near the highway, train tracks, or airport?)
- ❏ Scenic environment (Are there trees for shade or is it a parking lot?)
- ❏ Facilities for children (playground, pool, miniature golf)
- ❏ Facilities for pets (Is there an additional fee, is there a pet area?)
- ❏ Cable or satellite TV hookup (Is there a fee?)
- ❏ Dataport for computer hookup (Is there a fee?)
- ❏ Laundry facility
- ❏ Shower and flush toilet facilities

Sweet Dreams: Choosing Your Campground

Make a list of the campgrounds where you'd like to stay and check with them directly or online for their quoted price. Remember prices may be quoted by the day, week or month.

Campground & page	Location	Internet	Tel. (local)	Tel. (Toll-free)	Quoted rate

Campground Checklist

Here's a checklist of things to inquire about when booking your campground, depending on your needs and preferences.

- ☐ Hookup facilities (full or partial; electric amperage available)
- ☐ Site size (width and length, pull-through, or back-in)
- ☐ Noise (Is the campground near the highway, train tracks, or airport?)
- ☐ Scenic environment (Are there trees for shade or is it a parking lot?)
- ☐ Facilities for children (playground, pool, miniature golf)
- ☐ Facilities for pets (Is there an additional fee, is there a pet area?)
- ☐ Cable or satellite TV hookup (Is there a fee?)
- ☐ Dataport for computer hookup (Is there a fee?)
- ☐ Laundry facility
- ☐ Shower and flush toilet facilities

Places to Go, People to See, Things to Do

Enter the attractions you would most like to see and decide how they'll fit into your schedule. Next, use the "Going My Way" worksheets that follow to sketch out your itinerary.

Attraction/activity	Page	Amount of time you expect to spend there	Best day and time to go

Places to Go, People to See, Things to Do

Enter the attractions you would most like to see and decide how they'll fit into your schedule. Next, use the "Going My Way" worksheets that follow to sketch out your itinerary.

Attraction/activity	Page	Amount of time you expect to spend there	Best day and time to go

Going "My" Way

Day 1

Campground_____ Tel._____

Morning_____

_____

Lunch_____ Tel._____

Afternoon_____

_____

Dinner_____ Tel._____

Evening_____

_____

Day 2

Campground_____ Tel._____

Morning_____

_____

Lunch_____ Tel._____

Afternoon_____

_____

Dinner_____ Tel._____

Evening_____

_____

Day 3

Campground_____ Tel._____

Morning_____

_____

Lunch_____ Tel._____

Afternoon_____

_____

Dinner_____ Tel._____

Evening_____

_____

Going "My" Way

Day 4

Campground_____ Tel._____

Morning_____

_____

Lunch_____ Tel._____

Afternoon_____

_____

Dinner_____ Tel._____

Evening_____

_____

Day 5

Campground_____ Tel._____

Morning_____

_____

Lunch_____ Tel._____

Afternoon_____

_____

Dinner_____ Tel._____

Evening_____

_____

Day 6

Campground_____ Tel._____

Morning_____

_____

Lunch_____ Tel._____

Afternoon_____

_____

Dinner_____ Tel._____

Evening_____

_____

Going "My" Way

Day 7

Campground_____ Tel._____

Morning_____

_____

Lunch_____ Tel._____

Afternoon_____

_____

Dinner_____ Tel._____

Evening_____

_____

Day 8

Campground_____ Tel._____

Morning_____

_____

Lunch_____ Tel._____

Afternoon_____

_____

Dinner_____ Tel._____

Evening_____

_____

Day 9

Campground_____ Tel._____

Morning_____

_____

Lunch_____ Tel._____

Afternoon_____

_____

Dinner_____ Tel._____

Evening_____

_____

Notes

Index

• D •

• E •

• G •

Garland, Judy (actress), birthplace (MN), 256
gas leak detectors, 67–68
Gatchell Memorial Museum (WY), 296–297
Gatlinburg Outdoor Resorts (TN), 161–162
generators, 68
George E. Orh Arts Center (MS), 179
George Eastman House (NY), 134, 137
German village (OH), 236, 242
Getty Museum (CA), 352, 356–357
Giovanni's Fish Market (CA), 367
global positioning systems (GPS), 102
glossaries
  New Mexico chile dishes, 325–326
  RV and campground terms, 408–410
Gold Beach (OR), 333
Golden Age Passport, 58, 99
Golden Eagle Trading Co. (NM), 374
Golden Lamb Inn (OH), 235, 247–248
Golden Shore RV Park (CA), 393
Goo Goo Clusters (TN), 206
Good Sam Club, 60, 99, 100, 105
GPS (global positioning systems), 102
Grand Canyon (AZ), 375
Grand Canyon Railway (AZ), 375, 378
Grand Rapids, MN, 256
gray water holding tanks, 74
Grayton Beach State Recreation Area (FL), 174, 183
Great Lakes Aquarium (MN), 258
Great Passion Play (AR), 274, 278
Great Smoky Mountains National Park (TN), 10, 156–157, 164
"green" RVing, 13–14
Greyhound Bus Origin Center (MN), 256, 260
Grizzly Discovery Center (MT), 301
Gross Vehicle Weight Rating (GVWR), 77–78
Guadalupe Peak (TX), 316
Guggisberg Cheese Co. (OH), 236, 249
Gulf Coast drive
  campgrounds, 170, 180–184
  driving route, map, 171–177

food and beverages, 171, 175, 184–187
getting to area, 190
highlights, 18–19, 177–180
planning and packing, 170–171
services and information, 188
Gulf Islands National Seashore (MS), 174, 177–178, 181
Gulf State Park (AL), 176
guns, traveling with, 106

• H •

Hallmark Visitors Center (MO), 396
hamburger restaurants (Route 66), 373, 385–386
hand signals, 64
handicapped RVers. *See* disabled RVers
Handicapped Travel Club, 60
Handy, W.C. (musician), birthplace (AL), 11, 196, 200
Hardin Big Horn Valley KOA (MT), 306
Harraseeket Lunch & Lobster Co. (ME), 113, 126
Harris Beach State Park (OR), 333, 344
Harry London Chocolates Factory (OH), 237, 249
Hathorne Point (ME), 118
Haystack Rock (OR), 336
Hearst Castle (CA), 357–358
Herkimer Diamond KOA (NY), 133, 141, 143
Herkimer Diamond Mines (NY), 133, 140
Herschell Carrousel Factory Museum (NY), 136, 138
Herschell Spillman carrousel (CA), 361
Hillbillee's Café (OK), 373, 387
Hinze's Barbecue (TX), 227
The Hitching Post (CA), 353, 366–367
Hockey Hall of Fame (MN), 11, 256, 261
Hocking Hills State Park (OH), 236, 245–246
holding tanks, cleaning, 74
Homolovi State Park (AZ), 385
hook-up procedures, 96–97